To Stuart Grozbean:
an unbounded
source of personal and
professional
inspiration,
Joe – 3/01

Second Edition

DETECTING MALINGERING AND DECEPTION

Forensic Distortion Analysis

PACIFIC INSTITUTE SERIES ON FORENSIC PSYCHOLOGY
Edited by Harold Hall

With the support of Pacific Institute for the Study of Conflict and Aggression, Kamuela, Hawaii

Titles in this Series

Second Edition

DETECTING MALINGERING AND DECEPTION

Forensic Distortion Analysis

Harold V. Hall
Joseph G. Poirier

CRC Press
Boca Raton London New York Washington, D.C.

Library of Congress Cataloging-in-Publication Data

Hall, Harold V.
    Detecting malingering and deception : the revised forensic
distortion analysis / Harold V. Hall, Joseph G. Poirier.—2nd ed.
       p. cm. — (Pacific Institute series on forensic psychology)
    Includes bibliographical references and index.
    ISBN 0-8493-2325-8 (alk. paper)
    1. Malingering. 2. Deception. 3. Medical jurisprudence—United
States. I. Poirier, Joseph G. II. Title. III. Series.
RA1146 .H34 2000
614′.1—dc21

00-010342
CIP

© 2001 by CRC Press LLC

No claim to original U.S. Government works
International Standard Book Number 0-8493-2325-8
Library of Congress Card Number 00-010342
Printed in the United States of America 1 2 3 4 5 6 7 8 9 0
Printed on acid-free paper

Dedication

To my wife, Jerilynn Ono Hall
— H.V.H.

To my wife, Elizabeth A. Poirier,
and my children, Joseph III and Jessica E.
— J.G.P.

"Tell a man there are 300 billion stars in the universe and he'll believe you. Tell him a bench has wet paint on it and he'll have to touch to be sure."

— Jaeger's Facts

"Trust everybody; but always cut the cards."

— Finley Peter Dunne's Credo

"No matter where or what, there are makers, takers, and fakers."

— Kegley's Principle of Observation

"Toothaches tend to occur on Saturday nights."

— Johnson–Laird's Law

"Tell the truth and you won't have so much to remember."

— Abraham Lincoln

"An honest answer can get you into a lot of trouble."

— Welch's Caution

"I have seen the truth, and it makes no sense."

— G.K. Chesterton's Observation

"The man who sees little always sees less than there is to see; the man who hears badly always hears something more than there is to hear."

— Nietzsche

"The greatest way to live with honor in this world is to be what we pretend to be."

— Socrates, 470–399 B.C.

"A truth told with bad intent beats all the lies you can invent"

— William Blake

"As I grow older, I pay less attention to what men say. I just watch what they do."

— Andrew Carnegie

"No man can for any considerable time wear one face to himself and another to the multitude, without finally getting bewildered as to which may be true."

— Nathaniel Hawthorne, *The Scarlet Letter*

"It takes less time to do a thing right, than it does to explain why you did it wrong."

— Henry Wadsworth Longfellow

"Many of us believe that wrongs aren't wrong if it's done by nice people like ourselves."

— Unknown

"Tell the truth and you don't have to remember anything."

— Mark Twain

"A half truth is a whole lie."

— Jewish Proverb

"The least initial deviation from the truth is multiplied later a thousandfold."

— Aristotle

"Truth fears no questions."

— Unknown

"I hate mankind, for I think myself one of the best of them, and I know how bad I am."

— Samuel Johnson

"Character is much easier kept than recovered."

— Thomas Paine

Table of Contents

About the Authors

Harold V. Hall is the Director of the Pacific Institute for the Study of Conflict and Aggression located in Kamuela, Hawaii. He has served as a consultant for a wide variety of criminal and civil justice system agencies, including the Federal Bureau of Investigation, the National Bureau of Prisons, the U.S. Secret Service, and district and circuit courts at both the state and federal levels. Dr. Hall is a diplomate in both forensic psychology and clinical psychology from the American Board of Professional Psychology and is a fellow of the American Psychological Association. He was elected Distinguished Practitioner, National Academy of Practice in Psychology. He has investigated and trained others in deception analysis since the late 1960s in Hawaii, on the continental United States, and in Europe.

Joseph G. Poirier is the Clinical Director of the Child and Adolescent Forensic Evaluation Service (CAFES), Health and Human Services, Montgomery County Government, Rockville, Maryland. For 30 years, he has also been the codirector of the Circuit Court Mental Health Service, Prince Georges County, Maryland. He has testified as an expert witness in federal court and in district and circuit courts in a number of states. Dr. Poirier maintains a clinical-forensic private practice in Silver Spring, Maryland. Dr. Poirier is triple board certified in forensic psychology, clinical psychology, and family psychology by the American Board of Professional Psychology. He is also a fellow of the American Psychological Association.

Preface

Scholars and clinicians have commented on deception for at least two millennia. As we enter the current millennium, interest in the role of deception in human behavior continues with increased enthusiasm. What new things do we have to offer in this second edition of the book? The conceptual underpinnings of the Forensic Distortion Analysis (FDA) model continue as in the original volume. Virtually every chapter has been updated with new studies and investigations from the past decade. New to this edition of the book is a significantly expanded developmental perspective in the form of several new chapters addressing the ontogeny of deceptive behavior in nonhumans and humans. The developmental approach affords an enriched understanding of the etiological dynamics of deception.

An awareness of the continuing evolution in this field is our contribution. Five generations of deception-detecting methods can be identified, two of which are utilized today by most practitioners. The first generation consists of all those judgmental methods, which rely on observing/talking to the possible deceiver and/or significant others. Observation of the person's behavior in different contexts is part of this basic method. Accuracy rates for this first-generation set of measures range from almost zero to somewhat better than chance, depending upon a host of situational and interpersonal factors.

The second generation of deception detection includes objective methods with accuracy rates substantially and consistently above chance. However, they are still by no means awe-inspiring, falling somewhere in the 60 to 85% accuracy range. The validity indices of the Minnesota Multiphasic Personality Inventory (MMPI) and the polygraph for arousal responses to crime-related stimuli are two examples in this category.

A third generation of methods has recently emerged in focal areas such as forced-choice testing and neurocognitive assessment. Accuracy rates exceed 90% under the right conditions. Hypothetical models, which may eventually lead to a general theory of deception, have been proposed and constitute the fourth generation. The fifth generation is the product of technological developments including the computerization of data far surpassing the speed and memory limitations of the past. Included in this fifth generation are developments in medical technologies, the most notable of which is DNA research, which provide a variety of psychophysiological measures far more precise than currently possible with polygraph techniques.

Although this book is more of an applied book than a learned treatise, a model of deception that has utility for the evaluator is presented. The proposed model covers (1) targets of the faker, (2) response styles shown, and (3) methods to detect the deception. It will take the reader far beyond the basic differentiation between malingering vs. defensiveness as the two modes of distortion. The model proposes, for example, a fluctuating response mode as a distinct possibility, where the assessee may shift faking strategies during a single evaluation period. It is hoped the forensic evaluator will find useful methods that can be applied to a variety of deception-related settings and situations.

This book has three general aims: (1) to summarize historical and current information on distortion detection, (2) to present guidelines for detecting distortion that take into account the variable accuracy rates of different methods of deception detection and that consider the varying contexts in which distortion analysis may be relevant, and (3) to stimulate further research on effective methods of deception detection. The review of current detection methods includes experimental and judgmental methods as well as replicated and objective methods. The inclusion of these less accurate methods is not intended as an endorsement of their use by the practicing clinician, but rather as an impetus for refinement and development, which may eventuate in methods that are more useful.

The database of the authors consists of a review of hundreds of articles and books on deception and direct evaluation of several thousand forensic clients over the last 30 years. New areas of deception have continued to emerge, with items on a reading list of source material now numbering in the thousands. This book attempts to address the focal issue of detecting distortion in forensic contexts; yet it is the authors' sense that all of the material included in the book contributes to a vigorous discussion of deception detection. Several caveats are in order:

1. All cases in this book are disguised to protect the identity of relevant parties.
2. Legal citations are included to illustrate trends and controversies in the law and are not intended to represent precedents in any particular jurisdiction. Locally applicable law should be reviewed to determine practices and standards in particular cases.
3. The state of the art in deception analysis remains only slightly better than crude. It is tempting to press current methods into immediate service; yet caution should reign. This book is as much about prospects for the future as it is about practical guidelines for the present. Nevertheless, recommendations and guidelines for the practicing clinician are offered throughout the book, even when such counsel is simply to ignore a particular method.
4. This book requires readers to examine their decision processes in regard to deception. Yet, many forensic professionals are reluctant to change their biases and values with regard to deception, especially when loss of self-esteem or prestige is equated with giving up cherished beliefs.
5. A common complaint is that proper deception analysis requires much time and effort, burdening the busy professional even more. This is an increasingly accurate observation, but the authors have no sympathy for this problem. The days of administering an MMPI and a Rorschach to a client and thereby knowing everything there is to know about the person are gone forever.
6. Forensic evaluators are beginning to integrate the conceptual principles of forensic detection analysis (FDA) with emerging psychometric instruments of ever-improving sophistication and empirical validity. Similarly, the availability of new psychophysiological methods and DNA procedures offer astonishing new possibilities of adjunctive technology to FDA.
7. There are virtually no concepts or procedures in mental health that are sufficiently empirically grounded to warrant opinions expressed in absolutes. This is particularly true for virtually all the topical areas covered in this book. Yet, some forensic clinicians routinely couch their opinions in absolutes and this can be very compelling on the witness stand, especially to naive triers of fact. This circumstance should not be misused as a justification to respond in like manner.

The authors acknowledge the following individuals, many of whom have generously supplied time, ideas, manuscript reviews, and encouragement for the first edition of the book: Steven Alm, Esq., U.S. Attorney, Office of the U.S. Attorney, Honolulu, Hawaii; the late Edward C. Brennan, Ph.D., Scranton, Pennsylvania; James Craine, Ph.D., Consultant, Hawaii State Neuropsychology Service; Frederick Lee Hall III, Esq., Veterans' Administration, Honolulu, Hawaii; William Kilauano, Vietnam Vet Center, Honolulu, Hawaii; James I. Morrow, MGySgt, USMC (Ret.), Tucson, Arizona; Terri Needels, Ph D, Private Practice, Honolulu, Hawaii; Eugene Shooter, Ph.D., Independent Practice, Washington, D.C., and Udo Undeutsch, Ph.D., University of Cologne, Germany.

The authors also acknowledge the collegial support and input of the following individuals for this second edition: Susan Carney, Gustavo Goldstein, M.D., Ellen Levin, D.W.S., Gila Nordman, L.C.S.W., Zrinka Tomic, all affiliated with Montgomery County, Maryland, Department of Health and Human Services; Stuart Grozbean, Esq., Independent Practice, Rockville, Maryland; Sandy Scheele, Gaithersburg, Maryland; and Robin J. Derwin, L.C.S.W. and Clara Fratantuono, both of the Prince George County, Maryland, Circuit Court.

Permission is gratefully acknowledged from *Child Development* and *Forensic Reports*, the source of a number of databased articles relevant to faked memory, to reproduce a variety of tables and figures. Contents of several other articles first appeared in the *American Journal of Forensic Psychology* and are so indicated. The American Psychiatric Press agreed to allow presentation of base rate data on hysterical pseudo-seizures, a vexing problem in deception analysis. John E. Reid and Associates allowed the reproduction of "The 9 Steps of Interrogation, In Brief," even though the authors have pronounced misgivings about using deception to uncover deception (see Chapter 14). Scrutinizing methods at close quarters represents the first step toward understanding and limiting such techniques.

This second edition of the book is the work of Drs. Hall and Poirier who sincerely acknowledge the major contributions of Dr. David A. Pritchard to the first edition.

Many thanks are due to students and colleagues who have attended workshops and case conferences on deception. Appreciation is expressed to the staff of the National Institute of Justice, which has spent much time and effort in generating deception-related base rate data, especially in regard to violence and substance abuse.

Harold V. Hall
Kamuela, HI
May, 2000

Joseph G. Poirier
Rockville, MD
May, 2000

Introduction

Deception refers to inducing a false belief in another. Deception is often successful and rewarded when undetected, and victims of deception are subject to its influence even when they know they are being duped. False praise and adoration, as well as concealing dislike and loathing, allow smooth interaction with others — a social lubricant. Friends, lovers, and family members lie to one another with regularity. Business people and politicians distort as part of their natural interactions with others. "In everyday life it is usually possible for the performer to create intentionally almost any kind of false impression without putting himself or herself in the indefensible position of having told a clear-cut lie. Communication techniques such as innuendo, strategic ambiguity, and crucial omissions allow the misinformer to profit from lies without, technically, telling any" (Goffman, 1959, p. 62).

Lying as a form of deception begins at a very early age. As presented in Chapter 2, at what age children are developmentally able to understand and engage in deceptive behavior is a very controversial issue among researchers. It is known that the ability to deceive is acquired early in life, and there is research associating the capacity for deception with the neurological maturation of the prefrontal cortex. Among other behavioral functions, the prefrontal cortex is believed to be where the executive function is neurologically localized (Zelazo, Carter, Reznick, & Frye, 1997). Executive function is a neurological construct that integrates various aspects of problem-solving behavior with the capacity for making volitional decisions. Deception is one possible behavioral outcome to resolving a problem situation. The ability to be deceptive begins in childhood and continues unabated into adolescence and adulthood. Deceptive behavior cuts across all socioeconomic tiers, educational groupings, career lines, and workplace settings and is seen in every area of human activity.

Nash (1976) provided a natural history of confidence games in America. Documented accounts include that of Dr. John Tennant of Virginia, one of a long line of "quacks" in this country, who provided rattlesnake root to cure pleurisy (1800). Some of the more bizarre, but successful, medical schemes in the 19th century included the two-part pill for tuberculosis. Here, the first part of the pill turned the urine bright green and frightened the person into taking the second part, made of licorice and saw palmetto. The litany of fraud continued with feeding bone-thin cattle herds salted food to fatten them before a sale (1815), fake inheritance con games (1835), bogus stock issuances (1854), police payoffs (1870), selling "sucker lists" to mail-order houses (1881), and the start of the "wire" — obtaining the results of a horse race before the bookmakers (1898). David Mauer's *The American Confidence Man* (1974), A. A. Leff's *Swindling and Selling* (1976), and Darwin Ortiz's *Gambling Scams* (1990) each provide additional descriptions of how the con game works.

False presentations of self and deliberate distortions of intentions are part of the fabric of social life. From innocuous efforts to "make a good impression" to complicated schemes of fraud to terrifying acts of violence, deception is an integral part of social interaction. The social science literature is replete with analyses of and commentaries on the varieties of human deception.

Between one third and two thirds of high-school and college students cheat (Collison, 1990a, b), with the majority of college faculty having observed such cheating (Jendrek, 1989). More than 85% of college students were found to be deceptive to their partners, almost all with regard to other relationships and with the justification that they wanted to protect their partners (Shusterman & Saxe, 1990). In the authors' experiences, much research with human subjects incorporates misleading, incomplete, or blatantly false instructions, rationalized by the belief that true knowledge of experimental procedures by subjects would bias results.

Confidence games and white-collar crime include forgery, counterfeiting, fraud, embezzlement, bribery, theft of services and trade secrets, smuggling, tax evasion, and now computer fraud. Always, the deceiver's position of fiduciary trust, power, or influence has provided the opportunity for exploitation. *The Dictionary of Criminal Justice Data Terminology* (U.S. Department of Justice, 1981) defines white-collar crime as:

> Nonviolent crime for financial gain committed by means of deception by persons whose occupational status is entrepreneurial, professional or semiprofessional and utilizing their special occupational skills and opportunities. Also, nonviolent crime for financial gain utilizing deception and committed by anyone having special technical and professional knowledge of business and government, irrespective of the person's occupation. (p. 215)

One very common but hidden form of white/blue-collar crime is theft by employees. Base rate studies of theft-at-work problems indicate that 26 to 42% of employees admit to stealing from their job, depending on whether the setting is a retail business, hospital, manufacturing company, fast-food restaurant, or supermarket (see reviews by Camara & Schneider, 1994; Dalton, Wimbush, & Daily, 1994; Jones & Terris, 1990). These investigators cite statistics that show (1) a $1.8 billion increase in industry inventory shrinkage from 1982 to 1987 and (2) a 50% reduction in shrinkage over an 18-month period during which integrity testing was initiated in a home improvement center (Jones & Terris, 1990). In general, employee theft is a prevalent problem that results in huge financial losses, and the thieving employees are almost never caught (Slora, 1989). An estimated 2 to 5% of each consumer dollar is necessary to offset losses from employee theft (Touby, 1994).

Baseline data for employee theft is very difficult to establish because of multiple variables. Businesses can accurately identify total cost of inventory loss, but determining exactly how the loss occurred is difficult. All loss by theft is illegal and the involved players cannot be expected to be forthcoming. Inventory losses, for example, can be due to internal theft by employees or to external loss by shoplifting or fraudulent claims regarding shipped merchandise (Green, 1997). The situation presents a thorny problem to the investigator. How can baseline data be accurately collected when criminal charges and individual job security are at stake (Camara & Schneider, 1994)?

Wimbush and Dalton (1997) recently described a unique design to estimate employee theft baseline data. The approach would appear to have implications for forensic assessment. The authors conducted a study involving over 750 employees. The research approach assured complete anonymity for the participants. Three protocols were utilized: a conventional survey instrument, a randomized-response technique (RRT), and an unmatched count technique (UCT). The conventional survey instrument asked questions about theft by the respondent and co-workers in the workplace and otherwise collected no further data. The RRT protocol asked the same questions about workplace theft as the conventional survey, but first the subjects would flip a coin. If the coin landed heads and if the subject had engaged in theft, a box on the form would be checked; otherwise, the box was left unchecked. Based on the 50% probability of the coin toss outcome, the theft rate could be statistically prorated. The third protocol of UCT required two groups of subjects and two differently formatted sets of questions. The two sets of questions included the same inquiries as the conventional survey and several additional innocuous inquiries. The two formats were unmatched, and the UCT baseline estimates were based on the "aggregation of correct statements" regarding the target issue (for further discussion of UCT, see Dalton, Wimbush, & Daily, 1994).

Wimbush and Dalton (1997) found marked convergence of baseline findings between the RRT and UCT data. The participants acknowledged employee theft exceeding 50%. Predictably, most acknowledged employee theft was at the lowest theft level (i.e., less than $10), such that if this theft level were eliminated from the data the overall employee theft rate would have been reduced by 50%. The authors noted that this estimate was very consistent with estimates in the theoretical literature. This study described a unique research approach to the problem of deception. The study allowed the direct assessment of a known area of human reliance on deception without the deception of the perpetrator participants (see ethical guidelines for research, American Psychological Association, 1992).

Virtually all forms of violence involve deception. In burglary, concealment, hiding the actual, and blending into the environment are commonplace. Robbery often involves faking "good," shown by innocuous approach behaviors, followed by faking "bad," such as when the robber pretends to hold a pistol to the victim's back. Kidnapping also uses a combination of faking good and bad, as when the location of the victim is concealed, coupled with threats to harm the victim for noncompliance. Victims and their significant others can ill-afford to test whether the perpetrators are bluffing and, in some instances, are not sophisticated enough to be able to do so. Child sexual abuse relies on a calculated seduction of the child victim into trusting the older perpetrator.

Rape often involves substantial stalking and verbiage designed to lull the victim into complacency, and usually occurs at night or behind visual barriers. Date rape involves considerable trauma to the victim in spite of acquaintance with the rapist. Some serial rapists use a combination of faking good and bad, as Ted Bundy did when he concealed his intent to kill and had victims carry his books to his car because of his "broken" arm.

Just as in everyday life, deception is successful in many types of violence, perhaps partially explaining why the report rate is so low. People do not report what they believe will not result in direct action by authorities. Many violent offenders interviewed by the writers speak of how easy it is to commit violence and get away with it. They usually get caught when they do not practice deception, when they become substance intoxicated or impulsive, and when the critical processes necessary for high-grade deception are impaired. Even murder, often considered a crime of passion and therefore easily solved, has a 70 to 80% clearance rate where the probable perpetrator is identified and brought into custody. At the outset, this means that about 20 to 30% of the murders in this country are successfully concealed in terms of the identity of the killers.

Detecting Malingering and Deception: The Revised Forensic Distortion Analysis (FDA) focuses on the detection of deception in one important situation: the forensic evaluation. To date, the clinical/forensic literature has not yielded a lucid, organized approach to the overall analysis and detection of faked behavior in forensic situations. Although individual techniques for detecting deception in the forensic evaluation have been evaluated (Rogers, 1988, 1997), no organized plan of detection has been offered. As this edition of the book attempts to establish, the field is slowly inching forward with new, creative, and increasingly effective methodologies in a variety of areas, but a universally relevant, unifying model is still lacking.

This book discusses and demonstrates individual clinical and testing methods that may be applied readily to a wide variety of forensic situations. But more importantly, it suggests a framework for integrating data on deception from multiple sources. Application guidelines and common errors to avoid in deception analysis are presented to forensic evaluators of various disciplines in the civil and/or criminal justice systems. The focus is on the overall problems of detecting deception, supporting one's conclusions, and communicating findings, rather than on specific techniques alone.

A sound method of deception analysis is proposed whereby the most likely target symptoms and response styles of the client are scrutinized, which then suggest specific detection methods. Topics in this book include (1) a general model of deception analysis; (2) applications in civil and criminal law; (3) psychometrics and structured interviewing; (4) forms and report language; (5) denied or minimized conditions: amnesia, dangerousness, sensory loss; (6) specific malingered conditions: pain, psychosis, post-traumatic stress; and (7) recent advances in the detection of deception: forced choice, explicit alternative testing, and neurocognitive assessment.

FDA is defined generically as a set of interlocking procedures designed to answer focal questions relevant to deception. The definitional inclusion of *forensic* in FDA refers to the application of psychological principles to civil and criminal law; the word *distortion* implies that nondeliberate distortion must be considered before offering statements regarding intentional deception.

The purposes of FDA are as follows:

1. To examine the reliability and validity of database information;
2. To detect the possible existence of misrepresentation;
3. To determine the response style(s) utilized by the client;
4. To determine the magnitude of distortion;
5. To place symptoms, behaviors, or mental conditions associated with deception into clear perspective;
6. To offer a model of understanding and accounting for discrepancies and distortions;
7. To generate hypotheses for further evaluation/investigation;
8. To communicate the decision path and the findings of FDA to the referral source;
9. To eventually standardize the deception analysis process.

Metaphorically, FDA is an attempt to induce meaning from nebulous forms within shadows in an effort to distinguish illusive response styles within equally illusive mental conditions and psychological patterns. As difficult as it may sound, however, distortion analysis is possible.

PROFESSIONAL MISCONCEPTIONS REGARDING DECEPTION

Throughout the history of the mental health/law disciplines, beliefs about faking have been characterized by ignorance and vanity. People are naive about deception. They believe that they can tell if someone is deceiving them and that it does not happen very often. Actually, people are lousy at lie-catching. That is why deception is generally successful. Although successive advances in distortion analysis have dispelled some misconceptions, others persist as follows:

1. *Most spoken words and behavior can be taken at face value*. Actually, as shall be seen, most people distort, either unintentionally or intentionally. Popular surveys reveal that over 90% of average Americans say that they lie regularly (Gates, 1991). Many forensic professionals believe that distortion does not usually occur. They do not look for it. In the helping disciplines, false negatives may be less of an issue, but it is a problem when forensic issues are involved. Malingering has been confirmed or suspected in more than 20% of criminal defendants, with another 5% showing substantial unintentional distortion (Rogers, 1988). The deception rates for litigants in civil actions may be even higher.
2. *Malingering, when it does occur, means that the faker is mentally sick*. Desperate people often resort to desperate measures to survive or adapt. A person who fakes insanity is not necessarily mentally ill, but may want to avoid prison, a soul-destroying place under the best of conditions. As will be discussed, malingerers in general have good reality contact and are not psychotic. This myth may have been reinforced by the need to see psychopathology in liars when defendants or clients are misdiagnosed.
3. *The evaluator cannot be fooled (other people can)*. A favorite trick in cross-examination of experts is the following (Ziskin, 1981, p. 100):
   Q. And it is possible for an individual to deceive you, isn't it?
   A. Yes, it is possible, but I don't think that I am fooled very often.
   Q. Well, if someone was successful in fooling you, you wouldn't know that he or she had fooled you, would you?
   Melvin Belli, the famed litigator attorney, recounts a case where a woman allegedly slipped on a greasy sauce on the floor of a restaurant, suffering a crippling hand injury. She was the ideal witness, "everybody's grandmother," giving a pitiful account about how she could no longer play the church organ until she bolted out of the courtroom when the defense attorney showed how she collected $500,000 on a similar case in Florida. Belli used this case to illustrate how honest his clients are, and how he was duped for the first time in 60 years of practicing law (Gates, 1991).

Traditionally, health and legal professionals have not been very good at detecting faking (Ekman & O'Sullivan, 1991). Worse yet, an inverse relationship has been suggested from research: the greater the confidence, the lower the accuracy in detecting faking. Recent investigations have raised promise, however, that with certain professional groups and with specialized training, deception detection can be significantly enhanced (Ekman, O'Sullivan, & Frank, 1999).

The writers would like to believe that they are not fooled by forensic clients, given their experience and knowledge of the literature. The fact is that they would be fooled frequently without cross-validating data and standardized testing. A recent case illustrates this point:

> Defendant Stardowsky, examined for criminal responsibility, stated to the examiner that the glow in the right side of his brain was quite clearly unequal to that in the left hemisphere. Forces of good (FOG) and forces of the enemy (FOE) operated in the jail where he was incarcerated for robbery. "The police hacked off my arms and legs; it's a good thing I didn't try to get away." Visual hallucinations of personages were affirmed, providing the basis for his Prolixin medication and schizophrenic diagnosis by the correctional facility medical staff. Several days later, the investigating probation officer revealed that the defendant's mental problems had never been raised as an issue in his 100-plus burglaries and robberies over the last 10 years. His parents pointed out that the accused had been playing the FOG and FOE story since the fourth grade, but only when he wanted to get out of trouble.

4. *The* Diagnostic and Statistical Manual, *4th ed. (DSM-IV) criteria for malingering allow for deception analysis.* DSM-IV states that malingering should be diagnosed if any combination of the following is shown (American Psychiatric Association, 1994, p. 683):

(1) medicolegal context of presentation, e.g., the person's being referred by his or her attorney to the physician for examination;

(2) marked discrepancy between the person's claimed stress of disability and the objective findings;

(3) lack of cooperation during the diagnostic evaluation and in complying with the prescribed treatment regimen;

(4) the presence of Antisocial Personality Disorder.

However, these criteria are clinically inadequate. They fail to distinguish distorting influences such as evaluation anxiety and fatigue from deliberate deception; they emphasize exaggeration and fabrication of symptoms to the neglect of denial and defensiveness; they associate deliberate deception with a personality type rather than with a person in a situation. The reader is cautioned not to use the DSM-IV operational definition of malingering (Rogers, 1990).

5. *Some conditions, such as amnesia, hallucinations, and post-traumatic reactions, are easily faked and nearly impossible to prove.* As will be presented, empirical methods can detect faked amnesia with varying degrees of accuracy. Hallucinations are hard to disprove; yet base rates for comparison and decision criteria are available to assist the evaluator. Post-traumatic stress disorder (PTSD) can be assessed by psychometrics or arousal methods with built-in features to assess deception.

6. *Detecting faking is an art and cannot be taught.* Actually, the reverse appears to be true. Following a few simple rules increases the accuracy rate substantially. Deception analysis is a trainable skill. Workshops and clinical experiences over the years reveal that the average professional can be taught to adequately detect faking in a relatively short period.

Instructional material on deception analysis is embedded in the evaluation of (1) fitness to proceed and criminal responsibility (Hall, 1985, 1986); (2) post-traumatic stress disorder (Hall &

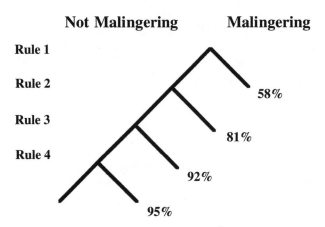

Not Malingering   **Malingering**

Rule 1

Rule 2   58%

Rule 3

                                              81%

Rule 4

                                        92%

                              95%

FIGURE I.1 Classification of pseudo-malingerers using multistage rules.

Hall, 1987); (3) neuropsychological impairment (Hall & McNinch, 1988; Hall & Sbordone, 1993); (4) mitigating defenses to murder (Hall, 1990); and (5) dangerousness (Hall, 1982, 1984; Hall et al., 1984). Detection tools include the MMPI, MMPI-2, and MMPI-A as part of a comprehensive evaluation (Shooter & Hall, 1989; Pope, Butcher, & Seelen, 2000), as well as process guidelines for deception analysis as a specific focus of inquiry (Hall, 1985; Paulsen & Hall, 1991).

Forced-choice testing and its later variants for deception provide a quick example of teaching others to detect deception. Learning a few statistical decision rules allows the evaluator to obtain a high degree of accuracy in assessing faked memory deficits. A series of investigations highlights the ease of learning how to administer the procedure and to interpret results (Hall & Shooter, 1989; Shooter & Hall, 1990; Hall et al., 1991). Figure I.1 shows the cumulative (nonoverlapping) accuracy with which pseudo-malingering subjects in these three studies can be classified. By using one decision rule, only 58% of the subjects were correctly identified as "malingering." However, using multiple decision rules in a sequential strategy increased the positive hit rate to 95%.

APPLICATIONS

Deception analysis is a foundational issue in applied forensics. Table 1 presents a number of clinical/forensic situations in which deception is a key issue (Hall, 1990). The emphasis of this book is on civil and criminal law applications.

DECEPTIVE SIGNS

What are the signs of deception? What do evaluators look for? Traditionally, the two most common factors are consistency and history. Does the subject present an inconsistent story of relevant events? Is there a positive history of misrepresentation? Unless inconsistencies are specific and replicable, they are of small value in demonstrating deception. Knowing that the assessee deceived others in the past is likewise of little help. Almost everyone has a substantial history of misrepresentation. High-achievement-oriented children (i.e., future leaders of society) actually seem to cheat more than their peers, perhaps to maintain their high status and other rewards that come from performing well academically (Grinder, 1961; Mischel & Gilligan, 1964). Adults are no better, as the above evaluations demonstrated. Modern society appears to offer daily opportunities for distortion of the truth. Skill at faking may even be positively related to success in some professions, at least in Western society.

Too many false positives emerge when applying the historical criteria — erroneously describing individuals as deceptive. This holds true when there is a history of criminality. Previous arrests,

TABLE 1
Applications of Deception Analysis

Criminal	Civil	Clinical
Identification of perpetrators	Competency exams	Selection for treatment
Competency to proceed	Witness credibility	Readiness for discharge
Criminal responsibility	Child custody and divorce actions	Treatment motivation
Dangerousness prediction	Personal injury and wrongful death	Transference and countertransference
	Employment screening and dishonesty	Honesty of collaterals
	Eligibility for disability benefits	Community monitoring of treatment

charges, convictions, or incarceration for crimes may not be helpful in determining whether the individual is at present deceiving in a specific context. Associating a history of maladaptive behavior with current faking is conceptually hazardous in another sense. A circular quality to utilizing history and mental illness or criminality emerges. Faking is seen as a symptom of maladaptation; proof that a person is mentally ill or criminal is taken as an indication of a tendency to distort and deceive. All this violates a basic premise of this book — that deception is adaptive and both cross- and intrasituation specific.

History, however, can be validly scrutinized in two ways. Are there contradictions between the reported and actual history of an individual? Differences are suspicious after mitigating factors, such as head trauma or drunkenness, are taken into account. The second way history can be scrutinized concerns whether or not a close "goodness of fit" exists between the relevant act and method (e.g., providing drugs to minors to obtain sex) and previous acts of the same kind.

A model of deception is presented in this book. Briefly, the evaluator first considers target symptoms of the faker selected in congruence with goal achievement. A veteran may malinger the intensity of his or her PTSD to obtain a higher service-connected compensation. Another may deny a history of violence to receive a lighter sentence for assault. A plaintiff may fake memory loss to obtain a large monetary settlement. A defendant may fake insanity to achieve exculpation and, hence, avoid penal incarceration. The task for the evaluator is to tap into these cognitive targets to determine whether they have led to faked or honest behavior.

The second part of the model deals with the response patterns of the deceiver, which fortunately cluster into variations of concealing the real or presenting the fake. The following response patterns seem most indicative of faking:

1. *A rapid improvement when external incentives change or when weak environmental triggers are presented.* A waxing or waning of response intensity is suspicious when it is in harmony with environmental events such as when the deceiver knows he or she is being observed.
2. *Response patterns not congruent with neuropsychological or psychological conditions or symptoms.* This often involves the violation of anatomical laws (e.g., loss of feeling across widely separated sites allegedly due to spinal injury rather than according to expected deficits). Neuropsychological principles may also be suspiciously disregarded (e.g., loss of crystallized knowledge in presence of ability to learn and short-term recall skills).
3. *Critical behaviors during the interview such as absurd responses, unlikely combinations, and contradictory responses.* Although not definitive by themselves, these critical behaviors should alert the evaluator to conduct a more intensive search for indicators of deception.

Detection methods are the third and last part of the FDA model. These include (1) variation from expected performance (e.g., errors on simple questions, violation of learning curves, deviant scores on parallel testing), (2) validity indicators (e.g., random patterns, subtle vs. obvious discrepancies), (3) failure on tests specifically designed to assess deception (e.g., Explicit Alternative Testing, tests of illusory difficulty), and (4) clinical intuitive hypotheses based on forensic training and experience.

For each faked condition discussed in this book, a synopsis of methods is provided at the end of the chapter. This will provide explicit guidelines on detecting deception. New directions, which may have fundamental impact on FDA, are discussed. This includes neurocognitive assessment and computerized versions of forced choice, utilizing multiple decision rules. In the final analysis, it is hoped that a practical method of detecting deception will emerge from this inquiry.

As a starting point, this book attempts to equip the evaluator with data and procedures to answer relevant questions concerning deception. Several critical questions in every assessment of deception are as follows:

1. Am I properly trained to conduct an FDA? Have ethical issues in this case been considered?
2. What events triggered a referral for a deception analysis? What happened at that time?
3. Did unintentional distortion occur during the critical forensic event or evaluation? What is the source of that distortion and how was it measured?
4. Has the assessee engaged in deliberate deception? How is that known? Is the deception associated with the past, the present, or both?
5. What is the magnitude of the faking? Quantitatively or qualitatively, how can I demonstrate the degree of faking uncovered?
6. Does the present deception differ from that shown previously by the assessee? What is the assessee's history of deception in similar situations?
7. What are the possible inducements to deceive for this particular forensic situation?
8. What is the deception response style shown by the client? Behaviorally, which variation of malingering or defensiveness is shown?
9. Who were, are, or will be the most likely targets of deception?
10. Which feedback mechanism can I suggest to assist future evaluators of this person's possible deception?
11. How can I fairly and accurately represent this person's possible deception to the referring party or trier of fact?

REFERENCES

American Psychiatric Association. (1994). *Diagnostic and statistical manual of mental disorders* (4th ed., rev.), Washington, DC: Author.

American Psychological Association. (1992). Ethical principles of psychologists and code of conduct. *American Psychologist, 47*, 1597–1611.

Camara, W. J., & Schneider, D. L. (1994). Integrity tests: Facts and unresolved issues. *American Psychologist, 49*, 112–119.

Collison, M. N.-K. (1990a). Apparent rise in students' cheating has college officials worried. *Chronicle of Higher Education*, A33–A34.

Collison, M. N-K. (1990b). Survey at Rutgers suggests that cheating may be on the rise in large universities. *Chronicle of Higher Education*, A31–A32.

Dalton, D. R., Wimbush, J. C., & Daily, C. M. (1994). Using the unmatched count technique (UCT). *Personnel Psychology, 47*, 817–828.

Ekman, P., & O'Sullivan, M. (1991). Who can catch a liar? *American Psychologist, 46*(9), 913–920.

Ekman, P., O'Sullivan, M., & Frank, M. G. (1999). A few can catch a liar. *Psychological Science, 10*(3), 263–266.

Gates, M. (1991). It's healthy to always be honest (Wait, we lied!), *Newhouse News Service*, Honolulu Star-Bulletin, Honolulu, HI.

Goffman, E. (1959). *The Presentation of Self in Everyday Life*. Garden City, New York: Doubleday.

Green, G. S. (1997). *Occupational Crime* (2nd ed.). Chicago: Nelson-Hall.

Grinder, R. (1961). New techniques for research in children's temptation behavior. *Child Development, 32,* 679–688.

Hall, H. V. (1982). Dangerousness prediction and the maligned forensic professional: Suggestions for estimating true basal violence. *Criminal Justice and Behavior, 9,* 3–12.

Hall, H. V. (1984). Predicting dangerousness for the courts. *American Journal of Forensic Psychology, 2,* 5–25.

Hall, H. V. (1985). Cognitive and volitional capacity assessment: A proposed decision tree. *American Journal of Forensic Psychology, 3,* 3–17.

Hall, H. V. (1986). The forensic distortion analysis: A proposed decision tree and report format. *American Journal of Forensic Psychology, 4,* 31–59.

Hall, H. V. (1990). *Truth or lies: Guidelines for detecting malingering and deception.* Psychological Consultants and Forest Institute of Professional Psychology Workshop, East-West Center, University of Hawaii, Honolulu.

Hall, H. V., Catlin, E., Boissevain, A., & Westgate, J. (1984). Dangerous myths about predicting dangerousness. *American Journal of Forensic Psychology, 2,* 173–193.

Hall, H. V., & Hall, F. L. (1987). Post-traumatic stress disorder as a legal defense in criminal trials. *American Journal of Forensic Psychology, 5,* 45–53.

Hall, H. V., & McNinch, D. (1988). Linking crime-specific behavior to neuropsychological impairment. *International Journal of Clinical Neuropsychology, 10,* 113–122.

Hall, H. V., & Sbordone, R. (Eds.). (1993). *Forensic neuropsychology of executive deficits: Civil and criminal law applications.* Orlando, FL: Paul M. Deutsch Press.

Hall, H. V., & Shooter, E. (1989). Explicit alternative testing for feigned memory deficits. *Forensic Reports, 2,* 277–286.

Hall, H. V., Shooter, E., Craine, J., & Paulsen, S. (1991). Explicit alternative testing for claimed visual recall deficits: A trilogy of studies. *Forensic Reports, 4*(3), 259–279.

Jendrek, M. P. (1989). Faculty reactions to academic dishonesty. *Journal of College Student Development, 30,* 401–406.

Jones, J. J. & Terris, W. (1990). Integrity testing for personnel selection: An overview. *Forensic Reports, 4,* 117–140.

Leff, A. A. (1976). *Swindling and selling.* New York: The Free Press.

Mauer, D. (1974). *The American confidence man.* Springfield, IL: Charles C Thomas.

Mischel, W., & Gilligan, C. (1964). Delay of gratification, motivation for the prohibited gratification, and response to temptation. *Journal of Abnormal Social Psychology, 4,* 411–417.

Nash, J. R. (1976). *Hustlers and con men.* New York: M. Evans & Co.

Ortiz, D. (1990). *Gambling scams.* New York: Carol Publishing.

Paulsen, S., & Hall, H. V. (1991). Common sense process factors in deception analysis. *Forensic Reports, 4,* 37–39.

Pope, K. S., Butcher, J. N., & Seelen, J. (2000) *The MMPI, MMPI-2, MMPI-A in court: A practical guide for expert witnesses and attorneys.* Washington, DC: American Psychological Association.

Rogers, R. (Ed.). (1988). *Clinical assessment of malingering and deception.* New York: Guilford Press.

Rogers, R. (1990). Models of feigned mental illness. *Professional Psychology: Research and Practice, 21,* 3, 182–188.

Rogers, R. (Ed.) (1997). *Clinical assessment of malingering and deception.* New York: Guilford Press.

Shooter, E., & Hall, H. V. (1989). Distortion analysis on the MMPI and MMPI-2. *Bulletin of the American Academy of Forensic Psychology, 10,* 9.

Shooter, E., & Hall, H. V. (1990). Explicit alternative testing for deliberate distortion. Towards an abbreviated format. *Forensic Reports, 4,* 45–49.

Shusterman, G. & Saxe, L. (1990). *Deception in romantic relationships.* Unpublished manuscript. Brandeis University, Boston.

Slora, K. (1989). An empirical approach to determining employee deviance base rates. *Journal of Business and Psychology, 4,* 199–219.

Touby, L. (1994). In the company of thieves. *Journal of Business Strategy, 15*(3), 24–35.

U.S. Department of Justice (1981). *Dictionary of Criminal Justice Terminology*. (2nd ed., NCJ-76939), p. 215. Washington, DC: Bureau of Justice Statistics.

Wimbush, J., & Dalton, D. R. (1997). Base rate for employee theft: Convergence of multiple methods. *Journal of Applied Psychology, 82*(5), 756–763.

Zelazo, P. D., Carter, A., Reznick, J. S., & Frye, D. (1997). Early development of executive function: A problem-solving framework. *Review of General Psychology, 1*(2), 198–226.

Ziskin, J. (1981). *Coping with psychiatric and psychological testimony* (3rd ed., Vols. 1–2). Beverly Hills, CA: Law and Psychology Press.

Part I

Background, Theory, and Method in Deception Analysis

1 Foundational Issues in Deception

Deception in various forms is a pervasive phenomenon among living organisms. This chapter, reviews deception in human affairs as a background to the primary focus of deception in forensic applications. Chapter 6 examines deception in nonhuman organisms to understand the most rudimentary features of deception and how such phenomena offer ontogenetic clues to the understanding of human deception. Subsequent chapters examine the human developmental stages of understanding and engaging in deception. Psychophysiological and nonverbal correlates of deception will also be reviewed.

Deception is widespread in human affairs. Although they are the subject of historical exposure and reviling, conjuring, confidence games, and psychic fraud are still popular ventures (Wiseman, 1996). Some of these activities are offered in recreational form, such as at carnivals and community fairs. Other forms of these activities involve high-stake, white-collar crime. Still other variations are media-promoted puffery; millions of public dollars are bilked for gain of the promoters. From the con man to the politician, the cheating spouse, the delinquent adolescent, and the military strategist, things are made to appear other than they actually are. Such deception in everyday life has been raised to a high art in contemporary society.

This chapter explores a variety of perspectives on deception, which help to define the scope, context, and study of human deception. Second, the chapter describes police and military deception as examples of the most developed, systematic use of deception. Third, the chapter discusses deception in the socialization process and its pervasive effect on personality. Fourth, the chapter looks at the ethics of deception as debated by moral philosophers and professional organizations. Last, the chapter presents suggestions for evaluating and using research results on deception.

A single, coherent field theory of deception is possible if it can interface across disciplines and account for the entire range of faking and falsehood. Once classification and theory building have begun, application and prediction can better proceed. Thus, this chapter considers deception from a variety of human perspectives. The strategies of police and military planners provide a systematic description of successful deceptive practices in socialization and serve as a reminder that everyone is both a giver and a receiver of deception. The views of ethicists will aid in evaluating the use of deception to detect the deceivers, and a review of principles of research interpretation will help to distinguish theory building from applied detection. There can be no deception without an entity to deceive. As a corollary, all falsehood is interactional and all interpersonal transactions are subject to deception. Intentional deception always involves representing the target's situation, maintaining the target as somehow appealing, and keeping it apart from the truth.

Psychologists, psychiatrists, and others in the helping professions have, with few exceptions, performed miserably in understanding this phenomenon. Prior to the 1990s, researchers in the social sciences ignored deception or viewed it as situation dependent. Other investigators see it as a stable trait cutting across many contexts. Actually, it may be both. Trait conceptualizations of human behavior have validity. Crime profiling is built entirely on trait descriptors of the perpetrator from crime scene characteristics, for example, and has yielded some remarkable solutions in individual cases. Since the early 1990s, and now entering the 21st century, there has been a significant surge of interest, both theoretical and empirical, in deceptive behavior. For forensic clinicians much of this new interest can be traced to developments in the legal arena, such as landmark cases dealing with violent crime and risk assessment (see Chapter 23), child abuse and family violence (see Chapter 7), sexual harassment (see Chapter 10), and violence by adolescents (see Chapter 8).

Interest in the problem of deception has also captured the disfavored eye of the public. Deception in marital/significant-other relationships has received considerable exploitive media attention as well as the attention of researchers interested in effective repair strategies (Aune, Metts, & Hubbard, 1998). The deliberate deception regarding HIV transmission and AIDS risk factors has created heightened professional and public concern about this problem (Brody, 1995; Latkin, Vlahov, & Anthony, 1993; Latkin & Vlahov, 1998).

The long-standing perception of the political world as being rife with deceptive practice has become a passively accepted tradition. A rash of high-profile scandals by popular political figures, e.g., the Kennedy brothers, President Nixon, President Clinton, has brought considerable attention to prominent national political figures in recent years. Moore (1996) commented on the "rhetorical subterfuge" of Senator Bob Packwood's public response to charges of sexual misconduct. Moore lamented that such maneuverings diluted any effectual response by the public who should be the most potent critics.

Self-deception intertwines with deception as deliberate falsity merges with unintentional distortion. The lines get fuzzy in the literature and in practical application. For the most part, it does not matter what type of distortion one is dealing with if testable hypotheses are generated from the evaluation.

Cross-disciplinary concepts and methods are used in this book to understand deception. These include ideas from biology, philosophy, neuropsychology, developmental psychology, industrial psychology, cognitive science, and sociology. Statistics and probability theory are employed when appropriate. As was discussed in the introductory chapter, industrial psychology researchers have developed promising new data collection approaches with the problem of employee theft based on *randomized response* and *unmatched count* techniques. The binomial probability distribution, as another example, provides the underpinnings for forced-choice testing. Thus, as will be expanded upon later, if a claimant asserts loss of sensory ability as a compensable disorder due to an auto accident, the evaluator can compare total responses to expected responses. Detection rates for faking are quite favorable, now in excess of 90% for a variety of subpopulation groups.

Historically, most investigation in deception was in detection technology-observational schemes, paper-and-pencil tests, polygraphy, "truth" serum, and so forth. The justification ranged from the cost of dishonest employees to the need of governments to conceal information for security reasons. In mental health, the justification was to provide better treatment, but the revenue-driven goals of managed care in the 1990s created additional justification to identifying both providers and consumers who attempted to deceive the carrier. In forensic contexts, the evaluation of litigants has been justified by the need to provide the trier of fact with accurate information. In more recent years, this forensic justification has been expanded by public demand to protect the community from offenders, both adult and juveniles, who have histories of violent and/or predatory behavior.

The assertion by some that near absolute prediction (of deception) accuracy can never be achieved may be an endangered assumption. Saxe (1991) predicts, for example, that such development is a fantasy because honesty is situational and because "[i]ndividuals have too many options available to encode their thoughts for us to be able to probe what they choose to hide." Technologies from the 1980s, such as DNA fingerprinting and P300 wave analysis, are nearly 100% accurate. The latter method is based on brain waves associated with stimulus familiarity rather than arousal, as in polygraphy, voice stress analysis, and penile plethysmography (Farwell, 1990; Farwell & Donchin, 1986, 1988, 1989).

DNA sampling of bodily fluids and tissues became vogue with the circumstances of the O.J. Simpson trial. Now 5 years later, and at the turn of the century, there is a national impetus to make DNA analysis the premier forensic tool of the 21st century. At present, all states require DNA samples from sex offenders, 40 states require samples for offenses against children, and 35 states for murder (Gugliotta, 1999). The DNA sampling requirements for other offenses vary widely from state to state. In the midst of the scurry over DNA analysis, defense attorneys are noting implicit infringement of Fourth Amendment rights to privacy. At the current time, there are few laws or guidelines regulating DNA sampling, although this will clearly change as use of the technology continues to expand. At present, a DNA sample can be used and then stored indefinitely; one obvious fear is the use/misuse of a stored sample in a subsequent legal matter other than that for which it was originally intended.

In October 1998, the FBI opened a national DNA database; the combined DNA database (CODIS) currently contains approximately 184,000 samples. This compares diminutively to the 226 million fingerprint cards of the FBI Criminal Justice Information Services Division (Gugliotta, 1999). The growth of CODIS in the near future is predicted to be exponential. The FBI fingerprint database, in the meantime, has not entered obsolescence. The FBI recently inaugurated a computerized fingerprint analysis system called the Integrated Automated Fingerprint Identification System (IAFIS) (Walsh, 1999). This system greatly accelerates the tedious process of matching fingerprints with the 34 million (i.e., of the total 226 million database) fingerprint cards that have been submitted over the years by law enforcement agencies. The IAFIS will greatly enhance timely criminal checks and civil background checks. The FBI receives approximately 50,000 requests per day for fingerprint checks, divided approximately evenly between criminal cases and civilian background checks. It is important to note that the foregoing technologies, albeit impressively accurate, are still indirect, after-the-fact measures of human deception in criminal matters. Direct assessment of the cognitive and volitional processes involved in deception is the nub of real deception assessment. Nonetheless, an unrelenting advance of technological developments is enhancing knowledge of deception detection.

In an effort to address some on these looming problems prompted by the advances of DNA technology, Attorney General Janet Reno directed the National Justice Institute to establish a commission to study the most effective ways to use DNA evidence. The National Commission on the Future of DNA Evidence was created in 1998 (Asplen, 1999).

Forensic professionals and investigators face a moral dilemma much like researchers and practitioners in the physical sciences in their development of more accurate technologies. The increased tendencies by institutions and individuals to exploit others through deceptive means should cause real concern to the practicing professional. This issue of "too little" vs. "too much" accuracy and at what cost, in terms of intrusiveness, has raised multiple concerns. It is not ethically appropriate for deception researchers to "deceive" suspected "deceivers" justified in the name of research, or justified in the forensic effort to determine the "truth." The quest to detect deception requires a prudent balancing of seeking accuracy with diligent adherence to ethical mandates. This critical theme will be reiterated throughout this book.

PROTO-THEORY AND EARLY WORK ON DECEPTION

Deception has traditionally been viewed as ubiquitous and adaptive in nature (see Dessoir, 1893; Binet, 1896; Jastrow, 1900). Some early conceptualizations viewed deception as originating in a universal instinct in the context of natural selection. Triplett (1900), a fellow at Clark University, explored magical tricks as his model for deception, stating that conjuring:

> [R]ests upon a universal instinct of deception — a biological tendency appearing throughout the animal world from simple forms to the highest orders, which acts as a constant force in the process of natural

selection — as a means of preserving the self or species. This instinct, blind enough at the beginning, and to be classed as a deception only by reason of its effect, in the higher orders becomes implicated with an ever-increasing intelligence, ending with the conscious deceptions of man which in him, find their widest range and their highest form. (p. 441)

According to Triplett, human deception traces its roots to mimicry, and conjuring is just one manifestation. In addition to revealing the secrets of known magical tricks in specific detail, Triplett commented on deceiver and target characteristics. The production of passive attention in the target was seen as essential for effective deception, implying that successful deception covaried with increased suggestibility of the target. The effect of conjuring should never be announced, and no trick should be presented twice, lest the target "catch on."

The best deceivers were seen as self-confident, highly disciplined, competent, socially graced, and given to planning. They should never rest on their laurels, and to achieve the best effect, should present deceptions in graduated form — each one more impactful than the previous. Thus, a strong achievement orientation is required. Triplett saw every teacher as some sort of conjurer, presaging qualities found in today's successful professionals. The same traits are mentioned today in describing excellent therapists, investigators, and forensic professionals across many disciplines.

Psychological work on deception emerged in the early 1900s before its promise ebbed. In a thought-provoking review of the deception literature, Hyman (1989) described the demise and resurgence of interest in this area as follows:

Human deception deals with the correspondences between internal representations and external reality. The behavioristic psychology that dominated American psychology from the early 1900s until the cognitive revolution in the late 1950s had no room for mentalism of any kind, including the intentionalism inherent in psychology of deception. Although those early accounts relied heavily on the prevailing associationalistic psychology, the principles they illustrate have aged surprisingly well and harmonize with the contemporary view of cognitive psychology. (p. 133)

Principles of deception discussed by Hyman from the early works include:

1. Perceptions are inferred from sensory input and are therefore subject to distortion. People have perceptual guidelines regarding what constitutes reality, usually based on the most probable event, and deceivers capitalize upon these expectations.
2. Knowledge of deception does not equal action to escape, avoid, or expose falsehood. The early literature is replete with examples in which deception was seen as positive (e.g., "white lies") or actually sought after (e.g., as in a magic show).
3. The notion of the invited inferences has relevance. A deceiver should lead targets into the desired outcome rather than tell them what they should believe or what the result will be.

Rogers (1990a) restated the adaptive nature of deception:

Inclusion criteria for the classification of malingering are shaped and largely predetermined by our explanatory theories. Current theories have postulated the motivation to malinger is either the product of under-lying psychopathology (pathogenic model) or criminal backgrounds (DSM III-R model). I have proposed a third model that malingering is typically an adaptive response to adverse circumstances which may best be understood in the context of decision theory. (p. 327)

Later in this chapter, still more recent commentary by Rogers regarding his efforts to refine thinking regarding appropriate contemporary models of malingering will be described.

DECEPTION AND MENTAL HEALTH PRACTITIONERS

In an effort to document the pervasive nature of deception the authors are, alas, compelled to acknowledge that even their mental health brethren are not immune from its sinister reach. The mental health delivery system is modeled after the medical system in many ways, and this includes record-keeping and fee-reimbursement procedures. The medical field has long been under scrutiny because of erroneous or falsified medical reports and illicit billing practices. The mental health field has also had to contend with these problems that can lull practitioners into deceptive practice. The elusive nature of psychological symptoms and the progressively restrictive climate of managed care reimbursement is an inducement for mental health practitioners to engage in the practice of fraudulent claims (Kirk & Kutchins, 1988; Maesen, 1991).

Part of the problem arises because mental health syndromes and services are not as readily defined as those in physical health. The removal of a diseased organ is relatively easy to document with a pathology report. Similarly, the surgical procedure lends itself to objective description. By comparison, the psychotherapeutic treatment of a recurrent depressive disorder is far more intangible in terms of syndrome definition and what will be involved to provide adequate diagnosis and treatment. The difficulties involved in defining psychological syndromes will be revisited in later chapters that deal with the likelihood of deception in claims of psychological injury (Chapter 10) and malingered pain (Chapter 12).

There is also a problem when insurance coverage does not reimburse for certain kinds of treatments; common examples are marital and family therapies, which are not viewed as necessary to treat bona fide "medical conditions." Pope (1990) addressed ethical issues regarding deceptive record keeping and billing as psychological practice expands into the hospital setting. The ethical perils of deceptive or perceived deceptive practice facing forensic mental health clinicians are also well documented (Bersoff, 1995, 1999; Canter et al., 1994; Poirier, 1999).

DECEPTION AND THE POLICE

Undercover and interrogation activities by police authorities are notorious examples of deception activities that society passively accepts as legitimate. In the landmark *Miranda v. Arizona* (1966) case, the court was sufficiently concerned with the risks of interrogation to establish the still-standing precedent of defendants' being warned of their rights prior to interrogation. Defendants are advised that whatever they say can be used against them. It should be noted that Miranda rights extend to all aspects of the pretrial process including court-ordered evaluations by mental health clinicians.

Undercover persons are solicited from the ranks of arrestees because they have valuable contacts in the criminal world. Selected arrestees are typically well known to the police from prior arrests. Defendants selected for undercover work are often without funds for legal representation. Also, the promise of mitigating consideration with respect to pending charges can be enticing to arrestees who are encouraged to cooperate even by legal counsel. Much of this activity occurs "unofficially," which adds considerable risk for undercover persons. The authors have also evaluated arrestees and defendants who were paid to do undercover work.

Interrogation activities are another example of calculated deception by police. Gudjonsson and Petursson (1991) suggested that three primary factors contributed to suspect confession: internal pressures, external pressures, and supporting data regarding the suspect's complicity. Leo (1996) reviewed data, conducted fieldwork observations, and participated in interrogation training courses; Leo concluded that the process of police interrogation could be best understood in terms of a confidence game. Interrogation was effective because of manipulation and the betrayal of trust. In spite of *Miranda* warnings and media exposure regarding interrogation tactics, defendants routinely succumb to police interrogation manipulations, raising a number of constitutional rights issues.

There is a substantial empirical database regarding the unreliability and lack of validity of police interrogation outcomes. Essentially, untrained police and observers are not able to accurately distinguish truthful from deceptive suspects (Ekman & O'Sullivan, 1991; Kassin, 1997; Kassin & Fong, 1999; McMahon, 1995). Interrogation tactics that employ trickery, manipulation, and deception are clearly subject to *false-positive* findings whereby innocent suspects will be deemed involved (Leo & Ofshe, 1998) and *false-negative* findings where complicit suspects will be judged not involved. Interrogation efforts begin with the interrogators' knowing a crime has occurred. The interrogators are, by definition, suspicious and have the expectation of interrogatees' engaging in deception. This prejudiced posture clearly lends itself to outcomes of finding suspects guilty (Burgoon et al., 1994).

It stands to reason that innocent suspects would be likely to be intimidated by coercive strategies. Most innocent suspects would experience an interrogation as highly stressful. For most people, the verbal and nonverbal signs of nervousness are essentially the same reactive signs of deceptive behavior. Usual and expected signs of nervousness by innocent suspects are likely to be misinterpreted as signs of intentional distortion or deception. It should be noted that this same circumstance is a primary basis of the unreliability of polygraph testing. By comparison, complicit suspects experienced in illicit activity and deception would be more likely to engage in effective reverse-deception during interrogation.

Police interrogation is a prejudicial procedure maintained by the feelings of the public and police officials confronted with the realities of serious crime. Interrogation is not always fair or objective to suspects. Is it appropriate to attempt to combat deceptive practice with interrogation strategies that involve deception? There are inherent risks for both criminal defendants and suspected defendants.

DECEPTION IN THE MILITARY

Deceptive practices in the military provide another excellent example of deception in contemporary society (Handel, 1977, 1982; Reit, 1978; Whaley, 1969, 1982; Wiseman, 1996; Wrangham, 1999). Vast sums of money have been spent by the federal government in the systematic study of operational deception, principles of which have been applied in modern American wars. The roots of current military thinking have their basis in the Old Testament of the *Bible*, Carl von Clausewitz's *On War* (translated in 1976), Chinese philosophers such as Sun Tzu's *Art of War* (translated in 1973), psychophysics, psychometrics, magic, and other sources.

Deceptive strategies are viewed favorably by the military. They serve as a force multiplier by magnifying the ostensible strength of friendly forces or by misdirecting the enemy in some other advantageous manner; cunning may be the only hope when friendly forces are understrength. An inverse relationship is usually found between the amount of deception employed and the strength of the military force. Deception is cheap in terms of labor and capital.

Finally, deception seems to work in most cases, given adequate planning, which accounts for its high favor and continued use. Handel (1982) stated:

> Since no effective measures to counter or identify deception have yet been developed, the inevitable conclusion is that deception — even if it does not achieve its original goals — almost never fails … and will therefore always favor the deceiver, the initiating party …. Perceptual and cognitive biases strongly favor the deceiver as long as the goal of deception is to reinforce a target's preconceptions or simply create ambiguity and doubt about the deceiver's intention …. Rationality dictates that a move which involves little cost and little risk of failure should always be included in one's repertoire. (p. 145)

The process of deceptive operations is most relevant to this book. Whaley (1982), and to some extent Handel (1982), describes a sequence of successful deceptive operations involving deception by hiding (i.e., termed *masking, repackaging, dazzling*) and by presenting the false (i.e., termed *mimicking, inventing, decoying*). The following descriptive sequence is presented with illustrations for military and forensic evaluations from the viewpoint of the litigant.

1. Select a long-range goal with a definable outcome.
   a. Military strategists try to win a war; tactically, a surprise invasion may be a long-range goal.
   b. Litigants in criminal settings may attempt to escape the consequences of their conduct; those in civil settings may desire a substantial cash settlement.
2. Determine how the target should respond and what it should think as a consequence.
   a. Movement in a certain direction to violate concentration and economy of forces may be a military objective. The enemy should think that a distinct advantage will accrue, such as cutting off opposing forces.
   b. Defendants in insanity trials may want the trier of fact to award them the Not Guilty by Reason of Insanity (NGRI) verdict. The trier of fact should think that the defendant is in need of psychiatric help but is not a criminal in personality or deed.
3. Decide what is to be hidden and what is to be falsely shown about the facts. Hiding and showing are best when they are presented simultaneously.
   a. Hiding the real involves passive deception. Descriptors include *covert*, *obscure*, *deny*, *minimize*, *mask*, *camouflage*, and others.
      i. Masking: Real objects or activities are put out of sight in this type of deception.
         — Smoke screens cover activities in combat.
         — Past violence consisting of predatory aggression may be denied by the defendant.
      ii. Repackaging: Disguise hides the real in this fakery.
         — A warship may be disguised as a freighter.
         — Conventional clothes may be worn by the defendant for a forensic evaluation in hopes of leading the examiner to conclude that the defendant is not associated with a criminal subculture.
      iii. Dazzling: Hides the real by confusion; the attempt is to blur a true pattern of events or responses.
         — Zigzag patterns are painted on war vessels.
         — Random patterns on testing or feigning confusion is sometimes seen in forensic clients.
   b. Presenting the false involves active attention and focused behaviors. Descriptors include *pretend*, *portray*, *profess*, *exaggerate*, *fabricate*, *invent*, and others. Successfully presenting the false is always based on successfully hiding the real.
      i. Mimicking: Involves fake imitation or copying.
         — Cooks posted as infantrymen bolster the apparent strength of combatants.
         — Forensic clients may learn symptoms from actual patients.
      ii. Inventing: Presents or creates something entirely new.
         — Rubber tanks and wooden guns may mislead the enemy into believing in a false capability.
         — Fabricating visual hallucinations may convince evaluators of a psychotic process.
      iii. Decoying: Inverts and distracts the attention of the opposition by falsely presenting a second pattern.
         — Diversion in one battle zone with an attack in another is frequently, almost routinely, employed by the military.
         — Entering psychotherapy to create a basis for civil litigation is frequently suggested to plaintiffs by retained attorneys.
         — Child sexual abuse suspect discloses for the first time a history of having been sexually abused.

4. Consider opportunity variables to set the plan into operation.
   a. Ordnance and backup equipment are made available for military operations.
   b. Factitious patients acquire the means to portray illness falsely; some aggressive defendants seek out the victim or witness to limit damaging testimony, or go to certain doctors whose outcomes are largely known beforehand.
5. Effect execution.
   a. Command and control units direct subordinate organizations to set the deceptive plan into action.
   b. Civil and criminal litigants execute the deception themselves; significant others occasionally attempt to deceive the evaluator at the behest of the defendant.
6. Send the distorted input to the target.
   a. Surrender leaflets must be read, seen as relevant, and construed with the intended meaning.
   b. The forensic evaluator must notice and see as genuine faked messages sent by the faker. Planning and rehearsal help increase believability.
7. Seek feedback on effectiveness of the deception effort.
   a. Outcome of battle and questioning of prisoners provide valuable insight into efficacy.
   b. Fakers frequently ask for feedback regarding how they have performed; defendants ask if they meet the criteria for lacking competency or criminal responsibility; and their untempered reactions to feedback can often be clinically telling.

According to various commentators on military deception, personality traits associated with good deceivers include imagination, practicality, knowledge of the relevant culture and history, and empathy, with the ability to see things from the target's viewpoint. Other traits include high competitiveness, individualism, and asociality, with operators and planners not being the traditional "company" person. Trait analysis appears to be ad hoc in the military studies and may actually have a weak or absent association with successful deception.

The dangers of military deception are much more convincing. The biggest error is self-deception — believing and acting on one's own distortions. Time and again, individuals and countries are seen to display unjustified arrogance because of a few initial successes. Wrangham (1999) distinguished between *military raids* and *military battles* based on whether or not one side has the opportunity to assess the other. Raids are more accurate in terms of objectives, and often more effective, because the other side's weaknesses are the basis of surprise attack. Battles, in contrast, are the failure of assessment with both sides holding erroneous positive illusions about their respective strength. The false-positive illusions according to Wrangham suppress inhibitory concerns and facilitate self-deceptive, favorable expectations. Although foolhardy, the self-deceptive process promotes the intensity of violence. This false illusory component of military deception would appear to be common to most forms of deceptive practice. Deception in both benign and harmful forms is the result of the deceivers' perceptions that they are capable of the deception effort, and that they are capable of instilling the false perception in the deceived. How often do people walk away from a car dealership in wonderment of the salesperson's pitch being so audacious and bold? On the other hand, how often do customers make purchases in acceptance of these strategies? How often do military and other world leaders wonder at the apparent stupidity of enemies overestimating their lethality in spite of evidence to the contrary?

Military lore reveals frequent examples of the deceived party recovering and eventually achieving the upper hand. Targets usually redouble their efforts when "faked out," improve their skills, and react to the adversary with greater determination. The deceivers' bluffs may be called and weaknesses exposed, their forces eventually defeated. A very real danger, then, is short-term success with deception, followed by a negative long-term impact.

Paradoxical findings emerge from the military literature and have relevance for the forensic evaluator. The more alert military planners are to deception, the more likely they are to be deceived.

Targets have fooled most evaluators creating skepticism about the truthfulness of the subjects. The more skeptical people are of the data, the more they rely on preconceptions, which may or may not be accurate in particular cases. Conversely, once a source is seen as credible, the harder it is for evaluators to disregard the data.

Countermeasures are possible, based on the assumption that deception can never be 100% successful, over time. The first is to keep open all channels of observation in regard to a situation. This corresponds in forensic evaluations to having a large and varied database, as clients may produce a consistent set of (distorted) data on one or two measures. This strategy increases "noise," or extra, nonusable data, but the evaluator can sift through this excess information with a variety of sound decision paths.

Generally, the better the reputation for honesty, the easier it is for countries, military personnel, or individuals to lie. Frequent use of deception is associated with loss of credibility. This yields another paradoxical finding. Honest and high-status people are the best liars because they are believed the most. Military officers and high-ranking civilian employees would fit into this category. Thus, they would be good deceivers in any planned operation.

A case in point was illustrated in the civil litigation of *Boyle v. United Technology* (1988). In *Boyle*, the Supreme Court reversed an earlier opinion by a federal district court upholding state (Virginia) tort law. Boyle was a copilot who died in a helicopter crash during a training exercise. The estate brought suit against the respondent alleging a defective emergency escape-hatch system. The Supreme Court found that the respondent, a private defense contractor, was shielded by the federal requirements for "military contractor defense." Kaun (1994) observed that the Court essentially limited the ability of citizens to litigate against private defense contractors, based on the dubious argument that there was a high degree of honesty in the federal procurement process and in particular in the weapons testing program.

Although not involving combat or warfare strategies, another application of deception in the military has involved the still touted "don't ask, don't tell" policy for gay men, lesbians, and bisexuals (Kavanagh, 1995). This problem continues as a thorny political and social conundrum.

In sum, the military literature on deception has some important lessons for the forensic evaluator. The military has clearly described the steps necessary for successful deception and has cataloged a variety of deceptive tactics that may be employed. Deception itself is not to be despised and may even be a mark of flexibility and empathy in the deceiver. Being oversensitive to possible deception may be as maladaptive as naively accepting appearances.

DECEPTION AND SOCIAL LIFE

American society embraces a strong ambivalence regarding deception and lying. Whereas misrepresentation in business is condemned, undercover tactics and "sting" operations by law enforcement agencies are tolerated and even applauded. Lying in the name of national security is an acceptable practice, while lying to protect one's privacy is a reason for dismissal from employment. Lying during union negotiations or budget hearings is a common, even expected, practice for which adjustments are automatically made. Social scientists are gaining a reputation for deceptive research practices, while their students are soundly punished for cheating in their classes. Electronic evangelists preach a rigid morality, while converting donations to the maintenance of a hypocritical lifestyle.

Deception in contemporary America is both tolerated and condemned. People transmit this ambivalence to their children and it is reinforced throughout development by cultural practices. Lying is one of the first interactive verbal behaviors to develop (Stouthammer-Loeber, 1986); it continues to be displayed and denied in adolescence and adulthood (Shusterman & Saxe, 1990).

As will be described in Chapter 7, children are exposed to the influences of deception in very early development. Children acquire a basic awareness of deceptive behavior and are tainted by social and cultural values regarding deception in ways that profoundly affect their lives. There is also a risk of forensic professionals' carrying these myths from childhood. Deception in forensic investigation can be inappropriately justified with the rationale that deception executed by a professional leads to a worthy end. Deception by offenders, on the other hand, is loathsome. From logical and pragmatic standpoints, it is foolhardy to expect that criminal defendants will not engage in deception to avoid imprisonment or other aversive outcomes. In civil contexts, personal injury and workers' compensation plaintiffs may feel that they not only deserve the possible financial reward, but that they need it to survive. Deception in this forensic context is also commonplace.

In the justice system context, the use of deceptive tactics by attorneys (Freedman, 1976) and by domestic mediators (Benjamin, 1995) is widespread, condoned, condemned, and arguably necessary.

> The effective management of conflict by a mediator requires the constructive use of deception. Rational discussion and logic are not sufficient to effect the changes in perspective required by disputing parties for conflicts to be settled. Deception is not only a normal but an essential activity for the survival and propagation of all life forms, including human beings. This is so even though the notion of deception has pejorative connotations, especially in Western culture where rational analysis is most highly valued. Mediators, in particular, from their intuitive understanding of conflict, must recognize the valid and necessary uses of deception. In this regard, the folkloric trickster figure provides an important model of the skills, strategies, and techniques needed by present-day mediators. (Benjamin, 1995, p.3)

Anger at being deceived may say more about the evaluator's self-beliefs than about the deceiver. It may also reflect overexposure to mythology in one's culture, providing the basis for a rigid and judgmental cognitive style.

In sum, the widespread ambivalence toward deception in American society likely pervades everyone's perceptions, attitudes, beliefs, and behaviors. Detecting deception in others requires a candid appraisal of its presence in one's own life and practices.

DECEPTION AND MORAL PHILOSOPHY

No one would argue that deception in plants and animals is immoral. Their deception can be evaluated solely on its consequences: it either has adaptive value or ensures survival or it does not. In humans, however, deception can become immoral in spite of advantageous consequences. Forgery, impersonation, consumer fraud, and perjury may all be adaptive and advantageous, but are nonetheless regarded as immoral and usually illegal.

Moral philosophers generally agree that deception which produces intended or foreseen harm is wrong. The deceptive act itself may be morally neutral — as in keeping a secret (Bok, 1989b), but the intentional harm that follows condemns the entire enterprise. Failing to reveal defects in a car, switching brand labels on a consumer product, or concealing limitations in one's skills are not immoral per se, but become wrong from the harm that follows. At the very least, deceptive practices unfairly alter the choices of the deceived by obscuring alternatives, the costs/benefits of those alternatives, or the probabilities of desired outcomes. Thus, potentially injurious consequences are one basis for evaluating the ethics of human deception.

A more hotly debated issue is whether certain deceptions by humans are wrong in themselves, irrespective of their intended or foreseeable consequences. The debate has focused on deceptive statements (i.e., lying) rather than on all types of deception. St. Augustine, St. Thomas Aquinas, Immanuel Kant, and John Wesley are among those who have argued that lying is always wrong and admit of no exceptions. Statements made with the intent to deceive may differ in the harm they cause, but they are always wrong, even if just in a technical sense. The condemnation of all forms of lying generally rests on its violation of natural law (i.e., abuse of purpose of human ability in communication), its threat to that interpersonal trust that is necessary for society's survival, or its affront to the dignity of other persons (Fagothey, 1967). Each of these arguments elevates a greater good above any outcome that might accrue from a lie.

The sweeping rejection of all lies has led to provocative debates about its implications. Why, for example, is it justifiable to use force in self-defense, while it is unjustifiable to lie for the same reason? Should a would-be assassin be directed to the intended target to avoid lying to the assassin about the victim's whereabouts? Should a lie be avoided if it would ensure the salvation of a million souls?

Such debate has produced logical subdivisions of lies, which allow important distinctions among lies while at the same time preserving the categorical condemnation. St. Thomas Aquinas, for example, distinguishes mortal from venial lies and argues that forgiveness of the latter is easier than of the former. Some scholastics have defined lies strictly in terms of the discrepancy between one's "mind" and one's statements. This distinction permits liars to use silent statements to themselves to reverse the apparent intent of their spoken words (akin to crossing one's fingers behind one's back while lying to another). Still other philosophers define a group of intentional misstatements, which are justified because the deceived has no right to know the truth.

Utilitarian philosophers, on the other hand, do not categorically censure lying. For them, the ethics of a lie are determined by balancing the positive and negative consequences of the lie. Some deceptive statements to some people under some circumstances are morally acceptable (even preferable) and other lies to other people under other circumstances are morally repugnant. This situational ethics avoids the machinations needed to apply a categorical condemnation of lying to the real world.

However, the utilitarian view of lying has its own problems. First, it is frequently difficult in the real world to estimate the complex costs and benefits associated with a lie. Everyday indulgences in equivocation and deception, such as in employment applications and in doctor–patient communications, result in enormous monetary and personal costs (Robinson, Shepherd, & Heywood, 1998). Complex issues such as nuclear power, abortion, and the death penalty do not easily lend themselves to the simple calculation of costs and benefits; lies about these issues do not make the calculations any easier. Second, the situational justification of lying provides no mechanism for correcting the biases of the liar. Since the justification is essentially private, it is too easy for the would-be liar to first settle on the desired outcome (to lie or not lie) and then to adjust the calculations to support that alternative. Third, the utilitarian view of lying assumes that lying per se is morally neutral and is not accorded an initially negative weight (cost), which must be overcome by especially positive benefits. This neutral view of lying per se overlooks the inherent harm done to society when even justifiable lies are offered.

The moral philosophers have not provided a simple checklist or set of rules for evaluating lies. Their discussion, disagreement, and analysis, however, have provided a perspective, which must be considered in any discussion of human deception. Bok (1989a) offered a contemporary application of this perspective, which may serve as a guide to discussions throughout this book:

> [W]e must ask, first, whether there are alternative forms of action which will resolve the difficulty without the use of a lie; second, what might be the moral reasons brought forward to excuse the lie, and what reasons can be raised as counter-arguments. Third, as a test of these two steps, we must ask what a public of reasonable persons might say about such lies. (pp. 105–106)

These three questions assume that lying is a last resort, which must be justified by moral reasons acceptable to reasonable persons other than the would-be liar. While not resolving the centuries-old debates in moral philosophy, this perspective demands a stringent accounting of lying in strictly moral terms.

The authors are especially interested in applying the moral perspective to the methods used by professionals to detect deception and lying in others. Must clients be informed that one purpose of an evaluation is to assess the genuineness of their self-presentations? Should clients be informed that the sole purpose of a particular test is to detect malingering? Is it ethical for professionals to lie to detect deception in clients? Perhaps the published ethical statements of leading professional organizations will provide guidance on these questions. The *Ethical Principles of Psychologists* (American Psychological Association, 1990) states:

> Principle 8a. In using assessment techniques, psychologists respect the right of clients to have *full explanations of the nature and purpose of the techniques* in language the clients can understand, unless an explicit exception to this right has been agreed upon in advance [emphasis added].

The "Ethical Principles of Psychologists and Code of Conduct" (American Psychological Association, 1992) states:

> Standard 1.07. When psychologists provide assessment, evaluation, treatment, counseling, supervision, teaching, consultation, research, or other psychological services to an individual, a group or an organization, they first provide the patient or client with *appropriate information about the nature of such service*, and they later provide appropriate information about results and conclusions [emphasis added]. (p. 1602)

and

> Standard 2.09. Unless the nature of the relationship is clearly explained to the person being assessed in advance and precludes provision of an explanation of results (such as in same organizational consulting, preemployment or security ccreenings, and forensic evaluations), psychologists insist that an explanation of the results is provided using language that is reasonably understandable to the person assessed or to another legally authorized person on behalf of the client. Regardless of whether the scoring and interpretation are done by the psychologist, by assistants, or by automated or outside services, psychologists take reasonable steps to ensure that appropriate explanations of results are given. (p. 1605)

The *Specialty Guidelines for Forensic Psychologists* (Committee on Ethical Guidelines for Forensic Psychologists, 1991) states:

> IV.E. Forensic psychologists have an obligation to ensure that prospective clients are informed of their legal rights with respect to the anticipated forensic service, *of the purposes of any evaluation, of the nature of procedures to be employed*, of the intended uses of any product of their services, and of the party who has employed the forensic psychologist [emphasis added]. (p. 658)

The *American College of Physicians Ethics Manual* (American College of Physicians, 1998), in discussing disclosures to patients, states:

> To make health care decisions and work intelligently in partnership with the physician, the patient must be well informed. Effective patient-physician communication can dispel uncertainty and fear and can enhance healing and patient satisfaction. Information should be disclosed whenever it is considered material to the patient's understanding of his or her situation, possible treatments, and probable outcomes. This information often includes the costs and burdens of treatment, the experience of the proposed clinician, the nature of the illness, and potential treatments.
>
> However uncomfortable to clinician or patient, information that is essential to the patient must be disclosed. How, when, and to whom information is disclosed are important concerns that must be addressed.
>
> Information should be given in terms that the patient can understand. The physician should be sensitive to the patient's responses in setting the pace of disclosure, particularly if the illness is very serious. Disclosure should never be a mechanical or perfunctory process. Upsetting news and information should be presented to the patient in a way that minimizes distress (20, 21). If the patient is unable to comprehend his or her condition, it should be fully disclosed to an appropriate surrogate.

In addition, physicians should disclose to patients information about procedural or judgment errors made in the course of care if such information is material to the patient's well-being. Errors do not necessarily constitute improper, negligent, or unethical behavior, but failure to disclose them may. (p. 579)

These excerpts offer varying advice to the practicing professional. The 1989 statement by the American Psychological Association requires a "full explanation" of assessment services and techniques. This position would appear to prohibit deceptive practices (e.g., nondisclosure) as well as outright lying to clients. However, the revised statement by the same organization requires only "appropriate information about the nature of such services." Presumably, the practitioner is to decide personally what is appropriate for disclosure and what is not. This revised statement appears to allow nondisclosure of information to a client, if the practitioner deems such nondisclosure appropriate, but does not specifically address the ethics of lying to a client, even if such lying is deemed appropriate. Nonetheless, the debate on the ethical use of deceptive practice in psychological research has had a measurable impact. Nicks, Korn, and Mainieri (1997) reviewed journal articles in personality and social psychology from 1921 to 1994. They found rare use of deception in psychological research during the developmental years of social psychology into the 1930s; references to deception then occurred gradually and irregularly until the 1950s. From the 1950s to the 1970s, the use of deception increased dramatically. The authors attributed the increase to changes in experimental methods, the pursuit of realism in social research, and the influence of cognitive dissonance theory. Since the 1980s, there has been a decided decrease in the use of deception compared with the previous decades, which is related to changes in ethical standards and to federal efforts to regulate research.

The Forensic Psychologists' Ethical Standards statement obliges, without exception, the practitioner to inform clients of both the purpose of an assessment and the nature of procedures to be used. This position leaves little room for either nondisclosure or lying. The American College of Physicians' statement requires full disclosure to patients, except when the patient may be personally harmed by such disclosure. This statement seems to allow nondisclosure under limited circumstances, but to prohibit nondisclosure in general. The statement is ambiguous regarding the ethics of intentional misstatements to clients.

This variety of opinion represents the full spectrum of moral positions on full disclosure, from categorical rejection of deception by a practitioner to utilitarian acceptance of deception depending on the judgment of the practitioner. There appear to be no easy answers to the moral questions posed by deception and no agreement among thoughtful practitioners. Perhaps the most that individual practitioners can do is (1) be sensitive to the moral issues involved in the detection of deception, (2) consult with colleagues on the ethics of particular practices, (3) adopt consistent procedures that address the ethical issues involved, and (4) maintain constantly updated knowledge of evolving ethical standards and practice guidelines.

In summary, the ethics of human deception can always be evaluated in terms of its consequences, while the ethics of lying (as a special case of deception) must be evaluated differently. Before adopting deceptive practices (e.g., nondisclosure), the individual practitioner must evaluate the potential harm that the practice may cause. However, lying (intentional misstatement) has such general, negative consequences that it requires extraordinary justification before reasonable persons will condone it. The statements of various professional organizations differ on the ethics of deceiving clients through nondisclosure and are generally silent on the ethics of lying to clients.

EVALUATING AND USING RESEARCH RESULTS ON DECEPTION

Forensic experts commonly refer to the wealth of research supporting their conclusions, predictions, and opinions. Little distinction is made between research that supports a particular theory or conceptualization and research that supports an applied prediction or classification. Any discussion of research on deception must carefully separate research that supports "theories" of deception and deception detection from that which supports actual predictions of deception. Research on theories relevant to deception focuses on the validity of hypotheses regarding the process of deception or the process of deception detection, while research on the prediction of deception focuses on the validity of predictions of deception.

The practitioner concerned with detecting deception in particular cases needs to review the available research on deception. Only some of that research is immediately useful in the individual case. The following guidelines should be considered in evaluating research studies:

1. *There continues to be a fundamental problem with how models of deception and malingering have been historically framed.* In addressing this issue, Rogers (1990b, 1997) critiqued that all efforts to improve the reliability of clinical observation are significantly compromised, if feigned psychological disturbance cannot be accurately ruled out. Rogers dismissed the DSM-III-R and, currently, the DSM-IV definitions of malingering as "puritanical" because they embodied moralistic overtones. Furthermore, Rogers notes that the DSM definitions of malingering were based on assumed criteria as opposed to being based on any empirical paradigm.

As alternatives, Rogers (1990a, b, 1997) proposed an *adaptation model* and a *detection model*. In the adaptation model, malingering is the adaptive product of a perceived, aversive stressor. The stressor and the malingering response are variables that can be empirically measured. Another dependent variable is the mechanism of choice-making in weighing the expected utility of a malingered response against the probability of a desired outcome. Most recently, Rogers (1997) differentiated the pathogenic model (psychiatric disturbance), the criminological model (DSM), and the adaptation model as representing explanatory models. The explanatory models are distinct from detection or assessment models. Explanatory models characterize potential, antecedent variables of malingering, whereas the detection models take forensic assessment one step farther and attempt to identify actual malingering incident.

2. *A significant relationship between a variable and deception does not necessarily indicate that the variable is a good predictor of deception.* Some research findings bear on the processes of deception and deception detection rather than on the outcomes of deception detection. Research on impression management and self-presentation (e.g., Schlenker & Weigold, 1992) is clearly relevant to deception, but only some of the research is relevant to the accurate identification of individual deceivers. Ekman (1985) described how nonverbal behaviors, such as posture, tone of voice, and facial expression, may leak information about the truthfulness of a person. Such findings provide valuable information about the processes of deception, but do not provide reliable clues to deception in individual cases. Ekman (1985), for example, warned that these clues might be related in individual cases to genuine emotions or to the person's feelings about being suspected of lying. The practitioner is cautioned, "behavioral clues to deceit should only serve to alert you to the need for further information and investigation" (p. 189).

In general, research reports of mean differences between groups of "deceivers" and "non-deceivers" or of correlations between test scores and malingering do not provide justification for use of the reported measures for detection of deception in individual cases. Such group differences and correlations do not address the important question of predictive accuracy. Group differences on Rorschach variables, for example, do not reflect the accuracy of predictions made with a particular cutoff score.

Even when a research finding focuses on individual prediction rather than on group correlates, a statistically significant relationship does not necessarily indicate a good predictor. The value of a variable as a predictor of deception is determined by its effect size, not by its statistical significance (Cohen, 1977). Since the significance of a statistical relationship is determined in part by the sample size of the study, it is possible for a weak relationship (small effect size) to attain statistical significance. Such weak predictors will not prove useful in the prediction of individual cases. Good overall predictors of deception are those that show a large difference (effect size) between deceivers and nondeceivers.

3. *Some good predictors of deception are "locally" rather than "generally" valid.* Being bald is a good predictor that one is male, but having a full head of hair is not a good predictor of being female. Amount of head hair is a poor general predictor of sex, but being bald is a good local predictor of being male. In general, a variable may be unrelated to a criterion throughout its entire range, but still be related to the criterion within a local region of its range.

In deception research, a low value on a scale or the absence of a "sign" may be unrelated to truthfulness, whereas a high value or the presence of the "sign" may indicate deception. A low MMPI F-scale score, for example, tells one nothing about deceptiveness, but a high score increases the likelihood of deception. An anatomically impossible symptom predicts deception, but the presence of a plausible symptom does not predict a genuine disorder.

Such asymmetrical relationships between predictors and deception function to lower overall tests of statistical significance, which are based on the entire range of values of the predictor. Thus, it is possible for research results that yield nonsignificant or small effects nonetheless to discover good predictors of deception.

These "local" predictors of deception are most clearly revealed in decision tables rather than in t-tests or correlation coefficients. Decision tables relate ranges of values on the predictor (e.g., high, medium, low) to values on the criterion (e.g., deceptive, nondeceptive) (Wiggins, 1973). Such classification tables permit analysis of the relationship between successive local ranges of the predictor and the criterion rather than just the overall relationship between predictor and criterion.

4. *Different research comparisons have differing practical implications.* Published research on malingering typically involves group comparisons between (1) normal subjects instructed to "fake bad" and normal subjects instructed to respond normally, (2) normal subjects instructed to "fake bad" and genuine patients instructed to respond normally, or (3) patients suspected of malingering instructed to respond normally and genuine patients instructed to respond normally. These three types of comparisons yield widely varying accuracy rates and resulting scales, patterns, and cutoff scores are applicable to widely different evaluation situations.

For example, Leavitt (1987) reported that a measure of pain was 82% accurate in detecting normal subjects instructed to fake pain, but only 64% accurate in detecting genuine pain patients who were instructed to exaggerate their pain. Similarly, Berry, Baer, and Harris (1991) reported in a meta-analysis of MMPI indicators of malingering that the mean effect size for studies comparing normal subjects with normal subjects instructed to "fake bad" was 2.66. The mean effect size for studies comparing genuine patients with normal subjects instructed to "fake bad" was 1.86, the mean effect size for studies comparing genuine patients with patients instructed to exaggerate was 1.48, and the mean effect size for groups inferred to be malingering with other groups was 0.83. Thus, the accuracy of detection methods varies greatly with the type of discriminations being made.

The results of studies that compare normal subjects with normal subjects instructed to "fake bad" are most relevant to evaluation situations which themselves involve this comparison (e.g., detecting malingerers among job applicants). Studies that compare genuine patients with normals instructed to "fake bad" are most relevant to situations where malingerers are seeking admission to patient status. The results of studies that compare genuine patients with other patients instructed to exaggerate their symptoms are most relevant to situations where current patients are seeking additional treatment/attention/benefits. In terms of the MMPI results reported by Berry et al. (1991), MMPI indices of malingering are likely to be most accurate in situations where they are least needed (e.g., distinguishing genuine normals from faking normals) and to be less accurate in situations where they are needed most (e.g., distinguishing suspected malingerers from genuine patients).

As a final example, in a recent study Ekman, O'Sullivan, and Frank (1999) reported a group of federal law enforcement officers and a group of sheriffs to be significantly more accurate than other law enforcement peer groups in detecting laboratory deception. The greater prediction accuracy was attributed to the experience and special training of the federal officer group. In the same study, a group of psychologists "interested in deception" was more accurate in predicting deception than a control group of psychologists. The significance of the study was the selectively greater accuracy of two subsets of professionals in detecting deception. This finding supported earlier evidence (Ekman & O'Sullivan, 1991) that some professionals are very accurate in detecting deception. The current study demonstrated deception-detection accuracy with select psychologists. While an important study in the deception literature, the approach was a laboratory-based paradigm involving videotaped scenarios that were observed by the subjects. The subjects received financial bonuses if their enactments of truth or deception were believed. The bonuses were intended to ensure a "high-stakes" milieu. There are limits to the practical utility of laboratory analogue models.

5. *A good predictor is not necessarily a useful one*. Discovery of a good overall or local predictor of deception is necessary but not sufficient for useful prediction of deception. It must also be shown that the predictor is useful in the situation in which it is applied. Meehl and Rosen (1955) discussed the influence of base rates (prior probabilities) on errors in prediction. If deception is very rare or very frequent in a particular situation, a good predictor will nevertheless produce a large number of incorrect predictions. Indeed, if the base rate is low enough, a good predictor with even a low error rate can produce more incorrect than correct predictions.

Even a predictor that produces more correct than incorrect predictions in a particular situation may not be useful. A false prediction in one situation is not necessarily as serious as a false prediction in a different situation. Falsely predicting malingering in a neurological case may have more dire consequences than falsely predicting dishonesty in hiring. Indeed, Swets (1992) has argued that the best decision rule for any given test is strictly a function of the base rate of the condition being evaluated and the relative costs of false-positive and false-negative decisions. Without knowing anything at all about the accuracy of a particular test, sign, or other decision rule, it is possible to define its usefulness in given situations. In general, assessment procedures for malingering will be less useful in situations with a low base rate for malingering than in situations with a higher base rate for malingering. "That is, one should not make the positive decision very readily when the chances are great that the negative alternative will actually occur" (Swets, 1992, p. 525). In addition, conservative rules for predicting malingering will be more useful than liberal rules when the relative cost of falsely calling someone "malingering" is greater than the relative cost of falsely calling someone "genuine." These costs of misclassification may differ considerably from one situation to another, even when the assessment decision (e.g., neurological malingering vs. genuine impairment) and base rates are the same. For example, it can be argued that the costs of falsely calling "malingering" are greater when the decision is irreversible (e.g., in courtroom testimony) than when the decision is reversible (e.g., in treatment where new information continuously updates treatment plans).

Of course, evaluation of the costs of predictive errors depends on one's values and one's investment in the outcome. Whether refusal to hire an applicant falsely labeled as "dishonest" is evaluated positively or negatively depends on whether one is the employer or the applicant. But the difficulty of balancing competing interests does not minimize the effect of those disparate values on the prediction process. What would be helpful is a public discussion of the relative costs of mispredicting "malingering" and of mispredicting "genuineness" in real-world situations (e.g., medical diagnosis, eligibility for disability, need for involuntary treatment) as perceived by consumers, decision makers, institutions, and society in general. Such discussion would help to define the type of decision rules (conservative vs. liberal) appropriate to situations with different base rates of "malingering" (low vs. medium vs. high) and with different costs of misclassification (high false-positive costs vs. high false-negative costs).

A final factor in determining the usefulness of a malingering assessment procedure is the cost of administering the procedure. A procedure that appropriately minimizes costs of misclassifications for a given situation may not be useful if it is prohibitively expensive to administer. Most clinicians would be unwilling to spend 3 hours assessing the "genuineness" of a 1-hour screening evaluation. However, the same 3-hour assessment may be a bargain when the relative cost of a misclassification is high enough (e.g., selection of astronauts for long-term space missions). Similarly, equipment costs may offset the value of accurately classifying subjects. Buchwald (1965) presented a discussion of the impact of the cost of testing on decisions whether or not to use a test at all. In some situations, the cost of detecting "malingering" may be greater than the cost of tolerating undetected "malingerers."

6. *The accuracy of an individual prediction is all-or-none.* Statistics on the accuracy of predictions and classifications (e.g., valid positive rates, positive hit rates) always reflect the results of a series of decisions. An assessment procedure is used with a group of people and the accuracy of the procedure is determined for the entire group (i.e., for the series of individual decisions). This type of accuracy information provides an empirical basis for deciding which procedures, cutting scores, signs, or other decision rules to use for particular purposes. For a particular purpose, the procedure with higher accuracy is preferable to one with lower accuracy; for a particular assessment situation, one cutting score is more accurate than another cutting score; for a given set of classificatory costs, a less costly procedure is preferable to a more costly procedure.

None of these statistics, however, reflects the accuracy of a prediction in an individual case. When an assessment procedure for "malingering" has a positive hit rate of 80% (for a particular base rate), the probability that a person with a positive score on the procedure is actually malingering is not 0.80. The probability of an individual prediction being correct is always either 1.0 or 0.0. A prediction in an individual case is always either correct or incorrect. The positive hit rate, valid positive rate, etc. associated with a particular procedure refer only to the relative frequency of correct decisions among a series of decisions, not to the probability of being correct in a particular case.

However, the accuracy statistics associated with a particular procedure in a particular situation can be used in a logical argument to support the decision in a particular case (Movahedi & Ogles, 1976). Given that 80% of persons with a positive score on a malingering test are in fact malingering and given that Mr. Jones has a positive score on the test, it is "80% logical" that Mr. Jones is malingering. In other words, the claimed probability is a measure of the logical relationship between the premises and the conclusion and not a measure of the empirical truth of the conclusion. Given the following premises: 75% of persons with X, Y, and Z are malingering and Mr. Jones possesses X, Y, and Z, the proper conclusion is not that "there is a 75% chance that Mr. Jones is malingering," but rather that "it is 75% logical that Mr. Jones is malingering."

Alternatively, accuracy statistics can be regarded as a measure of the decision maker's confidence in an individual conclusion rather than as a statement about reality. A rational decision maker would have more confidence, for example, in an individual prediction based on a procedure with a positive hit rate of 80% than in an individual prediction based on a procedure with a positive hit rate of 50%. The proper conclusion in the above syllogism is that "I am willing to bet that Mr. Jones is malingering."

With either interpretation, an individual decision is empirically either correct or incorrect, but the decision maker has a rational basis for acting on the decision in this particular case.

In summary, research on deception is relevant to the actual detection of deception only when it presents results on the predictive accuracy of general or local predictors of deception in research groups similar to those with whom the detection method will actually be used. These results are best evaluated in decision or classification tables, which allow determination of the error rates associated with the predictor. Predictors with low error rates must then be evaluated in terms of their usefulness in particular situations. The usefulness of a procedure involves considerations of (1) the base rate of the condition being assessed in the situation where the procedure will be used, (2) the relative costs associated with false-positive and false-negative classifications, and (3) the cost of administering the procedure. The accuracy statistics for a given procedure can be used in a logical argument that assessment results in individual cases should be used as if they were empirically true.

SYNTHESIS

This chapter asserts that deception is a ubiquitous, adaptive, and potentially detectable phenomenon. Discussions are presented on deception in nonhumans, deception in the military, deception during socialization, and deception, ethics, and research findings on deception detection.

Deception in its most rudimentary form in animals involves either presentation of the false or concealment of the true by the deceiver and induces either attraction or avoidance in the deceived. The goal of animal deception is always adaptive. In its more developed forms in humans, deception has been elaborated into a systematic strategy for achieving specific objectives. Between these two extremes are shades of distortion that are nondeliberate and unintentional, but that nonetheless obscure the truth.

The spectrum of deception among humans may be evaluated for its adaptive or strategic consequences, but must also be considered from an ethical perspective. Even if deception produces important outcomes, can it be recommended as a moral practice to be encouraged by society? Both ethicists and professional organizations disagree on the morality of deception in general and lying in particular.

This ambivalence toward deception is reflected throughout our culture. Socialization practices, as illustrated in the fables and fairy tales communicated to our children, glorify the use of deception by the "good guys" and vilify its use by the "bad guys." As adults, we are quick to justify our deceptions in terms of our good intentions.

The forensic expert is not immune from these ambiguities and contradictions. Should a subject's deception be viewed as adaptive or immoral? Is the deception intentional or nondeliberate? Is it justifiable to lie to a subject in order to unmask his or her pretense? How can the expert be "objective" in evaluating the deceit of another? Does scientific research really support the opinion?

Although this book cannot answer these difficult questions, it can provide a framework for detecting deception in others. This framework makes explicit the data, assumptions, and decisions of the expert and therefore makes them available to public scrutiny. Others will then be in a position to agree, criticize, argue, and debate the expert's opinion.

LEGAL REFERENCES

Boyle v. United Technology, 487 U.S. 500 (1988).
Miranda v. Arizona, 384 U.S. 336 (1966).

REFERENCES

American College of Physicians. (1998). American College of Physicians Ethics Manual (4th ed.). *Annals of Internal Medicine, 128*, 576–594.

American Psychological Association. (1990). Ethical principles of psychologists. (Amended June 7, 1989). *American Psychologist, 4*, 390–395.

American Psychological Association. (1992). Ethical principles of psychologists and code of conduct. *American Psychologist, 47*, 1597–1611.

Asplen, C. H. (1999) Forensic DNA evidence: National Commission explores its future. *National Institute of Justice Journal* (238), 17–24.

Aune, R. K., Metts, S., & Hubbard, A. S. (1998). Managing the outcomes of discovered deception. *The Journal of Social Psychology, 138*(6), 677–689.

Benjamin, R. D. (1995). The constructive uses of deception: Skills, strategies, and techniques of the folkloric trickster figure and their application by mediators. *Mediation Quarterly, 13*(1), 3–18.

Berry, D., Baer, R. & Harris, M. (1991). Detection of malingering on the MMPI: A meta-analysis. *Clinical Psychology Review, 11*, 585–598.

Bersoff, D. N. (1995). *Ethical conflicts in psychology.* Washington, DC: American Psychological Association.

Bersoff, D. N. (1999). *Ethical conflicts in psychology* (2nd ed.). Washington, DC: American Psychological Association.

Binet, A. (1896). Psychology of prestidigitation. *Annual Report of the Board of Regents of the Smithsonian Institution*, 555–571. Washington, DC: U.S. Government Printing Office.

Bok, S. (1989a). *Lying: Moral choice in public and moral life.* New York: Vintage Books.

Bok, S. (1989b). *Secrets: On the ethics of concealment and revelation.* New York: Vintage Books.

Brody, S. (1995). Patient's misrepresenting their risk factors for AIDS. *International Journal of STD & AIDS, 6*(6), 392–398.

Buchwald, A. M. (1965). Values and the use of tests. *Journal of Consulting Psychology, 29*, 49–54.

Burgoon, J. K., Buller, D. B., Ebesu, A. S., & Rockwell. P. (1994). Interpersonal deception: II. The inferiority in deception detection. *Communication Monographs, 61*, 303–325.

Canter, M. B., Bennett, B. B., Jones, S. E., & Nagy, T. F. (1994). *Ethics for psychologists: A commentary on the APA ethics code.* Washington, DC: American Psychological Association.

Cohen, J. (1977). *Statistical power analysis for the behavioral sciences.* New York: Academic Press.

Committee on Ethical Guidelines for Forensic Psychologists. (1991). Specialty guidelines for forensic psychologists. *Law and Human Behavior, 15*, 655–666.

Dessoir, M. (1893). The psychology of legedermain. *The Open Court, 7*, 3599–3602, 3608–3611, 3616–3619, 3626–3627, 3633–3634.

Ekman, P. (1985). *Telling lies: Clues to deception in the market place, politics, and marriage.* New York: W. W. Norton.

Ekman, P., & O'Sullivan, M. (1991). Who can catch a liar? *American Psychologist, 46*, 913–920.

Ekman, P., O'Sullivan, M., & Frank, M. G. (1999). A few can catch a liar. *Psychological Science, 10*(3), 263–266.

Fagothey, A. (1967). *Right and reason: Ethics in theory and practice.* St. Louis, MO: C. V. Mosby.

Farwell, L. A. (1990). Personal communication.

Farwell, L. A., & Donchin, E. (1986). The "brain detector": P300 in the detection of deception [Abstract]. *Psychophysiology, 23*(4), 434.

Farwell, L. A., & Donchin E. (1988). Event-related potentials in interrogative polygraphy: Analysis using bootstrapping [Abstract]. *Psychophysiology, 25*(4), 445.

Farwell, L. A., & Donchin E. (1989). Detection of guilty knowledge with ERPs [Abstract]. *Supplement to Psychophysiology, 26*(4A), 439.

Freedman, M. H. (1976). *Lawyers ethics in an adversary system.* New York: Bobbs-Merrill.

Gudjonsson, G. H., & Petursson, H. (1991). Custodial interrogation: Why do suspects confess and how does it relate to their crime, attitude and personality? *Personality and Individual Differences, 12*(3), 295–306.

Gugliotta, G. (1999). A rush to DNA sampling: Vital police tool? Affront to liberty? Both? *Washington Post*, 1, A14.

Handel, M. I. (1977). The Yom Kippur War and the inevitability of surprise. *International Studies Quarterly, 21*(3), 461–502.

Handel, M. I. (1982). Intelligence and deception. *The Journal of Strategic Studies, 5*, 122–154.

Hyman, R. (1989). The psychology of deception. *Annual Review of Psychology, 40*, 133–154.

Jastrow, J. (1900). *Fact and fable in psychology.* Cambridge, MA: Riverside Press.

Kassin, S. M. (1997). The psychology of confession evidence. *American Psychologist, 52*(3), 221–233.

Kassin, S. M., & Fong, C. T. (1999). "I'm innocent": Effects of training on judgments of truth and deception in the interrogation room. *Law and Human Behavior, 23*(5), 499–516.

Kaun, D. E. (1994). Lying as a standard operating procedure: Deception in the weapons testing program. *Journal of Socio-Economics, 23*(3), 229–254.

Kavanagh, K. (1995). Don't ask, don't tell: Deception required, disclosure denied. *Psychology, Public Policy, & Law, 1*(1), 142–160.

Kirk, S. A., & Kutchins, H. (1988). Deliberate misdiagnosis in mental health practice. *Social Services Review, 62*, 224–237.

Latkin, C. A., & Vlahov, D. (1998). Socially desirable response tendency as a correlate of accuracy of self-reported HIV serostatus for HIV seropositive injection drug users. *Addiction, 93*(8), 1191–1197.

Latkin, C. A., Vlahov, D., & Anthony, J. C. (1993). Socially desirable responding and self-reported HIV infection risk behaviors among intravenous drug users. *Addiction, 88*(4), 517–525.

Leavitt, F. (1987). Detection of simulation among persons instructed to exaggerate symptoms of low back pain. *Journal of Occupational Medicine, 29*(3), 229–233.

Leo, R. A. (1996). Miranda's revenge: Police interrogation as a confidence game. *Law & Society Review, 30*(2), 259–288.

Leo, R. A., & Ofshe, R. (1998). The consequences of false confessions: Deprivations of liberty and miscarriages of justice in the age of psychological interrogation. *Journal of Criminal Law & Criminology, 88*, 429–496.

Maesen, W. A. (1991). Fraud in mental health practice: A risk management perspective. *Administration and Policy in Mental Health, 18*(6), 421–432.

McMahon, M. (1995). False confessions and police deception. *American Journal of Forensic Psychology, 13*(3), 5–43.

Meehl, P., & Rosen, A. (1955). Antecedent probability and the efficiency of psychometric signs, patterns or cutting scores. *Psychological Bulletin, 52*, 194–216.

Moore, M. P. (1996). Rhetorical subterfuge and the "principle of perfection": Bob Packwood's response to sexual misconduct charges. *Western Journal of Communications, 60*(1), 1–20.

Movahedi, S., & Ogles, R. (1976). Prediction and inference in criminology. *Criminology, 14*, 2, 177–188.

Nicks, S. D., Korn, J. H., & Mainieri, T. (1997). The rise and fall of deception in social psychology and personality research. *Ethics and Behavior, 7*(1), 69–77.

Poirier, J. G. (1999). Violent juvenile crime. In H. V. Hall & L. C. Whitaker (Eds.), *Collective violence: Effective strategies for assessing and interviewing in fatal group and institutional aggression* (pp. 183–212). Boca Raton, FL: CRC Press.

Pope, K. S. (1990). Ethical and malpractice issues in hospital practice. *American Psychologist, 45*, 1066–1070.

Reit, S. (1978). *Masquerade: The amazing camouflage deceptions of World War II.* New York: Hawthorn.

Robinson, W. P., Shepard, A., & Heywood, J. (1998). Truth, equivocation/concealment, and lies in job applications and doctor-patient communication. *Journal of Language & Social Psychology, 17*(2), 149–164.

Rogers, R. (1990a). Development of a new classification model of malingering. *Bulletin American Academy of Psychiatry and the Law, 18*(3), 323–333.

Rogers, R. (1990b). Models of feigned mental illness. *Professional Psychology: Research and Practice, 21*(3), 182–188.

Rogers, R. (Ed.). (1997). *Clinical assessment of malingering and deception.* New York: Guilford Press.

Saxe, L. (1991). Lying: Thoughts of an applied social psychologist. *American Psychologist, 46*(4), 409–415.

Schlenker, B., & Weigold, M. (1992). Interpersonal processes involving impression regulation and management. In M. Rosenzweig, and L. Porter (Eds.), *Annual review of psychology* (pp. 133–168). Palo Alto, CA: Annual Reviews, Inc.

Shusterman, B., & Saxe, L. (1990). *Deception in romantic relatoinships.* Unpublished manuscript. Brandeis University, Boston.

Stouthammer-Loeber, M. (1986). Lying as a problem behavior in children: A review. *Clinical Psychology Review, 6*, 267–289.

Swets, J. A. (1992). The science of choosing the right decision threshold in high-stakes diagnostics, *American Psychologist, 47*(4), 522–532.

Triplett, N. (1900). The psychology of conjuring deceptions. *The American Journal of Psychology, 11*(4), 439–510.

Tzu, S. (1973). *The art of war* (translated by S. B. Griffith), p. 133. New York: Oxford University Press.

von Clausewitz, C. (1976). *On war* (edited and translated by M. Howard & P. Paret), p. 203. Princeton, NJ: Princeton University Press.

Walsh, E. (1999, 24 August). Law and order: The Justice Department: FBI's fingerprint matching goes electronic. *The Washington Post*, sec. Federal Page, p. A15.

Whaley, B. (1969). *Stratagem: Deception and surprise in war.* Cambridge, MA: Center for International Studies, MIT.

Whaley, B. (1982). Toward a general theory of deception. *The Journal of Strategic Studies, 5*, 178–192.

Wiggins, J. (1973). *Personality and prediction: Principles of personality assessment.* Reading, MA: Addison-Wesley.

Wiseman, R. (1996). Towards a psychology of deception. *Psychologist, 9*(2), 61–64.

Wrangham, R. (1999). Is military incompetence adaptive? *Evolution and Human Behavior, 20*(1), 3–17.

2 Involuntary Distortion

Generally, all information relevant to forensic distortion analysis (FDA) comes from the actor, the one acted upon, and the context in which it occurs. Interdisciplinary and multisourced in nature, no discipline or school of thought has cornered the market on deception analysis. This does not mean that all the information must be gathered firsthand by the evaluator. In many cases, the issues surrounding FDA make it impossible for one discipline or individual to answer all the biological, psychological, and social questions in deception analysis. Deception analysis will typically involve at least some collaboration with other sources of data. Depending on the reliability of those sources, the information can be helpful or compromising to the FDA effort. Evaluators must remember that detecting deceptive behavior is not necessarily the same as detecting the truth regarding some type of crime or civil misdeed. Evaluators must also remember that forensic assessments are not assessments of morality or sin (Slovenko, 1995), although such questions may be part of a given evaluation.

THE EVALUATOR'S DATABASE

An adequate database for FDA requires information relevant both to the time of the evaluation and to the time of some past event. Thus, at the very least, the examiner must scrutinize two time periods. This is particularly important in light of the tendency of clients to fake differentially depending on the time period involved. Many criminal offenders, for example, fake bad for the time of the alleged crime only to fake good for the present, such as when the defendant applies for release from hospital incarceration. The database continues to expand until all referral questions are addressed. It is secured, protected against scrutiny, utilized again if needed, and eventually destroyed. In some forensic instances, information that is gathered from the postincident time period could be very important. For example, a criminal defendant's behavior in a holding cell or in a pretrial detention facility may be telling when there is a question of competency or criminal responsibility. The authors have had the experience of correctional officers' describing, "You know he only acts like that when somebody from the outside is around; the rest of the time he is perfectly all right."

The authors also recall a case situation involving serial incest that was only disclosed after several children had been abused.

> The defendant, who was the victim's father, presented medical reports that he was on disability from a back injury. Indeed, the father produced reports describing a suspected lower back injury. The radiographic findings, however, were ambiguous because of artifacts from a prior injury. The father was receiving workers' compensation benefits, he was taking heavy doses of pain medications, and he was attending thrice weekly physical therapy sessions. The father and his attorney contended that his lower back injury would make the alleged incest (i.e., sexual intercourse) impossible and noted that the records documented the father's complaint of the injury negating sexual activity between him and his wife.
>
> During the trial regarding the sexual abuse charges, the victim-daughters presented timelapse home videos of the father. The videos were originally made by the father to monitor his progress while laying a lengthy concrete walk at a family summer home. Prior to the trial and during a clinical/forensic

assessment of the youngest victim, the older siblings questioned whether they should introduce the obviously damming videos. The siblings were feeling guilty over "building a case" against their father. We encouraged the siblings that the clearly established serial nature of the alleged abuse warranted whatever measures necessary to prevent other youngsters from being abused. Three of the older siblings were married and had children. The videos were proved to be from the time of the father's alleged disability. The father was convicted in the sex abuse matter, and separate fraud charges regarding the disability claim resulted in denial of the claim and an administrative court decision that restitution payments were to be made.

As an initial step, the evaluator must gather information. Possible sources include:

1. Interviews of significant/knowledgeable others;
2. Behavioral observations of the possible deceiver in individual and group, structured and unstructured, stressful and nonstressful situations;
3. Functional analysis of previous (i.e., historical) deception;
4. Analysis of validity indicators on psychological testing;
5. Analysis of learning curves and expected performance in intellectual and neuropsychological methods;
6. Competence assessment;
7. Medical and laboratory analysis;
8. Neurological testing using PET, CT, and MRI technologies;
9. Semantic and transcript analysis;
10. Body "leakage" (i.e., nonverbal behavior) analysis;
11. Autobiographical materials (e.g., diaries, letters);
12. Records produced by others (e.g., military, school, job);
13. "Expunged" records in the state or federal archives;
14. Intervention paradigms designed to assess deceit by changing it; and
15. Base rate analysis for traits of groups in which the deceiver holds membership.

The analysis then proceeds to a synthesis of the findings. All known factors are considered; weights, if estimable, are given to the various factors. A judgment is rendered in terms of the evaluator's confidence in the findings and possible degree of accuracy. It is hoped that the synthesis is verifiable and replicable by independent examiners. A good working rule is that deception must be demonstrated, not simply arrived at by ruling out other possibilities.

The evaluator should recognize that "ground truth" for any event, free of camouflage and faking, stands by itself and can be measured. Adults caught up in disputed custody/supervision matters are subject to tremendous feeling states that may induce false statements and false accusations both on a voluntary and involuntary basis. Differentiating between what is voluntary from involuntary distortion makes evaluation of disputed domestic matters extremely difficult.

Murders are an unfortunate reality and can be solved despite attempts by perpetrators to conceal or disguise the event. Auto accidents may cause genuine neurological damage for the plaintiff, who might exaggerate the symptoms in an effort to collect compensation. The perceptions of witnesses can be colored by many variables, including excitement, stress, bias, and naivete. Normal persons have faked their way into hospitals (and residential programs) for various reasons (Rosenhan, 1973); abnormal individuals have faked their way out of these settings. Some people even fake symptoms in others, for example, in Munchausen by proxy. In all of these situations, a reality exists separate from the faking. This reality is called "ground truth."

Deception manifests itself in the ways the deceiver attempts to fool others within a certain context. Ground truth always represents itself as an interaction of the actor, the acted upon, and the context; deception represents a departure from what actually transpired in this three-entity

---

TABLE 2.1
Nondeliberate Distortion Factors

1. Reporting Person
   a. Stress
   b. Physical disability
   c. Limited intelligence
   d. Inattention
   e. Recall problems
   f. Psychosis
   g. Extreme affective state
2. Reported Event
   a. Too brief
   b. Physical barriers
   c. Weak intensity
   d. Distractions
   e. Figure-ground merging
   f. No stimulus uniqueness
3. Evaluation Errors
   a. Unreliable measures
   b. Invalid measures
   c. Inadequate training
   d. Leading questions/procedures
   e. Emotional evaluation contexts
   f. Assessed event in remote past

---

interaction. Unfortunately for the deceiver, deliberate deception takes energy, thought, and often-times reveals inconsistency. This can be uncovered with diligence and method.

NONDELIBERATE DISTORTION

Unintentional distortion of words or behavior is common. It must be considered before the individual's behaviors are understood and placed into perspective prior to the examiner concluding that deliberate deception has taken place. Nondeliberate distortion can be analyzed in terms of (1) the reporting person, (2) the reported event, and (3) evaluation methods. Table 2.1 presents the more common nondeliberate distortion factors. The examiner should scan this list routinely in every assessment of deception before conclusions are rendered.

For example, in a recent case that involved the defendant shooting a police officer in the abdomen with a large-caliber pistol, the officer experienced a gross stress reaction. The forensic report read as follows:

Nondeliberate distortion due to stress and other factors appears to have been operative to a significant degree.

Officer Jones reported, for example, during the instant offense, perceiving his alleged assailant as between 5'7" to 5'10" tall and weighing "far more" than 200 pounds (actually, the perpetrator stood 5'4" and weighed 180 pounds). Temporal events were seen as stretched out in duration. Some relevant details were not recalled, for example, the license plate number of the vehicle allegedly belonging to the defendant or the behavior of the nearby witness during the time of the shooting. This is not surprising. Research has shown that as people switch from normal states into General Adaptational Syndrome (GAS) behaviors that may be associated with threats to their lives or well-being, they become less attuned to details because they are more concerned with immediate safety needs. Generally, memory for details and sequences can be demonstrated, but recall is less clear than normal. Time estimates are especially vulnerable to exaggeration — in some studies by a factor of two and a half to one (e.g., see Buckhout, [1980]). Size and weight of the defendant are usually overestimated with poor recall of perpetrator's clothing, as with the officer-victim.

DISTORTION GUIDELINES

A dozen guidelines for the evaluation of unintentional distortion should be considered:

1. *Use multimodal methods.* Standardized interviews, observation, review of records, and interviews of significant others can yield valid results; however, the evaluator should not rely on insight alone based upon these traditional sources of information. If psychometric tests are administered, a battery of tests should be utilized. This addresses the issue of single tests vs. a composite battery. Often, evaluators search for a quick sample of faking on a standardized instrument. It is highly unlikely that a single test instrument will cover all parameters of deception. In addition, an inordinate amount of false negatives and positives may be generated. The choice of a battery should typically include measures for possible genuine problems as well as for deliberate deception. Faking often accompanies nondeliberate distortion, as the evaluation of the defendant who shot the police officer revealed:

> Nondeliberate distortion for the defendant may include a chronic condition of borderline retardation with specific learning disabilities. Specific chronic deficits noted on standardized testing two weeks before the instant offense included (a) a short attention span, (b) a borderline level of memory for general information, (c) a low average word knowledge (vocabulary) and social (common sense) comprehension, and (d) an inability to cognitively process visual stimuli due to selecting specific visual cues in a maladaptive or inaccurate manner. He was unable to effectively handle selective visual cues. He experienced excessive anxiety, tension, and emotional conflict. Results on another test indicated a limited visual awareness for noting essential details of the human figure and social immaturity, and (e) confusion when listening. The Detroit Tests of Learning Aptitude showed problem areas in auditory sequencing and vocabulary skills.
>
> The Durrell Listening Comprehension results were at the third grade level. In general, results from the most recent testing are in accord with ten years of previous evaluation results which suggest significant problems in attention, both visual and auditory stimulus processing and recall, and language comprehension. The defendant admitted lying to the police officer when he stated he had not been drinking beer and in regard to the ownership of the assault weapon. After the shooting, the defendant told bystanders that a nearby witness was the actual perpetrator. He then drove from the scene, covered his car with bushes in a ravine, and attempted to hide in the mountains.
>
> A standard clinical battery — Wechsler Adult Intelligence Scale-Revised (WAIS-R), Minnesota Multiphasic Personality Inventory–2 (MMPI-2), Sentence Completion Test (SCT), Bender-Gestalt Visual–Motor Test (BGVMT) and an interview — consistently revealed faking in this case. Tests designed specifically to detect faking can be included in a composite battery of tests in spite of the possibility that the assessee has considerable nondeliberate distortion.

2. *Start with the most valid information first.* Data considered first most influence the evaluator. Premature closure and/or attempts to confirm what the evaluator already believes may lead to incorrect conclusions. The evaluator can consider data with the highest "hit rates" for accuracy first and suspend his or her conclusions until all data (e.g., laboratory data for substance consumption at the time of the relevant event) are analyzed.

3. *Adhere to validated decision rules even when tempted to abandon them for a particular case.* Decision rules are more accurate than clinical judgment. Evaluators should ask why they are tempted to abandon the validated decision rules in the first place. What biasing factors may be operating?

4. *Think base rates.* Knowledge of base rates alerts the evaluator of deception regarding the general chances that certain events will occur. Literature will be cited later to provide base rate

information in deception analysis. It would be helpful, for instance, if the evaluator knew that between one third and one half of defendants malinger memory problems in murder cases, with a 25% overall rate of such malingering when pleading insanity. Almost 50% of substances are verbally underreported compared with the results of urinalysis; yet the percentages differ depending on the particular locality and substance involved. On a test of remote memory, people generally do not err on autobiographical questions even if they are brain injured. Further, base rate information is all that may be available to the evaluator in certain types of crimes, such as serial homicides where the perpetrator is unknown. For some types of unverifiable problems, such as suicide ideation and command hallucinations, base rate information may be the only data available to the evaluator as a springboard for deception analysis.

5. *Do not become overly focused on unique, salient, or unusual case features.* Some evaluators consider the behavior in question to be genuine when a psychopath cries during the rendition of the instant offense. Conversely, evaluators have viewed a rape victim as not being credible because she was a prostitute and a belly dancer.

6. *Do not fall prey to illusory associations between evaluation responses and supposed faking.* These unfounded associations include the following:

a. From the ancient literature, a burned tongue from a hot sword indicates deception.
b. Responses to white spaces on the Rorschach means oppositional tendencies.
c. A lucid and reasonable account of the crime under hypnosis spells genuineness.
d. The L (Lie) scale on the MMPI was developed as a measure of the test taker's credibility.

Evaluators should be wary of meaningless scores on tests measuring deception. Recall that:

- Scores regress toward the mean with extreme scores showing the greatest change upon retesting.
- Small samples frequently misrepresent population parameters. Unfortunately, most of the specific tests for malingering fall into this category.
- Scatter can be due to chance and thus not indicate deception or other relevant dimensions.
- Chance occurrences can be seen as ordered.
- The year when a test is normed affects the scoring pattern.
- Reliance on highly intercorrelated measures is frequent. Evaluators tend to confirm the same problems when they use redundant testing. For example, administration of the MMPI and the California Personality Inventory (CPI) produces the same results in deception analysis.

7. *Do not assess deception from DSM-IV criteria.* Making incorrect associations between a diagnosis and certain traits may result in falsely attributing faking or honesty. For instance, a diagnosis of Antisocial Personality Disorder does not always imply lying and a diagnosis of Adjustment Disorder does not automatically mean that the labeled person is telling the truth. In general, no mental condition automatically indicates deception or honesty. As discussed in the Introduction, the DSM-IV criteria for malingering are fatally flawed. Any forensic problem could be seen as malingering if the assessee was uncooperative or happened to be diagnosed as Antisocial Personality Disorder. The need for a marked discrepancy between the subject's presented deficits and outside findings is important. Unfortunately, DSM-IV provides no threshold criteria for evaluating such discrepancies.

8. *Do not fail to consider triggers to ostensibly concealing or uncooperative behavior.* Clients have bad days. The need to assess over several sittings is important. Evaluators may have atypical days. Frustration or stress unrelated to the evaluation may be communicated to the assessee, who may show countertransference as a result. The evaluator, who may report distorted results, may overlook the cause-and-effect relationship.

One trigger to distortion is commitment bias — the tendency to repeat a wrong answer if given a second chance to respond. It is operative when the subject wants to please the evaluator and believes that the assessor thinks a certain choice is correct. The client, for example, may pick out the wrong face again in a photo lineup because of this bias. Unconscious transference is another trigger. This occurs when a person seen in one situation is confused with another, such as when one sees the partial face of a person in a subway and concludes it was the defendant's face.

9. *List alternative hypotheses and seek evidence for each.* The evaluator should systematically list disconfirming and confirming data for each conclusion rendered. This may result in more accuracy; there is some evidence that evaluators who deliberate longer are most accurate.

10. *Do not fail to limit and operationalize conclusions.* The evaluator should note the confidence in results as well as indicate the degree of defendant distortion that may have occurred. A feedback mechanism to reassess results should be specified — for example, a readministration of the same measures when a forensic issue reemerges.

11. *Do not overload the referring party or trier of fact with data.* The average working memory holds about 7 bits of information at a time. There may be a decrease in accuracy in most people as a result of overload after that point. The writers try to give jurors no more than about a half dozen critical points in their attempts to synthesize their overall presentation in court.

12. *Make a deliberate effort to get feedback.* At a bare minimum, cross-validating information should validate findings on deception. The forensic professional should know his or her "hit rate" in court for acceptance of conclusions regarding deception. Jurors can be questioned following either a civil or criminal trial. Normative data regarding distortion and deception for one's area, practice, or circumstances should be systematically collected. Age, sex, educational level, and ethnic differences should be noted.

Hindsight bias should be avoided. This occurs when an evaluator believes, after the fact, that the outcome could have been easily detected. It can be demonstrated by asking evaluators to estimate their own accuracy levels and comparing them with known results. Foresight in FDA focuses instead on what comes next in a deception problem.

SYNTHESIS

Generally, nondeliberate distortion needs to be ruled out or taken into account before deception is considered. Ground truth may be misrepresented by both nondeliberate and deliberate deception.

The issues in separating deliberate from nondeliberate distortion are important for both the individual and society. In criminal trials, jurors appear less willing to exculpate and judges may be harsher in sentencing when the defendant has been caught at deception. In civil cases, awards may be reduced (or eliminated) for behavior seen as deceptive.

Evaluators should know the behavioral science literature on deception to reduce their own nondeliberate distortion. This exercise will serve to keep one humble. The literature on deception is incomplete and fragmentary up to 1990. Since 1990, and now into the new millennium, there has been an increasing number of empirical investigations regarding deception and malingering, but the clinical/forensic methods remain rather rudimentary. Even worse, there is continued use of invalid or marginally acceptable techniques to establish that deception has occurred. These include the traditional clinical interview, forensic hypnosis, drug-assisted interviews, and some arousal methods, such as the voice stress analyzer and penile plethysmography. These methods are not held in high esteem in this book mainly because, for the most part, their scientific validity is still lacking or is disappointing.

The purpose of this chapter will be well served if the evaluator of deception follows a few simple guidelines as presented. Ground truth is that abstract absolute in forensics; it is the Holy Grail that forensic evaluators pursue. Separating one from ground truth is distortion, both intentional and unintentional. In a post hoc analysis of deception, unintentional distortion must be ruled out or accounted for first, as it may explain the evaluation findings. The forensic evaluator should routinely check for factors and events associated with nondeliberate distortion and report upon these in consultation or trial testimony. Failure to do so renders conclusions regarding intentional deception meaningless.

REFERENCES

Buckhout, R. (1980). Eyewitness identification and psychology in the courtroom. In G. Cooke (Ed.), *The role of the forensic psychologist* (pp. 335–339). Springfield, IL: Charles C Thomas.

Rosenhan, D. L. (1973). On being sane in insane places. *Science*, *179*, 250–358.

Slovenko, R.(1995) *Psychiatry and criminal responsibility.* New York: Wiley.

3 The Applied Forensic Distortion Analysis Model

Forensic distortion analysis (FDA) mandates a scrutiny of the actor, oneself as evaluator, and the context in which the distortion occurs. To comment upon possible faking by a murderer, one must be intimately familiar with the homicide. To state that cerebral insult stems from a car accident, one should know how the person typically behaved prior to the alleged trauma. To claim that a rehabilitation client is deliberately sabotaging therapy because of secondary motives, one must be aware of one's own countertransference, an insidious and often overlooked source of self-deception.

This chapter focuses further on the FDA model by discussing (1) the symptoms targeted for deception that may reflect goal formulation and perhaps planning on the part of the faker, (2) behavioral output in the form of typical styles of deceptive responding, and (3) the means used to understand and measure these response patterns. Figure 3.1 presents these aspects of deception analysis.

TARGET SYMPTOMS

As a rule, fakers choose target symptoms in accordance with the direction of their vested interests. People choose what they think will work to accomplish their goals. Much knowledge of psychological and medical conditions has been publicized in the media. Thus, actual neuropsychological symptoms may be selected for bogus head trauma. Amnesia may be chosen when a gap in memory is self-serving in a violent crime. Targets are not to be confused with goals, which may include anything from avoiding prison to obtaining a monetary reward. Targets are short term in nature; goals represent the ultimate objective of the faker.

Selecting a target means that the faker makes assumptions about both ground truth and distortion. Psychosis cannot be faked without having an idea of how a psychotic person behaves. This gives the evaluator an advantage by putting the onus for performing on the deceiver.

Targets can change as a function of many factors, such as opportunity, fatigue, and evaluator behavior. The goal, however, usually remains the same (e.g., wanting compensation for a back injury). Some targets are nonverifiable, particularly suicidal ideation, pain, hearing voices, and trauma-related nightmares. Finally, targets are often based on partially real deficits and represent an exaggeration of deficits rather than pure fabrication. The best lie is the partial truth.

A simple method for listing cognitive targets is presented in Table 3.1. All the major dimensions of deception in terms of targets are covered. The *behavioral* category includes verbal or motor acts as targets. *Somatic or psychosomatic* targets and symptoms include a broadband category of physical signs. *Sensation* refers to faked deficits in vision, hearing, smell, taste, touch, temperature, pressure, balance, and pain. *Affect* can involve autonomic and/or emotional events that may be distorted. *Cognitive* problems include deficits in attention, memory, language, and thinking. *Interpersonal* deficits involve faking when reporting upon the interaction with others. Table 3.1 also presents clinical examples of target symptoms.

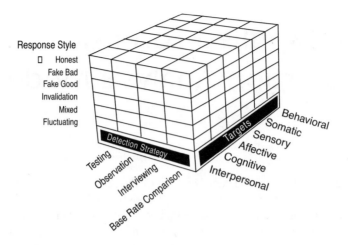

FIGURE 3.1 Three-dimensional model of distortion analysis.

TABLE 3.1
Targets of Deception

Category	Examples
Behavioral	
Motor	Slowness/agitation
Verbal	Mutism; aphonia
Somatic/psychosomatic	
Central nervous system	Epileptic seizures; paralysis
Other systems	Factitious arthritis; muscle weakness
Sensation	
Visual	Visual hallucinations; partial blindness
Auditory	Hearing voices; deafness
Tactile	Intense or persisting pain
Taste	Gustatory insensitivity
Smell	Olfactory hallucinations; loss of smell
Imagery	
Perception	Flashbacks; illusions
Rapid eye movement (REM) sleep	Nightmares; night terrors
Affect	
Autonomic	Anxiety; rage
Emotional	Lability; major depression
Cognitive	
Attention	Stupor; unconsciousness
Memory	Amnesia; recall problems
Language	Aphasia; word salad
Thinking	Schizophrenia; dementia
Interpersonal	
Social	Imposture; Munchausen by proxy

TABLE 3.2
Response Styles

1. Honest	Attempts to be accurate within own frame of reference; may show nondeliberate distortion
2. Faking bad	Exaggeration or fabrication of symptoms and negative features; denial and/or minimization of positive traits/events; misattribution of deficit to false cause
3. Faking good	Minimization and/or denial of symptoms and behaviors; exaggeration or fabrication of positive points; misattribution of blame to outside source
4. Invalidation	Attempts to render the evaluation meaningless
5. Mixed	Combination of styles within same evaluation period
6. Fluctuating	Change of style within or between evaluation period(s)

In sum, targets involve any short-term objectives which, when reached, are in the direction of the faker's stake. The targets (1) may change over time, during the evaluation, and/or subsequent to the evaluation; (2) may be specific or broadband in focus (e.g., tics or dementia); (3) are based upon cognitive schemes, experience, sophistication, and available disguises; (4) must be differentiated from nonfaked behaviors; and (5) can be translated into discrete response styles that can be measured.

RESPONSE STYLES OF DECEPTIVE BEHAVIOR

Response styles are the second part of the FDA model. The heart of FDA is in the analysis of response styles. Only through behavior can one infer deception. Response styles are connected to targets in the nature of cause and effect even though targets can be quickly conceived of or yield poor (i.e., detectable) patterns of behavior. The basic response styles for deception are presented in Table 3.2.

HONEST RESPONDING

Despite the focus of this book, most individuals have built-in prohibitions against deliberate deception. In forensic intervention settings, many clients are distressed psychologically or physically and just want to be well again. Returning to work or a meaningful lifestyle is a powerful reinforcer; most clients believe that nondeceptive behavior is proper and essential to achieve these goals.

In the criminal arena, defendants, witnesses, and significant others are reminded of their moral duty, which is reinforced by legal sanction, for truth telling. Possible charges relating to perjury and hindering prosecution add incentive to tell the truth. For defendants, malingering is strongly suspected in about 20% of the cases (Rogers, 1988). This means that the vast majority of defendants are not engaging in blatant deception, even when their liberty is at stake.

In the civil arena, the most notorious of settings with regard to eliciting deception for monetary gain, there may be a fear of being detected for one's fakery. Depositions are taken and oaths are administered in a judicial attempt to reduce deception. For some situations, such as workers' compensation, a theoretical question emerges of why people would fake to obtain a fraction of their normal pay.

Honest responding does not equal cooperation with the evaluator. Noncooperation can occur for a variety of reasons — from dislike of the evaluator to circumstances of the setting. Witnesses and significant others are often only minimally cooperative. They may claim that they are too busy, or make it clear that they do not want to become involved, or may be biased in favor of or against the accused.

Nondeliberate distortion does occur in the presence of truth telling. The brain-damaged or psychotic subject may give what he or she believes to be an accurate portrayal of events. Recall that nondeliberate distortion caused by stress may occur in the majority of people (Buckhout, 1980).

The following case illustrates honest responding for an individual accused of attempting to sexually assault a 25-year-old school teacher:

> Mr. Tanaka displayed few evidences of deliberate deception as suggested by (1) the congruence between pathological test signs and clinical behavior (e.g., both showing perseveration, bizarre statements); (2) acceptable range of responses on measures helpful in detecting faking bad and faking good (e.g., MMPI and forced-choice testing); (3) expected learning deficits with increased task difficulty (e.g., on neuropsychological testing); (4) similarity of scores on different subtests or test items of equal difficulty (e.g., digits forward and backward obtained on WAIS-R and Wechsler Memory Scale); (5) congruence of volunteered information with the physical evidence and victim and witness statements; (6) concordance of mental condition at the time of assessment with crime behavior, and (7) volunteering of much self-incriminating data.
>
> There were suggestions of considerable nondeliberate distortion for both the time of the evaluation and the alleged offenses. Immediate, short-term, and long-term recall showed contamination with psychotic features when compared with cross-validating data. Concrete answers were given to many queries with prompting needed to extract responses, which were later determined to be correct. His sense of time was substantially impaired compared with cross-validating data. He further displayed an inability to see his mistakes during testing, corresponding to historical behavior which showed poor judgment at home and on the job. His WAIS-R score revealed borderline intelligence with deficits in all areas of intellectual functioning, including vocabulary, computational, informational, and verbal associational skills.
>
> In general, for both the time of the evaluation and the instant offenses, the accused showed little deliberate, but considerable nondeliberate, distortion. Cross-validation with other database sources was necessary to determine credibility parameters.

FAKING BAD

Faking bad, also known as malingering, deceit, prevarication, false imputation, and simulation, always involves fabrication of nonexistent problems or the exaggeration of actual pathology. Denial or minimization of good points in an attempt to look worse than one actually is may also occur. As with any response style, malingering can coexist with genuine deficits. The writers' experience is that malingering associated with real problems should alert the evaluator that one is not dealing with an either–or situation.

Many faking bad patterns are possible. Table 3.3 presents a dozen of the more common patterns of faking bad encountered in clinical/forensic evaluation. Frequency data are lacking for most of these faking subtypes. Data on faked recall problems using a forced-choice format, however, suggest that many of the subtypes are common among successful fakers (Hall & Shooter, 1989; Shooter & Hall, 1990). These include randomizing (28%), perseveration (19%), fabrication (16%), fractionalizing (9%), and disengagement (9%). For unsuccessful fakers, the same response subtypes emerged, but in a different order or magnitude. Results showed that randomizing (9%), perseveration (5%), fabrication (41%), fractionalizing (20%), and disengagement (13%) were clearly detectable as response strategies. For both successful and unsuccessful fakers, the full gamut of the subtypes presented on Table 3.3 was represented.

FAKING GOOD

Also known as defensiveness and dissimulation, faking good is the exact opposite of faking bad. Faking good always involves denial or minimization of problems in the direction of one's vested interests. Fabricating and exaggerating positive points are also frequent. Second to honest responding, faking good is probably the most common distortion strategy utilized. Indeed, most people minimize and deny or exaggerate their positive points to adapt to the social environment. Otherwise, most marriages, businesses, and other relationships involving people would not last.

TABLE 3.3
Faking Bad Response Styles

Style	Behavioral Strategy	Examples
1. Verbal fabrication	Claims a nonexistent problem	"I have ringing in my right ear."
2. Verbal exaggeration	Amplifies real problem	"I'm more forgetful than usual."
3. Verbal denial	Disclaims an ability	"I can't smell anything."
4. Verbal minimizing	Downplays an ability	"I can walk only one block."
5. Misattribution	States deficit due to false cause rather than true etiology	Claiming developmental learning disability caused by a vehicular accident
6. Behavioral fractionalizing	Shows crudely estimated fraction of ability	Hand grip scores only half of ability
7. Behavioral approximating	Gets a close, but not exact, answer	"6 + 6 = 13; 7 × 3 = 22"
8. Behavioral infrequency	Sprinkles errors throughout performance on graduated scale	Errors on WAIS-R Comp. and Vocab. on initial items
9. Behavioral disengagement	Shows confusion and frustration — may give up	Claims total inability during blindfolded period of the Tactile Performance Test
10. Impulsivity	Answering quickly, presents first thing on mind	Poor on Arith. and Block Design compared to untimed performance
11. Perseveration	Persists with one response mode regardless of feedback	Alternates errors on WCST or Explicit Alternative Testing
12. Randomizing	No consistent pattern of errors	Speech Perception Test errors due to deliberate inattention

In faking good, the deceiver cannot do better than his or her true ability. Thus, faking good cannot occur on intelligence, neuropsychological, and other ability tests because clients cannot do better than their true best performance. The exception to this rule is taking performance-enhancing drugs, such as anabolic steroids or stimulants, to increase vigilance and motor speed. Some substances, such as antianxiety drugs, are occasionally used to cover anxiety during an interview and to project an image of confidence to the evaluator.

It is possible to fake good on personality measures and in interviews. One may affirm a fraction of the pathological items on the MMPI, or engage in self-praise during an interview. In general, the five most commonly used methods of faking good are:

1. Denial   "I didn't drink alcohol."
                      "I don't have a memory problem."
2. Minimizing   "I snort coke only on Wednesday nights."
                      "I do poorly on tests like this."
3. Fabrication   "I have run a mile in less than 4 minutes."
                      "I have a parasensory ability which allows me to discern the truth."
4. Exaggeration   "Nobody cooks as good as I."
                      "I'm considered a virtuous person."
5. Misattribution   "I beat my wife because I was grieving over my friend's death."

Faking good is difficult to demonstrate when it involves concealing the real. It places the onus on the evaluator to demonstrate the existence of that which is denied or minimized. Cross-validation is essential in these cases. The following illustrates defensiveness in a case involving a 26-year-old defendant accused of savagely beating his ex-girlfriend into a coma.

During the second interview on October 9, 1990, the defendant blamed the victim, acquaintances of the victim, his own attorney, and the court for slanting the "truth" and refusing to allow him to tell the whole story. He declined to take psychological tests, citing again issues of trust. Intellectually bright, verbal, and persistent in his efforts to dominate the interview, this brown-haired, brown-eyed male utilized cognitive strategies of minimization, denial, and withholding of information to convey a picture that this whole affair (i.e., the instant offense and events leading up to it) was a romantic feud that should best be simply forgotten by the court so he can go on with his life.

In regard to minimization and denial, examples included stating that (1) he hit the victim only once, consisting of an open-handed slap with his left hand, during the February 3, 1990 assault which caused brain damage to the victim, despite statements by two witnesses to the contrary. (2) He has never "attacked" the victim, only "hit" her on occasion. He affirmed the December 1988 assault, but stated that he hit the victim in the ribs two to three times at that time because she allegedly told him she had been sexually unfaithful with a previous boyfriend. (3) He placed an ice pick through a jacket on the victim's door, stating to the examiner that he was only returning the jacket and that no threat was intended. In retrospect, he can now see how the victim reacted with fright to this and other behaviors of his. (4) He threw a rock through the victim's window in October 1989 only to "wake her up," not to frighten her. (5) He never intended to pull the victim's hair out on October 6, 1989 and that he grabbed her head to get her attention; earlier in the day, the victim had reportedly walked into his apartment and destroyed two or three paintings with an umbrella. Even though he was angry at the victim, the hair-pulling allegedly occurred because the victim pushed his hand away, thus in essence pulling her own hair out. (6) He has never had a really serious drug problem; however, he stated later that while in California, he injected heroin 15 to 20 times, smoked it many other times, and committed crimes with eventual incarceration for those crimes, which were related to drug procurement activities. Records from California revealed that his daily heroin addiction cost about $200.

Many other examples exist. Suffice it to say that the defendant may not be a credible source of information due to distortion methods of (1) minimization, (2) denial, (3) projection of blame, and (4) withholding information to project a positive picture of himself. He denied feelings of anger toward the victim. Finally, he stated that he did not want his relatives contacted in connection with this case.

INVALIDATION

The evaluator may not know the reasons for a client's invalidating the evaluation by some tactic(s), thus rendering it meaningless. Conclusions cannot be reached when this occurs. Examples include (1) not reporting for the evaluation; (2) reporting for the evaluation, but having to leave after a half hour to avoid being fired from work or because of a sick spouse; (3) showing up substance-intoxicated; (4) becoming nauseous and sick in the middle of an interview; or (5) leaving too many unanswered items on MMPI. The evaluator must then perform the evaluation at another time or change data collection strategies to counter attempts at invalidation.

MIXED RESPONSE STYLES

Mixed response styles within one evaluation involve faking good and faking bad. How is it possible to have both malingering and defensiveness within one evaluation? The person may be extraordinarily sensitive about sexual behavior, for example, thinking (wrongly, of course) that this is none of the evaluator's business, yet attempting at the same time to exaggerate pain reactions to reap a financial reward in a civil suit. Clinically, they may say, "I am here to assess my pain, not my lifestyle." On the MMPI, overendorsed depression and other traits associated with pain may be seen, but anger, distrust, and suspicion may be downplayed.

FLUCTUATING RESPONSE STYLES

Suggestions are beginning to emerge that changes in response strategies occur within the same evaluation period. A common one, found in testing for feigned amnesia, is faking bad at the beginning of evaluation and then showing honest responding as fatigue sets in or as clients begin to believe that they have given themselves away. Honesty in the beginning of the interview, with faking bad as the evaluation progresses, is occasionally seen. This is a sign that the client may think the examiner can be duped.

A second fluctuating style involves presenting different styles during different time periods. The defendant may claim psychosis at the time of the instant offense to escape criminal liability, yet deny problems for the present to obtain release from hospitalization. A civil litigant may fake good concerning problems before an accident but fake bad for the present to assert damages. This suggests that evaluation procedures must be geared toward both the past and the present.

In general, there is no escape from considering possible deceptive responses, for it is only through behavior that faking can be understood and measured. Fakers select targets that serve overriding goals in the direction of their interest. By acting to achieve those targets, fakers create response patterns, which can be scrutinized by the evaluator.

DETECTION STRATEGIES

The last part of the FDA model deals with detection methods. The overall strategy of the evaluation is to gather information about the actor, the one acted upon, and the context of deception, all within a systematic, comprehensive approach, which is then tailored to the assessment needs of the individual examined.

For example, in testing for claimed cerebral deficits because of an auto accident involving problems with specific sensory skills such as numbness and agnosia, the evaluator would first use a neuropsychological battery. Specific claimed problems not measured on the battery, such as loss of smell and "frontal" problems, would then be tested.

Nontesting approaches that yield high reliability can be utilized. Structured interviews and interviews of significant/knowledgeable others for cross-validation of claimed deficits, for example, are very helpful. Observation, to determine whether claimed deficits correspond to actual behavior, may be utilized. The forensic community holds inpatient hospitalization for observation of deceptive response patterns in high regard. This method builds in multiple measures over time to evaluate the assessee. Figure 3.2 presents the authors' opinions of the clinical efficacy of selected methods for detecting deception.

In regard to detection methods, the evaluator should keep in mind that no one method is 100% accurate; the methods should be used in combination with one another. The examiner should use methods that are broadbanded, standardized, and flexible within the evaluation. Methods must

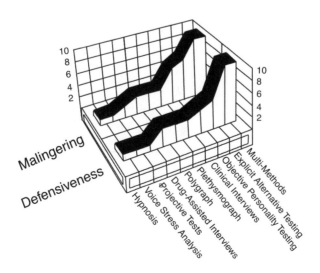

FIGURE 3.2 Clinical efficacy of deception detection methods.

eventually be geared specifically toward symptoms/targets. As discussed, they are operative for at least two periods of time. Few referral sources are particularly interested in deception only at the time of the evaluation. Last, built-in feedback and replication features are necessary to assess the effectiveness of the methods.

SYNTHESIS

In sum, the FDA model may assist the evaluator in focusing on the possible deceiver's target symptoms and response patterns. Detection methods can be broadbanded to illuminate targets and responses, and to provide testable hypotheses for further inquiry. Evaluation for deception must be general in the beginning and tailored to individual and specific questions as they arise.

REFERENCES

Buckhout, R. (1980). Eyewitness identification and psychology in the courtroom. In G. Cooke (Ed.), *The role of the forensic psychologist* (pp. 335–339). Springfield, IL: Charles C Thomas.

Hall, H. V., & Shooter, E. (1989). Explicit alternative testing for feigned memory deficits. *Forensic Reports*, 2, 277–286.

Rogers, R. (Ed.). (1988). *Clinical assessment of malingering and deception*. New York: Guilford Press.

Shooter, E., & Hall, H. V. (1990). Explicit alternative testing for deliberate distortion: Towards an abbreviated format. *Forensic Reports*, 4, 45–49.

4 Evaluation Process Guidelines

The traditional training of most mental health clinicians usually does not imbue the sense of caution and level of analytic inquiry that is necessary in forensic assessments. The effective FDA attitude is not skepticism, nor mistrust or antagonism. Any of these clinician attitudes will inevitably convey to interviewees and result in distorted and biased findings. Such attitudes will also become predictable fodder for any later cross-examination designed to impeach the evaluator's credibility. The proper approach is one of constant but respectful wariness for the possibility of deliberate and nondeliberate distortion. At the same time, there must be a vigilant effort to solicit the most accurate data possible. The evaluators must always respect the rights of interviewees to conduct themselves, as they deem necessary during examinations. Forensic clinicians are first data collectors; it is not their responsibility to conduct psychotherapy, to gather evidentiary information, or to correct the ills of the world (Greenberg & Shuman, 1997). Armed with the proper attitude, effective FDA requires proper preparation for the evaluation, conducting a proper evaluation, and proper follow-up after the evaluation. It is very important to understand that the forensic evaluator's work product in most instances is the written report. Learning how to write professional, quality reports is a critical aspect of the forensic clinician's training and ultimate working expertise.

The importance of careful and comprehensive preparation in any forensic assessment cannot be adequately stressed. By definition, every clinical/forensic assessment entails the probability of distortion, both deliberate and nondeliberate, as well as a combination of the two. The vigilant clinician will be best prepared to detect distortion, but, of course, the effort is never foolproof. Preparation must involve a thorough review of all available background data and materials. If critical background information is known to be missing, then every effort should be made to access it. The final report should always have a listing of all materials reviewed, persons interviewed, data examined, etc. Similarly, if there is known to be information that could not be accessed, that should be noted also. The effort is to document the clinician's database as accurately as possible.

The time to begin to prepare for standing up to cross-examination begins at the point of referral. The adversarial cross-examination means that the opposing attorney will make every possible effort to impeach the expert's testimony. The authors have had the experience of a comprehensive evaluation being cast in a dubious light with the opposing attorney's proffer that a prior report was not incorporated into the assessment. Another circumstance is not being able to access prior records because defense counsel advises the client not to provide consent. In this instance, the report should cite the reason for the inability to access material and the trier of fact will then have to make a determination how to proceed.

Not having accurate or complete background materials is just one area in which the expert's testimony is subject to impeachment (see Chapter 24). Citing all background materials that were relied upon, as well as those materials that were inaccessible (and why they were inaccessible) is the safest approach for the potential expert witness. The primary reason for the thorough background review, however, is to prepare the clinician for FDA.

A set of evaluation process guidelines by Paulsen and Hall (1991) is recommended and presented in Table 4.1.

TABLE 4.1
Process Factors in Deception Analysis

Suggestion	Rationale
Prior to the Evaluation	
1. Remain vigilant to possibility of assessee distortion	Knowledge of high-risk groups and distortion literature is essential
2. Assess examiner distortion, including that which is unintended	Examiner distortion is common (e.g., wrong assumptions, bias)
3. Maintain independence from referral party	Closeness with referral party suggests bias
4. Gather source data relevant to subject/incident	Objective data must be reviewed to ask incident-specific questions
5. Prepare a standardized distortion battery	There is no substitute for battery evaluation completeness
6. Schedule the evaluation	Generally, distortion increases with time since the incident
During the Evaluation	
7. Orient client to evaluation process and disposition	Written and signed orientation forms are recommended to refute later claims of evaluation bias
8. Tape the evaluation, with knowledge of client	This assists evaluator's recall and is the basis for possible replication
9. Conduct an open-ended interview	Broad questions force assessee to work out details
10. Eventually focus on critical distortion issues	Binary-type questions force assessee to take a stand
11. Sprinkle questions with known answers throughout interview	Known deviation from "ground truth" is helpful to assess distortion style
12. Use multiple assessment methods	Validity and examiner credibility will be increased
After the Evaluation	
13. Modify the evaluation as appropriate	Flexibility of examiner response may increase database (e.g., quickly presented questions)
14. Confront client with suggestions of distortion	Providing opportunity to change story may resolve discrepancies
15. Evaluate validity of each data source	Cross-validating sources are subject to distortion
16. Assess nondeliberate distortion of client	Rule out unintentional distortion before ruling in deception
17. Rule in deliberate distortion	Deception should be explicitly demonstrated
18. Differentiate between incident and evaluation distortion	Distortion always refers to two different points in time
19. Identify distortion along different points of time subsequent to incident	Fluctuating response styles suggest deception
20. Report incomplete or invalid data	Referral source needs to know if complete database is utilized
21. Determine whether uncovered distortion is relevant to referral questions	Genuine impairments are often associated with deception
22. Reflect the decision process in the report	How the examiner arrived at conclusions is central to distortion
23. Describe adequacy of process	Explicitly stating that distortion data warrant the conclusions is helpful
24. Delimit scope of distortion-related conclusions	Degree of certainty and temporal limitations should be specified
25. Make recommendations for case disposition	Further evaluation may be indicated (e.g., inpatient observation)
26. Identify a feedback mechanism	Later retesting for distortion is a frequent issue
27. Retain all data regarding distortion	Baseline material may be used for reanalysis

BEFORE THE EVALUATION

The following case, which won a $500,000 award for the plaintiff, illustrates errors on the part of the defendant, the State of Hawaii Health Department, which could have been avoided with proper preparation before an evaluation of a patient's readiness for discharge.

> A 28-year-old white male paranoid schizophrenic began hallucinating, hearing the voice of a spirit urging him to hurt people, particularly his family members who were responsible for his involuntary hospitalization. There was a history of repeated assaults on family members with threats to kill. After 2 weeks, the patient was partially stabilized on antipsychotic medication. However, episodic outbursts of rage, shown by head banging and chair throwing, continued. The patient was overheard saying that he belonged in the hospital and that, if released, he would physically hurt his family. For the next 3 days, he went to great lengths to deny and minimize symptoms, finally stating that he had "learned his lesson" and was ready to return home.
>
> The psychiatrist noted that the patient had "achieved insight" and made arrangements for discharge, which unfortunately did not include informing the patient's parents of his return to the community. The patient went to his family's home unannounced, refused to take his medication, and quickly deteriorated. A week later, he stabbed his mother in the heart with a 12-inch kitchen knife, lacerated his niece and nephew on the legs and arms, and plunged the knife into his sister's torso, leaving the blade embedded.

The forensic report submitted in this case concluded with the following:

> In sum, a prediction of violent behavior with a decision to continue preventive hospitalization was expected, required, and approved behavior by the authorities. There was no way for the State Hospital to escape the obligation of assessing the risk of violence prior to the patient's release from the hospital. Dr. Trevane should have been aware of a multitude of signals from the patient and from other sources that the patient posed a substantial risk of violence at the time of release. Dr. Trevane further ignored the extant professional literature on the subject, disregarded his own observations in deciding to release the patient, and used factors in his decision-making process that bore little, if any, relationship to whether future violence would occur.
>
> The staff did not have in their possession, or were otherwise not aware of, the contents of retrievable documentation regarding the patient's past violence and thus completely failed to uncover a history of dangerousness, escapes from previous inpatient psychiatric programs, noncompliance in taking medication, and other critical factors that must be considered in predicting dangerousness.
>
> They believed the patient when presented with his falsehoods, and they did not believe or ignored him when he stated that he should not return to his family upon release. The staff should have known that he was a substantial risk of danger to his family in particular, that the opportunity to inflict violence through the use of a knife was available and precedented in both the patient's recent and remote history, and that consideration of inhibitory factors such as preparing or even notifying the family of his release and ensuring treatment compliance was important in preventing and/or controlling violence. The acute and chronic physical and mental trauma suffered by the victims were created by the patient's violence of May 15, 1988 in the nature of cause and effect.

In this case, a number of factors were neglected. First, hospital staff should have been alerted to the possibility of defensiveness, particularly after the patient changed his mind and stated that he wanted to go home. Florid psychosis usually does not disappear in several days; rather, it dissipates gradually. The basal history of violence was neglected, and there was strong evidence that the staff was unaware of the patient's previous dangerousness and/or future anticipated triggers of violence. No psychometric testing was conducted. Ward notes by nursing and social work staff did not appear to have been read by program planners. In sum, very basic errors in evaluating the patient's claim of readiness for release were made through inadequate preparation before the formal evaluation for release.

DURING THE EVALUATION

One of the factors to be dealt with during an evaluation is the occurrence of disruptions, distractions, and sabotage of the evaluation process.

> A 38-year-old white male defendant reported for the sanity evaluation with his (loud) wife, a neighbor, and a friend, despite specific instructions from the writer to come alone.
>
> A review of court records had revealed a lengthy criminal past with known attempts to manipulate evaluators in the direction of leniency.
>
> The solution to this problem involved psychometrically testing the accused while his significant others were being interviewed individually. They were also given instructions to write down what they knew of the accused's history and the instant offense involving an alleged assault on the wife. After 3 hours of evaluation and the collection of much forensic data, the accused and his significant others were released from evaluation.

In matters where police authorities have been involved, the police reports can be very important sources of information. Often times, police reports provide the only source of information about the accused's psychological state at the time of a critical incident. Clinicians must bear in mind that the police reports are investigation documents, and police are trained to write reports that will support anticipated prosecutions.

Significant others are often given checklists to complete in addition to their other tasks. These include the Mooney Problem Check List, Post-Traumatic Stress Disorder checklists, and a structured history form, all regarding the accused. Basic background information is collected about the party supplying the information to assess his or her credibility. Orientation procedures, of course, are followed in gleaning information from significant others to counteract later claims of examiner distortion. The evaluator is advised to outline clearly the evaluator's role and objectives, as well as the limits of confidentiality. If it becomes apparent during an assessment that the subject has lost sight of the evaluator's role, the subject should be reminded. A common problem is inter-viewees' being lulled by the rapport of the assessment process and making incriminating statements or offering personal opinions that they would not make if they recalled, at the moment, the objective, impartial role of the forensic clinician. If interviewees complain later, as they predictably will, the evaluator is portrayed as having a malevolent interest. Evaluators must treat all witnesses with the same rights and privileges as the defendant, including the right to cease questioning.

The evaluation should start on a general level to tap into the assessee's stream of conscious-ness and style of thinking. Police commonly interrupt the interrogation of the accused before obtaining broadbanded information, thus losing the chance to observe the arrestee mentally working out details to the questions. Sometime during the initial part of the evaluation, the first in a pair of parallel test forms can be administered, followed by the second test toward the end of the session. These parallel test procedures include repeated measures of receptive vocabulary (e.g., Peabody Picture Vocabulary Test), visual recall (e.g., California Memory Test), and auditory discrimination (e.g., Auditory Discrimination Test), or other tests if the skills tapped by those tests are relevant to the issue of deception in a particular case. For example, the Shipley Institute of Living Scale or the Ravens Progressive Matrices can be administered to the accused in a sanity screening. This provides for parallel administration later or for comparison with WAIS-R scores. Regression equations permit prediction of WAIS-R IQ scores from both the Shipley and the Ravens tests.

Flexibility of response is especially important. One client refused to operate the hand dyna-mometer, claiming that it was a test for "physical therapy," but he agreed to do finger tapping. Although these tests are not sensitive to the same parts of the cortical motor system, both yield an indication of motor ability. Some individuals refuse a recommended CT scan but are agreeable to the MRI, which actually shows more details in terms of cerebral encephalopathy.

TABLE 4.2
Confrontation during Analysis for Deception

1. Assessor summarizes evaluation behaviors	"Are you saying that you do not recall anything about what happened on that night?"
2. Eliciting more complete information	"Tell me more about the reasons for your earlier [psychiatric] hospitalization."
3. Giving a chance to change self-report	"Looking back on what you said about the voices, do you obey them all the time? When don't you do what they say?"
4. Giving a chance to resolve discrepancies	"I'm wondering why you don't remember what you said yesterday about the accident."
5. Allowing client to admit to distortion	"If your ex-wife [boss, victim, etc.] were to describe your truthfulness, what would she [or he] say and why?"

The authors start with a structured interview format to lower threat. In sanity evaluations, the accused is oriented to the task, asked about identifying information, questioned on fitness to proceed, and then asked to describe the day of the instant offense in detailed sequence.* The instant offense is probed again to fill in missing time periods, behaviors, and other important details. It is during this stage of the process that data from the background information can be of immense value to the clinician. Posing hypotheticals, challenging the assessee's account, and confrontation can be utilized to allow the assessee a chance to resolve discrepancies. The evaluator should understand that the purpose of confrontation is to obtain more information, not to present an overview of evaluation findings to the defendant. Another caution is not to employ confrontation in a derogatory or oppositional manner such that the defendant complains, thereby setting the stage for dismissal or impeachment of the evaluation. Table 4.2 presents five methods of confrontation, and examples of each.

In sum, it is acceptable to ask the defendant to resolve discrepancies between the following:

1. What is written vs. what is stated orally.
2. What was said or done earlier in evaluation vs. what is being said or done now.

AFTER THE EVALUATION

A retrospective check for completeness is essential before the assessee is dismissed. A common problem by examiners is failure to recognize that data about deception must be relevant to time periods other than that of the evaluation.

Many forensic evaluations reviewed by the writers for various purposes have large amounts of data on distortion for the time of the evaluation but very little on that which connects to the critical event in question. In some instances, information about the defendant's behavior following the critical incident is essential. This is illustrated in the following case example involving an adolescent sexual offender.

Ivan was 17 years old and a senior in high school; he was identified as talented and gifted in the first 2 years of high school. During the summer between his sophomore and junior years, he became heavily involved with cannabis and other hallucinogens. He also became involved with girls, something he had previously shunned. He solicited girls usually a year or two younger than himself with a punk rock

---

* As pertinent to the situation (e.g., in court-ordered assessments of criminal matters), the defendant is always reminded of his or her *Miranda* rights. That is, the assessment is not confidential, and a report will be forwarded to the requesting judicial authority; defendants have the right to remain silent, the right to have legal counsel provided if they cannot afford to retain an attorney, and the right to have their attorney present.

image and free cannabis. A former girlfriend introduced Ivan to two of her girlfriends, both of whom had no prior experience with drugs or sex.

Ivan and the three girls became a foursome and gradually they began to engage in hallucinogen-induced weekend sexual orgies with Ivan being the focus of the girl's attentions. As with most adolescent dating, jealousy triangles emerged among the three girls and Ivan delighted in instigating bickering and actual physical altercations. Ivan then introduced bondage behavior into the sexual activities. One weekend Ivan took the youngest of the three girls for an evening drive. In addition to cannabis, Ivan brought alcohol; both the girl and Ivan were heavily intoxicated.

The evening ended in tragedy. The girl died from strangulation from implements used in an apparent bondage ritual; these implements were found with the body. The next day, police discovered the girl's nude body, partially submerged in a nearby stream. An autopsy showed strangulation to be the cause of death and reflected the victim's extreme intoxication.

The evening of the incident, police followed up on citizen complaints of a nude, male adolescent running through the neighborhood screaming, and had picked up Ivan. The police transported a bloodied and hysterical Ivan to an emergency room. He was sedated and treated for multiple abrasions and contusions.

The following day Ivan explained to the police that several adult males accosted him and the victim. The intruders haphazardly disrobed Ivan and beat him "to teach him a lesson." Ivan was not sure what the intruders did with his female friend. Police investigators determined that it was possible that intruders came upon the scene; the secluded area was well frequented by adolescents who engaged in the consumption of alcohol and illicit substances. Suspiciously, there was no evidence of Ivan's clothes or the victim's clothing. Ivan was charged in the matter. The treating medical staff later testified that Ivan's injuries were more consistent with his running or being dragged through underbrush as opposed to his having been pummeled.

A defense-retained clinician opined that Ivan was not criminally responsible due to an acute psychotic state induced by chronic and habitual substance abuse. One of the authors was court-ordered to evaluate Ivan regarding the issue of criminal responsibility. During the course of the evaluation and while interviewing the investigating police detectives, the clinician was invited to visit the crime scene. The visit to the crime scene took place approximately 2 months after the incident. In the intervening period, the season had changed abruptly from summer to fall and the leaves had fallen from surrounding trees. After a fruitless hour and a half search and survey, one of the police detectives happened to look up into the surrounding trees and observed what appeared to be a plastic trash bag. The bag was almost 30 ft off the ground but readily retrieved by the officer by climbing a series of branches. The bag contained the victim's and Ivan's clothes. Subsequently, Ivan confessed to the crime.

The discovery of the telling evidence in the Ivan case example was somewhat serendipitous. The case, nonetheless, illustrates the relevance of perpetrator behavior following the critical incident. The discovery of the well-hidden plastic bag dispelled the argument of a confused psychotic state, which purportedly had rendered Ivan from being criminally responsible.

Information relevant to distortion about the critical incident includes (1) verbal statements about capacities vs. self-control at the time of the instant offense, (2) blood alcohol concentration (BAC) vs. self-reported alcohol ingestion, (3) comparing observations of witnesses to those provided by the client, and (4) statements about past behavior that violate known diagnostic criteria, or can be demonstrated to be false. Table 4.3 lists other process factors when assessing for deception. Table 4.3 is an important tool for the forensic examiner of deception and distortion. Retrospectively, the examiner ensures that he or she has covered all the bases in deception analysis.

The importance of an adequate database prior to the clinical assessment has already been stressed. The evaluator must also approach the post-hoc decision tree with a firm grasp of the database. Next, nondeliberate distortion must be ruled out or taken into account.

Deliberate distortion must then be examined in witnesses and significant others, the accused, and the evaluator. Eventually, the subject's deception style must be identified. Last, conclusions regarding deception are presented.

The evaluator's report must first be able to state explicitly that the database was sufficient to draw conclusions to a reasonable degree of psychological certainty. If the assessment findings are

---

TABLE 4.3
Retrospective Forensic Decision Analysis Steps

A. Forensic database
   1. Multisourced
   2. Interdisciplinary
B. Rule out/account for nondeliberate distortion
   1. Reporting person
   2. Reported event
   3. Evaluation errors
C. Rule in deliberate distortion
   1. Examiner factors
   2. Individual examined
   3. Cross-validating sources
D. Determination of response style
   1. No distortion
   2. Faking good
   3. Faking bad
   4. Invalidation of results
   5. Mixed style
   6. Fluctuating style
E. Conclusions
   1. Sufficiency of data
   2. Degree of deception
   3. Confidence in judgment
   4. Likely targets of deception
   5. Temporal limits
   6. Feedback mechanism
   7. Intervention recommendations

---

not able to satisfy this criterion, then the report should acknowledge this and not proceed with any pertinent opinions about deception. If the assessment findings cannot meaningfully address the issue of deception, then opinions regarding other ultimate issues must either be qualified or result in no opinion.

Second, the degree of deception uncovered should also be specified. Table 4.4 presents degree factors for faking bad and faking good. Whatever the response style, the degree of deception uncovered must be specified.

Third, the confidence level of the evaluator's judgment about deception needs to be specified. Base rates and empirical support, as Table 4.5 shows, should validate one's conclusions whenever possible.

Fourth, likely victims and contexts in which deception occurs should be considered. History is the best predictor. The best guesses are those types of victims and settings in which the assessee was rewarded for past deception.

Fifth, the temporal limits of the report, as well as a feedback mechanism to assess opinions, need to be stated as the following illustrates: "The opinion that the accused is currently malingering psychotic symptoms to a moderate degree is valid for 1 year, after which a reassessment using inpatient observation and psychometric testing is recommended." It behooves evaluators to be very conservative with such temporal estimates, because human behavior can be capricious. Intervention recommendations are given when appropriate. The assessee should be treated for nondeliberate distortion as deficits may affect the ability and motivation to deceive.

Examples where treatment would be appropriate follow:

TABLE 4.4
Degree of Deception Uncovered

	Faking Bad	Faking Good
1. Negligible	No evidence of deception	No evidence of deception
2. Minimal	Basically honest but with some exaggeration of symptoms or minimization of strengths	Basically honest with some minimization of negative behaviors and/or exaggeration of positive attributes
3. Mild	Exaggeration of several critical symptoms and/or minimization of several positive behaviors	Minimization of several critical symptoms or exaggeration of several critical positive attributes
4. Moderate	Creation or fabrication of several critical symptoms or denial of several critical positive behaviors	Denial of several critical factors or fabrication of several critical positive attributes
5. Considerable	Creation or fabrication of a wide range of critical symptoms or denial of a wide range of positive behaviors	Denial of a wide range of critical behaviors or fabrication of a wide range of positive attributes
6. Extreme	Faked or denied behaviors are absurd with absolutely no basis in reality	Denied or fabricated behaviors are patently obvious and can be easily demonstrated

1. Intensive psychotherapy for a child victim preempts assessment for deception. This holds true for all victims, but it is possible to question them during the treatment process.
2. Some fakers have severe associated problems such as psychosis, borderline retardation, and brain damage. They may need treatment for these disorders as well as assessment for deception.
3. Factitious disorders, variants of faking bad, are usually associated with severe psychopathology, such as willingness to alter the body chemically to assume the role of a hospitalized patient.

The literature offers sparse validation of factitious disorders as an independent diagnosis as opposed to a specific variation of malingering. Rogers, Bagby, and Vincent (1994) compared SIRS records of subjects diagnosed with factitious disorders with primarily psychological symptoms to 25 suspected malingerers. There were no consistent differences between the records of the two groups. The authors suggested use of the factitious disorder diagnosis only on a provisional basis.

Evaluators should keep gathered data for as long as necessary — usually for a minimum of 5 to 10 years after an evaluation. Clinicians must be aware of and abide by local statutory requirements for retention of records as well as the provisions of the APA Ethical code. Following a criminal or

TABLE 4.5
Confidence in Evaluation Findings

1. Negligible	The examiner has no confidence in evaluation findings; the probability of valid findings in terms of classifying the person is 0 to 10%
2. Minimal	Findings are congruent with theory and yield some information about distortion, but there is much conflicting and/or insignificant data; the probability of valid findings in terms of accurately classifying the person is 11 to 25%
3. Mild	The probability of valid findings in terms of accurately classifying the person is 26 to 50%
4. Moderate	The probability of valid findings in terms of accurately classifying the person is 51–75%
5. Considerable	The probability of valid findings in terms of accurately classifying the person is 76–89%
6. Near certain	Findings are supported by research and theory and can be replicated upon reevaluation, using the same test procedures; accuracy is from 90 to 100%

civil action, data should not be released to anyone unless written permission from the original referring party is obtained. A criminal case may have to be retried if an appeal is successful. Finally, it should be noted that clinicians who do forensic work are highly vulnerable to ethical complaints and malpractice torts; the retention of forensic records must take into consideration statute of limitation provisions for ethical complaints and tort actions.

REFERENCES

Greenberg, S. A., & Shuman, D. W. (1997). Irreconcilable conflict between therapeutic and forensic roles. *Professional Psychology: Research and Practice, 28*(1), 50–57.

Paulsen, S., & Hall, H. V. (1991) Common sense process factors in deception analysis. *Forensic Reports, 4*(1), 37–39.

Robison, J. C., Gitlin, N., Morrelli, H. F., & Mann, L. J. (1982). Factitious hyperamylasuria: A trap in the diagnosis of pancreatitis. *The New England Journal of Medicine, 306*, 1211–1212.

Rogers, R., Bagby, R. M., & Vincent, A. (1994). Factitious disorders with predominantly psychological signs and symptoms: A conundrum for forensic experts. *Journal of Psychiatry and the Law, 22*(1), 91–106.

5 Deception and Nonverbal Behavior

Nonverbal behavior is communication without words including the nonlinguistic aspects of verbal behavior. It is a form of human communication that holds critical considerations for the detection of deception (DePaulo, 1994; DePaulo & Kirkendol, 1989; DePaulo & Rosenthal, 1979a, b; DePaulo, Rosenthal, Green, & Rosenkrantz, 1982; DePaulo, Zuckerman, & Rosenthal, 1980). Nonverbal behavior as a mode of deliberate or nondeliberate communication is a very pervasive and powerful mode of communication. Nonlinguistic behavior is language, albeit language without words. Every form of social interaction incorporates nonverbal behavior as a defining dynamic. Many everyday situations (Ekman & Frank, 1993), for example, engaging salespersons (DePaulo & DePaulo, 1989; Ekman, 1985), management and personnel operations (DePaulo et al., 1989; DePaulo & Pfeifer, 1986; Ekman, 1985), and social situations with intimate others (DePaulo, Stone, & Lassiter, 1985a; Ekman, 1985), involve nonverbal cues designed to effect deception. Nonverbal communication may not always be conscious or deliberate, but the actor through practice and experience can craft and modify expertise with nonverbal behavior (DePaulo, 1988; DePaulo & Kirkendol, 1989; DePaulo, Kashy, Kirkendol, Wyer, & Epstein, 1996). The instigation and effectiveness of deception is significantly influenced by deceiver motivation to manipulate receiver perception (DePaulo, 1988; DePaulo, Lanier, & Davis, 1983; DePaulo, Lassiter, & Stone, 1982; DePaulo, Lemay, & Epstein, 1991).

Forensic clinicians are generally more concerned with deliberate deception compared with nondeliberate deception. Nondeliberate deception usually connotes less harm to self or others, and generally, nondeliberate deception conveys no culpability. In actual practice, however, it is usually difficult to discern deliberate from nondeliberate deception. Nonverbal behavior can be an important aid to the trained evaluator in helping to make meaningful those discernments.

One variation of nondeliberate deception can be self-deception, and there are clinical scenarios in which self-deception can be very detrimental. Siegrist (1995) found depression and public self-consciousness to be correlated with self-deception in a student population. The suggestion is that depression and/or low self-esteem may induce self-deception as a coping mechanism. This is a dynamic often observed by treating clinicians. Individuals hold, or share with others, an illusory interpretation of a problem. The interpretation results in a less-than-realistic grasp of the problem situation. Forensic clinicians may encounter the dynamic intertwined with a serious forensic issue. A good forensic example is disputed custody/visitation matters where the extent of parental self-disillusionment can be impressive. Another forensic example is in criminal matters when family members cannot believe that a son or daughter has committed a serious criminal act in spite of overwhelming evidence. In these situations the nonverbal cues of the involved parties can be very telling and the forensic evaluator must be alert to alternative interpretations of deceptive behavior.

Nonlinguistic behavior is, therefore, an integral aspect of every human behavior and a very critical component of FDA. Distortion analysis is a primary method in the forensic detection of deception (Paulsen & Hall, 1991). Analysis of distortion between verbal and nonverbal behavior is an important component of that method. The problem is that nonverbal behavior can be incredibly elusive. When nonverbal behavior occurs, it is generally not very apparent to the observer. In fact,

---

TABLE 5.1
Nonverbal Signs of Deception

1. Increased body movement
2. Gaze aversion
3. Less assertive and dominant
4. Higher voice pitch
5. Longer latency of responses, reticence
6. More speech errors and higher pitch
7. Circumstantiality, vagueness
8. Terser answers
9. Posture noncongruent with portrayed emotion
10. Self-grooming responses
11. Prolonged inappropriate smiling
12. More negative remarks
13. Distractibility
14. Greater interest in test results
15. Increase in illustrators (e.g., hand motions)

---

nonverbal behavior is so prevalent that it is often overlooked or ignored. For the knowing, alert, and sensitive observer, nonverbal behavior can be very useful in interpersonal interactions in general, and in the detection of deception in particular. Skill in detecting and accurately reading nonverbal behavior is the stock in trade of many politicians, carnival game operators, psychotherapists, religious leaders, and others. At the same time, nonverbal behavior is difficult to measure and for most people difficult to decode accurately in a reliable manner. As this chapter will demonstrate, nonverbal communication is subject to myriad independent variables that can, and do, synergistically interact with one another.

TRADITIONAL NONVERBAL LEAKAGE ANALYSIS

Freud addressed nonverbal signals relating to deception when he stated, "He that has eyes to see and ears to hear may convince himself that no mortal can keep a secret. If his lips are silent, he chatters with his fingertips; betrayal oozes out of him at every pore" (1959). The literature on "body leakage," represented in part by Ekman and Friesen (1969, 1972b), Ekman, Friesen, and Sherer (1976), Kraut (1978), and DePaulo (1992), reflects that a wide array of nonverbal behaviors has been associated with deception.

Knapp, Hart, and Dennis (1974), based on videotaped interviews of 140 undergraduate military veterans, found a number of significant correlates of deception: uncertainty, vagueness, nervousness, reticence (total words and probes), dependence, and negative effect (i.e., eye duration, group references, disparaging statements). Knapp saw these six styles as natural, common traits of all people, with liars exceeding the bounds of convention.

Ekman (1980, 1985), DePaulo, Stone, and Lassiter (1985a), and others (Hall, 1986) suggest additional signs and some corrections. These findings place a greater emphasis on the motor behavior that deceivers show (Table 5.1).

Generally, liars are easier to detect in their fakery when:

1. Strong emotions are experienced by the deceiver during the interview.
2. Severe sanctions can be applied to the faker for lying.
3. The interviewer and liar share common values, culture, language, and/or are personally acquainted.

4. The interviewer has information that only the perpetrator would know.
5. An audience is present that is skeptical about the truthfulness of the deceiver.
6. The deceiver's personality predisposes him or her to fear, guilt, or "duping delight."
7. The interviewer has a reputation for being fair-minded, but difficult to deceive.
8. The interviewer is biased in the direction of believing that the deceiver is a liar or "no good," or is subject to emotion during the interrogation, although both of these increase the chances of false positives (i.e., nonliars being branded as liars).

On the other hand, Ekman (1985) stated that lie catching is especially difficult when:

1. The deceiver's story is rehearsed.
2. Deception involves hiding the true, as opposed to presenting the false.
3. There is benefit or gain from the lie.
4. The target would ordinarily trust the judgment of the deceiver, especially if the target had been successfully lied to previously by the liar.
5. The lie is authorized, and the target is a stranger.
6. The interviewer must conceal skepticism of the deceiver, as the cognitive focus may be on concealment instead of on the deceiver.
7. The liar is practiced in deception, is inventive, clever, articulate, and has good recall skills.
8. The liar consistently moves facial muscles to make conversational points.
9. The liar is self-deceived and believes in his or her lie, or is a psychopath.
10. The interviewer is the type of person who denies, avoids, and represses, expressing positive views toward most people.
11. The lie catcher receives some benefit from not exposing the deception.

Preliminary guidelines were proffered by Ekman (1985). The face, arms/hands, and legs/feet, in that order, have the capacity to send information with a reverse pattern in actually showing the leakage. The feet/legs are considered a good source of leakage when it occurs. The face, so easily controlled for many people, serves primarily as a distractor to the evaluator. The face reveals deception from so-called "microfacial" movements; however, these are often very difficult to detect. They represent the true, brief facial emotions before they are disguised.

Based on the foregoing, fakers tend to concentrate on self-control of facial movements but tend to neglect the limbs. Peripheral movement is rarely involved in positive deception; one would look for lies of omission rather than commission in the hands, for example. Examination of verbal content may be more revealing of actual events than nonverbal behavior. This finding has implications for forensic training and practice. Reading transcripts or listening to voice tapes of defendants may yield more information than attending to available visual cues. This would partially counteract fakers who "ham," or histrionically exhibit "honest" behaviors. The criminal justice system is replete with examinees of this description. Finally, accuracy of detection seems to bear little relationship to the ability to deceive others. People are generally more consistent at successful lying than they are in detecting lies.

CONTEMPORARY VIEWS OF NONVERBAL BEHAVIOR AND DECEPTION

De Paulo (1992) reviewed the history of research regarding nonverbal behavior as reflecting internal states to include nonverbal behavior designed to achieve deception. DePaulo described a range of variables that have been empirically demonstrated to influence nonverbal behavior. These include (1) cultural factors, (2) practice effect, (3) experience, (4) physical features (e.g., attractiveness), and (5) personality styles (e.g., anxious, defensive, acquiescence, assertive).

Research with nonverbal behavior has been conducted primarily from the social psychology perspective and remains rudimentary in terms of having an empirical basis for routine forensic application. Nonetheless, a variety of new nonverbal studies offers a fascinating and potentially very useful perspective on deception and malingering. This section of the chapter focuses on the deliberate/nondeliberate use of nonverbal behavior by deceivers.

De Paulo (1992) postulated there are "hard-wired links between the elicitation of certain basic emotions and the triggering of facial muscles that produce expressions of these emotions" (p. 207). If this hypothesis proves to be accurate, there are very clear implications for forensic research. The "hard-wired links" notion suggests that nonverbal behavior has the potential to convey telling cues regarding the emission of nondeliberate distortion. Similarly, nonverbal behavior has the potential to tip off to the examiner the presence of deliberate distortion.

As has been emphasized in earlier chapters, there is a fundamental interpersonal dimension in all deception. There must be a source and a receiver of the deception. Every FDA must account for the role of nonverbal behavior in the actor's presentation and in the witness's understanding and interpretation of that nonverbal input. This is no small challenge. To some extent, nonverbal behavior is the result of autonomic physiological events over which the actor has little, if any, control. In some instances, the actor may not even be aware of nonverbal behavior. For many years now, the general public has been aware of "Freudian slip" behavior, and it has become a social convention to comment on such slips when they occur. The potential for distortion, miscommunication, and misinterpretation with all nonverbal behaviors is enormous. The ultimate forensic question is what variables impinge on nonverbal behavior for purposes of self-presentation. How much control over nonverbal behavior does the actor have? One critical variable in the overall deception paradigm is whether the deceiver has direct interaction with the observer(s) (Burgoon et al., 1999); these particular variables are reviewed later in the chapter.

The manifestations of nonverbal behavior are multifaceted and, therefore, can be ambiguous for both the actor and the observer. This attribute is the main variable that makes polygraph testing so potentially useful, but at the same time notoriously unreliable (Bashore & Rapp, 1993; Bradley & Cullen, 1993; Bradley, MacLaren, & Carle, 1996). The ambiguity of nonverbal behavior poses problems for the forensic evaluator in terms of, first, accurate detection and, second, accurate interpretation.

De Paulo (1992) indicated that nonverbal behavior can be deliberately self-presentational in entirety, or be in partial or complete disguise. For example, an expert witness in testifying before a jury may purposefully alter nonverbal cues. The expert may perceive that the jury is becoming bored or inattentive and deduce that the jury perceives him or her as being too wordy or too officious. In response, the expert may purposefully alter nonverbal cues, such as relaxing his or her posture or attempting to attenuate nonverbal contact with specific jurors. The expert may deliberately attempt to nonverbally convey, or not convey, being under stress as a means of garnering jury favor. Such calculated behavior alterations at some point can constitute deception but, in conventional usage, the presenter's legitimate effort is to accentuate self-presentation to others. In another context, defendants or forensic subjects can attempt to manipulate their self-presentation deliberately to achieve covert deception objectives. The potential for simulation of basic emotions exists even when the actor is not experiencing the emotion in question. Simulation of emotions is the training and desired virtuoso of many aspects of the arts and theater. It is also the polished ability of many others. Politicians, religious leaders, psychotherapists, salespersons, parents, con artists, and criminals ply human targets in both positive and negative ways.

Based on her review of a large corpus of empirical studies primarily from the social psychology perspective, DePaulo (1992) proposed three phases of self-presentational nonverbal behavior. The first phase consists of the initial intentions of the actor, but is limited by certain constraints primarily involving cultural factors. For each of the three phases, different variables can influence the style and the effectiveness of the nonverbal communication. The three phases and the pertinent variables are outlined in Table 5.2.

TABLE 5.2

Variables Influencing Self-Presentational Nonverbal Behavior

Phases of Self-Presentational Nonverbal Behavior	Influencing Variables
First Phase: Actor frames the original intention of nonverbal behavior	• Cultural and subcultural variations • Situational variables • Actor's knowledge of relationship between internal states and nonverbal behavior
Second Phase: Actor's enactment ability, which can be improved by practice and experience	• Physical characteristics • Range and level of expressive cues • Personal style • Motivational constraints • Emotional constraints • Spontaneous expressive ability • Level of self-esteem and confidence • Constraints on appraisal and ability to modify self-presentation
Third Phase: Skill(s) to appraise and modify nonverbal performance in the future	• Legibility of nonverbal expression by perceiver • Actor's nonverbal posing skill • Sensitivity in execution of nonverbal behavior

Note: Adapted from "Nonverbal Behavior and Self-Presentation," by B. M. DePaulo, 1992, *Psychological Bulletin,* 111(2), 203–243.

The spectrum of human experience that can be communicated through nonverbal behavior is impressively broad. DePaulo (1992) described these functions as spanning eight groups. The eight groups and examples of each are summarized in Table 5.3.

In a fascinating report from the neurobehavioral perspective, Modell, Mountz, and Ford (1992) described neurological findings of a male patient with a 10-year history of lying in a variety of situations ranging from trivial to serious. According to single-photon emission computed tomography brain scanning, the patient had right hemithalamic dysfunction. Noting the hypothesized

TABLE 5.3

Range of Human Experience Conveyed by Nonverbal Behavior

Function	Examples
1. Physical states	Illness, exhaustion, tension, pain, sleep, death
2. Cognitive states	Thoughtful, pensive, brooding, befuddled, insightful, perplexed
3. Emotion	Excitement, surprise, happiness, glumness, overwhelmed, eagerness, fear, alertness, disappointment, glee, fright, enthusiasm, infatuation
4. Moods	Depressed, buoyant, dejected, hypomanic, anticipant, rejected, jealous
5. Values	Patriotism, loyalty, trustworthiness, piety, faithfulness, spirited, paternal, maternal, sociable, agreeable
6. Opinions	Agreement, disagreement, assent, dissent, approval, disapproval, intolerance
7. Personality disposition	Obsessive, perfectionist, picky, macho, dainty, affable, friendly, insolent
8. Psychopathologies	Manic, antisocial, paranoid, intoxicated, comatose, disoriented, depressed, psychotic

Note: Adapted from "Interpersonal Deception: VIII. Further Analysis on Nonverbal and Verbal Correlates of Equivocation," by D. B. Buller, J. K. Burgoon, A. L. Buslig, & J. F. Roiger, 1994, *Journal of Language and Social Psychology,* 13(4), 396–417, see text.

roles of the thalamus and associated brain regions in modulating behavior and cognition, the authors attributed the patient's history of lying to the thalamic dysfunction.

INTERACTIONAL CHARACTERISTICS OF NONVERBAL BEHAVIOR

Researchers have been consistent in reporting that, in general, there is no single behavioral profile of a deceiver's strategy (Buller et al., 1994; Burgoon, Buller, & Guerrero, 1995). Behaviors associated with deception are strongly influenced by a variety of interpersonal variables. In a study of videotapes of adults, alternatively telling the truth and then lying, no clear deception profile emerged (Buller et al., 1994). The subjects noted that their deception efforts were influenced by the type of deception involved (e.g., falsification, concealment, and equivocation), the perceived level of suspicion of the receiver, and the perceived degree of familiarity with the receiver (Buller et al., 1994; Burgoon et al., 1995).

In an effort to capture these very important aspects of deception as particularly applied to nonverbal behavior, Buller and his colleagues proposed the Interpersonal Deception Theory (IDT) (Buller, Strzyzewski, & Hunsaker, 1991; Burgoon & Buller, 1994; Burgoon et al., 1994, 1995, 1999). IDT postulates that interactive deception differs from noninteractive deception in fundamental ways. Interactive deception results from the combined influences of deceiver goals, social skills, and mutual influence processes involving feedback and interaction dynamics between the deceiver and the receiver. According to IDT (Burgoon & Buller, 1994), deceivers evidence the following interactional characteristics:

1. More uncertainty and vagueness;
2. More nonimmediateness and reticence;
3. More negative affect;
4. More arousal and noncomposure;
5. Generally a poorer impression compared with truth tellers;
6. More formal and submissive behavior; and
7. Kinesiac relaxation and pleasantness which is variable in line with apparent manipulative self-image management efforts.

Burgoon et al. (1999) summarized that deceivers adapt to communications (i.e., verbal and nonverbal) from receivers with reciprocal or compensatory displays. Low involvement by deceivers produces negative feedback from receivers. This negative feedback, in turn, instigates more behavioral adjustments than are necessary with high involvement deceivers. The postinteractive judgments of receivers about deception or truth are directly related to deceiver behavioral displays.

The effectiveness of deceptive behavior is a complicated function of the degree of intimacy between the deceiver and the recipient. Bond et al. (1992) proposed an *expectancy violation* model as a basis for a judge's assessment of deceitful behavior. According to the model, lay judges perceive deception when nonverbal behavior violates normative expectations. Several experiments were designed to test the model. In each experiment, lay judges observed videotapes of actors exhibiting atypical nonverbal behaviors such as arm or leg raising, staring, and head tilting. Two subject groups, American undergraduates and an illiterate group of natives from Pune, India, both associated higher levels of deception with actors exhibiting "weird" nonverbal behavior. The study demonstrated that judges discern deception based on discrepancies between verbal and nonverbal behavior. The authors proposed that intimate relationships, as opposed to stranger-to-stranger circumstances, significantly influence the expectancy violation model.

In intimate relationships, deception can be very consequential because it impacts directly on the very underpinnings of the relationship. In intimate relationships, the partners know each other in exquisite detail and minor changes are detected and interpreted. Thus, in intimate situations only minor indicators are perceived to implicate deception. This observation has obvious implications for forensic clinicians that evaluate disputed domestic matters. In intimate relationships, the gender and physical attractiveness of deception targets are influential variables in the intensity and effectiveness of the actor's deception (DePaulo, Stone, & Lassiter, 1985b).

Aune, Aune, and Buller (1994) operationalized levels of personal relationships in terms of the length of intimate relationships among college student subjects. They found that for negative emotions, there was a relationship between intensity of emotional expression and experienced emotional intensity emotion. They found no relationship for perceived appropriateness of emotions and level of relationship development for either positive or negative emotions.

One factor demonstrated to interpersonally effect the production of nonverbal behavior is probing inquiries posed by receivers. Buller et al. (1989) described a study with 239 undergraduate students. The subjects served as *sources* or *receivers*. The receivers interviewed sources regarding responses to a personality scale. After 1 min of interaction, one half of the receivers probed the sources for additional information. The probing introduced a number of changes in the nonverbal behavior of the sources, several of which differentiated between deceivers and truth tellers. The investigators suggested that the probing might have engendered suspicion or uncertainty. Deceptive sources were motivated to modify their nonverbal behavior in an attempt to mask deception-related cues and simulate truthfulness. The probing did not improve the ability of receivers to detect deception; the probing receivers perceived all sources to be truthful.

In a follow-up study utilizing the same experimental design, sources were divided into strangers and friends (Buller, Strzyzewski, & Comstock, 1991). Also introduced was the variable of induced suspicion with one half of the sources. Deceptive sources concealed deceit by masking arousal cues and simulating demeanors were more positive. The study found that none of the variables of probing, suspicion, or familiarity improved the detection of deception. Levine and McCornack (1996) critiqued the "probing effect" hypothesis of Buller et al., suggesting that the receivers could more simply attribute the receiver's response to behavioral adaptation.

Nonverbal behavior occurs by itself and is always an accompaniment of verbal behavior. When nonverbal and verbal behaviors are discrepant, most observers have elevated levels of suspicion. The best deceivers are those who can align nonverbal and verbal behavior even when the two are actually discrepant in the deceiver's experience. Researchers have studied nonverbal aspects of linguistic behavior and found that many cues can be sensitive cues of discrepancy. Buller et al. (1994) described fluency, dominance, formality cues, time spent talking, response latency, smiling, nodding, and linguistic immediacy cues to be reliable in helping to differentiate truthful from untruthful statements. In contrast to truthful statements, equivocal (i.e., deceptive) statements were less clear and less conversationally complete.

In another study, the believability of deceivers was enhanced by increased social skills (Burgoon, Buller, & Guerrero, 1995). The deceiver's perception of the level of suspicion of the receiver and familiarity with the receiver, were strong determinants of the deceiver's nonverbal behaviors. The interpersonal determinates of nonverbal behavior in deception are summarized in Table 5.4.

Research psychologists have long been skeptical of observer ability to detect truth from lying accurately based on either verbal or nonverbal behavior or a combination of the two (DePaulo et al., 1982). At the same time, researchers have pursued the analysis of nonverbal behavior as a fruitful approach to the detection of deception. Traditional studies have reflected that accuracy rates of judging deception based on nonverbal behavior cues have been no better than chance (Bond et al., 1992). Earlier studies utilizing judges with various expertises have also yielded essentially chance accuracy rates (Ekman, 1985; Ekman & O'Sullivan, 1991).

In spite of the poor accuracy rate in detecting deception through nonverbal behavior, there has been a persistent thread of research attempting to unlock the secrets of nonverbal behavior as mirroring real inner states. In particular, Ekman and his colleagues since the late 1960s have doggedly pursued the mysteries of nonverbal communication (Ekman & Friesen, 1969a, b). Into the early 1970s, the effort continued exploring various parameters influencing nonverbal behavior. Cultural influences were explored (Ekman, 1972, 1977; Ekman & Friesen, 1982b, 1987) and there

TABLE 5.4
Deception and Interactional Determinants of Nonverbal Behavior

Deception Type	Enhancing Deceiver Qualities	Deceiver Attributes that Assist Detection	Receiver Expertise	Relational Familiarity
1. Falsification	• Fluency • Positive affect • Less hesitant • Conveying believability • Dominance • Formality cues • Time spent talking • Response latency • Smiling • Nodding • Linguistic immediacy cues	• Less socially skillful • Uncertainty and vagueness • Nonimmediate and reticent • More negative affect • More arousal and noncomposure • Poor impression compared with truth tellers • More formal and submissive • Manipulative self-image effort	• For most receivers suspiciousness generally helps detection accuracy • With experts suspiciousness will often impair detection accuracy • Question strategy assists or aggravates inaccuracy	• Preinteractional and interactional features • Familiarity intensifies truth-bias especially when interviewers are suspicious
2. Equivocation	• All above and, • Particularly sensitive to deceiver social skill			
3. Concealment	• All in item 1 above and • Using a concealment strategy			

Note: Adapted from "Interpersonal Deception: VIII. Further Analysis on Nonverbal and Verbal Correlates of Equivocation," by D. B. Buller, J. K. Burgoon, A. L. Buslig, & J. F. Roiger, 1994, *Journal of Language and Social Psychology,* 13(4), 396–417, see text.

was an ongoing effort to introduce precision into the meaning and measurement of nonverbal behavior (Ekman, 1976, 1981, 1992; Ekman & Friesen, 1974, 1976, 1988). By the mid-1970s Ekman had begun to focus primarily on facial and linguistic tonal and inflection cues (Ekman & Friesen, 1972a, 1975, 1978, 1980, 1982a) and this has continued to be his emphasis to the present (Ekman, 1989, 1990, 1994; Ekman & Friesen, 1988; Ekman & O'Sullivan, 1991; Ekman, Roper, & Hager, 1980).

In laboratory studies, there is evidence that observers are more accurate in detecting deception than are conversational participants (Buller, Strzyzewski, & Hunsaker, 1991). By definition, conversational participants are more directly drawn into the deceptive interaction and have less ability to detach from cognitive and communication requirements in an interaction. Participants attributed more truth to sources than did observers, and participants were less accurate detectors than were observers. Even when not advised of the deception variable, observers relied more on accurate nonverbal cues than did participants. When advised of the deception manipulation, participants relied on inaccurate facial cues, whereas observers relied on inaccurate vocal cues.

Recent studies by Ekman and his colleagues (Ekman, O'Sullivan, & Frank, 1999; Frank & Ekman, 1997) and others (deTurck & Miller, 1990) have suggested that coaching of certain professionals in nonverbal deception indicators (primarily facial muscle movements and speech tones and inflections) can produce accuracy rates in the 70 to 100% range. In a laboratory study, Ekman, O'Sullivan, Friesen, & Scherer (1991) assessed measures of vocal behavior and body movement as increasing the accuracy of subjects to detect lying from truthfulness. Subjects were instructed to use three designated behavioral measures in making their determinations: two kinds of smiles and voice pitch. The judges' accuracy rate was an impressive 86%. Similar high accuracy rates were demonstrated with judges, Secret Service agents, and ("deception-interested") clinical psychologists (Ekman, O'Sullivan, & Frank, 1999).

SYNTHESIS

The role of nonverbal behavior in forensic behavioral analysis is still in the early stages of usefulness. The evidence is rather clear that nonverbal behavior complements linguistic behavior, but not always in a symmetrical way. Such asymmetry between nonverbal and verbal behavior is precisely the potential utility of nonverbal cues in forensic analysis. Researchers have described a variety of nonverbal cues and behaviors that can signal deception, but not with any reliability from one deception situation to another. The data also indicate that deception ability can improve with practice and experience.

For the uninitiated and inexperienced, deception probably induces arousal, which then results in discrepant nonverbal cues. This situation is probably well illustrated in the naive efforts of a young child to deceive parenting figures. In normative situations, the parents readily detect the child's efforts and thereby reinforce the child's trepidation about being discovered. The child is even more reactive with the next effort of deception. In the normative situation, when the child is repeatedly successful in deception, the deception effort becomes practiced, self-satisfying, and unfortunately self-reinforcing.

It is probably not serendipitous that the most common nonverbal cues of deception are focused in the face. On a day-to-day basis, the face is the most visible part of the body. The face is our naked front. Somehow people have learned as a social species to center their nonverbal reactivity in the facial muscles. Certainly other parts of the body emit nonverbal cues, but thus far the research suggests that facial cues hold the most valid information for detecting deceit. This does not equate, as has been seen, to the use of facial expression as the most valued indicator of deception. Many observers miss the cues provided by the face.

This chapter has highlighted the incredibly diverse nature of nonverbal communication. Given that diversity, and as DePaulo (1992) observed, it is impressive that the research has been able to establish any reliable cues of deception. It is apparent that humans can regulate nonverbal behavior for deceptive purposes. Expressed in operational terms, one can control nonverbal behavior for self-presentational purposes. This is what actors and others do to fulfill professional roles and, one hopes, for benevolent purposes. In some situations, however, modification of nonverbal self-presentation is for the purpose of deliberate and malicious deceit. Every FDA must account for this possibility even if our detection and interpretive abilities regarding nonverbal behavior remain rather primitive.

REFERENCES

Aune, K. S., Aune, R. K., & Buller, D. B. (1994). The experience, expression, and perceived appropriateness of emotions across levels of relationship development. *Journal of Social Psychology, 134*(2), 141–150.

Bashore, T. R., & Rapp, P. E. (1993). Are there alternatives to traditional polygraph procedures? *Psychological Bulletin, 11*(3), 3–12.

Bond, C. F., Omar, A., Pitre, U., Lashley, B. R., Skaggs, L. M., & Kirk, C. T. (1992). Fishy-looking liars: Deception judgment from expectancy violation. *Journal of Personality and Social Psychology, 63*(6), 969–977.

Bradley, M. T., & Cullen, M. C. (1993). Polygraph lie detection on real events in a laboratory setting. *Perceptual and Motor Skills, 76*(3, Pt 1), 1051–1058.

Bradley, M. T., MacLaren, V. V., & Carle, S. B. (1996). Deception and nondeception in guilty knowledge and guilty actions polygraph tests. *Journal of Applied Psychology, 81*(2), 153–160.

Buller, D. B., Burgoon, J. K., Buslig, A. L., & Roiger, J. F. (1994). Interpersonal deception: VIII. Further analysis on nonverbal and verbal correlates of equivocation. *Journal of Language and Social Psychology, 13*(4), 396–417.

Buller, D. B., Comstock, J., Aune, R. K., & Strzyzewski. K. D. (1989). The effect of probing on deceivers and truthtellers. *Journal of Nonverbal Behavior, 13*(3), 155–170.

Buller, D. B., Strzyzewski. K. D., & Comstock, J. (1991). Interpersonal deception: I. Deceivers' reactions to receivers' suspicions and probing. *Communication Monographs, 58*(1), 1–24.

Buller, D. B., Strzyzewski, K. D., & Hunsaker, F. G. (1991). Interpersonal deception: II. The inferiority of conversational participants and observers. *Communication Monographs, 58*(1), 25–40.

Burgoon, J. K., & Buller, D. B. (1994). Interpersonal deception: III. Effects of deceit on perceived communications and nonverbal behavior. *Journal of Nonverbal Behavior, 18*(2), 155–184.

Burgoon, J. K., Buller, D. B., Dillman, L., & Walther, J. B. (1995). Interpersonal deception: IV. Effects of suspicion on perceived communication and nonverbal behavior dynamics. *Human Communication Research, 22*(2), 163–196.

Burgoon, J. K., Buller, D. B., Ebesu, A. S., & Rockwell, P. (1994). Interpersonal deception: V. Accuracy in deception detection. *Communication Monographs, 61*(4), 303–325.

Burgoon, J. K., Buller, D. B., & Guerrero, L. K. (1995). Interpersonal deception: IX. Effects of social skills and nonverbal communication on deception. *Journal of Language and Social Psychology, 14*(3), 289–311.

Burgoon, J. K., Buller, D. B., White, C. H., Afifi, W., & Buslig, A. L. S. (1999). The role of conversational involvement in deceptive interpersonal interactions. *Personality & Social Psychology Bulletin, 25*(6), 669–683.

DePaulo, B. M. (1988). The motivational impairment effect in the communication of deception: Replications and extensions. *Journal of Nonverbal Behavior, 12*, 177–202.

DePaulo, B. M. (1992). Nonverbal behavior and self-presentation. *Psychological Bulletin, 111*(2), 203–243.

DePaulo, B. M. (1994). Spotting lies: Can humans learn to do better? *Current Directions in Psychological Science, 3*, 83–86.

DePaulo, P. J., & DePaulo, B. M. (1989). Can attempted deception by salespersons and customers be detected through nonverbal cues? *Journal of Applied Social Psychology, 19*, 1552–1557.

DePaulo, P. J., DePaulo, B. M., Tang, J., & Swaim, G. W. (1989). Lying and detecting lies in organizations. In R. A. Giacalone & P. Rosenfeld (Eds.), *Impression management in the organization* (pp. 377–393). Hillsdale, NJ: Erlbaum.

DePaulo, B. M., Kashy, D. A., Kirkendol, S. E., Wyer, M. M., & Epstein, J. A. (1996). Lying in everyday life. *Journal of Personality and Social Psychology, 45*, 1096–1103.

DePaulo, B. M., & Kirkendol, S. E. (1989). The motivational impairment effect in the communication of deception. In J. Yuille (Ed.), *Credibility assessment* (pp. 51–70). Norwell, MA: Kluwer Academic.

DePaulo, B. M., Lanier, K., & Davis, T. (1983). Detecting the deceit of the motivated liar. *Journal of Personality and Social Psychology, 45*, 1096–1103.

DePaulo, B. M., Lassiter, G., & Stone, J. (1982). Attentional determinants of success at detecting deception and truth. *Personality and Social Psychology Bulletin, 8*, 273–279.

DePaulo, B. M., LeMay, C., & Epstein, J. (1991). Effects of importance of success and expectations for success on effectiveness of deceiving. *Personality and Social Psychology Bulletin, 17*, 14–24.

DePaulo, B. M., & Pfeifer, R. L. (1986). On-the-job experience and skill at detecting deception. *Journal of Applied Social Psychology, 16*, 249–267.

DePaulo, B. M., & Rosenthal, R. (1979a). Ambivalence, discrepancy, and deception in nonverbal communication. In R. Rosenthal (Ed.), *Skill in nonverbal communication* (pp. 204–248). Cambridge, MA: Oelgeschlager, Gunn, & Hain.

DePaulo, B. M., & Rosenthal, R. (1979b). Telling lies. *Journal of Personality and Social Psychology, 37*, 1713–1722.

DePaulo, B. M., Rosenthal, R., Green, C. R., & Rosenkrantz, J. (1982). Diagnosing deceptive and mixed messages from verbal and nonverbal cues. *Journal of Experimental Social Psychology, 18*, 433–446.

DePaulo, B. M., Stone, J. L., & Lassiter, G. D. (1985a). Deceiving and detecting deceit. In B. R. Schlenker (Ed.), *The self and social life* (pp. 323–370). New York: McGraw-Hill.

DePaulo, B. M., Stone, J. L., & Lassiter, G. D. (1985b). Telling ingratiating lies: Effects of target sex and target attractiveness on verbal and nonverbal deceptive success. *Journal of Personality and Social Psychology, 48*, 1191–1203.

DePaulo, B. M., Zuckerman, M., & Rosenthal, R. (1980). Humans as lie detectors. *Journal of Communication, 30*, 129–139.

deTurck, M. A., & Miller, G. R. (1990). Training observers to detect deception. *Human Communication Research, 16*, 603–620.

Ekman, P. (1972). Universals and cultural differences in facial expression of emotion. In J. K. Cole (Ed.), *Nebraska symposium on motivation* (pp. 207–283). Lincoln, NE: University of Nebraska Press.

Ekman, P. (1976). Movements with precise meanings. *Journal of Communication, 26*, 14–26.

Ekman, P. (1977). Biological and cultural contributions to body and facial movement. In J. Blacking (Ed.), *The anthropology of the body* (pp. 39–84). San Diego, CA: Academic Press.

Ekman, P. (1980). Asymmetry in facial expression. *Science, 209*, 833–836.

Ekman, P. (1981). Mistakes when deceiving. *Annals of the New York Academy of Sciences, 364*, 269–278.

Ekman, P. (1985). *Telling lies: Clues to deceit in the marketplace, politics, and marriage.* New York: Norton.

Ekman, P. (1989). The argument and evidence about universals in facial expressions of emotion. In H. Wagner & A. Manstead (Eds.), *Handbook of psychophysiology: The biological psychology of the emotions and social processes* (pp. 143–164). New York: Wiley.

Ekman, P. (1990). Duchenne's smile: Emotional expression and brain physiology II. *Journal of Personality and Social Psychology, 58*, 342–353.

Ekman, P. (1992). Facial expressions of emotion: New findings, new questions. *Psychological Science, 3*, 34–38.

Ekman, P. (1994). Strong evidence for universals in facial emotion: A reply to Russell's mistaken critique. *Psychological Bulletin, 115*, 268–287.

Ekman, P., & Frank, M. G. (1993). Lies that fail. In M. Lewis & C. Saarni (Eds.), *Lying and deception in everyday life* (pp. 184–200). New York: Guilford Press.

Ekman, P., & Friesen, W. A. (1969). Nonverbal leakage and clues to deception. *Psychiatry, 32*, 88–105.

Ekman, P., & Friesen, W. A. (1969). The repertoire of nonverbal behavior: Categories, origins, usage, and coding. *Semiotica, 1*, 49–98.

Ekman, P., & Friesen, W. A. (1972a). *Emotion in the human face.* New York: Pergamon.

Ekman, P., & Friesen, W.A. (1972b). Hand movements. *Journal of Communication, 22*, 353–374.

Ekman, P., & Friesen, W. A. (1974). Detecting deception from the body or face. *Journal of Personality and Social Psychology, 29*, 288–298.

Ekman, P., & Friesen, W. A. (1975). *Unmasking the face: A guide to recognizing emotions from facial clues.* Englewood Cliffs, NJ: Prentice-Hall.

Ekman, P., & Friesen, W. A. (1978). *The facial action coding system*. Palo Alto, CA: Consulting Psychologists Press.

Ekman, P., & Friesen, W. A. (1980). Facial signs of emotional experience. *Journal of Personality and Social Psychology, 39*, 1125–1134.

Ekman, P., & Friesen, W. A. (1982a). Felt, false and miserable smiles. *Journal of Nonverbal Behavior, 6*, 2389–252.

Ekman, P., & Friesen, W. A. (1982b). What are the similarities and differences in facial behavior across cultures? In P. Ekman (Ed.), *Emotion in the human face* (2nd ed.) (pp. 128–143). Cambridge, England: Cambridge University Press.

Ekman, P., & Friesen, W. A. (1987). Universals and cultural differences in the judgments of facial expressions of emotion. *Journal of Personality and Social Psychology, 53*, 712–717.

Ekman, P., & Friesen, W. A. (1988). Smiles when lying. *Journal of Personality and Social Psychology, 54*, 414–420.

Ekman, P., Friesen, W. A., & Scherer, K. R. (1976). Body movement and voice pitch in deceptive interaction. *Semiotica, 16*, (1) 23–27.

Ekman, P., & O'Sullivan, M. (1991). Who can catch a liar? *American Psychologist, 46*(9), 913–920.

Ekman, P., O'Sullivan, M., & Frank, M. G. (1999). A few can catch a liar. *Psychological Science, 10*(3), 263–266.

Ekman, P., O'Sullivan, M., Friesen, W. V., & Scherer, L. R. (1991). Invited article: Face, voice, and body in detecting deceit. *Journal of Nonverbal Behavior, 15*(2), 125–135.

Ekman, P., Roper, G., & Hager, J. C. (1980). Deliberate facial movement. *Child Development, 51*, 886–891.

Frank, M. G., & Ekman, P. (1997). The ability to detect deceit generalizes across different types of high-stake lies. *Journal of Personality and Social Psychology, 72*(6), 1429–1439.

Freud, S. (1959). Fragment of an analysis of a case of hysteria (1905). In *Collected Papers* (Vol. 3; pp. 13–146). New York: Basic Books.

Hall, H. V. (1986). The forensic distortion analysis: Proposed decision tree and report format. *American Journal of Forensic Psychology, 4*(3), 31–59.

Knapp, M. L., Hart, R. P., & Dennis, H. S. (1974). An exploration of deception as a communication construct. *Human Communication Research, 1*(1), 15–29.

Kraut, R. E. (1978). Verbal and nonverbal cues in the perception of lying. *Journal of Personality and Social Psychology, 36*(4), 380–391.

Levine, T. R., & McCornack, S. A. (1996). Can behavioral adaptation explain the probing effect? Rejoinder to Buller et al. *Human Communication Research, 22*(4), 604–613.

Modell, J. G., Mountz, J. M., & Ford, C. V. (1992). Pathological lying associated with thalamic dysfunction demonstrated by [-super(99m)Tc]HMPAO SPECT. *Journal of Neuropsychiatry and Clinical Neurosciences, 4*(4), 442–446.

Paulsen, S., & Hall, H. V. (1991). Commonsense clinical process factors in deception analysis. *Forensic Reports, 4*(1), 37–39.

Siegrist, M. (1995). Inner speech as a cognitive process mediating self-consciousness and inhibiting self-deception. *Psychological Reports, 76*(1), 259–265.

Part II

The Developmental Context of Deception

6 Deception in Nonhumans

Beginning in the early 1990s the comparative psychology literature began to evidence a pattern of proposal and rebuttal studies regarding the "deception hypothesis" as applied to nonhuman species. Essentially, there are two camps of thought. One camp has advocated certain species-specific behaviors as representing deceptive behavior that occurs with implied intentionality; the other camp disputes such anthropomorphic interpretations offering explanations that are more naturalistic. The debate will undoubtedly continue, but for the purposes here, the two opposing camps of thought are not critical. At least for the present, comparative psychology researchers are not expected to resolve questions about human deception.

The comparative studies are fascinating and, in some instances, the interspecies parallels are striking. Plant/animal studies are examined for those parallels and for the insights that they may offer. The quest is neither to anthropomorphize the lesser species, nor to dehumanize the unique qualities of human deception (Mitchell & Hamm, 1997). The reader should note how the very language in describing nonhuman deceptive behavior subtly invites a humanized interpretation of a given behavior. For example, in one study described below, ants acquire the chemical identification marker unique to an alien ant colony. According to the authors, this enabled the "chemically camouflaged" ants to enter the alien nest unchallenged and "rob" food. The words *camouflaged* and *rob* connote deliberate, intentional efforts by the ant(s) to assume a false identity, deceive, and then rob the members of the alien colony.

The investigation of plant and animal activity leads to implications for theory and practice. There are forms of deception that occur in the plant and animal worlds that have clear parallels in human faking. The findings in nonhumans allow tightening of the behavioral factors in descriptions of deception and elucidation of the cognitive intent factors that may be employed. Last, principles from plant and animal deception will eventually be available to be integrated into an eventual meta-theory of deception.

A simple model of consummated deception involves the following sequence (Hyman, 1989; Mitchell, 1986; Whaley, 1982):

1. Organism "A" emits or conceals a stimulus.
2. Organism "B" picks up or misses the input. Misperception takes place.
3. Organism "A" obtains a favorable outcome or avoids an unpleasant consequence.

Here, "A" communicates to "B" a false or distorted message by emitting or concealing information. It is an untruthful message because it suggests an event of importance to "B" that will or will not occur. Successful deception results in a desirable outcome for "A," depending on whether the message is misperceived by "B," thus sustaining the deceptive patterns of "A."

An apparently desirable outcome for both "A" and "B" results from the preliminary analysis. There are simple examples that come from plant life. In Hawaii a variety of plant life, commonly called "sleeping grass," folds up when touched, assuming the appearance of limp, smaller vegetation. While no one would suggest that the plant is deliberately distorting, apparent reward for both plant and possible eater of vegetation are operative. The plant stays alive and the eater avoids ostensibly dead, unattractive food. In successful deception, the deceived behaves as if the false state of affairs had rewarding or punishing consequences.

Another dramatic form of plant life activity that appears to mimic deceptive behavior comes from the plant commonly known as the Venus fly trap (*Drosera adelae sarracenia purpurea gibbosa*). The flytrap plant is indigenous to the southeastern United States and was once sold as a novelty item until special harvesting controls were enacted because the plant was becoming endangered. The plant is "carnivorous" in that it secretes an enzyme that dissolves protein. Small insects are "lured" to pitcher-shaped pods by sweet nectar emitted by the plant. When the insect lands on the pods, sensors cause the pods to close quickly; the insect is trapped for leisurely consumption by the plant.

Examples of "deceptive behavior" from the animal kingdom are still more striking, and begin to suggest an intentionality and deliberateness comparable to actual human deception. Caution is clearly the watchword, however. Although plant and animal studies can be very instructive, generalizing among different levels of species regarding any behavior has limitations. Caution is particularly apropos with such a complex behavioral phenomenon as deception.

Insects, such as butterflies with predator eyes on their wings, may fool their would-be eaters into believing that they are a danger, thus living to fly another day. The butterfly's predators may employ deception applicable to their own species. Small stomatopod crustaceans (*Gonodactylus bredini*) were observed to engage in "bluffing behavior" to ward off fellow crustacea as they competed to inhabit abandoned bony cavities (Adams & Caldwell, 1990). Newly molted, the vulnerable crustacea evidenced a threat display even though their soft flesh status would not enable them to withstand or deliver aggressive blows. The frequency of the "bluffing" was observed to be positively related to the size of the opponent. The bluffing was most effective when the intruders were smaller than the resident, but still effective when the intruder exceeded the size of the resident by up to 15%. The investigators reported that, in the laboratory setting of the study, when the crustaceans fought twice, they appeared to modify their fighting–bluffing behavior according to the nature of their earlier encounter.

The characteristic behavior of male stickleback fish that guard nests containing eggs has been popularized in nature series media (e.g., *National Geographic*). The male fish engage in "distraction displays" to ward off intruders. With sufficient intrusions, the fish bury the eggs in sand for protection. Whoriskey (1991) investigated the fish distraction behavior to see if it was male-intrusion specific, that is, a sexual deception to ward off other males, as opposed to an instinctual "foraging" behavior unrelated to the sex of the intruder. The experimental design involved introducing all males, all females, and mixed males and females intruder groups. The distraction behavior was evidenced with all the intruder groupings supporting the foraging hypothesis. The author noted that the male-intruder groups did produce more territorial intrusions than the all-female groups. It was also noted that hatchling survival was better in mixed and all-male trials than with the all-female trials.

Ants recognize nest mates by detecting a common chemical marker unique to the ant colony. Breed et al. (1992) described how acquisition of the chemical camouflage marker enabled neotropical ants to enter and rob food from other target colonies. The authors described intercolony thievery that resulted in the mutual transfer of considerable quantities of food. Also interesting was the observation that the acquired chemical camouflage would be unique to specific thief ants who would then specialize in pilfering from the target alien colony. The pilfering would be successful because the target colony would not detect the acquired chemical camouflage of the alien ants.

Another example of startlingly deceptive behavior in the insect world comes from sugarcane rootstock borer weevils (*Diaprepes abbreviatus*). Harari and Brockman (1999) reported that apparent "homosexual" behavior by females of the inch-long borer beetle was in actuality a ruse designed to attract the largest male mates. The researchers noticed that the females of the species tended to mount other females. Further observation revealed that the mounting behavior attracted the largest male beetles that were likely to mate equally with both females. The females were similar in appearance to males except they were somewhat larger. The males were attracted to females primarily by sight. The authors concluded that by gravitating to mounting females, the males were likely to be able to mate with at least one female. The authors also noted that their explanation was consistent with that of all known cases of female mounting behavior in the insect world. Male insects are not readily able to distinguish females from other males; the males are drawn, therefore, to females in copulating pairs. Mounting females are thereby improving their opportunity to mate with large males.

As with the Hawaiian grass example above, birds that "cry wolf" (Munn, 1986) provide another example of mutual possible reward in deceptive behavior. Two species of birds, *Lanio versicolor* and *Thamnomanes schistogynus*, give a predator alarm call to scare off other birds, thus obtaining an unrestricted access to anthropoids in the area. Here, "A" gets food and "B" expects to preserve its life by escape.

The message by "A" must be believed to be effective. A balance between truth and falsehood must be achieved. Bond (1989), an ethnologist who writes of animal conflict, asserts that aggressive displays are a balance of the advantages of deception and the disadvantages of effecting skepticism in the receiver.

Bond (1989) received corroborating data for his hypothesis by using a numerical simulation model, finding that an equilibrium level of deceit was described, even when "B" was unaware of the degree of deception by "A."

Deception among birds may be unintentional, yet effective. Trained pigeons misreported the correct color of a light associated with a reward to a fellow pigeon also taught the procedure, thus obtaining more reward for themselves (Lanza, Starr, & Skinner, 1982).

The deception hypothesis has been controversially attributed to the mating behavior of pied flycatcher birds. Female flycatchers typically do not mate with already mated males. Stenmark, Slagsvold, and Lifjeld (1988) observed that already mated male pied flycatchers hide their mating status by singing in a secondary (non-nest) territory, thus increasing the probability of obtaining a second mate. The females would mate with already mated males when the females were apparently unaware that the male had mated in another territory. This observation led to the deception hypothesis being ascribed to the male flycatcher. Specifically, the hypothesis was that the males hid their existing mating status and deceived females into polygyny.

To further test the hypothesis, Searcy, Eriksson, and Lundberg (1991) introduced a stimulus female bird to already mated and unmated males. The stimulus female resulted in increased, characteristic mating behavior by both already mated and nonmated males. The authors concluded that the similar behaviors of the two male groups in response to the female-stimulus supported the deception hypothesis. Slagsvold and Dale (1994) observed the mating behavior of the flycatchers by videotaping at nest boxes being defended by males. There were 19 polygynous matings, 16 of which occurred either by females visiting only mated males or because a competitor had taken over the male's primary nest box. Of the females who had visited, both mated and unmated males, the majority chose unmated males. The authors concluded that their findings lent little support to a deception hypothesis. They indicated that the females were able to detect male mating status, but sometimes parsimoniously chose males who were mated because of the demands of having to search further. It also appeared that females were drawn to male quality (i.e., plumage color and age), irrespective of mating status, but mating status was a more dominant variable.

In another bird study, Boland, Heinsohn, and Cockburn (1997) observed white-winged choughs (*Corcorax melanorhamphos*). These birds live in groups; breeding usually occurs between one dominant pair. Subsequently, all birds in the group cooperate in rearing the young. The authors observed that usually younger members of the group would retrieve food and consume the food themselves instead of feeding the food to the nestlings. This behavior was most likely to occur when the young birds returned to the nest and were not being observed by other group members. Later, the errant birds were more likely to engage in supplemental care of the nestlings. The authors concluded that the young white-winged choughs "acted deceptively" by simulating helping behaviors but not at the expense of sacrificing their own supply of food.

Carlsson (1991) hypothesized deceptive courting behavior by male Tengmalm owls. Carlsson observed the singing behavior of male owls over a 2-year period; the male singing behavior was territorial and associated with female recruitment. Owl mating behavior is affected by food availability. The 2-year period of the study coincided with a peak abundance of small rodents (voles); voles are a preferred owl food. Male owls are characteristically site-tenacious, but when food was abundant, in addition to primary nest holes, they would begin singing at secondary nest holes. The author suggested that the secondary nest hole singing was an effort by "deception" to attract unmated females into polygynous breeding.

In a subsequent response, Sonerud (1992) disputed the "deception hypothesis" with Tengmalm owls. Sonerud offered the explanation that the bigynous behavior of male Tengmalm owls was instinctual and designed to preserve the species. The male owls would feed two females at the same rate during egg laying and incubation, as an adaptation to the high incidence of nest predation from the time of the pristine boreal forest. If the primary nest were lost to a predator, the male could allocate its energies to feed the secondary nest. These two owl studies highlight the ongoing controversy of anthropomorphizing animal behavior when explanations that are more parsimonious are possible.

It should not be surprising that deception behavior in animals is usually associated with objectives of species survival. Deceptive behavior is employed to ward off enemies, to attract the opposite sex, and to nurture and protect offspring. Male chickens use food calling when no edible food is present to attract hens to the area (Gyger & Marler, 1988). In yet another instance of cautioning against overinterpretation, Moffat and Hogan (1992) questioned published accounts of hens using food calls in a selective and deceptive manner with chicks. The investigators reinforced Burmese red jungle fowl (*Gallus gallus spadiceus*) chicks to a maternal food call. The study utilized two food-call designs. One was a highly preferred food item (a mealworm), and the other a less-preferred food (chick crumbs). The chicks initially approached the food call to the preferred food with faster response time, that is, regardless of reinforcement contingencies. By the third day the chicks responded faster to whatever food call was reinforced. The authors interpreted that the results indicated the preexisting preferences to food stimuli were clearly modified in the chicks by functional experience.

The subtlety of deceptive behavior may increase as mammals are scrutinized, illustrated by the following:

> Cougar, the cat of one of the authors and his wife, is allowed to remain on a ledge alongside the dining table provided she does not attempt to obtain food from the table. She has been well-trained in this "paws off" behavior over the years. When a particularly tasty fish dinner was served one evening, Cougar's attention was riveted at once. She moved toward the fish, only to be verbally admonished, so she returned to her original sitting position on the ledge. Feigning indifference and immobility, her eyes on the wall, she lay down and opened her mouth in a wide yawn. Her front left paw reached up as in a stretch, but instead of retracting it, her paw came to rest on the fish, spread out in a gripping posture. Her eyes, by this time, were on the fish, the yawn no longer in evidence.

Is this deception? Perhaps Cougar merely wished to stretch and found herself in a good position to obtain food. The authors do not know, yet believe that deception did indeed take place. This belief appears to have predictive power in regard to Cougar's behavior in similar situations. She cannot be trusted totally to act in a nondeceitful fashion when her keeper's food is available.

Intentionality at some level becomes more probable when lower primates are scrutinized for deceptive behavior. The tactical deception of familiar baboons *Papio ursinus* by peers has been illustrated (Bryne & Whiten, 1985). Deception in pongoid apes has been observed to include (1) use of camouflage, (2) feigning moods and curiosity, and (3) giving false motor signals to others (De Waal, 1986). In another primate study, the researcher observed the social behavior of a group of captive lowland gorillas consisting of two adult males, one female, and her infant (Mitchell, 1991). The males would attempt repeatedly to interact with the infant. The mother would intervene in an effort to thwart the males' intrusions. During an 81-hour period, the researcher observed 21 instances of deceptive distracting behavior by the mother in an effort to ward off the adult males' curious behavior toward the infant.

Mangabey monkeys (*Cercocebus torquatus torquatus*) were studied in a socially competitive paradigm (Coussi-Korbel, 1994). The experimenters hid food in the presence of particular animals. An informed young male repeatedly lost his food to a dominant male. After such misfortunes, the young male developed a pattern that when he was informed of the hidden food, he would move via an indirect route to the food. This behavior served purposefully to mislead the dominant male to the young male's advantage. When the dominant male was also informed, the young male observed the dominant male taking the food and would head straight to the remaining hidden food source. The author suggested that the young males use of an indirect route when he was informed could not be considered the expected response to a competitive situation but rather was a behavior evidencing "tactical deception."

Brown capuchin monkeys (*Cebus apella*) were observed to engage in deceptive pointing and withholding communication about the location of hidden food (Mitchell & Anderson, 1997). Three of the monkeys pointed to the food in the presence of a cooperative trainer; another monkey withheld communication to peers in the presence of a competitive trainer. The authors suggested that the monkey's behavior was explainable in the learning theory concepts of conditional discrimination and response inhibition.

More ominously, there is evidence that lower primates can and have engaged in warfare with their kin. Invasion of another territory, use of surprise and concealment, attacks on other chimpanzees using superior methods (e.g., coordinated movements, group attacks), and eventual extermination or chasing away of all males in the conquered territory have been documented. The perpetrators were all chimpanzees of the famous Gombe Colony in Tanganyika, studied by primatologist Jane Goodall for more than 10 years. Chimps in captivity at the famous Arnheim Zoo in the Netherlands have been shown to murder other chimps (Greene & Dewar, 1985). Deception and planning appeared to play an integral part in the violence.

Animal deception reveals two primary response tendencies, faking good and faking bad, both of which operate in any given deception to varying degrees. The former occurs when organisms deny, minimize, or conceal traits/events that would be noxious, dangerous, or otherwise unpleasant to the target. Faking good also includes the pretense to have positive traits: tiger stripes blending this predator into the background, an alligator hiding all but its nose and eyes under the water, and apes using foliage to conceal their presence from their enemy all fit this criterion. Hiding the real, masking, camouflaging, blurring old patterns, and subtracting from the customary are further possibilities. Faking good always involves looking benign, better, or more attractive than one is in order to achieve a given outcome.

Faking bad is showing the false by pretending to have negative traits, or denying the genuinely positive to obtain a particular goal. Other descriptors include fabrication, exaggeration, conjuring, and mimicking, keeping in mind that a new pattern is copied or invented. Harmless snakes with skin patterns of poisonous vipers, birds that "cry wolf," and buffalo that stamp their feet and snort before a fight with a peer in mating season may fit this criterion. Faking bad always involves looking worse, more dangerous, sick, or negative than one is to accomplish some task or to obtain a desired outcome.

Presenting the false and concealing the real are present to some degree in both faking good and faking bad. For deception of either type to occur, the deceived must have engaged in withdrawal or approach, depending on perception of the false event. Mixed forms of faking good and bad

TABLE 6.1
Deceptive Styles in Animals

Action	Faking Good	Faking Bad
D presents stimulus (shows the false)	T sees as reward if deception true (e.g., cat playing with mouse)	T sees a punishment if deception true (e.g., birds that " cry wolf")
D removes stimulus (hides the real)	T sees as reward if deception true (e.g., tiger stripes)	T sees a punishment if deception true (e.g., opossum feigning death)

Note: D = deceiver; T = target.

appear with regularity. The fox may fake good by concealment and hiding, only to feign death when trapped and exhausted.

Playing dead or wounded may be the prototype of human malingering. The literature presents data spanning the phylogenetic scale:

- Plants that, upon touch, appear lifeless and limp;
- Carnivorous plants that have sophisticated luring qualities (odor and structure) to attract and entrap insect quarry;
- Spiders, coleopters, and caterpillars that roll up into a ball when trapped;
- Ants that adopt chemical olfactory markers to enter and rob from stranger ant nests;
- Fish that appear dead when caught, only to swim away if set back in the water;
- Plovers and other birds that feign a broken wing to draw predators away from the nest;
- Opossums, foxes, and red squirrels feigning death when no escape seems possible;
- Monkeys, chimpanzees, apes, and baboons feigning death when defeated by peers or when near death.

In sum, the literature on animal deception provides a partial base upon which to build a general theory of human deception. The range and diversity of deceptive responses and the conditions under which they occur are paralleled in humans. A microanalysis of deceptive animal behavior also leads into potentially fruitful areas such as primal response tendencies involving all deception faking good and faking bad. By necessity, deception, in its simplest form, represents an interactional phenomenon. A recipient organism must react in the desired manner. To trigger this reaction, there must be a "germ of truth" or "glimmer of hope" that serves as a stimulus to attract the organism to be deceived. The creation of this "sliver of attraction" constitutes the real art of deception. Both the plant and animal kingdoms have impressive examples of how nature artfully creates this expectation of having some need filled by the intended deceived. This review of nonhuman examples of deception has metaphorically illustrated the "Barnum effect" (i.e., "there is a sucker born every minute") (Beins, 1993) in plant and animal nature. Table 6.1 illustrates a model of animal deception.

Perhaps the most fundamental lesson from this review of deception in nonhuman species is how deception evolves, in every instance, as a survival tool. The quest is not to deceive, but to meet a survival need, and deception becomes a means to meeting that need. With nonhumans, the deception is a nondeliberate by-product of species survival. With higher mammals such as the apes, the question of intentionality, admittedly, becomes a little more ambiguous. In contrast to nonhuman deception, deception at the human level can involve deliberateness, cunning, and malicious intent. Rationality in humans allows survival goals to be determined that go beyond fundamental necessities. Humans can choose to pursue substances of abuse, money, sexual aberrations, and myriad forms of quackery. All of these pursuits are cognitively and emotionally justified to be essential for existence, and therein lies an important element in understanding the dynamic of humans engaging in deliberate deception.

Deception in nonhuman species is a fascinating glimpse into very primitive forms of deception and serves as an important backdrop to the primary focus of this book on human deception. The next chapter reviews the developmental evolution of deception in children. Deception in both nonhumans and in children provides invaluable insight into the sophisticated levels of deception evidenced by adult humans.

REFERENCES

Adams, E. S., & Caldwell, R. L. (1990). Deceptive communication in asymmetric fights of the stomatopod crustacean *Gonodactylus bredini*. *Animal Behaviors, 39*(4), 706–716.

Beins, B. C. (1993). Using the Barnum effect to teach about ethics and deception in research. *Teaching of Psychology, 20*(1), 33–35.

Boland, C. R. J., Heinsohn, R., & Cockburn, A. (1997). Deception by helpers in cooperatively breeding white-winged choughs and its experimental manipulation. *Behavioral Ecology & Sociobiology, 41*(4), 251–256.

Bond, A B. (1989). Toward a resolution of the paradox of aggressive displays: I. Optimal deceit in the communication of fighting ability. *Ethology, 81*(1), 29–46.

Breed, M. D., Snyder, L. E., Lynn, T. L., & Morhart, J. A. (1992). Acquired chemical camouflage in a tropical ant. *Animal Behavior, 44*(3), 519–523.

Byrne, R. W., & Whiten, A. (1985). Tactical deception of familiar individuals in baboons (*Papio ursinus*). *Animal Behavior, 33*(2), 669–673.

Carlsson, B. (1991). Recruitment of mates and deceptive behavior by male Tengmalm's owls. *Behavioral Ecology & Sociobiology, 28*(5), 321–328.

Coussi-Korbel, S. (1994). Learning to outwit a competitor in mangabeys (*Cercocebus torquatus torquatus*). *Journal of Comparative Psychology, 108*(2), 164–171.

De Waal, F. (1986). Deception in the natural communication of chimpanzees. In R. Mitchell & N. Thompson, (Eds.), *Deception: Perspective on humans and nonhuman deceit* (pp. 527–529). Albany, NY: State University of New York.

Green, C., & Dewar, S. (1985). *The ascent of the chimps*. Film by New Wilderness III, Inc. Distributed by Prism Entertainment Corp., Los Angeles, CA.

Gyger, M., & Marler, P. (1988). Food calling in the domestic fowl. *Gallus gallus*: The role of external referents and deception. *Animal Behavior, 36*(2), 358–365.

Harari, A., & Brockman, H. J. (1999). Male beetles attracted by female mounting. *Nature, 401*(6755), 762–763.

Hyman, R. (1989). The psychology of deception. *Annual Review of Psychology, 40*, 133–154.

Lanza, R. P., Starr, J., & Skinner, B.F. (1982). "Lying in the pigeon." *Journal of the Experimental Analysis of Behavior, 38*(2), 201–203.

Mitchell, R.W. (1986). A framework for discussing deception. In R. W. Mitchell & N. S. Thompson (Eds.), *Deception: Perspective on human and nonhuman deceit* (pp. 3–40). Albany, NY: State University of New York.

Mitchell, R. W. (1991). Deception and hiding in captive lowland gorillas. *Primates, 32*(4), 523–527.

Mitchell, R. W., & Anderson, J. R. (1997). Pointing, witholding information, and deception in capuchin monkeys (*Cebus apella*). *Journal of Comparitive Psychology, 111*(4), 351–361.

Mitchell, R. W., & Hamm, M. (1997). The interpretation of animal psychology: Anthropomorphism or behavior reading? *Behaviour, 134*(3–4), 173–204.

Moffat, C. A., & Hogan, J. A. (1992). Ontogeny of chick responses to maternal food calls in the Burmese red junglefowl (*Gallus gallus spadiceus*). *Journal of Comparative Psychology, 106*(1), 92–96.

Munn, C. A. (1986). Birds that "cry wolf." *Nature, 319*(6049), 143–145.

Searcy, W. A., Eriksson, D., & Lundberg. A. (1991). Deceptive behavior in pied flycatchers. *Behavioral Ecology & Sociobiology, 29*(3), 167–175.

Slagsvold, T., & Dale, S. (1994). Why do female pied flycatchers mate with already mated males: Deception of restricted mate sampling. *Behavioral Ecology & Sociobiology, 34*(4), 239–250.

Sonerud, G. A. (1992). Nest predation may make the "deception hypothesis" unnecessary to explain polygyny in the Tengmalm's owl. *Animal Behavior, 43*(5), 871–874.

Stenmark, G., Slagsvold, T., & Lifjeld, J.T. (1988). Polygyny in the pied flycatcher, *Ficedula hypoleuca*: A test of the deception hypothesis. *Animal Behavior, 36*(6), 1646–1657.

Whaley, B. (1982). Toward a general theory of deception. *The Journal of Strategic Studies, 5*, 178–192.

Whoriskey, F. G. (1991). Stickleback distraction displays: Sexual or foraging deception against egg cannibalism. *Animal Behavior, 41*, (6), 989–995.

7 Children and Deception

There is a two-step developmental process in the human acquisition of deceptive behavior. *First*, the child must understand the concept of deception, and only then can the *second* step of the child's engaging in deceptive behavior occur. From the very beginning, deception is a complicated behavior at the human level. A child's ability to employ deception evolves from the child's maturation through intertwined stages of cognitive, affective, and interpersonal development. During age 3 to 4 years, the child's cognitive ability matures into a behavioral epistemology; that is, the child becomes capable of functional theory of knowledge (Wellman, 1990). By the time this occurs, the child is not only aware of himself or herself as differentiated from others but is also aware of his or her environment.

Hoogenraad and McKenzie (1995) traced this developmental process according to maternal accounts. The authors documented the reports of 100 mothers who recorded their observations of children who ranged in age from 3 to 7 years. It is this developmental base of cognitive–emotional maturation that enables the children to begin to manipulate others and their environment.

Children's manipulative efforts can be informed, constructive, and altruistic, but they can also be cunning and deceptive. It is the challenge of parents and society to guide the child through this developmental process in a wholesome and productive manner. Obviously, people do not always accomplish this objective, and youngsters learn very early how to engage in deception. The interest in children and deception is threefold: first, how early development contributes to use and reliance on deception in later development; second, how children can be used deceptively by self-serving adults; and third, how children who engage in deception impact on participation in court proceeedings as respondents* and as witnesses.

The recent research regarding children's understanding of deception has focused on ages 3 through 6 years as being a critical age range when the child conceptually grasps the deception and also begins to engage deliberately in deceptive behavior. This is not, of course, to suggest that the child's grasp of deception during these years approaches the complexity of an adult's.

There are two common forensic circumstances where the potential for deception in children is encountered. The first circumstance is children who are respondents in delinquency matters. During the decade of the 1990s even younger children have been respondents in juvenile deliquency matters (Poirier, 1999a). The second circumstance is children who appear as witnesses in different types of courtroom proceedings. The surge of child sexual abuse cases, in particular, has created considerable controversy regarding the suggestibility of children as witnesses in the courtroom (for reviews, see Ceci & Bruck, 1993; Bruck & Ceci, 1997; Bruck, Ceci, & Hembrooke, 1998). Much of this controversy has been spurred on by developmental psychologists who have challenged the historical notion that children are not reliable as witnesses (Myers, 1995). The situation has resulted in two serious problems: the overreporting on abuse that has not occurred and the underreporting of abuse that has occurred (Bruck, Ceci, & Hembrooke, 1998).

---

* *Respondent* is the juvenile justice system term for a youngster charged with a crime. Respondent is equivalent to the adult system term *defendant*. The traditional effort in the juvenile justice system is to recognize the basic difference, in terms of cognitive ability and emotional maturity, between children and adults. Thus, the difference in terminology and the hopeful acknowledgement that perhaps juvenile offenders are more malleable to change compared with adult defendants.

It has been only in the past 15 years that developmental researchers have begun to unravel the mysterious process by which humans learn to engage in deception. The surge of interest in the developmental evolution of lying and telling the truth is attributable to a number of factors These factors include the developmental research of children's suggestibility and, perhaps more notably, changes in case law and statutes permitting a more liberalized use of children as witnesses in the courtroom (Lee et al., 1997).

DECEPTION AND DEVELOPMENT

Children's exposure to deceptive behavior comes from many sources, some of which are timeworn and venerable means of helping children to mature. These sources include Biblical stories, nursery rhymes, fairy tales, fables, lullabies, and songs. As children become older, cartoons, computer games, and other media fare perpetuate the same exposure in even more vivid and graphic ways. It is through these multisensory inputs that caretakers, and the media, inculcate the values of good and evil in children. This process begins in the cradle and continues unabated to adulthood. It is in like manner that children learn about deception.

Many nursery rhymes capture themes of trickery and resultant pathos in human existence. It is commonplace experience for children of all cultures to be exposed to the singsong repetition of nursery rhymes and lullabies. Consider, for example, the influences engendered by the endearing rhymes of "Little Boy Blue," "Little Bo-Peep," "Pussy in the Well," "Jack and Jill," "What Are Little Boys and Girls Made of?" "Who Killed Cock Robin?" "Rock-a-bye, Baby," "Humpty Dumpty," and " Mother Goose."

In the children's fable "Puss and Boots" (Charles Perrault), a fake drowning is concocted to convince a king that Puss's master, the Marquis de Carabas, needed to be saved. Puss subsequently threatens to "chop into fine pieces" any worker in the area who would not lie by affirming that the Marquis indeed owned a large, attractive tract of land. Puss then murders the real landowner, pretending to be awed by the latter's abilities. The Marquis, who is aware of the deception, is rewarded with the land, marries the murdered king's daughter, and makes Puss the prime minister.

The heroine's sisters in "Beauty and the Beast" (Madame Leprince de Beaumont), who rubbed onions in their eyes in order to cry, illustrate faking bad. In "Cinderella," also by Charles Perrault, the wicked stepmother pretends to be nice to Cinderella until she marries Cinderella's father, then heaps work and abuse on her. Not to be outdone, Cinderella yawns and pretends to have been asleep when opening the door for her stepfamily returning from the ball, when in actuality, she had just returned from the ball herself.

Deception is presented in children's stories in other cultures as well. In the Russian fable, "Finn, the Keen Falcon," the heroine attempts to hide a diamond pin in a piece of pie dough, but is observed by her jealous sisters. The Sea King's daughter in the Japanese fable, "Urashima and the Turtle," changes into a turtle to see if a fisherman would eat her, thereby proving that he had a good heart when he did not do so.

Virtually all popular fairy tales and fables told to children by their caretakers contain substantial deception by one or more of the principal actors. In these stories, deception is usually successful for those who initiate it. Bad people, usually involving those with self-centered or base motives, do "bad" deception; "good" deception is performed by the heroes and heroines and is justified in terms of their righteousness and object goal. "Good" faking always triumphs over "bad" deception.

Children are exposed to these powerful messages about deception during critical periods of development. Children form early notions about interactions with others and in doing so work through the Eriksonian issues of trust, autonomy, and initiation (Erikson, 1963). Identification with the hero or heroine who deceives may allow children to successfully work through basic mistrust, shame, doubt, and guilt by creating illusions of reality upon which they can operate. A smoother fit into the adult world can be anticipated and perhaps is the principal function of learning fables.

Both positive and negative effects emerge from this incidental learning. The differences between good and evil, base and altruistic, crazy and normal are not at all clear and appear to vary as a function of antecedents, the act itself, and the consequences of the deed, whether intended or not. Without ascribing to a relativistic view of morality, children taught the absolutes of virtue and favorable outcome, and provided with role models who have the same characteristics (and win on top of that), may lack flexibility of thought and action when encountering reality. Unlike the view of Pinocchio's nose, much deception is nonverifiable, with unintentional distortion and deliberate deception merging in overlapping and nonmeasurable ways.

More insidiously, an identification of self with the good — that is, the hero or the heroine — may take place from exposure to these fairy tales and fables. One may come to believe that deception is carried as a virtuous by-product of this basic goodness. Self-righteousness may result. The etiology of deceptive behavior in humans is a learned behavior as far as is known. Only very recently have there been efforts to investigate deceptive behavior empirically in terms of familial and cultural factors, which are clearly also major influences in children's acquisition of an appreciation of deception. Perhaps in the future, studies will shed light on whether or not there are genetic factors that contribute to a person's potential for acquiring and engaging in deceptive behavior.

EMPIRICAL STUDIES OF DECEPTION AND DEVELOPMENT

Piaget (1929) was among the first to observe and document that children differed from adults in their understanding of lies and truth. A developmental psychologist, Piaget had a special interest in cognition. Piaget's hypotheses about children acquiring a moral awareness were based on their maturating cognition (Burton & Strichartz, 1991; Quinn, 1988). Piaget presented pairs of scenarios to children depicting actors engaging in verbal communication ranging from exaggeration to lying. The children would then be asked to make "moral judgments" about how "naughty" the communications were because they were not the truth. In Piaget's view, children younger than 7 years were not able to comprehend the true nature of lies. In the young child's perception, misstatements and false statements were lies; likewise, young children could not discriminate between an actual mistake and a deliberate attempt to be deceitful. Piaget found that younger children based their judgments on how much the actor's statements varied from actuality and whether punishment was involved when lies were told. Children could not grasp the actor's intentionality as a factor in their judgments until around 11 years of age. Piaget (1929, 1959) suggested that children in late childhood do not clearly know the difference between the internal (e.g., psychic) and the external (e.g., environmental). He viewed children as having difficulty recalling the origins of their knowledge. Markman (1979) found that 12-year-old children have difficulty seeing factual inconsistencies without prompting.

In reviewing the relevant research on memory, Johnson and Foley (1984) found children to be credible. They argued that generally children's recall, while less developed than that of adults, did not possess many of the deficits typically imputed to children's recall (e.g., fusing fantasy with fact). Extending these findings, Burton and Strichartz (1991) found that children were less likely than older children and adults to lie because of extenuating circumstances, and that in their naivete, children were likely to be motivated to be honest or more honest than adults.

Some pre-1990s studies suggested that with specific forms of memory children were more reliable than adults. For example, children may recall visual information better than verbal information (Duncan, Whitney, & Kunen, 1982). Marin et al. (1979) found that children as young as 5 years were no less competent than adults in their accuracy on a photograph identification task. King and Yuille (1987) reported that children under the age of 6 years were less accurate, compared with older children, in photograph identification. Thus, children as young as 5 or 6 may prove to be reliable witnesses when asked to identify target persons visually. A second view held that children had poor recall, were uncritical, and were very suggestible. Younger children were seen as viewing lying as being amoral (Kohlberg, 1981). Children's motives for lying may include obtaining attention, escaping punishment, and/or receiving material rewards. Children at younger ages may create a fantasy in order to have someone else to blame.

In a study involving 142 preschoolers and kindergartners, Haugaard et al. (1991) found that children grasped definitions of truth, but the findings also raised concerns about the reliability of children's eyewitness memory. As an aside, it should be noted that formative issues regarding children's memory intertwine with the child's evolving cognition. Clinical assessment of adult recall of childhood experiences must take into consideration this developmental facticity. This observation has direct relevance to the problem of recovered adult memories of childhood sexual abuse being subject to distortion (Ackil & Zaragoza, 1998; Rubin, 1996).

In spite of the accuracy of young children on photograph identification tasks, Parker and Carranza (1989) found that when children (mean age = 9 years) were given the option "none of the above" in a photograph identification task, they were less likely than adults to reject all the photographs. Children in the age range of 6 to 8 years may use more lax criteria for identifying suspect photographs than do older children. When the correct photograph is present in the line-up, children as young as 6 appear to be no less accurate than adults in selecting the correct photo, but when the correct photograph is absent, these children are more likely than adults to select an incorrect photograph.

A developmental view of children as witnesses recognizes the wide variability in developmental processes with children of different ages. This information must be considered in assessing a child's veracity. The most relevant findings attribute potential for distortion to a multitude of developmental processes, including sensation and perception, cognition, memory, language acquisition, moral awareness, social and emotional maturity, and achievement levels. Accordingly, developmentalists have consistently recommended advanced training in child development to help evaluators detect the truth in individual cases (Goodman, 1984; Lamb, Sternberg, & Esplin, 1995). Goodman (1984) described examples of how knowledge of a child's use of words could assist in detecting perpetrators of sexual abuse when those verbalizations are understood in a developmental context.

TARGET BEHAVIORS, AGE, AND DECEPTIVE BEHAVIOR

Deceptive behavior with children is a function of their age and respective abilities. Selected accounts of developmentally related distortion from age 4 to age 12 are presented below. These age-range summaries illustrate the typical developmental progressions of deception-related capacities in children; children mature through these phases at individualized rates.

Ages 0 to 3

Terr (1985) described the potential usefulness of infant testimony to astute clinicians who directly observe the responsiveness of infants to parenting figures. In situations where infants had been traumatized or where parentage was at issue, clinical observation of attachment behavior could be very revealing. In some instances, it is not feasible or advisable to rely directly on observations of the infants' behavior. The child's response may not be reliable because of the passage of time; the courtroom would be a threatening situation for most young childen; and observers, to include sitting judges, may not have the ability to accurately interpret a young child's response. "Whenever the expert witness's history, observations, examination, and supporting information concerning the baby are strong and complete enough to bypass the infant's own testimony, such a substitution is to be encouraged" (Terr, 1985, p. 321).

Traditionally, children younger than 4 years have been considered unreliable as witnesses because of their proclivity to interweave fantasy and reality in everyday experience. Opposing attorneys, for example, will mock, "How can the court accept the testimony of someone who still belives in the tooth fairy?" Infants and toddlers have primitive cognitive ability, but anyone experienced in working with very young children knows that they evidence awareness of others in unique and characteristic ways. Very young children express nonverbal awareness and attachment particularly with significant others. Similarly, very young children can make very nonverbally evident their displeasure with someone unfamiliar or distrusted.

Ages 3 to 4

Empirical studies have consistently identified the age range of 3 to 5 years as the age when children begin to grasp the concept of deception. By the age of 4 years, children understand false beliefs and deceptive ploys (Sodian et al., 1991). The 4-year-olds are able to attempt to create a false belief in others (Ruffman et al., 1993). Prior to age 4, children can engage in deception-like behavior, although not in a very sophisticated manner (Hala, Chandler, & Fritz, 1991; Lewis et al., 1989; Rice et al., 1997; Siegal and Peterson, 1994, 1996; Siegal, 1998; Sullivan & Winner, 1993; Zaitchik, 1991).

Perner and Wimmer (1985, 1987, 1988; Wimmer & Perner, 1983) conducted seminal studies regarding children and deception. They described first-order reasoning where the child is aware of a social circumstance involving two other people, e.g., Sue and Harry (Wimmer & Perner, 1983). In a subsequent study (Perner & Wimmer, 1985), they investigated the age that children could differentiate "embedded" thinking in others. Embedded thinking refers to the child's being able to comprehend the notion of another person's having an awareness of a third person's mental state. Being able to grasp the intention of another actor is a critical component of understanding deception. Second-order reasoning (Perner & Wimmer, 1985) would be the child's awareness that " Sue thinks that Harry feels …" or "Harry believes that Sue understands.…" Children understand deception when they conceptually grasp that the victim's false belief is what makes the victim vulnerable to deceit (Peskin, 1996). Age 3 to 6 is the period during which children make this cognitive leap.

Table 7.1 depicts the characteristics of first- and second-order reasoning in detail and summarizes the proposed ages of onset by different researchers. The data illustrate the divergent findings across researchers within a very narrow range of development. These findings have resulted in an array of still-evolving theoretical explanations and novel research paradigms.

Ruffman et al. (1993) use a modified Wimmer and Perner (1983; Perner & Wimmer, 1988) model with 3- and 4-year-old youngsters. They concluded that children age 4 and younger had difficulties with deception tasks primarily because of cognitive deficiencies. The children could understand how clues could affect an actor-onlooker in a story to have a false belief as long as the false belief was consistent with the story context. The children would have difficulty, however, when trying to grasp how a clue could actually induce the onlooker to have a false belief that would lead the deceived person to change his or her behavior, e.g., withhold negative consequences. This is a subtle but very important distinction between a child's conception of deception compared with that of an older child or an adult. Younger children may understand that deceptive behavior can be

---

TABLE 7.1
Age of Onset for First- and Second-Level Reasoning in Children by Different Researchers

Level of Reasoning	Functional Ability	Verbal Examples	Researcher(s)
First order	Child's capacity to understand another person's perception of a social situation	"He perceives"; "she perceives"; "they think"	Occurs at ages 3–5 years (Perner & Winner, 1985)
Second order	Includes first-order reasoning plus capacity to ascribe second-order thinking to another person	"He believes that she thinks that …"; "she perceives that they feel that …"	Occurs at ages 4–5 years (Sullivan, Zaitchin, & Tager-Flusberg, 1994; Peskin, 1996) Occurs at ages 5–6 years (Wellman, 1990)

a means of avoiding negative consequences, but they do not understand how deception can be used to induce the deceived persons to alter their behavior. Young children, therefore, may be able to enact deceptive behavior superficially but not with any purposeful intent in terms of achieving a desired goal, or avoiding negative consequences for themselves.

Polak and Harris (1999) replicated an earlier paradigm (Lewis, Stanger, & Sullivan, 1989) of asking youngsters not to touch a toy in a box when the experimenter left the room. The researchers found that most of the preschoolers (ages 2 to 5 years) in the experimental group touched the toy and then denied doing so. The youngsters were therefore able to engage in deception of a misdeed, but were less effective feigning ignorance of the contents of the toy box. The act of feigning ignorance was interpreted to be a more-sophisticated level of deception.

Krause and Saarnio (1993) conducted a study with 3- to 5-year-olds investigating the children's understanding of whether objects were edible in terms of appearance. The 4- and 5-year-olds clearly understood the edibleness of nondeceptive objects, but the 3-year-olds did not. All the youngsters had problems with deceptive objects (i.e., a magnet that looked like candy); the children made correct judgments of the nonedibilty of the magnets only 50% of the time.

Siegal and Peterson (1996, 1998) used teddy bears as actors and presented children with scenarios of the bears lying, not lying, or being mistaken about bread that was edible or moldy. The researchers investigated the abilities of 3-, 4-, and 5-year-olds to discriminate deception from being mistaken. These researchers prudently cautioned that children's failure to distinguish deception from mistakes must take into account the artificiality of the setting. That is, the younger children's difficulties in the posed tasks may have been due to extraneous conversational or contextual factors. Children's responses to laboratory-contrived scenarios may also reflect the children's personalized concerns as opposed to the intended scientific purpose of the researchers. Siegal and Peterson found that many of the 4- and 5-year-olds and even some of the 3-year-olds could differentiate deception from mistaken beliefs by actors in the food contamination scenarios. The authors suggested that since food ingestion was central to children's self-interests, the study involved an inherently motivating element that may have been the basis for the higher discrimination rates in their study.

Numerous researchers (Flavell, Green, & Flavell, 1986; Rice et al., 1997; Sullivan & Winner, 1993) have postulated a *correspondence bias* in young children. Correspondence bias refers to the child's tendency to adopt a single representation of an object that, for whatever reason, is most acceptable to the child at the moment. Thus, if a child perceives an object as a block of wood, it is difficult for the child to accept that the object may in fact be made of plastic or rubber. Researchers have suggested that correspondence bias is the reason young children may have difficulty grasping false-belief tasks (Rice et al., 1997). A proposed alternative explanation was that young children do not have sufficient information-processing ability because of neuropsychological immaturity. That is, the child cannot grasp the concept of two conflicting reality identities about the same object at the same time (Rice et al., 1997).

There is evidence (Chandler, Fritz, & Hala, 1989; Rice et al., 1997; Saltmarsh & Mitchell, 1998; Sullivan & Winner, 1993) that correspondence bias in children can be overcome if the false-belief task is presented in the explicit context of a deception scenario. The context of deception may put the children on alert that alternative explanations of the false-belief task should be considered.

Carlson, Moses, & Hix, (1998) conducted a series of studies with 3- and 4-year-olds and found that the children's difficulties with false-belief tasks were due less to conceptual difficulty and more to a lack of inhibitory control. That is, the children could not disinhibit cognitive conflicts to grasp a false-belief situation. If an object looked like food in terms of its sensory characteristics, then young children would not entertain the possibility of the object's being (intentionally) disguised to appear as food.

Russell et al. (1991) compared the abilities of 3- and 4-year-olds to 7- to 27-year-old subjects with autism engaging in a strategic deception task. The subjects tried to win chocolates and had to point to an empty or to a baited box. The correct strategy was to point to the empty box. Children who were 4 years old would quickly grasp the correct strategy. The 3-year-olds and the subjects with autism, however, would consistently point to the incorrect box. The authors theorized that the 3-year-olds and the autistic subjects persisted with a "false-belief" strategy because they could not inhibit knowledge about desired-object location to shift epistemic strategy. Inhibitory control is one aspect of neurological executive function and has been linked as a critical capacity to children's abilities to understand deceit (Hughes, 1998). Reinecke et al. (1997) also investigated the similar limitations of adolescents with autism being able to grasp deception strategies.

Youngsters this age are resistant to noncoercive suggestion (Lamb, Sternberg, & Esplin, 1995), but are susceptible to misleading postevent information (Lampinen & Smith, 1995). In comparison with adults, youngsters this age are not able to correct for false information due to deliberate deception by the source.

Ages 4 to 5

Annon (1987) suggested that all capacities considered, some 4-year-olds could be qualified as witnesses. According to Annon, the 4-year-old is in a transition period and can be considered a competent witness with proper, nonleading questions. This opinion regarding 4-year-olds is based on the assumption that youngsters this age have the ability to differentiate fact from fantasy. At the present time, the 4-year-old cutoff is not widely adopted by either clinicians or the courts.

In a review article, Ceci and Bruck (1993) reported that in approximately 88% of the studies that compared preschoolers to older children or to adults, the preschoolers were the most vulnerable to suggestion. In a study addressing children's competence to take the oath, 4-year-olds with histories of being maltreated recognized the immorality of lying, but tended to identify all statements as the "truth" (Lyon & Saywitz, 1999). In the same study, 5-year-olds could correctly differentiate truthful statements from lies, but could not define the meaning of "lie" or "truth." The authors suggested that children's oath-taking competence is underestimated because of linguistic and motivational difficulties.

Relevant to the potential for deliberate distortion, various studies show that between 21 and 49% of children in this age group evidence lying behavior (Stouthamer-Loeber, 1986). Stouthamer-Loeber cites statistics regarding the reasons for lying. Avoiding punishment is the main reason for children in this age group to lie. According to the subjects' mothers, avoidance of punishment comprised 44% of all excuses. Other reasons include confusion (15%), self-gain (14%), playing or having fun (10%), and protecting self-esteem (6%).

The previously cited Perner and Wimmer (1985) study presented stories to children of different ages. The stories portrayed person-actors in different social scenarios. The children would have to respond to inquiries designed to measure whether they grasped the levels of social interactions depicted in the stories. The authors concluded that children could not understand second-order reasoning (i.e., attributed mental states in the story characters) until age 6 to 7 years. It is important to recognize that the child's ability to understand that second-order reasoning is a critical element in the child's ability to understand complex social interactions.

Deceptive behavior is a complex social interaction involving the deceiver and the deceived. Deception makes a social interaction not what it overtly appears to be. To comprehend deception, the child must be able to grasp the capacity of one person's being covertly aware of another person's mental state. Deception occurs when that covert awareness of another person's mental state is inaccurate because of the intention of the other person to deceive. Understanding deceptive behavior is, therefore, a sophisticated, developmental ability whereby the child must grasp both the cognitive intent and the volitional decision of the deceiver.

Sullivan, Zaitchik, and Tager-Flusberg (1994) replicated the Perner and Wimmer research. The original stories were modified; the stories were shortened and made less complex. The research also incorporated a new story design. The new stories introduced an explicit deception theme. Prior research (Sullivan & Winner, 1993) determined children's ability to perceive false-belief circumstances was facilitated by the story line's having a deception context. For example, deception-based stories portrayed a mother misleading a child about a birthday gift in order to surprise the child. The child-actor, meanwhile, discovered the gift, thereby taking away any element of surprise.

These findings reflect that preschoolers and kindergartners are capable of second-order reasoning whereby the children correctly identified story subject's attributing mental states to other story characters. For younger children, there was an identifiable, intermediary step where children would first recognize a story-actor as being ignorant of an event as opposed to the child's understanding the actor as having a false belief about the event. It was easier for children to comprehend an actor's being ignorant compared with comprehending that the actor had a false belief. The developmental window for children's being able to grasp the difference between the actor being's ignorant and being deceptive was less than 2 years. In contrast to the earlier finding by Perner and Wimmer (1985) that ages 6 to 7 years was the critical age range, the current authors hypothesized that the ages 4 to 5 years actually marked the emergence of a child's ability to grasp the meaning of embedded mental states in others. As maturation continues and a child's information-processing capacity progresses, this second-order reasoning ability becomes more sophisticated.

Children from 4 to 6 years of age are at a critical stage with cognitive, memory, and social developmental factors being highly interactive and prominent in the child's growth curve. Accordingly, youngsters this age are very vulnerable to bias influence induced during interpersonal activity. This has obvious implications for forensic clinicians evaluating youngsters in this age group. In a laboratory study, Lepore and Sesco (1994) found that 4- to 6-year-olds produced misleading reports about their interactions with both familiar and unfamiliar adults when prompted to do so by an opinionated adult interviewer.

Ages 5 to 6

Children in this age group do not differ significantly from adults on answering simple "yes–no" questions, correctly identifying photographs of confederates, or being misled by leading task instructions or questions (Marin et al., 1979). In general, Marin's data revealed that eyewitness identification was poor along all age ranges, from childhood to adulthood (25 to 50% of subjects were unable to recognize a target male from six photographs). The number of incorrect items (as opposed to not guessing) increased linearly with age. Marin et al. summarized the findings by stating that children are no less accurate than adults in responding to direct objective questions but are less capable in giving narrative descriptions of target events. In other words, the children in this age group said little but were accurate in their representations of events. Further, 5- and 6-year-old children are generally unable to hide their deception by controlling facial expressions, voice tone, and speech content (Feldman & White, 1980; Morency & Kraus, 1982).

Although children by the ages of 5 and 6 years have an essential cognitive grasp of deceptive behavior, their discriminatory ability regarding the subtleties of deception is still evolving. Winner and Leekam (1991) presented stories to 5- to 7-year-olds. The stories ended in either deceptive or ironic statements. Correct judgments by the subjects were keyed to their correct understanding of the speaker as wanting the listener to believe them or not. Speaker intonation (sarcasm for irony; sincerity for the lie) was not a discerning variable in the children's judgment accuracy. The main finding was that the children in this age group accurately perceived the speaker's intention. This replicated earlier findings of 5- to 7-year-old children's being able to grasp second-order reasoning (i.e., second-order intention in the deceptive actor). The earlier studies used story figures as the deceivers; the current study used a live speaker and produced comparable findings.

In a study of eyewitness memory (Leippe, Romanczyk, & Manion, 1991), 5- to 6-year-olds had less complete free recall and made more errors compared with 9- to 10-year-olds and adults. Likewise, the 5- to 6-year-olds were inferior to adults in correctly identifying photographs of a "touching" intruder in a laboratory setting. The children failed to identify the intruder six of ten times, and made false identifications once out of four times. The latter finding was a 23% false identification rate, an obviously worrisome forensic finding in terms of young children's witness performance. Even with 5-year-olds, cognitive interviewing procedures have been reported to improve recall, although the youngsters were susceptible to misleading suggestions (Hayes & Delamothe, 1997)

Ages 6 to 7

In terms of nondeliberate distortion, Chance and Goldstein (1984) stated, "Face recognition of familiar faces under conditions that permit a clear view of the whole face is quite good, even in children as young as six years." Children of this age tend to be concrete, with literal interpretations of words and phrases (Ackerman, 1981). These children can also read four or more words, add two single-digit numbers, write ten words from memory, and spot missing parts in a picture (Blau, 1986).

Children in this age group can detect inconsistent information (Ackerman, 1983). They may contradict a person's stating inconsistent information, usually when the speaker is discredited or is of low status. Children as deceivers are usually detected by untrained others, yet still have some control over their nonverbal responses (Feldman & White, 1980). In general, children in this age group judge lies not by intent, but by whether statements invite punishment or involve forbidden actions or things (Piaget, 1965).

In the forensic setting, most children by the age of 6 years will be able to provide competent testimony assuming capable, nonprejudicial interviewing (Lamb, Sternberg, & Esplin, 1994). The ability to differentiate statements as truthful or as lies coupled with the inability to define the difference between "truths" and "lies" persisted from the age of 4 years to the age of 7 years (Lyon & Saywitz, 1999). Using a sample ($N = 86$) of second graders (i.e., 6- to 7-years-old), cognitive interviewing elicited 64% more correct information in initial interviews and 46% more in a second interview compared with a standard interview (McCauley & Fisher, 1995). Cognitive interview procedures improved recall (Hayes & Delamothe, 1997)

Ages 7 to 8

Children in this age group see lies as untrue statements (Piaget, 1965). Mistakes are still labeled as lies, but dirty or obscene words are not seen as lies, as they were with younger children. A child in this age group can (1) keep secrets for longer than 1 day, (2) attend to a stimulus, such as a lecture, for up to a quarter hour, (3) repeat five digits, and (4) give simple definitions (Blau, 1986). Malingering of a physical or psychiatric disorder by young children is rare (Quinn, 1988). There is evidence that latency age children (7 to 12 years) and adolescents engage in malingering (Greenfield, 1987).

As with younger children, the recall memory of 7- to 8-year-olds can be enhanced with cognitive interviewing techniques (Saywitz, Geiselman, & Bornstein, 1992). Hayes and Delamothe (1997) observed that children younger than 7 years require extended exposure to cognitive interviewing techniques to obtain maximum recall enhancement. Children 8 years and older compared equally to adults in perceived confidence and credibility, even when subjected to cross-examination (Luus, Wells, & Turtle, 1995).

Ages 8 to 9

Children in this age group can do all the above. They still may not see all of the conflicting information between successive statements (Markman, 1979). The recall of 9- to 11-year-old children was improved with cognitive interviewing procedures, although children at this age remained susceptible to misleading suggestions (Hayes & Delamothe, 1997).

Ages 9 to 10

Piaget (1959, 1965) described that children 10 years old and older could grasp the intentionality of a deceitful effort, but still could not grasp the subtleties of deception, as could an adult. Youngsters in this age range "can [successfully] fool their peers, adult strangers, and at times, their parents" (Quinn, 1988). Children from 9 to 12 years can fake believable neuropsychological deficits. Faust, Hart, and Guilmette (1988) found that none of 42 professional evaluators detected malingering in three children who had been instructed to fake bad. The neuropsychologists diagnosed abnormality with 93% accuracy; 87% stated that cortical dysfunction was indicated by test results. In a study of eyewitness accuracy, Leippe, Romanczyk, & Manion (1991) found that 9- and 10-year-olds have recognition accuracy similar to that of college students.

Ages 10 to 11

At this age, disguised, briefly seen, and previously unfamiliar faces can be much better recognized (Chance & Goldstein, 1984). Children younger than 10 years are largely unreliable in this ability. There is a shift at this age to a focus on the intent of lying. Piaget (1965) pointed out that these children focus on intent in lying and give adult definitions of prevarication. The recall of youngsters in this age group was significantly enhanced with cognitive interviewing techniques (Saywitz, Geiselman, & Bornstein, 1992). These youngsters evidenced especially pronounced recall improvement with cognitive questioning about an irrelevant event compared with younger children. This finding has obvious implications for real-life situations wherein children this age could benefit from select practice interviewing that would not prejudice inquiries about specific forensic events.

In a study involving 98 10-year-olds, Braginsky (1970) investigated the effect of Machiavellianism ("Mach") on lying. He found that high-Mach subjects (exploitive, manipulative) clearly gave more false information, distorted true information, concealed, presented incomplete sensory data, and acted in other misleading ways to influence the target person. Gender differences emerged in that high-Mach boys were best at telling lies of commission while the girls used omission to their advantage. In terms of ability to deceive strangers, fourth and fifth graders have the ability to deceive adults if given adequate incentive (Allen & Atkinson, 1978).

Ages 11 to 12

Social factors are increasing influences by this age; not only are these youngsters influenced by social interactions, they now actively pursue social contact particularly with peers and they are interpersonally assertive. Preteen children can give an explanation why criminals are locked up, avoid deliberately embarrassing others, control their anger, keep secrets as long as appropriate, and practice other forms of self-control (Blau, 1986). Generally, they justify the prohibition against lying in terms of trust and fairness (Peterson, Peterson, & Seeto, 1983).

OTHER DEVELOPMENTAL DETERMINANTS OF DECEPTION

Ceci and Bruck (1993) posited three "families" of factors as being important in the suggestibility of children: cognitive, biological, and social. Researchers have explored a number of sociocultural variables influencing children's developmental acquisition of deception knowledge and ability. Parenting styles have been described as influencing children's ability to be deceptive. In one study (Cole & Mitchell, 1998) with 57 youngsters, single-parent stress was cited as a major predictor of children's being able to convincingly verbalize an act of deception (expressive deception). In the same study, socioeconomic status was predictive of the children's understanding that the mind was capable of being deceived. The conditions of parents being incarcerated or parents having been involved in criminal behavior have been noted to influence children's awareness of deception (Gabel, 1992).

Family characteristics (Cole & Mitchell, 1998; Thomas, Booth-Butterfield, & Booth-Butterfield, 1995; Poirier, 1996) and social factors (Kawakami, 1995) have been cited as important determinants of deceptive behavior in children. The broad role of sociocultural variables has also been extensively explored (Aune & Waters, 1994; Bartolmew, 1994; Dunn et al., 1991; Lee et al., 1997; Siegal & Peterson, 1994, 1995, 1998). It has been suggested, for example, that different cultures may promote greater verbal communication to children that encourages more awareness of mental states (Siegal & Peterson, 1995).

Children's developmental grasp of deception is directly related to neurological maturation (Anderson, 1998; Dennis et al., 1998; Sodian et al., 1991; Thatcher, 1992). The skills necessary for goal-directed and purposeful activity (i.e., executive function) are mediated by the prefrontal and frontal cortices of the brain (Anderson, 1998). The maturation of the right cortical hemisphere, in particular, is felt to influence a child's ability to moderate interactions with the environment in a practical sense, and has been suggested to underlie the child's ability to understand deception (Siegal & Peterson, 1996).

SYNTHESIS

The literature suggests that conclusions regarding distortion in children should be geared toward developmental abilities and individual circumstances. It is naive to believe that a child is credible or noncredible without taking into account both nomothetic and ideographic information within a developmental perspective. Both unintentional distortion (i.e., developmental capacities) and deliberate misrepresentation must be considered in evaluating the credibility of child witnesses (Bruck, Ceci, & Hembrooke, 1998).

The potential combinations of nondistortion and deliberate and nondeliberate distortion in child witnesses are often difficult to untangle. Because of emerging cognitive and emotional capacities, the differentiation between deliberate and nondeliberate distortion is not always developmentally precise. Consider the accessory-to-sex syndrome where the child coerced into sex is pressured to keep quiet and to deny any sexual activity if questioned (Burgess & Holmstrom, 1985). After repeated assaults, the child tends to repress the unpleasant aspects of the activity, even if prodded by investigators. Is this deliberate or unintentional distortion? The same may be true of Munchausen syndrome by proxy (Meadow, 1982; Palmer & Yoshimura, 1984), in which a child, usually a preschooler, is ordered to remain silent about an illness or injury, which is fabricated by the caretaker. Is the child's contribution to the ruse due to developmental incapacities or to intentional misrepresentation?

Ceci and Bruck (1993) summarized the research exploring what conditions motivate children to lie or to tell the truth. They identified five categories of motivation that have been studied:

1. Lying and truth telling to avoid punishment;
2. Lying and truth telling to sustain a game;
3. Keeping promises;
4. Lying and truth telling for personal gain;
5. Lying and truth telling to avoid embarrassment.

CHILDREN AND THE JUDICIAL SYSTEM

There are three typical ways that children and adolescents become involved in forensic matters. Each scenario connotes a different *response pattern* and each is reviewed in turn. Children are our heritage and our future; they are always gullible and vulnerable. Regardless of the forensic circumstances, the foremost concern in any assessment involving children is protecting the child's welfare. Whether children are witnesses or respondents, the issues of the child's credibility and veracity are always central concerns. Additionally, every child involved in the legal arena is exposed to powerful pressures that heighten the likelihood of both intentional and nonintentional deception. This dynamic occurs because our culture rightfully holds such high regard for the rights and welfare of our children. Not only are the children vulnerable to distortion, but also parents, family members, and others. The first way that children can become involved in the legal system is as respondents in juvenile delinquency matters in the juvenile court. Just as with adult criminal defendants, the primary challenge with youngsters charged with delinquent acts is the respondent's veracity. Even very young children can be acutely aware of social taboo forces associated with asocial behavior. Although usually more naive than adults in clinical presentation, children involved in delinquency matters, especially with those with serious crimes, can pose formidable deception problems (Oldershaw & Bagby, 1997). In most jurisdictions children involved in serious crimes (e.g., murder, armed robbery, and rape) can be charged as adults and tried in the adult court where dispositional penalties are far more severe than in the juvenile court. Grisso (1998) has provided an overview of the forensic assessment of juvenile offenders.

In recognition of the growing problem of juvenile crime, the American Psychological Association formed a Commission on Violence and Youth in May 1991 (Gentry & Eron, 1993). The commission has a specific focus on preventive and rehabilitative interventions. In 1996, the Coordinating Council on Juvenile Justice and Delinquency Prevention (CCJJDP, 1996) proposed an eight-objective nationwide action plan to combat juvenile delinquency.

Statistics reflect that since the early 1990s, the age of youngsters charged with serious crimes has dipped into the preteen years (Tatem-Kelley et al., 1997; Sickmund, Snyder, & Poe-Yamagata, 1997; Poirier, 1999a). This increase of children's being involved in serious crime has been attributed, in part, to a rise in gang crime (Poirier,1999a). With very young children, the issues of competency to stand trial and criminal responsibilty for the offense are always in question. The specific problems of deception with competency and criminal responsibilty are addressed in depth in Chapters 17 and 18, respectivly.

The second way that a child can enter the legal system is as victim/witness in juvenile delinquency, adult criminal, civil, or domestic court matters. Children who are victims of abuse or neglect compose the most common category of children being called as witnesses. When children have been physically, sexually, or psychologically abused, or when they have been subjected to neglect, the law provides for the courts to step in and assume responsibility for the child. The legal principle involved is that of *parens patriae* (literally "parent of the country") and is a vestige of old English law when kings had sovereign control of their kingdom. The application of *parens patriae* could include "termination of parental rights" and adoption proceedings.

The third way that children become involved in the courts is as innocent, but very affected, parties in domestic court matters. Typically, these are divorce and contested custody/visitation matters.

The foregoing three categories are somewhat artificial in that some situations may involve more than one category, and different jurisdictions will have different criteria and different adjudication procedures. In all legal proceedings involving children, there are two probative concerns for the court. These two issues then become focal concerns for the forensic clinician. Both issues encompass the potential of deception. These issues are the child's *competence as a witness* and the child's *credibility as a witness*. Competency as a child witness denotes having sufficient developmental maturity to be legally fit; being competent has to do with the child's developmental qualifications to render meaningful testimony. In contrast, credibility is the perceived veracity or, in legal terms, the worthiness of belief of the witness. In legal proceedings, the child witness must first be deemed competent as a witness; then, and only then, the trier of fact judges the child's credibility. Competence addresses whether a child will be admitted as a witness; credibility addresses how much weight will be given to the child's testimony. A witness, therefore, can be competent but render noncredible testimony, or a witness can be incompetent but render credible testimony.

Prior to the 1990s, most U.S. jurisdictions did not allow expert testimony on the reliability or credibility of child witnesses (McGough, 1991), because such testimony may itself be unreliable (*Utah v. Rimmasch*, 1989). However, a few courts have permitted such testimony (McGough, 1991).

More recently, there have been additional cases of the courts allowing children to testify as professional methods of credibility analysis have improved. As will be described, there have also been recent judicial attempts to remedy the problems associated with child witness testimony.

Expert opinions on the reliability of children's complaints influence law enforcement efforts and also child welfare agencies in their investigations for prosecution of child physical or sexual abusers. Experts are also influential in their formulation of opinions on other substantive questions (e.g., parental fitness, allegations of parental violence, allegations of child sexual abuse by parental figures, and child parental preference) based on their assessment of a child's believability. Competence and credibility of the child witness present different problems regarding deception. The remainder of this chapter focuses on these two assessment issues.

DECEPTION AND CHILD WITNESS COMPETENCY

If the volume of case law citations, psychological studies, and theoretical opinions is any indication, the question of competence of child witness testimony has been a very popular and controversial topic since the early 1980s (Bruck & Ceci, 1993; Hudson & Fivush, 1991; Lamb, Sternberg, & Esplin, 1995; Myers, 1995). The vast majority of these references have been related to children who have been sexual abuse victims and brought into legal proceedings as witnesses. Meyer and Geis (1994) suggested that the voluminous research on children as witnesses has overshadowed the more important issue of how to detect whether children are lying when they say they have been victimized. In terms of applied forensic practice, there are two primary issues: the first is the inherent limitations of a child's reporting and memory; the second is the positive and negative impact of suggestive interviewing techniques (Bruck, Ceci, & Hembrooke, 1998). Additionally, it is important to recognize that, aside from the fact that the state of the art is not such that one can always accurately detect deception, the ultimate legal question of a witness's being credible is the task of the trier of fact, that is, the judge or jury.

In most jurisdictions, there are three essential elements for a child to be a competent witness, the child must understand:

1. The need for telling the truth, as opposed to speaking mistruth (Burton & Strichartz, 1991);
2. The need to recall and relate facts accurately and objectively;
3. Being under oath.

The assessment of a child's competence to be a witness involves questions about the child's understanding of honesty and lying. The focus is not on the accuracy of particular memories, or the susceptibility of the child to adult influence, or the motives of the child. Rather the focus is on the general capacity of the child to distinguish truth from lies and to subscribe to the importance of truth telling.

Historically, the prevailing assumption was that the mnestic and communicative abilities of young children were too immature to allow competent testimony. However, the U.S. Supreme Court in *Wheeler v. U.S.*, (1895) ruled that young children as a group cannot be declared incompetent, but each child's capacity to testify must be evaluated individually by the court. Under this rule, children are presumed to be incompetent to testify, but that presumption can be overcome in a particular case by evidence to the contrary. In all jurisdictions a child under the age of 10 can be allowed to testify if that child knows the difference between a truth and a lie; in some jurisdictions the child must also have the capacity to recall past incidents (Haugaard et al., 1991). Rule 601 of the Federal Rules of Evidence eliminated the presumption of incompetence of child witnesses and at least 13 states have adopted similar rules (Goodman & Reed, 1986). Under these new rules, children are presumed to be competent witnesses unless evidence to the contrary is offered.

Developmental psychologists have demonstrated that children clearly have different conceptions of truth and lying compared with adults. In general, children define lies more broadly than do

TABLE 7.2
Percentages of Subjects at Each Age Level Who
Defined Given Types of Statements as Lies

	Age				
Statement	5	8	9	11	Adult
Exaggeration	60	85	88	95	50
Age guess	55	45	20	8	5
Directions guess	90	69	65	48	30
White lie	80	95	95	88	92
Practical joke	75	72	75	65	50
Altruistic lie	95	100	95	87.5	80
Swearing	38	12	8	15	2
Self-protective/neutral lie	100	100	100	100	98
Self-protective/punished lie	98	100	100	100	100
Self-protective/believed lie	92	98	100	100	98

Note: From "Developmental Changes in Ideas about Lying," by C. Peterson, J. Peterson, & D. Seeto, 1983, *Child Development, 54*, 1529–1535. With permission.

adults. Below the age of 7, children typically conceive of lies as "bad words," words which can be expected to bring negative reactions from adults. "Naughty" words, swearing, cursing, as well as deliberate untruths, are all regarded as lies. Children 5 to 7 years old begin to differentiate "bad words" from untrue statements. Inaccurate statements, whether due to ignorance, mistake, or a deliberate intent to mislead, are all categorized as lies. Not until after the age of 7 do children typically consider lies as inaccurate statements intentionally designed to mislead. Table 7.2 presents the percentage of children at different age levels who categorized different statements as lies. The statements included "bad words" (e.g., swearing), exaggerations, mistakes, justified inaccuracies (i.e., altruistic lies), and intentionally misleading statements followed by differing consequences (i.e., punishment or no punishment). The results generally support the view that young children employ a broader definition of lies than do older children and adults.

Table 7.3 shows that children's likelihood of admitting to lying increases as a direct function of age; an inverse relationship is seen between age and viewing lying as always wrong. In terms of consequences, older children see that lying is more likely to destroy trust and create guilt, even though punishment is less apt to follow lying.

ASSESSMENT STRATEGIES

Several studies (Davies, Tarrant, & Flinn, 1989; Goodman & Reed, 1986; Leippe, Romanczyk, & Manion, 1991) described children younger than 7 years to have poorer memories than adults, especially in nonfamiliar circumstances, but young children also demonstrate weaker memory even when there is prolonged exposure to environmental stimuli. The forensic implication is that, in both casual bystander scenarios and familiar witness scenarios, children will be less competent witnesses than adults.

Memory jogging with 7- to 8-year-olds and 10- to 11-year-olds resulted in significantly improved recall of correct facts (Hayes & Delamothe, 1997). Saywitz, Geiselman, and Bornstein (1992) utilized staged tasking and incorporated measures to ensure motivated subject participation (i.e., rewards). The study also involved forensically relevant tasks. An interview based on cognitive psychology principles served as a guided memory search to provide "explicit retrieval strategies, specific retrieval cues, and strategies for organizing information" (p. 746). In a review of studies

---

TABLE 7.3
Percentages of Subjects at Different Age
Levels Responding to Questions about Lying

Question/Statement	Age			
	5	8	9	11
I have never told a lie	75	42	35	0
Lying is always wrong	92	88	78	28
What happens when lies are told:				
Punishment	80	70	75	28
Guilt	0	2	2	22
Destroys trust	10	25	20	48
Don't know	10	2	2	2

Note: From "Developmental Changes in Ideas about Lying,"
by C. Peterson, J. Peterson, & D. Seeto, 1983, *Child Devel-*
opment, 54, 1529–1535. With permission.

---

through the early 1990s, Ceci and Bruck (1993) concluded that the extreme positions of children's being summarily not competent as witnesses or being as competent as adults were untenable:

> In light of the full corpus of data that we have reviewed, these extreme opinions are not supported by the available research. This research shows that children are able to encode and retrieve large amounts of information, especially when it is personally experienced and highly meaningful. Equally true, however, is that no good will be served by ignoring that part of research that demonstrates potentially serious social and cognitive hazards to young child witnesses if adults who have access to them attempt to usurp their memories. Inattention to the full corpus of empirical data will only forestall efforts to improve the way child witnesses are treated and delay needed research into ways of optimizing young children's testimonial accuracy through better interviewing techniques and judicial reform. (p. 432)

In a study investigating the memory of children and adults over a long interval (i.e., 2 years), children's long-term memory was not associated with decreased accuracy (Poole & White, 1993). The children were, however, susceptible to distortion with repeated and specific questioning. Generally, competence to testify improves gradually with the child's age. Children under the age of 3 years lack the memory and communication ability to be competent witnesses. A child's competency rapidly improves through preschool and early school years such that by 6 years many youngsters will meet competency criteria assuming capable and nonsuggestive investigation/eval-uation (Lamb, Sternberg, & Esplin, 1994). Children who are 4 to 6 years of age, however, are especially vulnerable to thier testimony being prejudiced (Bruck, Ceci, & Hembrooke, 1998; Lepore & Sesco, 1994). The testimony of children this age can be tainted by extraneous social influences (deliberate or nondeliberate), including particularly investigation and interview interactions. The continuous repetition of a child's story of abuse (e.g., in separate interviews with parents, social workers, investigators, psychologists, attorneys) may reinforce a perceptual experience, which is subsequently recalled in rich, vivid, and convincing detail (Pynoos & Eth, 1984). It is also important to consider the child victim's conditioning history when evaluating the child's recollections of abuse. Past conditioning (e.g., hydrophobia) may explain parts of their reaction to an alleged crime (e.g., "freaking out" when placed into water).

Questions about a particular child's competence to testify are largely questions about non-deliberate distortion. One who is incapable of recognizing a lie cannot be said to lie deliberately; one who is unable to recall the past cannot be accused of deliberate distortion. Children's perceptions are strongly influenced by input from others, and accordingly children are very vulnerable to tainted perceptions and tainted memory that is deliberately or nondeliberately instilled by others. Ackil and Zaragoza (1998) investigated children's susceptibility to forced confabulation. The children viewed a movie clip and then were "forced" to respond to inquiries about an event in the movie clip that did not occur. A week later, first grade, third/fourth grade, and college level subjects all had false memories for details that they were forced to fabricate earlier. Predictably, children were more susceptible to this form of memory tainting than adults.

A major stumbling block regarding child sexual abuse victims' testifying as witnesses was removed by the U.S. Supreme Court ruling in *Maryland v. Craig* (1990). Prior to *Craig*, there was a critical constitutional issue that presented a significant hurdle in having child sex abuse victims testify in the courtroom and confront directly the accused. The Constitutional issue was the Sixth Amendment right of defendents to confront their accuser. The Court ruled that children could testify by closed-circuit television to protect them from the emotional duress of having to confront the accused in an open courtroom. The court's assumption in "shielding" the child witness was that the child would be less emotionally stressed and thereby able to be more communicative; in this manner the truth-telling objective of the adversarial process would be served (Montoya, 1995).

No doubt reflecting the spirit of the times regarding testimony from children, a number of states rapidly incorporated the *Craig* provisions (Davies & Wescott, 1995). By the end of 1990, videotaped testimony by child witnesses was permitted in 37 states, one-way closed-circuit television was allowed in 24 states, and two-way systems were authorized in 8 states (Small & Melton, 1994). Montoya (1995) critiqued the *Craig* decision and advocated the position that physical confrontation promotes truth telling and shielding promotes deception. Montoya offers an excellent conceptual summary of the pitfalls of interaction between a child witness and the overzealous expert witness.

Myers (1995) decried what he viewed as a "new era of skepticism regarding children's credibilty" (p. 387), which he attributed to three sources:

1. Popular media, which changed in the late 1980s from an advocacy posture to describing child abuse adjudications with characterizations of "climate of hysteria" and "Salem witchcraft trials";
2. Professional literature, which has been biased and misleading irrespective of claims of objectivity (see, especially, Ceci & Bruck, 1993 and Bruck & Ceci, 1993);
3. The New Jersey Supreme Court decision in *State v. Michaels* (1994), which held that, under certain conditions, a defendant may request a pretrial taint hearing to challenge investigatory interviews of child witnesses.

Myers's concerns about *Michaels* casting a disfavorable light on child witness testimony were not supported by Lamb, Sternberg, and Esplin (1995). These authors observed that the testimony of the children witnesses in *State v. Michaels* were so tainted as to be without value to the judicial proceedings, and they lauded the input of an amicus brief by Bruck and Ceci (1993) that cited the sources of contamination of the children's apparently damning testimony.

Are jurors inherently biased by negative stereotypes that a child witness's testimony is unreliable? Studies surveying adult beliefs have suggested that, generally, adults share this pessimistic prejudice (Ross et al., 1991). Luus, Wells, and Turtle (1995) conducted a study involving college students judging transcribed testimony by 8-year-old and adult witnesses in response to a videotaped mock crime. They found that there was a stereotyped bias against the child witnesses, but when judges were permitted to view the entire testimony of the children, the judges found them to be as equally confident and believable as the adults. Given the limits of the findings being generalized to an actual courtroom situation, the authors noted the cross-examination of the children did not support the contention that children would succumb to the pressure such that their perceived confidence or credibilty would be compromised.

TABLE 7.4
Factors Contributing to Mnestic Problems in Children

1. Neuropsychological maturation is a fundamental determinant in the child's mnestic ability.
2. The potential for distortion can be attributed to the complex interaction of a number of developmental processes (Goodman, 1984; Lamb, Sternberg, & Esplin, 1995).
3. Children's capacity to store and recall information is less than that of adults.
4. Children are more accurate in recognition than free recall (Leippe, Romanczyk, & Manion, 1991).
5. Children have more difficulty than adults in retrieving long-term memory events (Brown, 1979; Haugaard, Repucci, Laird, & Nauful. 1991).
6. Cognitive interviewing techniques improve children's recall (Hayes & Delamothe, 1997; Saywitz, Geiselman, & Bornstein, 1992).
7. Children are as accurate as adults in answering objective central questions, but are less accurate than adults in answering suggestive, peripheral questions (Bruck, Ceci, & Hembrooke, 1998; Cecci & Bruck, 1993; Goodman & Reed, 1986).
8. The presence of a postevent interviewer with strong preconceived notions of what happened may "lead" children to alter or supplement their recollections (Lampien & Smith, 1995; Lepore & Sesco, 1994).
9. Leading questions in general increase the chances that memory will be distorted (Lamb, Sternberg & Esplin, 1995; Marin et al., 1979; Poole & White, 1993).
10. Postevent questions of any kind may distort memory (Ackil & Zaragoza, 1998; Cohen & Harnick, 1980).
11. Once a distortion occurs, it appears to be accepted as part of reality and is difficult to change in favor of a more accurate memory of the actual event (Loftus & Davis, 1984).
12. Structured interview protocols may offer standardization of child witness interviews, as well as greater reliability of testimony (Bruck, Ceci, & Hembrooke, 1998).

ASSESSMENT ISSUES — CHILD WITNESS CREDIBILITY

Once a child has been found legally competent to be a witness, then and only then, does the issue of the child's credibility arise. The terms *reliability* and *credibility* are not synonymous, although they can be related in a given situation. Reports can be very reliable and accurate, but deemed not credible. Conversely, reports can be inaccurate but judged to be reliable (Bruck, Ceci, & Hembrooke, 1998). Credibilty refers to the believabilty the trier of fact places on the child's testimony. Reliabilty or consistency refers to the accuracy of a written report.

Do children lie? How accurate is the child's independent recollection of critical events? How susceptible are the child's recollections to influence by significant others? How resistant to leading and suggestive questioning are the child's communications about critical events? The answers to these and related questions determine the weight that a judge or jury should give to the child's testimony in deciding questions of fact. To begin with, childen do lie (Kaplan, 1990). Just as with adults, children lie to achieve some personal goal. Children are also very susceptible to lying to help achieve the goal of a significant other, such as a parent.

The credibility of a child's testimony may be affected by the developmental capacities of that child. Mnestic errors in children may be attributable to a number of factors. These factors are summarized in Table 7.4.

A novel and promising child competency assessment tool has been described by Lyon and Saywitz (1999). The assessment approach involves a series of pictorial figures portraying pairs of male or female child figures looking at commonplace objects (e.g., doll, dog, cookie, pizza). The subject is instructed that one child figure will tell a lie and the other will tell the truth. A stimulus object depicts the correct object, in cartoon fashion, one child figure portrayed as "thinking" of the correct figure and the other figure as "thinking of an incorrect figure." The subject is instructed that one figure, "says it's a doll," and the other "says it's a dog." The child is asked to identify which figure has told the "truth" and which the "lie." Later pictures depict social scenes with one child figure telling a lie and the other telling the truth; the child subject is asked which figure is "gonna get in trouble." The instrument assesses the child's ability to differentiate truth from a lie and also to understand the consequence of telling a lie.

DETECTION ISSUES — FALSE CHILD ABUSE ALLEGATIONS

The assessment of false allegations of child sexual abuse has received a great deal of attention in the last decade (Bruck, Ceci, & Hembrooke, 1998; Lamb, 1994; Lamb, Sternberg, & Esplin, 1995; Mikkelsen, Gutheil, & Emens, 1992; Walker, 1990). Young children readily learn the social and legal power of sex abuse allegations. Children involved in disputed custody/visitation matters are also very susceptible to psychological forces inducing false sex abuse allegations by a desperate or malicious parental figure (Kaplan, 1990; Myers et al., 1989). Older children can falsify sex abuse allegations in an effort to have authorities remove them from parental care (Quinn, 1988).

In sexual abuse cases especially, the notion is that data presented by children exceed their capacity to fabricate. Indeed, this factor is a component of a detection method called criteria-based content analysis (Raskin & Esplin, 1991a), which will be described later. Groth (1980) reported that of 147 children referred for polygraph testing from 1969 to 1974, only one child was found to have lied in regard to sexual abuse episodes. According to this view, denial of unpleasant experiences by children is regarded as more likely than fabrication. Berliner and Barbieri (1984) stated in regard to sexual victimization: "Our clinical experience indicates that many children who report being assaulted actually underreport the amount and type of abuse; exaggeration is rare" (p. 86). Green (1986) stated in agreement that false denials are common but that false accusations are rare. False accusations may occur when the child is "brainwashed" by vindictive parents, is projecting his or her own sexual fantasy, or is seeking revenge. Green offered criteria for distinguishing false from real claims of sexual abuse (Table 7.5).

Jones and McGraw (1987) studied 576 reports of child abuse and determined that most of the reports from children were reliable (70%) with only a small proportion being unreliable (8%). Examination of the unreliable reports suggested several commonalities: lack of emotion and detail and the presence of coercion. In some cases, inappropriate pronouns were used ("they" instead of "I," "we" instead of "me"). Custody/visitation disputes often triggered false allegations. Parents

TABLE 7.5
Characteristics of True and False Cases of Child Sexual Abuse

True Cases	False Cases
Delayed, conflicted disclosure, often with retractions	Disclosure easy and apparently spontaneous
Disclosure usually accompanied by painful and depressive affect	Disclosure with absence of negative affect
Child uses age appropriate sexual terminology	Child may use adult sexual terminology
Child initially reticent to discuss abuse with mother or others	Child discusses the abuse when prompted by mother — child checks with mother
Child rarely will confront father with the allegation, even with mother present	Child will often confront father with allegation in mother's presence
Child usually fearful in father's presence, congruent with ideation unless molestation was gentle and nonthreatening	Discrepancy between the child's angry accusations and the apparent comfort in his presence
Mothers often depressed; no other specific psychopathology	Prominent paranoid and hysterical psychopathology in mothers
Child usually demonstrates signs and symptoms of child sexual abuse syndrome	Child might be sexually preoccupied, but does not exhibit signs and symptoms of child sexual abuse

Note: From "True and False Allegations of Sexual Abuse in Child Custody Disputes," by A. Green, 1986, *Journal of the American Academy of Child Psychiatry, 25*, 449-456. With permission.

falsely accused the other parent more often than the alleged child victim would so accuse (9 parental-complainants out of 21 compared to 5 child-complainants out of 21; 7 complainants of unknown origin).

A substantial percentage of both children and adults involved in incidents of child abuse have histories of preexisting post-traumatic stress disorder (PTSD). Jones and McGraw (1987) made the cogent point that the use of explicit detail by an alleged victim with previous PTSD cannot be used as a criterion of truth. The previous trauma may have supplied much detail, which is then substituted for the instant offense. Similarly, Goodwin, Cauthorne, and Rada (1980) reported that all ten of their adopted girl subjects who were caught lying had been physically and emotionally abused in other settings. They lied about their adoptive mothers' allegedly dressing them in rags and were seen as having the "Cinderella Syndrome" by the investigators. They were essentially crying for help and thus were not engaging in malingering or deliberate deception.

Marx (1996) described the problem of child sexual abuse victims' recanting allegations. Recanting is a very common problem and poses yet another dimension of deception analysis for clinicians (Summit, 1983). Is the recanting an admission of a false allegation or the result of the child victim succumbing to overwhelming pressure from many sources if the allegation is truthful? Children victims are often exposed to unrelenting interviewing, some of which can be very intimidating. Throughout, the child's credibility is at issue and this is made very apparent. Often there is familial and social pressure. If, for example, a parent is determined to have committed abuse, then the marital relationship will be significantly impacted; if the offending parent is removed from the home or incarcerated, then there is usually significant financial impact on the family unit.

The assessment of the credibility of child sex abuse victims can be quite difficult for a variety of reasons, including the child's emotional reaction to the trauma. Reliance by the courts on evaluations of child abuse victims by psychologists and other mental health professionals has become increasing more commonplace (Walker, 1990). With this trend has come one controversy after another about both the competence and reliability of the child witness and the validity of such evaluations (Bruck, Ceci, & Hembrooke, 1998; Melton & Limber, 1989; Meyers, 1991). A related and equally complex problem for the forensic clinician is the assessment of the juvenile sexual offender (Poirier, 1999b).

Poirier (1991) described the difficulties of assessing disputed custody/visitation matters where even very young children become caught up in allegiance conflicts between parenting figures. The outcomes of disputed custody matters involve high stakes and this lends to intense emotions between the contesting parental sides. There is probably no other forensic situation more prone to distortion and outright deception.

During the 1990s, complaints of child sexual abuse by an opposing parent in disputed custody/visitation matters unfortunately became a vogue litigation strategy. In some disputed custody matters, it is very difficult to discern between children simply struggling to cope with a difficult family dynamic and youngsters capably malingering an allegience to one parental side.

Still more recently, the problem of false allegations of child sex abuse in disputed custody matters has been supplemented by false or distorted allegations of parental violence. The unassailable assertion is that children are negatively impacted by parental violence (e.g., spouse abuse, sibling abuse, aggressive behavior) whether or not the child has been a victim of the purported violence. A generic allegation of parental violence does not capture the same judicial skepticism as allegations of child sexual abuse. Allegations of parental violence are, however, often equally as difficult to substantiate, or refute, as parental sex abuse allegations, and the bench is left with no meaningful alternative but to tentatively assume the allegations to be accurate in order to protect the child. Protective stipulations are set in place, often for indeterminate periods of time, and often resulting in more traumas for the child/children and the family system. The literature reflects recent attempts to describe practices in child custody evaluations (Keilin & Bloom, 1986; Ackerman & Ackerman, 1997, 1999) and this remains a fertile area of forensic practice needing far more empirical investigation.

TABLE 7.6
Questions for Potential Child Witnesses

1. What is a lie? Can you tell me what a lie is?
2. Why is it naughty to tell a lie?
3. Is it a lie to call someone a bad name? Is it a lie to call someone a "fool"?
4. I'm going to tell you a story. There were two little boys and they each broke a cup. The first boy says it wasn't him. His mother believes him and doesn't punish him. The second boy says it wasn't him. But his mother doesn't believe him and punishes him. Are both boys equally naughty? Which boy is naughtier?
5. I'm going to tell you another story. Two children bought some eggs for their mother. But they played on their way home and broke the eggs. The first child broke 12 eggs; the other child broke only 1. When they got home, they told their mother that a big dog had jumped on them and broke the eggs. Was that telling lies? Were both the lies equally naughty? Which of these two lies is naughtier?
6. One day a mother told her little boy, "If anyone knocks on the door, tell them I'm not home. I don't want to see anyone today." A little later, a policeman knocks on the door and asks to speak to the mother. The little boy says, "Mama isn't home." Did the boy do the right thing? Why? Was it a lie he told? (A big lie or a little lie? Should he be punished for telling the lie?)

Table 7.6 presents some questions that the authors have found useful in assessing a child's understanding of lying. Answers to these questions may help a court decide if the child is legally competent to testify as a witness in a proceeding. The questions deal with the child's spontaneous definition of lying and understanding of the moral wrongness of lying. They require the child to distinguish between "bad words" and lies. They help determine whether lies are perceived as intrinsically wrong or as wrong because of their consequences. Finally, they pose a moral dilemma for the child (lying to a policeman or disobeying mother), which may be relevant to some cases in which children are asked to be witnesses. Similar questions may be constructed with facts or scenarios more similar to the cases in which child witnesses are asked to appear.

Forensic analysis of a child's credibility requires assessment of (1) the reliability of the memory and thinking skills of the child, including the ability to separate fact from fantasy; (2) the ability and inclination of the child to deliberately present falsehoods; (3) the influence of adults (including the examiner) on the child's testimony; and (4) the extent of corroborating data — if there is no corroboration of a child's allegation, there is usually no prosecution of the case.

Blau (1986) presented suggestions on enhancing the validity and completeness of later testimony by children in court. These included:

1. Know who talked to the child about the instant offense before you did.
2. Have corroborated facts separated from conjecture prior to your evaluation of the child.
3. Allow free recall without disruption.
4. Use language with which the child is familiar. Be simple and concrete.
5. Find out the child's mental age and gear questions to the appropriate level and ability.
6. Interview/test in 10- to 15-min sessions with rest and play in between.
7. The sequence of the questions should be "what," "who," "when," and "where."

It is not enough simply to ask objective questions of children because such questions can be leading. Goodman and Reed (1986) distinguished between objective and nonleading, and objective and misleading questions. Objective and nonleading questions concern facts about time, place, appearance, and actions (e.g., was there a TV set in the room?). Objective and misleading questions involve incorrect facts about time, place, appearance, and actions (e.g., how big was the TV set in the room?). Bruck, Ceci, and Hembrooke (1998) offered the following definition, "Suggestive interviews are now conceived of as a complex commingling of motives, threats, and inducements, which may appear in the form of misleading questions, but not always" (p. 141). Goodman and

Reed found no differences between children and adults in their responses to objective and non-leading questions, but found a significant effect for age on objective and misleading questions. Children were less likely than adults to disagree with the misleading suggestion or to answer that they did not know.

Quinn (1988) presented another checklist for the evaluation of deception in children. These questions are geared more toward issues of developmental and mental states:

1. Does the child have the developmental capacity to deceive?
2. Is there a history of persistent lying?
3. Does a mental disorder exist that would cause distortion or deception?
4. Is there a psychosocial stressor that would cause lying?
5. Has deception guilt decreased or deception apprehension increased?
6. Is the child pursuing a nonmoral (understandable) objective like lying in order to remain with one parent?
7. Is an adult lying for the child or distorting the child's communication?
8. Does a complaint or symptom presented by the child agree with well-recognized criteria?
9. Have interviewing errors contributed to distortion, for example, assuming that abuse has taken place?

A clinical method (criteria-based content analysis, or CBCA) to assess misrepresentation in witness's statements was described by Raskin and Esplin (1991a). Based on the earlier work of Undeutsch (1984, 1989) in Germany, this method proposes an analysis of the content of witness's statements obtained during a timely and noncontaminating interview. The statements are analyzed for their logical structure, their degree of organization, the quantity of details, and 16 other characteristics. In a preliminary study of the method, the authors reported 100% accuracy in discriminating between "confirmed" cases of child sexual abuse and "doubtful" cases. However, Wells and Loftus (1991) raised many questions about the methodology and interpretation of this study. They most importantly note that CBCA does not include age-related criteria based on developmental differences in the use of language, thus leaving the examiner without guidance in considering the age of the child victim witness. They decided, "strong conclusions about truth or lying based on the current, rather small amount of empirical research is premature" (p. 170). Raskin and Esplin (1991b) countered that "we do not advocate the use of CBCA as the basis of expert testimony that a child is or is not truthful.... [P]roper interview techniques combined with CBCA and statement validity assessment analysis are best employed as investigative tools to increase the quantity of information available to decision makers, such as police investigators, caseworkers, attorneys and prosecutors" (p. 173).

Socially "disapproved" behavior is frequently seen in victims. In repeated assaults, they may enjoy some aspects of the perpetrator's behavior (e.g., prolonged clitoral stimulation, payment of "hush" money). Victims are reluctant to share these experiences, which, in their thinking, add to their contribution to the wrongdoing. An experienced clinician will try to uncover these behaviors, if they exist, for two reasons: (1) they add to the veracity of the account and (2) they are targets for later treatment.

Spontaneous corrections and additions are to be expected in the retelling of the true account by a victim. In contrast, a deceiver may rigidly attempt to hold on to a story and show little variation in presentation or content — that is because the deceiver's story is a product of thought and deliberation. Psychometric evaluation is important to establish the child's functional capacities and limitations. Information on current intellectual functioning, academic achievement levels, and neuropsychological performance can provide the necessary background against which to evaluate suspicious symptoms and complaints in children. Adolescents with adequate reading skills can provide valuable self-reports of symptoms and complaints, against which to compare the results of interviews and observations. However, scales and indices of response distortions on "adult" inventories (e.g., F-K and Dissimulation Scale scores on the MMPI) have not been validated on inventories taken by adolescents and therefore should not be interpreted. Self-report scales with adolescents must be taken at face value and then compared with data from interviews, history, observation, and collateral sources.

Saywitz and Synder (1996) described a new and promising approach to the problem of evaluators tainting the testimony of children witnesses' testimony. In a preliminary study, these investigators found that a "narrative elaboration" intervention resulted in a 53% improvement of spontaneous recall compared with a control group. Two age groups were employed, 7 to 8 years and 10 to 11 years. The narrative elaboration procedure involved six experimental procedures designed to enhance the children's memory in a laboratory setting:

1. Memory strategy instruction;
2. Organizational guidance according to category cues;
3. External memory aids (e.g., pictorial cues);
4. Rationale for strategy usefulness;
5. Practice with feedback;
6. Reminders to use new strategies on subsequent trials.

The obvious advantages of the narrative elaboration approach are that it could be adapted for use with different age groups and that it relies entirely on enhancing the child's inherent abilities as opposed to enhancing the child's recollections.

Bruck, Ceci, and Hembrooke (1998) summarized that a number of interview protocols including "narrative elaboration" are in preliminary stages of development. The protocols are all designed to engender greater standardization and reliabilty in the investigative interviewing of a child witness/victim. Bruck also emphasized that the single most important need was for additional training programs designed to improve the general levels of competence in individuals who interview children. That competence must entail a sensitivity to children's capacities at different ages, and an awareness of interviewing techniques that elicit information, but that at the same time do not taint the child's recollections.

SUMMARY

The assessment of a child's competence to be a witness involves the straightforward evaluation of that child's understanding of truthfulness and of the necessity of telling the truth during the legal proceeding. The focus is on the child's capacity to reason about truth and deceit and willingness to answer questions honestly. In actual practice, the evaluation of a child's competence is not always straightforward or uncomplicated. By contrast, the assessment of a child's credibility as a witness is a more complex endeavor. The assessment of credibility must address the child's (1) capacity to recall, recognize, and communicate accurately; (2) capacity to deceive without detection; (3) resistance to the influence of others; and (4) possible motives for lying. Indications of distortion may be gleaned from (1) admissions of deception, (2) statements inconsistent with collateral information, (3) evidence of the influence of others in previous interviews, (4) observation of behavioral clues of lying, and (5) psychometric tests of current capacities.

Bruck, Ceci, and Hembrooke (1998) summarized the follow conditions to obtain maximum reliability when interviewing children:

1. Interviews conducted by unbiased, neutral interviewers;
2. Number of interviews held to a minimum;
3. Number of leading questions kept to a minimum;
4. Absence of threats and bribes;

5. Absence of peer pressure;
6. Interviewers trained to understand age differences in children's suggestibility.

The evaluator needs to be flexible in assessing possible deception in children, using a variety of clinical, observational, and psychometric approaches. As always, deception is not verified until it can be corroborated and cross validated using multiple sets of data.

Once a child cognitively grasps the meaning of deception, the child will then undertake to engage in deceptive behavior. Further empirical unraveling of that developmental process will provide additional clues to the ongoing refinement of the Forensic Distortion Analysis (FDA) model in its application to both children and adults.

LEGAL REFERENCES

Maryland v. Craig, 110 S. Ct. 3157,3169 (1990).
State v. Michaels, 642 A.2d 1372 (NJ 1994).
Utah v. Rimmasch, 775 P.2d 388, Sup. Ct. of Utah, (May 17, 1989).
Wheeler v. U.S., 159 U.S. 523 (1895).

REFERENCES

Ackerman, B. P. (1981). Young children's understanding of a speaker's intentional use of a false utterance. *Developmental Psychology, 17*, 472–480.

Ackerman, B. P. (1983). Speaker bias in children's evaluation of the external consistency of statements. *Journal of Experimental Child Psychology, 35*, 111–127.

Ackerman, M. J., & Ackerman, M. C. (1997). Custody evaluation practices: A survey of experienced professionals (revisited). *Professional Psychology: Research & Practice, 28*(2), 137–145.

Ackerman, M. J., & Ackerman, M. C. (1999). "Custody evaluation practices: A survey of experienced professionals (revisited)": Notice of clarification to Ackerman and Ackerman (1997) article. *Professional Psychology: Research & Practice, 30*(6), 599.

Ackil. J. K., & Zaragoza, M. S. (1998). Memorial consequences of forced confabulation age differences in susceptibility to false memories. *Developmental Psychology, 34*(6), 1358–1372.

Allen, V., & Atkinson, M. (1978). Encoding of nonverbal behavior by high-achieving and low-achieving children. *Journal of Educational Psychology, 70*, 17–28.

Anderson V. (1998). Assessing executive functions in children: Biological, psychological, and developmental considerations. *Neuropsychological Rehabilitation, 8*(3), 319–349.

Annon, J. (1987). The four-year-old child as competent witness. *American Journal of Forensic Psychology, 5*, 17–21.

Aune R. K., & Waters, L. (1994). Cultural differences in deception: Motivations to deceive in Samoans and North Americans. *International Journal of Intercultural Relations, 18*(2), 159–172.

Bartholomew, R. E. (1994). Disease, disorder, or deception? Lathah as a habit in a Malay extended family. *Journal of Nervous and Mental Disease, 182*(6), 331–338.

Berliner, L., & Barbieri, M. (1984). The testimony of the child victim of sexual assault. *Journal of Social Issues, 40*, 78–89.

Blau, T. (1986). The credibility of children as witnesses. Paper presented at the Second Annual Symposium in Psychology and Law of the American College of Forensic Psychology, Sanibel Island, FL.

Braginsky, D. (1970). Machiavellianism and manipulative interpersonal behavior in children. *Journal of Experimental Social Psychology, 6*, 77–99.

Brown, M. R. (1979). *Legal psychology.* Indianapolis, IN: Bobbs-Merrill.

Bruck, M., & Ceci, S. (1993). Amicus brief for the case of *State of New Jersey v. Michaels* presented by Committee of Concerned Social Scientists. Supreme Court of New Jersey, Docket & num; 36, 633. (Reprinted in *Psychology, Public Policy, and Law, 1*, 1995, 272–322.)

Bruck, M. R., & Ceci, S. J., (1997). The suggestibility of young children. *Current Directions in Psychological Science, 6*(3), 75–79.

Bruck, M. R., Ceci, S. J., & Hembrooke, H. (1998). Reliability and credibility of young children's reports: From research to policy and practice. *American Psychologist, 53*, 136–151.

Burgess, A., & Holmstrom, L. (1985). Accessory-to-sex: Pressure, sex and secrecy. In A. Burgess, A. Groth, L. Holmstrom, & S. Sgroi (Eds.), *Sexual assault of children and adolescents* (pp. 85–98). Lexington, MA: Lexington Books.

Burton, R. V., &. Strichartz, A. F. (1991). Children on the stand: The obligation to tell the truth. *Journal of Developmental and Behavioral Pediatrics, 12*(2), 121–128.

Carlson, S. M., Moses, L. J., & Hix, H. R. (1998). The role of inhibitory processes in young children's difficulties with deception and false belief. *Child Development, 69*(3), 672–691.

Chandler, M., Fritz, A. S., & Hala, S. (1989). Small-scale deceit: Deception as a marker of two-, three-, and four-year-olds' early theory of minds. *Child Development, 60*(6), 1263–1277.

Ceci, S. J., & Bruck, M. (1993). Suggestibility of the child witness: A historical review and synthesis. *Psychological Bulletin, 113*, 403–439.

Chance, J., & Goldstein, A. (1984). Face-recognition memory. Implications for children's eyewitness testimony. *Journal of Social Issues, 40*, 69–85.

Cohen, R. L., & Harnick, M. A. (1980). The susceptibility of child witnesses to suggestion. *Law and Human Behavior, 4*, 201–210.

Cole, K., & Mitchell, P. (1998). Family background in relation to deceptive ability and understanding of the mind. *Social Development, 7*(2), 181–187.

Coordinating Council on Juvenile Justice and Delinquency. (1996). *Combating violence and delinquency: The National Juvenile Justice Action Plan.* Washington, DC: Office of Juvenile Justice and Delinquency Prevention.

Davies, G., Tarrant, A., & Flin, R. (1989). Close encounters of the witness kind: Children's memory for a simulated health inspection. *British Journal of Psychology, 80*(4), 415–429.

Davies, G., & Wescott, H. (1995). The child witness in the courtroom: Empowerment or protection? In M. Zaragoza, I. Graham, G. Hall, R. Hirschman, & Y. Ben-Porath (Eds.), *Memory and testimony in the child witness* (pp. 199–213). Newbury Park, CA: Sage.

Dennis, M., Barnes, M. A., Wilkinson, M., & Humphreys, R. P. (1998). How children with head injuries represent real and deceptive emotion in short narratives. *Brain and Language, 61*(3), 450–483.

Duncan, E., Whitney, P., & Kunen, S. (1982). Integration of visual and verbal information on children's memories. *Child Development, 53*, 1215–1223.

Dunn, J., Brown, J., Slomkowski, C., Telsa, C., & Youngblade, L. (1991). Young children's understanding of other people's feelings and beliefs: Individual differences and their antecedents. *Child Development, 62*(6), 1352–1366.

Erikson, E. H. (1963). *Childhood and society* (2nd ed.). New York: W. W. Norton.

Faust, D., Hart, K., & Guilmette, T. (1988). Pediatric malingering: The capacity of children to fake deficits on neuropsychological testing. *Journal of Consulting and Clinical Psychology, 56*, 578–582.

Feldman, R., & White, J. (1980). Detecting deception in children, *Journal of Communication, 30*, 121–139.

Flavell, J., Green, F. L., & Flavell, E. R. (1986). Development of knowledge about the appearanceeality distinction. *Monographs of the Society for Research in Child Development, 51*(1), 1–68.

Gabel, S. (1992). Children of incarcerated and criminal parents: Adjustment, behavior and prognosis. *Bulletin of the American Academy of Psychiatry and the Law, 20*(1), 33–45.

Gentry, J., & Eron, L. D., (1993). American Psychological Association Commission on violence and youth. *American Psychologist, 48*(2), 89–89.

Goodman, G. (1984). The child witness. Conclusions and future directions for research and legal practice. *Journal of Social Issues, 40*, 157–175.

Goodman, G., & Reed, R. (1986). Age differences in eyewitness testimony. *Law and Human Behavior, 10*, 317–332.

Goodwin, J., Cauthorne, C., & Rada, R. (1980). Cinderella syndrome: Children who simulate neglect. *American Journal of Psychiatry, 137*, 1223–1225.

Green, A. (1986). True and false allegations of sexual abuse in child custody disputes. *Journal of the American Academy of Child Psychiatry, 25*, 449-456.

Greenfield, D. (1987). Feigned psychosis in a 14-year-old girl. *Hospital and Community Psychiatry, 38*, 73–77.

Grisso, T. (1998). *Forensic evaluation of juveniles.* Sarasota, FL: Professional Resource Press.

Groth, N. (1980). The psychology of the sexual offender: Rape, incest and child molestation. Workshop presented by Psychological Associates, Charlotte, NC.

Hala, S., Chandler, M., & Fritz, A. S. (1991). Fledging theories of mind: Deception as a marker of three-year-olds' understanding of false belief. *Child Development, 62*(1), 83–97.

Haugaard, J., Repucci, N., Laird, J., & Nauful, T. (1991). Children's definitions of the truth and their competency as witnesses in legal proceedings. *Law and Human Behavior, 15*, 3, 253–271.

Hayes, B. K., & Delamothe, K. (1997). Cognitive interviewing procedures and suggestibility in children's recall. *Journal of Applied Psychology, 82*(4), 562–577.

Hoogenraad, K., & McKenzie, B. E. (1995). Maternal reports of children's deceptive behavior. *Australian Journal of Psychology, 47*(1), 42–46.

Hudson, J. A., & Fivush, R. (1991). As time goes by: Sixth graders remember a kindergarten experience. *Applied Cognitive Psychology, 5*(4) 347–360.

Hughes, C. (1998). Executive function in children: Links with theory of mind and verbal ability. *British Journal of Developmental Psychology, 16*(2), 233–253.

Johnson, M., & Foley, M. (1984). Differentiating fact from fantasy: The reliability of children's memory. *Journal of Social Issues, 40*, 76–92.

Jones, D., & McGraw, J. (1987). Reliable and fictitious accounts of sexual abuse to children. *Journal of Interpersonal Violence, 2*, 27–45.

Kaplan, J. M. (1990). Children don't always tell the truth. *Journal of Forensic Science, 35*(3), 661–667.

Kawakami, K. (1995). Deception in children. *Japanese Journal of Child and Adolescent Psychiatry, 36*(3), 223–231.

Keilin, W. G., & Bloom, L. J. (1986). Child custody evaluation practices: A survey of experienced professionals. *Professional Psychology, 17*, 388–346.

King, M., & Yuille, J. (1987). Suggestibility and the child witness. In S. Ceci, D. Ross, & M. Toglia (Eds.), *Children's eyewitness memory* (pp. 24–35). New York: Springer-Verlag.

Kohlberg, L. (1981). *The philosophy of moral development.* San Francisco: Harper & Row.

Krause, C. M., & Saarnio, D. A. (1993). Deciding what is safe to eat: Young children's understanding of appearance, reality and edibleness. *Journal of Applied Developmental Psychology, 14*(2), 231–244.

Lamb, M. E. (1994). The investigation of child sexual abuse: An interdisciplinary consensus statement. *Family Law Quarterly, 28*, 151–162.

Lamb, M. E., Sternberg, K. J., & Esplin, P. W. (1994). Factors influencing the reliability and validity of statements made by young victims of sexual maltreatment. *Journal of Applied Developmental Psychology, 15*, 255–280.

Lamb, M. E., Sternberg, K. J., & Esplin, P. W. (1995). Making children into competent witnesses: Reactions to *Amicus Brief In re Michaels. Psychology, Public Policy, and Law, 1*(2), 438–449.

Lampinen, J. M., & Smith, V. L. (1995). The incredible (and sometimes incredulous) child witness: Child eyewitnesses' sensitivity to source credibility cues. *Journal of Applied Psychology, 80*(5), 621–627.

Lee, K., Cameron, C. A., Xu, F., Fu, G., & Board, J. (1997). Chinese and Canadian children's evaluations of lying and truth telling: Similarities and differences in the context of pro- and antisocial behaviors. *Child Development, 68*(5), 924–934.

Leippe, M. R., Romanczyk, A., & Manion. A. P. (1991). Eyewitness memory for a touching experience: Accuracy differences between child and adult witnesses. *Journal of Applied Psychology, 76*(3), 367–379.

Lepore, S., & Sesco, B. (1994). Distorting children's reports and interpretations of events through suggestion. *Journal of Applied Psychology, 79*(1), 108–120.

Lewis, M., Stanger, C., & Sullivan, M. W. (1989). Deception in 3-year-olds. *Developmental Psychology, 25*, 439–443.

Lewis, M., Sullivan, M., Stanger, C., & Weiss, M. (1989). Self development and self-conscious emotions. *Child Development, 60*, 146–256.

Loftus, E. F., & Davis, G. (1984). Distortions in the memory of children. *Journal of Social Science, 40*, 51–67.

Luus, C. A. E., Wells, G. L., & Turtle, J. (1995). Child eyewitnesses: Seeing is believing. *Journal of Applied Psychology, 80*(2), 317–326.

Lyon, T. D., & Saywitz, K. J. (1999). Young maltreated children's competence to take the oath. *Applied Developmental Science, 3*(1), 16–27.

Marin, B. V., Holmes, D. L., Guth, M., & Kovac, P. (1979). The potential of children as eyewitnesses. *Law and Human Behavior, 3*, 295–305.

Markman, E. (1979). Realizing that you don't understand: Elementary school children's awareness of inconsistencies. *Child Development, 50*, 643–655.

Marx, S. P. (1996). Victim recantation in child sexual abuse cases: The prosecutor's role in prevention. *Child Welfare, 75*(3), 219–233.

McCauley, M. R., & Fisher, R. P. (1995). Facilitating children's eyewitness recall with the revised cognitive interview. *Journal of Applied Psychology, 80*(4), 510–516.

McGough, L. (1991). Commentary: Assessing the credibility of witness' statements. In Doris, J. (Ed.), *The Suggestibility of Children's Recollections* (pp. 165–167), Washington, DC: American Psychological Association.

Meadow, R. (1982). Munchausen syndrome by proxy and pseudoepilepsy [Letter to the editor]. *Archives of Disease in Childhood, 57*, 811–812.

Melton, G., & Limber, S. (1989). Psychologist's involvement in cases of child maltreatment. *American Psychologist, 44*, 1225–1233.

Meyer, J. F., & Geis, G. (1994). Psychological research on child witnesses in sexual abuse cases: Fine answers to mostly wrong questions. *Child and Adolescent Social Work Journal, 11*(3), 209–220.

Mikkelsen, E. J., Gutheil, T. G., & Emens, M. (1992). False sexual-abuse allegations by children and adolescents: Contextual factors and clinical subtypes. *American Journal of Psychotherapy, 46*(4), 556–570.

Montoya, J. (1995). Lessons from Akiki and Michaels on shielding child witnesses. *Psychology, Public Policy, and Law, 1*(2), 340–369.

Morency, N., & Kraus, R. (1982). The nonverbal encoding and decoding of affect in first and fifth graders. In R. Feldman (Ed.), *Development of nonverbal behavioral skills* (pp. 212–226). New York: Springer-Verlag.

Myers, J. E. B. (1991). Comment on Melton and Limber. *American Psychologist, 46*(1), 81–82.

Myers, J. E. B. (1995). New era of skepticism regarding children's credibility. *Psychology, Public Policy, and Law, 1*(2), 387–398.

Myers, J. E. B., Bays, J., Becker, J., Berliner, L., Corwin, D., & Saywitz, K. (1989). Expert testimony in child sexual abuse litigation. *Nebraska Law Review, 68*, 1–145.

Oldershaw, L., & Bagby, R. M. (1997). Children and deception. In R. Rogers (Ed.), *Clinical assessment of malingering and deception* (pp. 153–166). New York: Guilford Press.

Palmer, A. J., & Yoshimura, G. J. (1984). Munchausen syndrome by proxy. *Journal of the American Academy of Child Psychiatry, 23*(4), 504–508.

Parker, J., & Carranza, L. (1989). Eyewitness testimony of children in target-present and target-absent lineups. *Law and Human Behavior, 13*(2), 133–149.

Perner, J., & Wimmer, H. (1985). "John thinks that Mary thinks that ..." Attribution of second-order beliefs by 5- to 10-year-old children. *Journal of Experimental Child Psychology, 39*(3), 437–471.

Perner, J., & Wimmer, H. (1987). Young children's understanding of belief and communicative intention. *Pakistan Journal of Psychological Research, 2*(1–2), 17–21.

Perner, J., & Wimmer, H. (1988). Misinformation and unexpected change: Testing the development of epistemic-state attribution. *Psychological Research, 50*(3), 191–197.

Peskin, J. (1996). Guise and guile: Children's understanding of narratives in which the purpose is pretense. *Child Development, 67*(4), 1735–1751.

Peterson, C., Peterson, J., & Seeto, D. (1983). Developmental changes in ideas about lying. *Child Development, 54*, 1529–1535.

Piaget, J. (1929). *The child's conception of the world*. New York: Harcourt, Brace & Co.

Piaget, J. (1959). *Judgment and reasoning in the child*. Totowa, NJ: Littlefield Adams.

Piaget, J. (1965). *The moral judgment of the child*. New York: Free Press.

Poirier, J. G. (1991). Disputed custody and concerns of parental violence. *Psychotherapy in Private Practice, 9*(3), 7–23.

Poirier, J. G. (1996). Violence in the family. In H. V. Hall (Ed.), *Lethal violence 2000: A source book on fatal domestic, acquaintance, and stranger aggression* (pp. 259–292). Kamuela, HI: Pacific Institute for the Study of Conflict and Aggression.

Poirier, J. G. (1999a). Violent juvenile crime. In H. V. Hall & L. C. Whitaker (Eds.), *Collective violence: Effective strategies for assessing and interviewing in fatal group and institutional aggression* (pp. 183–212). Boca Raton, FL: CRC Press.

Poirier, J. G. (1999b, August). The mental health/judicial interface: Taboo dynamics and collaboration strategies with the juvenile sex offender. In R. T. Saunders (Chair), Professional Collaboration in Independent Practice. Symposium conducted at the Annual Meeting of the American Psychological Association, Boston, MA.

Polak, A., & Harris, P. L. (1999). Deception by young children following noncompliance. *Developmental Psychology, 35*(2), 561–568.

Poole, D. A., & White, L. T. (1993). Two years later: Effects of question repetition and retention interval on the eyewitness testimony of children and adults. *Developmental Psychology, 29*(5), 844–853.

Pynoos, R., & Eth, S. (1984). The child as witness to homicide. *Journal of Social Issues, 40,* 44–51.

Quinn, K. (1988). Children and deception. In R. Rogers, (Ed.), *Clinical assessment of malingering and deception* (pp. 104–119). New York: Guilford Press.

Raskin, D., & Esplin, P. (1991a). Assessment of children's statements of sexual abuse. In Doris, J. *The Suggestibility of Children's Recollections* (pp. 153–164), Washington, DC: American Psychological Association.

Raskin, D., & Esplin, P. (1991b). Commentary: Response to Wells, Loftus and McGough. In Doris, J. *The Suggestibility of Children's Recollections* (pp. 172–176), Washington, DC: American Psychological Association.

Reinecke, D. R., Newman, B., Kurtz, A. L., & Ryan, C. S. (1997). Teaching deception skills in a game-play context to three adolescents with autism. *Journal of Autism and Developmental Disorders, 31*(6), 127–137.

Rice, C., Koinis, D., Sullivan, K., Tager-Flusberg, H., & Winner, E. (1997). When 3-year-olds pass the appearance-reality test. *Developmental Psychology, 33*(1), 54–61.

Ross, D. F., Dunning, D., Toglia, M., & Ceci, S. J. (1991). The child in the eyes of the jury: Assessing mock juror perceptions of the child witness. *Law and Human Behavior, 14,* 5–23.

Rubin, L. J. (1996). Childhood sexual abuse: False accusations of "false memory." *Professional Psychology: Research and Practice, 27*(5), 447–451.

Ruffman, T., Olson, D. R., Ash, T., & Keenan T. (1993). The ABC's of deception: Do young children understand deception in the same way as adults? *Developmental Psychology, 29*(1), 74–87.

Russell, J., Mauthner, N., Sharpe, S., & Tidswell, T. (1991). The "windows task" as a measure of strategic deception in preschoolers and autistic subjects. *British Journal of Developmental Psychology, 9*(2), 331–349.

Saltmarsh, R., & Mitchell. P. (1998). Young children's difficulty acknowledging false belief: Realism and deception. *Journal of Experimental Child Psychology, 69*(1), 3–21.

Saywitz, K. J., Geiselman, R. E., & Bornstein, G. K. (1992). Effects of cognitive interviewing and practice on children's recall performance. *Journal of Applied Psychology, 77*(5), 744–756.

Saywitz, K. J., & Snyder, L. (1996). Narrative elaboration: Test of a new procedure for interviewing children. *Journal of Consulting and Clinical Psychology, 64*(6), 1347–1357.

Sickmund, M., Snyder, H. N., & Poe-Yamaguta, E. (1997). *Juvenile offenders and victims: 1997 update on violence-statistics summary.* Washington, DC: Office of Juvenile Justice and Delinquency Prevention.

Siegal, M. (1998). Preschoolers' understanding of lies and innocent and negligent mistakes. *Developmental Psychology, 34*(2), 332–341.

Siegal, M., & Peterson, C. (1994). Children's theory of mind and the conversational territory of cognitive development. In C. Lewis & P. Mitchell (Eds.), *Children's early understanding of the mind: Origins and development* (pp. 427–455). Hillsdale, NJ: Erlbaum.

Siegal, M., & Peterson, C. (1995). Memory and suggestibility in conversations with young children. *Australian Journal of Psychology, 47*(1), 37–41.

Siegal, M., & Peterson, C. (1996) Breaking the mold: A fresh look at children's understanding of questions about lies and mistakes. *Developmental Psychology, 32*(2) 322–334.

Siegal, M., & Peterson, C. C. (1998). Preschooler's understanding of lies and innocent and negligent mistakes. *Developmental Psychology, 34*(2) 332–341

Small, M., & Melton, G. (1994). Evaluation of child witnesses for confrontation by criminal defendants. *Professional Psychology: Research and Practice, 25*(3), 228–233.

Sodian, B., Taylor, C., Harris, P., & Perner, J. (1991). Early deception and the child's theory of mind: False trails and genuine markers. *Child Development, 62*, 468–483.

Stouthamer-Loeber, M. (1986). Lying as a problem behavior in children: A review. *Clinical Psychology Review, 6*, 267–289.

Sullivan, K., & Winner, E. (1993). Three-year-olds' understanding of mental states: The influence of trickery. *Journal of Experimental Child Psychology, 56*(2), 135–148.

Sullivan, K., Zaitchik, D., & Tager-Flusberg, H. (1994). Preschoolers can attribute second-order beliefs. *Developmental Psychology, 30*(3), 395–402.

Summit, R. (1983). The child sexual abuse accommodation syndrome. *Child Abuse & Neglect, 7*, 177–193.

Tatem-Kelly, B., Huizinga, D., Thornberry, T. P., & Loeber, R. (1997). *Epidemiology of serious violence.* Bulletin. Washington, DC: U.S. Department of Justice, Office of Justice Programs, Office of Juvenile Justice and Delinquency Prevention.

Terr, L. (1985). The baby as a witness. In D. H. Schetky & E. P. Benedek (Eds.), *Emerging issues in child psychiatry and the law* (pp. 313–323). New York: Brunner/Mazel.

Thatcher, R. W. (1992). Cyclical cortical reorganization during early childhood. *Brain and Cognition, 20*, 24–50.

Thomas, C. E., Booth-Butterfield, M., & Booth-Butterfield, S. (1995). Perceptions of deception, divorce disclosures, and communication satisfaction with parents. *Western Journal of Communication, 59*(3), 228–245.

Undeutsch, U. (1984). Methods in detecting assessee misrepresentation. Paper presented at the European Military Psychologists' Conference, Nuremberg, Federal Republic of Germany.

Undentsch, U. (1989). The development of statement reality analysis. In J. C. Yuille (Ed.), *Credibility Assessment* (pp. 101–119). Dordrecht, the Netherlands: Klewer.

Walker, L. E. A. (1990). Psychological assessment of sexually abused children for legal evaluation and expert witness testimony. *Professional Psychology: Research and Practice, 21*(5), 344–353.

Wellman, H. (1990). *The child's theory of mind.* Cambridge, MA: MIT Press.

Wells, G., & Loftus, E. (1991). Commentary: Is this child fabricating? Reactions to a new assessment technique. In J. Doris *The Suggestibility of Children's Recollections* (pp. 168–171), Washington, DC: American Psychological Association.

Wimmer, H., & Perner, J. (1983). Belief about beliefs: Representation and constraining function of wrong beliefs in young children's understanding of deception. *Cognition, 13*(1), 103–128.

Winner, E., & Leekam, S. (1991). Distinguishing irony from deception. *British Journal of Developmental Psychology, 9*(2), 257–270.

Zaitchik, D. (1991). Is only seeing really believing? Sources of the true belief in the false belief task. *Cognitive Development, 6*(1), 91–103.

8 Deception and Adolescents

Adolescence is generally regarded as the 13th through the 17th years of human development, although some developmentalists extend adolescence through age 19. The importance of adolescence as a formative stage of human development was foreshadowed by Freud and brought into prominence by the neoanalysts (Blos, 1962). The forensic clinician observes in the adolescent the remnants of childhood naivete, and the emerging adult capacity for deceptive behavior.

There have been few studies regarding deceptive behavior with younger adolescents. Most such research consists of individual case studies. Greenfield (1987), for example, described a hospitalized 14-year-old girl who feigned psychosis. Adolescents are far more perceptive and shrewd than children, and it is simply not realistic to present adolescents with some of the comparatively simplistic, experimental, deception paradigms that were reviewed in the last chapter with children.

The ethical issue of confidentiality in research with children is straightforward; all research must have the informed consent of parents or guardians. In principle, the issue of confidentiality in research with adolescents is also straightforward; that is, parental/guardian consent is necessary. In practice, however, the situation with adolescents can be vexing because the parents of adolescents are not always as accessible as is usually the case with younger children. Ethical problems can arise because adolescents engage in adult-level behavior, and many live adult lifestyles.

Research can be complicated by questions of sensitivity to the adolescent's privacy, and the temptation for researchers to employ deceptive strategies to obtain truthful or accurate data (Phillips, 1994). Brink (1995) reported that most adolescents and adults (17 to 44 years) responding to an anonymous questionnaire regarding sexual behavior stated that they would tell the truth about most items, but that an important minority stated they would not.

As any psychotherapist who works with adolescents can attest, perhaps the most formidable issue is their characteristic personal sensitivity to being caught up in situations in which they may be deceived, embarrassed, or humiliated. This important developmental dynamic plays out in the adolescent's behavior at home, in school, and in the community. Similarly, the dynamic is operative in psychotherapy and can make treatment with adolescents very challenging. The same dynamic will be evident in efforts to engage adolescents in empirical investigations. Any empirical study exploring deception with adolescents is ripe for ethical complaints. For these reasons, many of the empirical studies dealing with deception in adolescence have involved older adolescents.

In Western cultures, adolescence is regarded as a tumultuous period of development. The process of leaving the protected period of childhood is in itself scary, but it is compounded by the struggles of becoming autonomous and trying to define future goals. There is the challenge of interacting and competing with peers who are going through the same process. The adolescent must also endure the changes brought on by puberty, complete the difficult time of the academic process, and function adequately in the community and the workplace. Yet another potent struggle for adolescents is resolving issues of sexual identity and coping in a meaningful fashion with early dating relationships.

TARGET BEHAVIORS — ADOLESCENT DECEPTION DYNAMICS

Erikson (1963) described the primary developmental hurdle of adolescence as working through a meaningful self-identity, or as Erikson conceptualized it, the task of achieving a healthy identity vs. identity diffusion. To the extent the adolescent successfully works toward a meaningful self-identity, there is a sense of positive self-esteem, leading the way to successful maturation to adulthood. The period of adolescence is a range of developmental hurdles. The travails of adolescence coupled with the typical sensitivities of adolescents offer many opportunities and temptations to engage in deception.

The target behaviors of deception for the adolescent are intertwined with the developmental challenges of pubescence and beyond. The adolescent's struggle to achieve and nurture a healthy self-esteem has been described as one prominent factor in the adolescent's use of deception (Lowenstein, 1994). Kashy and DePaulo (1996) reported that undergraduates who told more lies were manipulative and more concerned with social presentation. Those who told fewer lies were more highly socialized and reported higher quality same-sex relationships. A study by Newton and Duda (1993) examined the self-perceived causes of success by adolescents. In response to inquiries about being successful in tennis, both male and females coupled strong ego orientation with success. This was especially true for the males; the female subjects cited the coincident need to deemphasize external factors to include specifically deceptive tactics.

DePaulo et al. (1996) and DePaulo and Kashy (1998) conducted a series of studies with a group of undergraduates and adult community members. The subjects recorded diaries documenting their social interactions and lies for 1 week. The college students acknowledged telling two lies per day contrasted to one lie per day by the community members. The subjects reported more self-centered lies than other-centered lies except in women dyads where other-centered lies were more prevalent. The subjects also noted that the lies were usually not planned and that they did not regard the lies as serious. There was agreement that relationships characterized by lying behavior were less pleasant and less intimate. The findings reflected that subjects told fewer lies to significant others and subjects reported more feelings of discomfort with telling lies to significant others. Lies to significant others also differed qualitatively from lies to acquaintances and strangers. With significant others, lies were more "altruistic" as opposed to self-serving. The study found also that lies to significant others were more likely to be discovered.

Studies of adolescent sexual behavior abound and are all suspect with respect to truthful reporting. Some adolescents will underreport and still others, often males, will overreport. As with most forms of deception, the situational context determines usage and form of the distortion. In a situation of competitive male peers, for example, a male adolescent may be inclined to exaggerate sexual activity; the same adolescent interacting with an attractive coed might be inclined to underestimate sexual activity. With parental or other adult figures, the same male adolescent may have still other estimates of sexual activity.

In a series of studies with university students enrolled in a human sexuality class, Knox and colleagues collected self-reported, anonymous data. Male and female subjects reported similar frequencies for intercourse and oral sexual activity. The male and female subjects reported significantly different frequencies for masturbation and number of sexual partners (Knox & Schacht, 1992). Of the university students, 92% reported use of lying behavior with potential sexual partners. The most frequent lies were about the number of prior sexual partners (most typically giving a lower number than was actually the case), the evaluation of the just occurring sexual interaction, and the extent of the feelings for the current partner (Knox et al., 1993).

A number of studies have explored the use of deception by adolescents in dating activities. Peterson (1996) asked adolescent and adult subjects to respond to written scenarios depicting men and women couples engaging in six types of deception (blatant lying, white lies, failed lies, omission, distortion, and half truths). Relationship satisfaction by all subjects was negatively correlated with subjects' or their partners' use of deception. In a survey study, college students perceived that relationships that were mutually satisfactory (win–win) were more likely to persist, compared with imbalanced (win–lose) relationships; no students felt that mutually unrewarding relationships would continue (Knox et al., 1995). Younger undergraduates (less than 19 years) were also more likely to believe in "love at first sight," and that "love conquers all," compared with older undergraduates (20 years and older) (Knox, Schacht, & Zusman, 1999). Romanticized perceptions by the collegiate respondents were positively correlated with current involvement in a love relationship. Fischer (1996) assessed attitudinal predictors of verbal deception and coercive behavior in dating with college males. The multiracial sample comprised 673 subjects. Only 0.02% of the subjects acknowledged having used threat or force and 25% acknowledged lying to have sex. Four predictors of lying were cited: (1) greater sexual experience, (2) excessive alcohol consumption, (3) greater belief in a woman's token "no," and (4) greater hostility.

RESPONSE STYLES

Adolescents are tempted to become involved in deceptive behavior as a natural product of the life challenges of their age. Adolescence is a period when self-esteem burgeons with possibility and at the same time is exquisitely vulnerable. Adolescence is a developmental window for working through a healthy awareness of the potency of human deceptive behavior. It is also a developmental window for acquiring an immature, and in some instances pathological, style of coping with life challenges through deception. Clinical/forensic assessment must involve examination of the adolescent's response styles of appreciating, engaging in, and managing deceptive behavior.

In a psychoanalytic case study with abused, adopted adolescents, Wilkinson and Hough (1996) described how clearly unbelievable stories told to a therapist enabled the adolescents to cope with painful and perplexing loss of continuity when the adolescents were removed from their homes. In therapy, the adolescents' lies became "narrative truths" for them. Only sensitive treatment could enable the adolescents to give up the deception and acknowledge the painful truth of their situation.

Adolescents are in a limbo area between childhood and adulthood. They are old enough to work, to drive motor vehicles, to vote, and to join the military. They are not old enough to purchase or consume alcoholic beverages legally. These circumstances lead to the prevalent problem of adolescents utilizing false ID cards and other forms of deception to obtain alcohol (Schwartz et al., 1998). Unfortunately, such deceptive practice is commonplace and even considered machismo in the adolescent culture. If adolescents are involved in illicit substance abuse, the reliance on deceptive behavior is even more sophisticated and devious (Chait & Perry, 1992; Lather, Vasudeva, & Verma, 1997). In a review of multiple studies, McCann (1998) described an average of 15% of adolescents found to malinger psychiatric disorders in mental health settings for a variety of manipulative purposes.

Following are the age level characteristics of adolescents with respect to their awareness and use of deceptive behavior:

Ages 13 to 14

An adult level of resistance to false suggestions is achieved by early adolescence (Ceci & Bruck, 1993, 1995). In terms of nondeliberate distortion, this age group remembered both familiar and unfamiliar faces as well as adults (Chance & Goldstein, 1984). Deliberate distortion is well entrenched by this age in social and achievement settings and situations. In a study of 46 boys, Mischel and Gilligan (1964) found widespread cheating in a temptation paradigm. In a study with 86 Australian girls of late primary school age, Moore (1995) reported significant use of deception and denial relating to pubertal and menarche status. The subjects described attitudes about menstruation as characterized by embarrassment, discomfort, and ambivalence about growing up.

In a study with religious and secular (public) high school students in grades 9 through 12, Bruggeman and Hart (1996) compared moral reasoning levels and the incidence of lying and cheating. The results reflected a surprisingly high level of dishonest behavior in two high-incentive lying and cheating tasks. The two groups of students did not differ in moral reasoning level or in incidence of dishonest behavior.

Ages 15 to 17

At this age, adolescents perceive lying as a significant social problem. Vidoni, Fleming, and Mintz (1983) noted that the 504 eighth graders tested ranked lying in the upper 15th percentile among social problems and viewed lying as being as serious as did teachers and clinicians. Peterson, Peterson, and Seeto (1983) see adults as more lenient than teens in their moral evaluation of lying. Those of this age group are similar to adults in this respect. In an experimental task, adolescents 15 years and older, as well as adults, were swayed to alter their attitude by perceived combined high status and high power based on whether the subjects functioned as an ordinary subject or as a coexperimenter. Participating as an ordinary subject was defined as connoting low status and low power.

The previous chapter observed that, with children, the level of cognitive sophistication was an important factor in the understanding of deception. In a study with 17-year-olds and adults, Millar and Millar (1997) found that truth bias about a perceived task was more pronounced with low cognitive capacity than with high cognitive capacity. High-cognitive-capacity subjects witnessed a veracity scenario undistracted; low cognitive capacity was determined by subjects' doing math problems as they witnessed the scenario.

As with adults, adolescents are confronted on a daily basis with the opportunity to engage in deceptive behavior. Especially in interpersonal relationships, adolescents must deal with problems of self-esteem and wanting to be part of their social milieu. Parents and other authority figures must struggle with the throes of an adolescent attempting to achieve maturity, but constantly stumbling with childlike behaviors and strategies in doing so. The temptations to engage in lying and manipulative behaviors are very powerful forces for every teenager. In the ideal, most adolescents work through this period of development in a positive manner. One of the primary dynamics, even in young people who come from wholesome backgrounds in which parenting figures impart strong values, is succumbing to peer influences that tout situational justifications for being less than truthful (Backbier, Hoogsstraten, & Meerum, 1997). In contemporary culture, many adolescents do not satisfactorily resolve the use of deceit to avoid or cover up consequences of poor judgment and misbehavior. This is a primary etiology of adult deception.

Several studies have explored how adolescents strive to cope with this truth/deception-choice aspect of their developmental status in day-to-day life; 15% of high school students, 14% of college freshman, and 24% of teenage drug abusers acknowledged use of false ID cards and other forms of deception to purchase alcohol (Schwartz et al., 1998). Similar to adult co-respondents, adolescents 16 years and older acknowledged use of "white lies" in intimate relationships. The most frequent justification for using deception was to avoid conflict (Peterson, 1996).

Legally, most jurisdictions recognize the 18th birthday as the age of majority. In the judicial system, adolescence is not formally recognized as distinct from childhood. Although there are isolated exceptions, in most jurisdictions everyone 18 years of age and younger is a juvenile. With many adolescents, the capacity for deception is every bit as effective as what can be mustered by adults, although generally adolescent deception does not have the practiced and experienced quality that can be evident in adults.

ADOLESCENT OFFENDERS AND DECEPTION

Violent adolescent offenders and adolescent sexual offenders as groups represent the extreme end of the adolescent continuum with respect to potential for deception. In the adolescent, the forensic clinician sees both the remnants of childhood naivete and the clear emerging potential of adult-quality capacity for deceptive behavior. Juveniles who commit illegal acts are juvenile delinquents. Juveniles also enter the juvenile judicial system when they are victims of abuse or neglect. Juvenile delinquents and juvenile victims of abuse and neglect offer a fertile bed for concerns regarding credibility, deception, and malingering.

As with children, when adolescents are victims of a life circumstance such as an accident, illness, or human folly, society has traditionally tended to adopt a benevolent and protective posture. For many years, juvenile courts pursued a philosophy of rehabilitation of juvenile offenders as contrasted to a punitive philosophy. These social standards were extended to adolescent offenders until approximately the early 1990s when crime statistics began to reflect alarming trends of youth being involved in increasingly serious crimes at increasingly younger ages (Browning et al., 1999). These trends have resulted in harsher approaches with adolescent offenders (Poirier, 1998). Juvenile courts were established nationally, beginning in the 1920s, with the recognition that the legal needs of children and adolescents could not be adequately met in the adult court. According to National Institute of Justice statistics, there has been a modest but consistent drop in the national average of serious crime for all age groups each year since 1995 (Poirier, 1998). Nonetheless, the problem of serious crime by youngsters has captured public outcry and political momentum. Local and federal courts are exploring alternative legal definitions of chronic and serious juvenile offenders and looking to impose more substantive sentencing dispositions.

Childhood and adolescence are seminal stages of development for understanding and engaging in deceptive behavior. A few youngsters unfortunately leave childhood already adept at patterns of deliberate deception and manipulation. It is in the adolescent stage of maturation where sophisticated adult behaviors that have been existentially introduced in childhood are integrated into the workings of a healthy psyche. Conversely, adolescence can result in ingrained, maladaptive behavior patterns that persist for life.

Stouthamer-Loeber (1986) found a widespread frequency of deceptive behavior with delinquent youths. Woods (1993) described a sadistic adolescent sex offender with an extensive history of sexual acting out that was effectively contrived to be absent to minimal with family members and involved professionals. The adolescent eventually acknowledged deliberate lies and manipulations.

A significant amount of pre-teenage involvement in criminal activity is related to youth gangs. Data reflect that youngster involvement with gangs significantly increases the likelihood of involvement in serious crime (Battin-Person et al., 1998; Browning, Thornberry, & Porter, 1999; Howell & Decker, 1999; Moore and Terrett, 1998, 1999). An estimated one half of serious crime committed by juveniles involves youth gangs (Poirier, 1998). Prevalence data reflect boys to be significantly more involved in violent crime compared with girls (Kelley et al., 1997). For the years 12 to 15, however, girls come closer to the serious violence rate of boys. All types of violent juvenile crime involve the potential for deception. Juvenile perpetrators will deny their own complicity in offenses. Unique to this age group, where gang activity is frequent, youthful offenders will prevaricate about the involvement of peers.

The probability of deception with an adolescent offender exists in direct proportion to the adolescent's history of acting-out behavior and delinquent acts. A repetitive history of asocial behavior, by definition, encompasses a pattern of escalating reliance on deceptive and exploitive behavior with others. For this reason alone, adolescence is a last critical period for interrupting what can become a lifetime behavioral cycle of antisocial activity.

Cultural taboos regarding inappropriate sexual behavior are pervasive and very powerful social forces. Forensic clinicians will encounter potent challenges in attempting to unravel deception with juvenile sexual offenders. These taboos are particularly powerful when children are the victims of inappropriate sexual behavior. Taboo dynamics impose powerful incentives for deception. The vast majority of juvenile sexual offenders are male (90+%) and the modal age is 14 years (Ryan, 1991). Juvenile sexual offenders will characteristically deny any complicity, even in the face of overwhelming evidence. They will also be strongly supported in these denials by family members. In incest circumstances, the taboo dynamics are even more commanding. A juvenile sex offender who denies complicity will not be responsive to intervention, nor will the family.

Historically, society has struggled with the problem of inappropriate sexual behavior when the victim(s) and the perpetrators(s) are minors. "Experimental" sexual behavior among children and adolescents, while frowned upon, did not receive particular attention from the public or the judicial system. Beginning in the late 1960s, society began to adopt a more strident posture with the problem of juvenile sexual offenders (Marshall, 1996; Poirier, 1999; Ryan & Lane, 1997). The rapid progression of juvenile substance abuse, the parallel progression of increasingly violent behavior by juveniles, and society's attention, generally, to child sex abuse victims were significant factors in recognition of the problem of juvenile sexual offenders.

Statistics documenting the prevalence of juvenile sex offenses vary widely. Barbaree, Hudson, and Seto (1993) summarized that the best available data suggested that 20% of all rapes and 40% of child sexual abuse were perpetrated by adolescent males. The same authors noted a high incidence (approximately 50%) of adult male sexual offenders who began their sexual offending in adolescence. It is important to recognize that the label of juvenile sexual offender is not a clinical notion, but rather a legal concept. The juvenile sexual offender is a youngster who commits a sexual offense. As with adult offenders, the range of juvenile sex offenses covers a wide variety of behaviors and can involve a multitude of comorbid factors such as family dysfunction, substance abuse, psychiatric disorder, and aggressive behavior. Similarly, the offense circumstances can encompass many scenarios and many types of victims.

Clinicians working with juvenile sexual offenders must have a thorough grounding in child/adolescent clinical work, a working familiarity with the judicial system, and expertise with the vagaries of the adversarial process. Varieties of effective intervention strategies have been developed for working with juvenile sexual offenders and their victims, as well as affected family members. These strategies have encompassed public education, identification and investigation methods, adjudication procedures, clinical assessment, and clinical treatment modalities. Unique to the problem of juvenile sex offenders has been the creation of collaboration models among police authorities, social work investigators, judicial authorities, juvenile service workers, and a wide variety of direct service clinicians.

It is too simplistic to conceptualize the problem of juvenile sex offending in traditional clinical terms. Intervention from prevention through identification, assessment, treatment, and follow-up must incorporate an understanding of the cultural taboo that surrounds the problem of sexual offenses. The cultural taboo phenomenon affects every aspect of approaching the problem. Sometimes the impact is very subtle, sometimes the impact is very overt, but it is always pervasive. In terms of developing effective intervention plans, the investigation/evaluation process is critical. A major concern with juvenile sex offenders is the established chronicity of the pedophile sexual abuse cycle (Lane, 1991). If the juvenile sexual offender persists in denial and deception, then no intervention will be worthwhile and there is high probability of abuse occurring and reoccurring.

ADOLESCENTS AND DISPUTED DOMESTIC MATTERS

Adolescents are just as prone as children to being caught up as witnesses in disputed domestic adjudication matters. Drawn by intense emotions, adolescents will establish an allegiance with one parent over the other, often based on justifications other than parental fitness. Disturbed family dynamics only exacerbate usual and expected turmoil in parent/adolescent relationships. Adolescents also rely on relationships with parenting figures to work through issues of role model, sexual identity, and differential male/female personality attributes and values. A rare adolescent can put aside all these issues and assume an objective posture regarding concerns of parental fitness. In actual practice, the issue of witnessing by adolescents in disputed custody/visitation matters is sometimes moot because of the parent's status. That is, a parent has engaged in untoward behavior that has compromised the children's welfare, or the parent presents with mitigating circumstances such as serious mental or physical illness. The courts frequently ask forensic clinicians to assess preferences of adolescents regarding parental figures. These assessments require a thoughtful approach. Evaluation of disputed domestic matters is a minefield of ethical issues for the clinician. These issues include complex questions of confidentiality, dual relationships, and professional boundaries (Poirier, 1991).

DETECTION STRATEGIES

Deceptive behavior with all age groups is a function of situational variables that affect possible outcomes for the actor. The higher the motivation to achieve or avoid a specific outcome, the greater the likelihood of deception. When engaging in deceptive behavior, the majority of adolescents presents with less naivete and simplicity compared with children, but with less sophistication compared with adults. A conventional clinical interview is not very useful with young children, but with caution can be utilized with adolescents. The clinician must attenuate the use of clinical procedures with the developmental needs of the patient. Most adolescents can meaningfully engage in the usual verbal repartee of an interview format. Garnering the interest, trust, and meaningful cooperation of the adolescent is an entirely separate challenge.

Most adults, including those who are court-involved or court-referred will approach clinical interviews with a serious and concerned attitude. Adolescents generally do not offer the clinician such luxury of self-motivated cooperation and concern. One way to maximize adolescent motivation in forensic assessments is to include a "family assessment" component in the evaluation. Adolescents, especially those who are court-involved, will frequently challenge the clinical assessment with attitudinal issues of testiness, defiance, belligerence, uncooperativeness, indifference, and the like.

There are several structured interview formats available for conducting a diagnostic/forensic assessment with the adolescent. McCann (1998) summarized the usefulness of structured interview instruments noting the limited validation studies of the instruments for adolescents. Given the validity concerns, McCann suggested use of these instruments as *collaborative* as opposed to *definitive* assessment tools. The Structured Interview of Reported Symptoms (SIRS; Rogers, Bagby, & Dickens, 1992) has modified cutoffs for adolescents (Rogers, Hinds, & Sewell 1996). McCann also suggested the Psychopathy Checklist-Revised (PCL-R; Hare, 1980, 1991). The PCL-R is not a deception instrument per se, but may be useful in gathering pertinent data about the adolescent to assist with making a clinical determination regarding deception. A primary disadvantage with the PCL-R is the lengthy period of time required for proper administration and scoring.

The attraction of psychometrics as a reliable approach to detecting deception and malingering extends to the adolescent population. Adolescent offenders can be very vexing to the juvenile justice system, leading to an unbridled acceptance of psychometric data. Psychometrics carries an aura of objectivity and validity to the unsophisticated that is rarely warranted. Forensic clinicians must be appropriately wary and utilize the multifaceted evaluation approach advocated throughout this book.

A mainstay objective personality test for adolescents is the Minnesota Multiphasic Personality Inventory-Adolescent (MMPI-A; Archer, Maruish, & Imhof, 1991). The MMPI-A is a derivative of the MMPI and has benefited from the reputation of its parent MMPI as a useful forensic tool (Pope, Butcher, & Seelen, 2000). The MMPI-A requires a seventh-grade reading level and has been normed for 14- to 18-year-olds. It is a very useful instrument for assessing deception and malingering because, like its predecessor the MMPI, it has several validity and response style scales.

Adolescent deception was investigated comparatively with the MMPI-A, SIRS, and the Screening Index of Malingered Symptoms (SIMS) (Rogers, Hinds, & Sewell, 1996). In this study, the commonly used MMPI-A scales of F, F1, and F2 were not found to be effective. The F-K >20 index, however, was an effective discriminant measure. Utilizing adult criteria cutoffs, the SIRS yielded moderate positive predictive effectiveness and excellent negative predictive power. As a screen, the SIMS was moderately effective. A two-stage discriminant analysis offered support for the incremental validity of a combined SIRS and MMPI-2 evaluation of adolescent feigning.

Also useful with adolescents is the Millon Adolescent Clinical Inventory (MACI; Millon, & Davis, 1993). McCann (1998) described four Modifier Indices on the MACI that are pertinent to the assessment of deception and malingering. These self-report style scales are Reliability (V), Disclosure (X), Desirability (Y), and Debasement (Z). McCann noted that the MACI Modifier Indices have limited empirical validation to date and, therefore, should be used with appropriate caution.

The significant limitations of direct measures of deception and malingering on psychological tests, combined with characteristic adolescent guardedness, require clinicians to rely adroitly on assessment information beyond the instrument data itself. Grisso (1998) noted that clinician observations of subjects behavior during the administration of psychological testing can be very useful in assessing malingering. The Rorschach inkblot technique offers an excellent example of an instrument that has limited, direct forensic validity, but affords interactive opportunity between examiner and examinee that can be quite helpful in terms of generating useful interactional data with a perplexing adolescent. Unlike the pen and pencil self-administering objective instruments, projective techniques generally require an extended and structured period of examiner/examinee interaction that can produce worthwhile data regarding the adolescent's demeanor and social style.

When the formalized administration rules are adhered to, the Exner Rorschach system provides this structured interaction. During forensic assessment, many adolescents evidence a defensive style that can be accompanied by misleading response style and affect. Some adults, when caught up in the stress of a forensic assessment, will also display such avoidant or hysterical defensive styles, but it is characteristic of many adolescents under the stress of a forensic assessment. Clinicians who are attuned to the vagaries of adolescence can productively incorporate these dynamics into the forensic examination.

Adolescents involved in serious juvenile justice matters will sometimes dramatically and tellingly react to the loose structure of the Rorschach format. This occurs in the absence of any prior history of psychopathology. Adolescent Rorschach productions can be extreme, atypical, and sometimes accompanied by raw affective responses that are not otherwise evidenced, for example, during clinical interviewing. When confronted with such discrepancies in their performance, adolescents will often acknowledge deviant responding. Stymied adolescents will suggest that they misunderstood the original instructions, that they had a sudden urge to indulge a creative whim, or similar explanation. Such seemingly minute miscues can be invaluable sources of further inquiry for the astute clinician.

The foregoing situations offer very subtle clinical data that must be carefully integrated into the assessment findings. No assessment opinion of whether or not an adolescent is malingering would ever rest solely on such encapsulated behaviors. Forensic work with adolescents can be very difficult and the clinician must rely on whatever resources are available and useful.

With adolescent sexual offenders, cultural sexual taboos generate considerable motivation for denial, collusion, and deception. This potential for deception exists for the adolescent offender and just as strongly for family members and in many instances for professionals previously involved with the offender. Assessment of the juvenile sexual offender must incorporate a comprehensive review of developmental and familial factors. These include the usual array of clinical issues, and, in addition, there should be a comprehensive review of the perpetrator's history for any victimization of the perpetrator, substance abuse, impulsivity, aggression, and prior offenses. There must also be a thorough review of the perpetrator's psychosexual history; collaborating this history can become a very sensitive pursuit and the evaluator must employ considerable discretion.

Varieties of assessment tools for juvenile sex offenders have been described. These instruments range from traditionally available psychological tests such as the 16PF (Grossman, Haywood, & Wasyliw, 1992), the Beck Depression Inventory (Becker et al., 1991), the Jesness Inventory (Oliver, Hall, & Neuhaus, 1993), the MMPI (Grossman et al., 1992; Lanyon, 1993). The literature also reports newly developed instruments including self-report inventories such as the Adolescent Sexual Interest Card Sort, the Adolescent Cognition Scale, and the Multiphasic Sex Inventory (Bourke & Donohue, 1996). Investigators have also devised follow-up questionnaires for offenders who have completed treatment (Bremer, 1992).

The perils of assessment with adolescents were offered in a study of adolescents faking believable deficits during neuropsychological evaluation. Guilmette and Arkes (1988) found that three adolescents (15 to 17 years old) were able to fool all 60 neuropsychologists when instructed to fake brain damage. None of the evaluators detected malingering. On an even more disheartening note, the neuropsychologists appeared overconfident in their judgments.

REFERENCES

Archer, R. P., Maruish, M., & Imhof, E. A. (1991). Psychological test usage with adolescent clients. *Professional Psychology: Research and Practice, 22*, 247–252.

Backbier, E., Hoogsstraten, J., & Meerum, T. K. (1997). Situational determinants of the acceptability of telling lies. *Journal of Applied Social Psychology, 27*(12), 1048–1062.

Barbaree, H. E., Hudson, S. M., & Seto, M. C. (1993). Sexual assault in society: The role of the juvenile offender. In H. E. Barbaree, W. L. Marshall, & S. M. Hudson (Eds.), *The juvenile sex offender* (pp. 1–24). New York: Guilford Press.

Battin-Person, S. R., Thornberry, T. P., Hawkins, J. D., & Krohn, M. D. (1998). *Gang membership, delinquent peers, and delinquency behavior.* Bulletin. Washington, DC: U.S. Department of Juvenile Justice, Office of Justice Programs, Office of Juvenile Justice and Delinquency Prevention.

Becker, J. V., Kaplan, M. S., Tenke, C. E., & Tartaglini, A. (1991). The incidence of depressive symptomatology in juvenile sex offenders with a history of abuse. *Child Abuse and Neglect, 15* (4), 531–536.

Blos, P. (1962). *On adolescence: A psychoanalytic interpretation.* New York: First Free Press.

Bourke, M. L., & Donohue, B. (1996). Assessment and treatment of juvenile sex offenders. *Journal of Child Sexual Abuse, 5*(1), 47–70.

Bremer, J. F. (1992). Serious juvenile sex offenders: Treatment and long-term follow-up. *Psychiatric Annals, 22*(6), 326–332.

Brink, T. L. (1995). Sexual behavior and telling the truth on questionnaires. *Psychological Reports, 76*(1), 218.

Browning, K., Huizinga, D., Loeber, R., & Thornberry, T. P. (1999). *Causes and correlates of delinquency program* (OJJP Fact Sheet No. 100). Washington, DC: Office of Juvenile Justice and Delinquency Prevention.

Browning, K., Thornberry, T., & Porter, P. K. (1999). *Highlights of findings from the Rochester Youth Development Study* (OJJDP Fact Sheet No. 103). Washington, DC: Office of Juvenile Justice and Delinquency Prevention.

Bruggeman, E. L., & Hart, K. J. (1996). Cheating, lying, and moral reasoning by religious and secular high school students. *Journal of Educational Research, 89*(6), 340–344.

Ceci, S. J., & Bruck, M. (1993). Suggestibility of the child witness: A historical review and synthesis. *Psychological Bulletin, 113*(3), 403–439.

Ceci, S. J., & Bruck, M. (1995). *Jeopardy in the courtroom: A scientific analysis of children's testimony.* Washington, DC: American Psychological Association.

Chait, L., & Perry, J. L. (1992). Factors influencing self-administration of, and subjective response to, placebo marijuana. *Journal of Addictive Diseases, 3*(6), 545–552.

Chance, J., & Goldstein, A. (1984). Face-recognition memory. Implications for children's eyewitness testimony. *Journal of Social Issues, 40*, 69–85.

DePaulo, B. M., & Kashy, D. A. (1998). Everyday lies in close and casual relationships. *Journal of Personality & Social Psychology, 74*(1), 63–79.

DePaulo, B. M., Kashy, D. A., Kirkendol, S. E., Wyer, M. M., & Epstein, J. A. (1996). Lying in everyday life. *Journal of Personality & Social Psychology, 70*(5), 979–995.

Erikson, E. H. (1963). *Childhood and society* (2nd ed.). New York: Norton.

Fischer, G. (1996). Deceptive, verbally coercive college males: Attitudinal predictors and lies told. *Archives of Sexual Behavior, 25*(5), 527–533.

Greenfield, D. (1987). Feigned psychosis in a 14-year-old girl. *Hospital and Community Psychiatry, 38*, 73–77.

Grisso, T. (1998). *Forensic evaluation of juveniles.* Sarasota, FL: Professional Resource Press.

Grossman, L. S., Haywood, T. W., & Wasyliw, O. E. (1992). The evaluation of truthfulness in alleged sex offenders' self-reports: 16PF and MMPI validity scales. *Journal of Personality Assessment, 59*(2), 264–275.

Guilmette, T., & Arkes, H. (1988). Neuropsychologist's capacity to detect adolescent malingerers. *Professional Psychology: Research and Practice, 19,* 508–515.

Hare, R. D. (1980). A research scale for the assessment of psychopathy in criminal populations. *Personality and Individual Differences, 1,* 111–117.

Hare, R. D. (1991). *The Hare Psychopathy Checklist–Revised manual.* North Tonawanda, New York: Multi-Health Systems, Inc.

Howell, J. C., & Decker, S. H. (1999). *The youth gangs, drugs, and violence connection bulletin.* Washington, DC: U.S. Department of Juvenile Justice, Office of Justice Programs, Office of Juvenile Justice and Delinquency Prevention.

Kashy, D. A., & DePaulo, B. M. (1996). Who lies? *Journal of Personality and Social Psychology, 70*(5), 1037–1051.

Kelley, B. M., Huizinga, D., Thornberry, T. P., & Loeber, R. (1997). *Epidemiology of serious violence.* Washington, DC: Office of Juvenile Justice and Delinquency Prevention, Office of Justice Programs, U.S. Department of Justice. Juvenile Justice Bulletin.

Knox, D., & Schacht, C. (1992). Sexual behaviors of university students enrolled in a human sexuality course. *College Student Journal, 26*(1), 38–40.

Knox, D., Schacht, C., Holt, J., & Turner, J. (1993). Sexual lies among university students. *College Student Journal, 27*(2), 269–272.

Knox, D., Schacht, C., Turner, J., & Norris, P. (1995). College students' preference for win–win relationships. *College Student Journal, 29*(1), 44–46.

Knox, D., Schacht, C., & Zusman, M. E. (1999). Love relationships among college students. *College Student Journal, 33*(1), 149–151.

Lane, S. (1991). The sexual abuse cycle. In G. D. Ryan & S. L. Lane (Eds.), *Juvenile sexual offending* (pp. 103–142). Lexington, MA: Lexington.

Lanyon, R. I. (1993). Validity of MMPI sex offender scales with admitters and nonadmitters. *Psychological Assessment, 5*(3), 302–306.

Lather, A. S., Vasudeva, P., & Verma, P. (1997). A study of drug abuse among students as related to personality variables. *Journal of the Indian Academy of Applied Psychology, 23*(1–2), 43–49.

Lowenstein, L. F. (1994). Why children lie: How to prevent and curtail it. *Criminologist, 18*(1), 11–22.

Marshall, W. (1996). Assessment, treatment, and theorizing about sex offenders. *Criminal Justice & Behavior, 23,*(1), 162–199.

McCann, J. T. (1998) *Malingering and deception in adolescents: Assessing credibility in clinical and forensic settings.* Washington, DC: American Psychological Association.

Millar, M. G., & Millar, K. U. (1997). The effect of cognitive capacity and suspicion on truth bias. *Communication Research, 24*(5), 556–570.

Millon, T., & Davis, R. D. (1993). The Millon Adolescent Personality Inventory and the Millon Clinical Inventory. *Journal of Counseling and Development, 71*(5), 570–574.

Mischel, W., & Gilligan, C. (1964). Delayed gratification, motivation for the prohibited gratification, and response to temptation. *Journal of Abnormal Social Psychology, 4,* 411–417.

Moore, S. M. (1995). Girls' understanding and social construction of menarche. *Journal of Adolescence, 18*(1), 87–104.

Moore, J. P., & Terrett, C. P. (1998). *Highlights of the 1996 National Youth Gang Survey* (OJJDP Fact Sheet No. 86). Washington, DC: Office of Juvenile Justice and Delinquency Prevention.

Moore, J. P., & Terrett, C. P. (1999). *Highlights of the 1997 National Youth Gang Survey* (OJJDP Fact Sheet No. 97). Washington, DC: Office of Juvenile Justice and Delinquency Prevention.

Newton, M., & Duda, J. L. (1993). Elite adolescent athletes' achievement goals and beliefs concerning success in tennis. *Journal of Sport and Exercise Psychology, 15*(4), 437–448.

Oliver, L. L., Hall, G. C. N., & Neuhaus, S. M. (1993). A comparison of the personality and background characteristics of adolescent sex offenders and other adolescent offenders. *Criminal Justice and Behavior, 20*(4), 359–370.

Peterson, C. (1996). Deception in intimate relationships. *International Journal of Psychology, 31*(6), 279–288.

Peterson, C., Peterson, J., & Seeto, D. (1983). Developmental changes in ideas about lying. *Child Development, 54,* 1529–1535.

Phillips, S. R. (1994). Asking the sensitive question: The ethics of survey research and teen sex. *IRB: A Review of Human Subjects Research, 16*(6), 1–7.

Poirier, J. G. (1991). Disputed custody and concerns of parental violence. *Psychotherapy in Private Practice, 9*(3), 7–23.

Poirier, J. G. (1998). Juvenile delinquency and violent crime. In L. C. Whitaker & H. V. Hall (Eds.), *Collective violence: Effective strategies for assessing and interviewing in fatal group and institutional aggression* (pp. 183–212). Boca Raton, FL: CRC Press.

Poirier, J. G. (1999, August). The mental health/judicial interface: Taboo dynamics and collaboration strategies with the juvenile sexual offender. In R. T. Saunders (Chair), American Psychological Association Annual Meeting, Boston, MA.

Pope, K. S., Butcher, J. N., & Seelen, J. (2000). *The MMPI, MMPI-2, & MMPI-A in court: A practical guide for expert witnesses and attorneys* (2nd ed.). Washington, DC: American Psychological Association.

Rogers, R., Bagby, R. M., & Dickens, S. E. (1992). *Structured Interview of Reported Symptoms: Professional manual*. Odessa, FL: Psychological Assessment Resources.

Rogers, R., Hinds, J. D., & Sewell, K. W. (1996). Feigning psychopathology among adolescent offenders: Validation of the SIRS, MMPI-A, and SIMS. *Journal of Personality Assessment, 67*, 244–257.

Ryan, G. (1991). Juvenile sex offenders: Defining the population. In G. D. Ryan & S. L. Lane (Eds.), *Juvenile sexual offending* (pp. 3–8). Lexington, MA: Lexington.

Ryan, G., &. Lane, S. (Eds.). (1997). *Juvenile sex offending: Causes, consequences, and corrections*. San Francisco: Jossey-Bass.

Schwartz, R. H., Farrow, J. A., Banks, B., & Giesel, A. E. (1998). Use of false ID cards and other deceptive methods to purchase alcoholic beverages during high school. *Journal of Addictive Diseases, 17*(3), 25–33.

Stouthamer-Loeber, M. (1986). Lying as a problem in children. *Clinical Psychology Review, 6*, 267–289.

Vidoni, D., Fleming, N., & Mintz, S. (1983) Behavior problems of children as perceived by teachers, mental health professionals and children. *Psychology in the Schools, 20*, 93–98.

Wilkinson, S., & Hough, G. (1996). Lie as truth in abused adopted adolescents. *Psychoanalytic Study of the Child, 51*, 580–596.

Woods, P. (1993). Overview of an adolescent sadistic sex offender. *Issues in Criminological & Legal Psychology, 19*, 33–36.

9 Deception and Elderly People

There are several unique considerations with regard to the ability of elderly people to understand and engage in deceptive behavior. Elderly people are at the opposite end of the human developmental continuum from children, but both present with some similar issues regarding deception. The chronological age that marks the beginning of the elder years is a topic of ongoing discussion. The authors have arbitrarily adopted the definitional age of 65 years and older recognizing that many people achieve this age, and much older, without any significant psychological impairment. For the purpose of this study of deception, developmental and environmental factors associated with very late adulthood are of more interest than is the issue of chronological age. These topics concerning the twilight phase of human development are the interests of social gerontologists; they offer a final backdrop to the study of developmental themes with deception.

Crime statistics reflect that elderly people commit a very small number of serious crimes. Exceptions to this are crimes of elder abuse and elder neglect, which, surprisingly, are perpetrated primarily by elderly spouses (Poirier, 1996). When elderly people are involved in serious crimes, the issues regarding deception are similar to those with all adults, but there is the added clinical issue of aging having a negative impact on cognitive and memory functioning.

Forensic clinicians are often called upon to evaluate the testamentary capacity (i.e., ability to competently make a will) of an elderly person. Testamentary capacity evaluations can involve issues of deception by both the elderly person and perhaps more frequently by family members driven by greed regarding inheritances.

One unique forensic application of deception and elderly people is their vulnerability to cons and scams. This is a particular problem for those who reside in the community, but has not been an unknown problem with the those who reside in assisted-care and/or nursing home placements. A typical scenario is for a con artist to create some type of ruse prompting the elderly person to withdraw monies from the bank either to help the con artist with some crisis or in the hopes of receiving a large monetary award. Telemarketers perpetrate another common form of this type of elderly abuse. Plying the loneliness of elderly people with initially friendly telephone conversation, the telemarketers are deceptive in aggressively marketing some product, which is expensive and often useless to the elderly victim.

The human aging process results in predictable changes in cognitive and volitional functioning. The timing and extent of these changes are not predictable on an individual basis. Neurobehavioral decline occurs as a function of normal aging, and secondary to particular illnesses (e.g., cerebrovascular accident) associated with this developmental period. Organs and organ systems inevitably begin to succumb to age; the circulatory and neurological systems are especially vulnerable. Dementia in one stage or another is a common issue, as is memory loss. Elderly people also present with age-related problems of depression and hopelessness that can be quite incapacitating. These represent an overview of the peripheral challenges presented in the assessment of the elderly person.

A number of environmental variables have been associated with healthy and content lifestyles for elderly people. Being in good physical health and being married are two well-established factors (Rapkin & Fischer, 1992). Being widowed or having struggled with long-standing disadvantages in education, job status, and socioeconomic achievement are negative factors associated with healthy psychological status of elderly people. These same factors can be psychological inducements to distortion, fabrication, and deception with the older person.

Elderly people are more sensitive to poverty and crime in their community. Because of their age and related declines in strength and mobility, crime becomes more visible and more worrisome to them. Depending on the elderly person's/couple's life circumstances, poverty becomes a real and looming concern. Stories have been written and movies made about these strident themes in the lives of elderly people.

Social stereotypes of the elderly population are many (for a review, see Hummert, 1990), and there are cross-cultural variations. Younger people can be impatient and intolerant with the concerns of elderly people. Compared with the interests and goals of younger segments of the population, the complaints of elderly people are frequently viewed as trivial and insignificant. Such intolerance with the concerns of elderly people only serves to accentuate the self-perception of them as being useless and lonely.

The majority of the elder population who enter health care channels do so, ostensibly, because of physical health problems. Research has demonstrated a high incidence of comorbid depression associated with elders involved in primary care. The estimates of comorbid syndromal depression in elderly people vary from 15 to 45% (Rapp, Smith, & Britt, 1990). Comorbid depression is also known to increase the risk of further medical morbidity (Williamson & Schultz, 1992). Depression in the elderly person is frequently undetected and this problem involves a multitude of factors. One obvious issue is the lack of proper training with professionals who work with elderly people to look for subtle depressive symptoms. There are also patient-generated factors. Williamson and Schultz noted the role of psychosocial variables affecting the self-report of complaints of depression by elderly people. Motivated by concerns about financial status, feelings of control and self-worth, and usual desire to be able to continue to live in the community, the elderly person will minimize, withhold information, and actually prevaricate regarding depressive symptoms.

An important application of deception dynamics with the elderly population involves health care personnel, usually physicians and nurses, who work with terminally ill elderly persons and who must make decisions whether or not to advise patients of their actual health status. The usual justification for not advising the patient or the family is that full disclosure will make an already difficult situation more traumatic. A variety of issues come into play including the philosophy and mentality of the institution, the personal philosophies of the health care providers, and their interpretations of ethical principles. Tuckett (1998) conducted a study of nurses' strategies about informing patients of foreboding physical health issues. The strategies ranged from telling the "truth, the whole truth," to "titrating" information, to altogether withholding information. The author concluded, "It does seem that nursing stands amidst this world of deception as a practice prone to speaking half-truths, omitting details, misleading through evasion, failing to disclose by 'fobbing off' a client, simply not telling and/or giving partial insights by controlled release of information" (p. 293).

As noted (Chapter 1), such relative applications of ethical considerations may avoid immediate criticism of a given circumstance, but hardly address the fundamental problem. As is reflected throughout the chapters of this book, the ethical conundrums of actual and quasi-deceptive behaviors by professionals are many and thorny.

TARGET BEHAVIORS

In general, the elderly person is just as capable of engaging in deception as any younger person. Elderly people can be actor-deceivers in any of the activities described in the chapters of this book.

A majority of the elderly population enters retirement years on fixed-income living standards. They must use their resources discreetly and resourcefully. Because of these circumstances, there are a significant number of elderly people who resort to minor criminal activity (e.g., theft, shoplifting, trespassing, and embezzlement) as a means of survival. Subgroups among these offenders include elderly "street persons" and/or the unhospitalized elderly mentally ill person. Forensic clinicians who work for local courts will encounter members of these latter two groups on a regular basis. The usual referral questions are competency, criminal responsibility, and dispositional recommendations.

Evaluation of the elderly people poses unique challenges both to the court and to the clinician. Justice will prevail, but dispositional recommendations must be based on a compassionate review of the elderly defendant's circumstances and resources. Clinicians can make valuable interventions by knowing community resources and effecting appropriate referrals. The common problem is that resources for the elderly population are often meager.

Elderly people who are of means present another array of forensic circumstances involving deception. As time goes on and the likelihood of estate settlement becomes more imminent, beneficiaries will began to posture. There will be innuendo or accusations of incompetence to manage their affairs currently or to make a proper will. Civil court actions follow and forensic clinicians are often asked to conduct assessments to provide guidance to the bench.

RESPONSE PATTERNS

For the forensic clinician, the elderly person can present with an unnerving mixture of "fake bad" and "fake good" response patterns. The forensic assessments may involve elderly persons in criminal, civil, or domestic legal matters. The most challenging forensic scenarios involve elderly people who present with cognitive or memory impairments. To begin with, such impairments invoke concerns regarding competency, and assuming competency, there will be questions regarding distortion being deliberate or nondeliberate.

DETECTION STRATEGIES

Old age is accompanied by cognitive decline that is sometimes apparent and heart-rending to the patient and to the family. The functional capacities of elderly persons, who in their younger years were very bright, educated, and accomplished, can be devastated by the maladies associated with the aging process. One example is patients with stroke who can suffer a wide range of cognitive impairments. Patients with Alzheimer's disease (AD) are even more striking examples because of the slow, progressive, and inevitable clinical course. Empirical understanding of the nuances of the neurobehavioral ravages of AD is still unfolding (Cronin-Golomb et al., 1992; Winograd et al., 1999).

Patients with early-stage dementia typically have awareness of their progressive cognitive loss. That awareness is frightening and depressing. At some point, the family or other involved caretakers have no choice but to intervene and initiate legal steps to have the patient declared incompetent. In some situations, the need is to protect the patient from self-inflicted harm or danger. In other circumstances, the need is to protect someone dependent on the patient, such as a child or elderly spouse; another common scenario is the endangered welfare of a pet.

The courts will ask forensic clinicians to assess the *testamentary capacity* of an elderly person. Testamentary capacity is a legal concept and essentially refers to having the cognitive ability to manage personal affairs meaningfully, particularly financial affairs. The usual application of testamentary capacity is the ability to assist in the preparation of a will and to attest to its accuracy. The following case example was such an assessment and provides an illustration of FDA in the context of assessing an elderly person:

Case of Mrs. Green — A number of years ago, one of the authors was contacted by a Circuit Court Judge who indicated that he was hearing a matter involving the testamentary capacity of a 74-year-old woman who was residing in a nursing home. Prior to entering the nursing home, Mrs. Green had prepared a will essentially leaving her substantial estate to her two daughters. A son, who was in his late 40s, would receive a token "dollar" benefit. The judge requested, "I would like you to do all those tests that you do because this is going to be a very contested matter when it enters trial and there is no doubt that it is going to trial."

The son was contesting his mother's mental competence at the time of signing her will. The son and his attorneys asserted that Mrs. Green had experienced a series of cerebrovascular accidents that had rendered her not only physically disabled, but also mentally incompetent. The current will had been prepared following Mrs. Green's second stroke, and shortly after she entered the nursing home. According to the son, his mother had regressed mentally and essentially had the "mind of a child."

One evening 2 weeks later, we went to the nursing home prepared to conduct the evaluation to include the administration of a battery of cognitive and neuropsychological instruments. As we entered the front lobby and introduced ourselves to a receptionist, a gentleman quickly approached and introduced himself as Mrs. Green's son. Mr. Green was in his late 40s but he presented with decidedly weathered features; he appeared to be in his mid-50s. He was uncomfortably attired in a shirt and tie, clothing that was worn, unclean, and ill-kept. Mr. Green's hygiene was also less than adequate.

Mr. Green expressed his good fortune in coincidentally being in the waiting room and recognizing our name when we spoke to the receptionist. Mr. Green advised that he visited his mother regularly because he was very concerned with her welfare. He made no mention of contesting his mother's mental abilities. Mr. Green did note that he and his attorney would cooperate in whatever way possible.

We proceeded to the nursing station to review Mrs. Green's medical chart. The essential history was confirmed. Most recently, Mrs. Green was described as having episodes of apparent personality change in which she would occasionally behave in a childlike manner. She had a panoply of physical health problems, but now, nearly 2 years later since her third and last stroke, the records described that most of the time she was mentally alert, cooperative, and friendly. From the nursing notes, it was clear that Mrs. Green was well liked by the nursing staff.

As we were reading the clinical record, a charge nurse introduced herself. The nurse reported that she had become concerned on Mrs. Green's behalf. Her concern was because Mrs. Green would always be upset with the recent round of daily visits from her son. Mr. Green had suddenly begun to visit his mother on a regular basis, after having visited on only two or three prior occasions in the nearly 2 years of Mrs. Green's stay in the nursing home. The nurse related that for the preceding 2 weeks (i.e., coinciding with the court order for the current assessment), Mr. Green would arrive each evening at approximately 5:30 p.m. He would go to his mother's room for approximately 1 or 2 min and then proceed to the waiting room area where he would remain for approximately $2^1/_2$ hours. The nurse stated that on several of these visits, staff reported Mr. Green to evidence the odor of alcohol, but he had never presented as obviously intoxicated in his behavior.

We found Mrs. Green asleep in her bed. She awoke with a smile and interacted in a "little girl" manner; she was coy, deferring to the examiner, and she spoke in a soft, high-pitched voice. We explained to Mrs. Green the purpose of the visit. During the next 10 min, Mrs. Green asked four times who we were and why we were visiting her. During this discussion, she repeatedly observed the remaining food on her dinner tray; we offered to open a plastic dessert carton. She observed our activity carefully. She asked if we would open another small carton and place the whipped cream on her Jell-O, which we proceeded to do. We then attempted to feed her. She smiled, abruptly took the spoon, and commented, "That's all you need to do, Mister. I can feed myself, thank you very much."

Mrs. Green's behavior became more serious and intense. She questioned, once more, why we had come to see her. We explained the Circuit Court Order and provided her with a copy; we explained the fact that we would prepare a written report. We elected to proceed with the administration of the verbal subtests from an intelligence scale (WAIS). Mrs. Green performed very capably throughout and, in the end, achieved a verbal I.Q. of 124. Her level of performance was consistent across the subtests.

Mrs. Green became progressively more relaxed, brighter in her disposition, and more interactive. Midway through the cognitive testing, she stated, "Can I say something?" We paused with the testing and invited Mrs. Green to speak her mind. Mrs. Green expressed, "I know why you're here. It is all about my son. I want you to go back and tell the judge that my will is exactly the way I want it. My daughters have always been the ones to take care of me since my husband died. After my first stroke, my eldest daughter took me in. She, her husband, and her children have been very good to me. Before my husband died, he tried to help my son grow up. My son has a problem with alcohol. Over the years he has terrorized my entire family. I am still afraid of him. He has been coming here every night for the past couple of weeks. I am sure it is because he knew you were coming. Before my husband died, he gave my son two pieces of property that he still owns. I insisted that my husband put the properties in trust so that he cannot sell them until he is 65. I think that is what he's living off, but he has never really worked. Whatever money he gets, he takes to drink and to gambling. I gave a lot of thought to my will and my attorney followed my instructions. I do not want that changed."

Mrs. Green expressed that since incurring her disabilities, she was very frightened of her son's temper. When she first entered the nursing home, her son had visited her and verbally intimidated her about changing her will. Mrs. Green expressed that she had learned to feign incompetence by assuming a childlike bearing with her son in an effort to avoid his unpredictable wrath, which was usually coincident with his having consumed alcohol. She stated that she also feigned incompetence with her son's attorneys and with anyone she suspected to be involved with her son. She acknowledged that she had initially suspected the current clinician to be sent by her son.

Nearly 2 hours later, we completed the assessment with Mrs. Green. We elected not to administer all the test instruments since Mrs. Green was clearly competent. As we were leaving, Mr. Green was still waiting. Mr. Green clearly was anticipant of some type of feedback. We advised him perfunctorily that we would prepare a report and it would go directly to the judge. The report was carefully crafted to avoid contributing further to any family dissension. We were later advised that the court hearing was very abbreviated. The judge cited our report and declared that Mrs. Green met the criteria for having testamentary capacity. Mrs. Green's will was a valid reflection of her desires and of her competent attempt to manage her affairs.

The case of Mrs. Green offers an example of how the forensic clinician must integrate bits and pieces of apparently inconsistent information. FDA is an effort to reconstruct a given forensic scenario so those distorted elements are accounted for, thereby rendering a meaningful understanding of the circumstance and laying the foundation for a defensible expert opinion regarding the legal issues.

PSYCHOMETRIC ASSESSMENT OF ELDERLY PERSONS

The forensic assessment of elderly people utilizing psychometric instruments is essentially similar to that of adults in general. The major precaution would be the utilization of correct age norms as applicable to a given instrument. Clinicians must be sensitive to the special problems of clinical presentation that elderly people may present. In particular, this includes the high probability of performance-impairing depression, confabulated responses to mask impairment, and the special sensibilities of an elderly person who is aware of, and embarrassed by, emerging impairments.

The assessment of cognitive functioning in elderly people has a direct bearing on the elderly person's basic capacity to detect, understand, and engage in deceptive behavior. Now at the other end of the developmental spectrum, most of the earlier maturational considerations with children and adolescents remain quite relevant. The impact of aging can return some elderly persons to a childlike level of deceptive behavior. Their efforts to engage in the steps in deception are naive and immature, and they are very vulnerable to being victimized by the deception of others.

Psychological assessment of cognitive abilities and neuropsychological assessment assume that mitigating factors have been eliminated or accounted for. With elderly people, this means that interference from fatigue, medications, potential influence of depression and other affective symptoms, and possible impacts of medical problems need to be addressed. These factors must be either eliminated to the extent possible or, at least, considered in review of the assessment findings.

Distinct cognitive profiles indicative of the presence and severity of depressive symptoms have been described in neuropsychological testing with elderly people (Boone et al., 1995). Depression profiles were marked by subtle weaknesses in visual memory and nonverbal intelligence, but with verbal skills maintained. Increased severity of depression was marked by mild weaknesses in information-processing speed and executive skills, but with memory, intelligence, language skills, constructional ability, and basic attention unaffected.

Malec et al. (1995) described a study of a large group ($N = 376$) of nonclinical elderly subjects. The investigators examined clusters of psychometric profiles in an effort to identify elderly subjects, who were at risk for future cognitive decline. The study found that relative cognitive impairments as captured in the psychometric data were not reasonably predictive of future cognitive decline. It is important to emphasize that this study involved only elderly subjects with no current symptoms or complaint of cognitive impairment. The findings point to the inadequacy of current psychometric instruments to identify at-risk elderly. Psychometrics are more effective in identifying elderly people with cognitive deficits, and mapping the extent and severity of those deficits. There is also impressive accuracy in identifying the neurological localization of some deficit syndromes.

Later chapters will address in greater depth the issues of assessment of deception and malingering in specific clinical syndromes. Several of these chapters (e.g., Chapter 10, Malingered Neuropsychological Deficits; Chapter 11, Faked Pain; and Chapter 16, Competency and Deception) will have particular relevance for the elderly person.

SYNTHESIS

The review of deception issues with the elderly population completes the human developmental spectrum. It is likely that there is a transgenerational component to human deceptive behavior. It is not clear, however, if this is due to genetic factors, environmental factors, or both. Forensic clinicians who work with children and families can readily observe patterns of reliance on deception being carried through family generations. With this likelihood, consideration of transgenerational transmission of deceptive behavior patterns is added to FDA.

The elderly person has endured years of exposure to human deception in all spheres of life. At present, there is no mega-study data reflecting whether there is any long-term psychological impact of engagement in, or exposure to, patterns of human deception. Is there an impact, for example, if a person lives his or her life predominantly as a deception-actor or deception-victim?

Perhaps the ever-increasing numbers of individuals incarcerated for serious crimes provide one relevant database in terms of those who engage as deception-actors. Perhaps elderly people who have been recurrent deception-victims are another database. In any event, these are little more than philosophical and moral inquiries at this point, but the prevalence of depression and despair in the elderly members of our culture causes one to ponder the questions.

There is a definite impact on the child's understanding and use of deception based on a number of experiential factors. These factors include the child's being exposed to deceptive behavior and being taken advantage of by deceptive behavior. What is the impact of lifelong experience with the human capacity for deception for a person who enters maturity? Erikson (1963) stated that the ego challenge for the person entering maturity was to achieve *ego integrity* vs. *despair*. According to Erikson, the developmental challenge for elderly people is to be able to accept their life, their accomplishments, their failures, and their finality. For the elderly person who has coped and achieved through life based on a lifestyle characterized by deception, this would appear to be a formidable task. Similarly, the elderly person who enters maturity bitter in the perception of having been chronically victimized by human deceit will have difficulties achieving ego integrity. As a final commentary to the developmental review of deceptive behavior, Erikson's observation is acknowledged: "And it seems possible to further paraphrase the relation of adult integrity and infantile trust by saying that healthy children will not fear life if their elders have integrity enough not to fear death" (p. 269).

REFERENCES

Boone, K. B., Lesser, I. M., Miller, B. L., Wohl, M., Berman, N., Lee, A., Palmer, B., & Back, C. (1995). Cognitive functioning in older depressed outpatients: Relationship of presence and severity of depression to neuropsychological test scores. *Neuropsychology, 9*(3), 390–398.

Cronin-Golumb, A., Keane, M. M., Kokodis, A., Corkin, S., & Growdon, J. H. (1992). Category knowledge in Alzheimer's disease: Normal organization and a general retrieval deficit. *Psychology and Aging, 7*(3), 359–366.

Erikson, E. (1963). *Childhood and society* (2nd ed.). New York: Norton.

Hummert, M. L. (1990). Multiple stereotypes of elderly and young adults: A comparison of structure and evaluations. *Psychology and Aging, 5*(2), 182–193.

Malec, J. F., Smith, G. E., Ivnik, R. J., Petersen, R. C., & Tangalos, E. G. (1995). Clusters of impaired normal elderly do not decline cognitively in 3 to 5 years. *Neuropsychology, 10*(1), 66–73.

Poirier, J. G. (1996). Violence in the family. In H. V. Hall (Ed.), *Lethal violence 2000: A source book on fatal domestic, acquaintance, and stranger aggression* (pp. 259–292). Kamuela, HI: Pacific Institute for the Study of Conflict and Aggression.

Rapkin, B. D., & Fischer, K. (1992). Personal goals of older adults: Issues in assessment and prediction. *Psychology and Aging, 7*(1), 127–137.

Rapp, S. R., Smith, S. S., & Britt, M. (1990). Identifying comorbid depression in elderly medical patients: Use of extracted Hamilton Depression Rating Scale. *Psychological Assessment, 2*(3), 243–247.

Tuckett, A. (1998). "Bending the truth": Professionals' narratives about lying and deception in nursing practice. *International Journal of Nursing Studies, 35*, 292–302.

Williamson, G. M., & Schulz, R. (1992). Physical illness and symptoms of depression among elderly outpatients. *Psychology and Aging, 7*(3), 343–351.

Winograd, E., Goldstein, F. C., Monarch, E. S., Peluso, J. P., & Goldman, W. P. (1999). The mere exposure effect in patients with Alzheimer's disease. *Neuropsychology, 13*(1), 41–46.

Part III

Deception Analysis in
Civil Contexts

10 Civil Law and Deception

Deception is relevant to all forensic settings and situations where expert opinions on mental state are proffered. All legal forums require a valid foundation (database) for expert opinions, and deception by a client affects the validity of that foundation. This chapter considers applications of deception analysis in particular areas of civil law. Civil claims of psychological damage or trauma where malingering must always be suspected are of special interest. Specific techniques for assessing faked organic deficits, pain, and post-trauma reactions — common targets of civil claims — are addressed in subsequent chapters.

Civil claims of mental injury, trauma, or defect may be broadly categorized into tort claims and eligibility claims. Tort claims allege that a personal injury was caused to the plaintiff (personal tort) or to the plaintiff's property (property tort) by the negligence or intentional act of the defendant. The defendant would be another person or business, although in cases where there are claims and counterclaims, the distinction between plaintiff and defendant can become blurred. Injuries are compensable through awards for the actual damages sustained and, sometimes, for punitive damages, as well. Theoretically, tort claims cover all losses and there are no limits to the financial awards. In recent years, however, the courts have become concerned about frivolous claims and extravagant damage awards. Accordingly, in many jurisdictions maximum limits for tort claims have been established.

Eligibility claims allege that the claimant satisfies current criteria for special assistance from a government program. The eligibility claims systems evolved, historically, because of the complex, adversarial, fault-oriented tort system. Examples of disability assistance programs include Social Security Supplemental Income for disabled persons, workers' compensation, and Veterans Administration programs. These disability programs are alternatives to the tort claim system; they are no-fault in application and based on functional loss, that is, loss of earning capacity.

Tort claims are originally tried in state and federal inferior courts and are decided based on a judicial decision process. Eligibility claims are originally heard before administrative boards or tribunals and outcomes are the result of an administrative process as compared with the judicial process of tort actions. The threshold legal questions, rules of evidence, rules of procedures, and burdens of proof differ between these two types of forums, as do the types of outcomes. Frequently, cases that begin as eligibility matters can evolve into tort actions.

The following discussion outlines the features of these two classes of claims. Special attention is given to issues involving claims of psychological injury or disability (Hall, 1990; Hall & Hall, 1991; Lees-Haley, 1985). In all of these types of claims, distortion and outright malingering of complaints is a significant probability. Our primary interest in civil actions is the meaningful assessment of any contributory elements of distortion or malingering (Lees-Haley, Williams, & English, 1996; Weissman, 1990).

TORT CLAIMS

Under the law, all persons owe a duty of care to each other that can logically be expected from ordinary, reasonable, and prudent persons. A tort is simply an injury to one's person, interests, reputation, or property that is caused by a breech of that duty. The primary goal of tort law is to compensate injured parties for damages caused by breach of certain commonly recognized duties. As a historical example, many of the very first cases of applied U.S. tort law involved claims by passengers against the early railroad systems. The early railroads were not very reliable for a variety of reasons including the weather, faulty equipment, damage by buffalo herds, and raids by Indians.

The successful prosecution of a tort claim requires proof that: (1) a personal injury occurred, (2) the injury was the result of the defendant's negligence or intentional act, or (3) the injury should have been foreseen by the defendant. The distinction between negligent torts and intentional torts is important, because the former allow awards only for actual damages suffered, while the latter also permit punitive damages.

Tort claims involve huge financial considerations both in terms of court resources and damages. In a study of tort trials by U.S. District Courts in 1994–1995, 3,356 cases were decided with 42.5% resolved in the favor of the plaintiff (Press & DeFrances, 1997). The median award to plaintiffs was $140,000; 17.9% of the cases involved awards of over $1 million, and 8.6% of the cases had awards of over $10 million. The largest portions of the high-end awards were for medical malpractice cases. In a follow-up study, Litras and DeFrances (1999) described a modest drop in the number of tort trials for 1996–1997. This decrease was attributed to a decline in certain types of personal injury cases, specifically marine, medical malpractice, and motor vehicle cases. Otherwise, the tort trial data for the 1994 and 1997 years were comparable. In 1997, damages were awarded to 87% of the plaintiffs in personal injury matters with 17% of these plaintiffs receiving $1 million dollars or more; 26% of the medical malpractice claims were for $1 million or more.

In a study of 1992 civil jury decisions comprising 12,026 cases in large counties (DeFrances et al., 1995), medical malpractice claims accounted for 11% of the jury decisions. The median recovery in all these cases was $52,000, with $2.7 billion being awarded by juries. In the medical malpractice cases, hospitals were the defendants in 72% of the cases involving awards of $1 million or more. The states have different rules regarding contributory negligence, but in the 1992 data, 13% of the jury-decided cases determined plaintiffs to have contributed to loss or injury for $84 million. These data illustrate the context of financial stakes from which involved parties can be readily induced to engage in deceptive and malingered behavior.

Malpractice is a particular and relevant application of tort law to professionals who do not meet the standard of care for providing services as established by their discipline. From the legal perspective, professionals have a duty of care based on their particular training and experience, which, in turn, is the basis for the professional relationship. Malpractice claims, therefore, introduce an additional element into the proof requirements. A malpractice claim must demonstrate a breech of the professional duty of care according to the prevailing standards for the profession.

The issue of deception in tort claims speaks to the question of the existence or severity of the alleged injury. If the defendant can show that no injury was actually suffered, then the claim has been successfully defended. If the defendant can show that the actual injury suffered is less severe than claimed, then the size of any damages may be reduced accordingly.

Civil courts have shown a combination of reluctance and fear in accepting opinions that a plaintiff is malingering. In *Miller v. United States Fidelity and Guaranty Co.* (1957), the court stated:

> The principle that courts will stigmatize a claimant as a malingerer only upon positive and convincing evidence justifying such a conclusion is so well embedded in our jurisprudence as to preclude the necessity for specifications.

The damage done to the plaintiff's reputation is one reason for this reluctance to accept opinions of malingering. Another is the logic of the economic situation. In both *King Mining Co. v. Mullins* (1952) and *Sutcliffe v. E. I. Dupont De Nemours & Co.* (1948), the courts found it difficult to believe that the plaintiffs would sacrifice relatively well paying jobs to fake an injury for a mere fraction of the amount of their pay. The courts want neither to label one as a malingerer, nor to allow recovery for malingering to take place.

Juries appear to become very rigid, however, when they feel the plaintiff may have attempted to dupe them. In *Freeman v. Bandlow* (1962), plaintiff was an elderly passenger who exited a bus in a careless manner and was hit by the defendant's auto. The jury awarded the plaintiff only $280 — the amount of a doctor's bill. The court noted as follows:

> The plaintiff alleged that he was severely injured in the area of the neck and back, suffered great physical and mental pain, which will continue in the future, and sustained temporary and permanent diminution of income and earning capacity. There was little doubt as to defendant's negligence, but the record reflects considerable doubt as to the cause, nature and extent of plaintiff's pathological condition during the two-year interim between the collision and the trial of the case early in 1961 [and] there was substantial expert opinion testimony tending to show that plaintiff's injuries were grossly exaggerated and that he was largely a malingerer and was not, in fact, appreciably disabled as a result of his mishap. (pp. 548–549)

Controversy over the latitude of the courts in allowing either direct or indirect testimony regarding malingering has continued to the present day. There is an entire area of disability law dealing with the admissibility of collateral sources of income for plaintiffs. The collateral source rule essentially holds that a plaintiff's recovery need not be offset by other sources of income. In cases where malingering is an issue, collateral source evidence can be very prejudicial to the plaintiff's case. In a landmark case addressing the discretion of courts to permit testimony regarding malingering, the U.S. Supreme Court ruled against a lower court allowing such testimony (*Eichel v. New York Cent. R.R. Co.*, 1963). In *Eichel*, the court opined, "[i]nsofar as the evidence bears on the issue of malingering, there will generally be other evidence having more probative value and involving less likelihood of prejudice than the receipt of a disability pension" (p. 317).

Eichel was decided before the current Federal Rules of Evidence were enacted. Rule 403 of the Federal Rules conferred "broad discretion upon the district court to weigh unfair prejudice against probative value" (709 F.2nd at 741). In *Savoie v. Otto Candies, Inc.* (1982), the court found that the adjudicatory analysis in *Eichel* was consistent with Rule 403. More recently, in *McGrath v. Consolidated Rail Corporation* (1998), the federal court ruled that the lower court did not abuse its discretion by permitting testimony regarding malingering. The court found:

> As its motion in limine to admit the collateral source evidence argues, Conrail offered the evidence of McGrath's disability payments on the issue of McGrath's credibility. Specifically, Conrail presented collateral source evidence to show McGrath's lack of motivation for returning to work. In allowing Conrail to question McGrath about collateral source evidence, the district court, on several occasions, issued cautionary instructions to the jury, advising it to consider the evidence only on the issue of malingering. In one instance where McGrath's tax return was admitted into evidence, the court specifically noted that "any references in there to [collateral] sources of income are not to reduce any compensation he may receive here or to increase it, but only on the issue of his motivation to go back to work .... (p. 96)

Aside from judicial restraints in the use of collateral source information in cases of suspected malingering, collateral data are invaluable for the forensic clinician. It is conceivable that the court may later deem any such data utilized in a forensic assessment inadmissible, but this is true for virtually any information that is part of the forensic database. Attorneys have a responsibility to protect their client's legal interests, and can attempt to have any information they perceive as prejudicial ruled inadmissible.

The courts have made clear that, absent evidence of malingering, awards can be made under many conditions for psychological trauma in the absence of physical injury. "Loss of consortium" as one application of psychic harm has been consistently recognized as compensable (*Metropolitan Dade County v. Reyes et al.*, 1996; *Byerley and Byerley v. Citrus Publishing*, 1999). The courts have also recognized delayed-onset symptoms, for example, symptoms appearing in adulthood stemming from childhood trauma. In *Teater v. State of Nebraska* (1997), the appeals court overturned a lower court decision that a claim was time-barred because it was made well after a 2-year statute of limitations had been exceeded. The claimant was an adult who had been placed as a child by the Department of Social Services in a foster home. As a child, her foster father continually subjected Ms. Teater to sexual assaults from the age of 6 to the age of 14. The plaintiff's claim was not made until 22 years after the first reported abuse. The claim was that Ms. Teater suffered permanent psychological injury and that the State of Nebraska had been negligent in providing adequate safeguards. Expert witnesses differed regarding whether the alleged sexual abuse had ever occurred, and regarding any injuries (i.e., damages).

The experts in *Teater* were opining from having reconstructed psychological events over 20 years earlier. This is an imposing task even under ideal circumstances. It could legitimately be argued that the state of the art of the mental health profession is not even close to being able to do what was called for in this case. At the optimum, only a very qualified best "guess" could be reasonably offered. The adversarial process has little patience, however, with other than "reasonable degree of certainty" opinions that are expressed with apparent certitude, and therein lies a fatal hazard for many mental health expert witnesses. In its analysis of *Teater*, the appeals court found:

> The focus is not on when the injured party recognizes whose negligence is responsible for the injury, but rather, the statute of limitations begins to run on the date on which the party holding the cause of action discovers or, in the exercise of reasonable diligence, should have discovered the existence of the injury.
>
> Thus, Teater's cause of action did not accrue on the date she alleged she discovered the actual nature of her relationship with her foster parents. Rather, Teater's cause of action accrued on the date of the discovery of her injuries. (p. 761)

A relatively recent area of emphasis in personal injury claims is the introduction of claims of sexual harassment in both tort and eligibility claim actions. Sexual harassment claims have appeared with increasing frequency as stand-alone claims or as simultaneous actions in tort and eligibility claims (see, *Underwood v. NCUA*, 1995; *Neal v. Director, D. C. Department of Corrections*, 1996; *Nichols v. American Nat'l. Ins.*, 1999).

An overview of the complex problems faced by the courts in adjudicating sexual harassment complaints was offered in the appeals case, *Underwood v. NCUA* (1995). *Underwood* was a complicated matter, originally beginning as a workers' compensation claim, and evolving into a tort action that was appealed. The matter involved Underwood's employment with a credit union, and a sexual liaison between Underwood and the plaintiff, who was a supervisor. Subsequently, Underwood filed claims of physical injury, emotional distress, and a claim of sexual harassment. The case was complicated further by the fact that, in the midst of the original proceedings, the credit union went into liquidation. Receivership was assumed by NCUA, the defendant in the immediate appeal action. In its decision the court determined:

> [T]he fact that appellant's common tort claim for emotional distress is premised on the same events that underlie her Human Rights Act claim for sexual harassment profoundly affects the analysis. As a result, her alleged disability "clearly" falls outside the WCA [Workers' Compensation Act] definition of disabling injuries as a matter of law, and appellant is thus free to file suit for emotional distress in Superior Court rather than submitting that claim to DOES [Department of Employees Services]. (p. 626)

In its decision, the court also left "for another day" several issues inherent, but not immediately actionable, in *Underwood*. These other issues included the situation where a claim of emotional distress is grounded only in part on sexual harassment, and also the situation in which one co-worker inflicts sexual harassment and another co-worker inflicts separate, but simultaneous, harassment of another kind. The *Underwood* matter demonstrates the potential judicial complexities of a civil claim, and serves to alert the forensic clinician of how convoluted such matters can be in terms of deception. A litigant, for example, may begin with a bona fide, work-related physical health problem, but end up malingering the severity of those symptoms, and also be induced to malinger or exaggerate psychological symptoms, as well as claim sexual harassment, or any combination thereof.

Numerous tort cases have emerged reflecting the court's dependence on testimony from mental health experts regarding claims of psychological damage/trauma, but then being overwhelmed and confused by apparently divergent and contradictory expert opinions (see *Lowery v. Miller, Van Rybroek, Maier, & Roach*, 1990). One working factor in this situation may not so much be the disparate views of mental health experts, as opposed to attorneys using the adversarial process to polarize what in an actual clinical setting may be working opinions regarding diagnosis, personality dynamics, and treatment needs. Yet another major change in civil litigation was introduced by *Daubert v. Merrell Dow Pharmaceuticals, Inc.*, (1993). In *Daubert*, the U.S. Supreme Court gave trial judges a "gate-keeping" function to decide whether or not scientific expert testimony was sufficiently reliable to be admissible. The trial judges are empowered with wide discretion to make this determination. In *Nichols v. American Nat'l. Ins.* (1999), the appeals court cited *Daubert* and ruled inadmissible the testimony of an expert witness psychiatrist. The court stated that the psychiatrist's testimony regarding the claimant's "psychiatric credibility" based on "theories" of recall bias, secondary gain, and malingering did not meet the *Daubert* criteria for having a scientific basis. The court also noted that, moreover, the issue of the claimant's credibility was exclusively the purview of the jury anyway.

Table 10.1 lists numerous judicial principles, which have continued to emerge in civil case law over the years. An inspection of this table reveals that considerable conceptual latitude is shown toward the plaintiff when he or she is attempting to recover for nonverifiable (i.e., mental) states.

ELIGIBILITY CLAIMS

Eligibility claims require evidence that the claimant satisfies current criteria for admission to special government programs developed to assist eligible persons. These programs differ from entitlement programs, since the applicant must prove that special eligibility criteria are satisfied. There does not have to be a total disability for compensation to be awarded. The largest eligibility programs include the Social Security Supplemental Income (SSI) Program, the Social Security Disability Insurance (SSDI) Program, Workers' Compensation Programs, and Veterans Administration Disability Assistance Programs.

SSDI provides cash assistance to currently disabled workers, and their dependents, who have contributed to social security taxes according to a statutorily set minimum work period. SSI provides a minimum income to the needy disabled (regardless of whether or not they paid social security taxes in the past). Both programs require proof that the applicant has a medically determinable impairment that interferes with the ability to engage in substantial gainful work and that can be expected to last for at least 12 months (Social Security Administration, 1986). Each state's Disability Determination Service makes original decisions regarding eligibility. Adverse decisions are appealable to the federal court system.

Some, but not all, mental disorders are considered impairments for purposes of determining eligibility for these Social Security programs. Organic mental disorders, schizophrenia, paranoia, and other psychotic disorders, affective disorders, mental retardation and autism, anxiety-related disorders, somatoform disorders, personality disorders, and substance addiction disorders are eligible disorders in adults. Chronic brain syndrome, psychosis of infancy and childhood, functional nonpsychotic disorders, and mental retardation are eligible disorders in children. However, the criteria used to define these categories are not necessarily the same as those in related categories of the DSM-IV. Griffin et al. (1996) estimated one fifth of Social Security disability claims to be compromised by malingering.

Workers' compensation programs provide compensation or insurance for injuries arising in the course and scope of employment, regardless of whether the injury was due to the negligence or

TABLE 10.1
Personal Injury Litigation

Principle	Representative Case
Recovery of damages possible for mental or emotional injuries if linked to compensable physical trauma	*Sinn v. Byrd* (1979)
Physical trauma frequently causes emotional sequelae	*Murphy v. Penn Fruit Co.* (1980)
Physical trauma frequently causes associated residual pain	*Tramutola v. Bortine* (1973)
Expert testimony required if physical trauma or associated psychological injuries are not a matter of common knowledge	*Foley v. Kibrick* (1981)
Expert psychiatric/psychologic testimony required establishing link between physical injury and schizophrenia	*Pagan v. Dewitt P. Henry Co.* (1976)
Expert psychiatric/psychologic testimony required establishing link between physical injury and psychoneurosis	*Hess v. Philadelphia Transp. Co.* (1948)
Expert testimony not required for pain and suffering	*Jones v. Miller* (1972)
Successful cases depend on requirement of reasonable medical certainty	*Bell v. New York City Health & Hosp. Corp.* (1982)
Psychologists can relate pain to organic cause if malingering ruled out	*Buckler v. Sinclair Ref. Co.* (1966)
Recovery for psychological injuries in absence of physical injury possible if intentionally inflicted	*Nickerson v. Hodges* (1920)
Recovery for psychological injuries in absence of physical traumata possible if another party injured or died	*Landreth v. Reed* (1978)
Recovery for psychological injuries in absence of physical traumata possible if injured party in "zone of risk"	*Tobin v. Grossman* (1969)
Neuropsychologist can testify to organic basis of cognitive deficits caused by exposure to toxic chemicals	*Morris v. Chandler Exterminators* (1991)
Expert witness testimony inadmissible because it did not meet current scientific standard (i.e., *Daubert*), and because it addressed conclusion (claimant credibility) that is exclusive function of jury	*Nichols v. American Nat'l. Ins.* (1998)
Plaintiff or defendant may use videotaped expert witness deposition made by either side	*Ross v. Hobbs* (1998)

intentional fault of the employer. The amount of compensation is set by a fixed schedule according to the degree of loss. Youngjohn (1991) estimated that malingering might compromise as many as one half of all workers' compensation cases.

Federal employees are covered under the Federal Employees Compensation Act; seaman are covered by the federal Jones Act; longshoremen are covered by the federal Longshoremen's and Harbor Workers' Compensation Act. In addition, each state has its own employee compensation program with varying coverage, rules, and compensation schedules. These local acts should be consulted for specific information on the operation of workers' compensation programs in each locale. Adverse decisions are appealable to either the federal or state court systems.

The Veterans Administration (VA) offers programs of medical and mental health treatment to honorably discharged veterans on a priority basis (Campbell & Tueth, 1997). The availability of these services depends on current VA resources; eligibility depends on one's status at the time of discharge, and whether the disorder is "service-connected." In addition, the VA administers a program of monetary payments to veterans (and their dependents) who are totally or partially disabled by a service-connected disability. Regional Offices of Jurisdiction, whose decisions are appealable to the Board of Veterans Appeals, determine eligibility for disability payments and the degree of disability. Decisions of the Board of Veterans Appeals are appealable to the U.S. Court of Veterans Appeals.

All of these types of eligibility claims are vexed with problems of malingering (Beal, 1989; Braverman, 1978; Hall, 1990; Hall & Hall, 1991; Lipman, 1962; Rickarby, 1979; Wasyliw & Cavanaugh, 1989; Williams, Lees-Haley, & Djanogly, 1999). For example, the U.S. Department of Veterans Affairs, *Physician's Guide for Disability Evaluations*, 1985 Ch. 1, Sec. II, Para. 1.14, 1.16 and 13.6(f), 13.6(g) (1985), 1B11-56, states as follows:

> Physicians encounter some veterans or other claimants who are not capable of reliably participating in examinations because they are too ill physically or mentally to provide an accurate report of current symptoms or current level of functioning. Some veterans may exaggerate their disabilities, while others, particularly older veterans, may deny or be unrealistic in reporting the extent of their disablement.

A selection of cases and holdings for Social Security and Workers' Compensation determinations is presented in Tables 10.2 and 10.3.

Generally, the claimant in administrative hearings is given much leeway in demonstrating disability. Although malingering per se is not grounds for denial of eligibility, it may likely be a contentious element in many claims. In *Board of Trustees of Fire and Police Employees Retirement System of City of Baltimore v. Ches* (1982), a police officer claimant was held to be disabled from an August 1, 1977 rear-end accident in his police car despite medical testimony of his malingering (pretending to be ill or injured to avoid work). In *Transit Authority of River City v. Vinson* (1985), collateral evidence of social security disability and insurance benefits paid to a plaintiff after an accident was excluded where the court felt that the jury would be misled by evidence of malingering. In *Cockrell v. U.S.* (1934), the plaintiff's deliberate failure to obtain work to avoid discontinuance of a VA disability was admissible as evidence of malingering and in Board of Veterans Appeals (BVA) decision of March 17, 1978, Docket No. 77-36-991, feigned reactive depression was admissible evidence in a VA case. The essential feature of most eligibility programs is the adversarial nature of the disability determination evaluation. Claimants are presumed to be ineligible for services unless they can prove that their injury/disability satisfies current eligibility criteria.

TARGETS

Any deficit may be faked in the civil claims of psychological damage. Some types of traumas are more common sources of claims than others. As one example, mild head trauma is one of the most prevalent targets of civil claims (Binder, Rohling, & Larrabee, 1997). Although monetary compensation may be the prime motive for civil litigation, case law, behavioral science research, and the authors' clinical experience suggest other motives. One such incentive is the preservation of self-esteem in the face of the possible loss of major supports in life work and physical/mental health. Loss of function is generally associated with diminution in self-esteem. This triggers a search to rectify the situation or to at least place the disability in a different and less-threatening perspective. For many cases of malingering, unintentional distortion may occur.

Lees-Haley (1988, p. 196) described these nondeliberate factors in civil claims in terms of the following progression: (1) a physical or psychological trauma occurs; (2) this trauma causes genuine transient effects such as pain, anxiety, and depression; and (3) the patient develops a combination of reactions during treatment, including (a) hysterical reactions to real and imagined problems, (b) hypochondriacal reactions to real and imagined problems, (c) genuine side effects of prescribed medications, (d) hysterical and hypochondriacal reactions to the side effects, and (e) secondary gain. Throughout this process, the patient learns the "language" of stress disorder claims through interactions with attorneys, relatives, friends, health care providers, and others, including popular

TABLE 10.2
Social Security Disability

Principle	Representative Case
Ultimate test for compensation is whether claimant unable to engage in substantial gainful activity	*Lewis v. Weinberger* (1976)
Inability to work must be supported by objective clinical evidence; claimant's statements alone are insufficient	*Underwood v. Ribicoff* (1962)
Objective criteria for mental disorders exist infrequently	*Branham v. Gardner* (1967)
As a general rule, more weight should be given to opinion of treating clinicians than nontreating clinicians	*Wiggins v. Schweiker* (1982); *Morgan v. Commissioner SSA,* (1999)
Opinions by mental/health treatment providers, which reach disability standard, require substantial opposition data in order to deny claim	*Aubeuf v. Schweiker* (1981)
Weight accorded psychiatric opinion a function of database utilized	*Richardson v. Perales* (1971)
Administrative hearings to appeal adverse determination are not adversarial, with SSA not represented	*Ware v. Schweiker* (1982)
Expert psychologist opinion cannot be dismissed merely because it is contradicted by another doctor; it may be rejected only for "clear and convincing" reasons	*Baxter v. Sullivan* (1991); *Lester v. Chater* (1995)
Against purpose of SSA to deny benefits because of inability to obtain appropriate treatment	*Gordon v. Schweiker* (1984)
Expert opinion based on claimant's subjective report of symptoms can be disregarded if complaints have been properly discounted	*Brawner v. Secretary of Health and Human Servs.* (1988)
Administrative Law Judge (ALJ) has the responsibility to resolve conflicts and ambiguities between expert witness testimonies	*Magallanes v. Bowen* (1988)
Nonexamining expert opinion with "nothing more" does not constitute substantial evidence	*Pitzer v. Sullivan* (1990)
Expert psychologist testimony rejected because of suspect psychological test results due to claimant's alcohol ingestion prior to testing	*Andrews v. Shalala* (1995)
Credibility determinations are the province of the ALJ and must be based on substantial evidence	*Diaz v. Secretary of Health and Human Servs.* (1995)
ALJ erred in relying on testimony from an expert elicited by incomplete, hypothetical questioning as opposed to objective medical evidence	*Kepler v. Chater* (1995)
Treating or examining expert testimony cannot be rejected based on nontreating, nonexamining expert's testimony	*Roberts v. Shalala* (1995)
ALJ accepted "independent" expert testimony over treating clinician, whose testimony was untrustworthy because it varied from his treatment notes, was worded ambiguously, and was written in apparent attempt only to assist claimant in obtaining social security benefits	*Salee v. Chater* (1995)
ALJ appropriately rejected testimony of treating psychiatrist and examining psychologist based on substantial evidence	*Morgan v. Commissioner SSA* (1999)
Opposing psychologist expert witness testimony not contradictory, each report written in response to different questions; both opinions essentially supporting plaintiff's claims	*Regennitter v. Commissioner of the SSA* (1999)

TABLE 10.3
Workers' Compensation

Principle	Representative Case
Conversion reactions with unknown physical etiology recoverable	*American Smelting & Ref. Co. v. Industrial Commn* (1942)
No difference seen between physical and psychological injury if the result is disability	*Carter v. General Motors* (1960)
Recovery possible for psychological injuries in absence of physical trauma if another insurance party injured or died	*Bailey v. American General Insurance Co.* (1955)
Recovery for psychological injuries possible if another party committed suicide	*Wolfe v. Sibley, Lindsay & Curr & Co.* (1975)
Malingering is not compensable	*Swift & Co. v. Ware* (1936)
PTSD is compensable if related to relevant injury	*Allis Chalmers Mfg. Co. v. Industrial Commn.* (1974)
Expert testimony necessary to link mental diagnoses to injury claimed	*Andrus v. Rimmer & Garrett, Inc.* (1975)
Direct examination of claimant of mental injury by psychiatrist or psychologist required as a minimum	*Texas Employers Assn. v. Thames* (1951)
Rules of evidence are generally more relaxed	*Thom v. Callahan* (1975)
Requirement of reasonable medical certainty not necessary with opinions expressed in terms of probability	*Schope v. Red Owl Stores, Inc.* (1982)
In reference to claimant adhering to statute of limitations, medical reports alone, referring to possible psychiatric conditions, do not indicate that claimant is aware of such conditions	*McCurdy v. Mihm* (1993)
Earlier court erred when it did not resolve conflicting testimony between evaluating psychologist and treating psychiatrist, regarding whether or not claimant could understand he had a psychiatric problem	*Tatum v. Buckeye Steel Castings Co.* (1996)
A compensation claimant cannot transform employer delay of payments into an actionable tort alleging intentional infliction of emotional distress	*Montes De Oca v. Orkin Exterminating Co.* (1997)
No damages if court determines that employee knowingly or intentionally made false, misleading, or incomplete statements to secure workers' compensation benefits	*Painting v. Lessard* (1997)
Claim cannot be denied because claimant delayed seeking treatment for a personal injury because of a lack of insurance and lack of ability to pay	*Ramey v. Winn Dixie Montgomery, Inc.* (1998)
Employer/Carrier can conduct ex parte conference with health care providers, but not with expert medical advisor(s)	*Pierre v. Handi Van Inc., & Humana Workers' Compensation Services* (1998)
Employer not required to pay for treatment not authorized, or nonemergency, but ordered to pay for all psychological treatment after date claimant requested authorization for it	*Mayo Clinic and Johns Eastern Insurance Co. v. Tomblin* (1998)
Absenteeism may be misconduct and justify discharge, but not sufficient to deny unemployment benefits	*Roberts v. Diehl & Florida Unemployment Appeals Commission* (1998)
Appeals court permits maintenance of a sexual harassment suit independent of a separate workers' compensation claim	*Moniz v. Reitano* (1999)
Word "physician" in workers' compensation legislation encompasses Ph.D. clinical psychologists, but not as an independent medical examiner (IME); testimony of psychologist who conducted an IME and declared claimant to be malingering is inadmissible; testimony of second psychologist who did not conduct an IME is admissible, but should carry less weight than that of treating physician	*Ebi/Orion Group v. Blythe* (1998)

magazines. This knowledge influences the patient's view of symptoms and interpretations of other, irrelevant experiences.

Thus, fakers who are wholly conscious of their deception and who target specific symptoms for deception may be in the minority. Malingering associated with real conditions, representing an exaggeration rather than a fabrication, may represent the norm. Keep in mind that disability may be represented for different periods of time (e.g., for the time of an evaluation, for the past or future), adding to the difficulty of assessing disability claims.

RESPONSE STYLES

In a typology of deceivers within an industrial injury context, Braverman (1978) described several styles of malingering:

1. *"True," deliberate, or fraudulent malingerer.* This comprised less than 1% of Braverman's 2500 clients. Detection was simple as they were all persons with (a) gross psychopathology, (b) no binding ties within a migratory pattern, (c) intolerance for long diagnostic testing, and (d) a quick termination of the case once confronted with the possibility of malingering and (e) they were all men age 25 to 37.
2. *Cover-up or decoy malingerer.* Here the faker experienced real trauma (most likely to the head). The compensable disease, such as cancer, is misattributed to the genuine injury. Fear of death and a family history of the disease emerged as central dynamics. About 3% of Braverman's sample is accounted for by this type of deception.
3. *The hysterical malingerer.* Comprising about 31% of the patients and the largest proportion of the sample, malingering in this type stems from a hysteric process culminating in loss of hope and victim distress. Braverman stated:

   > By "hysteric malingering" reference is made to a condition which emerges following objective or threatened injury after the affected person (a) loses all hope of recovery to pre injury status; (b) begins to perceive himself with a new identification, namely, as "the injured," in which development of the "part" (injured) becomes more important than the "whole" (the intact residual). Reaction to the injured "part" may pervade the "intact residual"; and (c) becomes aware that his very sustenance is to be determined no longer by his previous capacity to work (now lost), but by the obligation the effects of his injury and incapacity impose upon society. (p. 38)

4. *The psychotic malingerer.* Comprising about 2% of the sample, this type usually has paranoid and bizarre features to his or her disability.
5. *The organic malingerer.* Composed largely of patients with Korsakoff syndrome and consisting of 2% of the sample, this type invents pathology due to the organic condition. Associated features included hypersuggestibility, shifting of symptoms, and uncertainty about the symptoms.

Braverman makes the valid point that work-related malingering is seldom planned in advance and is usually concocted after genuine injury and attendant loss of face occur. In anticipation of fluctuating response styles, he stated that malingering, like most other defenses to loss of face, waxes and wanes in accordance with environmental stimuli. Overall, as the above percentages suggest, he found that about one third of his 2500 clients engaged in psychotraumatic malingering.

Four types of response styles have been described by Lipman (1962):

1. Invention — The patient has no symptoms, but fraudulently represents that he has.
2. Perseveration — Genuine symptoms formerly present have ceased, but are fraudulently alleged to continue.

3. Exaggeration — Genuine symptoms are present, but the patient fraudulently makes these out to be worse than they are.

4. Transference — Genuine symptoms are fraudulently attributed to a cause other than the actual cause in fact. (p. 143)

In general, the response styles delineated by investigators describe one or more of the classic types propounded in this book. Applied to civil situations, these are as follows:

1. *Honesty*. Attempts to be accurate within one's perceptions. Here, deficits are portrayed as they are seen, even though nonintentional distortion, such as caused by stress, may be operative to a considerable degree.

2. *Faking bad*. Exaggeration or fabrication of symptoms and behaviors, or denial/minimization takes place to look worse than one is. Exaggerated back injuries, common and difficult to disprove, are placed into this category.

3. *Faking good*. Minimization or denial of symptoms and behaviors or exaggeration/fabrication of symptoms to look good. The claimant may try to hide the fact that illicit substances contributed to an auto accident or that safety equipment was not operative.

4. *Invalidation*. Attempts to render the evaluation meaningless (e.g., irrelevant, random responding). The claimant may feign cooperation with the retained expert but not report for appointments with the opposition expert.

5. *Mixed responding*. Combination of above within same evaluation period. The claimant may exaggerate back injury but deny alcohol problems.

6. *Fluctuating*. Change of response styles between or within evaluation periods. The claimant may start off honestly in order to become familiar with testing procedures, then switch to mixed responding, then to random responding as tiredness sets in.

DETECTION METHODS

Lees-Haley (1990, 1991a, b) has proposed several existing (Ego Strength) or new (Fake Bad, Credibility) scales from the Minnesota Multiphasic Personality Inventory item pool for use with civil litigants. However, these scales have not been widely used or cross-validated. In another study, Lees-Haley (1997) assessed the accuracy of MMPI-2 base rate variables for distinguishing malingering with personal injury plaintiffs. Drawing upon a large sample of 492 subjects, possible malingering was indicated in 20 to 30% of the sample based on the studied MMPI-2 validity measures (L, F, K, F minus K, Ds-r, Fake Bad, Ego Strength, Back F, Total Obvious minus Subtle, VRIN, and TRIN). The author described contaminating variables of coaching by attorneys and congruence between personality styles and the expected demands by plaintiffs of personal injury litigation.

Boccaccini and Brodsky (1999) reported a survey among 80 concurrent members of American Psychological Association Divisions 12 and 41. The psychologists were asked to describe psychodiagnostic instruments used in emotional injury assessments. The study found that test selection and the reasons for test selection were highly variable. The authors concluded that psychological experts need to select tests more carefully and to keep the *Daubert* criteria (i.e., *Daubert v. Merrell Dow Pharmaceuticals*, 1993) in mind.

In general, a large database is suggested for the detection of both intentional and unintentional distortion among civil litigants. One important database source is base rate information regarding specific complaints. Lees-Haley and Brown (1993), for example, described base rate data for neuropsychological complaints. The database should include information regarding the pretrauma psychological status of the plaintiff(s). It is also important to consider pretrauma risk factors known to predispose and/or exacerbate, post-trauma events. The FDA model suggests that any combination of methods — interviewing, testing, observation, base rate comparison — can be utilized. The next three chapters on faked brain damage, pain, and post-trauma reactions review techniques that may be used in the detection of deception in civil cases.

LEGAL REFERENCES

Allis Chalmers Mfg. Co. v. Industrial Commn., 57 Ill.2d 257, 31N.E.2d 280 (1974).

American Smelting & Ref. Co. v. Industrial Commn., 59 Ariz. 87,23 P.2d 163 (1942).

Andrews v. Shalala, 53 F.3rd 1035 (9th Cir. 1995).

Andrus v. Rimmer & Garrett, Inc., 316 So.2d 433 (La.Ct.App.1975).

Aubeuf v. Schweiker, 649 F.2d 107 (2nd Cir. 1981).

Bailey v. American General Insurance Co., 154 Tex. 430, 279 S.W.2d 315 (1955).

Baxter v. Sullivan, 923 F.2nd 1391, 1396 (9th Cir. 1991).

Bell v. New York City Health & Hosp. Corp., 104 N.E.2nd 872, 456 NYS2d 787 (1982).

Board of Trustees of Fire and Police Employees Retirement System of City of Baltimore v. Ches, 294 Md. 668, 452 A.2d 422 (Md. 1982).

Board of Veterans Appeals Decision March 17, 1978, Docket No. 77 991.

Branham v. Gardner, 383 F.2d 614 (6th Cir. 1967).

Brawner v. Secretary of Health and Human Servs. 839 F.2nd 432, 433-34 (9th Cir. 1988).

Buckler v. Sinclair Ref. Co., 68 Ill.App. 2d 283 216 N.E.2d 14 (1966).

Byerley and Byerley v. Citrus Publishing, Inc., 24 FLW D262 (1999).

Carter v. General Motors, 361 Mich. 577, 106 N.W.2d 105 (1960).

Cockrell v. U.S., 74 F.2d 151 (8th Cir. 1934).

Daubert v. Merrell Dow Pharmaceuticals 125 L. Ed.2d 469, 113 (S. Ct. 2786, 1993).

Diaz v. Secretary of Health and Human Services, 898 F.2d 774, 777 (10th Cir. 1995).

Ebi/Orion Group v. Blythe, 1998 Mont. 90 (Sup.ct. Mont. 1998).

Eichel v. New York Cent. R. R. Co., 375 U.S. 253 (U.S. Supreme Court 1963) (per curium).

Federal Rules of Evidence, 709 F.2nd 741.

Foley v. Kibrick, 12 Mass.App.Ct. 382, 425 N.E.2d 376 (1981).

Freeman v. Bandlow, 143 So.2d 547 (2d DCA Fla. 1962).

Gordon v. Schweiker, 725 F.2nd 231, 237 (4th Cir. 1988).

Hess v. Philadelphia Transp. Co., 358 Pa. 144, 56 A.2d 89 (1948).

Jones v. Miller, 290 A.2d 587 (D.C. 1972).

Kepler v. Chater. 68 F.3rd 387 (10th Cir. 1995).

King Mining Co. v. Mullins, 252 S.W.2d 871 (Ky App. 1952).

Landreth v. Reed, 570 S.W.2d 486 (Tex. Civ. App. 1976).

Lester v. Chater, 81F.3d 821, 835 (1995).

Lewis v. Weinberger, 541 F.2d 417, 420 (4th Cir. 1976).

Lowery v. Miller, Van Rybroek, Maier, & Roach, Lexis 677 (Court of Appeals, District Four 26 Jul, 1990).

Magallanes v. Bowen, 881 F.2nd 747, 751 (9th Cir. 1988).

Mayo Clinic and Johns Eastern Insurance Co. v. Tomblin, 23 FLWD1728 (1st DCA, 1998).

McCurdy v. Mihm, 363, 369, 624 N.E.2d 760 (Ohio App. 3d. 1993).

McGrath v. Conrail, No. 97-1063, 97-1064, 1998. Available at http://www.law.emory.edu/pub-cgi/p 2/12/1998, No. 97-1063 (U.S. Court of Appeals for the First Circuit Decided 12 February, 1998).

McGrath v. Consolidated Rail Corporation, 943 F. Supp. 95 (D. Mass. 1996), No. 97-1063, 1998, available at http://www.law.emory.edu/pub-cgi/p (District of New Hampshire/Eleventh Circuit aff'd, 1996/1998).

Metropolitan Dade County v. Reyes, et al., 21 FLW (Florida/Florida Supreme Court 19/December, 1996).

Miller v. United States Fidelity and Guaranty Co., 99 So.2d 511, 516 (La. App. 1957).

Moniz v. Reitano, 1999 Fla. App. Lexis 8051 (4th Cir. 1999).

Montes De Oca v. Orkin Exterminationg Co., 692 So. 2nd 257 (Fla. 3d DCA). Rev. denied, 699 So. 2d 1374 (Fla. 1997).

Morgan v. Commissioner SSA, 169 F.3d 595 (9th Cir. 1999).

Morris v. Chandler Exterminators, 409 S.E. Ed. 677 (Ga. Ct. App.) (1991).

Murphy v. Penn Fruit Co., 274 Pa. Super. 427, 418 A.2d 480 (1980).

Neal v. Director, D.C. Department of Corrections, U.S. Dist. Lexis 8874, (1996).

Nichols v. American Nat'l. Ins., 154 F3d. 875 8th Cir. (1999).

Nickerson v. Hodges, 146 La. 735, 84 So. 37 (1920).

Pagan v. Dewitt P. Henry Co., 27 Pa.Commw. 495, 365 A.2d 46 (1976).

Painting v. Lessard, 688 So. 2d 941 (Fla. 1st DCA 1997).

Pierre v. Handi Van Inc., & Humana Workers' Compensation Services, 23 FLWD2244 (1st DCA 1998).

Pitzer v. Sullivan, 908 F.2nd 502, 506n. (9th Cir. 1995).

Quint v. A.E. Staley Mfg. Co., No. 98-1300 (1st Cir. 3/15, 1999).

Ramey v. Winn Dixie Montgomery, Inc., 23 FLWD1111 (Fla. 1st 1998).

Regennitter v. Commissioner of SSA, Fed. R. App. P. 34(2)i 34 (9th Cir. R. 24/February, 1999) (Filed)

Richardson v. Perales, 402 U.S. 389, 407 (1971).

Roberts v. Diehl & Florida Unemployment Appeals Commission, 23 FLWD633 (Fla. 2nd DCA 1998).

Roberts v. Shalala, 66 F.3rd 179 (9th Cir. 1995).

Ross v. Hobbs, 23 FLW (Fla. 2nd DCA 1998).

Salee v. Chater, 83 F.3rd 322 (9th Cir. 1995).

Savoie v. Otto Candies, Inc., 692 F.2nd 363,371 (5th Cir. 1982).

Schope v. Red Owl Stores, Inc., 323 N.W.2d 801 (Minn. 1982).

Sinn v. Byrd, 486 Pa. 146, 404 A.2d 672 (1979).

Sutcliffe v. E. I. Dupont De Nemours & Co., 36 So.2d 874, 877 (La. App. 1948).

Swift & Co. v. Ware, 53 Ga.App. 500, 186 S.E. 452 (1936).

Tatum v. Buckeye Steel Castings Co., 1996 Ohio App. Lexis 2137 (10th Cir. 1996).

Teater v. State of Nebraska, 559 N.W.2nd 758 Lexis 70 (Neb./Supreme Court of Nebraska 1997).

Texas Employers Assn. v. Thames, 236 S.W.2d 203 (Tex. Civ. App. Ft. Worth 1951).

Thom v. Callahan, 97 Idaho 151 540 P.2d 1330 (1975).

Tobin v. Grossman, 24 N.Y.2d 609, 249 N.E.2d 419, 301 NYS2d 554 (1969).

Tramutola v. Bortine, 63 NJ 9, 304 A.2d 197 (1973).

Transit Authority of River City v. Vinson, 703 S.W.2d 482 (Ky. App. 1985).

Underwood v. NCUA, 665 A.2nd 621 (District of Columbia Court of Appeals 31 August, 1995) (No. 92-CV-840, No. 92-CV-936).

Underwood v. Ribicoff, 298 F.2d 850, 851 (4th Cir. 1962).

Ware v. Schweiker, 651 F.2d 408 (5th Cir. 1981), cert. denied, 455 U.S. 912 (1982).

Wiggins v. Schweiker, 679 F.2d 1387 (11th Cir. 1982).

Wolfe v. Sibley, Linday & Curr & Co., 36 N.Y. 505, 330 N.E.2d 603, 369 NYS 2d 637 (1975).

REFERENCES

Beal, D. (1989). Assessment of malingering in personal injury cases. *American Journal of Forensic Psychology, 7*(4), 59–65.

Binder, L. M., Rohling, M. L., & Larrabee, G. J. (1997). A review of mild head trauma. Part I: Meta-analytic review of neuropsychological studies. *Journal of Clinical and Experimental Neuropsychology, 19*, 421–431.

Boccaccini, M. T., & Brodsky, S. L. (1999). Diagnostic test usage by forensic psychologist in emotional injury cases. *Professional Psychology, 30*, 253–259.

Braverman, M. (1978). Post injury malingering is seldom a calculated ploy. *Occupational Health and Safety, 47*(2), 36–48.

Campbell, W., & Tueth, M. J. (1997). Misplaced rewards: Veterans Administration System and symptom magnification. *Clinical Orthopaedics and Related Research, 336*, 42–46.

DeFrances, C., Smith, S., Langan, P. A., Ostrom, B. J., Rottman, D. B., & Goerdt, J. A. (1995). *Civil jury case and verdicts in large counties* (Tech. Rep. No. NCJ-154346). Washington, DC: U.S. Department of Justice, Office of Justice Programs.

Griffin, G. A. E., Normington, J., May, R., & Glassmire, D. (1996). Assessing dissimulation among Social Security disability income claimants. *Journal of Consulting and Clinical Psychology, 64*, 1425–1430.

Hall, F. L., III. (1990). Materials on law of malingering. Unpublished manuscript.

Hall, F. L., III, & Hall, H. V. (1991). The law and psychology of malingering. Unpublished manuscript.

Lees-Haley, P. R. (1985). Psychological malingerers: How to detect them. *Trial, 21*, 68.

Lees-Haley, P. R. (1988). Unintentionally fraudulent claims for stress disorders. *Defense Counsel Journal, 55*, 194–197.

Lees-Haley, P R. (1990). Provisional normative data for a credibility scale for assessing personal injury claimants. *Psychological Reports, 66*, 3, 1355–1360.

Lees-Haley, P. R. (1991a). A fake bad scale on the MMPI-2 for personal injury claimants. *Psychological Reports, 68*, 1, 203–210.

Lees-Haley, P. R. (1991b). Ego strength denial on the MMPI-2 as a clue to simulation of personal injury in vocational neuropsychological and emotional distress. *Perceptual and Motor Skills, 72*, 3, 815–819.

Lees-Haley, P. R. (1997). MMPI-2 base rates for 492 personal injury plaintiffs: Implications and challenges for forensic assessment. *Journal of Clinical Psychology, 53*(7), 745–755.

Lees-Haley, P. R., & Brown, R. S. (1993). Neuropsychological complaint base rates of 170 personal injury claimants. *Archives of Clinical Neuropsychology, 8*, 203–209.

Lees-Haley, P. R., Williams, C. W., & English, L. T. (1996). Response bias in self-reporting history of plaintiffs compared with nonlitigating patients. *Psychological Reports, 79*, 811–818.

Lipman, F. D. (1962). Malingering in personal injury cases. *Temple Law Quarterly, 35*(2), 141–162.

Litras, M. F. X., & DeFrances, C. J. (1999). *Federal Tort Trials and Verdicts*, 1996–97 (Tech. Rep. No. NCJ 172855). Washington, DC: U.S. Department of Justice, Office of Justice Programs.

Press, A. H., & DeFrances, C. J. (1997). *Federal Tort Trials and Verdicts*, 1994–1995 (Tech. Rep. No. NCJ-165810). Washington, DC: U.S. Department of Justice, Office of Justice Programs.

Rickarby, G. A. (1979). Compensation neurosis and the psychosocial requirements of the family. *British Journal of Medical Psychology, 52*, 333–338.

Social Security Administration (1986). *Disability evaluation under Social Security*. Social Security Administration Publication No. 64-039.

U.S. Dept. of Veterans Affairs. (1985). *Physician's guide for disability evaluations* (1B11 56).

Wasyliw, O. E., & Cavanaugh, J. L., Jr. (1989). Simulation of brain damage: Assessment and decision rules. *Bulletin of the American Academy of Psychiatry & Law, 17*(4), 37–73.

Weissman, H. (1990). Distortions and deceptions in self-presentation: Effects of protracted litigation on personal injury cases. *Behavioral Sciences and the Law, 8*, 67–74.

Williams, C., Lees-Haley, P., & Djanogly, S. (1999). Clinical scrutiny of litigants' self-reports. *Professional Psychology: Research and Practice, 30*(4), 361–367.

Youngjohn, J. R. (1991). Malingering of neuropsychological impairment: An assessment strategy. *Journal for the Expert Witness, the Trial Attorney, and the Trial Judge, 4*, 29–32.

11 Malingered Neuropsychological Deficits

The assessment of malingered traumatic brain injury (TBI) is difficult for several reasons. To begin with, in spite of considerable research, there is little support for any type of "malingering profile" on neuropsychological tests (Franzen, Iverson, & McCracken, 1990; Heubrock & Peterman, 1998). Actual malingerers rarely acknowledge their deception, and, therefore, it is difficult to identify real-life malingerers for empirical comparison (Greiffenstein, Baker, & Gola, 1994). An additional complication is that many TBI situations are involved in criminal and/or civil litigation (Hart, 1995; Miller, 1998). For these reasons, clinicians must creatively rely on indirect measures of malingered TBI. Apparent inconsistencies, misrepresentations, and poor performance on neuropsychological instruments should always raise the suspicion of malingering (Franzen et al., 1990; Hart, 1995).

Neuropsychological symptoms are inherently subtle, especially when there are no observable physiological symptoms that accompany claimed psychological symptoms. Symptoms involving cognitive and memory deficits are good examples of the problem. Both cognitive (Sherman, Strauss, Spellacy, & Hunter, 1995) and memory (Mittenberg, Azrin, Millsaps, & Heilbronner, 1994) deficits can be malingered very effectively particularly when the malingerer has known someone with actual symptoms and/or when the malingerer makes the effort to educate him or herself about a syndrome.

One of the most functionally disabling consequences of brain injury, especially to significant others, is emotional changes and other noncognitive symptoms (Lezak, 1989; Youngjohn, Davis, & Wolf, 1997). Noncognitive sequelae (e.g., affect, activity-level, aggravation, frustration, hesitation, poor cooperation, and self-awareness) have long been recognized as consequences of TBI, but only recently have come under the serious scrutiny of neuropsychologists (Iverson, 1995; Satz et al., 1996).

Traditional individual neuropsychological measures have not been very useful in accurately discriminating malingerers from individuals with cerebral brain impairment (Greiffenstein, Baker, & Gola, 1994). In addition to adults, children and adolescents are also successful in mimicking cerebral dysfunction (Faust, Hart, & Guilmette, 1988a, b). It is more difficult to mimic patterns of neuropsychological dysfunction consistently and meaningfully. Neuropsychological findings must be valid in terms of patterns of neuropsychological functioning and must be consistent in terms of established patterns among neuropsychological measures. As an oversimplified example, brain trauma may impair recent memory, but leave intact long-term memory. Two or more tests of recent memory, however, should reflect similar findings.

All neuropsychological test measures are multidimensional and equivocally reflect isolated behaviors (Sherman et al., 1995). Recent research has been directed at investigating such patterns between and across modalities (Iverson & Franzen, 1996; Larrabee, 1991; Mittenberg et al., 1994; Sherman et al., 1995). Although far from foolproof, it is knowledge of such neuropsychological patterns and relationships that can assist the clinician in the detection of malingering. The forensic neuropsychologist is a scientist, a clinician, an investigator, and, in a very real sense, a detective.

The following case example illustrates the value of the neuropsychological perspective in the assessment of malingering:

Greg Lance is a 22-year-old, single Caucasian male acquitted by reason of insanity and civilly committed to the state hospital for the attempted murder, rape, and sodomy of a female tourist. He had an extensive history of assaultive behavior and other antisocial behavior extending back to early adolescence.

Exculpation was granted in 1988 on the basis of claimed epilepsy with associated amnesia at the time of the instant offenses, although this was never substantiated by the defense or proven otherwise by the prosecution. Ward notes during hospitalization contain examples of serious prevarication in order to leave the hospital grounds, have sex with incompetent psychotic patients, and "con" money from his peers. In examining his history, significant distortion of facts by Mr. Lance appears to have occurred since at least 1988. When questioned in 1989 about previous alleged suicide gestures, he finally admitted that the only instance occurred while in custody in 1988 as a ruse to change cells. During that year, the forensic hospital social worker, during a social intake, noted: "He has been observed in animated interaction and activity with other patients, but when speaking to staff, assumes a 'depressive' attitude" (July 29, 1988). He played the role of a depressed individual to the staff over a half-year period. During that time, Dr. Smith observed that "recent MMPI findings would strongly indicate that the patient is faking the symptoms of isolation and impoverishment of emotional experience. This evidence is supported by the fact that in unguarded moments, the patient exhibits the full range of affective state" (August 18, 1988).

Other suggestions of faking bad included (1) obtaining better scores on some intellectual subtests when allegedly mentally retarded than when "normal" — his Wechsler Adult Intelligence Test IQs rose from 57 to 116 over three separate administrations, from mentally defective to bright normal in 25 months; (2) during administration of different tests during the same general time period, showing the ability to perform multiplication and other complex mathematical manipulations on one test while exhibiting the inability to do simple addition problems on another test; (3) correctly identifying words such as *kayak, descend, bereavement, appraising,* and *amphibian* while showing the inability to define simpler words such as *winter, slice, conceal,* and *enormous,* (4) exhibiting inconsistent memory skills (digits forward, digits backward) over time instead of a consistently poor performance; and (5) reversing Performance and Verbal IQs at the superior mode of functioning at different times, instead of showing improvement within the dominant factor upon retesting.

Faking cerebral dysfunction has a long and infamous history. In civil law, faking central nervous system (CNS) damage is discussed by Miller and Cartlidge (1972):

Simulation and accident neurosis following injuries to the head and the spinal cord on a large scale are really disorders of the Industrial Revolution. Attention was first directed to them in Prussia, where the introduction of a national railway system evoked the first accident insurance laws in 1871 and 1884. Within a few years professional attention was drawn to the frequency with which malingering was encountered in civilians claiming severe disablement after minor industrial injury, and to the importance of financial gain as a motive. In Britain an exactly similar situation followed the Employers Liability Act of 1880 and the Workmen's Compensation Acts of 1898 and 1906. The epidemic of functional complaints that arose as a byproduct of this socially admirable legislation attracted the attention of many of the most eminent neurologists of the period. In less sophisticated hands it led to the creation of a group of new syndromes such as railway spine, which enjoyed a remarkable vogue for a few decades, until the courts tumbled to its nature and it promptly disappeared. (p. 580)

Successfully faking CNS deficits is predicated on knowledge of the characteristics and types of brain damage. The four main categories of organic brain syndromes (OBS) (Strub & Black, 1981) are (1) the acute confusional states, (2) the dementias, (3) the focal brain syndromes, and (4) the "symptomatic functional syndromes." The latter are organically based and resemble psychopathology (e.g., schizophrenic behavior in temporal lobe epilepsy; schizophreniform syndrome in chronic LSD abuse).

Subclinical pathology is often underdiagnosed or regarded as faked (Boll, 1985; Parker, 1990). The postconcussive syndrome (PCS), for example, is commonly mistaken for "compensation neurosis" despite the cluster of symptoms that appear with regularity whether or not economic gain is realized (Binder, 1986). The cluster of PCS includes headache, labile behavior, concentration problems, sleep disturbances, and diffuse residential effects. Normal people under high stress may also show OBS-like symptoms. Subsequent deficits remit quickly as the stress is eliminated.

Malingering brain damage has long been recognized in criminal forensic settings, despite an unwarranted belief that neuropsychological tests could not be malingered (Hart, 1995; Heaton, Smith, Lehman, & Vogt, 1978; Ziskin & Faust, 1988). This acceptance of the nonfakability of tests used to assess brain–behavior relationships occurred at a time when neuropsychologists were being granted expert witness status (*Jenkins v. United States,* 1961; *Buckler v. Sinclair Ref. Co.*, 1966). Despite recent challenges to neuropsychologists in court, their role remains crucial to the understanding of cerebral dysfunctions in defendants.

MODELS

Few models of feigning cerebral dysfunctions have been offered. One model was provided by Freedland (1982). Freedland's model incorporated five relationships on neuropsychological test batteries that could be analyzed for patterns of faking. These relationships are:

(a) Sophistication of the subject,
(b) Events to which the subject attributes his or her apparent dysfunction,
(c) Symptoms and problems which the subject intends to fake,
(d) Strategies used in attempting to fake believable deficits without getting caught, and
(e) Perceived risks and potential benefits

According to the model, faking subjects will selectively alter performance on tests and test items perceived to measure target symptoms. Thus, tests specifically designed to assess faking (e.g., MMPI validity indices) may not correlate with subject performance on other tests in the battery.

This chapter incorporates Freedland's concepts and focuses on the model presented in Chapter 3, which scrutinizes targets of the faker, response styles employed, and the detection strategies used to uncover feigned neuropsychological dysfunctions.

TARGETS

As an illustration, an examination of the criminal–civil case at the beginning of this chapter is in order. First, Lance could have chosen a multitude of targets in the direction of his vested interest. For example, to obtain his not guilty by reason of insanity (NGRI) verdict, Lance might have chosen to excuse the perpetrated violence by a condition known to create brain insult. The range of conditions causing (blameless) violence include (Hall & McNinch, 1989): (1) acute confusional states; (2) some degenerative conditions such as Huntington's disease, Alzheimer's disease, and alcoholic dementia; (3) head trauma, PCS; (4) toxic conditions caused by drugs, alcohol, medications, and some heavy metals; (5) neoplastic disease processes of the CNS; (6) seizure disorders such as psychomotor, complex-partial, and temporal lobe epilepsy; and (7) "borderland" organic mental disorders (see Strub & Black, 1981) such as the episodic dyscontrol syndrome.

As a working hypothesis, the defendant may have deliberately selected a seizure disorder to mimic. To obtain the NGRI verdict, he then faked bad on a wide range of intellectual, achievement, and ability tests. Lance may not have known that virtually any target can be selected and that it may change over time and be combined with other conditions such as a thought disorder. Yet, pathology was seen on both neuropsychological and psychological testing. The professional attempting to understand faked OBS in a particular person must realize that targets themselves are cognitive events, which are nonverifiable in nature. Thus, for the first part of the model, the basic questions are:

"Does the individual have a motive for faking?"
"What are the most likely targets of deception?"

In the instant case, the defendant had a motive for faking and, in fact, achieved his goal of admission to the state hospital as opposed to receiving a sentence of 20 years to life in prison. He appeared to choose targets that were broadbanded, conformed in part to his history, and were unverifiable.

In a study using the Halstead–Reitan Neuropsychological Battery (HRNB) on 52 brain-impaired patients and 202 normal subjects, Goebel (1989) determined the following strategies for faking from debriefing his 141 faking subjects:

Slowing performance or looking dull or confused	36%
Giving the wrong answer	30%
Showing motor incoordination	14%
Simulating memory impairment	2%
Ignoring stimuli	2%
Changing emotional state	1.5%
Stuttering	0.5%

Deterrents to faking are also important to consider. In all of the authors' investigations on deception with subjects instructed to fake, a small but significant proportion of the sample showed no deception. About 10% of Goebel's (1989) subjects did not fake despite instructions to do so, and 92% believed they could have done a better job of faking. Reasons for not faking or for thinking they could have done better include:

Unfamiliar with and unprepared for task	60%
Got too involved to fake	30%
Presence of the examiner	21%
Tests too easy to allow faking	20%

As a final note in regard to targets, the evaluator is urged to take into account a general caution by fakers in reaching their long-term goals. Freedland (1982) noted that fakers may selectively choose symptoms (e.g., unilateral vs. bilateral deafness) to avoid detection even though more serious symptoms would merit larger compensation.

RESPONSE STYLES

The following is a generic summary of strategies that fakers, including the defendant in the instant case, may employ in attempts to feign believable deficits on neuropsychological evaluations (Craine, 1981, 1990; Hall, 1985, 1990):

1. *Present realistic symptoms.* A deceiver will employ a "commonsense" or "popular" schema of what brain-damaged persons are like and will select symptoms that accord with that "naive" view (e.g., Aubrey, Dobbs, & Rule, 1989). Although the symptoms may appear realistic from this unsophisticated point of view, the expert evaluator will (one hopes) have a more objective and detailed view of "realistic" neurological symptoms.

2. *Distribute errors.* To cover their targets, fakers tend to make a deliberate number of mistakes throughout the evaluation rather than miss only difficult items. A balance is sought between

appearing fully functional (missing too few items) and appearing too impaired (missing too many items). Fakers attempt to control their errors as much as possible, but, in practice, they fail to maintain a "realistic" percentage of errors.

3. *Protest that tasks are too difficult and/or feign confusion and frustration.* The faker may feign confusion, anger, or other emotions superimposed upon adequate cooperation and task compliance. For example, a 22-year-old man convicted of rape and assault was observed by the neuropsychological technician on the Tactile Performance Test (TPT) as follows (total time = 21.9; memory = 5; localization = 1):

> Constantly complaining — "It's too hard," "This is too much" — Rt Block in hand — moving block over board — doing some exploration of spaces — getting fairly good messages — after 1st block inserted. Began to explore the whole board — getting fairly good messages but taking a lot time locating the correct block, thereby losing the location & needs to start again feeling the spaces [sic].

4. *Perform at a crudely estimated fraction of actual ability.* Speed may be deliberately decreased. The faker is generally knowledgeable of his or her true rate of responding but may decide to show a partial performance. The following evaluation illustrates this point for a 35-year-old Portuguese man accused of murder:

> The scores obtained on the neuropsychological battery would be compatible with a diagnosis of brain dysfunction, except that we have some grave doubts as to how motivated Jim was for these particular tests. He appears to have adequate fine motor speed, for example, but when he is given a test of Fine Finger Dexterity (manipulating small pegs), he is noted to purposely work very slowly in order to appear somewhat damaged in this respect. On most tasks that required speed, this client was noted to purposely work quite slowly in order to give a poor picture of his abilities. It may well be that he does have some minor brain dysfunction, but once we have noted that he has purposely performed poorly on some of these tests, we have serious doubts as to the legitimacy of any of the scores we obtained after that point.

The evaluator needs to search for other types of failures on easy test items. The WAIS-R items, for example, generally progress from easy to difficult. Fakers may try to distribute their errors throughout the subtest (or battery), not realizing that, for some tasks, successive items increase in difficulty. Failure on easy items, according to Craine, also occurs on graduated forced-choice tests. Deliberate errors are made on the (easy) items to which the answers are known. Random responses may occur when the faker encounters (difficult) items to which the answers are unknown. This means that the point between the known (and deliberately faked) items and the unknown items is very difficult to estimate. Thus, the evaluator needs to weight missed easy items more heavily than mistakes on difficult items. Easy items on the Aphasia Screening Test, which are particularly sensitive to faking, include (a) mispronounced words, (b) misspelled words, and (c) acalculia. All items on the Aphasia Screening Test, or a similarly constructed scale, should be passed by a normal person. If a client has difficulty with these easy items, other tests tapping the same skills should also show deficit responding.

5. *Errant affective style.* Many types of head traumas produce changes in characteristic affective styles. Patients with stroke are a common example and many laypersons have experienced elderly family members who have suffered strokes. Following trauma, there can be a generalized blunting of affect, increased or decreased affective sensitivity, loss of affective discrimination, and in some cases increased propensity for anger and rage. Deceivers may employ changes in affect as a part of their malingering strategy. This can be a difficult response style to detect, but is one more pattern of which the forensic clinician must be mindful. A telling clue may be if the subject demonstrates loss of prior ability to identify deceptive emotion in others. In a study with brain-injured children, Dennis et al. (1997) found inability to identify deceptive emotion to be associated with head injury at an earlier age and frontal lobe contusions. The authors distinguished

between emotions as felt and emotions serving as a cognitive framework for understanding the actions and mental states of others. The MMPI has been a mainstay component of neuropsychological test batteries (Lezak, 1995), and the MMPI-2 has been demonstrated to have comparable utility to the MMPI with neurological populations (Miller & Paniak, 1995; Mittenberg, Tremont, & Rayls, 1996). The MMPI-2 provides the neuropsychologist with valuable information about the patient's noncognitive functioning to include behavioral, emotional, and psychiatric issues. Also particularly useful in forensic circumstances are the MMPI-2 scales designed to indicate response bias. Lamb, Berry, Wetter, and Baer (1994) noted that the MMPI-2 is vulnerable to simulated closed head injury; MMPI-2 findings alone, therefore, cannot be relied upon as the sole indicator of malingering of head injury.

The role of possible financial gain in TBI matters is an important forensic issue, and one having direct relevance for FDA in litigated TBI matters. In one recent study (Berry et al., 1995), head-injured patients pursuing compensation were found to have higher MMPI-2 scale scores on HS, D, Hy, Pt, and Sc in comparison to head-injured patients not pursuing litigation. Another study (Youngjohn, Davis, & Wolf, 1997) with the MMPI-2 investigated the influence of severity of head injury with litigating and nonlitigating patients. Minor TBIs resulted in almost certain litigation. The findings implicated litigation as prompting MMPI-2 scale elevations that were indicative of increased concern with physical health and serious psychiatric symptoms. The research evidenced an important paradoxical finding; minor TBIs characteristically evidenced greater MMPI-2 psychopathology (on Hs, D, Hy, and Pt) compared with severe head injuries. A comparison of the groups suggested that the variable of litigation alone could not account for this disparity. The authors acknowledged the problem of further research comparing nonlitigating to litigating mild head injuries when the majority of mild head injuries result in litigation. They suggested evaluation of minor TBI patients directly from emergency rooms or review of emergency room records as an alternative strategy to access nonlitigation, minor TBI comparison groups.

Youngjohn et al. (1997) offered another possible explanation for the elevated MMPI-2 profiles with the minor TBI group. Perhaps the severe TBI patients evidenced a comparative lack of awareness of impairment (i.e., *anosognosia*) such that they underreported actual neurobehavioral symptoms. Clearly, there is a complex interplay of variables operative in these cases. These variables include the possibility of secondary gain, awareness of impairment depending on injury severity and, perhaps most importantly, preexisting personality pathology and psychosocial issues that predispose certain individuals to pursue litigation (Millis & Putnam, 1994).

Satz and his colleagues (Nelson, Drebing, Satz, & Uchiyama, 1998; Satz et al., 1996) described a new and promising instrument called the Neuropsychology Behavior and Affect Profile (NBAP). The NBAP is an inventory of behavioral and affective changes in brain-injured individuals as rated by peers. The profile has five clinical scales and four validity scales. The questionnaire has 106 items addressing explicit behaviors and emotions as being present or absent both now and prior to trauma. While offering a new tool in neuropsychological assessment, the primary drawback to the approach is its susceptibility to bias by the patient's peer reviewers. To address the peer bias issue a follow-up study (Satz et al.) developed four validity scales. The external validity of the NBAP was examined through a dissembling (i.e., levels of informed and malingering raters) paradigm. The four validity scales are as follows:

1. Atypical Postinjury Symptom (APS) scale is designed to detect endorsement by raters of atypical symptomatology; elevated scores on this scale would suggest possible symptom exaggeration.
2. Infrequency scale is analogous to the MMPI F scale and designed to detect deviant responses.

3. Contradictory scale is based on pairs of items opposite in meaning and similar to the MMPI-2 True Response Inconsistency (TRIN) scale.
4. Complementary scales consist of pairs of items that are similar in meaning.

The study found that combinations of the clinical and the validity scales could effectively differentiate among training levels of the dissemblers, that is, the coached raters who distorted (malingered) their ratings. The dissemblers in the study were made up of three groups with varying levels of neuropsychological training. The first group was composed of undergraduate introductory psychology course students. The second group was senior undergraduate psychology majors, and the third group was highly trained dissemblers (i.e., licensed clinical neuropsychologists).

The NBAP is an example of a sophisticated and structured application of neuropsychological data regarding noncognitive sequelae of TBI. When combined with usual batteries of neurocognitive instruments, the NBAP offers a potent adjunct to FDA with TBI cases.

Frederick (1997) described the Validity Indicator Profile (VIP), a two-alternative forced-choice (2AFC) procedure designed to identify when the results of cognitive and neuropsychological testing may be invalid because of malingering or other problematic response styles. The instrument comprises 100 problems that assess nonverbal abstraction capacity and 78 word-definition problems. The VIP attempts to establish performance as representative of the subject's overall capacity (i.e., valid or invalid). A valid performance is classified as "compliant," and an invalid performance is subclassified as "careless" (low effort to respond correctly), "irrelevant" (low effort to respond incorrectly), or "malingering" (high effort to respond incorrectly). Frederick and Crosby (2000) reported a cross-validation study with 152 nonclinical subjects, 61 brain-injured subjects, 49 subjects considered as being at risk for malingering, and 100 randomly generated VIP protocols. The nonverbal and verbal subtests of the VIP demonstrated overall classification rates of 79.8% (73.5% sensitivity and 85.7% specificity), and 75.5% (67.3% sensitivity and 83.1% specificity), respectively. The VIP is another promising instrument for the detection of malingering. The authors suggested that the instrument's fourfold classification scheme (i.e., cross-classification of high to low motivation and high to low effort) reduces problems with *false-positive* classifications.

DETECTION STRATEGIES

Detection strategies fall into several categories (Craine, 1990; Freedland & Craine, 1981; Hall, Shooter, Craine, & Paulsen, 1991). These include (1) lack of neurological fit, (2) searching for patterns of failures on easy items, (3) administering easy vs. difficult versions of similar tasks, (4) searching for departures from expected levels of accuracy on forced-choice tests, and (5) examining for test inconsistencies.

1. Lack of Neurological Fit

The question of neurological fit is whether reported history, presenting symptoms, or responses on neuropsychological tests or on individual test items make sense compared with what is known about the functional neurological systems involved. For single items or symptoms, does the assessee present signs that do not make sense neurologically, such as glove amnesia or hemiparesis ipsilateral, to a supposedly involved hemisphere? On multidimensional tests, does the assessee produce a pattern of scores (profile), which is consistent with known neuropsychological syndromes?

A comparison of epileptic seizures with faked seizures (Roy, 1989) illustrates the strategy of evaluating neurological fit. Feigned epilepsy is often superimposed on a history of genuine seizures. This accords with studies that show that simulation of brain and spinal cord injuries is frequently superimposed on tangible organic pathology (Miller & Cartlidge, 1972). Morgan, Manning, Williams, and Rosenbloom (1984) discovered disparities in eight (child) patients between the clinical

TABLE 11.1
Main Characteristics of Epileptic Fits and Hysterical Pseudoseizures

	Epilepsy	Hysteria
Attack pattern	Similar	Variable
Apparent cause	Absent	Emotional disorder
Frequency	Rarely more than one a day, except petit mal	Often, frequent, many a day
Others present?	Sometimes when alone; can be nocturnal	Only when other people are present (often relatives or consorts); rarely nocturnal
Where?	Anywhere	Indoors, usually at home
Warning	If present, often stereotyped	Variable, sometimes over breathing
Onset	Commonly sudden	Often gradual
Scream	At onset	During attack
Convulsion	Stereotyped tonic clonic phase	Variable, rigidity with random struggling movement
Biting	Tongue	Of lips, hands, and other people
Micturition	Very common	Very rarely (not never)
Injury	Fairly frequent	Infrequently (not never)
Talking during attack	Never	Frequently
Duration	A few minutes	Many minutes, but sometimes much longer
EEG	Abnormal during and between seizures	Normal during and between attacks

Note: From "Pseudoseizures: A Psychiatric Perspective," by A. Roy, 1989, *Journal of Neuropsychiatry, 1*, 69–71. With permission.

description and frequency of seizures at home vs. school. Fabrication of seizures began for some as early as age 5. The characteristics of genuine and faked seizures in this small sample are listed in Table 11.1.

Generally, persons who pseudoseize compared with those with genuine seizures have (1) a greater history of other relatives with mental illness; (2) a greater personal history of psychiatric disorder, including attempted suicide and sexual maladjustment; and (3) more claimed health problems, depression, and anxiety, and an increased likelihood of an affective disorder (Roy, 1989). Thus, there are many differences in history and symptoms, which helped to differentiate genuine from malingered seizures in this sample. These features, while not definitive, should raise suspicions of exaggeration or fabrication of seizures.

Another strategy is to compare the test profile of the assessee with that of a comparison group from the research literature. Is there goodness of fit between the claimant's profile and that of either "genuine" or "faking" research groups reported in the neuropsychological literature? Smith et al. (1989) used a hand dynamometer connected to a computer to measure peak force and force–time curves for subjects instructed to fake bad. These faked performances could be distinguished from normative performance with between 92 and 100% accuracy, depending on the particular statistic used for comparison.

Heaton et al. (1978) used an expanded Halstead–Reitan Neuropsychological Battery to distinguish between 16 volunteer malingerers and 16 genuine brain-injured patients. Stepwise discriminant analysis for this sample of subjects yielded two functions that achieved a hit rate of 100% (neuropsychological tests) and 94% (MMPI scales). However, when Thompson and Cullum (1991) applied these discriminant functions to a new sample, they were unable to discriminate between patients judged to have put forth their best efforts on the tests and patients judged not to have tried their best. The lack of replication is not surprising given the small number of subjects in the study and the small subject-to-variable ratio in the multivariate analysis.

Although the Heaton et al. (1978) discriminant functions do not appear to be generally useful, their results suggested particular tests which may be especially prone to faking. They reported the following differences on individual tests:

Head-Injury Group, Worse	Malingerers, Worse
Category Test	Speech-Sounds Perception Test
TMT, Part B (errors)	Finger tapping
TPT (total time, memory, location)	Finger agnosia, sensory suppressions, hand grip
	WAIS Digit Span
	Higher F scale and six clinical scales on MMPI

Thompson and Cullum (1991) also found individual tests capable of distinguishing faked from genuine performances. These include measures of sensory-perceptual, learning and memory abilities (Cullum, Heaton, & Grant, 1991). In a study of these same tests, Trueblood and Schmidt (1993) compared eight patients in a neuropsychological practice who failed a stringent test of malingering with eight patients who passed the test of malingering. They found that their malingering patients performed significantly worse than their matched controls on the WAIS-R Digit Span, Finger Tip Number Writing, and Speech Perception tests, but not on finger tapping, finger agnosia, sensory suppressions, or hand grip.

Mensch and Woods (1986) found that normal subjects instructed to "fake bad" on the Luria–Nebraska Neuropsychological Battery showed a discrepancy between the number of elevated clinical scales and the elevation of the pathognomic scale. The subjects generally showed more cerebral pathology on scales measuring specific neuropsychological functions than they did on the single scale most sensitive to brain dysfunction. Like the subjects in the Heaton et al. (1978) study, subjects performed most poorly on tests of sensory and motor functions and displayed longer response times. It is possible that impairment on sensorimotor and timed tasks is most consistent with lay conceptions of how brain-injured patients perform.

The following case illustrates the above detection methods for a 45-year-old taxicab driver involved in litigation after an accident. Malingering was diagnosed based upon the following:

a. On the WAIS-R, he obtained a VIQ of 65 and a PIQ of 70. Several years before, he achieved an FSIQ of 110 with comparable verbal and performance abilities.

b. On an auditory discrimination test, he obtained a score equal to that of a 6-year-old child. Upon retesting with a parallel form 1 hour later, he obtained a normal score, showing a 300% improvement.

c. On a memory test, he displayed an inability to remember his age and the institution and city in which he was evaluated, responses obtained by less than 1% of the normative sample.

d. He obtained the minimal possible score on a test tapping visual, logical, verbal, and other kinds of memory. This score is compatible with such conditions as severe diffuse brain damage, but not with the memory skills the accused clinically demonstrated outside the test context.

e. He obtained a score on a forced-choice scale designed to test deception that was compatible with recognizing the visual stimulus but choosing not to report it.

f. There was a lack of fit between his clinical demeanor and a condition of dementia.

g. He previously exhibited faking while being tested for cerebral impairment similar to that claimed in the present case.

In this case the lack of fit between expected neurological performance and (1) presenting symptoms and (2) obtained test results revealed so many inconsistencies that the cumulative weight of the evidence supported a diagnosis of malingering.

2. Retesting or Comparison Strategies

a. Easy vs. difficult versions of similar tests

The faker may not understand that a second testing may be easier or more difficult than the first. Thus, fakers may perform similarly on the two versions whereas nonfakers would perform differently.

The Dot Counting Test (DCT) illustrates this method. Cards A, B, and C (consisting of massed dots) are more difficult than their counterparts, Cards, D, E, and F (consisting of clusters of dots), even though the two sets have the same number of dots to count. Administration of the two sets of the DCT may yield such inconsistent results that only a conscious attempt to control performance can explain them.

Another test with built-in easy vs. difficult items is the Auditory Discrimination Test (ADT) (Language Research Associaton, 1958). Initial administration of the ADT involves informing the assessee that words will be read, two at a time, and that the task is to say whether the two words are the same or different (e.g., tub–tub, lack--lack, web–wed, leg–led, chap–chap). A second form presents same or different word pairs of similar difficulty and number ($N = 40$) as the first form (e.g., gear–beer, cad–cab, bug–bud). In terms of threshold values, the faker may not realize that normals can miss many of the "same" items (<15), but should miss only a few of the "different" items (>4) before the performance appears suspicious. Comparison of the "hit rates" for same vs. different items may detect a suspicious asymmetry in the types of items missed.

> Claiming brain damage and psychosis in connection with the alleged murder of his cellmate, defendant Marcos was tested four times with both forms of the ADT. His performance ranged from normal to markedly impaired, with proportionally more "different" than "same" items missed in the abnormal performances. During the testing, he would interrupt the evaluator, saying it was time for him to see his other doctor.

Caution should be exercised, however, in deciding that failures of "easy" items within a test are more characteristic of deliberate distortion than of genuine responding. Mittenberg, Hammeke, and Rao (1989) examined the distribution of intratest scatter among brain-damaged and normal subjects on the Vocabulary, Comprehension, and Similarities subtests of the Wechsler Adult Intelligence Scale–Revised (WAIS-R). Their results suggested quite high cutoff scores (e.g., more than six failed items interpolated among passed items) for distinguishing brain-damaged subjects from normal subjects. If intratest scatter is to be used as an index of "faking bad" as well as an index of brain damage, then the cutoff scores for distinguishing actual brain damage from malingered brain damage would have to be even higher than those for distinguishing brain damaged from normal subjects. In a later study, Mittenberg, Theroux-Fichera, Zielinski, and Heilbronner (1995) compared selected WAIS-R subtest score differences between a group of recruited simulators and a mild-head-injury group. A significant discriminant function was identified and the cutoffs differentiated the two groups. The TBI group showed negligible differences between Vocabulary and Digit Span subtest performance. The simulators performed better on Vocabulary compared with Digit Span. The authors acknowledged the limitation of their experimental cutoff scores being used with actual clinical populations.

Whether failing more "easy" items than "difficult" items on a particular test is indicative of "faking bad" is, despite its commonsense appeal, always an empirical question. The distributions of intratest scatter among normal subjects, genuinely impaired subjects, and "faking" subjects must be explicitly compared to determine the usefulness of intratest scatter as an indicator of "faking." Gudjonsson and Shackleton (1986) described a statistical method for analyzing responses to easy vs. difficult subtests on the Raven's Standard Progressive Matrices (RSPM) and presenting cutoff scores for distinguishing faked from nonfaked performances. Their technique tests for a lack of expected decrease in subtest scores across the five, increasingly more difficult subtests of the RSPM. Their technique may have applicability to other tests with subtests differing in difficulty level or with "easy" and "difficult" forms.

b. Parallel testing

Repeat administrations of the same test or administration of a parallel form of a test should yield similar performances. The faker may not understand that a repeat of the test will be given and, therefore, may have difficulty replicating the previous performance. Faked scores in general are less stable than genuine scores.

The Peabody Picture Vocabulary Test (PPVT) as a test of receptive vocabulary is an example. Clients often have difficulty obtaining the same score on a parallel form even when the testing is administered a short time later.

c. Deviations from predicted scores

The evaluator can compare performance on predicted scores on a test with actual performance on that test. For example, regression equations have been developed to predict WAIS-R scores from scores on the Shipley–Hartford Institute of Living Scale (Zachry, 1986; Weiss & Schell, 1991), Raven's Progressive Matrices (O'Leary, Rusch, & Guastello, 1991) and the National Adult Reading Test (Willshire, Kinsella, & Pryor, 1991). A faker's obtained score on the WAIS-R may fall outside the confidence interval predicted from one of these three other tests.

The Shipley–Hartford and Raven's Matrices in particular are useful screening measures of intelligence because they take only a short time to administer. In addition, the Shipley–Hartford provides alternate forms, that will yield information on test–retest performance as well as giving an estimated WAIS-R IQ. Impaired nonfaking subjects should obtain WAIS-R IQ scores similar to those predicted by these two tests.

3. Certain Test Characteristics

a. Inconsistencies across similar items or tasks

Within the same test, the faker may not pay attention to item similarity and, therefore, not perform in an identical fashion. A less stable performance on similar items is frequently seen in fakers, just as with parallel tests. On tests with repeated trials of the same task (e.g., finger tapping, dynamometer), intertrial variability also increases with faking. However, it should be remembered that the reliability of item-level scores is much lower than the reliability of scale-level scores. Therefore, less confidence should be placed in item-level or trial-level inconsistencies than in scale-level inconsistencies.

b. Failure to show learning

Fakers often do not show expected learning curves (or may perhaps even show deterioration) across repeated trials of a task. The Mirror Tracing Test (Andreas, 1960; Millard, 1985) illustrates this expectation. The subject is told to trace the path between the two solid lines of a maze while viewing the maze in a mirror. An error is counted each time the subject's pencil touches a guideline. If the subject crosses the line, he or she must reenter at the same point; otherwise, a reentry counts as a second error. Faking may be suspected if the expected bilateral transfer of training (improved performance with the opposite hand after training with one hand) does not occur, if the expected improvement over trials (learning curve) is not apparent or if the total time exceeds five min.

4. Departures from Expected Accuracy

Forced-choice testing and forced-choice reaction time testing provide powerful methods of assessing deception of deficits. These tasks are all so easy that even severely impaired persons should perform satisfactorily. Departures from expected levels of performance provide a measure of a conscious attempt to manipulate performance.

Jensen (1980, pp. 686–698) described the use of forced-choice reaction time (RT) as a measure of faking. The subject is presented with an apparatus containing a push-type micro switch ("home") with eight additional push-switches arranged in a semicircle above the "home" button. Above each of the eight switches is a signaling light. The subject is instructed to depress the "home" button and wait for a warning tone. Within 1 to 4 s of the warning tone, one of the signal lights is illuminated and the subject is asked to move the finger from the "home" button "as quickly as possible" to the switch below the illuminated light. The subject's reaction time (measured in milliseconds) is the time between the onset of the signal light and the decompression of the "home" button.

Since a subject's average reaction time is considerably less than the recognition threshold (approximately 0.5 s), any intentional attempt to delay responding will dramatically and obviously shift the distribution of reaction times in the direction of longer latencies. Preliminary research showed that "when subjects are instructed to attempt voluntarily to fake less than their 'best' RT performance, they are remarkably unsuccessful. The subject's least conscious intention to respond less quickly than his or her 'best' RT puts the RT into an entirely different distribution with a *median about eight standard deviations removed from the median of the distribution of the subject's normal, unfaked RT. Faked RTs do not even fall within the normal distribution of individual differences in RT* [emphasis added]" (Jensen, 1980, p. 691).

These faked-choice reaction times are clearly distinguishable not only from the performances of normal subjects, but also even from the performances of subjects who were severely retarded (IQ < 40). They are also distinguishable from the large day-to-day variations in reaction times displayed by all subjects. Thus, the forced-choice reaction time test may provide nearly 100% accuracy in distinguishing persons who are consciously slowing their response times from even severely retarded persons whose reaction times are slower than normal.

It has yet to be determined how distinct deliberately slowed RTs are from those of patients with various neuropsychological deficits. Although Miller (1970) and van Zomeren and Deelman (1976, 1978) presented simple and forced-choice reaction times for groups of brain-injured patients, no study has yet compared such patients with other patients, with normal subjects, or with malingerers on the same reaction time task. Do apraxic patients perform similarly to severely retarded persons or are they more similar to deliberate fakers? Where does the distribution of RTs among patients with Alzheimer's disease fall in relation to normal and faked RTs? If RTs were as discriminating between known neurological groups and fakers as they are between persons who are severely retarded and fakers, a simple and effective (unfakeable?) detection method would be available to the practicing neuropsychologist.

Symptom Validity Testing (SVT) and Explicit Alternative Testing (EAT) attempt to measure faked sensory and recall deficits (Grosz & Zimmerman, 1965; Hall & Shooter, 1989; Pankratz, 1979, 1983, 1988; Pankratz, Fausti, & Peed, 1975; Theodor & Mandelcorn, 1973). EAT involves the presentation of stimuli whose perception or recognition is either affirmed or denied by the assessee. An interference period may be added if recall, rather than sensory perception, is the target of evaluation (see Chapter 19).

Almost no one should miss the presented items unless a genuine impairment exists. In the case of total impairment (e.g., total blindness or deafness), one's performance should approximate chance responding (50% accuracy with two-choice tasks). A significant deviation from chance responding is defined as an accuracy score with a probability less than some specified level (e.g., $p < 0.05$ or $p < 0.01$) as determined by the binomial distribution. For example, the one-tailed probability of obtaining fewer than 40 correct responses in 100 trials of a two-choice task is less than 2%. Achieving fewer than 36 correct answers would occur by chance less than twice in a thousand tests ($p = < 0.0019$).

Fakers usually assume that impaired performance requires less than 50% accuracy (Haughton, Lewsley, Wilson, & Williams, 1979; Pankratz, 1988). Persons genuinely impaired will usually guess randomly on EAT testing. Fakers do worse than chance because they intentionally suppress the correct answers on items for which they know the answers. Pankratz (1988) explains the basic problem for the faker on an EAT task:

A 50% hit rate is expected from any patient who declares at the outset that he or she cannot perceive the test stimuli in a two-alternative procedure. The untruthful patient is in a dilemma when confronted with repeated trials. If he or she holds to the denial and tries to manage the impression of a disability, then he or she runs the risk of revealing too much. On the other hand, if the deceptive patient properly identifies the cues, he or she openly admits that the deficit is not as severe as first claimed. In most clinical situations deceptive patients "guess" wrong too frequently.

In doing this, the final results are often below the probabilities of chance. Even when the final score is within normal limits, the response pattern may be incompatible with the notion that the stimulus did not register at all. (p. 185)

Pritchard (1992) has developed a computerized version of EAT that examines faked hearing, visual, or mnestic deficits. This is a 72-item forced-choice test that utilizes three sets of 24 trials each (Hiscock & Hiscock, 1989). A subject's total and subset performance may be compared with expected (theoretical) levels based on the binomial probability distribution. In comparing the performance of normal subjects instructed to feign a sensory or memory deficit and hospitalized psychiatric patients (including patients with organic mental disorders) instructed to try their best on this computerized version of EAT, Pritchard and Moses (1992) found that 66% of the pseudo-malingerers performed below expectation while 0% of the patients performed this poorly.

Evaluators can improvise applications of the EAT methodology for particular clinical problems. For example, in testing a 56-year-old male VA patient for alleged numbness of the entire body except for the spine, which was tender to touch, Pankratz, Binder, and Wilcox (1987) stated:

The patient was asked to close his eyes and guess which hand the examiner touched. After 34 trials he refused to continue; he made 27 errors. Application of the binomial theorem resulted in a score of 3.25, $P = < 0.0006$, one-tailed test.

The problem with EAT methodology is that it is too conservative. By considering as "faked" only those performances that are significantly below chance levels of responding, one is assuming that the person is attempting to mimic a complete loss of the tested function. For example, a completely blind person or a totally deaf person would respond with around 50% accuracy on a binary forced-choice test and performances significantly below this level would indicate an intentional underreporting of actual perceptions. However, most subjects do not claim a total loss of function and therefore would not be expected to perform significantly below chance levels. Hart, Guilmette, and Elliott (1991) reported that only 38% of their pseudomalingerers performed significantly below chance as defined by the binomial distribution. Pritchard and Moses (1992) found that only 66% of normal subjects instructed to feign a deficit performed below expectation. Similarly, Bickart, Meyer, and Connell (1991), Brandt, Rubinsky, and Lassen (1985), Haughton et al. (1979), and Iverson, Franzen, and McCracken (1991) found large false-negative rates when referring the performances of pseudomalingerers to the binomial distribution.

To detect those fakers who are presenting only a partial loss of function, Pritchard (1992) provided three alternative sets of interpretation rules. One set compared the subject's performance with chance levels based on the binomial distribution, a second set was empirically defined to maximize the positive hit rate (percentage of fakers who are called faking by the test), and the third set was empirically defined to maximize the negative hit rate (percentage of nonfakers who are called not faking by the test). This combination of theoretical and empirical rules may prove more useful in actual clinical practice than the sole use of interpretations based on the binomial probability distribution.

The Smell Identification Test (SIT) provides an illustration of forced-choice testing of faked sensory deficits. Developed by Doty and colleagues (Doty, Shaman, & Dann, 1984; Doty, Shaman, & Kimmelman, 1984) at the University of Pennsylvania, the 40-item SIT provides a quantitative measure of smell function in less than 15 min. The authors note that problems with the sense of smell are frequently associated with head trauma, with anosmia found in between 7 and 8% of cases.

The SIT may be useful when the assessee is suspected of malingering in regard to his or her sense of smell, such as when insurance/accident claims are filed. Four choices of smells are presented upon release of an odorant, yielding a 25% chance of accuracy in correctly identifying the designated smell, given total anosmia (10 out of 40). Most nonfaking patients will correctly identify 35 or more of the 40 odorants with females generally outscoring males at all age levels. Zero was the modal number of correct guesses for 158 men and women instructed to fake bad in the Doty, Shaman, and Kimmelman, (1984) study. Doty (1991) notes that under the assumption that $p = 0.25$, the probability of obtaining a score of zero by chance is one in 100,000; the chance of obtaining five or fewer correct on the SIT is less than 5 in 100. Those with genuine problems reflecting total loss of smell (i.e., anosmia) generally score around 10 at chance level due to essentially random responding. Patients with partial dysfunction have intermediate SIT scores. Patients with multiple sclerosis yield scores slightly above average; patients with Parkinson's or Alzheimer's disease produce scores that are significantly lower than average, but that are still substantially above the expected range for random responding.

The Victoria Symptom Validity Test (VSVT; Slick, Hopp, Strauss, & Spellacy, 1996) is a forced-choice instrument. The VSVT was designed to address the validity of reported cognitive impairments. The VSVT is computer-administered and consists of five-digit numbers of varying difficulty. One feature of the VSVT is an administration time of 10 to 15 min; another is its production of probability values (scores for valid, questionable, and invalid profiles). The test manual has a table of binomial probability values that is used to estimate the probability of obtaining the number of items correct out of the total numbers of items completed. Each testing produces a printout of normative values (for controls, a feigning group, a compensation-seeking group, and a non-compensation-seeking group). In a validation study the VSVT was found to be effective in detecting feigned memory impairment (Slick, Hopp, Strauss, & Thompson, 1997). This is a new instrument in need of additional normative data studies, but the initial validity and reliability data are encouraging (for a test review, see Lees-Haley, Dunn, & Betz, 1999).

CAVEATS

Forensic professionals attempting to understand faked brain damage do not appear to be aware of the rudimentary state of the art. Studies generally show that clinicians perform at chance to slightly above chance levels when asked to detect neuropsychological malingering (Ziskin & Faust, 1988; Heaton et al., 1978). Standard neuropsychological training is *not* sufficient to detect faking in spite of the usually high confidence neuropsychologists place on their opinions. Heaton et al. (1978) stated:

> On virtually all ability tests, the subject is told what is required in order to do well. At the same time, it usually becomes obvious what a bad performance entails, for example, be slow, make errors, fail to solve problems. Therefore, neuropsychological tests would seem intrinsically vulnerable to faking. (p. 900)

Although this holds true for sensory and mental status evaluation by neuropsychologists and psychiatrists, the courts have generally held neuropsychological testing in high esteem (Ziskin & Faust, 1988). Yet neuropsychologists need to learn that their training poorly prepares them for deception analysis. Neuropsychological tests can and have been faked and it is quite possible (and even likely) that those most prone to faking may have some genuine impairments. The question is not simply one of either faking or nonfaking; rather, the two coexist in many cases. Likewise, in actual clinical practice genuine symptoms may be distorted and/or exaggerated in intensity, frequency, and duration (Zielinski, 1995).

On the other hand, neuropsychologists' training does prepare them to read the literature and apply statistical guidelines. The clinical judgment of neuropsychologists in regard to detecting faking is poor while statistical decision making may not be. The development and cross-validation of such statistical decision rules should become a high priority in neuropsychological research and the use of such rules by clinical neuropsychologists should become commonplace.

A second caveat is that the evaluator should be wary of the traditionally accepted signs of hysteria and malingering, which actually may reflect cerebral dysfunction. Gould, Miller, Goldberg, and Benson (1986) surveyed the literature and found that the majority of clients (60 to 80%) thought to be hysteric or presenting neurological problems due to secondary gain actually suffered brain damage. In their own study of 30 consecutive neurology service admissions with acute structural brain disease, the encephalopathies confirmed by CT scans and other evidence, the following signs were revealed by the patients:

- History of hypochondriasis
- Secondary gain
- *La belle indifference*
- Nonanatomical sensory loss
- Split of midline by pain or vibratory stimulation
- Changing boundaries of hypalgesia
- Give-away weakness

All subjects showed at least one of the above signs, with most exhibiting three to four of them. The presence of these "malingering" signs in genuine patients means that they may be worthless for discriminating malingering. The lack of a comparison group in this study, however, prohibits the clear conclusion that these signs are not indicative of exaggerated or fabricated symptoms.

A third caveat concerns the need for multiple measures of distortion. When evaluating neuropsychological patients for forensic purposes, the authors use specific devices for detecting deception, in addition to a composite neuropsychological battery and as much historical and premorbid information as is available. Recall that the Bender-Gestalt was inappropriately used for decades by clinicians (and APA-approved training programs) as a sole measure of cerebral impairment. Bigler and Ehrfurth (1981) and others present convincing evidence, supported by CT scans, that this test misses genuine cerebral impairment. The high false-negative rate suggests the need for broadbanded neuropsychological testing with built-in devices for detecting deception. A further problem with the Bender-Gestalt is false positives. Bruhn and Reed (1975) found that the Pascal–Suttell and Canter scoring methods failed to differentiate fakers from those who are genuinely impaired. Because any distorted response is scored by these systems, they fail to differentiate among genuine disorders, situational influences (such as fatigue or boredom), peripheral disorders (such as peripheral neuritis), and malingering.

An instrument with a similar tradition as the Bender-Gestalt is the widely used Rey Fifteen Test (FIT; Rey, 1964). The FIT is a screening instrument designed to identify malingered memory complaints. To the examinee, the FIT initially appears to be more difficult than it actually is. The redundancy of simple character sets makes the memory task relatively simple, such that significant memory problems are necessary to generate actual deficit performance. Twenty years of studies (for a review, see Hart, 1995), mostly consisting of cutoff score refinements and adjustments, have indicated the FIT to be vulnerable to false-positive findings. The FIT is unique in its simplicity and brevity, but these same attributes render it not able to yield meaningful discriminant functions. "Although the FIT is popularly used due to the ease of administration and scoring, it is currently subject to significant criticism and may not stand up to scrutiny in court" (Hart, 1995, p. 58).

Caution is also in order with instruments that are still widely employed. Mattarazzo (1990) and Ryan, Paolo, and Smith (1992) cogently argue that WAIS-R Verbal-Performance discrepancies and subtest scatter are inadequate signs by themselves of cerebral dysfunction. Sherman et al.

(1995) noted the need for restraint in extrapolating conclusions regarding TBI from the WAIS-R's Verbal Comprehension, Perceptual Organization, and Freedom from Distractibility factors. Lees-Haley and Fox (1990) administered the Trail Making Test (TMT) and the MMPI to personal injury litigants with no known, or suspected, history of head injury. Using traditional TMT cutoff rates, the authors reported a high rate of false positives. Correlations between the MMPI and the TMT scores were consistent with the view that depression, as well as exaggeration of symptoms, interfered with TMT performance. The only adequate database for assessing neuropsychological deception is one that includes test and nontest data, contemporary and historical information, and third-party as well as first-person reports.

A fourth caveat involves the array of factors that are reviewed in assessing neuropsychological symptoms. In a study of base rate data regarding PCS with a large sample ($N = 1116$), neurological, psychological, and environmental variables were found to affect symptom presentation (Fox, Lees-Haley, Earnest, & Dolezal-Wood, 1995). The authors observed that neuropsychological test data must be reviewed in the context of a broad range of factors before PCS complaints are used as a basis for brain damage.

Additional cautions for neuropsychological assessment are presented by Wasyliw and Cavanaugh (1989), who state that evaluators should avoid:

> (1) "Blind" testing and interpretation (i.e., using a stock procedure regardless of the specifics or without review of prior history and evaluation); (2) lack of personality and psychopathology evaluation; (3) "gut" impressions of diagnosis or issues of malingering without clear objective or observational data; (4) conclusions as to organicity or malingering based on single tests, intelligence testing alone or performance on personality tests; (5) conclusions that loss or reduction in functioning has occurred without historical assessment of prior functioning; (6) prognostic conclusions based on testing performed prior to maximum recovery; (7) conclusions as to degree of recovery based on the client's self-description alone; and (8) conclusions that deficits were due to a specific historical incident, based on test data alone. (p. 382)

Wasyliw and Cavanaugh (1989) pointed out that to prove a personal injury case, the evaluator must demonstrate (1) the presence of encephalopathy; (2) damages in the form of behavioral, cognitive, or affective deficits; (3) a connection between the deficits and the encephalopathy; and (4) a causal connection between the encephalopathy and the allegedly tortious incident. Refutation of any of the four elements is sufficient to negate the total claim.

The same general requirements are found in criminal forensic neuropsychology. To demonstrate mental incapacity under the American Law Institute Standard of insanity, for example, the neuropsychologist must (1) diagnose an organic mental condition operative at the time of the instant offense, (2) demonstrate a cognitive and/or volitional impairment at the time of the alleged crime, and (3) connect the mental condition to the cognitive and/or volitional impairment. Refutation of any of these three factors suffices to disprove insanity.

In a 10-year review of research on the assessment of malingering in neuropsychological evaluations, Hart (1995) summarized:

1. The ability to systematically assess and detect malingering has advanced dramatically.
2. Poor performance on neuropsychological measures should not automatically lead to a conclusion of cerebral dysfunction.
3. Neuropsychologists are increasingly aware of attitudinal and motivational factors significantly affecting neuropsychological test performance. These factors must be systematically evaluated to come to the most accurate diagnosis.
4. Some available measures miss malingering because they are too simplistic; other measures incorrectly identify TBI as malingering.
5. Still needed is the development of measures that are both sensitive and specific to malingering.

6. A number of studies on malingering are empirically suspect because they rely on recruited simulators who are asked to fake symptoms. These studies represent artificial malingering constructs and it is questionable that they can be generalized to actual clinical/forensic applications. The slippery nature of real life malingering makes it likely that recruited malingerers will continue to be used particularly in the early development of instruments.

7. Available measures are imperfect, but, nonetheless, qualified use can lend credence to expert witness testimony. Reliance solely on "clinical impressions" regarding the accuracy of an examinee's test performance is no longer appropriate.

8. The assessment of malingering has brought us closer to developing instruments that assess motivation and basic level of effort as basic features of clinical presentation.

SUMMARY AND SUGGESTIVE SIGNS OF FAKING

Neuropsychological testing lends itself well to deception analysis. Fruitful areas of inquiry are plentiful within a composite battery, whose findings can then be integrated with data from other sources. Tests for cerebral functioning can be combined with personality tests, clinical observation, and cross-validating sources to provide conclusions regarding faking.

The following list presents signs suggestive of deception:

1. Failure on specific measures adapted to assess faking of cerebral impairment (e.g., illusorily difficult tests);
2. (a) Inconsistency between clinical/test behaviors and known neuropsychological syndromes (i.e., goodness of neurological fit); (b) Failure to exhibit impaired function outside the context of evaluation;
3. Skill performance changing on parallel testing;
4. Anterograde better than retrograde memory;
5. Approximate answers in interviews when concurrent testing reveals adequate skills;
6. Neuropsychological test results consistent with statistical rules for detecting malingering;
7. Similar or better performance on easy compared with difficult versions of the same test;
8. Less than accurate performance on forced-choice sensory, recall, and reaction-time tests;
9. No improvement where expected (e.g., absence of learning curve);
10. Test scores outside of predicted confidence intervals (e.g., actual WAIS-R Full Scale IQ outside the confidence interval predicted by the score on the Ravens Progressive Matrices);
11. Noncognitive behavior changes, which must always be explored and differentiated between malingering vs. genuine TBI.

Although not definitive in themselves, these factors are suggestive enough of distorted performance to justify a more intensive investigation of the possibility of malingering.

LEGAL REFERENCES

Buckler v. Sinclair Ref. Co., 68 Ill.App.2d 283, 216 N.E.2d 14 (1966).
Jenkins v. United States, 307 F.2d 637, 651, 652 (DC Cir. 1961).

REFERENCES

Andreas, B. G. (1960). *Experimental psychology.* New York: Wiley.
Aubrey, J., Dobbs, A., & Rule, B. (1989). Laypersons' knowledge about the sequelae of minor head injury and whiplash, *Journal of Neurology, Neurosurgery & Psychiatry, 52,* 7,842–846.

Berry, D. T., Wetter, M. W., Baer, R. A., Youngjohn, J. R., Gass, C. S., Lamb, D. G., Franzen, M. D., MacInnes, W. D., & Buchholz, D. (1995). Overreporting of closed-head injury symptoms on the MMPI-2. *Psychological Assessment, 7*(4), 517–523.

Bickart, W., Meyer, R., & Connell, D. (1991). The symptom validity technique as a measure of feigned short-term memory deficit. *American Journal of Forensic Psychology, 9*(2), 3–11.

Bigler, E., & Ehrfurth, J. (1981). The continued inappropriate singular use of the Bender Visual Motor Gestalt Test. *Professional Psychology, 12*, 562–569.

Binder, L. W. (1986). Persisting symptoms after mild head injury: A review of the postconcussive syndrome. *Journal of Clinical and Experimental Neuropsychology, 8*, 323–346.

Boll, T. (1985). Developing issues in neuropsychology. *Journal of Clinical and Experimental Neuropsychology, 7*, 473–484.

Brandt, J., Rubinsky, E., & Lassen, G. (1985). Uncovering malingered amnesia, *Annals of the New York Academy of Science, 44*, 502–503.

Bruhn, A., & Reed, M. (1975). Simulation of brain damage on the Bender Gestalt Test by college students. *Journal of Personality Assessment, 39*, 244–255.

Craine, J. (1981). *Faking on neuropsychological tests.* Paper presented at Hawaii Psychological Association, Honolulu, HI.

Craine, J. (1990). Minimizing and denying: A testing approach to feigned amnesia. In *Truth or lies: Guidelines for detecting malingering and deception.* Workshop by Psychological Consultants and Forest Institute of Professional Psychology, Honolulu, HI.

Cullum, C., Heaton, R., & Grant, I. (1991). Psychogenic factors influencing neuropsychological performance: somatoform disorders, factitious disorders and malingering. In H. Doerr, and A. Carlin (Eds.), *Forensic neuropsychology: Legal and scientific bases* (pp. 195–196), New York: The Guilford Press.

Dennis, M., Barnes, M. A., Wilkinson, M., & Humphreys, R. P. (1997). How children with head injury represent real and deceptive emotion in short narratives. *Brain and Language, 61*(3), 450–483.

Doty, R. L. (1991). Personal communication. University of Pennsylvania Smell and Taste Center, Philadelphia, PA.

Doty, R. L., Shaman, P. S., & Dann, M. (1984). Development of the University of Pennsylvania Smell Identification Test: A standardized microencapsulated test of olfactory function. *Physiology & Behavior, 32*, 489–502.

Doty, R. L., Shaman, P. S., & Kimmelman, C. P. (1984). University of Pennsylvania Smell Identification Test: A rapid quantitative olfactory function test for the clinic. *Laryngoscope, 94*, 176–178.

Faust, D., Hart, K., & Guilmette, T. J. (1998a). Neuropsychologists capacity to detect adolescent malingerers. *Professional Psychology: Research and Practice, 19*, 508–515.

Faust, D., Hart, K., & Guilmette, T. J. (1988b). Pediatric malingering: The capacity of children to fake believable deficits on neuropsychological testing. *Journal of Clinical and Consulting Psychology, 56*, 578–582.

Fox, D. D., Lees-Haley, P. R., Earnest, K., & Dolezal-Wood, S. (1995). Base rates of postconcussive symptoms in health maintenance organization patients and controls. *Neuropsychology, 9*(4), 606–611.

Franzen, M. D., Iverson, G. L., & McCraken, L. M. (1990). The detection of malingering in neuropsychological assessment. *Neuropsychological Review, 1*, 247–279.

Frederick, R. I. (1997). *Validity Indicator Profile manual.* Minnetonka, MN: NCS Assessments.

Frederick, R. I., & Crosby, R. D. (2000). Development and validation of the Validity Indicator Profile. *Law and Human Behavior, 24*, (1), 59–82.

Freedland, K., & Craine, J. (1981). Personal communication.

Goebel, R. (1989). Detection of faking on the Halstead–Reitan Neuropsychological Test Battery. *Journal of Clinical Psychology, 39*, 731–742.

Gould R., Miller, B., Goldberg, M., & Benson, D. (1986). The validity of hysterical signs and symptoms. *Journal of Nervous & Mental Diseases, 174*, 593–597.

Greiffenstein, M. F., Baker, W.J., & Gola, T. (1994). Validation of malingered amnesia with a large clinical sample. *Psychological Assessment, 6*(3), 218–224.

Grosz, H., & Zimmerman, J. (1965). Experimental analysis of hysterical blindness: A follow-up report and new experiment data. *Archives of General Psychiatry, 13*, 255–260.

Gudjonsson, G., & Shackelton, H. (1986). The pattern of scores on Raven's Matrices during "faking bad" and "non-faking" performance, *British Journal of Clinical Psychology, 25*, 1, 35–41.

Hall, H. V. (1985). Cognitive and volitional capacity assessment: A proposed decision tree. *American Journal of Forensic Psychology, 3*, 3–17.

Hall, H. V. (1990). Faking good and faking bad. In *Truth or lies: Guidelines for detecting malingering and deception.* Workshop by Psychological Consultants and Forest Institute of Professional Psychology, Honolulu, HI.

Hall, H. V., & McNinch, D. (1989). Linking crime-specific behavior to neuropsychological impairment. *International Journal of Clinical Neuropsychology, 10*, 113–122.

Hall, H. V., & Shooter, E. A. (1989). Explicit alternative testing for feigned memory deficits. *Forensic Reports, 2*, 277–286.

Hall, H. V., Shooter, E. A., Craine, J., & Paulsen, S. (1991). Explicit alternative testing: A trilogy of studies on faked memory deficits. *Forensic Reports, 4*(3), 259–279.

Hart, K. (1995). The assessment of malingering in neuropsychological evaluations: Research-based concepts and methods for consultants. *Consulting Psychology Journal: Practice and Research, 47*(4), 246–254.

Hart, K., Guilmette, T., & Elliot, M. (1991). Symptom validity testing as a method for malingering detection. Paper presented at the 11th Annual Conference of the National Academy of Neuropsychology, Dallas, TX.

Haughton, P. M., Lewsley, A., Wilson, M., & Williams, R. G. (1979). A forced-choice procedure to detect feigned or exaggerated hearing loss. *British Journal of Audiology, 13*, 135–138.

Heaton, R., Smith, H., Lehman, R., & Vogt. A. (1978). Prospects for faking believable deficits on neuropsychological testing. *Journal of Consulting and Clinical Psychology, 46*, 892–900.

Heubrock, D., & Peterman, F. (1998). Neuropsychological assessment of suspected malingering: Research results, evaluation techniques, and further directions of research and application. *European Journal of Psychological Assessment, 14*(3), 211–225.

Hiscock, M., & Hiscock, C. (1989). Refining the forced-choice method for the detection of malingering. *Journal of Clinical and Experimental Neuropsychology, 11*, 967–974.

Iverson, G. L. (1995). Qualitative aspects of malingered memory deficits. *Brain Injury, 9*(1), 35–40.

Iverson, G. L., Franzen, M. D., & McCracken, L. (1991). Evaluation of an objective assessment technique for the detection of malingered memory deficits. *Law and Human Behavior, 15*(6), 667–676.

Iverson, G. L., & Franzen, M. D. (1996). Using multiple objective memory procedure to detect simulated malingering. *Journal of Experimental Neuropsychology, 18*(1), 38–51.

Jensen, A. (1980). *Bias in mental testing.* New York: The Free Press.

Lamb, D. G., Berry, D. T. R., Wetter, M. W., & Baer, R. A. (1994). Effects of two types of information on malingering of closed head injury on the MMPI-2: An analog investigation. *Psychological Assessment, 6*(1), 8–13.

Language Research Association (1958). *The Auditory Discrimination Test.* Chicago, IL: Author.

Larrabee, G. J. (1991). Cautions in the use of neuropsychological evaluation in legal settings: Neuropsychological tests can be failed for reasons other than brain damage. *Neuropsychology, 4*, 239–249.

Lees-Haley, P. R., Dunn, J. T., & Betz, B. P. (1999). Test review: The Victoria Symptom Validity Test. *American Psychology-Law Society Newsletter, 19*(3), 12–16.

Lees-Haley, P. R., & Fox, D. D. (1990). Neuropsychological false positives in litigation: Trail Making Test findings. *Perceptual and Motor Skills, 70*(3, Pt 2), 1379–1382.

Lezak, M. (1989). Assessment of psychosocial dysfunctions resulting from head trauma. In M. Lezak (Ed.), *Assessment of the behavioral consequences of head trauma* (pp. 113–143). New York: Alan R. Liss, Inc.

Lezak, M. (1995). *Neuropsychological Assessment* (3rd ed.). New York: Oxford University Press.

Mattarazzo, J. (1990). Psychological assessment versus psychological testing: Validation from Bunet to the school, clinic and courtroom. *American Psychologist, 45*, 999–1016.

Mensch, A., & Woods, D. (19986). Patterns of feigning brain damage on the LNNB. *International Journal of Clinical Neuropsychology, 8*(2), 59–63.

Millard, R. W. (1985). *Application of selected measures for detecting neuropsychological impairment among alcoholics.* Unpublished doctoral dissertation, University of Hawaii, Manoa.

Miller, E. (1970). Simple and choice reaction time following severe head injury. *Cortex, 6*(1), 121–127.

Miller, L. (1998). Malingering in brain injury and toxic tort cases. In Wiley Law Editorial Staff (Ed.), *1998 Wiley expert witness update: New developments in personal injury litigation* (pp. 225–289). New York: Wiley.

Miller, H., & Cartlidge, N. (1972). Simulation and malingering after injuries to the brain and spinal cord. *Lancet, 1*, 580–584.

Miller H. B., & Paniak, C. E. (1995). MMPI and MMPI-2 profile and code type congruence in a brain-injured sample. *Journal of Clinical and Experimental Neuropsychology, 17*(1), 58–64.

Millis, S. R., & Putnam, S. J. (1994). The Recognition Memory Test in the assessment of memory impairment after financially compensated mild head injury: A replication. *Perceptual and Motor Skills, 79*(1, Pt 2, Special Issue), 384–386.

Mittenberg, W., Azrin, R., Millsaps, C., & Heilbronner, R. (1994). Identification of malingered head injury on the Wechsler Memory Scale–Revised. *Psychological Assessment, 5*(1), 34–40.

Mittenberg, W., Hammeke, T., & Rao, S. (1989). Intrasubtest scatter on the WAIS-R as a pathognomonic sign of brain injury. *Psychological Assessment: A Journal of Consulting and Clinical Psychology, 1*, 273–276.

Mittenberg, W., Theroux-Fichera, S., Zielinski, R. E., & Heilbronner, R. L. (1995). Identification of malingered head injury on the Wechsler Adult Intelligence Scale–Revised. *Professional Psychology: Research and Practice, 26*(5), 491–498.

Mittenberg, W., Tremont, G., & Rayls, K. R. (1996). Impact of cognitive function on MMPI-2 validity in neurologically impaired patients. *Assessment, 3*(2), 157–163.

Morgan, M., Manning, D., Williams, W., & Rosenbloom, L. (1984). Fictitious epilepsy. *Lancet, 2*(8396), 232–233.

Nelson, L. D., Drebing, C., Satz, P, & Uchiyama, C. (1998). Personality change in head trauma: A validity study of the Neuropsychology Behavoir and Affect Profile. *Achives of Clinical Neuropsychology, 13*(6), 549–560.

O'Leary, U., Rusch, K., & Gudstello, S. (1991). Estimating age-stratified WAIS-R IQs from scores on the Raven's Standard Progressive Matrices. *Journal of Clinical Psychology, 47*(2), 277–284.

Pankratz, L. (1979). Symptom validity testing and symptom retraining: Procedures for the assessment and treatment of functional sensory deficits. *Journal of Consulting and Clinical Psychology, 47*, 409–410.

Pankratz, L. (1983). A new technique for the assessment and modification of feigned memory deficits. *Perceptual and Motor Skills, 57*, 367–372.

Pankratz, L. (1988). Malingering on intellectual and neuropsychological measures. In R. Rogers (Ed.), *Clinical assessment of malingering and deception* (pp. 169–192). New York: Guilford Press.

Pankratz, L., Binder, L. M., & Wilcox, L. M. (1987). Evaluation of exaggerated somatosensory deficits with symptom validity testing [Letter to the editor]. *Archives of Neurology, 44*, 798.

Pankratz, L., Fausti, S. A., & Peed, S. (1975). A forced-choice technique to evaluate deafness in a hysterical or malingering patient. *Journal of Consulting and Clinical Psychology, 43*, 421–422.

Parker, R. (1990). *Traumatic brain injury and neuropsychological impairment*. New York: Springer-Verlag.

Pritchard, D. (1992). *Tests of neuropsychological malingering*. Orlando, FL: Paul M. Deutsch Press.

Pritchard, D., & Moses, J. (1992). Tests of neuropsychological malingering. *Forensic Reports, 5*, 287–290.

Rey, A. (1964). *L'examen clinique en psycholgic [The clinical examination in psychology]*. Paris: Presse Universitaires de France.

Roy, A. (1989). Pseudoseizures: A psychiatric perspective. *Journal of Neuropsychiatry, 1*, 69–71.

Ryan, J., Paolo, A., & Smith, A. (1992). Wechsler Adult Intelligence Scale–Revised intersubtest scatter in brain-damaged patients: A comparison with the standardization sample. *Psychological Assessment, 4*(1), 63–66.

Satz, P., Holston, S. G., Uchiyama, C. L., Shimahara, G., Mitrushina, M., Forney, D. L., Zaucha, K., Light, R., Asarnow, R., Drebing, C., Kline, A. E., van Gorp, W., Nelson, L. D., Foster, J., Fahy, J., & Namerow, N. (1996). Development and evaluation of validity scales for the Neuropsychology and Affect Profile: A dissembling study. *Psychological Assessment, 8*(2), 115–124.

Sherman, E. M. S., Strauss, E., Spellacy, F., & Hunter, M. (1995). Construct validity of WAIS-R factors: Neuropsychological test correlates in adults referred for evaluation of possible head injury. *Psychological Assessment, 7*(4), 440–444.

Slick, D. J., Hopp, G., Strauss, E., & Spellacy, F. J. (1996). Victoria Symptom Validity Test: Efficiency for detecting feigned memory impairment and relationship to neuropsychological tests and MMPI-2 validity scales. *Journal of Clinical and Experimental Neuropsychology, 18*(6), 911–922.

Slick, D. J., Hopp, G., Strauss, E., & Thompson, G. B. (1997). *Victoria Symptom Validity Test, Version 1.0., Professional manual*. Odessa, Fl: Professional Resource, Inc.

Smith, G., Nelson, R., Sadoff, S., & Sadoff, A. (1989). Assessing sincerity of effort in maximal grip strength tests. *American Journal of Physical Medicine & Rehabilitation, 68*(2), 73–80.

Strub, R., & Black, F. (1981). *Organic brain syndromes*. Philadelphia, PA: F.A. Davis Company.

Theodor, L. H., & Mandelcorn, M. S. (1973). Hysterical blindness: A case report and study using a modern psychophysical technique. *Journal of Abnormal Psychology, 82*, 552–553.

Thompson, L., & Cullum, C. (1991). *Pattern of performance on neuropsychological tests in relation to effort in mild head injury patients*. Paper presented at the 1991 meeting of the National Academy of Neuropsychology, Reno, NV.

Trueblood, W., & Schmidt, M. (1993). Malingering and other validity considerations in the neuropsychological evaluation of mild head injury, *Journal of Clinical and Experimental Neuropsychology, 15*(4), 578–590.

van Zomeren, A., & Deelman, B. (1976). Differential effects of simple and choice reaction after closed head injury. *Journal of Clinical Neurology and Neurosurgery, 79*, 2, 81–90.

van Zomeren, A., & Deelman, B. (1978). Long-term recovery of visual reaction time after closed head injury. *Journal of Neurology, Neurosurgery and Psychiatry, 41*, 452–457.

Wasyliw, O., & Cavanaugh, J. (1989). Simulation of brain damage: Assessment and decision rules. *Bulletin of American Academy of Psychiatry and Law, 17*, 373–386.

Weiss, J., & Schell, R. (1991). Estimating WAIS-R IQ from the Shipley Institute of Living Scale: A replication, *Journal of Clinical Psychology, 47*, 4, 558–562.

Willshire, D., Kinsella, G., & Pryor, M. (1991). Estimating WAIS-R IQ from the National Adult Reading Test: A cross-validation. *Journal of Clinical and Experimental Neuropsychology, 13*(2), 204–216.

Youngjohn, J. R., Davis, D., & Wolf, I. (1997). Head injury and the MMPI-2: Paradoxical effects and the influence of litigation. *Psychological Assessment, 9*(3), 177–184.

Zachry, R. (1986). *Manual for Shipley Institute of Living Scale*. Los Angeles, CA: Western Psychological Services.

Zielinski, J. J. (1995). Malingering and defensiveness in the neuropsychological assessment of mild traumatic brain injury. *Clinical Psychology: Science and Practice, 1*(2), 169–184.

Ziskin, J., & Faust, D. (1988). *Coping with psychiatric and psychological testimony* (4th ed.). Los Angeles: Law and Psychology Press.

12 Faked Pain and Loss of Sensation

The forensic assessment of malingered pain continues to be an elusive quest. It is not yet possible to differentiate in any reliable manner malingered representations of pain from actual pain. As a result, empirical approaches to detection of feigned pain remain reliant on intuitive measures (Craig, Hill, & McMurtry, 1999). The costs of fraudulent injury claims based on pain symptoms are enormous (James, 1998). The problem of fraudulent claims has resulted in a maze of recovery processes pitting claimants against insurers with both sides ultimately being penalized.

Psychological variables are fundamental, causative factors in pain perception. At present, the primary focus is on the experience of physical pain, but this is not to ignore the reality that psychologically based pain can also be an excruciating human experience. Miller (1992) described patient dishonesty in psychotherapy as the "Pinocchio syndrome" and suggested that lies in therapy were often motivated by the patient's need to camouflage painful psychological realities. The Pinocchio syndrome is often motivated by the patient's efforts to cope with feelings of guilt and anxiety. References throughout this chapter will document the efforts of Lees-Haley and his colleagues to champion the need for evaluators to exercise caution with the self-reports of personal injury claimants (Williams, Lees-Haley, & Djanogly, 1999)

One area of pain research has been assessing the ability of judges to detect pain deception subjectively. A common paradigm has been for judges to assess dissimulated pain manifested in nonverbal facial expressions (for a review, see Poole & Craig, 1992). In one laboratory study, judges were asked to differentiate facial expressions that displayed genuine pain, no pain, masked pain, and exaggerated pain (Hadjistavropoulos, Craig, Hadjistavropoulos, & Poole, 1996). The findings indicated that the judges' classification decisions were better than chance, but the error rate was still high. The level of the judges' confidence was consistent with their level of accuracy. The researchers suggested that systematic training regarding specific facial cues that were, and were not, reliable would probably improve the judges' accuracy. Galin and Thorn (1993) found that judges provided with facial action training and enhanced feedback did improve their ability to distinguish between genuine and distorted facial pain displays.

Judgments made by observers of displayed facial pain in experimental designs are tainted by a number of factors. Advanced warning of pain deception did not improve judges' accuracy but did result in more conservative or nonempathic judging styles (Poole & Craig, 1992). In another study, observer judgments were significantly biased by the subject's gender and physical attractiveness (Hadjistavropoulos, McMurtry, & Craig, 1996). Male patients and physically attractive patients were judged to be functioning better than female and physically unattractive patients.

Undergraduate nursing students were asked to judge pain experience based on videotapes of preterm and fullterm infants being exposed to heel incisions for blood-sampling procedures (Hadjistavropoulos, Craig, Grunau, & Whitfield, 1997). The findings indicated that viewing the incision procedure contributed uniformly to judgments of pain experience. Judgments based on infant facial expression produced the most variance, followed by bodily activity and gestational age.

The self-report of experienced pain by persons with intellectual disabilities is predictably not very reliable. LaChapelle, Hadjistavropoulos, and Craig (1999) described an attempt to rate objectively the pain experience of an intellectually disabled population who experienced intramuscular injections. The facial reactions of the subjects were recorded and subjected to observer judgments. The findings supported the validity of both objectively coded and observer-rated facial expressions as research tools in assessing pain levels with this disabled population.

Mere self-attention to somatic symptoms can significantly influence experience of neuropsychological symptoms. Participants in one study were told to attend to physical and psychological symptoms (Williams, Lees-Haley, & Price, 1998). Those instructed subjects evidenced more complaints of physical symptoms and reports of anxiety and depression, compared with controls who were not instructed. The findings support careful consideration of self-reported symptoms by assessors.

Two other factors significantly affecting the assessment of malingered pain are litigation and compensation. Studies have demonstrated that legal definitions and compensation criteria can and do influence pain syndrome presentation (Hadjistavropoulos, 1999; Lees-Haley, 1989, 1990; Lees-Haley & Fox, 1990). Researchers have found, for example, that patients in litigation consistently reported more favorable preinjury status compared with controls (Lees-Haley, Williams, & English, 1996; Lees-Haley et al., 1997). Such a response style by plaintiffs underscores the need for caution in approaching personal injury cases involved in litigation. Self-reported symptoms by plaintiffs are subject to response bias that must be considered in the assessment process. The biased response set does not necessarily implicate deceit over a reliable report.

One of the most important aids to neuropsychological assessment is awareness by the clinician of base rate data for given categories of symptoms (Dunn, Brown, Lees-Haley, & English,, 1993). Base rate studies of self-reported symptoms by personal injury claimants reflect spuriously high rates of reported symptoms (Lees-Haley, 1992; Lees-Haley, Williams, & English, 1996). These high rates of reported symptoms by personal injury claimants have led to some investigators' labeling the phenomenon as the "Barnum" effect (Lees-Haley, Williams, & Brown, 1993). The effect refers to ambiguous interpretations (nondeliberate distortion) of circumstances and symptom/effects based on individual personality differences. Another consideration is the relative ease involved with even naive, untrained individuals to mimic accurately a variety of psychiatric and neuropsychological symptoms, for example, mild brain injury, PTSD, major depression, and anxiety disorders (Lees-Haley & Dunn, 1994).

According to Stein (1972), professionals should be cautious in concluding that feigned pain indicates malingering:

> An expert may properly state his opinion that the pain is real, imagined or feigned. However, a claim that the plaintiff is malingering must be approached with great caution, since it necessarily implies that the plaintiff is practicing willful deception, if not perjury. "Malingering" may be defined as the deliberate, conscious feigning of pain by one who knows that he has no pain. The fact that there is no objective basis for the pain which the plaintiff claims falls far short of proving malingering. (p. 39)

According to this view, purely subjective claims of pain should not automatically be construed as fabricated or exaggerated. Imputation of conscious, intentional faking of pain requires more than the absence of tissue pathology or of functional impairment.

In *Boyd v. General Industries* (1987), the court held that a 47-year-old assembly-line worker who injured her back on the job in 1980 could recover for increased or prolonged disability due to subjective pain in view of the testimony of doctors that her experience of pain was real to her. Furthermore, plaintiffs may recover damages even if they engaged in willful deception, based on the principle that unrelated lying and distortion could accompany genuine deficits such as psychological pain. The court stated as follows:

> We have also said, however, that the Commission may not refuse compensation to a claimant simply because he is untruthful (*Guidry v. J & Eads Const. Co.* 1984). In the case at bar, Boyd's credibility

is only relevant on the issue of whether she is malingering, and the Commission's decision carries with it an implicit finding that she is malingering. As the Supreme Court stated in *Wilson & Co. v. Christman*: It goes without saying, and without the necessity for citation of cases, that true malingering is not a form of disability of any sort. It is a form of ability rather than disability. It is a form of ability to feign injury or disability that does not exist. Had appellee in this case been malingering his disability, the Commission might well have determined that he had none. (p. 755)

The *Boyd* court continued:

Here, there is no substantial evidence to support a finding of malingering. Dr. Hutt, upon whose testimony the Commission particularly relied, said that Boyd's perceptions of pain are "very real to her," and that there was no evidence of malingering or intentional distortion of perceived severity of pain. Dr. Bevilacqua stated that Boyd appeared "very sincere and reliable" and that "she has absolutely no insight into her obvious emotional conflicts."

Dr. Kaczenski said Boyd was not malingering. None of the many doctors who have seen Boyd have so much as suggested that she might be malingering. Although compensation claims predicated upon mental disorders must be carefully scrutinized in order to protect the employer against unwarranted claims, the danger of denying recovery to a deserving claimant must be guarded against with equal enthusiasm. *Royer v. Cantrelle* (1972).

To summarize, the evidence in this case clearly established that:

1. Boyd suffered a compensable but relatively minor back injury in 1980, which has now completely healed.
2. At the time of the injury she was neurotic, but without symptoms.
3. She now suffers pain, which causes her to be unable to work.
4. This pain is a symptom of her neurosis.
5. She is not malingering.
6. Her injury did not cause the neurosis — the neurosis was a pre-existing condition, and
7. Although the on-the-job injury did not "cause" her present pain in a medical sense, it was the precipitating event, which brought forth this symptom, and was therefore a legal cause of her resulting disability. For the foregoing reasons, this case is reversed and remanded to the Commission for a determination of the extent of Boyd's disability. (p. 755)

In contrast, in *Yager v. Labor and Industry Review, Sentry Insurance Company and Lands' End* (1999) the appeals court upheld the earlier finding of the Labor and Industry Review Commission (LIRC) of malingering by the plaintiff. The court cited the LIRC opinion:

The inconsistencies in the applicant's testimony as compared to her medical records undercuts her credibility. In addition the evidence indicated that the applicant had a history of preexisting neck, shoulder, and back problems which required treatment and were bothering her up until the day before the alleged incident on January 25, 1996. Given the medical evidence in the record, including the reports from Dr. Goodman and Dr. Marsh … the evidence was sufficient to raise a legitimate doubt that the applicant sustained a shoulder, neck, or back injury arising out of her employment … on January 25, 1996.

Defining pain and its possible deception is difficult. The standard definition suggests that pain is a response to noxious stimuli — those that produce or threaten to produce tissue damage. Yet, psychic pain produced by psychological stimuli may be just as distressing as purely physical pain to affected individuals. In many cases, there may be no difference between physical and psychological pain in reported intensity, frequency, or duration. Both intertwine to a considerable extent, with depression, anxiety, and frustration increasing experienced pain, and vice versa.

The most common types of chronic pain syndromes include (1) headaches — tension, migraine, vascular, and post-traumatic; (2) back pains — disk disease, spondylitis, osteoporosis, fractures; (3) psychologically induced pain — trauma, PTSD, etc.; and (4) others — myofascial pain, muscle spasm, and sympathetic dystrophies. These, of course, are types of disorders in which pain is the primary complaint.

In addition, headaches around the eyes can be also due to glaucoma, around the back of the neck to meningitis, and in the face to trigeminal neuralgia. Psychological pain is a common correlate of many DSM-IV (1994) conditions. These include the depressive and anxiety disorders, hypochondriasis and hysteria, and the organic mental disorders. The International Classification of Diseases (ICD, 1989) describes many pain-related diseases, including musculoskeletal disorders (e.g., osteoarthritis, Paget's disease), ischemic disorders (angina pectoris, claudication), neurological disorders (e.g., causalgia, coccydynia, scar pain), and miscellaneous categories such as chronic pancreatitis and temporomandibular joint syndrome.

In sum, pain may be either the defining or an associated feature of a disorder and may be due to either physical or psychological causes. It may be exaggerated or distorted without being totally fabricated. It may be genuine even when there is evidence of outright lying.

Recent court findings have focused on dispositional concerns with pain claimants, as compared with earlier cases that attempted to define and refine conditions under which pain claims met legal criteria. In *Keever v. Middletown* (1998), the plaintiff Keever was a disabled police officer who claimed that his alleged forced retirement amounted to a constructive discharge from duty and thereby violated disability statutes. The appeals court found that reasonable accommodations had been offered to the plaintiff. The count found invalid Mr. Keever's perception that his being offered a "desk job" was punitive. In another personal injury case stemming from on-the-job injuries, the employer argued that the plaintiff had not submitted to actual physical assessments of her incapacities to determine definitively if the claimed injuries were factual (*Quint v. A. E. Staley*, 1999). The court ruled that no court precedent existed to require Americans with Disabilities Act (ADA) plaintiffs to submit to such physical assessment. Instead, the court ruled that the plaintiff might rely on competent medical testimony to justify a personal decision to refrain from a life activity that could result in imminent risk of further injury.

The issue of plaintiffs' "subjective testimony" regarding claims of personal injury was addressed in *Smolen v. Chater* (1998). The court described that the administrative law judge (ALJ) must perform two stages of analysis in making a determination to accept or reject a claimant's subjective testimony regarding claimed symptoms. The two stages of analysis are as follows:

1. The Cotton Test (*Cotton v. Bowen*, 1986). The standard of this test requires that claimants who allege disability based on subjective symptoms must produce objective medical evidence of an underlying impairment that "could reasonably be expected to produce" the claimed symptoms. The evidence must also support a causal relationship between the impairments and symptoms.
2. Credibility Analysis. The standard of this test is the ALJ's finding no "affirmative evidence" that the plaintiff is malingering.

These two analyses outline a process for judges in personal injury cases to assess and try claims based on subjective pain symptoms. Nonetheless, the door remains open for malingering. Another obvious problem is the process of the ALJ's making a subjective determination about a subjective symptom.

NEUROLOGICAL/NEUROPSYCHOLOGICAL FACTORS

On a biological level, receptors to noxious stimuli are called nociceptors, which are needed for the perception of pain and are found both internally and on the surface of the skin. Together, the nociceptive and the antinociceptive pathways, which provide pain relief, constitute the beginning and end points of the body's response to physical pain. Peripheral sites and tracts converge on the spinal cord, in particular the substantia gelatinosa, consisting of nerve cells in the dorsal horn of the spine. Pain information is sent in ascending pathways to the brain. The "gate theory" (Melzack, 1973) of pain perception suggests that a limited number of pain signals enter the brain, and that there is a modulating influence on pain information and pathways descending from the brain. The primary modulating factor operating to reduce pain is the production of endogenous opiates. These are mainly amino acid chains (polypeptides) called endorphins, which emanate from CNS sites. Endorphin sites include, but are not limited to, the brain stem, especially the periaqueductal gray matter. Tolerance, withdrawal, and other morphine-like effects have been noted in regard to endorphins. In fact, much chronic pain could be due to a withdrawal reaction (due to depletion) to endogenous opioids, thus depriving the organism of relief from pain. Parker (1990) noted in this regard that pain is inversely related to presurgery B-endorphin levels.

The brain has few pain endings and cerebral lesions rarely cause pain. The exception is the (rare) thalamic pain syndrome, which may cause vague, difficult-to-localize pain. Strokes and surgery involving the thalamus create a burning sensation, contralateral from the lesioned site (Kaufman, 1985).

Dermatome analysis (Goldberg, 1987) may be relevant to the evaluation of pain deception. This involves the study of perceived pain or loss of sensation corresponding to the striplike projection areas of individual sensory nerve roots, which are distributed over the body similarly for most humans, and then relating them to reported pain in individual cases. In general, a sensory deficit involving an extremity (rather than a specific dermatome) suggests a lesion on a sensory tract within the CNS, whereas sensory deficits along a dermatome, especially when associated with localized pain, suggest a peripheral nerve lesion (Goldberg, 1987). CNS lesions, therefore, rarely produce a correspondence between dermatomes and areas of reported pain or loss of sensation.

PSYCHOLOGICAL/AFFECTIVE FACTORS

Both physical and psychic pain pathways involve the limbic system, thus associating sensory with affective information. Parker (1990) notes some psychological features of pain:

1. At low levels of arousal, pain may serve an informative function.
2. At high levels of arousal and stress, pain is accentuated.
3. Elevated tension and anger are associated with increased acute pain; chronic anxiety (e.g., "anxiety proneness") and depression are also associated with an increased perception of pain, as well as the presence of collateral physical impairment.
4. Increased pain is associated with inability to express one's feelings.

The usual psychological consequences of chronic pain include deteriorating self-esteem, irritation, sexual dysfunction, anger, and guilt. Depression may be a key psychological correlate of chronic pain (Griffith, 1990).

SOCIAL/CULTURAL FACTORS

Pain often functions as a signal to others for help and/or attention. Flor, Kerns, and Terk (1987) reported that the best predictor of self-reported pain was the person's perception of spousal reinforcement. Patients who viewed their spouses as solicitous, reported higher levels of pain and lower levels of activity. Increased dependency on others as a response to pain is common. A progressive withdrawal and isolation from others is seen in some cases. This process is exacerbated by a noted tendency for family, friends, and acquaintances to avoid people in pain. One reason for this avoidance is to reduce exposure to the unpleasant displays of the affected party. Loss of work may further reduce self-esteem and increase depression, as well as destroy the financial basis for the future of the individual.

Culturally, some persons are not encouraged to show pain responses (e.g., some Asian groups, Northern Europeans). Other groups are much more expressive (e.g., Mediterranean people, Polynesians). The evaluator needs to consider communication styles when assessing an individual's complaints of pain. In some individuals, apparently exaggerated complaints of pain may represent personal (e.g., histrionic) or subcultural (e.g., Mediterranean) styles of communication rather than evidence of intentional distortion.

TARGETS OF DECEPTION

Both pain and loss of sensation may be compensable losses. All chronic pain and sensation-loss syndromes can be targeted for deception. Although pain complaints are overrepresented in the lower-back area (where nerves are in abundance) (Griffith, 1990), reported pain can be widely distributed over the body. Lifestyle should be adversely affected with genuine pain. Thus, the evaluator needs to be alert to many targets of deception and to assess the entire lifestyle of the assessee.

Examples of potentially malingered pain include:

Behavior: Discrete motor behaviors associated with low back pain were shown by a 25-year-old male who engaged in vigorous exercise when not posturing weakness and immobility.

Somatic/psychosomatic: Pseudoseizures following an alleged painful aura-like experience were presented by a 32-year-old brick mason in an attempt to collect workers' compensation.

Sensation: Extreme reactivity to touch and pressure was shown on two point threshold tests by an 18-year-old burn patient 4 years after suffering minor (first-degree) burns.

Imagery: Painful images (flashbacks) of war were experienced by a 35-year-old male veteran even though it was determined that he had not been stationed in a combat area (see opening case in PTSD Chapter 13).

Affect: Anxiety lowered, rather than raised, perceived pain in a 45-year-old female seeking compensation for an accident involving a slight fall while disembarking from a marine craft.

Cognition: "Suicide" ideation and gestures of an unrealistic nature (hitting self with fists, trying to strangle himself) were shown by a 27-year-old in an alleged attempt to escape from a painful love relationship.

Interpersonal: Interpersonal manipulation was suggested by a 59-year-old when he required family members to wait on him after making up a history of painful heart attacks.

It is important to note genuine symptoms of pain, or signs associated with pain, which cannot be faked. These include (1) muscle atrophy and fasciculation, the latter consisting of a sometimes painful contraction of skeletal muscles in which groups of muscle fibers innervated by the same neuron contract together and (2) visual disturbances such as the pupillary light reflex, abnormal retinal appearance, ocular divergence, and nystagmus (Goldberg, 1987). All these should be considered involuntary in nature.

Evaluators should not confuse complainers with fakers. False positives are frequent in this (primitive) stage of pain analysis, as the following case demonstrates:

Lt. Arnold walked into the army mental health clinic stating that he had been referred by the internist to rule out psychological factors to a reported injury. This young officer explained that no medical cause had been found for a sharp, excruciating, but episodic pain in his lower back, first experienced when leading his platoon in calisthenics, and that he did not feel the examining physician believed him. Psychometric tests revealed many traits associated with hysteria including a substantial conversion "V" on the MMPI.

Subsequently, the lieutenant reported that the military physician, upon receiving the psychological test results, had accused the officer of malingering and ordered him back to the field. The psychologist referred the client to an osteopath who cleared up the problem in less than 15 minutes with spinal manipulation.

RESPONSE STYLES

Like targets, the kinds of behaviors associated with faking some aspect of pain include any responses that may yield a successful outcome for the faker. Honesty is common when there is no reason to fake or when cross-validating data are readily available to the evaluator. Faking good sometimes occurs when the client wishes to minimize or deny a more negatively perceived problem such as sexual dysfunction. This denial covaries with cultural upbringing and with contexts where the expression of pain may be disapproved (e.g., military, sports).

Malingering pain and faking sensory numbness may be linked to a payoff for the deceiver. Mixed and fluctuating responding can be exhibited, such as when one type of pain is exaggerated (e.g., backache) and another denied (e.g., headache), with both changing in the reported level of severity over time.

Help-seeking behaviors associated with pain and injuries are instructive to study. Peck, Fordyce, and Black (1978) studied a wide range of pain behavior in tort claim litigants. Only two conditions identified the possible fakers — they consulted fewer physicians and used more supportive devices (i.e., crutches, and prosthetics) that cost more than $200. As part of this study, Peck et al. found that claimants used less prescribed pain-relieving drugs than nonlitigants for the first month after the injury. By the sixth month, drug ingestion had dropped off sharply for both groups. In sum, the Peck et al. study suggests there are few differences between claimants and nonlitigants in help-seeking behaviors. If anything, those who had reason to fake seemed to avoid evaluators and treatment personnel. None of the following categories considered by these investigators should be regarded as indicative of faking: (1) number of hospital admissions, (2) length of stay in the hospital, (3) number of diagnostic procedures in the hospital, (4) help-seeking in regard to rehabilitative centers, (5) days lost from work, and (6) number of patient–physician contacts or specialists consulted.

In a study exploring a relationship between personality disorder diagnosis and malingering response style, a significant relationship was found between personality test validity scales and faking bad (Grillo, Brown, Hilsabeck, Price, & Lees-Haley, 1994). The investigators administered the MCMI-II and the MMPI-2 (F, K, L, F-K, O-S, Es, and FBS) to personal injury claimants. There was a positive relationship between Histrionic, Compulsive, Schizoid, Schizotypal, Paranoid, Borderline, Antisocial, Avoidant, and Passive-Aggressive personality disorders and fake bad elevations on validity indices. There was no such relationship between Dependent and Narcissistic personality disorders. The authors concluded that psychopathologic variables, and specifically personality disorders, as opposed to malingering, could account for symptom exaggeration in forensic settings. The next question is whether there is a comorbid relationship between certain personality disorders and malingering.

DETECTION STRATEGIES

Most evaluators of pain use a consistency model in determining faked pain. Yet, pain may be inconstant due to habituation, change in context, psychological modification, and other factors. This argues for a multifaceted approach to evaluation, with the hope that the results point in the same direction.

A few methods for detecting faked pain are as follows:

1. *Anatomical inconsistencies:*
   a. Pain vs. temperature: These sensations tend to coincide because they are located in the same nerve bundles. When the temperature sensation is preserved while there is a loss of pain sensation, the deficit is not considered organic in etiology. Kaufman (1985) reports that a lesion of the pain–temperature pathway (spinothalamic tract) will result in loss of pain–temperature sensation contralateral to and below the level of the lesion. This holds true whether the lesion is in the brain or in the spinal cord. Additionally, the loss of pain–temperature sensation in the right leg and loss of proprioception in the left leg suggest a single lesion on the spinal cord.
   b. Faked hemiparesis is clinically more common in the left limb than the right, perhaps because of the more frequent right-limb dominance. Often, there will be a short period of normal activity prior to the limbs "giving away" and the patient reassuming the paretic position.
   c. Fakers often have an incorrect belief about laterality of symptoms. This is exhibited when the faker describes right- or left-sided headaches in conjunction with other anomalies (e.g., hearing, sight, smell, and motor deficits) on the right side. The faker is not aware that contralateral and not ipsilateral deficits are expected from the suggested injury. Multiple lesions, causing unilateral symptoms, are required to account for the reported effects.
   d. Self-inflicted pain is usually avoided when there is voluntary control. In this sense, a person will not strike himself or herself when pretending to be in a coma or paretic. Neurologists will often use a "face-hand" test assessing alleged motor impairment, pulling the hand away from the face and suddenly letting it go.
   e. Motor inconstancies are suggested when impairments disappear under hypnosis or sodium amytal, or when the faker believes he or she is unobserved. Findings from hypnosis and drug interviews, however, should be considered weak evidence unless corroborated by independent data.
   f. Alleged pain imperception or loss of sensation is difficult to fake upon repeated bilateral stimulation. This is because fakers are relying on a subjective strategy rather than responding to the strength of the stimulus. Von Frey hairs, for example, can be used to test a faked sensory imperception bilaterally.

2. *Drug response discrepancies:* Some drugs have differing chemical composition, yet are similar in terms of effect on reducing pain. Thus, two tablets of aspirin (600 mg) are reported to have the same effect as a standard dose of Darvon, codeine, or Demerol (Kaufman, 1985). Suspected faking is associated with widely divergent pain relief from the two. This is a weak hypothesis until confirmed by cross-validating data suggesting malingering.

3. *Clinical interview behavior:* Data are lacking on interview behavior associated with faked pain. However, systems looking at faked pain and loss of sensation are beginning to be developed. Barkemeyer, Callon, and Jones (1989) have developed a malingering test for pain, loss of sensation, and other complaints. The full range of interviewing and evaluation behaviors is described in Table 12.1.

4. *Presence of psychometric signs:*

   a. Although the "conversion V" on the MMPI may or may not reflect a conversion based on a psychological conflict, it does suggest the clients' perceptions of their pain, their perceptions of affect related to their disability, and the degree of functional impairments (Tapp, 1990). This pattern is associated with a poorer prognosis for recovery and with the experience of acute, high-intensity pain. A hysterical overlay to exhibited pain may

TABLE 12.1
Barkemeyer-Callon-Jones Malingering Detecting Scale

I. Interview Behaviors

INSTRUCTIONS: For each of the behaviors described below, check those that occurred during your evaluation of the patient.

A. Introductory Phase: Spontaneous Comments by the Patient

_____   1. The patient expressed exaggerated confidence in the examiner's ability.

_____   2. The patient made statements or presentations that would appear in some way to enhance his position in society.

_____   3. The patient made denigrating statements about others in the immediate community.

B. History Taking Phase: Characteristics of the Patient's Presentation

_____   4. The patient focused on the severity of the reported problem.

_____   5. The patient focused on the impairment resulting from the reported problem.

_____   6. The patient's reasoning included no alternatives.

_____   7. The patient made temporal associations that are not known to represent cause-and-effect relationships.

_____   8. The patient described an atypical or very unlikely response to treatment.

_____   9. The patient denied responsibility for clearly voluntary acts.

_____   10. The patient presented a constellation of complaints that are not consistent with a recognized abnormality of an anatomical substrata.

_____   11. The patient's disability was emphasized during the examination to the exclusion of consideration of his abilities.

_____   12. The patient denied the ability to learn new skills to compensate for those lost.

C. History Taking Phase: Manipulation Attempts

_____   13. The patient cited another professional who allegedly agreed there was a problem.

_____   14. The patient described the prestige of other people who allegedly found a pathological process.

_____   15. The patient quoted an authority on the subject of the suspected pathological process.

_____   16. The patient used an irrational analogy to justify a claim of physical pathology.

_____   17. The patient threatened harm to himself or others if relief was not found.

_____   18. The patient overstated the examiner's authority for intervening on the patient's behalf.

_____   19. The patient implied there might be legal retaliation for a missed diagnosis of improper care.

D. Patient's Response to Questions

_____   20. The patient questioned the competence of the examiner.

_____   21. The patient gave an affirmative response to an inappropriate leading question.

E. Examination Phase

_____   22. Any physical effort resulted in enhancement of the patient's presentation of symptoms.

_____   23. The patient's responses during the examination did not support a physiological explanation.

F. Patient's Response to Disagreement

_____   24. The patient's response to the examiner's explanation suggested a distorted meaning of the examiner's statement.

_____   25. The patient demanded an explanation based on inadequate data.

_____   26. The patient questioned the examiner's motives.

II. Apparent Goals for Patient's Behavior

INSTRUCTIONS: Rate each of the following according to the likelihood of their correctness. If the statement appears to be correct in this instance, place a check mark beside it.

_____   27. The patient's complaints lead to the avoidance of a normal responsibility or a noxious activity.

_____   28. The patient's complaints result in the gain of either a concrete entity or an abstract quality.

_____   29. The patient's complaints result in the retention of either a concrete entity or an abstract quality.

Note: From Charles A. Barkemeyer, North Street Publishing Company, Baton Rouge, LA. Cutoff score of 7.6 on the 29 items revealed a hit rate of 95.1% (96.7% true positives and 90% percent true negatives). With permission.

be present. The hysteria may not be subject to control by the assessee and should not be considered deception by the evaluator.

Validity indices on the MMPI and other objective tests may be used to determine general response style. Indications of faking bad on the MMPI, for example, may suggest (but do not prove) that reported pain might also be exaggerated. Furthermore, pain is seldom experienced in the absence of other affective and psychological problems. These other problems should also be apparent in psychological test scores and profiles. In a study designed to determine the various MMPI-2 indicators of exaggeration, the profiles of 289 claimants from workers' compensation and personal injury cases were examined (Fox, Gerson, & Lees-Haley, 1995). The test indices that were reviewed included the intercorrelations of the F, F-K, MMPI Dissimulaton Scale-Revised, total of obvious minus subtle scales, Fake Bad Scale, VRIN, and TRIN. The relative sensitivity of the different scores was estimated according to various cutoffs. Factor analysis indicated that malingering could be evidenced as inconsistent responding and as symptom exaggeration. Not surprisingly, the study also found that patients evaluated at the request of plaintiff attorneys appeared to show a greater degree of symptom exaggeration and inconsistent responding compared with those referred by defense counsel.

b. An illness questionnaire developed in Australia by Clayer, Bookless, and Ross (1984) appears promising for the global assessment of distress. Validated on 164 male and female public utility workers, half of whom were instructed to fake a serious injury, and 82 male and female clients at a pain clinic, the questionnaire appeared effective in differentiating fakers from those experiencing distress that was neurotically determined. Base rates for normals and neurotics generally revealed an increasing percentage of item endorsement by the latter group. Fakers were very clearly differentiated from nonfakers (i.e., normals and neurotics) on 7 of the 62 total questions. Recalculating the data, the majority of fakers (64.2%) endorsed all the following questions compared with 27% of the nonfakers, with a 25 to 50% point spread between the two groups (mean difference = 36.8%) on each question:

- Do you care whether or not people realize you are sick?
- Do you find that you get jealous of other people's good health?
- Do you ever have silly thoughts about your health which you can't get out of your mind, no matter how hard you try?
- Are you upset by the way people take your illness?
- Do you often worry about the possibility that you have a serious illness?
- Do you often think that you might suddenly fall ill?
- Do you get the feeling that people are not taking your illness seriously enough?

c. The Millon Behavioral Health Inventory (MBHI; Millon, Green, & Meagher, 1979) attempts to measure responsivity to pain treatment as well as a host of basic coping and prognostic signs. The MBHI illustrates the great difficulty of measuring variables associated with distress. The 150-item true–false questionnaire yields 20 scores and a three-item validity scale. Test construction, reliability, and validity of the measure have been vigorously challenged (Allen, 1985; Lanyon, 1985).

d. Chronic pain self-report inventories. A number of self-report measures for chronic pain have been described. All these measures must be used with caution because of the potential for deliberate as well as nondeliberate distortion. Accordingly, none of these inventories should be considered to be a specific test for faking pain as no such reliable and valid measure exists. These checklist inventories may be useful in developing a broad database before arriving at conclusions.

The Pain Survey Checklist (PSCL) (see Appendix A) is one example of a self-report inventory. The PSCL is comprehensive, covering most known parameters of the pain experience. Significant others may be asked to fill out the checklist in regard to the patient independently, thereby providing information where follow-up assessment may be needed.

In a comparative study, Mikail, DuBreuil, and D'Eon (1993) reviewed the following nine commonly used self-report measures:

Oswestry Back Pain Disability Questionnaire
Pain Behavior Questionnaire
Beck Depression Inventory
State-Trait Anxiety Inventory
Coping Strategies Questionnaire
Pain Beliefs Questionnaire
McGill Pain Questionnaire
West Haven–Yale Multidimensional Pain Inventory
Life Impact Scale

Factor analysis identified five factors across the battery of inventories. The factors were General Affective Distress, Coping, Support, Pain Description, and Functional Capacity. The investigators reported that the combination of the Multidimensional Pain Inventory, the Beck Depression Inventory, and the McGill Pain Questionnaire best captured the pain experience with minimal overlap across instruments. The investigators also recommended that if anxiety were an issue with a specific pain case, the Trait Anxiety Inventory should be administered

The Chronic Pain Coping Inventory (CHIP; Jensen, Turner, Romano, & Strom, 1995; Hadjistavropoulos, MacLeod, & Asmundson, 1999) is another self-report checklist instrument. The CHIP is designed to provide measures of emotion-focused and task-oriented responses to injury (Hadjistavropoulos, Asmundson, & Norton, 1999). In terms of deception, all of these instruments are subject to the pitfalls of any self-reported data. The judicious use of such inventories may provide, however, records of the patient's post injury status. These data could also provide indirect measures of the patient's ongoing experience with pain and genuine commitment to rehabilitation.

  e. Other methods. Previously discussed methods for detecting malingering (e.g., analysis of learning curves, regression equations, parallel testing, explicit alternative testing) may be used in pain deception analysis, if those methods measure an associated feature of reported pain (e.g., loss of sensation).

5. *Inconsistency in community vs. evaluation behavior:* A detailed analysis of pain reportedly experienced outside the evaluation context is necessary for sound conclusions. This is based on two assumptions: (a) reduced motor activity level accompanies genuine pain and (b) the activity level shown during evaluation should be similar to that shown outside the evaluation session. Some impairment in work and in central love relationships should be reported with chronic pain. Is the claimant willing to have you speak with significant others? A refusal is suspicious. A list of specific questions that can be asked is provided in Appendix A. The same list can be given to different relatives and acquaintances to fill out independently of one another. Inconsistencies can be evaluated. A statement by significant others, for example, that nothing the claimant does changes reports of pain needs to be explored. The claimant needs to be asked what he or she does to reduce pain. The evaluator should explore statements of changes in pain in the absence of events, which would explain them.

Malingered pain is suggested when behavior in the community is inconsistent with complaints of pain.

A 32-year-old mail carrier was routinely administered psychological and medical exams as part of ongoing evaluation and treatment for an alleged neck injury reportedly caused by a fall due to an attacking dog on his route several years previously. Claimed discomfort in the neck area persisted in spite of normal MMPIs and physical/neurological exams over the years. Complaints abruptly ended when a full (and permanent) medical retirement was awarded. After retirement, the party was seen frequently on the golf driving range, engaging in strenuous exercise that only a few months previously had been reported impossible to perform.

6. *Lack of response to common interventions:* Almost all clients should show some pain relief with (a) biofeedback, (b) hypnosis, (c) mild analgesics, (d) psychotherapy for anger and arousal management, (e) relaxation exercises, (f) heat and ice, and (g) mild exercise. The client should show pain relief in his limbs or lower back with transcutaneous electrical nerve stimulation (TENS). TENS involves an electric stimulus being applied near the painful site, which has the effect of creating analgesia. Why a person with chronic pain would not show some improvement with these methods needs to be answered and integrated into evaluation findings.

INDICATIONS OF FAKED PAIN AND LOSS OF SENSATION

1. (a) Pain. Pain-free behaviors observed in community are absent or denied during evaluation, or
   (b) Loss of sensation. Behavior in community implies sensitivity which is absent or denied during evaluation.
2. Admission of exaggeration or fabrication.
3. Violation of anatomical laws involving dermatomes, pain vs. temperature loss, paresis, cerebral laterality, and motor functioning.
4. (a) Malingering on psychometric measures of psychopathology.
   (b) Failing tests specifically designed to assess faking.
5. Failure to show improvement when treated with typically effective interventions.

Research investigating the nature of pain syndromes continues to be a very challenging area of clinical practice (Lautenbacher & Rollman, 1999). The experience of pain is an inevitable and ubiquitous aspect of human existence. The evaluation, treatment, and management of pain is a very costly expense in the ongoing effort to achieve productive and functional lifestyles for all cross sections of socioeconomic strata (Block, Kremer, & Fernandez, 1999).

Perhaps an indication of the frustration with the challenge of forensic evaluations, some authors (Johnson & Lesniak-Karpiak, 1997) have suggested warning patients that simulation of symptoms may be detected. Such a warning is an ethically questionable assertion, given the current limitations in detecting pain deception. An additional consideration is that others (Youngjohn, Lees-Haley, & Binder, 1999) have noted that such warnings only serve to prevent detection of deception. When warned, malingers feign symptoms with less exaggeration and generally offer more believable presentation. Although still far from a refined art, the clinical differentiation of actual and falsified pain continues to be an area of active research. Craig, Hill, and McMurtry (1999) summarized that the most recent research regarding malingered pain provides the following evidence:

1. Genuine presentations of pain differ from deceptive presentations; the research challenges are to develop procedural methodologies that reliably distinguish these differences across various types of pain presentations and in real-life clinical situations.
2. Informed and careful observers-clinicians, as well as others, can discriminate genuine and deceptive presentations.
3. Empirically informed assessment approaches can be developed.

LEGAL REFERENCES

Boyd v. General Industries, 11 Ark. 103, 733 S.W.2d 750 (Ark.Ct.App. 1987), 244 Ark. 141, 424 S.W.2d.
Cotten v. Bowen, 799 F.2d 1403 (9th Cir. 1986).
Guidry v. J & Eads Const. Co., 11 Ark.App. 219, 669 S.W.2d 48 (1984).
Keever v. Middletown, 1998 FED App. 0167 (6th Cir. 1998) (No. 95-00716).
Quint v. A. E. Staley, 172 F.3d 1, *1999 U.S. LEXIS 4145 (1999).

Smolen v. Chater, 80 F.3rd 1273 (1998) (No. 94-35056).

Royer v. Cantrelle, 267 So.2d 601 (La.Ct.App. 3rd 1972), writ denied, 263 La. 626, 268 So.2d 680 (1972).

Yager v. Labor and Industry Review Commission, Sentry Insurance Company and Lands' End, 599 N.W.2d 666 (1999) (Wisc. App. LEXIS 631) (No. 98-2378).

REFERENCES

Allen, M. (1985). Review of Millon Behavioral Health Inventory. In J. V. Mitchell (Ed.), *The Ninth Mental Measurements Yearbook* (p. 1521). Lincoln, NE: University of Nebraska Press.

Barkemeyer, C., Callon, E., & Jones, G. (1989). *Malingering detection scale manual*. Baton Rouge, LA: North Street Publishing Company.

Block, A. R., Kremer, E. F., & Fernandez, E. (1999). *Handbook of pain syndromes: Biopsychosocial perspectives*. Mahwah, NJ: Erlbaum Associates.

Clayer, J., Bookless, C., & Ross, M. (1984). Neurosis and conscious symptom exaggeration: Its differentiation by the illness behavior questionnaire. *Journal of Psychosomatic Research, 28*, 237–241.

Craig, K. D., Hill, M. L., & McMurtry, B. W. (1999). Detecting deception and malingering. In A. R. Block, E. F. Kremer, & E. Fernadez (Eds.), *Handbook of pain syndromes: Biopsychosocial perspectives* (pp. 41–58). Mahwah, NJ: Erlbaum Associates.

Dunn, J. T., Brown, P. R., Lees-Haley, P. R., & English, L. T. (1993). Neurotoxic and neuropsychologic symptom base rates: A comparison of three groups. Paper presented at the 13th Annual Conference of the National Academy of Neuropsychology, Phoenix, AZ.

Flor, H., Kerns, R., & Turk, D. (1987). The role of spouse reinforcement, perceived pain, and activity levels of chronic pain patients. *Journal of Psychosomatic Research, 31*, 251–259.

Fox, D. D., Gerson, A., & Lees-Haley, P. R. (1995). Interrelationship of MMPI-2 validity scales in personal injury claims. *Journal of Clinical Psychology, 51*(1), 42–47.

Galin, K. E., & Thorn, B. E. (1993). Unmasking pain: Detection of deception in facial expressions. *Journal of Social and Clinical Psychology, 12*(2), 182–197.

Goldberg, S. (1987). *The 4-minute neurologic exam*. Miami, FL: MedMaster.

Griffith, J. (1990). *Pain management: Learning to live with ongoing pain and disability*. Paper presented at Hickam Air Force Base, Honolulu, HI.

Grillo, J., Brown, R. S., Hilsabeck, R., Price, J. R., & Lees-Haley, P. R. (1994). Raising doubts about claims of malingering: Implications of relationships between MCMI-II and MMPI-2 performances. *Journal of Clinical Psychology, 50*(4), 651–655.

Hadjistavropoulos, T. (1999). Chronic pain on trial: The influence of litigation and compensation on chronic pain syndromes. In A. R. Block, E. F. Kremer, & E. Fernandez, (Eds.), *Handbook of pain syndromes: Biopsychosocial perspectives* (pp. 59–76). Mahwah, NJ: Erlbaum Associates, Inc.

Hadjistavropoulos, H. D., Asmundson, G. J. G., & Norton, G. R. (1999). Validation of the Coping with Health, Injuries, and Problems Scale in a chronic pain sample. *Clinical Journal of Pain, 15*(1), 41–49.

Hadjistavropoulos, H. D., Craig, K. D., Grunau, R. E., & Whitfield, M. F. (1997). Judging pain in infants: Behavioural, contextual and developmental determinants. *Pain, 73*(3) 319–324.

Hadjistavropoulos, H. D., Craig, K. D., Hadjistavropoulos, T., & Poole, G. D. (1996). Subjective judgments of deception in pain expression: Accuracy and errors. *Pain, 65*(2–3), 251–258.

Hadjistavropoulos, H. D., MacLeod, F. K., & Asmundson, G. J. G. (1999). Validation of the Chronic Pain Coping Inventory. *Pain, 80*(3), 471–481.

Hadjistavropoulos, T., McCurty, B., & Craig, K. D. (1996) Beautiful faces in pain: Biases and accuracy in the perception of pain. *Psychology and Health, 11*(3), 411–420.

James, S. (1998). Malingering: Maze of recovery, money, and law confronts insurers. *Issues of Injury, 12*(3), 1–5.

Jensen, M. P., Turner, J. A., Romano, J. M., & Strom, S. E. (1995). The Chronic Pain Inventory: Development and preliminary validation. *Pain, 60*(2), 203–216.

Johnson, J. L., & Lesniak-Karpiak, K. (1997). The effects of warning on malingering on memory tasks in college samples. *Archives of Clinical Neuropsychology, 12*(3) 231–238.

Kaufman, D. (1985). *Clinical neurology for psychiatrists* (2nd ed.). Orlando, FL: Grune and Stratton.

LaChapelle, D. L., Hadjistavropoulos, T., & Craig, K. D. (1999). Pain measurement in persons with intellectual disabilities. *Clinical Journal of Pain, 15*(1), 13–23.

Lanyon, R. I. (1985). Review of Millon Behavioral Health Inventory. In J. V. Mitchell (Ed.), *The ninth mental measurements yearbook* (p. 1205). Lincoln, NE: University of Nebraska Press.

Lautenbacher, S., & Rollman, G. B. (1999). Somatization, hypochodriasis, and related conditions. In A. R. Block, E. F. Kremer, & E. Fernandez, (Eds.), *Handbook of pain syndromes: Biopsychosocial perspectives* (pp. 613–632). Mahwah, NJ: Erlbaum Associates.

Lees-Haley, P. (1989). Litigation Response Syndrome: How the stress of litigation confuses the issues in personal injury, family and criminal litigation. *Defense Counsel Journal, 56*(1), 110–114.

Lees-Haley, P. (1990). Contamination of neuropsychological testing by litigation. *Forensic Reports, 3*(4), 421–426.

Lees-Haley, P. (1992). Neuropsychological complaint base rates of personal injury claimants. *Forensic Reports, 5*(5), 385–391.

Lees-Haley, P., & Dunn, J. T. (1994). The ability of naive subjects to report symptoms of mild brain injury, post-traumatic stress disorder, major depression, and generalized stress disorder. *Journal of Clinical Psychology, 50*(2), 252–256.

Lees-Haley, P., & Fox, D. (1990). Neurological false positives in litigation: Trail Making Test findings. *Perceptual and Motor Skills, 70*, 1379–1382.

Lees-Haley, P. R., Williams, C. W., & Brown, R. S. (1993). The Barnum effect and personal injury litigation. *American Journal of Forensic Psychology, 11*(2), 21–28.

Lees-Haley, P. R., Williams, C. W., & English, L. T. (1996). Response bias in self-reported history of plaintiffs compared with nonlitigating patients. *Psychological Reports, 79*(3), 811–818.

Lees-Haley, P. R., Williams, C. W., Zasler, N. D., Marguilies, S., English, L. T., & Stevens, K. B. (1997). Response bias in plaintiffs' histories. *Brain Injury, 11*(11), 791–799.

Melzack, R. (1973). *The puzzle of pain*. New York: Basic Books.

Mikail, S. A., DuBreuil, S., & D'Eon, J. L. (1993). A comparative analysis of measures used in the assessment of chronic pain patients. *Psychological Assessment, 5*(1), 117–120.

Miller, M. J. (1992). The Pinocchio syndrome: Lying and its impact on the counseling process. *Counseling and Values, 37*(1), 25–31.

Millon, T., Green, C. J., & Meagher, R. B. (1979). The MBHI: A new inventory for the psychodiagnostician in medical settings. *Professional Psychology, 10*, 529–539.

Parker, R. (1990). *Traumatic brain injury and neuropsychological impairment*. New York: Springer-Verlag.

Peck, C., Fordyce, W., & Black, R. (1978). The effect of the pendency of claims for compensation upon behavior indicative of pain. *Washington Law Review, 53*, 251–264.

Poole, G. D., & Craig, K. D. (1992). Judgments of genuine, suppressed, and faked facial expressions of pain. *Journal of Personality and Social Psychology, 63*(5), 797–805.

Stein, J. A. (1972). *Damages and recovery — Personal injury and death actions* (Sec. 22). San Francisco, CA: Bancroft Whitney Co.

Tapp, J. (1990). A multisystems perspective on chronic pain. *Psychotherapy in Private Practice, 7*, 1–16.

Williams, C. W., Lees-Haley, P. R., & Djanogly, S. E. (1999). Clinical scrutiny of litigants' self-reports. *Professional Psychology: Research & Practice, 30*(4), 361–367.

Williams, C. W., Lees-Haley, P. R., & Price, J. R. (1998). Self-attention and reported symptoms: Implications for forensic assessment. *Professional Psychology: Research & Practice, 29*(2), 125–129.

Youngjohn, J. R., Lees-Haley, P. R., & Binder, L. M. (1999). Comment: Warning malingerers produces morre sophisticated malingering. *Archives of Clinical Neuropsychology, 14*(6), 511–515.

13 Post-Traumatic Stress Disorder and Deception

Post-traumatic stress disorder (PTSD) is a pathological form of persistent anxiety that is precipitated by a severe trauma. Psychiatric symptoms in reaction to extreme trauma have been described for centuries (Deykin, 1999; Kinzie & Goetz, 1996; Starcevic & Slavoljub, 1993). The prevalence of PTSD in returning Vietnam veterans prompted formal recognition of the syndrome in DSM-III-R (1980). The syndrome continues in DSM-IV (1994). For the past decade, PTSD has been a very popular area of research and there have been thousands of articles dealing with variants of PTSD clinical presentation. A very few of these articles have addressed malingering as a primary variable.

The syndrome of PTSD originally evolved from the postcombat experiences of World War II soldiers and concentration camp survivors who reacted with characteristic clusters of symptoms (Kinzie & Goetz, 1996). For some time, but especially over the past 10 to 15 years, the applicability of PTSD has been expanded to virtually every kind of trauma experience that could conceivably induce psychological stress. Victims of PTSD include individuals exposed to any of the overlapping categories of (1) consummated, attempted, and threatened violent crimes; (2) child and spouse abuse; (3) auto accidents involving severe injury; (4) industrial accidents; (5) civilian catastrophes; and (6) war and associated activities. The spectrum of PTSD interpretations is depicted in the studies summarized in Table 13.1.

While the expansion of PTSD applications is perhaps a tribute to the creativity of mental health professionals, there are other critical issues involved. PTSD is recognized in DSM-IV, rendering the disorder an identified psychiatric problem; as such, it is subject to managed care benefits coverage and, more to the point, it can be a compensable disorder in eligibility claims or in civil tort action.

A 42-year-old U.S. Air Force veteran, determined by the Veterans' Administration (VA) to have a 50% service-connected disability for schizophrenia, applied for PTSD-related VA compensation on the basis of alleged war service in Indochina. John M. claimed that he was in the Blue Berets, a special unit of the USAF trained for paramilitary and military police duties, and was stationed in the central highlands in Vietnam from 1966 to 1967.

John M. reported nightmares and flashbacks, which he linked to frequent fire fights, night patrols, and venturing into neighboring Cambodia on "special assignments." His history revealed sporadic employment since the military, four marriages accompanied by spouse abuse, and chronic substance dependence. He reported multiple instances of closed head trauma due to fighting over the years. John M. claimed that he obtained a Ph.D. in theoretical mathematics from Princeton University and an MFA from Yale University after serving in Indochina; however, when contacted by the evaluator, these institutions indicated that there were no records of the veteran. VA records revealed that John M. was stationed in Washington State at the time he claimed service in Vietnam. During the evaluation, he did not wish to discuss his USAF experience, stating that it brought back bad memories. Neuropsychological and psychological testing revealed no cerebral injury or psychosis, but a pronounced tendency to fake bad within a Mixed Personality Disorder. His claim was subsequently denied.

TABLE 13.1
The Spectrum of PTSD Applications

PTSD Clinical Presentation	Study
Accident-related pain, affective disturbance, and disability	Geisser et al. (1996)
Adolescent cancer	Pelcovitz et al. (1998)
Adolescent psychiatric inpatients	Koltec et al. (1998)
Adolescent survivors of a cruise ship disaster	Yule, Ten Bruggencate, & Joseph (1994)
Australian Vietnam veterans	O'Toole et al. (1998)
Bereaved children of the Oklahoma City bombing	Pfefferbaum et al. (1999)
Bereavement	Zisook, Chentsova-Dutton, & Shuchter (1998)
Bone marrow transplantation after breast surgery patients	Jacobsen et al. (1998)
Bosnian refugees, 1 year after resettlement in the United States	Weine et al. (1998)
Breast cancer treatment	Cordova et al. (1995)
Burn injury victims	Difede & Barocas (1999)
California toxic spill victims	Freed, Bowler, & Fleming (1998)
Children and adolescents	Cohen et al. (1998); Cuffe et al. (1998); Famularo et al. (1996); McCloskey & Walker (2000)
Children exposed to disaster	Anthony, Lonigan, & Hecht (1999)
Child sexual abuse victims and their mothers	Timmons-Mitchell, Chandler-Holtz, & Semple (1997)
Combat	Henning & Frueh (1997)
Combat-related head injury	Chemtob et al. (1998)
Concussions from motor vehicle accidents	Price (1994)
Criminal defense of Vietnam veterans	Higgins (1991)
Croatian soldiers at East Slavonian Front	Pozgain et al. (1992)
Dutch war veterans	Jongedijk et al. (1996)
Factitious PTSD in fishing disaster victim	Fear (1996)
Female Vietnam war veterans	Wolfe et al. (1994)
HIV victims	Kelly et al. (1998)
Holocaust survivors	Yehuda, Kahana, et al. (1995)
Incarcerated women with histories of childhood abuse	Zlotnick (1997)
Jewish adolescents' brief exposure to concentration camps	Silverman et al. (1999)
Khmer children survivors of the horrors of the Pol Pot regime (1975–1979)	Sack, Aim, & Dickason(1999)
Mass shooting survivors	North, Smith, & Spitznagel (1994)
Mild traumatic brain injury	Bryant & Harvey, 1998; Bryant, Mayou, & Lloyd-Bolstock (1997)
Mothers of pediatric cancer survivors	Manne et al. (1998)
Motor vehicle accident victims	Blanchard, Hickling, Taylor, Forneris, et al. (1995); Geisser et al. (1996)
Myocardial infarction	Kutz et al. (1994)
Nonsexual assault victims	Riggs, Rothbaum, & Foa (1995)
Peers of adolescent suicide victims	Brent et al. (1995)
Physician internships	Klamen, Grossman, & Kopacz (1995)
PTSD in elderly people	Weintraub & Ruskin (1999)
PTSD simulated to disguise opiate withdrawal	Salloway, Southwick, & Sadowsky (1990)
Rape victims	Resnick (1991)
Refugees with history of exposure to severe trauma	Ferrada-Noli et al. (1998)
Schizophrenia sufferers hospitalized involuntarily	Priebe, Brocker, & Gunkel (1998)
Southeast Asian refugees	Kinzie et al. (1990)
Surviving siblings and parents of unexpected childhood death	Appelbaum & Burns (1991)
Traffic accident victims	Koren, Arnon, & Klein (1999); Ursano et al. (1999)

TABLE 13.1 *(continued)*
The Spectrum of PTSD Applications

PTSD Clinical Presentation	Study
Trauma survivors	Shalev et al. (1997)
Traumatized police officers	Carlier et al. (1996)
Tortured POWs	Kozaric-Kovacic, Marusic, & Ljubin (1999); Neal, Hill, Hughes, Middleton, & Basuttil (1995)
Women hospitalized for eating disorders	Gleaves et al. (1998)
Women with childhood rape histories	Epstein, Saunders, & Kilpatrick (1997)
Work-related injury	Asmundson et al. (1998)
Veterans with spinal cord injuries	Radnitz et al. (1998)
Vietnam veterans	Jordan, Nunley, & Cook (1992); Orsillo et al. (1996); Weyermann, Norris, & Hyer (1996); Zatzick et al. (1997)
Vietnam veterans in prison	Sigafoos (1994)

PTSD AND THE LAW

PTSD-related personal injury and wrongful death claims are garnering large awards. In a $9,250,000 verdict for the wrongful death and emotional distress related to a traffic sign falling on their car and killing the plaintiffs' 3¹/₂-year-old daughter (Case No. 86-6149 [CL] I; Judge Jack H. Cook presiding), PTSD-related data influenced the high award. Zarin and Weitzman (1990) stated the following in their analysis of this Palm Beach County, Florida case:

> The treating psychiatrist testified as to the effect of unjust and violent circumstances. The plaintiff mother testified that every time she views her scar in the mirror or touches her scar, it causes a flashback of the vision of her daughter's face spilt [sic] in half. As of the date of trial, the plaintiff mother continued to experience multiple flashbacks on a daily basis of the vision of her daughter's face. (p. 6)

In a $780,000 verdict where a child was molested by a stranger inserting a finger into her vagina, the victim's PTSD and diminution in IQ were successfully asserted (*Barraza v. Jewelry Realty Corp.*, Index No. 22283/78: Judge Richard Rosenbloom, April 12, 1990.) Zarin and Weitzman (1990) state the following in their analysis of the case:

> The plaintiff's examining clinical psychologist testified that the assault caused a severe post-traumatic stress disorder which has continued to the present. The plaintiff was 19 at the time of the subject trial. The plaintiff's expert related that the plaintiff continues to experience nightmares, fear of traveling and fear of enclosed spaces. This expert additionally related that the incident caused a flat emotional affect, rendering the plaintiff unable to express emotions normally. The plaintiff's expert educational psychologist testified that the plaintiff scored within the low/normal range upon IQ testing. The expert maintained that the plaintiff's results in various sub-tests differed widely and contended that such an "inter-test score scatter" generally reflects emotional instability. The plaintiff's clinical psychologist concurred in this conclusion. (p. 6)

In criminal cases, PTSD is frequently asserted either as a basis for the insanity defense, as a basis for diminished capacity, or as a factor in mitigation of punishment.

BACKGROUND

PTSD has been given different names in the successive revisions of the American Psychiatric Association's Diagnostic and Statistical Manual (DSM):

DSM I (1952) Gross Stress Reaction
DSM II (1968) Adjustment Disorder of Adult Life
DSM-III (1980) Post Traumatic Stress Disorder
DSM-III-R (1987) Post Traumatic Stress Disorder
DSM-IV (1994) Post Traumatic Stress Disorder

The introduction of PTSD in DSM-III caused considerable legal and clinical concern. An "official" mental disorder such as PTSD that is recognized by most courts and insurance companies may be misused in civil and criminal litigation. PTSD is largely subjective and may be seen as an easy (and unverifiable) mental condition to serve the interests of litigants seeking monetary compensation or relief from punitive action. In addition, a professional may be reluctant to diagnose faked PTSD. In the case described at the beginning of this chapter, for example, evaluation of John M. followed at least a dozen previous mental assessments subsequent to his discharge from the military. The documentation that the claimant was in Washington State when he claimed he was involved in combat was available to all examiners, yet none questioned the genuineness of his claim.

DIAGNOSTIC CRITERIA AND ASSOCIATED DYNAMICS

With the introduction of DSM-III and in succeeding editions, the objective has been to define psychiatric syndromes based primarily on data from empirical studies. Prior versions of the DSM were problematic because of reliance on different theories of psychopathology, most notably psychoanalysis. Since DSM-III, changes in the criteria for a given psychiatric disorder have been based on new empirical developments. Accordingly, there have been ongoing modifications of PTSD criteria based on empirical data. Nonetheless, our understanding of PTSD has continued to be confounded by questions of nomenclature, etiology, and compensation (Kinzie & Goetz, 1996).

According to DSM-IV, a diagnosis of PTSD requires exposure to a traumatic event in which both of the following conditions are met: (1) the person experienced, witnessed, or was confronted with an event or events that involved actual or threatened death or serious injury, or a threat to the physical integrity of self or others; (2) the person's response involved intense fear, helplessness, or horror. (*Note:* In children, this may be expressed instead by disorganized or agitated behavior.)

The DSM-IV field trial findings suggested that PTSD was associated with symptoms tradition-ally ascribed to hysteria. These symptoms include problems with stimulus discrimination, self-regulation, and cognitive integration of experience (van der Kolk et al., 1996). The formal DSM-IV symptom criteria for PTSD span three specific areas. The *first* is persistent reexperience of the traumatic event to include recurrent and intrusive distressing recollections, dreams, and feelings. The reexperiencing may also be in the form of intense psychological distress, or physiological reactivity in response to internal or external cues that in some way serve to symbolize the traumatic event. The *second* cluster of symptoms is persistence avoidance of stimuli cues associated with the traumatic event. These can include efforts to avoid thoughts, feelings, conversations, activities, places, or people that arouse recollections of the traumatic event. Other symptoms in this cluster include restricted affect, inability to recall aspects of the traumatic event, and feelings of detachment or estrangement. DSM-IV added the symptom of a sense of foreshortened future to this cluster. The *third* cluster is persistent symptoms of increased arousal. The relevant indications include sleeping difficulties, irritability, anger outbursts, hypervigilance, exaggerated startle response, and difficulties concentrating. Minimal impact was found on three traditional PTSD instruments (Mississippi Scale for Combat-Related PTSD, MMPI–2 Pk PTSD, and Impact of Events Scale) because of the criteria changes from DSM-III-R to DSM-IV (Engdahl, Eberly, & Blake, 1996)

The development of PTSD is associated with the degree of life threat, for example, bone marrow transplantation for breast cancer (Jacobsen et al., 1998), and motor vehicle accident victims (Blanchard, Hickling, Taylor, Forneris, et al., 1995; Geisser, 1996). In a study with female rape victims,

Cascardi, Riggs, Hearst-Ikeda, and Foa (1996) investigated the consequences of the assault occurring in safe or dangerous environments and by "safe" vs. "dangerous" assailants. The rape victims reported more severe PTSD symptoms, and the most significant lifestyle changes, when the assault was in a safe location and perpetrated by a dangerous assailant. The authors suggested that assault brutality and violation of safety expectations were two key variables influencing the severity of post-trauma reactions in assault victims.

Symptom intensity levels are higher and PTSD more severe and long-lasting if the trauma is of human design (e.g., war), involves intrusive stimuli from the perpetrator and helplessness on the part of the victim (e.g., torture, rape), or sets off, or is associated with, a physical component (e.g., malnutrition, head trauma).

The traumatic event can be reexperienced by recurrent and intrusive recollections — "flashbacks" — of the event, recurrent nightmares, or suddenly behaving as if the traumatic event was present because of a presumed association with an environmental or mental event (e.g., dissociative states). The individual, for a time, pays exclusive attention to the dominant reality represented by the experienced imagery, feeling state, and/or ideation. PTSD is ruled out if reexperiencing of the trauma cannot be demonstrated by relevant behaviors or be established by diagnostically consistent self-report, observation, laboratory tests, or psychometric findings.

The experience of reliving the trauma, illusions, hallucinations, dissociative states, and intrusive recall may be organic in origin. Subsequent to a "biologically important event ... all recently active circuits may be 'printed'" (Livingston, 1985, p. 1270) by neurotransmitters.

Numbing of responsiveness to, or reduced involvement with, the external world usually begins not long after the traumatic event. An individual may show a diminished sex drive, feel disinterested in previously enjoyed pastimes, and complain of emotional isolation and distance from others. Affect is constricted, meaning that the previous range of emotion shown toward others or activities is narrowed, usually in the direction of showing little emotion. In particular, tenderness and caring appear to be absent or diminished compared with premorbid behavior.

The affected individual experiences autonomic arousal and related symptoms in the form of high anxiety, depression, and guilt. There is often a lack of insight regarding the reason for the impairment of memory or concentration. Attempts to suppress symptoms are often revealed in substance abuse, high geographic mobility, and avoidance of activities that resemble the original trauma.

PTSD also involves difficulty falling or staying asleep, irritability, outbursts of violence with fears of losing control, difficulty concentrating, and an exaggerated startle response.

Epidemiological data suggested that approximately 80% of PTSD cases meet the criteria for at least one other psychiatric disorder (Brady, 1997). The most frequent comorbid manifestations are affective disorders, other anxiety disorders, somatization, substance abuse, and dissociative disorders. The course and clinical presentation of PTSD, as well as the optimal treatment approach, can be significantly affected by comorbid disorders. The comorbidity issue also has significant forensic implications. It is critical that PTSD be differentially diagnosed from other similar mental conditions or that comorbid presentation is accurately identified. The key to this analysis is careful consideration of the onset and duration criteria of the disorder(s). Amir et al. (1997) noted the similarity of diffuse pain syndromes with PTSD cases that in actuality may be undiagnosed fibromyalgia syndrome. With comorbid PTSD and fibromyalgia, the patients reported more tenderness, more pain, lower quality of life, higher functional impairment, and more distress that is psychological.

PTSD can dissipate and then be diagnosed for a later time period, especially if symptoms of the first PTSD episode persisted more than 1 month, the temporal cutoff point suggested by DSM-IV. There is no durational limit to PTSD; it depends upon treatment resources, individual symptoms, and severity of the original trauma(s).

PTSD can occur with children, adolescents (Giacona et al., 1995), and adults (for a review of PTSD issues with children and adolescents, see Deykin, 1999). The American Academy of Child and Adolescent Psychiatry recently published practice parameters for the assessment and treatment of children and adolescents with PTSD (Cohen et al., 1998).

Based on interviews with 337 children from ages 6 to 12, McCloskey and Walker (2000) found that a significant number of children abused by family members, or who were exposed to certain single-event trauma, developed PTSD symptoms. In the study, the leading PTSD precipitants were death or illness of someone close to the child. Family violence and exposure to violent crime also prompted PTSD. In contrast, witnessing a motor vehicle accident or a drowning was not highly associated with PTSD manifestations. The data suggested that children who were targets of abuse were more likely to evidence PTSD compared with children who witnessed another family member being abused. The children with PTSD evidenced a high comorbidity for phobias, separation anxiety, and oppositional disorder.

Children and adolescents with PTSD evidenced poorer overall memory performance (measured with the Rivermead Behavioral Memory Test, RBMT) compared with controls (Moradi, Doost, Taghavi, Yule, & Dalgleish, 1999). The PTSD youngsters also performed more poorly on prospective and orientation items of the RBMT.

One new area of research with PTSD in children is the impact of victim PTSD distress on significant others. For example, with child sexual abuse victims, Timmons-Mitchell, Chandler-Holtz, and Semple (1997) described the victims' mothers as more prone to exhibit PTSD symptoms, if the mothers had been child sex abuse victims themselves. The secondary gain potentials of many PTSD circumstances make it a syndrome highly prone to both deliberate and nondeliberate deception. In DSM-IV, there were modest but significant changes in the DSM-III-R criteria. DSM-IV explicitly cautions, "Malingering should be ruled out in those situations in which financial remuneration, benefit eligibility and forensic determinations play a role" (p. 427).

A decision tree for PTSD, compatible with DSM III-R, was offered by Hall (1990). The DSM-IV changes in the criteria for PTSD utilizing Hall's decision tree model are depicted in Figure 13.1. A significant forensic problem with all PTSD cases is ruling out preexisting PTSD and ruling out comorbid psychiatric disorders. At the very least the preexisting and comorbid dynamics must be acknowledged and some effort made to factor out the relative etiological roles to the victim's current status. In one study dealing with civilian survivors of mass shootings, the rates of preexisting PTSD were high, but not predictive of postdisaster PTSD (North, Smith, & Spitznagel, 1994). In the same study, 50% of the women and 25% of the men were diagnosed with comorbid postdisaster psychiatric diagnoses, most notably major depression. Psychopathology was infrequent in subjects without PTSD.

The following case illustrates a particularly dramatic case of PTSD in family members:

On May 5, 1985 at around midday in his family residence, Jerry S., a single, unemployed, 23-year-old Filipino male, used a knife to destroy some family pictures and frames.

This behavior followed a long series of strange and potentially violent actions, including attacking the walls, doors, and living room table with a large knife, responding to auditory hallucinations, talking to the television, and threatening family members with a knife. When his father asked him for the knife, Jerry S. started shouting as though his deceased brothers were in front of him, then attacked his father. During the next few minutes, Jerry S. attacked four family members with the knife, including his sister and his 1½-year-old nephew, fatally stabbed his mother in the heart, and attempted to run his father down with an automobile. He then went to the residence of other family members, knife in hand, covered with blood, and asked them if they wanted to die. He was apprehended the following day by police after escaping from the scene of his violence. A list of the injuries and impact on the surviving victims is provided below:

1. Fred S. (the father) was stabbed or sliced multiple times in the torso, hand, and shoulder. The victim was hospitalized for 10 days at Sunrise Hospital and subjected to several operations for his life-threatening injuries. He was placed on psychotropic medication (Valium) upon release. Post-Traumatic Stress Disorder (PTSD) symptoms commenced soon after the assault and included sleep problems and poor appetite. PTSD symptoms were still reported several years later. Severe and chronic PTSD included the following:

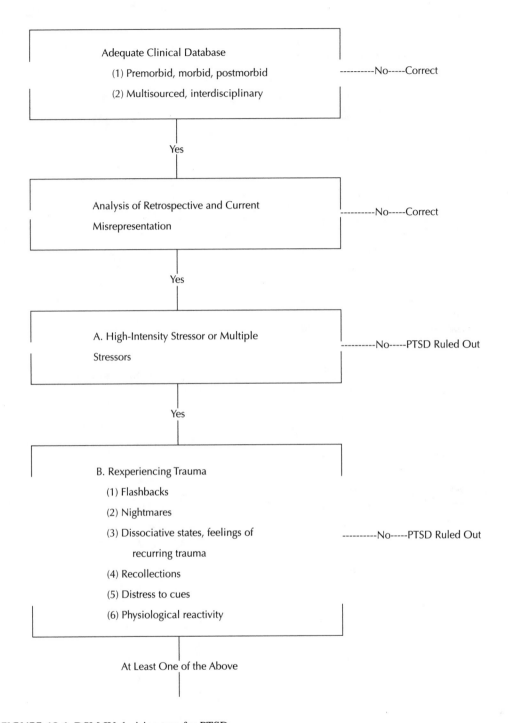

FIGURE 13.1 DSM-IV decision tree for PTSD.

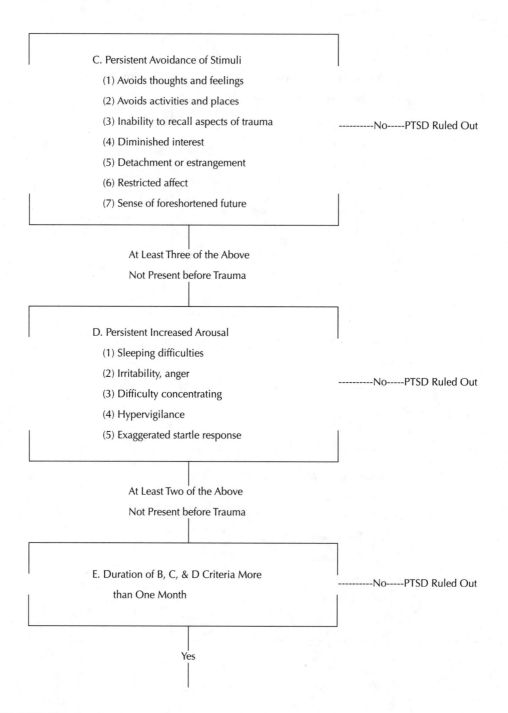

C. Persistent Avoidance of Stimuli

(1) Avoids thoughts and feelings

(2) Avoids activities and places

(3) Inability to recall aspects of trauma   ----------No-----PTSD Ruled Out

(4) Diminished interest

(5) Detachment or estrangement

(6) Restricted affect

(7) Sense of foreshortened future

At Least Three of the Above

Not Present before Trauma

D. Persistent Increased Arousal

(1) Sleeping difficulties

(2) Irritability, anger

(3) Difficulty concentrating   ----------No-----PTSD Ruled Out

(4) Hypervigilance

(5) Exaggerated startle response

At Least Two of the Above

Not Present before Trauma

E. Duration of B, C, & D Criteria More   ----------No-----PTSD Ruled Out

than One Month

Yes

FIGURE 13.1 *Continued*.

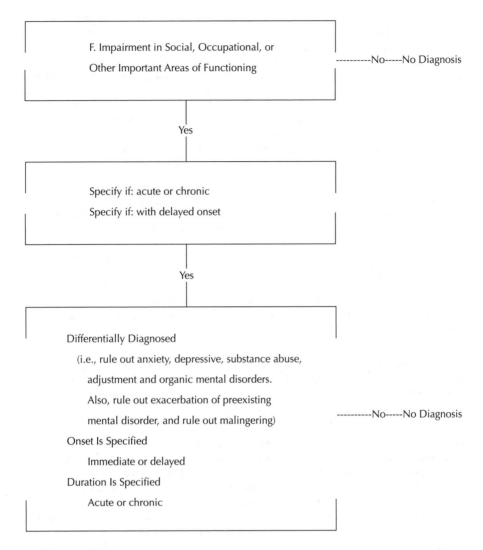

FIGURE 13.1 *Continued.*

a. Existence of a recognizable stressor that would evoke significant symptoms of distress in almost everyone. This included the sustained wounds, the thought that other family members would be killed or wounded, and later finding out about the multiple assaults and his wife's death.

b. Reexperiencing the trauma. This included frequent nightmares of the incident, vivid daytime memories of the assaults and killing of his wife, and panic attacks.

c. Numbing of responsiveness to or reduced involvement with the external world. This included a loss of interest in usual activities, problems in trusting others, and few, if any, leisure activities. Fred attempted to remain active in the yard to a limited degree as a coping mechanism for the incident, for example, continuing to plant the favorite vegetables of his wife in the family garden even though that was seen as unnecessary by other family members. He occasionally broke down in tears.

d. Relevant other symptoms. These included difficulty falling asleep; waking during the night, usually around 2 or 3 a.m. with continued wakefulness for the remainder of the day; startle responses; and avoidance of activities that reminded him of the incident including moving from the residence at which the violence took place.

2. Lucille L. was stabbed by her brother multiple times in the arm, back, and hand; some of her wounds were sustained when she attempted to keep the perpetrator away from her baby, Tom L. Some stab wounds were deep (e.g., right chest, $3^1/_2$-in. penetration; another wound $2^1/_2$ in. deep) with a confirmed pneumothorax (right chest) and a subsequent exploratory operation at Sunrise Hospital. PTSD symptoms commenced while she was in the hospital and included insomnia and obsessive rumination about the incident. She was given Dalmane for sleep intervention at a follow-up visit, with the medical observation that the patient appeared depressed. Lucille reported that for 2 months after hospitalization, she could barely move. For 4 months after the incident, she could not engage in housework, sex, socialization with others, or take care of her son Tom. PTSD symptoms reported in 1985 continued with only mild improvement through 1990. Inspection of pre-1985 medical records revealed that Lucille was a basically healthy person. Chronic PTSD is suggested as follows:

a. Existence of a recognizable stressor that would evoke significant symptoms of distress in almost everyone. This included for Lucille the sustained wounds, fear that her wounded child would die, knowledge of the assaults on family members including the death of her mother and the stabbing of her son.
b. Reexperiencing the trauma. This included vivid memories and flashbacks of the assaults and panic attacks where she became anxious, faint, dizzy, and behaviorally disorganized.
c. Numbing of responsiveness to or reduced involvement with the external world. For Lucille, this meant often feeling emotionally blocked, unresponsive, and/or unable to express her feelings.
d. Relevant other symptoms: Insomnia, waking up during the night, and excessive jumpiness were present.

3. Tom L., son of Lucille L., sustained stab wounds to the left side of his forehead, left thigh, and under his chin (all about 1-in. lacerations). Prolonged crying was witnessed up to and long after admission to the hospital. The possible onset of PTSD, shown by nightly crying (November 7, 1988) and sleep disturbances, included nightmares of a man attacking him (February 16, 1991).

4. Dolores S., aunt of the perpetrator, witnessed Jerry S. walk into her house with blood on his body and a knife in his hand. He walked up to and held Dolores' daughter, Ann, age 6 at the time, and asked her several times if she wanted to die. He then asked Mrs. S. several times if she wanted to die, demanded that she look at the blood on his body, and informed her that he had just killed his parents and sister. PTSD symptoms shown by Mrs. S. appeared in 1988 and 1991 and included (a) vivid memories of the incident, (b) difficulty falling asleep, (c) difficulty concentrating, (d) waking up during the night after dreaming of the incident, (e) difficulty with her short-term memory, particularly whether or not she had flushed the toilet and washed her hands, possible indications of guilt and anxiety, (f) excessive jumpiness, and (g) avoidance of activities that remind her of the incident. She was particularly obsessed about her children's safety when they are alone at home. Work was significantly disrupted because of inquiries from others regarding the incident and when Jerry was due to leave the State Hospital. She felt that the family name had been tarnished in their small communitity.

5. Vicenta P., mother of Dolores, witnessed most of the assault on Dolores prior to escaping from the house to get help. She believed that her daughter and granddaughter had been killed or wounded before finding out otherwise. Her PTSD symptoms included (a) vivid memories of the threatened killings, (b) panic attacks, (c) startle responses, (d) waking up early in the morning, and (e) avoidance of activities that reminded her of the incident.

6. Ann S., daughter of Dolores, whose life was threatened by the perpetrator, reported PTSD symptoms including (a) flashbacks and vivid memories of the threatened killing, (b) nightmares of the incident, (c) waking up during the night, and (d) avoidance of activities that remind her of the incident.

7. Pedro S., husband of Dolores, appeared to have suffered from secondary PTSD symptoms caused by the near-death experiences of his wife and daughter, fear that the perpetrator would return prior to

his apprehension, and the trauma of discovering that his mother had been killed and other relatives wounded by his wife's nephew . Symptoms included (a) vivid memories of the incident as related to him by his wife, child, and mother-in-law, and as he observed the scene prior to the arrival of the police and at the hospital where the victims were taken, (b) nightmares of the near death of his wife and daughter, (c) difficulty falling asleep with later mid-sleep cycle wakefulness, and (d) avoidance of activities that remind him of the incident.

In this case, some symptoms obviously related to the original trauma were not reported because they were not of at least moderate severity. Similarly, non-PTSD problems of a substantial severity, such as abdominal discomfort and severe headaches reported by some family members, were not reported because they are not diagnostic of PTSD.

Conservative interpretations of symptoms within the context of a comprehensive evaluation are a safeguard against overzealous diagnosis of PTSD. Not every complaint and symptom of a victim is a symptom of PTSD, and not every PTSD-relevant symptom is of sufficient severity to include in the diagnosis. The state attorney's office negotiated a half-million-dollar settlement on behalf of the victims in this case from the insurance carrier of the mental health group providing treatment services to the perpetrator at the time of the incidents. The amount of the settlement suggested that conservative claims of post-traumatic effects are more persuasive than a laundry list of every problem experienced by the victim.

Atkinson, Henderson, Sparr, and Deale (1982) describe some of the problems in diagnosing PTSD:

1. Professional bias against the diagnosis. Many clinicians believe that PTSD is not a bona fide disorder.

2. Adverse interactional styles between claimants and staff. An adversarial relationship between examining staff and clients with possible PTSD may reduce the accuracy of evaluation findings. This may occur in civil cases when defense experts examine plaintiffs and in criminal cases where court-appointed forensic evaluators may be viewed by claimants as adversaries.

3. Lack of corroboration of data. Information from significant others, as well as supporting documentation, is critical to cross-validate a PTSD diagnosis.

4. The "silent" claimant. Avoidance of PTSD-related memories is frequent in this condition, to the point of being a cardinal diagnostic sign. Denial and minimizing is often seen in genuine PTSD and, hence, should be a target of detection and measurement.

5. Exaggeration and falsification of data. Faking bad does occur. Once PTSD is asserted, the clinician is placed in a position of refuting the existence of symptoms that may not be directly verifiable.

6. "Partial" PTSD (stressors without full symptoms). Some persons exposed to substantial trauma satisfy some, but not all, of the DSM-IV criteria. In these cases, PTSD should not be diagnosed in spite of fragmentary signs in that direction. In the above case, the differentiation was made between those family members with full-blown PTSD and those having some PTSD symptoms, but not rising to the threshold of a mental disorder.

7. "Idiosyncratic" disorders (PTSD symptoms without the stressors). Sometimes, persons exhibit the arousal symptoms in PTSD when no original stressor of sufficient magnitude can be uncovered. If no stressors are revealed subsequently to justify a diagnosis of PTSD, other conditions may be considered (e.g., phobias, adjustment disorder).

8. Intervening stressors. There should be a clear time frame for the onset of PTSD and a distinct set of identifiable stressors. Multiple events, all capable of producing PTSD, can then be distinguished in terms of their consequences. PTSD may have been triggered by a stressor unrelated to the alleged claim (e.g., intervening domestic problems or bankruptcy rather than war experiences may be responsible for the PTSD).

9. Deviant social behavior. Some behaviors are considered part of PTSD when, in fact, they are features of social deviancy (e.g., criminality, lifetime tendency to avoid or exploit others). Care must be taken to differentiate between PTSD and psychopathic behavior. Genuine PTSD-related violence, for example, has a dissociative, perseverative quality which most likely reflects a reenactment of a previous traumatic event.

10. Either–or diagnostic judgment. PTSD may mimic other conditions or be combined with them. In fact, PTSD is often accompanied by substance abuse disorders, depression, and organicity, if criteria for those conditions are satisfied. The combination of alcohol abuse and PTSD is a case in point. PTSD-caused substance abuse, for example, yields an increase in flashbacks, nightmares, and other symptoms when alcohol is eliminated or reduced. In non-PTSD-related alcoholism, this effect is not seen. Alcohol abuse may be used to suppress PTSD signs and to maintain a facade of normality. When alcohol consumption stops, disturbing imagery returns, whereas in non-PTSD substance abusers, nightmares usually cease as a function of abstinence.

11. Impact on examiners. "Secondary PTSD" is often encountered in examiner/therapists who have frequent contact with PTSD clients. Mental health professionals can themselves develop PTSD symptoms by listening to affected persons, all without experiencing a personal trauma. The authors have noted the same contagious quality with family members of PTSD clients.

TARGETS

Any PTSD symptom may be targeted for deception since they are well known in the media. Genuine but mild PTSD sufferers may exaggerate symptoms, or those unaffected with the condition can fabricate symptoms. Selected PTSD symptoms can be targeted for denial. Symptoms may be chosen that are unverifiable in nature (e.g., flashbacks, nightmares, suicide ideation), are severe, or have a partial base in reality. As Lynn and Belza (1984) stated in reporting on seven Vietnam veterans suspected of faking PTSD in a VA hospital: "In analyzing the cases presented, one common denominator of factitious PTSD becomes apparent. Each patient had obviously acquired sufficient knowledge of PTSD to develop a tale best suited to his needs" (p. 700).

In terms of targets in actual clinical populations, the standard was set in the DSM-IV field trials of PTSD which studied 395 traumatized treatment-seeking subjects and 125 non-treatment-seeking subjects. The findings showed that PTSD dissociation, somatization, and affect dysregulation were highly interrelated. The subjects meeting the criteria for lifetime (as opposed to current) PTSD scored significantly lower on these disorders compared with those with current PTSD, and significantly higher than those who never had PTSD. Subjects who developed PTSD following interpersonal trauma as adults had significantly fewer symptoms compared with those who were traumatized as children. The adults traumatized as children also had significantly more PTSD symptoms than disaster victims (van der Kolk et al., 1996).

RESPONSE STYLES

Virtually every style of distortion is seen with PTSD. Honest responding is seen most often among fellow survivors and to a lesser extent with counselors or relatives. Denying and minimizing PTSD is abundant in genuine and severe cases. Faking good appears to function in an effort to maintain self-esteem and social acceptance. Faking bad is frequent, however. Mixed and fluctuating styles may occur as a function of changing motivations and goals.

In general, response styles of PTSD fakers present a varied picture and are probably not confined to war veterans. As Lynn and Belza (1984) stated:

Factitious PTSD, heretofore undocumented, is a not-uncommon entity that arose as a consequence of the Vietnam conflict. Though unrecognized in DSM-III, it probably has been in existence as long as PTSD itself. It presents another form of clinical deception for which the unsuspecting clinician must develop an index or degree of suspicion. So adept are factitious PTSD patients at their deception that even the most experienced physicians can find themselves fooled by the presenting complaints. (p. 699)

PTSD AND ORGANIC FACTORS

Although PTSD is etiologically related to a traumatic event, recent explanations have emphasized biological factors. This is based in large part on the DSM-IV diagnostic criteria B. (5) for PTSD (Pitman, Saunders, & Orr, 1994): "… physiological reactivity on exposure to internal or external cues that symbolize or resemble an aspect of the traumatic event" (p. 428).

The search for biological anchors to PTSD is based on the notion that trauma can alter the neurochemistry of the brain. Alternatively, preexisting neuroanatomic correlates may serve to heighten risk for exposure to combat-induced PTSD (Gurvits, Shenton, Hokama, & Ohta, 1996). Years after a trauma, heightened states of arousal may again trigger PTSD behaviors, illustrating classical respondent conditioning in a previously traumatized person (Franklin, 1988; Kolb, 1987, 1988; Lipton & Shaffer, 1988; van Der Kolk, 1988). McCaffrey, Lorig, Pendrey, McCutcheon, and Garrett (1993) examined EEG changes in response to trauma- and non-trauma-related odors with small groups ($N = 5$) of male Vietnam veterans and a comparison group. The simulated odor of burning hair produced the greatest EEG, self-report, and PTSD effects. The authors suggested that odor-induced EEG changes may be a useful measure of CNS functioning in the detection of Vietnam veterans with actual PTSD symptoms.

Affected CNS structures and functions implicated in PTSD may include the limbic system generally, projections of the septal-hippocampal complex (subserving anger control and memory), tyrosine hydroxylase production, alpha-2 inhibitory receptors (presynaptic), and excitatory receptors (postsynaptic). The catecholamines, dopamine, norepinephrine, and epinephrine have all been demonstrated to be elevated in Vietnam PTSD veterans compared with control subjects (Yehuda, Southwick, Giller, Ma, & Mason, 1992). Dopamine and norepinephrine (but not epinephrine) levels correlated with severity of PTSD symptoms. The authors concluded that the findings supported the hypothesis of enhanced sympathetic nervous system activation in PTSD, and that the increased sympathetic arousal may be closely linked to the severity of select PTSD symptom clusters. Yehuda, Boisoneau, Lowy, and Giller (1995a) postulated permanent changes in the regulation of the hypo-thalamic–pituitary–adrenal axis following exposure to trauma. This observation was based on dose-related changes in plasma cortisol and lymphocyte glucocorticoid receptors following the admin-istration of dexamethasone in groups of combat veterans with and without PTSD. Cortisol hyper-suppression appeared to reflect PTSD. The presence and severity of PTSD was measured by several instruments (i.e., the Structured Clinical Interview for Mental Disorders–III–Revised, or DSM-III-R; the Impact of Events Scale; the Figley PTSD Scale; the Combat Exposure Scale). In a related study, Holocaust survivors evidenced low levels of urinary cortisol decades after trauma exposure, suggesting that lower urinary cortisol levels were associated with significant PTSD symptoms and not due to exposure to the trauma per se (Yehuda et al., 1995b).

By utilizing more-advanced technology, the foregoing findings were confirmed in a study by Baker et al. (1999). Male combat veterans were tested by a technique of continuous sampling of cerebrospinal fluid (CSF) for corticotropin-releasing hormone (CRH) concentrations. CRH con-centration is intimately related to adrenocortical activity, which directly influences affective levels and depression in particular. Urinary-free cortisol excretion was also measured. The mean CSF/CRH levels were significantly greater in PTSD patients compared with normal subjects. The investigators correlated the neuroendocrine data with PTSD and depressive symptoms. Urinary-free cortisol excretion levels were negatively and significantly correlated with PTSD symptoms.

Other PTSD neuroendocrine relationships have also been reported. Serum thyroid studies have reported unusual thyroid profiles with PTSD. Wang and Mason (1999) described elevated levels of free triiodothyronine (T_3), total thyroxine (T_4), and thyroxine-binding globulin (TBG) in Vietnam veterans compared with controls. Commings, Muhleman, and Gysin (1996) described 58.3% of the 56 Vietnam veterans in their study as carrying the D_{2A1} dopamine receptor gene possibly conferring an increased risk to PTSD. Peripheral serotonin function measured by [^{3}H] paroxetine binding to blood platelets was not found to have any relationship to major depression symptoms in PTSD (Maguire, Norman, Burrows, Hopwood, & Morris, 1998). Elevated natural cytotoxicity was found with Vietnam combat veterans when PTSD was comorbid with depression (measured by the Beck Depression Inventory) (Laudenslager et al., 1998). Evidence of chronic neuroendocrine activation in women with PTSD related to child sexual abuse was reported by Lemieux and Coe (1995).

Other compelling neurologically based studies of PTSD have involved positron emission tomography (PET) to measure regional cerebral blood flow (rCBF) in patients with PTSD. One study involved women with histories of childhood sexual abuse (Shin et al., 1999). During PET, script-driven imagery was introduced. A traumatic condition, in comparison to a neutral control condition, reflected increased rCBF in the orbitofrontal cortex and anterior temporal poles for the subjects with PTSD. The comparison group exhibited rCBF increases in the insular cortex and the anterior cingulated gyrus. The PTSD group also exhibited greater rCBF decreases in bilateral anterior frontal regions, and singular decreases in the left inferior frontal gyrus. Bremner et al. (1999) examined PET recordings of rCBF with combat veterans exposed to traumatic pictures and sounds. The subjects with PTSD had decreased blood flow to the medial prefrontal cortex, an area postulated to have a role in regulation of affect through inhibition of amygdala responsiveness. There were also significant differences between subjects with PTSD and controls with rCBF findings in cortical areas involved in memory and visuospatial processing. Neuroscience is not yet sufficiently sophisticated to determine precisely what these neurological findings between the subjects with PTSD and the control subjects mean. What is significant, however, is that the PET recordings reflected specific and consistent differences. Perhaps future investigations will enable the use of such findings to discriminate actual from simulated PTSD.

Increases in CSF beta-endorphin (i.e., natural opioid) concentrations were found in PTSD combat veterans compared with normals (Baker et al., 1997). The authors acknowledged that their findings did not determine if the CNS opioid concentrations predated the traumatic stress, but the findings raised the hypothesis that the increased concentrations made the subjects with PTSD more vulnerable to dissociation.

There are also similarities between PTSD and traumatic brain injury (TBI), which feed speculations about organic components in PTSD and about delayed-stress reaction in TBI. Both involve acute signs and delayed effects. PTSD can involve symptoms similar to those stemming from cerebral insult (e.g., failing memory, difficulty in concentration, headache, and vertigo), while TBI usually involves emotional problems, such as elevated depression and anxiety, which are common in PTSD. Stuss and Benson (1986) point to possible anterior brain dysfunction when a markedly diminished interest in significant activities (i.e., "emotional numbness"), a feeling of detachment or estrangement from others, and a restricted range of affect, with a depressive sense of a foreshortened future, occur. Head injury was found to be more prevalent among PTSD combat veterans compared with veterans without PTSD (Chemtob et al., 1998). Head injury associated with PTSD also indicated more severe PTSD symptoms. The association of head injury and PTSD was not related to greater exposure to combat experience in the head injury group.

Weintraub and Ruskin (1999) investigated PTSD in elderly people. They noted that although dysfunctions of the adrenergic system and the hypothalamic–pituitary–adrenal axis have been implicated in the neurobiology of PTSD, there was no current evidence that such changes have any impact on the presentation of PTSD in the elderly population.

Price (1994) concluded that head traumas resulting in concussion could not logically be followed by claims of PTSD. By definition, concussions involve memory loss of events preceding the injury. He reasoned that if there is no memory of events preceding the injury, there could be no ruminating over the injury, no flashbacks of the trauma. Patients with PTSD are characteristically reluctant to discuss their trauma, show emotional agitation or withdrawal, and are bothered by flashbacks. In contrast, concussion patients discuss their injury, have no emotional upset in doing so, and are not troubled by flashbacks. Price concluded, therefore, if a concussion victim is unable to remember the accident, but subsequently claims PTSD, only the diagnoses of postconcussion syndrome or malingering should be considered.

The CNS activity of abused and nonabused children, measured by the impact of acoustic startle tones on EEG-evoked potentials, reflected significant differences between the two groups (McPherson, Newton, Ackerman, Oglesby, & Dykman, 1997). Essentially, the children with PTSD had greater specific (P2-N2 ERP) EEG intensity gradients compared with the nonabused subjects. The authors hypothesized that the results reflected heightened CNS processing of the startle stimulus intensity by children with abuse histories.

Psychophysiological arousal measures may sometimes be useful for detecting faked PTSD. Blanchard, Kolb, Pallmeyer, and Gerardi (1982) found a 95.5% hit rate using this method. Heart rate alone yielded a hit rate of 91% in differentiating subjects with true PTSD from controls. However, Gerardi, Blanchard, and Kolb (1989) examined 36 combat-experienced Vietnam veterans, half with and half without PTSD, on heart rate, blood pressure, peripheral surface temperature, forehead electromyogram (EMG), and skin resistance level. The group with PTSD could not significantly decrease their arousal to combat stimuli when requested to do so, while non-PTSD subjects could increase their physiological responses when asked to fake arousal to the combat stimuli. There were, therefore, no significant differences between the two groups on this measure. However, discriminant analysis revealed that subjects with PTSD could be distinguished from faking non-PTSD subjects by several measures. Diastolic blood pressure correctly classified 88.9% of all subjects ($\kappa = 0.79$) followed by heart rate (85.2%), systolic blood pressure (80.8%), and frontal EMG (70.4%).

In contrast to the Blanchard et al. (1982) finding that heart rate significantly discriminated between patients with PTSD and controls, Gerardi, Blanchard, and Kolb (1989) found that heart rate correctly classified only 76% of their sample. However, when heart rate difference scores from subjects with PTSD were compared with non-PTSD veterans, a 76 beats-per-min cutoff score correctly classified 83% of the subjects with PTSD and 89% of the non-PTSD veterans.

Only 22.2% of faking subjects were correctly identified, indicating that normals can fake PTSD-like heart rates when motivated to do so. Gerarldi, Blanchard, and Kolb (1989) then took both baseline heart rate (HR) and maximum HR responses on any particular trial into account at the same time. They stated:

> This rule stipulates that veterans without PTSD will have baseline HR < 67 bpm or a maximum HR response < 10 bpm.... [T]his decision rule correctly classified 16 out of 18 (89%) veterans with PTSD. For the veterans without PTSD, 6 out of the 9 (66.7%) attempting to fake PTSD, and 8 of the 9 (88%) remaining non-PTSD veterans (or 14/18 (77.8%) are correctly classified. Altogether, 30 out of the 36 (83.3%) veterans are correctly classified as PTSD and non-PTSD by this decision rule ($\kappa = .66$). (p. 235)

P1 midlatency auditory-evoked EEG potentials were recorded with male Vietnam combat veterans with PTSD (Gillette et al., 1997). Diminished P1 potentials were significantly correlated with the intensity of reexperiencing symptoms, e.g., nightmares and flashbacks. The authors suggested that the finding was supportive of a "sensory gating effect at the brainstem level" in PTSD and that the suppression effect may similarly influence other psychophysiological measures.

In addition to combat veterans, recent investigations have explored PTSD psychophysiological arousal measures with assault victims, motor vehicle accident victims and other civilian traumas

(Orr et al., 1993; Pitman, Saunders, & Orr, 1994; Shalev, Orr, & Pitman, 1993). Pitman, Saunders, and Orr (1994) summarized that across a broad range of studies, psychophysiological assessment was effective in correctly identifying 60 to 88% of PTSD cases. In contrast, 79 to 100% of non-PTSD cases were correctly identified.

The comparison of psychometric with psychophysiological measures of PTSD needs to be explored to revolve basic issues of accuracy and efficiency (Gerardi, Keane, & Penk, 1989). In one such investigation involving Vietnam veterans, 25 subjects with PTSD — 18 healthy subjects and 6 anxious subjects — completed psychometric tests, followed by measuring psychophysiological responses to combat imagery (Orr et al., 1990). Depending upon the test, 22 to 41% of the variance was common to both the psychometric and psychophysiological measures.

The MMPI-PTSD subscale yielded an optimal cutoff of 21, identifying 72% of the genuine PTSD subjects, 94% of the healthy subjects, and 86% of the anxious control subjects. The combined physiological measures identified 64% of the PTSD subjects, 94% of the healthy subjects, and 100% of the anxious control subjects.

The validity measures of the MMPI examined in the Orr et al. (1990) study — higher obvious than subtle item endorsement, F, F-K, and DS-R — were essentially useless because all of the factors correlated substantially with physiological responses. There was no motive for subjects to fake in this study. Finally, the items themselves have direct relevance to PTSD (e.g., F-scale items: "I have nightmares every few nights," "I believe my sins are unpardonable"). In sum, this study suggests that clinicians must return to observation, analysis of inconsistencies, and documented exposure to the original trauma to establish whether or not faking PTSD has occurred.

As Wilson (1989) stated, "Extreme stress affects organismic functioning directly on four interrelated levels: physiological, psychological, social-interpersonal, and cultural ... interrelated processes which influence each other in direct and subtle ways that constitute the essence of the mind–body relationship" (p. 21).

One study found both right and left hippocampi to be significantly smaller in subjects with PTSD compared with combat control and normal subjects (Gurvits et al., 1996). There were no significant differences in intracranial cavity, whole brain, ventricles, brain ratio, or amygdala. The two combat groups did evidence increased subarachnoidal cerebrospinal fluid. The authors suggested that since hippocampal volume was directly correlated with combat, traumatic stress might cause damage to the hippocampus.

Neurochemical and neuropsychological explanations of PTSD are interesting and progress continues in the refinement of their accuracy and clinical relevance. Nonetheless, they remain of limited application in forensic matters. At the current time, diagnoses of PTSD cannot be based solely on psychophysiological test findings (Pitman, Saunders, & Orr, 1994), but, if used prudently, can be an important adjunct in the forensic clinician's armamentarium.

In actual case situations, the role of psychophysiological and psychological factors in PTSD symptomatology is inseparable and the relative impact of each is not determinable. Clinicians will frequently find it very difficult to discern psychophysiological findings from preexisting personality impairments, intrapsychic conflicts, and social factors (Kinzie & Goetz, 1996). Consideration of all possible etiological origins of a PTSD case is an essential aspect of FDA. Often there are multiple possible etiological explanations, and the FDA clinician must account for the relative role of each with candor, based on reasonable empirical assessment.

PREDICTORS OF PTSD

One important area of consideration in any forensic analysis of PTSD is the clinician's understanding of comorbid variables predictive of the intensity and the course of PTSD. Most PTSD patients recover within 1 year of their traumatic experience. Those who remain ill for a year or more rarely recover completely (Freedman, Brandes, Peri, & Shalev, 1999). Established predictors can be useful in analyzing a case of PTSD in terms of whether or not the reported clinical history coincides with established predictors.

A number of operating variables have been established to be comorbidly associated with PTSD. These variables are summarized in Table 13.2.

Ehlers, Mayou, and Bryant (1998) described a longitudinal study with motor vehicle accident victims who were diagnosed with PTSD. The subjects had visited an emergency room shortly after the accident, and again at 3 and 12 months for follow-up. The prevalence rate of PTSD at 3 months was 21% and at 12 months 16.5%. Based on statistical analysis of frequency data from structured questionnaires completed by the patients, the authors described psychological predictors associated with PTSD symptoms. The PTSD psychological predictors are summarized in Figure 13.2.

In a longitudinal study by Freedman et al. (1999) it was found that depressive symptoms were the best predictors of PTSD at 4-month and 12-month post-trauma intervals. Simon (1999) described a PTSD Prognostic Checklist designed to assist mental health clinicians in evaluating the prognosis with a given case of PTSD. The checklist is based on consideration of a series of risk factors.

DETECTION

The last decade has seen continued investigation of a number of traditional PTSD psychological instruments and the development of numerous new PTSD scales. A number of the new instruments has been reported in the literature but received little to no additional attention in follow-up or replication studies (e.g., Dissociative Experiences Scale, Penn Inventory for PTSD). There is also ongoing controversy regarding specific instruments because investigators are not always able to replicate earlier findings. This problem has occurred with some of the time-worn instruments felt to have a degree of validity and reliability. Part of the difficulty is different investigators' using different PTSD populations. The dynamics of combat-related PTSD, for example, may be different from the dynamics of civilian motor vehicle accident–induced PTSD (McGorry, 1995). Another factor is that different investigators measure different aspects of PTSD or use different instruments to measure the same PTDS dimension. PTDS research will clearly continue into the future. The reader is cautioned that it is one thing to investigate the correlation between one PTSD instrument and another, or to investigate if an instrument correlates with DSM criteria. It is a far more imposing task for an instrument to be used to discern credible from simulated PTSD in actual clinical/forensic cases.

Although PTSD instruments remain at a relatively rudimentary stage, there have been promising developments. Assessment tools to gauge PTSD include tests geared to measure acute and cumulative stress, as well as other symptoms relevant to DSM-IV PTSD criteria. Measures reportedly sensitive to PTSD are listed in Table 13.3; the measures developed specifically for use with Vietnam veterans are distinguished from general measures of PTSD by an asterisk. The measures marked with a plus sign are touted to be sensitive to deception.

General stress tests, such as the Social Readjustment Rating Scale (SRRS; Holmes & Rahe, 1967) are useful. The authors typically have the assessee complete the SRRS for (1) the present extending back 1 year; (2) 1 year before the trauma, to capture an idea of premorbid functioning; (3) the time of the trauma and the year following the trauma, reporting the worst symptoms during this period; and (4) other times, depending on the remoteness of the original trauma. The spouse (or family members) is asked to complete ratings for the same temporal periods. Differences in reporting events are often revealing.

For war veterans, a base rate comparison of those with PTSD and those without the condition can be made. The Combat Exposure Scale provides a relevant measure for Vietnam veterans. Keane et al. (1989) built on previous efforts to develop a measure of the severity of prior combat exposure and produced a seven-item Likert-type scale with adequate reliability and discriminant validity.

Lund, Foy, Sipprelle, and Strachan (1984) offered the following advice for assessment of PTSD:

TABLE 13.2
Operating Variables and Risk Factors Associated with PTSD

Variable	Representative Studies
Alcohol abuse	Blanchard et al. (1996)
Biological and genetic factors	Yehuda (1999)
Childhood stressors (e.g., parental alcoholism, parental unemployment, parental strictness)	Emery et al. (1991); Donovan et al. (1996)
Chronic pain	Beckham, Crawford, et al. (1997)
Chronic pain, affective disturbance and disability	Geisser et al. (1996)
Civil litigation, e.g., workers' compensation, transportation accidents, crimes compensation, and compensation to relatives	Litigation is a contributing variable: Blanchard et al. (1996); Bryant & Harvey (1995)
	Litigation is not a contributing variable: Mendelson (1995); Mayou, Tyndel, & Bryant (1997); Bryant, Mayou, & Lloyd-Bolstoc (1997)
Cocaine dependence	Najavits et al. (1998)
Cognitive factors	Dunmore, Clark, & Ehlers (1999)
Combat-related guilt (survival guilt, guilt over acts of omission and commission, guilt about thoughts and feelings)	Henning & Frueh (1997)
Comorbidity — 80% of PTSD cases meet criteria for at least one other psychiatric disorder	Brady (1997); Weyermann, Norris, & Hyer (1996)
Depression, comorbid	Freedman et al. (1999)
Dissociation during or following trauma	Foa & Hearst-Ikeda (1996); Spiegel (1991); Koopman, Classen, & Spiegel (1994)
Elevated corticotropin-releasing hormone levels in combat PTSD	Baker et al. (1999); Yehuda, Boisoneau, et al. (1995)
Females more susceptible to PTSD	Ehlers, Mayou, & Bryant (1998); Kessler et al. (1995); Norris (1992)
Gerontological factors	Cuffe et al. (1998); Hankin et al. (1996)
Head injury	Chemtob et al. (1998)
Impaired ability of elderly people to cope with trauma	Weintraub & Ruskin (1999)
Low precombat intelligence	Macklin et al. (1998)
Maltreated children	Famularo et al. (1994)
Mothers of maltreated children	Famularo et al. (1994)
Negative parenting behavior predicting combat PTSD severity	McCranie et al. (1992)
Nicotine dependence	Beckham, Kirby, et al. (1997)
Perceived threat to life	March (1993); Mayou, Bryant, & Duthie (1993); Mayou, Tyndel, & Bryant (1997); Blanchard, Hickling, Taylor, & Loos (1995); Blanchard et al. (1996)
Persistent financial problems	Mayou, Bryant, & Duthie (1993); Mayou, Tydel, & Bryant (1997); Blanchard et al. (1997)
Persistent medical problems	Mayou, Bryant, & Duthie (1993); Mayou, Tydel, & Bryant (1997); Blanchard et al. (1997)
Preexisting personality disorder	Blanchard et al. (1996)
Preexisting psychiatric problems	Breslau et al. (1991); Smith et al. (1990); Blanchard et al. (1996)
Psychophysiological changes	Gurvits et al. (1996); Yehuda, Kahana, et al. (1995)
Psychosocial adjustment	McFall et al. (1990)
Reactions of intimate others to victim's trauma (i.e., mothers of child sex abuse victims)	Timmons-Mitchell, Chandler-Holtz, & Semple (1997)

TABLE 13.2 *(continued)*
Operating Variables and Risk Factors Associated with PTSD

Variable	Representative Studies
Self-reported interpersonal hostility	Beckham, Crawford, et al. (1997)
Substance abuse, comorbidity	Brown et al. (1998); Brown, Stout, & Mueller (1999); Saladin et al. (1995); Sharkansky et al. (1999); Wasserman et al. (1997)
Suicidal behavior after severe trauma	Ferrada-Noli et al. (1998)
Trauma severity	Blanchard, Hickling, Mitnick, et al. (1995)
Unconsciousness at trauma	Mayou, Bryant, & Duthie (1993); Blanchard et al. (1996)
Victim perception of assault safety	Cascardi et al. (1996)
Vietnam veterans physical health status, and somatization	Beckham, Crawford, et al. (1998)

> In diagnosing and treating PTSD, it is important to ask directly about concrete events. With Vietnam veterans, asking about low-scoring, common events and proceeding to rare, more traumatic events on the Combat Exposure Scale provides a brief and systematic way of exploring war experiences. (p. 1325)

PTSD malingerers could, of course, fabricate events associated with the scaled items. This possibility highlights the necessity for a comprehensive evaluation of possible PTSD, including psychological testing and cross-validating documentation.

The importance of knowing explicit details of the alleged original stressor is illustrated in *Pard v. U.S.* (1984) involving two (unsuccessful) claims totaling $9.5 million. The plaintiff, a Vietnam veteran, asserted that the VA had failed to diagnose his combat-related PTSD, which resulted in his assaultive behavior toward the police. Sparr and Atkinson (1986) reported on events of the civil trial, which culminated in a ruling that the VA was not negligent:

> At the 1984 trial, the government introduced testimony by three persons who served in Vietnam with the plaintiff: his commanding officer, a pilot, and a fellow crew chief. Their testimony made it evident that the plaintiff's helicopter was not a gunship but had been used for the administrative purposes of moving the commanding officer and his staff from place to place and for ferrying supplies. Members of the unit saw little, if any, combat. They had never been sent on missions to kill the enemy and had registered no confirmed kills. Testimony of his commanding officer demonstrated that no administratively assigned helicopter had ever been shot down during the time that the plaintiff was in Vietnam, and that no incident took place in which the plaintiff shot several children or any other Vietnamese people, civilian or military. The plaintiff had not been wounded by enemy bullets but had been injured when his own machine gun malfunctioned and a piece of the gun lodged in his arm. None of the men from the plaintiff's unit had heard of the incident in which the squad was supposed to have saved a general. Both the plaintiff's personal military record (Army 201 file) and the testimony at the trial made it plain that the plaintiff had not received the Distinguished Flying Cross or the Bronze Star. (p. 1018)

At the earlier (February 1980) criminal trial, the jury was not aware of these facts and returned a verdict of "not guilty by reason of insanity" due to PTSD.

Neuropsychological tests should be administered if traumatic brain injury is implicated. Are neuropsychological deficits showing up on testing? The best tests to use would include those tapping PTSD-related problems such as attention, vigilance, short-term memory, judgment, planning, and execution. Nondeliberate distortion must first be ruled out. Signs of deception can be detected from those presented in Chapter 11 on Malingered Neuropsychological Deficits.

Clinically, there is a noticeable tendency for malingerers of PTSD to avoid psychotic signs as part of their response strategy. Simulators usually do not report for any mandatory medical/psy-

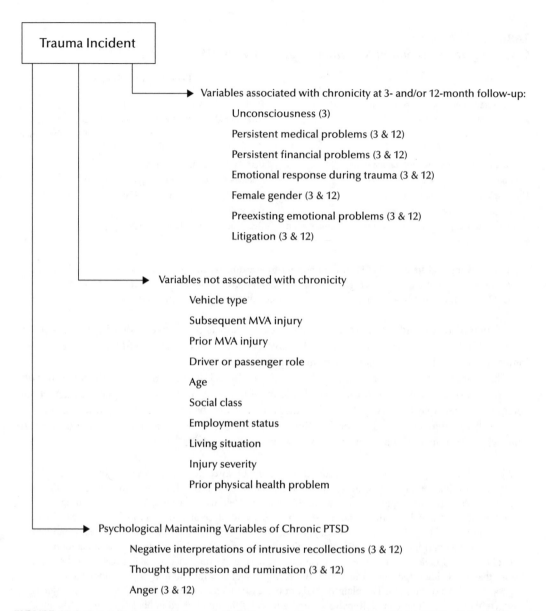

FIGURE 13.2 Psychological predictors of clinical course of motor vehicle accident PTSD. (Adapted from Ehlers, Mayou, & Bryant, 1998.)

chological examinations. Often, there is a history of sporadic employment and a claimed lack of ability to work with concurrent involvement in recreation. "Soft" signs of faked PTSD include (1) bringing up the trauma early in assessment/treatment as opposed to the reluctance of genuine PTSD victims to discuss symptomatology and traumatic events, (2) indignation rather than surprise or blandness when confronted with suspicions of distortion, and (3) absence of impulse control problems, often found in the client with genuine PTSD.

Resnick (1984, 1987, 1988a, b, 1997, 1999) discussed PTSD faked primarily, but not exclusively, by Vietnam veterans. His signs can be placed within the DSM-IV criteria for PTSD, as shown in Table 13.4, but may not be relevant to all categories of PTSD-affected individuals. One problem with these signs is the considerable overlap with genuine PTSD behavior. Resnick right-

TABLE 13.3
Psychometric Measures Sensitive to PTSD

Measure	Study
Impact of Event Scale (IOES)	Horowitz, Wilner, & Alvarez (1979)
Dissociative Experiences Scale (DES)	Bernstein & Putnam (1986)
Diagnostic Interview Schedule–PTSD	Helzer, Robins, & McEvoy (1987)
*Combat Exposure Scale	Lund et al. (1984)
*Figley PTSD Scale	Watson, Juba, & Anderson (1989)
*Jackson Structured Interview for PTSD	Malloy et al. (1983)
*PTSD Checklist	Kulka & Schlenger (1986)
*Mississippi Scale for Combat-Related PTSD	Keane, Caddell, & Taylor (1988)
*MMPI PTSD Scale	Keane, Malloy, & Fairbank (1984)
Minnesota Multiphasic Personality Inventory	Penk et al. (1981); Roberts et al. (1982); Fairbank, Keane, & Malloy (1983); Foy et al. (1984)
MMPI-2 PTSD Scale	Munley et al. (1995a); Scotti, Sturges, & Lyons (1996); Lyons & Wheeler-Cox (1999)
SCID and MMPI-2	Weyermann, Morris, & Hyer (1996)
+MMPI-F-scale	Jordan, Nunley, & Cook (1992)
+MMPI-2 validity scales and MCMI-II Modifier scales	Lees-Haley (1992)
Penn Inventory for PTSD	Hammarberg (1992)
+Structured Interview of Reported Symptoms (SIRS)	Rogers et al. (1992)
*Keane PTSD Scale of the MMPI	Scotti, Sturges, & Lyons (1996)
Rorschach	Frueh & Kinder (1994)
+Clinician-Administered PTSD Scale (CAPS-1)	Blake et al. (1995); Blanchard, Hickling, Taylor, et al. (1995)
+Personality Assessment Inventory (PAI)	Liljequist, Kinder, & Schinka (1998)
+Morel Emotional Numbing Test for PTSD (MENT)	Morel (1998)
Short Screening Scale for DSM-IV PTSD	Breslau et al. (1999)
*WZ-PTSD scale	Weathers et al. (1996)
Self-Rating Scale for PTSD (SRS-PTSD)	Carlier et al. (1998)
MMPI Acute PTSD Scale	Gaston et al. (1998)
MMPI Chronic PTSD Scale	Gaston et al. (1998)

Note: Scales marked with an asterisk (*) are designed specifically for use with (Vietnam) veterans; scales marked with a plus (+) appear to have sensitivity to deception.

fully emphasized the need for a thorough review of records and interview of the subject's spouse and family. In this regard, Resnick noted (1988b):

> The accessibility of specific DSM III-R criteria permit the resourceful malingerer to report the "right" symptoms. The assertion that individuals dream or think about a traumatic event should be verified by others who have heard them talk about it in situations that are not related to the litigation. In addition, the clinician must obtain a detailed history of living patterns preceding the stressor. For example, symptoms such as difficulty concentrating or insomnia may have been present before the traumatic event.
>
> Baseline activity in a typical week before the trauma took place should be compared with reported impairment at the time of the evaluation. The clinician must carefully examine the reasonableness of the relationship between the symptoms and the stressor, the time elapsed between the stressor and the symptom development, and the relationship between any prior psychiatric symptoms and current impairment. (p. 94)

The Wahler Physical Symptoms Inventory (WPS; Wahler, 1983) may be useful in evaluating physical complaints because it has a built-in decile table to examine item frequency. Overly high

---

TABLE 13.4
Traditional Signs of Faked PTSD

A. Clinical database
    1. Overidealization of functioning before trauma
    2. Evasiveness
    3. Uncooperativeness
    4. Understandable motive to fake PTSD
B. Stressor(s)
    1. Reporting of "incapacitating" prior injuries
    2. Emphasizing relationship of stressor(s) to symptoms
C. Reexperiencing trauma
    1. No nightmares or an unvarying repetitive theme
    2. Grandiose dreams with power themes
D. Numbed responsiveness/reduced involvement
    1. Poor work record
    2. Discrepant work and leisure activities
    3. Antisocial activities
E. Arousal symptoms
    1. Inconsistency in symptom presentation (relevant to memory and concentration problems)
    2. No guilt over involvement or surviving the stressor
    3. Anger at authority
    4. Admission of malingering or psychometric evidence or corroborative evidence of dissimulation

---

frequency endorsement (decile > 9) is unrealistic unless confirmed by results from the laboratory or medical examination.

Physical symptoms most frequently faked on the WPS include (1) severe headaches, (2) feeling hot or cold regardless of the weather, (3) difficulty sleeping, (4) numbness or lack of feeling in any part of the body, (5) feeling tired, (6) dizzy spells, (7) difficulty with appetite, and (8) poor health in general. The WPS is sensitive to exaggeration of real symptoms as well as pure fabrication.

Fairbank, McCaffrey, and Keane (1985) correctly classified 90% of patients with PTSD and subjects instructed to fake PTSD on the MMPI. Specifically, both the bogus and the genuine subjects produced elevations on the F-scale and a PTSD subscale, but the genuine subjects scored significantly lower than the fakers. These two predictor variables (F-scale, PTSD subscale) combined in a discriminant function to classify correctly 95.6% of the subjects who faked on PTSD. Essentially replicating this study, McCaffrey and Bellamy-Campbell (1989) found that the MMPI F-scale and PTSD subscale correctly classified 91.4% of their total sample with no fakers incorrectly classified. However, Perconte and Goreczny (1989) reported that a discriminant analysis of the F-scale and PTSD subscale correctly identified only 43.59% of the 39 subjects in their study. Their subjects consisted of Vietnam veterans being treated for PTSD, Vietnam veterans subsequently determined to have malingered PTSD, Vietnam veterans without PTSD, and mental health professionals instructed to feign PTSD. Degree of combat exposure emerged as the single best predictor of PTSD in this sample. In a related follow-up study, Perconte and Goreczny (1989) reported not being able to replicate the MMPI F-scale and PTSD subscales to discriminate PTSD veterans from controls in a clinical setting.

Perr (1986) pointed out that faking subjects in the Fairbank, McCaffrey, and Keane (1985) study were instructed in DSM-III symptoms. Fakers outside this context might not be so indoctrinated and may therefore produce less deviant (and more similar) scores. In rejoinder, Fairbank, McCaffrey, and Keane (1986) pointed out that the F-scale cutoff and the PTSD subscale should be used as adjuncts to interviewing, other testing, and possibly psychophysiological assessment.

Dalton, Tom, Rosenblum, Garte, and Aubuchon (1989) administered the Mississippi Scale for Combat-Related Posttraumatic Stress Disorder to 35 VA patients who were instructed to fake PTSD.

As a group these pseudomalingerers scored lower than a group of 30 inpatients in a PTSD treatment program, but 77% of the fakers nonetheless scored above the suggested cutoff score for inferring PTSD. Similarly, Lees-Haley (1989) found between a 52 and 80% misclassification rate on the MMPI PTSD scale among subjects instructed to fake a psychological disorder in the wake of a traumatic disorder. In a study investigating whether the high face validity of the Mississippi Scale for Combat-Related PTSD makes it vulnerable to faking, instructed controls were able to mimic the scores of subjects with PTSD (Lyons, Caddell, Pitman, Rawls, & Perrin, 1994). The PTSD veterans did have higher Mississippi Scale scores compared with the instructed controls. The authors recommended a change in the cutoff score to 121 as opposed to the originally recommended diagnostic cutoff score of 107.

McFall, Smith, Roszell, Tarver, and Malas (1990) reported convergent validity among the Mississippi Scale for Combat-Related PTSD, the Impact of Events Scale, and the PTSD subscale of the MMPI. The three instruments evidenced significant correlations across psychometric indices of PTSD symptoms as reflecting degrees of traumatic combat exposure and DSM-III-R diagnoses.

When Vietnam combat veterans, who were being financially compensated, were psychologically compared with those not compensated, the MMPI F-scale (Validity) discriminated between the two populations (Jordan, Nunley, & Cook, 1992). Essentially, the veterans seeking compensation were prone to symptom exaggeration as measured by the F-scale. The authors also reported that the F-score cutoff criteria for inpatient PTSD were higher than cutoff scores reported in previous studies that detailed findings chiefly with outpatient populations.

In a study designed to differentiate PTSD patients psychometrically from controls, Lees-Haley (1992) identified pseudo-PTSD patients as scoring $T = 65$ or higher on both the PK and PS PTSD subscales of the MMPI-2. Spurious PTSD was effectively identified utilizing the following MMPI-2 and MCMI-II cutoffs:

MMPI-2 — F > 62, F-K ≥ –4, Ego Strength (Es) ≥ 30, Fake Bad Scale (FBS) ≥ 24 (men),
   FBS ≥ 26 (women), total obvious minus subtle ≥ 90,
MCMI-II — Disclosure Scale (DIS) ≥ 60; Desirability Scale (DES) ≥ 60

Lyons and Wheeler-Cox (1999) reported that various MMPI-2 scales were useful in detecting malingering, but concurrence regarding cutoff scores was lacking.

Rogers' Structured Interview of Reported Symptoms (SIRS) was noted to be effective in detecting feigned PTSD (Rogers, Kropp, Bagby, & Dickens, 1992). Veterans with PTSD were compared on MMPI-2 scales with a veteran control group (Munley, Bains, Bloem, Busby, & Pendziszewski, 1995a). Significant univariate differences were found on two MMPI-2 subscales. The Keane PTSD scale (PK) and the Post-traumatic Stress Disorder Scale (PS) both produced higher scores in subjects with PTSD. The subjects with PTSD also had significantly higher univariate differences on the Anger Content subscale. Munley et al. (1995a) reported disappointing findings in an effort to distinguish accurately a PTSD group from a comparison non-PTSD group with the Millon Clinical Multiaxial Inventory–II (MCMI-II). Hyer, Boyd, Stanger, and Davis (1997) reported that the MCMI-II did discriminate between a PTSD group and a control group, but there were questions — including the MCMI-II profiles being influenced by an acquiescent response style — warranting further validation studies.

Weathers et al. (1996) described a new scale for assessing war zone–related post-traumatic stress disorder (WZ-PTSD). The WZ-PTSD scale was derived from the Symptom Checklist-90-R (SCL-90). The 25-item scale had excellent internal consistency, and signal detection analyses indicated its diagnostic utility to be equal to, or better than, several established PTSD scales.

One PTSD instrument that has stood the test of time is the Impact of Events Scale (Horowitz, Wilner, & Alvarez, 1979). Perkins and Tebes (1984) described that the construct validity of the Impact of Events Scale did not justify that the scale could distinguish genuine from simulated responses. In a study with undergraduate subjects, the scale did differentiate students who were recently traumatized by parental death from students who were informed to respond as if they had experienced the trauma. The Impact of Events Scale was used to explore PTSD symptom clusters of combat veterans from the war in the former Yugoslavia (Jovic, Knezevic, & Lecic-Tosevski, 1998). The findings suggested two different mechanisms of veterans coping with intrusive memories: (1) avoidance, which corresponds to a phobic pattern of behavior, and (2) dissociation, which relates to symptoms of psychological numbing and detachment.

Frueh and Kinder (1994) compared the Rorschach responses of Vietnam veterans with PTSD to students who were "role-informed malingerers" (RIMs). While there were some similarities between the RIM Rorschach responses and those of the veterans, the RIMs gave less complicated and overly dramatic responses. The RIMs were also less emotionally restrained, which the authors interpreted as an exaggerated sense of impaired reality testing.

One new PTSD instrument consists of a structured interview that is intended for experienced clinicians, but the authors tout that it can also be administered by appropriately trained paraprofessionals (Blake et al., 1995). The instrument is called the Clinician-Administered PTSD Scale (CAPS-1). The CAPS-1 yields both continuous and dichotomous scores for current and lifetime PTSD symptoms. According to the authors, the CAPS-1 appears to meet desired psychometric standards more uniformly than traditional instruments. Blanchard et al. (1995b) systematically varied the scoring rules of the CAPS-1 from liberal to conservative. The variations changed the sample diagnoses from 44 to 29%. A comparison of the excluded subjects (i.e., previously included) with the subjects with PTSD according to the conservative scoring reflected the still-included subjects to have significantly greater subjective distress and role impairment. Changes in the CAPS-1 scoring rules clearly had clinically significant impact on the incidence and severity of subjects diagnosed with PTSD.

Vietnam combat veterans diagnosed with and without PTSD were administered the Keane PTSD Scale of the MMPI. Scotti, Sturges, and Lyons (1996) reported the Keane PTSD scale to have excellent sensitivity in discriminating the two groups when the recommended cutoff score of 30 was used. The Structured Clinical Interview for the DSM-III-R (SCID) was used to diagnose PTSD in veterans and classify them into four groups: PTSD only, PTSD with mood disorders, PTSD with other anxiety disorders, and PTSD with mood and anxiety disorders (Weyermann, Norris, & Hyer, 1996). The subjects were also administered the MMPI-2. All groups had MMPI-2 elevations on scales F, 1, 2, 3, 4, 6, 7, 8, 0, PK, and PS, with peak elevations on scales 8, 7, and 2. The PTSD-only group scores were not significantly lower than the scores of the other groups.

Many personality-based instruments that attempt to differentiate PTSD from malingering rely on the finding that malingerers overexaggerate pathology, which inflates clinical scale scores above what is known to be normative for PTSD groups. Liljequist, Kinder, and Schinka (1998) used the Personality Assessment Inventory (PAI) (Morey, 1991; Morey & Lanier, 1998) to try to isolate a pattern of responding indicative of malingered PTSD. The responses of students asked to feign PTSD were compared with veterans. Seven PAI scales were found to distinguish the two groups reliably. The PAI responses of student simulators were also investigated in a study by Rogers, Sewell, Morey, and Ustad (1996). Naive (undergraduates with minimal preparation) and sophisticated (doctoral students with 1 week preparation) groups were compared with clinical groups of three specific disorders (schizophrenia, major depression, and generalized anxiety disorder). The PAI was moderately effective with naive simulators, but evidenced only modest effectiveness with the sophisticated simulators. A two-stage discriminant analysis, however, yielded a moderately high hit rate that exceeded 80%. This analysis was effective regardless of the feigned disorder or the level of simulator sophistication. The PAI was reported to be generally useful in detecting malingering with an inmate population from a corrections-based psychiatric hospital (Wang et al., 1997).

Morel (1998) described preliminary validation of a promising new instrument designed to detect PTSD. The Morel Emotional Numbing Test for PTSD (MENT) is a forced-choice instrument designed to detect response bias in assessments of PTSD. The preliminary study compared MENT responses among four groups of military veterans applying for monetary compensation for combat-related PTSD and two groups of hospitalized military veterans. The total N was 102. Veritable vs. suspect groupings were determined by examining MMPI-2 F-K dissimulation index scores. The suspect groups produced more MENT errors compared with the veritable group or the hospitalized group. Based on clinical decision rules, the overall efficiency in the MENT was an impressive 95.6%. The study was preliminary and subject to multiple empirical questions, most notably the reliance on the dissimulation index scores as a benchmark of suspect subjects.

Chi-square analysis of the MMPI yielded two derivative scales for diagnosing acute and chronic PTSD (Gaston, Branet, Koszycki, & Bradwejn, 1998). According to the authors, the MMPI Acute PTSD Scale and the MMPI Chronic PTSD Scale had respective 83 and 75% hit rates discriminating between samples of civilian acute and chronic PTSD as compared with controls. The authors reported that gender or types of traumatic events did not substantially influence the scales.

Carlier, Lamberts, Van Uchelen, and Gersons (1998) described a new PTSD instrument adapted from the Structured Interview for PTSD (SI-PTSD). The new instrument is an abridged version of the SI-PTSD and demonstrated satisfactory internal consistency and interjudge reliability when applied to a sample of 136 plane crash survivors. The instrument is based on a self-report format, however, which would suggest limited applicability in forensic settings. Another short-form PTSD instrument (Short Screening Scale for DSM-IV PTSD) based on the DSM-IV criteria was recently reported (Breslau et al., 1999). The authors report that a cutoff score of four or greater on the seven-symptom screening scale was 80% sensitive in identifying PTSD.

SUGGESTIONS OF FAKED PTSD

Malingered PTSD is suggested when any of the following occur in combination:

1. Reported PTSD symptoms conflict with (a) verified records or (b) cross-validating sources. The reported symptoms are more pathological and similar to PTSD than those yielded from (a) and/or (b).
2. Psychometric performance evidences significant distortion in the direction of faking bad on measures reflecting PTSD symptoms.
3. Laboratory measures reflect no difference in autonomic arousal when PTSD scenes are presented to the individual.
4. Assessee admits to faking PTSD and that condition is not suggested by other evaluation results.

SUMMARY

Knowledge of PTSD has improved immensely in the past 15 years. Empirical studies have contributed to a better understanding of the temporal parameters of PTSD syndromes. There also is a better grasp of what types of stressors contribute to the intensity of PTSD, and what factors influence the course of PTSD syndromes. There have been significant advances understanding the role of secondary gain factors as instigating and sustaining PTSD. There have been impressive findings with both physiological and psychological instruments designed to diagnose and classify subgroups of PTSD, including PTSD deception. There have been impressive efforts with instruments that appear to hold promise with detecting deception regarding PTSD. As this chapter has illustrated, however, PTSD is a diffuse, subtle, and complicated disorder that can clinically manifest itself in myriad ways. The complexity of PTSD makes it a disorder very vulnerable to malingering (Sweet & Sweet, 1999). It is incumbent upon the forensic clinician to screen very carefully for PTSD, to preserve the integrity of true cases of PTSD.

In spite of the advances, meaningful understanding of the roles of malingering and deception in the disorder remains elusive. There remain many critical issues to be resolved. For example, still undetermined in the etiology and course of PTSD are the precise roles of preexisting and/or comorbid disorders. The evidence suggests that these variables increase susceptibility to PTSD, and also affect intensity and duration of PTSD symptoms. In addition, the presence of such variables impacts on malingering and deception dynamics with PTSD. There needs to be more work with interdisciplinary approaches to detect deception of PTSD. Such efforts will involve collective input of individuals from a variety of fields, who then create a multisourced and interdisciplinary database. In the end, there are no accurate and reliable measures to help determine when deliberate and nondeliberate distortions begin and end with PTSD.

LEGAL REFERENCES

Pard v. U.S., 589 F. Supp. 518 (D. Ore., 1984).

REFERENCES

Amir, M., Kaplan, Z., Neumann, L., Sharabani, R., Shani, N., & Buskila, D. (1997). Posttraumatic stress disorder, tenderness and fibromyalgia. *Journal of Psychosomatic Research, 42*(6), 607–613.

Amundson, G. J. G., Norton, G. R., Allerdings, M. D., Norton, P. J., & Larsen, D. K. (1998). Posttraumatic stress disorder and work-related injury. *Journal of Anxiety Disorders, 12*(1), 57–69.

Anthony, J. L., Lonigan, C. J., & Hecht, S. A. (1999). Dimensionality of post-traumatic stress disorder symptoms in children exposed to disaster: Results from confirmatory factor analyses. *Journal of Abnormal Psychology, 108*(2), 326–336.

Applebaum, D. C., & Burns, G. L. (1991). Unexpected childhood death: Post-traumatic stress disorder and surviving siblings and parents. *Journal of Clinical Child Psychology, 20*(2), 114–120.

Atkinson, R., Henderson, M., Sparr, L., & Deale, S. (1982). Assessment of Vietnam veterans for posttraumatic stress disorder in Veterans Administration disability claims. *American Journal of Psychiatry, 139*, 1118–1121.

Baker, D. G., West, S. A., Nicholson, W. E., Ekhator, N. N., Kasckow, J. W., Hill, K. K., Bruce, A. B., Orth, D. N., & Geracioti, T. D. (1999). Serial CSF corticotropin-releasing hormone levels and adrenocortical activity in combat veterans with post-traumatic stress disorder. *American Journal of Psychiatry, 156*(4), 585–588.

Baker, D. G., West, S. A., Orth, D. N., Hill, K. K., Nicholson, W. E., Ekhator, N. N., Bruce, A. B., Wortman, M. D., Keck, P. E., & Geracioti, T. D. (1997). Cerebral spinal fluid and plasma beta-endorphin in combat veterans with post-traumatic stress disorder. *Psychoneuroendocrinology, 22*(7), 517–529.

Beckham, J. C., Crawford, A. L., Feldman, M. E., Kirby, A. C., Hertzberg, M. A., Davidson, J. R. T., & Moore, S. D. (1997a). Chronic post-traumatic stress disorder and chronic pain in Vietnam combat veterans. *Journal of Psychosomatic Research, 43*(4), 379–389.

Beckham, J. C., Kirby, A. C., Feldman, M. E., Hertzberg, M. A., Moore, S. D., Crawford, A. L., Davidson, J. R. T., & Fairbank, J. A. (1997b). Prevalence and correlates of heavy smoking in Vietnam veterans with chronic post-traumatic stress disorder. *Addictive Behaviors, 22*(5), 637–647.

Blake, D. D., Weathers, F. W., Nagy, L. M., Kaloupek, D. G., Gusman, F. D., Charney, D. S., & Keane, T. M. (1995). The development of a Clinician-Administered PTSD Scale. *Journal of Traumatic Stress, 8*(1), 75–90.

Blanchard, E. B., Hickling, E. J., Forneris, C. A., Taylor, A. E., Buckley, T. C., Loos, W. R., & Jaccard, J. (1997). Prediction of remission of acute posttraumatic stress disorder in motor vehicle accident victims. *Journal of Traumatic Stress, 10*, 215–234.

Blanchard, E. B., Hickling, E. J., Mitnick, N., Taylor, A., Loos, W., & Buckley, T. C. (1995). The impact of severity of physical injury and perception of life threat in the development of post-traumatic stress disorder in motor vehicle accident victims. *Behavior Research and Therapy, 33*, 529–534.

Blanchard, E. B., Hickling, E. J., Taylor, A. E., Forneris, C. A., Loos, W., & Jaccard, J. (1995). Effects of varying scoring rules of the Clinician-Administered PTSD Scale (CAPS) for the diagnosis of post-traumatic stress disorder in motor vehicle accident victims. *Behavior Research and Therapy, 33*, 471–475.

Blanchard, E. B., Hickling, E. J., Taylor, A. E., & Loos, W. R. (1995). Psychiatric morbidity associated with motor vehicle accidents. *Journal of Nervous and Mental Disease, 183,* 495–504.

Blanchard, E. B., Hickling, E. J., Taylor, A., Loos, W. R., Forneris, C. A., & Jaccard, J. (1996). Who develops PTSD from motor vehicle accidents? *Behavior Research and Therapy, 34,* 1–10.

Blanchard, E. B., Kolb, L. C., Pallmeyer, T. P., & Gerardi, R. J. (1982). A psychophysiological study of post-traumatic stress disorder in Vietnam veterans. *Psychiatric Quarterly, 54,* 220–229.

Brady, K. T. (1997). Posttraumatic stress disorder and comorbidity: Recognizing the many faces of PTSD. *Journal of Clinical Psychiatry, 58*(9, Suppl.), 12–15.

Bremner, J. D., Staib, L. H., Kaloupek, D., Southwick, S. M., Soufer, R., & Charney, D. S. (1999). Neural correlates of exposure to traumatic pictures and sound in Vietnam combat veterans with and without posttraumatic stress disorder: A positron emission tomography study. *Biological Psychiatry, 45*(7), 806–816.

Brent, D. A., Perper, J. A., Moritz, G., Liotus, L., Richardson, D., Canobbio, R., & Schweers, J. (1995). Posttraumatic stress in peers of adolescent suicide victims: Predisposing factors and phenomenology. *Journal of the Academy of Child and Adolescent Psychiatry, 34*(2), 209–215.

Breslau, N., Davis, G. C., Andreski, P., & Peterson, E. (1991). Traumatic events and posttraumatic stress disorder in an urban population of young adults. *Archives of General Psychiatry, 48,* 216–222.

Breslau, N., Peterson, E. L., Kessler, R. C., & Schultz, L. R. (1999). Short screening scale for DSM-IV posttraumatic stress disorder. *American Journal of Psychiatry, 156*(6), 908–911.

Brown, P. J., Stout, R. L., & Gannon-Rowley, J. (1998). Substance use disorder–PTSD comorbidity: Patients perceptions of symptom interplay and treatment issues. *Journal of Substance Abuse Treatment, 15*(5), 445–448.

Brown, P. J., Stout, R. L., & Mueller, T. (1999). Substance use disorder and post-traumatic stress disorder comorbidity: Addiction and psychiatric treatment rates. *Psychology of Addictive Behaviors, 13*(2), 115–122.

Bryant, B., Mayou, R. A., & Lloyd-Bolstock, S. (1997). Compensation claims following road accidents: A six year follow-up study. *Medicine Science and the Law, 37,* 326–336.

Bryant, R. A., & Harvey, A. G. (1995). Avoidant coping style and posttraumatic stress following motor vehicle accidents. *Behavior Research and Therapy, 33,* 631–635.

Bryant, R. A., & Harvey, A. G. (1998). Relationship between acute stress disorder and posttraumatic stress disorder following mild traumatic brain injury. *American Journal of Psychiatry, 155*(5), 625–629.

Carlier, I. V. E., Lamberts, R. D., Fouwels, A. J., & Gersons, B. P. R. (1996). PTSD in relation to dissociation and traumatized police offices. *American Journal of Psychiatry, 153*(10), 1325–1328.

Carlier, I. V. E., Lamberts, R. D., Van Uchelen, A. J., & Gersons, B. P. R. (1998). Clinical utility of a brief diagnostic test for post-traumatic stress disorder. *Psychosomatic Medicine, 60*(1), 42–47.

Cascardi, M., Riggs, D. S., Hearst-Ikeda, D., & Foa, E. B. (1996). Objective ratings of assault safety as predictors of PTSD. *Journal of Interpersonal Violence, 11*(1), 67–78.

Chemtob, C. M., Muraoka, M. Y., Wu-Holt, P., Fairbank, J. A., Hamada, R. S., & Keane, T. M. (1998). Head Injury and combat related post-traumatic stress disorder. *Journal of Nervous and Mental Disease, 186*(11), 701–708.

Cohen, J. A., & American Academy of Child and Adolescent Psychiatry Work Group on Quality Issues. (1998). Practice parameters for the assessment and treatment of children and adolescents with post-traumatic stress disorder. *Journal of the American Academy of Child and Adolescent Psychiatry, 37*(10, Suppl.), 4S–26S.

Commings, D. E., Muhleman, D., & Gysin, R. (1996). Dopamine D-sub-2 receptor (DRD2) gene and susceptibility to postraumatic stress disorder: A study and replication. *Biological Psychiatry, 40*(5), 368–372.

Cordova, M. J., Andrykowski, M. A., Kennady, D. E., McGrath, P. C., Sloan, D. A., & Redd, W. A. (1995). Frequency and correlates of posttraumatic-stress-disorder-like symptoms after treatment for breast cancer. *Journal of Counseling and Clinical Psychology, 63*(6), 981–986.

Cuffe, S. B., Addy, C. L., Garrison, C. Z., Waller, J. L., Jackson, K. L., McKeown, R. E., & Chilappagari, S. (1998). Prevalence of PTSD in a community sample of older adolescents. *Journal of the American Academy of Child and Adolescent Psychiatry, 37,* 147–154.

Dalton, J., Tom, A., Rosenblum, M., Garte, S., & Aubuchon, I. (1989). Faking on the Mississippi Scale for Combat-Related Posttraumatic Stress Disorder. *Psychological Assessment, 1*(1), 56–57.

Deykin, E. Y. (1999). Posttraumatic stress disorder in children and adolescence: A review. *Medscape Mental Health 4,* 4. Retrieved 1999 from the World Wide Web: http://www.medscape.com/Medscape/psychia-try/journal/1999/v.no 4/mh3048.deyk/mh3048.dey.

Donovan, B. S., Padin-Rivera, E., Dowd, T., & Dudley, D. (1996). Childhood factors and war zone stress in chronic PTSD. *Journal of Traumatic Stress, 9*(2), 361–368.

Difede, J., & Barocas, D. (1999). Acute intrusive and avoidant PTSD symptoms as predictors of chronic PTSD following burn injury. *Journal of Traumatic Stress, 12*(2), 363–369.

Dunmore, E., Clark, D. M., & Ehlers, A. (1999). Cognitive factors involved in the onset and maintenance of post-traumatic stress disorder (PTSD). *Behavior Research & Therapy, 37*(9), 809–829.

Ehlers, A., Mayou, R. A., & Bryant, B. (1998). Psychological predictors of chronic posttraumatic stress disorder after motor vehicle accidents. *Journal of Abnormal Psychology, 107*(3), 508–519.

Emery, V., Emery, P. E., Shama, D. K., Quiana, N., & Jassais, A. K. (1991). Predisposing variables in PTSD patients. *Journal of Traumatic Stress, 4*(3),325–343.

Engdahl, B. E., Eberly, R. B., & Blake, J. D. (1996). Assessment of post-traumatic stress disorder in World War II veterans. *Psychological Assessment, 8*(4), 445–449.

Epstein, J. N., Saunders, B. E., & Kilpatrick, D. G. (1997). Predicting PTSD in women with a history of childhood rape. *Journal of Traumatic Stress, 10*(4), 537–588.

Fairbank, J., Keane, T., & Malloy, P. (1983). Some preliminary data on the psychological characteristics of Vietnam veterans with PTSD. *Journal of Consulting and Clinical Psychology, 51*, 912–919.

Fairbank, J. A., McCaffrey, R. J., & Keane, T. M. (1985). Psychometric detection of fabricated symptoms of post-traumatic stress disorder. *American Journal of Psychiatry, 142*, 501–503.

Fairbank, J. A., McCaffrey, R. J., & Keane, T. M. (1986). On simulating posttraumatic stress disorder [Letter to the editor]. *American Journal of Psychiatry, 143*, 268–269.

Famularo, R., Fenton, T., Kinscherff, R., & Augustyn, M. (1996). Psychiatric comorbidity in childhood post-traumatic stress disorder. *Child Abuse & Neglect, 20*(10), 953–961.

Famularo, R., Fenton, T., Kinscherff, R., Ayoub, C., & Barnum, R. (1994). Maternal and child post-traumatic stress disorder in cases of child maltreatment. *Child Abuse & Neglect, 18*(1), 27–36.

Fear, C. F. (1996). Factitious post-traumatic stress disorder revisited. *Irish Journal of Psychological Medicine, 13*(3), 116–118.

Ferrada-Noli, M., Asberg, M. A., Ormstad, K., Lundijn, T., & Sundbom, E. (1998). Suicidal behavior after severe trauma. Part 1: PTSD diagnoses, psychiatric comorbidity and assessments of suicidal behavior. *Journal of Traumatic Stress, 11*(1), 103–112.

Foa, E. B., & Hearst-Ikeda, D. (1996). Emotional dissociation in response to trauma: An information processing approach. In L. K. Michaelson & W. J. Ray (Eds.), *Handbook of dissociation: Theoretical, empirical, and clinical perspectives* (pp. 207–224). New York: Plenum Press.

Foy, D., Sipprelle, R., Rueger, D., & Carroll, E. (1984). Etiology of PTSD in Vietnam veterans: analysis of premilitary, military and combat exposure influences. *Journal of Consulting and Clinical Psychology, 52*, 79–87.

Franklin, J. (1988). *Molecules of the mind: The brave new science of molecular psychology.* New York: Dell.

Freed, D., Bowler, R., & Fleming, I. (1998). Post-traumatic stress disorder as a consequence of a toxic spill in Northern California. *Journal Applied Social Psychology, 28*(3), 264–281.

Freedman, S. A., Brandes, D., Peri, T., & Shalev, A. (1999). Predictors of chronic post-traumatic stress disorder: A prospective study. *British Journal of Psychiatry, 174*, 353–359.

Frueh, B. C., & Kinder, B. N. (1994). The susceptibility of the Rorschach test to malingering of combat-related PTSD. *Journal of Personality Assessment, 62*(2), 282–298.

Gaston, L., Brunet, A., Koszycki, D., & Bradwejn, J. (1998). MMPI scales for diagnosing acute and chronic PTSD in civilians. *Journal of Traumatic Stress, 11*(2), 355–365.

Geisser, M. E., Roth, R. S., Bachman, J. E., & Eckert, T. A. (1996). The relationship between symptoms of post-traumatic stress disorder and pain, affective disturbance and disability among patients with accident and non-accident related pain. *Pain, 66*(2–3), 207–214.

Gerardi, R., Blanchard, E., & Kolb, L. (1989). Ability of Vietnam veterans to dissimulate a psychophysiological assessment for post-traumatic stress disorder. *Behavior Therapy, 20*, 229–243.

Gerardi, R., Keane, T., & Penk, W. (1989). Utility: sensitivity and specificity in developing diagnostic tests of combat-related post-traumatic stress disorder (PTSD). *Journal of Clinical Psychology, 45*, 5, 691–703.

Giacona, R. M., Reinherz, H. Z., Silverman, A. B., Pakiz, B., Frost, A. K., & Cohen, E. (1995). Traumas and PTSD in a community population of older adolescents. *Journal of the American Academy of Child and Adolescent Psychiatry, 34*, 1369–1380.

Gillette, G. M., Skinner, R. D., Rasco, L. M., Fielstein, E. M., Davis, D. H., Pawelak, J. E., Freeman, T. W., Karson, C. N., Boop, F. A., & Garcia-Rill, E. (1997). Combat veterans with post-traumatic stress disorder exhibit decreased habituation of the P1 mid-latency auditory evoked potential. *Life Sciences, 61*(14), 1421–1434.

Gleaves, D. H., Eberenze, K. P., & May, M. C. (1998) Scope and significance of posttraumatic symptomatology among women hospitalized for an eating disorder. *International Journal of Eating Disorders, 24*(2), 147–156.

Gurvits, T. V., Shenton, M. E., Hokama, H., & Ohta, H. (1996). Magnetic resonance imaging study of hippocampal volume in chronic, combat-related posttraumatic stress disorder. *Biological Psychiatry, 40*(11), 1091-1099.

Hall, H. V. (1990). PTSD in war veterans. Paper presented at the meeting of the Hawaii Psychological Association, Honolulu.

Hammarberg, M. (1992) Penn Inventory for Posttraumatic Stress Disorder: Psychometric properties, *Psychological Assessment, 4*(1), 67–76.

Hankin, C. S., Auberg, F. R., Gallagher-Thompson, D., & Laws, A. (1996). Dimensions of PTSD among older veterans seeking outpatient medical care: A pilot study. *Journal of Clinical Geropsychology, 2*(4), 239–246.

Helzer, J., Robins, L., & McEvoy, L. (1987). Post-traumatic stress disorder in the general population: findings of the epidemiological catchment area survey, *New England Journal of Medicine, 317*, 1630–1634.

Henning, K. B., & Frueh, B. C. (1997). Combat guilt and its relationship to PTSD symptoms. *Journal of Clinical Psychology, 53*(8), 801–808.

Higgins, S. A. (1991). Post-traumatic stress disorder and its role in the defense of Vietnam veterans. *Law & Psychology Review, 15*, 259–276.

Holmes, T. H., & Rahe, R. H. (1967). The social readjustment rating scale. *Journal of Psychosomatic Research, 11*, 213–218.

Horowitz, M., Wilner, N., & Alvarez, W. (1979). Impact of event scale: A measure of psychosomatic stress, *Psychosomatic Medicine, 41*, 209–218.

Hyer, L., Boyd, S., Stanger, E., & Davis H. (1997). Validation of the MCMI-III scale among combat veterans. *Psychological Reports, 80*(3, Pt 1), 720–722.

Jacobsen, P. B., Widows, M. R., Hann, D. M., Andrykowski, M. A., Kronish, L. E., & Fields, K. K. (1998). Post-traumatic stress disorder symptoms after bone marrow transplantation for breast cancer. *Psychosomatic Medicine, 60*(3), 366–371.

Jongedijk, R. A., Carlier, I. V., Schreuder, B. N., & Berthold, P. R. (1996). Complex post-traumatic stress disorder: An explanatory investigation of PTSD and DES NOS among Dutch war veterans. *Journal of Traumatic Stress, 9*(3), 577–586.

Jordan, R. G., Nunley, T. V., & Cook, R. R. (1992). Symptom exaggeration in a PTSD inpatient population: Response set or claim for compensation. *Journal of Traumatic Stress, 5*(4), 633–642.

Jovic, V., Knezevic, G., & Lecic-Tosevski, D. (1998). Relation between anxiety and dissociative symptoms in the clinical picture of posttraumatic stress disorder. *Psihijatrija Danas, 30*(2), 225–236.

Keane, T., Caddell, J. & Taylor, K. (1988). Mississippi Scale for Combat-Related Post-Traumatic Stress Disorder: Three studies in reliability and validity. *Journal of Consulting and Clinical Psychology, 56*, 1–6.

Keane, T., Fairbank, J., Caddel, J., Zimering, R., Taylor, K., & Mora, C. (1989). Clinical evaluation of a measure to assess combat exposure. *Psychological Assessment, 1*(1), 53–55.

Keane, T., Malloy, P., & Fairbank, J. (1984). Empirical development of an MMPI subscale for the assessment of combat-related PTSD. *Journal of Consulting and Clinical Psychology, 62*, 888–891.

Kelly, B., Raphael, B., Judd, F., Kernutt, G., Burnett, P., & Burrows, G. (1998). Post-traumatic stress disorder in response to HIV infection. *General Hospital Psychiatry, 20*(6), 345–352.

Kessler, R. C., Sonnega, A., Bromet, E., Hughes, M., & Nelson, C. B. (1995). Posttraumatic stress disorder in the National Comorbidity Study. *Archives of General Psychiatry, 52*, 1048–1060.

Kinzie, J. D., Boehnlein, J. K., Leung, P. K., Moore, L. J., Riley, C., & Smith, D. (1990). The prevalence of post-traumatic stress disorder and its clinical significance among South East Asian refugees. *American Journal of Psychiatry, 147*(7), 913–917.

Kinzie, J. D., & Goetz, R. R. (1996). A century of controversy surrounding posttraumatic stress-spectrum syndromes: The impact on DSM-III and DSM-IV. *Journal of Traumatic Stress, 9*(2), 159-179.

Klamen, D. L., Grossman, L. S., & Kopacz, D. (1995). Posttraumatic stress disorder symptoms in resident physicians related to their internship. *Academic Psychiatry, 19*(3), 142–149.

Kolb, L. C. (1987, August). A neuropsychological hypothesis explaining PTSD. *American Journal of Psychiatry, 144*(8), 989.

Kolb, L. C. (1988). A critical survey of hypotheses regarding post-traumatic stress disorders in light of recent research findings. *Journal of Traumatic Stress, 1*(3), 291–293.

Koltek, M., Wilkes, T. C. R., & Atkinson, M. (1998). The prevalence of posttraumatic stress disorder in an adolescent inpatient unit. *Canadian Journal of Psychiatry, 43*(1), 64–68.

Koopman, C., Classen, C., & Spiegel, D. (1994). Predictors of posttraumatic stress symptoms among survivors of the Oakland/Berkeley, Calif., firestorm. *American Journal of Psychiatry, 41,* 429–434.

Koren, D., Arnon, I., & Klein, E. (1999). Acute stress response and post-traumatic stress disorder in traffic accident victims: A one-year prospective, follow-up study. *American Journal of Psychiatry, 156*(3), 367–373.

Kozaric-Kovacic, D., Marusic, A., & Ljubin, C. (1999). Combat experience soldiers and tortured prisoners of war differ in the clinical presentation of post-traumatic stress disorder. *Nordic Journal of Psychiatry, 53*(1), 11–15.

Kulka, R., & Schlenger, W. (1986). *Report to the Office of Technology Assessment (OTA) on the status of the National Vietnam Veterans Readjustment Study: Review of clinical and preclinical studies.* Paper prepared at the Research Triangle Institute, P.O. Box 12194, Research Triangle Park, North Carolina, 27709.

Kutz. I., Shabitai, H., Solomon, Z., Neumann, M., & David, D. (1994). Posttraumatic-stress disorder in myocardial infarction patients: Prevalence study. *Israel Journal of Psychiatry & Related Sciences, 31*(1), 48–56.

Laudenslager, M. L., Aasal, R., Adler, L., Breger, C. L., Montgomery, P. T., Sandberg, E., Wahlberg, L. J., Wilkins, R. T., Zweig, L., & Reite, M. L. (1998). Elevated cytotoxicity in combat veterans with long-term post-traumatic stress disorder: Preliminary observations. *Brain, Behavior & Immunity, 12*(1), 74–79.

Lees-Haley, P. R. (1989). Malingering post-traumatic stress disorder on the MMPI. *Forensic Reports, 2,* 1, 89–91.

Lees-Haley, P. R. (1992). Efficacy of MMPI-2 validity scales and MCMI-II modifier scales for detecting spurious PTSD claims: F, F-K, Fake Bad scale, Ego Strength, Subtle-Obvious subscales, DIS, and DEB. *Journal of Clinical Psychology, 48*(5), 681–689.

Lemieux, A. M., & Coe, C. L. (1995). Abuse-related post-traumatic stress disorder: Evidence for chronic neuroendocrine activation in women. *Psychosomatic Medicine, 57*(2), 105–115.

Liljequist, L., Kinder, B. N., & Schinka, J. A. (1998). An investigation of malingering post-traumatic stress disorder on the Personality Assessment Inventory. *Journal of Personality Assessment, 71*(3), 322–336.

Lipton, M. I., & Schaffer, W. R. (1988). Physical symptoms related to PTSD in an aging population. *Military Medicine, 153*(6), 316.

Livingston, R. B. (1985). Neurophysiology. In J. B. West, (Ed.), *Best and Taylor's physiological basis of medical practice* (11th ed.; pp. 970–1295). Baltimore, MD: Williams & Wilkins.

Lund, M., Foy, D., Sipprelle, C., & Strachan, A. (1984). The combat exposure scale: A systematic assessment of trauma in the Vietnam War. *Journal of Clinical Psychology, 40,* 1323–1328.

Lynn, E., & Belza, M. (1984). Factitious posttraumatic stress disorder: The veteran who never got to Vietnam. *Hospital and Community Psychiatry, 35,* 697–701.

Lyons, J. A., Caddell, J. M., Pitman, R. L., Rawls, R., & Perrin, S. (1994). The potential for faking on the Mississippi Scale for Combat-Related PTSD. *Journal of Traumatic Stress, 7*(3), 441–445.

Lyons, J. A., & Wheeler-Cox, T. (1999). MMPI, MMPI-2 and PTSD: Overview of scores, scales and profiles. *Journal of Traumatic Stress, 12*(1), 175–183.

Macklin, M. L., Metzger, L. J., Litz, B. T., McNally, R. J., Lasko, N. B., Orr, S. P., & Pitman, R. K. (1998). Lower precombat intelligence is a risk factor for post-traumatic stress disorder. *Journal of Consulting & Clinical Psychology, 66*(2), 323–326.

Maguire, K., Norman, T., Burrows, G., Hopwood, M., & Morris, P. (1998). Platelet paroxetine binding in post-traumatic stress disorder. *Psychiatry Research, 77*(1), 1–7.

Malloy, P. F., Fairbank, J. A., & Keane, T. M. (1983). Validation of a multimethod assessment of posttraumatic stress disorders in Vietnam veterans. *Journal of Counseling & Clinical Psychology, 51*(4), 488–494.

Manne, S. L., Du Hamel, K., Gallelli, K., Sorgen, K., & Redd, W. H. (1998). Posttraumatic stress disorder among mothers of pediatric cancer survivors: Diagnosis, comorbidity, and utility of the PTSD Checklist as a screening instrument. *Journal of Pediatric Psychology, 23*(6), 357–366.

March, J. S. (1993). What constitutes a stressor? The criterion "A" issue. In R. T. Davidson & E. B. Foa (Eds.), *Posttraumatic stress disorder and beyond* (pp. 37–56). Washington, DC: American Psychiatric Press.

Mayou, R. A., Bryant, B., & Duthie, R. (1993). Psychiatric consequences of road traffic accidents. *British Medical Journal, 307,* 647–651.

Mayou, R. A., Tyndel, S., & Bryant B. (1997). Long-term outcome of motor vehicle accident injury. *Psychosomatic Medicine, 59,* 578–584.

McCaffrey, R. J., & Bellamy-Campbell, R. (1989). Psychometric detection of fabricated symptoms of combat-related posttraumatic stress disorder: A systematic replication. *Journal of Clinical Psychology, 45,* 76–79.

McCaffrey, R. J., Lorig, T. S., Pendrey, D. L., McCutcheon, N. B., & Garrett, J. G. (1993). Odor-induced EEG changes in PTSD Vietnam veterans. *Journal of Traumatic Stress, 6*(2), 213–224.

McCloskey, L. A., & Walker, M. (2000). Posttraumatic stress disorder common in children abused by family members. *Journal of the Academy of Child and Adolescent Psychiatry, 39,* 108–115.

McCranie, E. W., Hyer, L. A., Boudewyns, P. A., & Woods, M. G. (1992). Negative parenting behavior, combat exposure, and PTSD symptoms severity: Test of a person^event interaction model. *Journal of Nervous & Mental Disease, 180*(7), 431–438.

McFall, M. E., Smith, D. E., Roszell, D. K., Tarver, D. J., & Malas, K. I. (1990). Convergent validity of measures of PTSD in Vietnam combat veterans. *American Journal of Psychiatry, 147*(5), 645–648.

McGorry, P. D. (1995). The clinical boundaries of post-traumatic stress disorder. *Australian & New Zealand Journal of Psychiatry, 29*(3), 385–393.

McPherson, W. B., Newton, J. E. O., Ackerman, P., Oglesby, D. M., & Dykman, R. A. (1997). An event-related brain potential investigation of PTSD and PTSD symptoms in abused children. *Integrative Physiological & Behavioral Science, 32*(1), 31-42, 75-83.

Mendelson, G. (1995). Post-traumatic stress disorder as psychiatric injury and civil litigation. *Psychiatry, Psychology and Law, 2*(1), 53–64.

Moradi, A. R., Doost, H. T. N., Taghavi, M. R., Yule, W., & Dalgleish, T. (1999). Everyday memory deficits in children and adolescents with PTSD: Performance on the Rivermead Behavioral Memory Test. *Journal of Child Psychology & Psychiatry & Allied Disciplines, 40*(3), 357–361.

Morel, K. R. (1998). Development and preliminary validation on a forced-choice test on the response bias for post-traumatic stress disorder. *Journal of Personality Assessment, 70,* 299–314.

Morey, L. C. (1991). *Personality Assessment Inventory: Professional manual* [Brochure]. Tampa, FL: Psychological Assessment Resources.

Morey, L. C., & Lanier, V. W. (1998). Operating characteristics of six response distortion indicators for the Personality Assessment Inventory. *Assessment, 5*(3), 203–214.

Munley, P. H., Bains, D. S., Bloem, W. D., & Busby, R. M. (1995a). Post-traumatic stress disorder and the MMPI-2. *Journal of Traumatic Stress, 8*(1), 171–178.

Munley, P. H., Bains, D. S., Bloem, W. D., Busby, R. M., & Pendziszewski, S. (1995b). Posttraumatic stress disorder and the MCMI-II. *Psychological Reports, 76*(3, Pt 1), 939–944.

Najavits, L. M., Gastfriend, D. R., Barber, J. P., Reif, S., Muenz, R., Blaine, F. A., Crits-Christoph, P., Thase, M., & Weiss, R. D. (1998). Cocaine dependence with and without PTSD among subjects in the National Institute on Drug Abuse Collaborative Cocaine Treatment Study. *American Journal of Psychiatry, 155*(2), 214–219.

Neal, L. A., Hill, N., Hughes, J., Middleton, A., & Busuttil, W. A. (1995). Convergent validity of measures of PTSD in an elderly population of former prisoners of war. *International Journal of Geriatric Psychiatry, 10*(7), 617–622.

Norris, F. H. (1992). Epidemiology of trauma: Frequency and impact of different potentially traumatic events on different demographic groups. *Journal of Consulting and Clinical Psychology, 60,* 409–419.

North, C. S., Smith, E. M., & Spitznagel, E. L. (1994). Posttraumatic stress disorder in survivors of a mass shooting. *American Journal of Psychiatry, 151*(1), 82–88.

Orr, S. P., Claiborn, J. M., Altman, B., Forgue, D. F., de Jong, J. B., Pitman, R., & Herz, L. R. (1990). Psychometric profile of posttraumatic stress disorder, anxious, and healthy Vietnam veterans: Correlations with psychophysiologic responses. *Journal of Consulting and Clinical Psychology, 58,* 329–335.

Orr, S. P., Pitman, R. K., Lasko, N.. B., & Herz, L. R. (1993). Psychophysiological assessment of posttraumatic stress disorder imagery in World War II and Korean combat veterans. *Journal of Abnormal Psychology, 102,* 152-159.

Orsillo, S. M., Weathers, F. W., Litz, B. T., Steinberg, H. R., Huska, J. A., & Keane, T. M. (1996). Current and lifetime psychiatric disorders among veterans with war zone related post-traumatic stress disorder. *Journal of Nervous & Mental Disease, 184*(5), 307–313.

O'Toole, B. I., Marshall, R. P., Schureck, R. J., & Dobson, M. (1998). Posttraumatic stress disorder and comorbidity in Australian Vietnam veterans. *Australian & New Zealand Journal of Psychiatry, 32*(1), 32–42.

Pelcovitz, D. L., Libov, B. G., Mandel, F., Kaplan, S., Weinblatt, M., & Septimus, A. (1998). Post-traumatic stress disorder and family functioning in adolescent cancer. *Journal of Traumatic Stress, 11*(2), 205–221.

Penk, W. E., Robinowitz, R., Roberts, W. R., Patterson, E. T., Dolan, M. P., & Atkins, H. G. (1981). Adjustment difficulties among male substance abusers varying in degree of combat experience in Vietnam. *Journal of Consulting and Clinical Psychology, 49*(3), 426–437.

Perconte, S., & Goreczny, A. J. (1989). Failure to detect fabricated posttraumatic stress disorder with the use of the MMPI in a clinical population. *American Journal of Psychiatry, 147*, 1057–1060.

Perkins, D. V., & Tebes, J. A. (1984). Genuine versus simulated responses on the Impact of Event Scale. *Psychological Reports, 54*(2), 575–578.

Perr, I. (1986). On simulating posttraumatic stress disorder [Letter to the editor]. *American Journal of Psychiatry, 143*, 268.

Pfefferbaum, B., Nixon, S. J., Tucker, P. M., Tivis, R., Moore, V. L., Gurwitch, R. H., Pynoos, R. S., & Geis, H. K. (1999). Posttraumatic stress response in bereaved children after the Oklahoma City bombing. *Journal of the American Academy of Child and Adolescent Psychiatry, 38*(11), 1372–1379.

Pitman, R. K., Saunders, L. S., & Orr, S. P. (1994). Psychophysiologic testing for post-traumatic stress disorder. *Trial, 30*(4), 22–26.

Pozgain, I., Filakovic, P., & Perekovic, V. (1992). Posttraumatic stress disorder in Croatian soldiers at east Slavonian front. *Psychologische Beitraege, 34*(3–4), 258–263.

Price, K. P. (1994). Post-traumatic stress disorder and concussion: Are they incompatible? *Defense Law Journal, 43*(1), 113–120.

Priebe, S., Brocker, M., & Gunkel, S. (1998). Involuntary admission and post-traumatic stress disorder symptoms in schizophrenia patients. *Comprehensive Psychiatry, 39*(4), 220–224.

Radnitz, C. L., Hsu, L., Willard, J., Perez-Strumolo, L., Festa, J., Lillian, L. B., Walczak, S., Tirch, D. D., Schlein, I. S., Binks, M., & Broderick, C. P. (1998). Post-traumatic stress disorder in veterans with spinal cord injury: Trauma-related risk factors. *Journal of Traumatic Stress, 11*(3), 505–520.

Resnick, P. J. (1984). The detection of malingered mental illness. *Behavioral Sciences and the Law, 2*(1), 21–38.

Resnick, P. J. (1987). *The detection of malingered mental illness*. Workshop presented at the American Academy of Psychiatry and Law, Ottawa, Canada.

Resnick, P. J. (1988a). Malingered psychosis. In R. Rogers (Ed.), *Clinical assessment of malingering and deception* (pp. 34–53). New York: Guilford Press.

Resnick, P. J. (1988b). Malingering of posttraumatic disorders. In R. Rogers (Ed.), *Clinical assessment of malingering and deception* (pp. 84–103). New York: Guilford Press.

Resnick. P. J. (1997). Malingering of posttraumatic stress disorders. In R. Rogers (Ed.), *Clinical assessment of malingering and deception* (2nd ed.; pp. 130–152). New York: Guilford Press.

Resnick. P. J. (1999). *Clinical assessment of malingering and deception*. Course outline (Specialized Training Services, Inc., 9606 Tierra Grande, Suite 105, San Diego, CA, (619) 695-1313).

Resnick, H. S., Kilpatrick, D. G., & Lipovsky, J. A. (1991). Assessment of rape-related posttraumatic stress disorder: Stressor and symptom dimensions. *Psychological Assessment, 3*(4), 561–572.

Riggs, D. S., Rothbaum, B. O., & Foa, E. B. (1995). A prospective examination of symptoms of posttraumatic stress disorder in victims of nonsexual assault. *Journal of Interpersonal Violence, 10*(2), 201–214.

Roberts, W. R., Penk, W. E., Gearing, M. L., Robinowitz, R., Dolan, M. P., & Patterson, E. T. (1982). Interpersonal problems of Vietnam combat veterans with symptoms of posttraumatic stress disorder. *Journal of Abnormal Psychology, 91*(6), 444–450.

Rogers, R., Kropp, P. R., Bagby, R. M., & Dickens, S. E. (1992). Faking specific disorders: A study of the Structured Interview of Reported Symptoms (SIRS). *Journal Of Clinical Psychology, 48*(5), 643–648.

Rogers, R., Sewell, K. W., Morey, L. C., & Ustad, K. L. (1996). Detection of feigned mental disorders on the Personality Assessment Inventory: A discriminant analysis. *Journal of Personality Assessment, 67*(3), 629–640.

Sack, W. H., Him, C., & Dickason, D. (1999). Twelve-year follow-up study of Khmer youths who suffered massive war trauma as children. *Journal of the American Academy of Child & Adolescent Psychiatry, 38*(9), 1173–1179.

Saladin, M. E., Brady, K. T., Dansky, B. S., & Kilpatrick, D. G. (1995). Understanding comorbidity between PTSD and substance use disorder: Two preliminary investigations. *Addictive Behaviors, 20*(5), 643–655.

Salloway, S., Southwick, S. M., & Sadowsky, M. (1990). Opiate withdrawal presenting as post-traumatic stress disorder. *Hospital and Community Psychiatry, 41*(6), 666–667.

Scotti, J. R., Sturges, L. V., & Lyons, J. A. (1996). The Keane PTSD Scale extracted from the MMPI: Sensitivity and specificity with Vietnam veterans. *Journal of Traumatic Stress, 9*(3), 643-650.

Shalev, A. Y., Freedman, S., Peri, T., Brandes, D., & Sahar, T. (1997). Predicting PTSD and survivors: Prospective evaluation of self-report and clinician-administered instruments. *British Journal of Psychiatry, 170*, 558–564.

Shalev, A. Y., Orr, S. P., & Pitman, R. K. (1993). Psychophysiologic assessment of trauma surgery in Israeli civilian post-traumatic stress disorder patients. *American Journal of Psychiatry, 150*(620), 4.

Sharkansky, E. J., Brief, D. J., Pierce, J. M., Meehan, J. C., & Mannix, L. M. (1999). Substance abuse patients with post-traumatic stress disorder (PTSD): Identifying specific triggers of substance use in their associations with PTSD symptoms. *Psychology of Addictive Behaviors, 13*(2), 89–97.

Shin, L. M., McNally, R. J., Kosslyn, S. M., Thompson, W. L., Rauch, S. L., Alpert, N. M., Metzger, L. J., Lasko, N. B., Orr, S. P., & Pitman, R. K. (1999). Regional cerebral blood flow during script-driven imagery in childhood sexual abuse-related PTSD: A PET investigation. *American Journal of Psychiatry, 156*(4), 575–584.

Sigafoos, C. E. (1994). A PTSD treatment program for combat (Vietnam) veterans in prison. *International Journal of Offender Therapy & Comparative Criminology, 38*(2), 117–130.

Silverman, J. J., Singh, N. N., Carmanico, S. J., Lindstrom, K. A., Best, A. M., & Clearfield, S. (1999). Psychological distress and symptoms of post-traumatic stress disorder in Jewish adolescents following a brief exposure to concentration camps. *Journal of Child & Family Studies, 8*(1), 71–89.

Simon, R. I. (1999). Chronic post-traumatic stress disorder: A review and checklist of factors influencing prognosis. *Harvard Review of Psychiatry, 6*(6), 304–312.

Smith, E. M., North, C. S., McCool, R. E., & Shea, J. M. (1990). Acute postdisaster psychiatric disorders: Identification of persons at risk. In *American Journal of Psychiatry, 31*, 227–237.

Sparr, L., & Atkinson, R. (1986). Posttraumatic stress disorder as an insanity defense: Medicolegal quicksand. *American Journal of Psychiatry, 143*, 608–613.

Spiegel, D. (1991). Dissociation and trauma. In A. Tasman & A. E. Goldfinger (Eds.), *Review of psychiatry* (pp. 261–275). Washington, DC: American Psychiatric Press.

Starcevic, V., & Slavoljub, D. (1993). Post-traumatic stress disorder: Current conceptualization, an overview of research and treatment. *Psihijatrija Danas, 25*(1–2), 9–31.

Stuss, D., & Benson, D. F. (1986). *The frontal lobes*. New York: Raven Press.

Sweet, J. J., & Sweet, J. J. (1999). Malingering: Differential diagnosis. In J. J. Sweet (Vol. Ed.) & J. J. Sweet (Ed.), *Forensic neuropsychology* (pp. 255–285). Lisse, the Netherlands: Swets & Zeitlinger.

Timmons-Mitchell, J., Chandler-Holtz, D., & Semple, W. E. (1997). Post-traumatic stress disorder symptoms in child sexual abuse victims and their mothers. *Journal of Child Sexual Abuse, 6*(4), 1–14.

Ursano, R. J., Fullerton, C. S., Epstein, R. S., Crowley, B., Kao, T., Vance, K., Craig, K. J., Dougall, A. L., & Baum, A. (1999). Acute and chronic post-traumatic stress disorder in motor vehicle accident victims. *American Journal of Psychiatry, 156*(4), 589–595.

van der Kolk, B. A.. (1988). The trauma spectrum: The interaction of biological and social events in the genesis of the trauma response. *Journal of Traumatic Stress, 1*(3), 273–283.

van der Kolk, B. A., Pelcovitz, D. R., Roth, S., Mandel, F. S., McFarlane, A., & Herman, J. L. (1996). Dissociation, somatization, and affect dysregulation: The complexity of adaptation to trauma. *American Journal of Psychiatry, 153*(Suppl.), 83–93.

Wahler, H. J. (1983). *Wahler physical symptoms inventory*. Western Psychological Services, 12031 Wilshire Boulevard, Los Angeles, CA 90025.

Wang, E. W., Rogers, R., Giles, C. L., Diamond, P. M., Herrington-Wang, L. E., & Taylor, E. R. (1997). A pilot study of the Personality Assessment Inventory (PAI) in corrections: Assessment of malingering, suicide risk, and aggression in male inmates. *Behavioral Sciences and the Law, 15*(4), 469–482.

Wang, S., & Mason, J. (1999). Elevation of serum T-sub-3 levels and their association with symptoms in World War II veterans with combat-related posttraumatic stress disorder: Replication of findings in Vietnam combat veterans. *Psychosomatic Medicine, 61*(2), 131–138.

Wasserman, D. A., Havassy, B. E., & Boles, S. M. (1997). Traumatic events and post-traumatic stress disorder in cocaine users entering private treatment. *Drug and Alcohol Dependence, 46*(1–2), 1–8.

Watson, C. G., Juba, M. P., & Anderson, P. E. (1989). Validities of five combat scales. *Psychological Assessment, 1*(2), 98–102.

Weathers, F. W., Litz, B. T., Keane, T. M., Herman, D. S., Steinberg, H. R., Huska, J. A., & Kraemer, H. C. (1996). The utility of the SCL-90 for the diagnosis of war-zone-related post-traumatic stress disorder. *Journal of Traumatic Stress, 9*(1), 111–128.

Weine, S. M., Vojvoda, D., Becker, D. F., McGlashan, T. H., Hodzic, E., Laub, D., Hyman, L., Sawyer, M., & Lazrove, S. (1998). PTSD symptoms in Bosnian refugees 1 year after resettlement in the United States. *American Journal of Psychiatry, 155*(4), 562–564.

Weintraub, D., & Ruskin, P. L. (1999). Posttruamatic stress disorder in the elderly. *Harvard Review of Psychiatry, 7*(7), 144–152.

Weyermann, A. G., Norris, F. H., & Hyer, L. (1996). Examining comorbidity and post-traumatic stress disorder in a Vietnam veteran population using the MMPI-2. *Journal of Traumatic Stress, 9*(2), 353–360.

Wilson, J. (1989). The psychobiology of trauma. In J. P. Wilson (Ed.), *Trauma, transformation, and healing: An integrative approach to theory, research, and post traumatic therapy* (p. 21). New York: Mazel Publishers.

Wolfe, J., Schnurr, P. P., Brown, P. J., & Furey, J. (1994). Posttraumatic stress disorder and war-zone exposure as correlates of perceived health in female war veterans. *Journal of Counseling and Clinical Psychology, 62*(6), 1235–1240.

Yehuda, R. (1999). Biological factors associated with susceptibility to posttraumatic stress disorder. *Canadian Journal of Psychiatry, 44*(1), 34–39.

Yehuda, R., Boisoneau, D., Lowy, M. T., & Giller, E. L. (1995). Dose-related changes in plasma cortisol and lymphocyte glucocorticoid receptors following dexamethasone administration in combat veterans with and without posttraumatic stress disorder. *Archives of General Psychiatry, 52*(7), 583–593.

Yehuda, R., Elkin, A., Binder-Brynes, K., Kakana, B., Southwick, S. M., Schmeidler, J., & Giller, E. (1996). Dissociation in aging Holocaust survivors. *American Journal of Psychiatry, 153*(7), 935–940.

Yehuda, R., Kahana, B., Binder-Byrnes, K., Southwick, S. M., Mason, J. W., & Giller, E. L. (1995). Low urinary cortisol excretion in Holocaust survivors with posttraumatic stress disorder. *American Journal of Psychiatry, 152*(7), 982–986.

Yehuda, R., Southwick, S. M., Giller, E. L., Ma, X., & Mason, J. W. (1992). Urinary catecholamine excretion and severity of PTSD symptoms in Vietnam combat veterans. *Journal of Nervous & Mental Disease, 180*(5), 321–325.

Yule, W., Ten Bruggencate, S., & Joseph, S. A. (1994). Principal components analysis of the Impact of Events Scale in adolescents who survived a shipping disaster. *Personality & Individual Differences, 16*(5), 685–691.

Zarin, I., & Weitzman, L. (1990). *The National Jury Verdict Review and Analysis*, 5. Newark, NJ: Jury Verdict Review Publications, Inc.

Zatzick, D. F., Marmar, C. R., Weiss, D. S., Browner, W. S., Metzler, T. J., Golding, J. M., Stewart, A., Schlenger, W. E., & Wells, K. B. (1997). Posttraumatic stress disorder and functioning of quality of life outcomes in a nationally representative sample of male Vietnam veterans. *American Journal of Psychiatry, 154*(12), 1690–1695.

Zisook, S., Chentsova-Dutton, Y., & Shuchter, S. R. (1998). PTSD following bereavement. *Annals of Clinical Cancer, 10*(4), 157–163.

Zlotnick, C. (1997). Posttraumatic stress disorder (PTSD), PTSD comorbidity, and childhood abuse among incarcerated women. *Journal of Nervous & Mental Disease, 185*(12), 761–763.

Part IV

Deception Analysis in Criminal Contexts

14 Interviewing and Interrogation

This chapter discusses pretrial investigation of suspects and witnesses through interviewing and observation. Extant methods are effective to varying degrees. Academic researchers frequently claim that present methods of interviewing and interrogation yield too many false positives (innocent parties labeled as perpetrators). A number of sources have stressed the importance of corroborating the self-reports of suspected malingerers with reports made by other parties (Horvath, Jayne, & Buckley, 1994; Vrij, Semin, & Bull, 1996; Vrij & Winkle, 1993). Vrij (1993, 1994, 1995) reported studies with police detectives who viewed video fragments of confederates instructed to be truthful or lie in an interview with an actor dressed as a police officer. The detectives indicated their judgments of whether the confederates were lying or not. In one study (Vrij, 1994), the accuracy rate was no better than chance (49%); the author concluded that the detectives used the wrong cues to detect deception.

The conclusions in this chapter are based on the authors' experiences over the years with police departments and other investigative/enforcement agencies. It is important to note that, in general, *interviewing* refers to clinical interviews and assessment procedures and the term *interrogation* refers to investigation procedures used by police and others. Clinical interviewing is designed to generate clinical findings and hypotheses objectively. This is achieved through a process of regulating and managing clinical impressions (Schlenker, & Weigold, 1992); interviewing is usually not invasive, intimidating, or aggressive. Interrogation is an aggressive procedure and is designed primarily to generate evidence to be used in litigation. Extreme examples of interrogation procedures have been portrayed in Hollywood spy movies depicting aggressive questioning and brutal physical torture, as well as other exotic means of extracting desired information from withholding subjects. Clinical interviewing in forensic matters should be comprehensive, exacting, and rigorous; these objectives, however, are not tantamount to clinicians being exempt from usual ethical guidelines in delivering clinical services.

The literature on word association methods and interrogation-oriented interviews is relevant to an investigation. Also relevant is the corpus of data from Chapter 5 regarding nonverbal behavior. Police investigators are taught to be exquisitely sensitive to nonverbal behavior although not always in a reliable or empirically accurate manner. The evaluator should recall that interviewing is employed frequently in combination with other investigative approaches — forensic hypnosis, polygraphy, criminal profiling. All of these methods are relatively crude. Although the techniques can be very effective with sensitive, intuitive, well-trained police investigators, investigative teams persist in overutilizing them. At the very least, the serious evaluator of deception should be aware of methods from other disciplines that are designed to cut through denial and fakery. A significant difference between police methods and clinical approaches is the disdain for direct reliance on suspect-generated information by police investigations. As has been repeatedly cautioned throughout this book, such reliance is an acknowledged major weakness of psychological evaluation where deception is an issue. In contrast, the police investigation relies primarily on crime scene evidence and study of the suspect's *modus operandi*. The thesis here is that both approaches have value and both have limitations. Most forensic clinicians will have access to police investigative materials. It is important, therefore, for forensic clinicians to have a fundamental grasp of their value.

The final section of this chapter addresses ethical and legal implications of interrogation/investigation techniques. Existing, traditional methods need to be replaced and reconceptualized so that they are congruent with the needs of society and with the rights of interrogated individuals. The next chapter describes advances with police investigator "profiling" techniques, which is a step toward a more contemporary approach. Computerized methodologies have considerably enhanced the effectiveness of the profiling technique.

REACTION TIME AS A SIGN OF DECEPTION

In a case involving a confession for the rape, sodomy, and murder of two young Asian females and suspicion of a third murder, a 20-year-old radio repairman agreed to undergo comprehensive evaluation. For the unsolved third murder, the following methods were used and the following results were obtained:

> Words associated with key items and events surrounding the homicide known only to the perpetrator were completed. The victim was strangled with an orange scarf in a schoolroom, for example, so words such as "orange," "scarf," and "school" were selected. Words matched in frequency of occurrence were selected from the Lorge–Thorndike tables. A mixed list of 50 words was presented individually to the suspect, with instructions for him to associate a common word with the stimulus word. Delay in response time and emotional indicators were dependent variables. The suspect presented longer latencies of response to the critical words, evidencing facial twitching and other arousal signs as associated features. He declined to continue after 36 words, claiming that the test made no sense and that he was tired. The case on the third murder was subsequently dropped because of lack of evidence. The perpetrator was incarcerated on the first two murders. Years later, he told a cell mate that he had killed the victim in the unsolved murder; however, he related the information in a hypothetical manner such that he could not be prosecuted.

Word association methods were used extensively in the early part of the century to detect deception and concealment (Goldstein, 1923; Henke & Eddy, 1909; Leach & Washburn, 1910; Marston, 1920; Yerkes & Berry, 1909). Research was conducted on a variety of populations including college students, criminals, and military personnel. Despite their early promise, investigations of this sort became less popular as a result of many different influences.

Goldstein (1923) summarized this early research:

> The primary interest of the early workers in this field lay in the diagnosis of the emotional complexes underlying cases of hysteria and neurasthenia. The method was, however, also applied by Jung and Wertheimer in attempts to detect crime. In this use of the association-reaction method, the list of words used as stimuli contains words relating to the crime. The reaction time to these critical words was found to be lengthened in the case of those criminals who attempted deception by avoiding responses which implicated them in the crime.

Although subject to methodological criticisms, these early investigations frequently uncovered where subjects had concealed objects. Among the findings from this early work were:

1. Reaction words were suggested by objects in the room or by earlier words in the series. Fakers used recent input to distort. A perseverative quality was indicated.
2. A small subset of subjects came up with shorter reaction times (termed "negative" subjects), which could be controlled by inclusion of neutral words equivalent in difficulty and frequency. In some cases, a mixed pattern was observable (i.e., both negative and positive types), again detectable by a controlled comparison.

3. Fear and anger accounted for the discrepancies from expected performance. Stress was seen to create a momentum of its own with awareness of anger or fear generating further abnormal latencies. Fear was associated with longer latencies and anger with shorter ones.

4. Most subjects had a plan to deceive. For longer latencies, they planned to go slower and welcomed opportunities and distractions to lengthen the reaction times. This was contingent upon awareness by the faker that the method was tapping deception.

5. For shorter latencies and in anticipation of the "hamming" style of deception discussed later, Marston (1920) stated the following:

> I believe it will be commonly recognized that there are individuals among our acquaintances who can lie faster and more fluently than they can tell the truth.... The behavior of the negative type subjects, as noted by the experimenter, was almost wholly calm, confident, and showed a high degree of intellectual concentration. The guilty flush was almost altogether absent and the manner of the subject was usually more convincing upon deceptive lists than upon truthful ones. In the negative type, we find the successful liar.

Interestingly, later experimentation showed that the negative types were not conscious of their deception (Goldstein, 1923). In contrast, subjects with longer latencies felt guilty and were aware when they were deceiving and relaxed when they were responding naturally. They showed more hesitation, confusion, and arousal.

CORROBORATION AS A CLINICAL/FORENSIC TOOL

A number of clinical sources (Hall, 1982; Resnick, 1997; Shapiro, 1999) have emphasized the need to corroborate the self-reports of suspected malingerers with the independent reports of other parties involved in the malingering scenarios. Depending on the nature of the malingered behavior, collateral reports may be gathered from past or current circumstances. For example, if a criminal defendant is suspected to be malingering hallucinations, it would be important to gather information from the defendant's prior history to determine if psychotic experience was previously reported by the defendant. If the suspected malingering involves the defendant's self-report of the instant offense, then gathering of other eyewitness accounts would be vitally important.

Corroborating data should be discreetly incorporated into the evaluation process, and any limitations in its utility should be candidly acknowledged. Rogers (1990) aptly pointed out that subjective reports of corroborators might also be distorted. Discrepancies between the reports of suspected malingerers and the reports of corroborating others, therefore, are not necessarily indicative of anything. Varying perceptions of involved parties (i.e., suspect, victims, witnesses, and police investigators) are characteristic of criminal matters. Another prime example of such discrepant views by involved parties is disputed custody/visitation matters (Poirier, 1991). Disputed domestic matters in general involve intense, and usually bitter, negative emotions such that the credibility of wholesome individuals who are usually very reliable becomes hopelessly tainted. In these circumstances, forensic formulations can be caught up in a frustrating and fruitless pursuit trying to arrive at meaningful conclusions when the database is limited to subjective reports.

Unfortunately, expert witness reliance on such limited data is all too commonplace in important matters such as arriving at dispositional recommendations regarding criminal defendants and those involving custody/visitation, child abuse/neglect findings, and termination of parental rights dispositions. Judicial proceedings will rely on an opposing expert witness rendering opinions based solely on the expert's subjective interpretation of the credibility of the parties who have provided their subjective interpretations. The circumstances have justifiably resulted in the expert witness testimony of mental health professionals being viewed with considerable skepticism by the public and the judiciary.

INTERROGATION/INVESTIGATION INTERVIEW DYNAMICS

There has been an effort by researchers to understand the dynamics of police investigator interview techniques. The impetus for this study comes from several sources not the least of which is the question of how these techniques may compromise a suspect's legal rights. There is also interest in developing and refining these techniques so they are more useful and effective.

During the 1990s, retraction of incriminating admissions became a commonplace phenomenon in criminal investigations. Defense attorneys capitalized on mounting public concern with complaints of police brutality and coercion and argued that initial admissions of guilt or incriminating statements by suspects were the product of police intimidation. Gudjonsson (1990) investigated the psychological characteristics of 100 individuals who retracted self-incriminating admissions during interviews with police investigators. Based on psychometric findings, the retracting subjects were described as having generally lower cognitive ability and higher scores on scales of suggestibility, compliance, and acquiescence compared with controls. In a later study of prison inmates who claimed to have made false confessions during police interviews, the false confessors were reported to have more antisocial features on psychometric testing compared with controls (Sigurdsson & Gudjonsson, 1996). Further, a subgroup of the false confessors had elevated suggestibility and confabulation scores. A parallel study with 108 juvenile offenders found no reports of false confessions.

The objective of undercover officers is to infiltrate groups suspected of criminal activity. To achieve this, undercover agents must engage in purposeful, staged deception. Based on interviews with 18 undercover narcotic agents, Jacobs (1992a) described a deception typology consisting of four primary components:

1. Rehearsal
2. Appearance manipulation
3. Verbal diversion
4. Physical diversion

The role-deception tactic used by police agents has been referred to as a new application of "dramaturgical theory" (Jacobs, 1992a, b, 1997). Jacobs (1997) conducted semistructured interviews with 24 undercover officers to identify the methods used to introduce themselves into desired criminal circles. The undercover officers described their use of "contingent ties," that is, the use of established relationships with informants to then employ role deception (i.e., undercover officers as criminals) to integrate themselves into relationships with criminal elements. Also important was the use of linguistic devices such as street parlance and idioms to curry favor toward the undercover officers. The inference is that undercover agents may be able to ply their understanding of the social psychology of individuals with antisocial dynamics to infiltrate groups involved in criminal activity.

These considerations and strategies have been described by undercover narcotics agents involved in covert drug transactions (Jacobs, 1992a). Ethnographic interviews were conducted with 35 undercover narcotic agents who described the concept of "interaction as infiltration." The agents would effect role performances based on their knowledge of the target group's social structure and by use of verbal and nonverbal machinations necessary to achieve sufficient deception for infiltration. The writers suggested that the methods of the undercover officers embody broader sociological relevance than simply police work. As an example, Hessing, Elffers, Robben, and Webley (1993) conducted a study of interviews with individuals claiming unemployment benefits. The fraudulent claimants were less educated, were more socially alienated, were more inclined to take risks, and had generally more receptive attitudes toward a variety of kinds of fraud.

Sexual offenders faced with sentences that will compromise their freedoms for significant periods are highly motivated to be deceptive during investigations and, for that matter, during clinical assessments, as well. The authors have experienced this to be a problem even with juvenile sexual offenders. The particular ability of sexual offenders to engage in deception appears, in part,

---

TABLE 14.1
Guidelines for Interrogating Suspects

Isolate suspect from all intrusions and resources.
Keep suspect immobile as much as possible.
Establish dependence on the part of the suspect.
Examiner is friendly, concerned, and firm.
Ask open-ended questions for new information.
Proceed from the general to the specific.
Precise questions are asked for concrete data.
Occasionally ask questions randomly to upset faking patterns.
Summarize statement in sequence of events.
Suspect verifies each part of summarized sequence material.
Suggest excuses to crime to suspect before suspect spontaneously mentions them.
Project indifference to criminal behavior of suspect ("Everybody does it").
Induce stress when appropriate (e.g., initially).
Provide relief after an admission, then induce stress again; repeat the cycle.
Continue until a confession is obtained.

Note: Adapted from *The Gentle Art of Interviewing and Interrogation: A Professional Manual and Guide,* by R. F. Royal, & S. R. Schutt, 1976, Englewood Cliffs,
NJ: Prentice-Hall.

---

to be related to years of prior awareness of social taboos regarding sexual misconduct (Poirier, 1999). By the time of actual criminal activity, sexual offenders are already well postured to be deceptive. Happel and Auffrey (1995) addressed this problem with sexual offenders presenting before clinician-staffed prison "Therapy Review Boards." Noting the sexual offenders' "dance of denial," misrepresenting their involvement in a sexual offense(s), the authors proposed that a three-person model for review boards was more valuable than individual sources of information regarding sexual offenders.

CRIMINAL INVESTIGATION APPROACHES

Royal and Schutt (1976) typify an investigative approach through interviewing. Their method is based upon the assumptions that (1) induced stress in examinees is desirable because reason decreases as emotions increase; (2) polite, respectful examiner behavior can yield confessions and reduce invalid or illegal findings; and (3) the deceptive suspect will eventually trip himself or herself up. Implicit assumptions are that most people are dishonest and that almost all suspects actually committed the crime for which they are interviewed.

Their method involves detecting lies, discrediting alibis, and "pumping up" the quality of incriminating evidence. Fear of punishment, and of bringing shame upon the family, as well as other similar methods, is utilized to motivate the suspect. Table 14.1 presents some of their recommended techniques used, of course, in conjunction with other forensic methods.

A structured approach to interviewing is recommended by Reid & Associates in books, articles, and seminars (1986). Many investigative agencies endorse these methods in their fieldwork. Guidelines to truthful vs. deceptive suspects are presented in Table 14.2, followed by a sequential process recommended by Reid and Associates (1986; 1988).

CONFRONTATION

In this initial step, the suspect is accused of a crime (e.g., "John, evidence shows that you murdered Mrs. Jones in her house last night"). The purpose of the accusation is to increase anxiety and

TABLE 14.2
Differentiating Truthful from Deceptive Suspects (Reid System)

Truthful	Deceptive
Eye contact direct and continuous	Eye contact erratic and indirect when threatened
Facial expressions vary from anger to surprise	Facial expressions vary from fear to passive/blank
Increased anger with continual accusations	Difficult to rouse to anger
More likely facial flushing	More likely blanching
Minimal body movements	More frequent and extreme body movements
Leans toward interrogator	Turns away from interrogator
Less use of barriers	More use of barriers (e.g., arms crossing chest)
Infrequent self-grooming responses	Frequent self-grooming responses
Responds without delay unless question requires thought	Evasive or nonresponsive
More information about case reduces arousal	No change or increased tension with more case information
Cooperates with investigation	Noncooperation comes in various forms
Prompt, with no hesitancy in delaying termination	Arrives late and desires to leave early
Task oriented and interested in unresolved issues	More likely presents physical problems, complaints, crying, etc.
Task oriented	Emphasizes truthfulness
Some memory loss expected	Selective memory loss or too good recall
Direct	Excessive use of qualifiers
Smooth execution of words and sentences	More likely "tongue-tied" or otherwise disorganized answer
Easy to spot	Harder to determine
Denials become stronger as interrogation continues	Denials weaken as interrogation continues

stress in the suspect. A transition step is often introduced here with the addition of a warm and supportive investigator.

THEME DEVELOPMENT

The suspect's anxiety is reduced by continually plying him with rationalizations for his crime until one is workable (e.g., to suspect in wife-beating case: "Everyone pushes around his wife a little"). The idea is to prompt a confession without fear of recrimination. The seriousness of the crime is minimized, blame is projected onto the victim, and the suspect is provided with a positive image.

REJECTION

Theme development continues in this stage with denials being cut off by the interrogator (e.g., "I know what you want to say, but let me share this with you ..."). The interrogator meets objections by the suspect that the suspect could not have committed the crime by character support. The suspect may state that he is a family man, for example, and could never jeopardize that status by sexually assaulting his daughter. The interrogator then supports the notion of his good character by relating it back to theme development (e.g., "Our investigation shows that you are a good and decent family man, John. I'm sure this is the only time this has occurred in your life").

ACCEPTANCE

The defenses of the suspect begin to diminish. Cues that the suspect is tiring include muscle relaxation, slumped posture, dropping of eyes, and crying. Tears are considered a good sign because they signify that the suspect's defenses are breaking down. The interrogator is advised to press on with the attack, calling the suspect by his or her first name, touching and invading the personal space of the suspect, and using other means.

ALTERNATIVES

Two or more offense scenarios are presented to the suspect, with the option of selecting one that will inculpate him (e.g., "Your stepdaughter says that this has been going on for years. Is this true or was it a one-time thing?").

The following are alternatives presented to a therapist suspected of fraudulent billing practices:

> If this is something where you have built your entire practice on falsified billing statements, and this is just one of thousands, I am going to have to spend weeks going through your records, contacting clients, and insurance companies to verify each bill. But, if this was something that just started a little while ago, you can save me a lot of time by telling me that. I'm really hoping that this was just an isolated incident, wasn't it?

CLOSURE

This involves expanding any admission to the crime into a legally acceptable format. Support of the accused with no recourse to leading questions is used. Follow-up questions with no note taking until details of the crime are known are encouraged.

There should be both oral and written confessions, with audio and videotapes of the statements. A formal statement is taken with all legal points in mind. These include (1) obtaining a witness, (2) *Miranda* warnings, (3) the suspect giving both a general and a detailed presentation of the offense, (4) use of exact words, (5) correction of errors being initialed by the suspect, and (6) signatures by all parties.

OTHER METHODS

The above is presented not as recommended procedure by the practicing clinician, but as an illustration of commonly used interrogation techniques by investigative agencies in this country. Deception is used by the interviewers throughout these methods — the personalizing of the suspect, the minimizing of wrongdoing, the gap of time deliberately placed between signing of a waiver of rights and the interrogation, and other gimmicks and ploys.

The "Mutt and Jeff" technique is a classic police interrogative technique. Here, the more cynical, aggressive, and usually older officer feigns anger at the suspect while the more liberal, sympathetic, and usually younger or female officer attempts to wheedle a confession out of the suspect. Reid and Associates (1988) object to this method, not on moral grounds, but because most suspects recognize the methods and the confession may be rendered inadmissible in court.

Other methods of manipulation presented by Reid and Associates (1988) include (1) discussing the suspect in the third person, "roping" him or her into the content in order to set up alternatives; (2) repeatedly breaking the body boundary space to induce threat and then relief; (3) presenting to the suspect aspects of the victim that can be blamed for the crime.

The above methods raise ethical concerns. First, the target's life may be in danger. The authors know of no investigative agency that routinely builds in deprocessing procedures and psychiatric safeguards following interrogation. The investigators appear to be playing junior psychologist or psychiatrist — diagnosing the suspect, but having no skill (or even interest) in intervening if the person becomes destabilized. Suspects remain a part of the community until they are convicted and they are entitled to fair treatment. A final concern is that the suspect's view of the legal process may be tarnished forever and an increased alienation from police may be the result.

The second harmful effect is the corrosive influence these techniques have on police officers in particular. Police become overly suspicious of the citizens they have sworn to protect, thus predisposing them to make false positive errors in spite of their experience with crime. Cynicism and hostility abound with the belief by officers that most people would commit crimes if they could "get away with it" (Bartol, 1983, p. 59). Later, the cynicism expands from the public to the police system and its failings, and eventually becomes directed against life itself (Niederhoffer, 1967). Niederhoffer found that cynicism among police increases in proportion to the length of service. As a response, police officers withdraw from the public, forming cliques of drinking buddies, becoming more distant, cold, angry, and authoritarian, and developing a dogmatic attitude toward life. There are increases in substance abuse, depression, family problems, and difficulties with authority figures.

The community itself feels the third harmful effect. The many interviews that end in confessions through dubious practices may not alter the overall effect of crime; however, an increasing alienation of the community may result, as shown by the Rodney King case in Los Angeles in 1991. Recall that most encounters between police and citizens are initiated by citizens, rather than by police. Black (1971) found a ratio of 6 to 1. This fact alone suggests that community acceptance of the police is imperative. Feeley and deTurck (1998) noted the confusion caused by some deceptive communications being tacitly sanctioned and other communications not being sanctioned.

A reconceptualization is in order. The central issue is detecting deception while preserving the integrity of both the suspect and the police. To do this, the authors recommend abandoning lies and manipulation and, instead, practicing the following:

1. Psychologically screen police applicants not only to avoid the misfits, but also to obtain officers who are warm, compassionate, and flexible thinkers.
2. Rotate shifts and duties so that interrogators will have to perform patrol duty and other routine police assignments.
3. Introduce mandatory therapy for all officers and teach them the skills to reduce stress in themselves and in one another. Every department should have a psychologist on the staff.
4. Use noninvasive deception methods that only the perpetrator can respond to, such as word association tests and forced-choice testing. Eliminate methods and techniques that are unreliable or that violate the integrity of the suspect.
5. Develop the attitude that not all cases involving deception can be solved. The short-term gain in obtaining a confession may not outweigh the long-term harm to police officers and to the community.

REFERENCES

Bartol, C. R. (1983). *Psychology and American law.* Belmont, CA: Wadsworth Publishing Co.

Black, D. (1971). The social organization of arrest. *Stanford Law Review, 23,* 1087–1111.

Feeley, T. H., & deTurck, M. A. (1998). The behavioral correlates of sanctioned and unsanctioned deceptive communication. *Journal of Nonverbal Behavior, 22*(3), 189–204.

Goldstein, E. R. (1923). Reaction times and the consciousness of deception. *The American Journal of Psychology, 34*(4), 562–581.

Gudjonsson, G. H. (1990). One hundred alleged false confession cases: Some normative data. *British Journal of Clinical Psychology, 29*(2), 249–250.

Hall, H. V. (1982). Dangerousness prediction and the maligned forensic professional: Suggestions for estimating true basal violence. *Criminal Justice and Behavior, 9,* 3–12.

Happel, R. A., & Auffrey, J. J. (1995). Sex offender assessment: Interrupting the dance of denial. *American Journal of Forensic Psychology, 13*(2), 5–22.

Henke, F. G., & Eddy, M. W. (1909). Mental diagnosis by the association reaction method. *The Psychological Review, 16*(5), 399–409.

Hessing, D. J., Elffers, H., Robben, H. S., & Webley, P. (1993). Media or greedy? The social psychology of individuals who fraudulently claim unemployment benefits. *Journal of Applied Social Psychology, 23*(3), 226–243.

Horvath, F., Jayne, B., & Buckley, J. (1994). Differentiation of truthful and deceptive criminal suspects in behavior analysis interviews. *Journal of Forensic Sciences, 39*(3), 793–807.

Jacobs, B. A. (1992a). Drugs and assumption: Undercover infiltration and dramaturgical theory. *Human Relations, 45*(12), 1293–1310.

Jacobs, B. A. (1992b). Undercover deception: Reconsidering presentations of self. *Journal of Contemporary Ethnography, 21*(2), 200–225.

Jacobs, B. A. (1997). Contingent ties: Undercover drug officiers' use of informants. *British Journal of Sociology, 48*(1), 35–53.

Leach, H. M., & Washburn, M. F. (1910). Some tests by the association reaction method of mental diagnosis. *The American Journal of Psychology, 21*(1), 162–167.

Marston, W. M. (1920). Reaction-time symptoms of deception. *Journal of Experimental Psychology, 3*, 72–87.

Niederhoffer, A. (1967). *Behind the shield: The police in urban society.* New York: Doubleday.

Poirier, J. G. (1991). Disputed custody and concerns of parental violence. *Psychotherapy in Private Practice, 9*(3), 7–23.

Poirier, J. G. (1999). The mental health/judicial interface: Taboo dynamics and collaboration strategies with the juvenile sexual offender. In R. T. Saunders (Chair), *American Psychological Association Annual Meeting.* Boston, MA: APA.

Reid, J. E. & Associates, Inc. (1986). 1986 seminar schedule, The Reid technique of interviewing and interrogation. Based on over 200,000 successful interviews and interrogations by Reid & Associates, Inc., Chicago.

Reid, J. E. & Associates, Inc. (1988). *The investigator, 4*(2). Chicago: Author

Resnick. P. J. (1997). Malingering of posttraumatic stress disorders. In R. Rogers (Ed.), *Clinical assessment of malingering and deception* (pp. 130–152). New York: Guilford Press.

Rogers, R. (1990). Models of feigned mental illness. *Professional Psychology: Research and Practice, 21*(3), 182–188.

Royal, R. F., & Schutt, S. R. (1976). *The gentle art of interviewing and interrogation: A professional manual and guide.* Englewood Cliffs, NJ: Prentice-Hall.

Schlenker, B., & Weigold, M. (1992). Interpersonal processes involving impression regulation and management. *Annual Review of Psychology, 43*, 133–168.

Shapiro, D. L. (1999). *Criminal responsibilty evaluation: A manual for practice.* Sarasota, FL: Professional Resource Press.

Sigurdsson, J. F., & Gudjonsson, G. H. (1996). The psychological characteristics of "false confessors." A study among Icelandic prison inmates and juvenile offenders. *Personality & Individual Differences, 20*(3), 321–329.

Vrij, A. (1993). Credibility judgments of detectives: The impact of nonverbal behavior, social sales, and physical characteristics on impression formation. *Journal of Social Psychology, 133*(5), 601–610.

Vrij, A. (1994). The impact of information and setting on detection of deception by police detectives. *Journal of Nonverbal Behavior, 18*(2), 117–136.

Vrij, A. (1995). Behavioral correlates of deception in a simulated police interview. *Journal of Psychology, 129*(1), 15–28.

Vrij, A., Semin, G. R., & Bull, R. (1996). Insight into behavior displayed during deception. *Human Communication Research, 22*(4), 544–562.

Vrij, A., & Winkle, F. W. (1993). Objective and subjective indicators of deception. *Issues in Criminological and Legal Psychology, 20*, 51–57.

Yerkes, R. M., & Berry, C. S. (1909). The association reaction method of mental diagnosis. *The American Journal of Psychology, 20*, 22–37.

15 Criminal Profiling

Forensic professionals have been increasingly involved in crime profiling in the last few decades (Annon, 1995; Brussel, 1968; Douglas, Burgess, Burgess, & Ressler, 1992; Groth, 1979; Hazelwood & Douglas, 1980; Holmes, 1989; Holmes & Holmes, 1998; Homant & Kennedy, 1998; McCann, 1992; Ressler, Burgess, & Douglas, 1988; Rider, 1980; Tamura et al., 1998a, b; Turco, 1990). Profiling involves the analysis of crime scene characteristics to eliminate unlikely suspects and narrow the search for a perpetrator. These characteristics of the crime scene may yield information about the general traits or characteristics of the perpetrator of the crime. An organized crime scene, for example, may suggest that the perpetrator has an organized lifestyle, is meticulous, careful, intelligent, and given to planning. Profiling is but one more alternative to the problem of deception that is inherent in every criminal act. Often, there is positive correlation between the seriousness of a crime and the degree of deception involved. As with most investigatory methods, training and experience produce the most efficient and valid findings (Pinizzotto & Finkel, 1990).

The Behavioral Science Unit (BSU) of the FBI has amassed a vast database on convicted killers. The BSU has also contributed methods for analyzing crime scenes, victims, and other forensic evidence. The most comprehensive data held by BSU are those involving serial murders, serial rape, sexual homicides, child molestations, and ritualistic crimes (Annon, 1995; Burgess, Douglas, & Burgess, 1997). While the focus of profiling in this chapter is with violent criminals, the profiling approach has been utilized in a variety of civilian and criminal applications; these are summarized in Table 15.1.

It is important to recognize the distinctions between the investigation processes involved in crime profiling, in clinical assessment, and in clinical/forensic assessment. Crime profiling begins with a crime scene and methodically attempts to develop a physical/psychological profile of the perpetrator. Clinical assessment begins with a patient presenting with complaints; the clinician then attempts to develop a diagnostic profile and treatment plan. Clinical/forensic assessment begins with the referral of a suspected or admitted perpetrator, and information about a crime. The forensic clinician's task is to conduct an evaluation integrating clinical assessment techniques with knowledge of forensic issues and arrive at an opinion regarding a forensic concern (i.e., competency, criminal responsibility, malingering, dangerousness, etc.). At one end of the spectrum, police investigators conduct their investigatory work deductively (i.e., drawing conclusions about particulars from general premises) from crime scene hard evidence (Turvey, 1998). In contrast, the clinician works primarily from an inductive approach (i.e., drawing a general conclusion from particulars). Both approaches have something to offer to an investigatory effort and the forensic clinician should strive to work from an integration of these two approaches.

The accumulation of data about crime scenes and about victims to describe probable characteristics of perpetrators constitutes the wealth of information contained in "base rates." Such information is useful in narrowing the range of potential suspects, but it also forms a "background" against which distortion analysis may be performed. Is this suspect typical of others charged with the same offense? If not, what are the differences? Is the suspect genuinely atypical or is there substantial distortion in the suspect's self-presentation? The general methods of criminal profiling are therefore useful in formulating hypotheses about a suspect during evaluation, in "raising

TABLE 15.1
Profiling Applications

Application	Study
Predicting patients' response to psychotherapy	Leon et al. (1999)
Profiling child sexual abusers	Haywood et al. (1994); Murphy & Peters (1992)
Profiles of parent child abductors in custody and access disputes	Cole & Bradford (1992)
Profiles of disruptive and nondisruptive kindergarten boys	Larivee et al. (1994)
Profiles of juvenile offenders in custody	Thornton, Cookson, & Clark (1990)
Profiles of sexual offender characteristics and victim ages	Kuznestov, Pierson, & Harry (1992)
Random violence offenses in Japan	Tamura et al. (1998a, b)
Typologies of rapists' speech	Dale, Davies, & Wei (1997)
DNA profiling of criminals	Brockman & Humphreys (1998); Knoppers (1993)
Serial murder and serial rapist profiles	Annon (1995); Holmes (1991); Myers et al. (1993)
Homocide profiles	Burgess, Douglas, & Burgess (1997)
Profiles of sexual homocide perpetrators	Annon (1995); Burgess, Douglas, & Burgess (1997); Hazelwood & Douglas (1980); Holmes (1991)
Profiles of ritualistic crime perpetrators	Annon (1995)
Social, demographic, and land use profiles of high-crime areas	Hirschfield & Bowers (1997)
Temperment and character profiles of incarcerated criminals	Kozeny, Tisanska, & Meznik (1998)
Profile factors associated with probation sucess or failure	Sims & Jones (1997)
Profiles of terrorists	Smith & Morgan (1994)

suspicions" regarding distortions by the suspect and in assessing the genuineness of a particular suspect's behavior during evaluation.

Criminal profiling is most helpful in (1) sex-related assaults and homicides; (2) unique homicides such as those involving torture, mutilation, evisceration, and ritualistic violence; (3) assassination; (4) child molestation and abduction; (5) fire setting, arson, and bombing; and (6) extortion. Terrorist threats can also be analyzed through the psycholinguistic aspects of notes or recorded conversations (Miron & Goldstein, 1979; Miron & Pasquale, 1978).

Bizarre crimes lend themselves to profiling because of the distinct patterns that emerge, thus narrowing the pool of potential suspects to manageable proportions. In general, the behavior of the perpetrator in any given crime determines whether profiling can be used.

The BSU has a computerized profiling system, the results of which are available to local police departments on request (Ressler et al., 1988). Douglas et al. (1992) described subtypes of murders, arsons, and sexual assaults based on this system. Characteristics of several hundred rapists and rape murderers are shown in Tables 15.2 and 15.3.

Generally, the process of crime profiling focuses on the following:

1. Primary profiling inputs, from evaluation of the criminal act, crime scene, victim, and significant/knowledgeable others;
2. Secondary inputs involving suppositions on time, location, acceleration, and other factors;
3. Crime assessment in terms of the overall reconstruction and dynamics of the crime;
4. Development of a profile (see Pinizzotto & Finkel, 1990, for one of the few empirical studies of the process of developing criminal profiles);
5. Investigation and comparison of characteristics to a suspect pool; and
6. Possible apprehension.

Some crimes are solved by this process (Ressler, 1990; Ressler et al., 1988); many others are resolved by "dumb luck," involving the victim's escaping or the perpetrator's being arrested on another charge.

TABLE 15.2
FBI Base Rates for Serial Rapists

Stable employment	54%
Married at least once	71%
Served in military	1%
Above average on intelligence tests	52%
Average or better socioeconomic status	54%
Sexual abuse as child	76%
Physical abuse as child	38%
Collected pornography as child	36%
Witnessed sexual violence by others	25%
Compulsive masturbation	54%
History of voyeurism	68%
History of fetishism	41%
History of cross-dressing	23%
History of obscene phone calls	38%
History of sexual bondage	26%
Selected victim because of availability	98%
Selected victim because of gender	95%
Selected victim because of age	66%
Selected victim because of location	66%
Selected victim because of race (Caucasian)	63% (88–93%)
Victim a targeted stranger	80–88%
Victim raped at home	45–52%
Mean number of rape convictions	7.6
Mean number of actual rapes consummated	27.8

Note: Collected from "The Serial Rapist: His Characteristics and Victims, Part I: Conclusion," by R. Hazelwood, & J. Warren, 1989, *FBI Law Enforcement Bulletin, 1,* 10–25.

The process is somewhat similar to that used by forensically oriented clinicians to diagnose and treat offenders. Collected data are scrutinized, reconstruction of behavioral patterns and lifestyle is conducted, and hypotheses are formulated. Priorities for treatment are established, and intervention is implemented, all in a feedback loop with ongoing and continual assessment.

Another way to analyze the process of profiling is by following a traditional scientific method. This includes (1) identification of the problem and collection of facts, (2) creation of preliminary hypotheses, (3) the collection of additional facts, (4) formulating the investigative hypotheses, (5) deducing further consequences, (6) testing the consequences, and (7) application. An illustration follows.

DEFINING THE FORENSIC PROBLEM

The forensic problem is often framed in the referral question and has, as its basis, a group of facts, which do not have a ready or acceptable explanation without analysis and synthesis. An actual illustration is chosen that utilizes a forensic task (criminal profiling) and a means to assess the utility of the sequence (narrowing the range of possible perpetrators). The illustration starts with the body of a letter of referral received several months after the instant offenses:

As we discussed on the telephone today, our office wishes to retain your consultation services in relationship to an unsolved murder-rape-kidnapping that occurred on October 8, 1991 in Port Hueneme,

TABLE 15.3
FBI Base Rates for Serial Rape/Murderers

Male	100%
White	92%
Poor high school grades	60%
Average or better intelligence	80%
Stable socioeconomic status of parents	86%
Poor relationship with male caretakers	72%
Pornography exposure as child	81%
Intact family as child	85%
First rape fantasies, at age ~12 to 14	50%
Assaultive to adults (adolescent)	86%
Stealing (adolescent)	81%
Isolation as child/adolescent	71%
Chronic lying as child/adolescent	71%
Enuresis as child/adolescent	68%
Fire setting as child/adolescent	56%
As adult, one to six sexual assaults not resulting in apprehension	57%
As adult, >25 unapprehended assaults	21%
As adult, acquittals for previous sex offenses	35%
Behaviors/events during escalation stage	
Stress increase before killing	100%
Preoccupation with murder	100%
Fantasy intensifies	100%
Increase in hostility and anger	46%
Increase in frustration	50%
Increase in agitation	43%
Increase in excitement	41%
Common suspected or actual work problems	65%
Plans killing	50%
Open to opportunities for killing	34%
Drinks prior to violence	49%
Takes drugs prior to violence	35%
Conflict with a woman	59%
Conflict with parents	53%
Financial problems	48%
After the murder, follows investigations in media	46%
Introjects self in investigation	20%
Disposes of body, conceals	58%
Exposes body of victim at disposal site	42%
Victim nude or partially clothed	72%
Obtains souvenirs from victim	27%
Has sex with victim after death	42%
Returns to crime scene	27%
Returns to crime scene to relive the fantasy	26%
Returns to crime scene to gauge progress of police	19%

Note: Collected from *Sexual Homicide: Patterns and Motives,* by R. Ressler, A. Burgess, & J. Douglass, 1988, Lexington, MA: Lexington Books.

California (see enclosed police reports). Briefly, the victim, Tanya B. R., a 24-year-old Caucasian seamstress for a local firm, was abducted at a bus stop at Main and Roan Streets and was dragged into a nearby hillock area, where she was raped and murdered.

We can establish a foot trail from the bus stop to the hillock, but the perpetrator's footprints are indistinct due to poor soil conditions. Witnesses on several buses observed only one party near the victim at the approximate time of the instant offenses, with descriptions centering on either a Caucasian or Chicano male wearing military fatigues, being of a height between 5'6" and 5'11," weighing between 130 and 160 pounds, and appearing to be in his late teens or early 20s. It should be added that there are approximately 40,000 military personnel stationed in this area at any one time, representing all branches of the military.

Evidence shows that the victim's throat was cut with a broken wine bottle, possibly occurring after both anal and vaginal penetration by the perpetrator (no semen was found). The trail of blood extends from the hillock into a small ravine 20 to 30 ft away, where the victim's head and upper chest were crushed by a 50-pound boulder being dropped or possibly thrown from a vertical position. As far as we can tell, no money was taken, but the victim's photographic identification was missing.

Please let us know if you would consider involvement in this case. If you are able to go to the crime scene, we can arrange for the police evidence specialist to be there. All the physical evidence, minus the victim's body, can be returned to the crime scene to reenact the appropriate elements. We can then process the case with the investigation team.

Thank you very much, and I look forward to hearing from you.

Sincerely,
Chief Detective
Oxnard Police Department

It is very important for the forensic clinician to recognize that responding to such a request imposes a very special and atypical role on the clinician. Essentially, the clinician forms a working alliance with the police investigators and by inference with the prosecutorial arm of the jurisdiction in question. This is an appropriate and ethical role for the forensic clinician; the critical point is for the clinician to maintain very clear awareness of his or her role with all involved parties. It would, for example, be ethically inappropriate for the clinician to introduce himself or herself as "Dr. A." and purposefully or inadvertently lull a criminal defendant into thinking that the clinician is there in some advocacy role for the defendant. Indeed, there are an increasing number of mental health professionals who specialize in police work and many major jurisdictions now have institutionalized full-time positions for such professionals.

PRELIMINARY HYPOTHESES

The key consideration at this phase is to suspend judgment until a great deal of data has been obtained. In particular, the evaluator should steer clear of assumptions of psychopathology because of the bizarreness of the violence. The evaluator may otherwise go down a blind alley early in the evaluation process.

Yet, some opinions must be formulated before the forensic evaluation can proceed. In this case, the assumptions were made that:

1. The instant offenses were crimes.
2. Similar crimes have yielded apprehension of some criminals who were eventually detected.
3. Criminals are of different personality types depending on previous criminality, developmental history, intelligence, employment and educational factors, and a host of other variables.

4. Personality types and background features of criminals can be measured and assigned to distinct profile types. In this regard, Megargee and Bohn (1979) have such a system of classifying criminals on the basis of their Minnesota Multiphasic Personality Inventory (MMPI) responses. To date, thousands of criminal offenders have been measured, with 95% of the criminal population assigned to one of the ten discrete types. The Megargee taxonomy is important because it has been determined to be reliable and valid (e.g., Edinger, 1979). Of considerable interest for forensic evaluators are the associated background characteristics that come with each profile type. Note that the MMPI data substitutes, in part, for the FBI system of base rate comparison.
5. The perpetrator in this case left suggestions at the crime scene and/or from observation that could be used to formulate a tentative profile.
6. The tentative profile type can yield descriptive traits or leads for investigation, ultimately reducing the number in any suspect pool.

COLLECTING ADDITIONAL FACTS

The forensic evaluator collects as much data as possible in regard to the perpetrator, victim, and crime scene in order to describe the interactions of the three that were operative at the time of the crime. Data may be historical in nature (e.g., developmental history of the victim), instant offense related (e.g., physical evidence at the crime scene), molar in scope (e.g., assumed perpetrator traits), or molecular in focus (e.g., specific autopsy results), as long as the crime is better described. These additional facts may lead to new hypotheses, which must be investigated, if only to rule them out as competing explanations.

Relevant to the victim in the criminal profiling case described above, data were collected on her background, lifestyle, and physical characteristics. Generally, she was quite ordinary and conservative in nature, with no criminal record, a high school education, and 1 year of technical education in textiles. This 24-year-old woman was unmarried, with a long-term boyfriend whose movements were accounted for during the period of the crime. She was living at home with her parents and was waiting at the bus stop, on her way home, when the attack occurred. There were no distinguishing features to her appearance, with a medium build (5'5," 130 pounds) and plain looks, as described by friends and family. Her clothing consisted of a gray dress and black jacket. The principal themes that emerged about the victim included unobtrusiveness, conservativeness, and high conventionality.

Relevant to the crime context, the location was a bus stop at a busy intersection next to a vacant lot with a hillock in its center, approximately 30 yards from the bus stop. The time of the crime was estimated at 8:30 a.m., plus or minus 15 minutes. Trees hid from view the hillock and the adjacent small ravine where the victim was dragged.

Relevant to the possible perpetrator, general characteristics were available from the investigation reports. Extrapolating from crime scene and victim data, a probable profile type was constructed. First, this perpetrator was seen as a hostile, insensitive man (possible MMPI elevations on Scales 4 and 6), with poor social skills, who was probably clumsy around people (MMPI profiles elevation on Scale 0). He traversed a good distance from the bus stop to consummate the deed and therefore may be manic or hyperactive under stress (high Scale 9). Perhaps the perpetrator was not concerned about disease from the victim, or cleanliness (low on Scales 1, 2, and 3). Some stress can be assumed due to the time of the day, the busy intersection, no similar crimes before in the area, and the disorganized manner of the crime (high F and 8).

Investigators riding the bus route and questioning riders around the time of the offense compiled a list of approximately 300 suspects. The assumption was made that the suspect rode the bus and that the crime scene was possibly located between his residence and job site.

FORMULATING THE HYPOTHESIS

All facts or assumed facts needed to solve the problem may not be on hand at this stage, yet a synthesis of the data must be performed. What is needed is a hypothesis that will account for all data and will lead to further inquiry.

Putting all speculations together, the possible perpetrator fits the profile of a disorganized psychopath. The perpetrator would be of average or lower intelligence, not psychotic, yet deeply antisocial and passive in coping with stress. His interpersonal skills are intact but he lacks reciprocity toward others and is immature. Previous criminality was probably not extensive, as it would have been detected during the military screening process. Also, the instant offense was "sloppy" in its commission, requiring both a throat cut and a crushing blow with a boulder to "finish the victim off." Triggering stimuli included possible alcohol consumption, but since the incident occurred in the morning, the abuse was possibly chronic or, at least, episodic in pattern. Other stress could be anticipated, the most likely (and most common) explanation being that there may have been problems in this individual's central love relationship. Most likely, therefore, the possible perpetrator was married or had a girlfriend with whom he was in conflict. The profile the possible perpetrator most likely fits (Megargee's Group How) included a person from the rural, as opposed to the city, area. Additional characteristics would be second or later-born as opposed to firstborn or the only child in the family, a high school education or less, a strong possibility of substance abuse tendencies, and eventual problems and resentment against authority.

In short, the final hypothesis involved the profile of a chronically sociopathic, nonpsychotic, but somewhat passive individual. Alcohol and relationship triggers may have been operative. He picked out a target of opportunity to aggress upon. He did not care about consequences to the victim, or the busy crime context; thus, one must remove those two primary factors as contributing to the violence that occurred. Most likely, the victim's behavior represented a displaced target of aggression, and he, therefore, probably did not know the victim previously.

Other characteristics of the disorganized type include (1) lives/works near the crime scene and (2) has a minimal change in lifestyle (Ressler et al., 1988). Based on these factors, the perpetrator could be expected to have remained in the area of the rape/murder.

DEDUCING FURTHER CONSEQUENCES

The hypothesis must be checked for degree of predictiveness. It should point beyond known data to new areas where confirmatory information can be obtained regarding its accuracy. The new facts help confirm, deny, or render moot the final hypothesis.

The possible perpetrator in the instant case was hypothesized to be in a state of high stress, with displaced aggression toward the victim. This meant that other violence within the same geographic area may have functioned in the same way as the instant offense, although perhaps not resulting in homicide. Unprovoked and unexplained stranger violence toward females was sought with the sexual motive seen as secondary. Police files were checked, and one such event that fit this picture emerged. A 35-year-old Caucasian woman was walking along a park trail not far from the site of the present murder. A lone perpetrator with a description closely fitting that of the possible perpetrator in the instant case passed her. He then turned around, walked back, and punched her in the mouth for no apparent reason. Additional data, as gleaned from that victim, included the perpetrator's height (5'10"), weight (140 to 150 pounds), race (Caucasian), and enlisted military clothing, with no recall of identifying marks or insignia.

The 300-person suspect pool was scrutinized in terms of the above characteristics. These included height, weight, race, previous criminality, place of origin, ordinal position, enlisted status, and other factors, which could be verified. The list of 300 was narrowed down to 10 males who fit the pattern.

TESTING THE CONSEQUENCES

The deductions or inferences from the hypothesized type require some means of verification; in other words, there must be a way to see if the deductions that can be derived from any hypothesis can be affirmed. Observation and oral interview can be used for this stage.

In the instant case, investigators staked out all ten individuals. The identification card of the victim was found in the garbage bin of the apartment complex in which one of the suspects lived. All ten individuals were brought in and questioned, followed by a polygraph examination. One suspect, the one who lived in the apartment complex where the identification card was found, failed the polygraph. Five-point fingerprint identification was found on the broken wine bottle and matched this perpetrator's prints. When confronted with this evidence, the individual confessed to the crime.

APPLICATION

This involves the application of the hypothesis for the original purpose. In this case, the perpetrator was brought to trial, charged with rape and murder, and subsequently released on technicalities. He was suspected in at least one other similar crime some years prior to this, but there was insufficient proof to charge him in that matter. The case was dismissed when it was determined that the police had not properly informed him of his rights, and, therefore, his confession was not admissible. The other evidence was circumstantial.

GENERALIZATION

Regardless of the ultimate outcome, all forensic evaluations must follow a sequence of stages. This applies to most problems in forensic psychology, from criminal profiling to insanity evaluations to violence predictions. A problem is defined, and the evaluator works toward a hypothesis and application of that hypothesis.

Several caveats apply. First, to apply the procedure, the investigator must be free from bias and moral values that would contaminate the accuracy of the data collection efforts. But is that ever possible? Often, this requires that the forensic evaluator undergo a rigorous self-examination.

In pure form, the above procedure can be used for focal problems, such as criminal profiling, but when most forensic issues involve value-laden opinions relevant to risk, criminal responsibility, or some other global type of issue, the task becomes less specific and more subject to moral bias. Evaluators are typically biased in the direction of suspiciousness. Falsely accepting that there is no difference between the suspect and the universe of confirmed perpetrators is a cardinal error.

PROFILING ORGANIZED RAPE/MURDERERS

This section focuses on traits associated with rape/murderers of the organized type. All traits stem from the authors' experiences, the FBI system, and the clinical/forensic literature (for a review, see Holmes, 1991). Keep in mind the above considerations for profiling in general. For organized rape/murderers (almost all male) in particular, the number of victims (usually, but not always, female) often runs into the double figures. Serial murderers do not "burn out" of their own accord; in this sense, their assaults are self-generated. "Clumping" occurs in that there is usually a spree of killing followed by long durations between series. Much self-control and premeditation is shown. The world of the serial sexual killer was described in considerable qualitative and quantitative detail by the previously described BSU of the FBI (Ressler et al., 1988). Based upon several serial cases, the FBI data, and training in homicide, the authors propose the following traits associated with organized rape/murderers:

Developmental traits (birth to approximately 18 years of age). The developmental history of the organized serial rape-murderer can be characterized by family instability, poor bonding with significant others, emotional isolation from others, underachievement, and the emergence of violent sexual fantasies and behaviors.

Family:
1. White or dominant racial/ethnic group membership in area.
2. Poverty not a significant factor but low-middle socioeconomic status.
3. Family moves frequently in early years; minimal attachment to the community.
4. Mental illness or history of criminality in at least one parent; alcohol abuse very common.
5. Family is intact (two-parent) in early years.
6. Inconsistent parental discipline.
7. Sexually repressed environment with possible covert sex abuse of offspring by father.
8. Frequent arguments in home.

Father:
9. Uninvolved with perpetrator; perpetrator feels emotional coldness toward father.
10. Unskilled, blue-collar but steadily employed.
11. Moderate likelihood of father leaving family unit before perpetrator grows up.

Mother:
12. Dominant and hostile parent.
13. Perpetrator experiences most physical and psychological abuse from mother.
14. Strong dislike toward mother, coupled with ambivalent feelings of tolerance and hate.

Siblings:
15. Compete with each other for rewards in an emotionally deficit environment; perpetrator often given responsibility for care of siblings.

Animals:
16. Animal cruelty, including mutilation and torture.
17. Perpetrator has developing interest in firearms and activities, such as hunting, which provide opportunity for safe aggression.

Perpetrator:
18. Unknown prenatal problems.
19. First or second born, or oldest son.
20. School problems in pattern of underachievement (low grades, discontinuation of school with above-average intelligence).
21. Turns mentally inward where he can gain control.
22. Isolates self from others, weak attachments to other family members and peers.
23. Not physically unattractive; no distinguishing physical handicaps/defects which set him apart.
24. Emergence of violent/sadistic fantasies that become functionally autonomous (i.e., independent) of initial need to go inward to gain control from overwhelming stress.
25. Preference for autoerotic sex.
26. Heterosexual sex on low frequency with developing interest in degradation of females.
27. High comorbidity with ADD.
28. Fire setting; arson incidents.
29. High comorbidity with a variety of soft psychiatric symptoms and personality traits including borderline, passive–aggressive, narcissistic, and schizoid.

Adult traits (after approximately 18 years of age to late middle age). The adult period is characterized by a continuation of many of the above behavioral patterns and violent fantasies, eventually crystallizing into a set of fixed attitudes. These are as follows:

1. Devaluation of people. He remains emotionally distant from others, self-centered in thinking, and perceives others as objects rather than as unique, positive, and important.
2. World viewed as unjust. Projection of blame for misdeeds and shortcomings can be expected, as others have primarily caused his problems. He perceives himself as having been "ripped off" and exploited in his early years and believes that others do not acknowledge his assets in adulthood. He has learned to cover this attitude (and the others) and may, in fact, verbalize self-blame when deemed congruent with vested interests. Social skills can be described as superficial, and others often view him as friendly and unobtrusive but distant.
3. Authority and life viewed as inconsistent. He does not trust authority figures. Male figures are especially distrusted and disliked. The ambivalence, interspersed with hate, continues toward females, especially those in a position to influence or control his behavior.
4. Autoerotic preference. Preferred isolated sex experiences include interest in pornography, compulsive masturbation, fetishism, and voyeurism, alone or in combination. Isolated sex is usually interspersed with heterosexual intercourse, and the perpetrator is usually living with a partner.
5. Obsession and dominance through aggression. Violence-related fantasies and sexual activities become increasingly frequent, especially so during periods of interpersonal stress, but also continue during periods of low conflict with others. At this point, the fantasies are internally generated, controlled, and concealed from others in their expression. The mate usually is the recipient of requests to engage in violent or potentially violent sexual activities (e.g., bondage, slapping), but is rarely the target of the consummated homicide, primarily because the acts are under the control of the perpetrator and the chances of apprehension are high.
6. Fantasy is reality. The perpetrator equates his inner with his outer world, although he is rarely psychotic. A decision is made to act out on the violent sex fantasies, and may be followed by a lag period of several years to several decades. Opportunity variables then achieve importance.

Family:
1. May be married or have a girlfriend. The female is the nondominant member of the dyad and may be many years younger than the perpetrator.
2. Poverty is not a significant factor, but a pattern of underachievement continues.
3. Family moves frequently.
4. Mental illness may be in family, but criminality is low grade in terms of arrests, or is undetected. May not be known to police, especially if family moves frequently. Mental health treatment is rarely sought.
5. Sadistic impulses may be shown toward mate in less than lethal fashion (e.g., requests or acts relating to bondage, anal sex, physical violence to mate during sex). Bizarre sex (hanging wife upside down on hook while she fellates him) and power themes emerge, with perpetrator in dominant role.

Peers/Work:
6. Adequate social skills.
7. Often seen as personable, friendly, socially competent, but distant.
8. Passive-aggressive in interpersonal style:
   a. Not seen as demanding;

  b. Reluctant to express negative/angry feelings;
  c. Denies and is uncomfortable with anger;
  d. Distortion by omission if possible rather than proactive lying.
9. Has few close male friends; a socially adept loner.
10. Thrives on omnipotence and power usually achieved by indirect means. He prides himself on his intelligence and ability to manipulate others.
11. Seen as helpful toward others.
12. A steady job at one location is unlikely:
  a. Usually absent or poor military history;
  b. Skilled work preferred.

Perpetrator Traits:
13. Psychometrics show distinct strengths and problems:
  a. IQ is above average and may be superior;
  b. Projectives (Rorschach, TAT) suggest much suppressed violence;
  c. Objective testing (e.g., MMPI-2) shows elevated distress scores (e.g., high F) and social alienation patterns (e.g., high O);
  d. Signs do not show brain damage or psychosis; some symptoms of depression and inferiority and inadequacy;
  e. Above-noted psychopathology usually not picked up during clinical interviewing as opposed to psychometric testing.
14. Pleasant general appearance.
15. Height and weight within normal limits.
16. White or member of dominant ethnic group in area.
17. Energies funneled into fantasies of aggression and mastery over others.
18. In mid-20s or early 30s at time of first series of murders.

PERPETRATOR'S ASSAULT CYCLE

An individual's typical assault cycle for particular crimes is the behavioral equivalent of recurring physical evidence, although not as easily measurable. That is, cognitive, affective, behavioral, and interactional themes emerge that remain remarkably constant across particular types of crimes. They may differ from each other primarily in terms of environmental circumstances, such as triggering stimuli and opportunity factors.

A standard assault cycle is presented in Figure 15.1. The cycle consists of a baseline period of (1) adult traits and circumstances, (2) an escalation or triggering phase, (3) the actual violence, (4) a recovery phase, and (5) a return to baseline. The assault cycle is strengthened and modified by previous assaults, usually making future violence more likely, easy, and rewarding for the perpetrator.

The typical assault cycle for serial rape/homicides is unique. The baseline period (Stage 1) is represented by the adult traits and events listed in the previous section. The triggering or escalation stage (Stage 2) consists of the following:

1. Stress is experienced due to conflict or disappointment with the perpetrator's mate, work situation, or other factors, such as financial problems.
2. Anniversary triggers reflecting negative events may fuel the accelerating process (e.g., death of a close family member, divorce from previous wife).
3. The perpetrator feels inferior more than usual as a result.
4. Violent fantasies increase; he sees violence as a means to regain self-esteem, mastery, and enjoyment. Yet, self-control is high; there are no sudden explosions of rage. If the perpetrator resists his compulsion during this stage, high tension and other arousal symptoms (e.g., headaches, gastrointestinal tract upset) may occur.

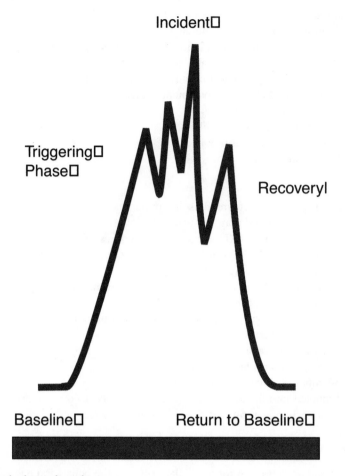

FIGURE 15.1 Standard assault cycle.

5. He begins to abuse alcohol or, to a much lesser extent, drugs. Arguments increase with his mate, and he begins to engage in escapist activities, such as taking walks or drives.
6. He has a vehicle in good working order.
7. Planning and rehearsal for the violence preoccupies much of his time. Enactment of fantasies is also rehearsed, which includes the fate of the victim. The rape/murder is calculated and preplanned. The intent is to abuse and torture the victim, thereby gratifying himself.
8. Cruising or stalking victims in various areas, usually not too far from his home or work site, takes place. Many victims are considered, but only a few are chosen, since the perpetrator has particular tastes. Vulnerability of the victims is important. The first victim in a series, for example, may be physically more vulnerable than the others due to size, weight, or other factors. The first victim in a series may be of a different race than later victims in the series. The first victim's race usually matches the perpetrator's race. As the perpetrator recognizes his own strength, this becomes less important as the series progresses. Hence, a considerable amount of time may be devoted to the escalation and search process.
9. He becomes more secretive, concealing, and provides excuses for his whereabouts to others.
10. A rape/murder kit is assembled, consisting usually of a weapon and a means of binding or immobilizing the victim. Gagging and blindfold material and instruments of torture

are sometimes part of the rape-murder kit. Precautions are taken against discovery of the assembled kit.

11. Clothing that would not intimidate and may even win the confidence of the victim (e.g., work uniform, business suit, casual clothes) is chosen. The perpetrator may impersonate vocations of others in his dressing.
12. Just prior to the violence, a victim who meets the perpetrator's requirements and is within his staked-out or patrolled area is finally selected.
13. He almost always engages in verbal interaction. His demeanor is not suspicious.
14. There is an attempt to establish a pseudo-relationship, which may include offering the victim a ride or otherwise assisting her.
15. After the pseudo-relationship is established and the opportunity to aggress with conceal-ment is available, the rape/murder kit weapon is brandished.
16. The weapon is usually not used initially, if at all, and the victim is often promised no harm if she cooperates.
17. The victim is immobilized through binding, fear, or some other means. Control is now firmly in the hands of the perpetrator.
18. Substance abuse will instigate and/or exacerbate all of the above activity.

The actual violence portion of the assault cycle (Stage 3 of the cycle) is characterized by high self-control, mounting excitement, sadism, and the victim's death. The victim is bound or immo-bilized at this point. The eroticized aggression can take place now without fear of discovery. The death of the victim is prolonged as the perpetrator feeds off the pain cues of the victim taking place often over a period of hours or even days if the opportunity allows.

1. This is a sadistic rape, as opposed to a power or anger rape. Sadistic rapes constitute less than 5% of the three main types of rapists (i.e., see Groth, 1979).
2. Initially, the mood of the perpetrator is controlled. Mounting excitement is seen, espe-cially when the victim resists in any manner. The perpetrator may continue to degrade the victim until she resists, as this provides pain cues that are rewarding to the perpetrator. He may be without an erection until the victim's resistance begins. Look for suggestions of biting, burning, whipping, slapping, or strangulation. Slow strangulation is possible, with some perpetrators reviving the victim to prolong the ordeal.
3. Sexual areas (breasts, buttocks, genitalia, and anus) are specific foci of abuse. He may use a stick or other implement to penetrate the victim's orifices, possibly masturbating at the same time. Frequently, items 2 and 3 are combined, as when the perpetrator vaginally penetrates the victim with his penis while slowly strangling or striking the victim.
4. Ritualistic or bizarre acts are frequent. The perpetrator may clip the hair of the victim, wash her body, force her to dress in some way, or demand any variety of "kinky" sex.
5. Finally, the perpetrator works himself into a frenzy of rage and lust, fueled by the pain cues of the victim. The actual killing of the victim is the ultimate orgasm, and the perpetrator attempts to conjoin the two. Repeated rape-murders perfect the unison of these two behaviors.

The next stage of the assault cycle for the serial murderer is the recovery phase (Stage 4). The perpetrator now has a dead body on his hands. He is late for work, home, or some other activity, and must cover his tracks. Precautions are taken against discovery, such as ensuring that the weapon from the rape/murder is not left at the crime scene. The site of the rape/murder is often tidied up — blood and fingerprints from the victim being a first priority for removal. The victim may be totally or partially redressed.

Remembrances of the victim are collected and set aside for later enjoyment or as a gift to "loved" females (e.g., his mother or girlfriend). The perpetrator almost always disposes of the body at a location other than the crime scene, but again in his own "turf" — that is, in the general proximity of home/work sites. The best "dumping" sites are those that are isolated (unpopulated areas), corrosive (e.g., fresh but especially salt water; open or shallow graves allowing for body decomposition), or consuming (e.g., fire, acid pits), the latter infrequently chosen due to availability factors. The symbolic significance of certain dumping sites (e.g., water points) as signifying possible guilt, redemption, need for cleansing, or some other despairing motive, is usually weak and unhelpful hypothesis.

The return to the baseline portion of the assault cycle (Stage 5) is characterized by a lack of remorse for the rape/murder, prodigious efforts at concealment, and resurgence of fantasy, now fueled by the memorabilia of the victim coupled with masturbation. These are hidden in his special place but can be easily retrieved. Newspaper accounts of the crime are read avidly and often clipped out for retention. Almost always, he is aware that he will kill again. The acted-upon rape/murder fantasy now provides a sense of purpose and fulfillment. Within a series of rape/murders, fantasies of his previous homicides contribute to subsequent killings. He thinks of means to perfect the phases of the assault cycle. Other events during this stage include:

1. Repetitive sadistic attacks may be interspersed with consenting encounters.
2. He may contact the police to assist in their search of the perpetrator or victims. All this is rehearsed mentally and provides more excitement to the perpetrator as well as helping him learn the status of the investigation or alter its outcome. He also believes that if he does not contact the police, he may be selected as the logical final suspect, due to many factors.
3. If questioned by the police, he will more likely than not deny the crimes. He may have elaborate excuses for each bit of evidence. Remember that he is manipulative of others and is accomplished at deception. He also considers himself superior to the interrogator(s).
   a. He may show distress or depression when questioned about the instant offenses within a context of ostensible cooperation. Look for body leakage, especially upper arm and hand movements associated with lying, as compared with known data (e.g., see Ekman, 1985, for target illustrators, emblems, manipulators, and other clues to deceit). These signs can be used to gather hypotheses about unknown data, for example, where to search for his rape/murder kit. The forced-choice methodology can be used to demonstrate statistically his involvement in the killing.
   b. He may have an erection during the portion of the interview that triggers recollections of the rape/murders. Consider interviewing where the full body of the perpetrator can be observed.
   c. These perpetrators often relate better to male interviewers, rather than female interviewers, toward whom they feel hate.
   d. There is a tendency to ramble on when allowed. Often, there is a subtle quality of omnipotence during the interview, as if he were comfortable in knowing that no one knew of the rape/murders except himself and that he had the ability to explain away the evidence.
   e. If psychiatrically hospitalized during the general time of the interview, he will most likely show "No Mental Disorder" (see DSM-IV, 1994). Suggestions of low psychological disorganization will emerge upon interviewing and observation.
4. The perpetrator often leaves town or changes his job after a series of rape/murders.

In returning to baseline, the perpetrator assumes all prior traits (see Adult Trait discussion) with an enhanced chance of committing another series. Intervals of many years between series are well known, contrasted to the relatively close temporal period of the homicides within a series.

Look within a series to determine whether each assault cycle for each victim was well formulated — that is, with no evidence of learning new methods of procuring, attacking, and disposing of a victim. If not, there is a possibility that a previous series was committed, perhaps in another jurisdiction.

RAPE/MURDER BASE RATES

The preceding sections should make it clear that rape/murderers have certain characteristics, and that these can be differentiated on the basis of primary factors. The organized vs. disorganized crime scene differentiation is the primary split. Culling together all sources, the differences between organized and disorganized perpetrators and crime scene characteristics are shown in Table 15.4.

Hall (1999) noted that deception occurs at every stage of the lethal violence sequence. It is critical to evaluate a given crime scenario for deception elements from a temporal perspective. The violence sequence emanates from a baseline background, continues through a triggering phase, to the violence incident, through a recovery phase. Perpetrators may use a mix of faking good or faking bad strategies and in all likelihood will strategically shift from different deceptions at opportune points in the violence sequence.

RANDOM VIOLENCE OFFENDER PROFILES

A particularly virulent form of violence is so-called "random violence," that is, violence lacking an identifiable motive. In most instances, random violence will meet the criteria for constituting disorganized crimes. This type of violence is a universal occurrence, but has been a particular problem in Japan during the past decade. The problem in Japan has received notoriety because of a number of random violence outbreaks in metropolitan areas with large-scale victim consequences. The Japanese word *Torima* translates to English as "nonspecific-motive attacking" and is the word the Japanese use to refer to the phenomenon of random violence.

Tamura et al. (1998a, b) studied the characteristics of perpetrators of random violence committed in Japan from January 1994 to July 1997 in an effort to develop a basis for criminal personality profiling. The database was police investigation reports. The study examined the cases of 28 subjects and classified the subjects by the scope of the attack (i.e., single, spree, or serial type offenders), sociodemographic features, weapons used, timing of attacks, arrest circumstances, and personality type. The subjects were 26 males and 2 female Japanese adolescents and adults. A number of the subjects evidenced major (schizophrenia and mental retardation) and minor psychiatric disorders. Some of the subjects were determined to have experienced stimulant-induced psychosis.

PROFILING AND THE COURTS

The courts have reached varied results regarding the admissibility of expert evidence regarding whether or not defendants or victims fit certain "profiles," but the trend has clearly been not to admit such testimony (*State of Delaware v. Floray*, 1997). The findings of various court decisions are summarized in Table 15.5.

The typical justifications of the courts for suppressing profiling testimony have been fourfold:

1. Profiling data are character evidence, which in most courts is impermissible.
2. Profiling data are not relevant.
3. Profiling data are impermissible because they invade the province of the jury regarding the ultimate issue of fact.
4. It is not based upon data that are reasonably relied upon by members of the scientific community.

TABLE 15.4
Sexual Homicides: Perpetrators and Crime Scene Characteristics

Organized	Disorganized
Average or higher intelligence	Average or lower intelligence
Socially skilled	Socially immature
Adequate work history	Poor work history
Sexually competent	Sexually incompetent
Firstborn or eldest son	Minimal birth order status
Father's work stable	Father's work unstable
Inconsistent discipline in childhood	Harsh discipline in childhood
Lives with intimate other	Living alone
Lives/works away from crime scene	Lives/works near crime scene
Keen interest in news media	Minimal interest in news media
Changes lifestyle to avoid detection	Minimal change in lifestyle
Heavy use of alcohol	Minimal use of alcohol
Significant stress triggers violence	Minimal situational stress
Weapon brought and taken from scene	Weapon found and left at scene
Victim a targeted stranger	Victim or location of crime known
Controlled conversation	Minimal conversation
Controlled mood during crime	Anxious mood during crime
Use of ruse or con to lure victim into vulnerable position	More likely direct attack and kills quickly
Scene reflects planning and overall control	Scene reflects impulsivity and disarray
Ritualistic and planned quality	Symbolic and spontaneous quality
Victim patterning, shares common traits with others	Victim attacked in her routine activities
Specific areas of body damaged and cause death	Specific areas of body targeted for mutilation after death
Sexual torture before death	Sexual mutilation after death
Sexual acts before death	Sexual acts after death
Restraints likely with demands for submission	Restraints not likely
Crime control reflective of obsessive–compulsive lifestyle	Crime disorganization reflective of lifestyle
Controlled perseverance likely (e.g., continuous choking of victim to prolong sexual assault)	Uncontrolled perseverative responses likely (e.g., continuous slashing/stabbing, bite marks)
Death scene and crime scene are separate	Death scene and crime scene are same
Less likely destruction of face	Destruction of face more likely
Hides body	No attempt to conceal body
Alters crime scene, conceals/destroys evidence	More likely leaves crime scene intact
Fingerprints/footprints not likely	Fingerprints/footprints likely
Less likely insertion of items into victim's orifices	Inserts items into victim's orifices
Body dumped at another site	Body left at scene
Relies on own or victim's vehicle	Relies on public transportation
Does not take souvenir, article, or clothing	Takes souvenir, article, or clothing
Blood smearing or other unusual acts less likely	Blood smearing, cannibalism, anthropophagy more likely
Less likely to return victim's items to grave site	May return souvenir to grave site

SUMMARY

The crime profiling process — essentially a base rate comparison approach — describes a sequence of clinical/forensic activities used to uncover concealment of offenses. The state of the art is extremely rudimentary, yet cues have been provided leading to the identification of perpetrators. The process of crime profiling illustrates the wealth of information contained in statistical base rates and the value of such information in forming "empirical stereotypes" of offenders against which to compare individual suspects. Such empirical stereotypes could also prove useful in describing typical cases of mental disorders and in evaluating the self-presentations of individual clients.

TABLE 15.5
Summary of Court Decisions Regarding the Admissibilty of Profiling Expert Witness Testimony

Legal Citation	Profile Data	Court Finding
Cohn v. State (1993)	Psychological profile of child victim of	Generic testimony of behavior
Duckett v. State (1990)	sexual abuse	displayed by child sexual abuse
		victims permitted
Hall v. State (1985)	Pedophile profiles	Assumption that defendant matches
State v. Maule (1983)		the profile, must be guilty, is
State v. Percy (1986)		inadmissible
State v. Clements (1989)	Child molester profile	Admissibility reversed
Pennell v. State (1991)	Serial murder profile	Profile testimony permits defendant to
		be accused by a witness who was not
		present at any of the crimes
People v. Stoll (1989)	Profile as sign of "deviance or	Admissible as character evidece by
	abnormality"	specific statutory provision
People v. Watkins (1989)	"Personality type" profile as evidence	Inadmissible
	of defendant likely to commit armed	
	robbery	
Gregory G. Sarno, Annotation,	Pedophile profile	Not admissible
Admissibility of Expert Testimony as		
to Criminal Defendents Propensity		
toward Sexual Deviation (1985 &		
1996 Supp.)		
State of Delaware v. Floray (1997)		
Turgate v. Commonwealth, Ky. (1995)		
*State v. Cavallo (1982)	Pedophile profile	Scientific literature does not support
State v. Michaels (1993)		conclusion that there is a reliable
*United States v. St. Pierre (1987)		profile of a "typical" sexual offender
State v. Screpesi (1991)	Pedophile profile	Profile evidence not introduced as
		such, but as testimony; state did not
		pose defendant as child abuser
State v. Tucker (1990)	Pedophile profile	Expert can define profile
		characteristics, but cannot state
		profile is consistent or inconsistent
		with crime having occurred
United States v. Powers (1996)	Profile of fixated pedophile	Defendant fitting the profile is not
		relevant to defendant commiting the
		crime
Williams v. State of Texas (1994)	Profile of someone likely to engage in	Inadmissible
	telephone harrassment	

* It should be noted that these cases were decided under *Frye v. United States* (1923), which was superseded by Federal Rules of Evidence 702 and *Daubert v. Merrell Dow Pharmaceuticals, Inc.*, (1993).

In a study of the validity research with criminal profiling, Homant and Kennedy (1998) described an excellent summary of the contemporary status of profiling techniques:

1. Crime scene profiling is a separate and distinct process from psychological profiling and from offender profiling.
2. It may be possible to generalize from various behavioral aspects of a crime scene to some characteristics of the perpetrator.

3. There is some evidence that it may be possible to type offenders and crime scenes as organized or disorganized.
4. The organized/disorganized typing may be related to certain aspects of offender personality.
5. There is evidence that those who are FBI-trained in profiling are more effective.
6. The evidence for the validity of profiles remains weak.
7. Profiling should not be relied upon to the exclusion of other alternatives.
8. There is need for more specific validity research.
9. Profiling should not be generalized beyond its original purpose of providing leads and focusing investigations.

The authors would add to the foregoing list the myriad ethical responsibilities that accompany appropriate use of profiling procedures. The principal areas of ethical concern would include competency, confidentially (Brockman & Humphreys, 1998; Knoppers, 1993), and appropriate use of findings and general subject welfare.

There is an ongoing effort to use computers to store, manage, codify, and interpret criminal profile data (Holmes & Holmes, 1996). Computerization should also help rectify the problem that empirical research has lagged far behind the rush to profile, and the lack of an organized knowledge base (Grubin, 1997). These significant shortcomings have been recognized by the judicial system. Nevertheless, profiling is a promising tool in criminal investigations. Profiling offers a means of understanding and defining the psychological mechanisms that contribute to criminal behavior. At the present time, however, the limitations of profiling make it of questionable value in the courtroom and it behooves law enforcement and clinical expert witnesses to be extremely judicious in attempting to use profiling data to formulate ultimate opinions.

LEGAL REFERENCES

Cohn v. State, 849 S. W.2d 817 (Tex. Crim. App. 1993).
Ducket v. State, 797 S. W.2d 906 (Tex. Crim, App. 1990).
Gregory G. Sarno, Annotation, Admissibility of Expert Testimony as to Criminal Defendant's Propensity toward Sexual Deviation, 42 A.L.R. 4th 937 (1985 & 1996 Supp.).
Hall v. State, Ark. App. 309, 692 S.W. 2d 769 (1985).
Pennell v. State, Del., Supr., 602 A. 2d 48 (1991).
People v. Stoll, Cal. Supr,. 49 Cal. 3d 1136, 738 P 2d 698, 265 Cal. Rptr. 111 (1989).
People v. Watkins, Mich. App., 176 Mich. App. 428, 440 N. W. 2d 36, 37 (1989).
State v. Clements, Kan. Supr. 770 P.2d 447 (1989).
State v. Cavallo, N.J. Supr., 88 N.J. 508, 443 A.2d 1020, 1023 (1982).
State of Delaware v. Floray, 715 A.2d 855,*,1997 Del. Super. Lexis 272.
State v. Maule, Wash. App., 15 Ark. App. 287, 667 P. 2d 96 (1983).
State v. Michaels, N.J. Super. App. Div., 264 N.J. Super. 579, 625 A. 2d 489, 508 (1993).
State v. Percy, Va. Supr. 146 Vt. 475, 507 A.2d 955 (1986).
State v. Screpesi, Del. Supr., 611 A.2d 34 (1991).
State v. Tucker, App., 165 Ariz. 340, 798 P.2d 1349 (1990).
Turgate v. Commonwealth, Ky. Supr., 901 S. W. 2d 41 (1995).
United States v. Powers, 4th Cir., 59F. 3rd 1460, 1470 (1995), cert. denied, 116 S. Ct. 784 (1996).
United States v. St. Pierre, 8th Cir., 812 F.2d 414, 420 (1987).
Williams v. State of Texas, 895 S. W.2d 363,*, 1994 Tex. Crim. App. Lexis 135.

REFERENCES

American Psychiatric Association. (1994). *Diagnostic and statistical manual of mental disorders* (4th ed.). Washington, DC: Author.

Annon, J. S. (1995). Investigative profiling: A behavioral analysis of the crime scene. *American Journal of Forensic Psychology, 14*(4), 67–75.

Brockman, B., & Humphreys, M. (1998). Criminal Evidence (Amendment) Act 1997. Compromised ethics: Consequences of compulsory DNA sampling from psychiatric patients. *Journal of Forensic Psychiatry, 9*(2), 245–247.

Brussel, J. A. (1968). *Casebook of a crime psychiatrist.* New York: Dell.

Burgess, A. W., Douglas, J. E., & Burgess, A. G. (1997). Classifying homicides and forensic evaluations. *Crisis Intervention & Time-Limited Treatment, 3*(3), 199–215.

Cole, W. A., & Bradford, J. M. (1992). Abduction during custody and access disputes. *Canadian Journal of Psychiatry, 37*(4), 264–266.

Dale, A., Davies, A., & Wei, L. (1997). Developing a typology of rapists' speech. *Journal of Pragmatics, 27*(5), 653–669.

Douglas, J., Burgess, A. W., Burgess, A. G., & Ressler, R. (1992). *Crime classification manual.* New York: Lexington Books.

Edinger, J. (1979). Cross-validation of the Megargee MMPI typology for prisoners, *Journal of Consulting and Clinical Psychology, 47*(2), 234–242.

Ekman, P. (1985). *Telling lies.* New York: Norton.

Groth, A. (1979). *Men who rape: The psychology of the offender.* New York: Plenum Press.

Grubin, D. (1997). Offender profiling. *Journal of Forensic Psychiatry, 6*(2), 259–263.

Hall, H. V. (1999). Overview of lethal violence. In H. V. Hall (Ed.), *Lethal violence: A sourcebook on fatal domestic, acquaintance and stranger violence* (pp. 1–52). Boca Raton, FL: CRC Press.

Haywood, T. W., Grossman, L. S., Kravitz, H. M., & Wasyliw, O. E. (1994). Profiling psychological distortion in alleged child molesters. *Psychological Reports, 75*(2), 915–927.

Hazelwood, R. R., & Douglas, J. E. (1980). The lust murderer. *FBI Law Enforcement Bulletin, 49*, 61–68.

Hazelwood, R., & Warren, J. (1989). The serial rapist: His characteristics and victims, Part I: Conclusion. *FBI Law Enforcement Bulletin, 1*, 10–25.

Hirschfield, A., & Bowers, K. J. (1997). The development of a social, demographic and land use profiler for areas of high crime. *British Journal of Criminology, 37*(1), 103–120.

Holmes, R. M. (1989). *Profiling violent crimes.* Newbury Park, CA: Sage.

Holmes, R. M. (1991). *Sex crimes.* Newbury Park, CA: Sage.

Holmes, R. M., & Holmes, S. T. (1996). *Profiling violent crimes: An investigative tool* (2nd. ed.). Thousand Oaks, CA: Sage.

Holmes, R. M., & Holmes, S. T. (1998). *Contemporary perspectives on serial murder.* Thousand Oaks, CA: Sage.

Homant, R. J., & Kennedy, D. B. (1998). Psychological aspects of crime profiling: Validity research. *Criminal Justice & Behavior, 25*(3), 319–343.

Knoppers, B. M. (1993). Confidentiality in genetic testing: Legal and ethical issues in an international context. *Medicine & Law, 12*(6–8), 573–582.

Kozeny, J., Tisanska, L., & Meznik, J. (1998). Dotaznik temperametovych a charakterovych rysu TCI: Profil osob ve vykonu trestu [Temperament and character inventory TCI: Profile of incarcerated persons]. *Ceskoslovenska Psycholgie, 42*(3), 218–226.

Kuznestov, A., Pierson, T. A., & Harry, B. (1992). Victim age as a basis for profiling sexual offenders. *Federal Probation, 56*(2), 34–38.

Larivee, S., Parent, S., Charlebois, P., & Gagnon, C. (1994). L'interaction du profil intellectuel et de la turbulence a l'ecole primaire comme predicteur de la delinquance autorevelee [The interaction between the intellectual profile and the disruptiveness at the primary school as a predictor of self-reported delinquency]. *Psychological Belgica, 34*(1), 1–31.

Leon, S. C., Kopta, S. M., Howard, K. I., & Lutz, W. (1999). Predicting patients' responses to psychotherapy: Are some more predictable than others? *Journal of Consulting & Clinical Psychology, 67*(5), 608–704.

McCann, J. T. (1992). Criminal personality profiling in the investigation of violent crime: Recent advances and future directions. *Behavioral Science & the Law, 10*(4), 475–481.

Megargee, E., & Bohn, M. (1979). *Classifying criminal offenders: A new system based on the MMPI.* California: Sage.

Miron, M., & Goldstein, A. (1979). *Hostage.* New York: Pergamon Press.

Miron, M., & Pasquale, A. (1978). Psycholinguistic analysis of coercion. *Journal of Psycholinguistic Research, 7*, 95–120.

Murphy, W. D., & Peters, J. M. (1992). Profiling child sexual abusers. *Criminal Justice & Behavior, 19*(1), 24–37.

Myers, W. C., Reccoppa, L., Burton, K., & McElroy, R. (1993). Malignant sex and aggression: An overview of serial sexual homicide. *Bulletin of the American Academy of Psychiatry & the Law, 21*(4), 435–451.

Pinizzotto, A., & Finkel, N. (1990). Criminal personality profiling. *Law and Human Behavior, 14*(3), 215–233.

Ressler, R. (1990). *Crime profiling.* Workshop presented by FBI at Hickam USAF Base, Honolulu, HI.

Ressler, R., Burgess, A., & Douglas, J. (1988). *Sexual homicide: Patterns and motives.* Lexington, MA: Lexington Books.

Rider, A. (1980). The firesetter: A psychological profile. *FBI Law Enforcement Bulletin, 49*, 1–23.

Sims, B., & Jones, M. (1997). Predicting success or failure on probation: Factors associated with felony probation. *Crime & Delinquency, 43*(3), 314–327.

Smith, B. L., & Morgan, K. D. (1994). Terrorists right and left: Empirical issues in profiling American terrorists. *Studies in Conflict and Terrorism, 17*(1), 39–57.

Tamura, M., Watanabe, K., Suzuki, M., Sano, K., Watanabe, S., & Ikegami, S. (1998a). 1/Criminal profiling of "Torima" nonspecific-motive attacking: I. Research on perpetrators of random violence in Japan. *Reports of National Research Institute of Police Science, 39*(1), 1–11.

Tamura, M., Watanabe, K., Suzuki, M., Sano, K., Watanabe, S., & Ikegami, S. (1998b). 1/Criminal profiling of "Torima" nonspecific-motive attacking: II. Estimating the perpetrator's traits through analysis of the nature of random violence offenses in Japan. *Reports of National Research Institute of Police Science, 39*(1), 12–20.

Thornton, D., Cookson, H., & Clark, D. (1990). Profiles of the youth custody population: Dependencies, delinquencies and disciplinary infractions. *Issues in Criminological & Legal Psychology,* No. 15, 7–23.

Turco, R. N. (1990). Psychological profiling. *International Journal of Offender Therapy & Comparative Criminology, 34*(2), 147–154.

Turvey, B. E. (1998). Deductive criminal profiling: Comparing applied methodologies between inductive and deductive criminal profiling techniques. Knowledge Solutions Library [On-Lline]. Available: http://www.corpus-delicti.com/Profiling_law.html.

16 Forensic Hypnosis

The first record of an American court of law admitting testimony that was obtained hypnotically was in 1846. Gravitz (1995) described that the case involved a murder trial in which the allegations against the defendant were not supported by the evidence and a verdict of not guilty was determined. Since then, hypnosis has continued as a source of considerable forensic dispute.

When there is question of deception in a forensic matter, hypnosis could conceivably assist with clarifying victim, witness, and defendant testimony. The problem is with the reliability of hypnotically produced recall. Even in the 1846 trial, Gravitz noted in the expert testimony of Amariah Brigham that hypnosis can produce an amalgam of fact and distortion. Brigham stressed that some hypnotic subjects were more vulnerable to distortion than others. These were observations that remain accurate today in terms of the forensic limitations of hypnosis.

Authorities have traditionally agreed that there are no reliable physiological determinants that unequivocally differentiate between the hypnotic and normal waking states (Barber, 1965c; Gorten, 1949; Hilgard, 1965). As will be reviewed, however, recent studies have indicated that certain physiological measures are reasonably reliable in measuring deception in the laboratory setting (for a review, see Kinnunen, Zamansky, & Block, 1994). Historically, it was necessary for researchers in the field of hypnosis to define the state of hypnosis in terms of particular displayed behaviors, given a specified set of conditions (i.e., procedures used, induction techniques employed, etc.). For example, researchers (Hilgard, 1965; Weitzenhoffer, 1963) have contended that some evidence for the hypnotic state exists when individual suggestibility is increased. It is in this light that certain types of behavior, such as catalepsy, ideosensory activities (e.g., hallucinations), ideomotor activities (e.g., arm levitation), automatic writing, dissociation, age-regression, anesthesia, and posthypnotic suggestion have been considered to be hallmarks of the hypnotic trance (Erickson, 1944; Kroger, 1963; Weitzenhoffer, 1963).

Clinicians have long recognized the insidious potential of hypnotic dynamics especially with vulnerable individuals. In an interesting commentary, Beahrs (1999) described the response pattern of trauma victims who perceive others in their lives as being dichotomized into groups of allies or enemies. Trauma serves to induce and intensify this paranoid perceptual style. The behavior is seen with traumatized patients who tend to unite in "tightly knit in-groups" that according to the writer resemble cults. The members of the groups unite in the denigration of others as enemies. Among the in-group members, polarized beliefs are shaped by suggestive interactions that resemble the effect of hypnotic suggestion. This phenomenon described by Beahrs is but one example of the distorting potential of hypnosis and why its use in forensics must involve due caution.

Usually included in the category of hypnotic markers is hypnotically induced amnesia (Clemes, 1964; Hammer, 1954; Scott, 1930; Spanos, James, & deGroot, 1990; Weitzenhoffer, 1963; Williamsen, Johnson, & Ericksen, 1965). Eyewitness testimony without hypnosis is known to be very vulnerable to distortion from a variety of influences and to include misleading suggestions during interrogation (Lindsay, 1990). The recovery and restoration of memory loss with eyewitnesses, for example, constitutes the most frequent use of hypnosis in forensic practice (Miller & Stava, 1997).

Despite the accumulated evidence supporting the contention that amnesia is a reliable index of hypnosis, early laboratory research (Barber & Calverly, 1966) cast doubt on the typicality of memory distortions attributed to hypnosis. In essence, it is questioned whether the hypnotic state is either necessary or sufficient to elicit mnestic distortions. Moreover, most of the early studies have been attacked on methodological grounds, contending that when proper controls are absent (such as including a waking condition in the design and isolating the role of motivating instructions to the subjects), no valid inferences concerning hypnotic phenomena can be made (Barber, 1965a, b; Parker & Barber, 1964). In prototypic investigations, Hall (1969) and Thorne and Hall (1969) found that amnesia was elicited as easily in the waking state as under hypnosis. In their investigation, the Harvard Group Scale of Hypnotic Susceptibility (HGSHS) was administered to 667 undergraduate students. Out of this original group, 120 subjects of high and low hypnotic susceptibility were asked to participate in the experimental procedures. Each subject was randomly assigned to one of six treatments, which varied in terms of the type of amnesia suggestion given (authoritarian or permissive) and the kind of motivational procedure employed (hypnotic and waking motivation, and waking nonmotivation). Each procedure started with instructions to learn well a list of paired associates. After a period of time and in conjunction with one of three motivational procedures, the subjects were given a suggestion to forget what they had previously been instructed to learn. A partially related Word Association Test (WAT) was presented to discern the relative effectiveness of the memory suggestion and analyzed in terms of word response (WR) and reaction time (RT) scores. Statistical analysis of the data suggested the following. (1) Association responses were differentially affected by susceptibility level. High susceptibility subjects tended to forget more in terms of WR scores than low susceptibility subjects. (2) Task motivation to forget the paired words was more effective in terms of WR scores than instructions to forget without task motivation. Within the task-motivated procedures, there was no difference in amnesia performance between the hypnotic and waking groups. (3) Type of suggestion did not differentially affect association responses. All except the second finding conformed to popular hypnotic theories. In general, it would not be predicted that hypnotic-like behavior can be produced as readily in the waking compared with the "trance" state.

Since hypnosis as a psychological state is inferred from its manifestations and since these manifestations may be produced in nontrance states, the question of deception by subjects during hypnotic recall is important to consider. Can subjects successfully feign a hypnotic trance and its manifestations (e.g., amnesia)? Investigators have found differences between faking and genuine subjects in tasks tapping memory skills (Orne, Sheehan, & Evans, 1968; Spanos, Radtke, Bertrand, Addie, & Drummond, 1982; Worthington, 1979). The Orne et al. (1968) study, as an example, found that subjects given posthypnotic instructions ran their hands through their hair when they were cued with the word *experiment*. Fake subjects responded only to the experimenter; genuine subjects responded to a secretary outside the research room, thus showing response generalization to hypnotic stimuli.

Faking amnesia during recall may create unusual features, which the evaluator can note. Spanos et al. (1982) found that recall is not disorganized in genuine hypnosis. The large majority of subjects who faked loss of the target words organized their recall in a manner detectable by the experimenter.

In sum, hypnosis appears to create mnestic changes (e.g., amnesia or enhanced recall), but so do other methods that merely require focusing and concentration. All behaviors elicited in hypnosis, including amnesia and enhanced recall, can be replicated in the waking state. Some means of detecting faked hypnosis have been proffered, which occasionally have been replicated in other studies. Some suggested signs of faked hypnosis are presented in Table 16.1.

Later research (Brandt, Rubinsky, & Lassen, 1985; Coe, 1989; Kihlstrom, 1980; Kinnunen, Zamansky, & Block, 1994; Spanos, 1986; Spanos, James, & deGroot, 1990; Spanos, Quigley, Gwynn, Glatt, & Perlini, 1991) has consistently suggested that the hypothesis of hypnotic amnesia cannot be adequately explained in terms of deception. Brandt, Rubinsky, and Lassen (1985) and later Spanos, James, and deGroot (1990) found that subjects hypnotized to be amnestic consistently recognized words at above-chance levels that they had failed to recognize during amnesia testing. In comparison, subjects simulating amnesia had below-chance recognition for the same task. This finding suggested, therefore, that below-chance performance on recognition memory tasks might provide an indicator of detecting simulated amnesia in forensic samples.

TABLE 16.1
Traditional Signs of Simulation in Hypnosis

More Likely Faking if:	Example
1. Susceptibility scale scores change upon repeated testing	Genuine subjects' Harvard or Stanford scale scores remain stable over time
2. Increased arousal creates variable performance	Genuine subjects show steady improvement in performance from stupor to arousal
3. Distress tolerance deceased	Prolonged arm levitation without tiring is unusual
4. Atypical ocular movements	Genuine subject moves eyes and head; faker tracks moving object with fixed head
5. Increased arousal state	Elevated pulse and respiration rate (unless suggested by hypnotist)
6. Suggested acts are discontinued when hypnotist leaves	Toe-tapping to music in fakers ceases after experimenter creates sham interruption
7. Negative hallucinations create atypical behavior in forced-choice situations	Stumbles or stops in front of "invisible" chair; genuine subjects will walk around it
8. Logical thinking guides responses to hypnotist	Fakers will not affirm feeling in hand suggested to be numb despite later contrary instructions

In a study of hypnotically induced pseudomemories, Sheehan, Statham, and Jamieson (1991) found that the reporting of pseudomemories was very sensitive to variables of hypnotist skill, stimulus features, type of memory test, and reliably administered instructions. An investigation by Spanos et al. (1991) had subjects witness a videotaped shooting. Immediately after viewing the film, the subjects were interrogated and then interrogated again several days later. Prior to the second interrogation, half of the subjects received hypnotic suggestion for enhanced memory recognition. The findings reflected no differences between hypnotic subjects and controls in identification accuracy of offender mug shots. The hypnotic subjects, however, expressed more confidence in their misidentifications. In a third session, subjects who had correctly identified a mug shot returned and were examined and cross-examined in a mock courtroom setting. Half of these subjects underwent pretrial preparation (PRP) aimed at building confidence. When coupled with PRP, hypnotic subjects maintained relatively high certainty in their testimony. With cross-examination, the hypnotic subjects were as likely as controls to disavow their earlier testimony. In contrast, PRP induced substantial resistance to recanting earlier testimony.

One experimental effort to evaluate deception in hypnosis used electrodermal skin conductance response (SCR) as the dependent variable (Kinnunen et al., 1994). SCR was chosen over other physiological measures — e.g., blood pressure, heart rate, respiration, galvanic skin response (GSR), skin potential response (SPR), oxygen saturation level, blood volume, breathing amplitude, and breathing cycle time — because it has been shown to be the most effective somatic indicator of deception in the laboratory. The study compared the SCR responses of deeply hypnotized subjects with nonhypnotized subjects in response to a guilty knowledge technique (GKT). In the GKT, subjects are asked to lie about the identity of a stimulus they have privately selected beforehand from among a series of stimuli. In this study, the GKT was referent to subjects' actually experiencing, or not, suggested effects (e.g., arm levitation; amnesia for a symbol). The SCR findings indicated that 89% of the hypnotized subjects' reports met the criteria for truthfulness, whereas only 35% of the simulators' reports met the criteria. Thus, the majority of the hypnotized subjects experienced the effects conveyed by hypnotic suggestions.

In another study, hypnotizable subjects were exposed to a baseline and a hypnotic-deafness condition (Perlini, Haley, & Buczel, 1998). The subjects were required to rate the intensity of a pure tone 10 seconds following completion of the tone. The hypnotized subjects were found to bias their responses according to demand instructions. When the subjects received bogus holographic feedback challenging the veracity of their loudest ratings, subjects tended to recant their original biased responses. The findings suggested that the hypnotized subjects evidenced reporting bias indicative of purposeful deception. Clearly, expectancy variables are important hypnotic outcome determinants. Kirsch and Baker (1993) described expectation effects with hypnotic and placebo-induced analgesia.

In still another laboratory study, subjects were given suggestions for arm levitation and for visual, auditory, tactile, and taste hallucinations (Perugini et al., 1998). The suggestions were administered twice by audiotape to a "highly suggestible" group of students and a "low suggestibility" group of simulators. In one administration the subjects were (mis-)led to believe they were alone, when, in fact, their behavior was surreptitiously recorded on videotape and observed on a video monitor. During the other administration, an experimenter who had not been informed about group assignment openly observed the subjects. When unaware that they were being observed, simulators were significantly less responsive to suggestion and engaged in substantially more role-inappropriate behavior. In contrast, the responsiveness of nonsimulating students was not affected by the presence of an experimenter, and they exhibited little role-inappropriate behavior even when they were alone. The authors concluded that the behavior of the suggestible subjects reflected internally generated changes (i.e., due to hypnosis), and was not due to simple intentional compliance (i.e., faking).

EVIDENTIARY PROBLEMS

It should come as no surprise that the pretrial use of hypnosis has substantial problems. Diamond (1980) presents critical questions pertaining to the hypnotist, the subject, and hypnosis itself. First, is the hypnotist trained, experienced, and certified in practicing hypnosis? Can he or she detect faked hypnosis, avoid planting suggestions in the mind of the subject, and distinguish fact from fiction after the trance state? Last, is it possible to have confidence in presented opinions beyond a reasonable degree of scientific certainty?

Questions also arise concerning the subject. Can a hypnotizable person ever be free of heightened suggestibility and, if not, can even waking memories be free from their projections and fantasies? Does the richness of hypnotic recall indicate truthfulness, or must memories be verified by corroborating data? After the hypnotic trance, do subjects continue to distort information and do they believe in their own hypnotically produced fabrications?

Last, Diamond suggests one ask whether hypnosis can ever be truly recorded or observed, because it is largely an internal event. In the final analysis, and with all of its flaws, is hypnosis any better than more conventional techniques such as interviewing and interrogation? Not wanting to lose hypnosis altogether as a tool in forensic work, Spiegel and Spiegel (1984) suggested that hypnosis could be used in some forensic instances as a "diagnostic probe." They suggested further that hypnosis had usefulness as a treatment tool, as a test of motivation, and as an important diagnostic tool in terms of a subject's responsiveness to systematically measured hypnotic induction.

FORENSIC HYPNOSIS APPLICATIONS

Hypnosis in the forensic setting has been used to enhance eyewitness memory (for a review, see Kebbell & Wagstaff, 1998). Gravitz (1997) described the use of hypnosis as an investigative technique with child witnesses and victims. A number of variables has been identified as having a critical bearing on efforts to enhance eyewitness testimony hypnotically. Variables of subject suggestibility and subject and hypnotist levels of confidence as affecting eyewitness accuracy have been investigated in laboratory settings (Py & Fernandes, 1995) and in actual forensic matters (Wagstaff, 1996). These studies have reflected divergent findings of the efficacy of hypnosis in enhancing eyewitness testimony.

Tayloe (1995) presented a case report of a 50-year-old man who was on trial for murdering his wife in a non-U.S. jurisdiction. The man claimed no memory of events surrounding the crime, although the circumstantial evidence was compelling. Hypnosis was used to recover the man's memory. In only a second hypnotic session, the man recalled that he shot his wife while attempting to kill himself in front of his wife. The information dramatically altered the outcome of the trial. Six months later the man was released and subsequently was successful in committing suicide. The investigator suggested that the case demonstrated how extremely emotional circumstances can be actively repressed from conscious memory and that those memories can later be accurately recalled during hypnosis.

Offering an alternative strategy to hypnotic enhancement of eyewitness testimony, Kebbell and Wagstaff (1998) noted that "cognitive interviewing" procedures enhanced recall by 35% and avoided the possibility of memory distortion associated with hypnosis. These investigators suggested that hypnosis with eyewitnesses may be effective solely because hypnotic interviewers have better psychological, clinical, and interpersonal skills compared with police officers.

Anecdotal information regarding the misuse of hypnotic techniques abounds. Knowledge of hypnotic induction techniques is readily available to laypersons, and it is well established that a small percentage of the population is highly suggestible. Highly suggestible subjects can be vulnerable to even inept induction attempts. In addition to ethical complaints and civil litigation against qualified professionals who use hypnosis, there is a regular flow of litigation complaints regarding misuse of hypnosis by nonprofessionals. Vingoe (1998) described the legal case of a man accused of raping his stepson's 15-year-old girlfriend after inducing hypnosis. It is quite plausible that the victim's plight was secondary to hypnosis lowering her inhibitions, although other factors could have contributed to the alleged rape as well.

Another non-U.S. jurisdiction case report involved a criminal rape trial in which neither the alleged male perpetrator nor the woman victim had any memory of the sex act (Neal, Scott, & Grimsbo, 1993). A hypnotic interview with the man also met with his denials of any recollection of the incident. The man was found not guilty in spite of the prosecutor's contentions that a rape had occurred while the woman was unconscious. A jury found the man not guilty, reportedly in the belief that the victim's and the perpetrator's lack of memory was due to alcohol-induced blackouts.

There are clinicians who have advocated for "legal controls" of hypnosis (Stanley, 1994). The argument is that legal sanctions are necessary to address the misuse of hypnosis by lay practitioners and also stage performers. Perhaps an even more troubling misuse of hypnosis, however, has been the hypnotic interviews of eyewitnesses by police investigators, which frequently result in false information against alleged perpetrators (Gibson, 1995; Wagstaff, 1996).

Hypnosis can present difficulties because of suggestibility problems with many psychiatric diagnostic categories. Notable are hysterical and borderline syndromes, and the controversial multiple personality disorder (MPD; Lewis & Bard, 1991). Coons (1991) described actual case studies that evidenced iatrogenic creation of MPD "symptoms" through hypnotic and nonhypnotic cuing that were then used as a basis for lack of criminal responsibility. Arguably, other syndromes may negatively impact on suggestibility, for example, paranoid, psychotic, and organic syndromes. In each of these situations there can be specific clinical issues, specific concerns with malingering and distortion, and legal evidentiary problems.

CASE LAW

The legal consensus is that hypnotically induced testimony is unreliable and therefore inadmissible (Giannelli, 1995; Milne, 1992; Spiegel & Spiegel, 1987). Essentially for the past 25 years, the courts have uniformly rejected the admissibility of out-of-court statements made by individuals subjected to hypnosis. Very recent case law decisions, however, have begun to make exceptions particularly with "refreshed testimony" of witnesses (Newman & Thompson, 1999).

The basic problem with hypnotic testimony is that it is both a procedure and a state, which relies on suggestion. The suggestion may create pseudomemories, which may confuse the trier of fact in the determination of a case. In questioning experts, courts are aware that there is no extant method to determine faked vs. genuine hypnosis. A precedent case law decision regarding hypnotic testimony was made in the Supreme Court of Minnesota in 1980 (*State v. Mack,* 1980). In *Mack,* the court ruled that under the *Frye* test (*Frye v. U. S.,* 1923) hypnosis was not a recognized scientific technique and therefore hypnotic testimony was not admissible. *Mack* established a per se exclusion of hypnotically induced testimony that has since been essentially adopted in most American jurisdictions (Perry, 1997). The per se exclusion has been similarly applied by the courts to the polygraph as an index of deception.

A number of states have set out rules that differentiate between memories produced (1) prior to hypnosis, (2) within the hypnotic trance administered during pretrial investigation, and (3) during hypnosis administered as therapy to victims, witnesses, or a defendant. These rules are important to consider because they may affect the use of other focusing, suggestive, or relaxation techniques in forensic settings and situations.

In spite of the prevailing trend, some states have ruled that hypnotically produced memory is admissible under certain conditions (*Harding v. State,* 1968; *Kline v. Ford Motor Co.,* 1975; *State v. Hurd,* 1981; *United States v. Adams,* 1978; *United States v. Miller,* 1969). Generally, these courts have held that cross-examination enables a jury to evaluate hypnosis in terms of its effect on the credibility of the witness (see Table 16.2).

TABLE 16.2
Cases on Forensic Hypnosis

Biskup v. McCaughtry (1994)	Prosecutors use of hypnotically refreshed testimony does not automatically violate Sixth and Fourteenth Amendments
Borawick v. Shay (1995)	Hypnotically refreshed recollections of sexual abuse possibly admissible based on "totality-of-the-circumstances approach"
Harding v. State (1968)	Testimony based on hypnosis admissible, with weight for trier of facts (since overruled)
Radcliff v. Commonwealth (1995)	Affirmed trial courts per se inadmissibility of videotape of murder defendant's hypnotic testimony
Rock v. Arkansas (1987)	U.S. Supreme Court disagreed with *People v Shirley,* and upheld admissibility of murder defendant's hypnotic testimony that refreshed defendant's recollection of crime scene
United States v. Miller (1969)	Defendant entitled to new trial due to nondisclosure to defense of hypnosis; jury must be aware of hypnosis
United States v. Adams (1978)	Hypnosis process should be considered in terms of weight, as opposed to admissibility
State v. Hurd (1981)	Testimony based on hypnosis permissible if stringent criteria set by court are met
State v. Mena (1981)	Hypnosis so unreliable that hypnotically induced testimony should be excluded until *Frye* test requirements met
People v. Shirley (1982)	Hypnosis renders witnesses incompetent to testify on any matters covered during hypnosis
State v. Collins (1982)	Witnesses can testify as to facts recalled from hypnosis
State v. Armstrong (1983)	Hypnosis did not render inadmissible subsequent identification of defendant or in-court testimony of events covered during trance state
Commonwealth v. Kater (1983)	Hypnosis fails the *Frye* test; the proposed standards are not workable
Harker v. Maryland (1986)	Hypnosis may be useful in developing leads in criminal investigations
People v. Hughes (1983)	Witnesses can testify as to facts recalled prior to hypnosis
Radcliff v. Commonwealth (1995)	Videotape of murder defendant's hypnotic interview carries great risk of confabulation and not admissible
Rock v. Arkansas (1987)	Hypnosis does not guarantee accuracy of recall
State v. Mack (1980)	Hypnosis per se not admissible under *Frye* test

In *State v. Hurd* (1981), a variant rule was adopted making hypnosis admissible provided that very stringent criteria were met. In doing so, the court was appalled that, among other events, the witness in question was hypnotized in the presence of a third party (a police officer) who even asked questions during the trance state. The court noted that hypnosis renders subjects vulnerable to suggestion, creates loss of critical judgment, and has a tendency to confound genuine with hypnotic memories.

Hurd lays out the requirements in order for hypnotically induced evidence to be considered admissible. At a minimum, Orne (1979) standards should be met: (1) the hypnotist should be a psychiatrist or psychologist trained in hypnosis; (2) the hypnotist should be independent of the defense or prosecution; (3) all transactions between hypnotist and subject, as well as between referring party and hypnotist, must be recorded; (4) a prehypnotic interview covering the instant offense or tort event must take place; and (5) only the hypnotist should be present prior to, during, and after the hypnosis. Other requirements set forth in *Hurd* include determining whether hypnosis is appropriate, based on expert testimony, and the "amenability of the subject to hypnosis." Finally, the burden of establishing admissibility by clear and convincing evidence should be on the party who tenders the hypnotically influenced testimony.

Some courts have permitted witnesses to testify as to facts occurring prior to the induction of hypnosis (*Commonwealth v. Kater*, 1983; *People v. Hughes*, 1983; *State v. Collins*, 1982). In *Hughes*, for example, the New York Court of Appeals held that, although the victim's posthypnotic recollections were inadmissible at a rape trial, she would not necessarily be precluded from testifying about events recalled before the induction of hypnosis. However, the prosecution was admonished for failure to give the defendant pretrial notice of its intention to call a witness who had previously been hypnotized in connection with the case. The state was seen as having the burden of proving that the hypnotized witness would be reliable.

Viewing hypnosis as a hopeless contaminant of memory, other courts have invoked a bright-line rule that witnesses are incompetent to testify on any matters covered in hypnosis (*People v. Shirley*, 1982; *Polk v. State*, 1981; *State v. Mena*, 1981). *Shirley* disallowed testimony even when the recall was recorded on other sources. This view holds that hypnosis simply does not meet the basic requirement set forth in *Frye v. United States* (1923), because hypnosis is not generally accepted as reliable in the scientific community. Against collective mainstream legal thought, Graham and Kabacy (1990) argued that the rule of *Frye* should apply to those aspects of scientific knowledge based on education but not on aspects of knowledge based on experience.

Shirley would abolish hypnosis in the courtroom even if strict procedural safeguards are built into the evaluation of hypnosis. The court noted that the stringent *Hurd* requirements are geared toward preventing the hypnotist from exploiting subject hypersuggestibility in hypnosis and do not prevent (1) hypnotically related loss of critical judgment, (2) false confidence in memory, and (3) confusion of real and confabulated memories.

In an ironic twist, *Shirley* would allow for the investigative use of hypnosis (e.g., recalling a license plate number), but not for the fruits of that inquiry if the hypnotic trance were successful. Likewise, treatment of post-trauma reactions by hypnosis would eliminate victims from testifying in court on instant matters. Justice Klaus, in a concurring and dissenting opinion, notes that the defendant would be prevented from testifying if hypnotized for forensic evaluation or treatment.

Klaus stated, "it is a mistake to adopt a sweeping 'per se' rule that the majority proposes — excluding virtually all testimony of a witness who had undergone pretrial hypnosis" (p. 46) without further investigation into the merits and demerits of the method. Finally, he makes the cogent argument that other forms of memory evaluation — such as eyewitness testimony — in general, have similar problems in reliability and validity.

According to Giannelli (1995), these divergent opinions fall within three points of view:

1. "Credibility" approach, which essentially leaves the reliability issue in the hands of the jury.
2. "Discretionary admission" approach, which leaves the reliability issue to the trial judge.

TABLE 16.3
Totality-of-the-Circumstances Evidentiary Approach

Consideration Factor	Consideration	Rationale
First	Evaluate the purpose of the hypnosis	Hypnosis during therapy less likely to induce confabulation than when used to refresh witness memory of an accident or crime
Second	Evaluate whether the witness received any suggestions from the hypnotist or others prior to or during hypnosis	Key information subject to suggestibility
Third	Determine presence or absence of a permanent record that can help ascertain whether suggestive procedures were used	Hypnotic sessions should be audio or videotaped
Fourth	Evaluate if the hypnotist was appropriately qualified by training and psychology or psychiatry	Self evident
Fifth	Evaluate whether corroborating evidence exists to support the reliability of the hypnotically refreshed memories	Consistency between corroborating evidence and hypnotic testimony
Sixth	Subject's hypnotizability may be relevant	Highly hypnotizable subjects may be more prone to confabulation and more susceptible to suggestion
Seventh	Consider any expert evidence in the light of the reliability of the procedures used in the case	Unorthodox procedures may contaminate the hypnotic productions
Eighth	Pretrial evidentiary hearing to enable the presentation of expert evidence and to test credibility through cross-examination	Desirable procedure
Ninth	Party attempting to admit the hypnotically enhanced testimony bears the burden of persuasion	The court must be convinced that the balance tips in favor of admissibility

Note: Adapted from *Borawick v Shay,* 68 F.3d 597 (U.S. App. 1995).

3. "Procedural safeguards" approach, which limits the application and extent of hypnotic procedures (e.g., see Orne, 1979).

A recent case decision by U.S. Court of Appeals for the second circuit has underscored a fourth variation (*Borawick v. Shay*, 1995; Anonymous, 1996) that has been frequently adopted by the federal courts. In *Borawick*, the court found that the rule of admissibility of hypnotic testimony should be flexible and based on a "totality-of-the-circumstances approach." This approach has been endorsed by a number of investigators (Campbell, 1997; Colwick, 1995; Perry, Orne, London, & Orne, 1996; Scheflin, 1994, 1997; Udolf, 1990) as being the most in accord with the current empirical status of hypnosis. The points of consideration under this totality approach as suggested by the *Borawick* court are outlined in Table 16.3.

A number of courts have addressed the issue of the admissibility of hypnotic testimony in terms of the defendants' rights as guaranteed by the U.S. Constitution (particularly, the Fifth, Sixth, and Fourteenth Amendments). These Constitutional considerations were reviewed by Newman and Thompson (1999); they are summarized in Table 16.4.

In 1993, the U.S. Supreme Court overturned the *Frye* standard in *Daubert v. Merrell Dow Pharmaceuticals Inc*. The ultimate impact of *Daubert* regarding the admissibility of hypnosis awaits full interpretation in trial courts. In *Borawick v. Shay*, the court observed:

TABLE 16.4
Constitutional Issues with Hypnosis

Amendment	Provision	Hypnosis Issue
Sixth[a]	Right to confront witnesses	Defendant does not have access to witness's prehypnotic, uncontaminated memories
	Right to impartial jury	Hypnotic witness may be strongly convinced of testimony and appear more credible to trier of fact
		There are common misconceptions regarding the effectiveness and potency of hypnosis that could unduly prejudice the trier of fact
Fifth[a]	Individual cannot be compelled to witness against himself in a criminal trial	Hypnosis may induce defendant to make an "involuntary" or coerced confession
	Right to testify in one's own behalf	Area of controversy for courts (see Table 16.3)

[a] The Fourteenth Amendment applies the protections of these Amendments to the individual states.

Note: Adapted from "Constitutional Rights and Hypnotically Elicited Testimony," by A. W. Newman, & J. W. Thompson, 1999, *Journal of the American Academy of Psychiatry & the Law, 27*(1), 149–154.

First, by loosening the strictures on scientific evidence set by Frye, Daubert reinforces the idea that they should be a presumption of admissibility of evidence. Second, it emphasizes the need for flexibility in assessing whether evidence is admissible. Rather than using rigid "safeguards" for determining whether testimony should be admitted, the courts' approach is to permit the trial judge to weigh the various considerations pertinent to the issue in question. Third, Daubert allows for the admissibility of scientific evidence, even if not generally accepted in the relevant scientific community, provided its reliability has independent support. Finally, the court expressed its faith in the power of the adversary system to test "shaky but admissible" evidence, *Daubert, 113 S. Ct. at 2798,* and advanced a bias in favor of admitting evidence sure of that solidly and indisputably proven to be reliable. (p. 606)

In sum, hypnosis currently is not viewed favorably by the majority of trial courts, but there are emerging judicial trends making allowances for the admissibility of hypnotic testimony in some instances. Perhaps research and clinical application in the new millennium will yield a still more receptive posture by the judiciary. In the meantime, the forensic evaluator is encouraged to utilize hypnosis discreetly in accord with prevailing local judicial guidelines. In addition, other memory-enhancing methods — general relaxation, motivation to do well, and instruction in cognitive focusing — are available to the practitioner. These latter approaches may equal hypnosis in recall effectiveness, but do not carry the stigma of possibly creating distortion in the very data it is attempting to recover or refresh.

A final comment is warranted on a troublesome clinical/forensic application that in some instances can incorporate hypnotic procedures. The problem area involves recall of child sexual abuse for the first time while in therapy. The recall of repressed memories of childhood sexual abuse has resulted in a number of well-publicized legal suits against professionals (Watkins, 1993). The validity of recovered memories, especially when involving such a sensitive topic as child sexual abuse, is very controversial and very prone to generating grievance actions against clinicians. This is particularly true when the memories are elicited by suggestion-based techniques to include hypnosis, but also guided imagery, dream interpretation, survivor's groups, and bibliotherapy. There can likewise be difficulties in conventional psychotherapy when inferences of prior "abuse" are made from presented symptoms or from interventions designed to overcome "denial" and a history of sexual abuse is (suggestively) interpreted as an explanation (Feldman-Summers, 1996). In a survey of 133 families accused by an adult child of abuse, the families appeared to be functional, intact, and successful (Wakefield & Ungerwager, 1992). The one feature common in the sample was purported recovered memories in adult children, all having been in therapy.

LEGAL REFERENCES

Biskup v. McCaughtry, 20 F.3d 245 (7th Cir. 1994).

Borawick v Shay, 68 F.3d 597 (U.S. App. 1995).

Commonwealth v. Kater, 388 Mass. 519, 447 N.E.2d 1190 (1983).

Daubert v. Merrell Dow Pharmaceuticals, 125 L. Ed. 2d 469 (S. Ct. 2786, 1993).

Frye v. United States, 293 F.1013 (DCCir. 1923).

Harding v. State, 5 Md.App. 230, 246 A.2d 302 (1968).

Harker v. Maryland, 800 F.2d 437 (4th Cir. 1986).

Kline v. Ford Motor Co., 523 F.2d 1067 (9th Cir. 1975).

People v. Hughes, 59 N.Y.2d 523, 453 N.E.2d 484, 466 N.Y.S.2d 255 (Ct. App. 1983).

People v. Shirley, 31 Cal.3d 18, 181 Cal.Rptr. 243, 641 P.2d 775 (1982).

Polk v. State, 48 Md.App. 382 427 A.2d 1041 (Md. 1981).

Radcliff v. Commonwealth, No. 0987-93-1 WL 332217 (Va. Ct. App., 1995).

Rock v. Arkansas, 483 U.S. 44 (L. Ed. 2d 37, 107 S. Ct. 2704, 1987).

State v. Armstrong, 110 Wis.2d 555, 329 N.W.2d 386 (1983).

State v. Collins, 132 Ariz. 180, 644 P.2d 1266 (1982).

State v. Hurd, 432 A.2d 86 (N.J. 1981).

State v. Mack, Minn., 292 N.W.2d 764 (1980).

State v. Mena, 128 Ariz. 226, 624 P.2d 1274 (1981).

United States v. Adams, 581 F.2d 193 (9th Cir. 1978).

United States v. Miller, 411 F.2d 825 (2nd Cir. 1969).

REFERENCES

Anonymous. (1996). Legal decision: Borawick v. Shay. *Cultic Studies Journal, 13*(1), 2–25.

Barber, T. X. (1965a). The effects of "hypnosis" on learning and recall. *Journal of Clinical Psychology, 21,* 19–25.

Barber, T. X. (1965b). Experimental analysis of "hypnotic" behavior: A review of recent empirical findings. *Journal of Abnormal Psychology, 70,* 132–154.

Barber, T. X. (1965c). Physiological effects of "hypnotic suggestions": A critical review of recent research (1960–1964). *Psychological Bulletin, 63,* 201–222.

Barber, T. X., & Calverly, D. S. (1966). Toward a theory of "hypnotic" behavior: Experimental analysis of suggested amnesia. *Journal of Abnormal Psychology, 71,* 95–107.

Beahrs, J. O. (1999). Posttraumatic polarization in psychiatry and law. *Journal of the American Academy of Psychiatry & the Law, 27*(2), 335–343.

Brandt, J., Rubinsky, E., & Lassen, G. (1985). Uncovering malingered amnesia. *Annals of the New York Academy of Sciences, 444,* 502–503.

Campbell, P. (1997). Admissibility and per se exclusion of hypnotically induced recall in American courts of law. *International Journal of Clinical and Experimental Hypnosis, 45*(3), 266–279.

Clemes, S. R. (1964). Repression and hypnotic amnesia. *Journal of Abnormal and Social Psychology, 69,* 62–69.

Coe, W. C. (1989). Posthypnotic amnesia: Theory and research. In N. P. Spanos & J. F. Chaves (Eds.), *Hypnosis: The cognitive-behavioral perspective* (pp. 110–148). Buffalo, NY: Prometheus.

Colwick, E. (1995). Hypnotically recalled testimony: Issues facing courts in their determination of its admissibility in civil sexual abuse cases. *Law & Psychology Review, 19,* 183–210.

Coons, P. M. (1991). Iatrogenic and malingering of multiple personality disorder in the forensic evaluation of homicide defendants. *Psychiatric Clinics in North America, 14*(3), 757–768.

Diamond, B. (1980). Inherent problems in the use of pre-trial hypnosis on a prospective witness. *California Law Review, 68,* 313.

Erickson, M. R. (1944). An experimental investigation of the hypnotic subject's apparent ability to become unaware of stimuli. *Journal of General Psychology, 31,* 191–212.

Feldman-Summers, S. (1996). Litigation pitfalls for the psychologist whose client "first remembers" childhood sexual abuse during therapy. *Women & Therapy, 19*(1), 109–122.

Giannelli, P. C. (1995). The admissibility of hypnotic evidence in U. S. Courts. *International Journal of Clinical & Experimental Hypnosis, 43*(2), 212–233.

Gibson, H. B. (1995). A further case of the misuse of hypnosis in a police investigation. *Contemporary Hypnosis, 12*(2), 81–86.

Gorten, B. E. (1949). The physiology of hypnosis. *Psychiatric Quarterly*, 317–343; 547–585.

Graham, E., & Kabacy, R. E. (1990). Expert testimony by psychologists: Novel scientific evidence. *Law & Psychology Review, 14*, 71–85.

Gravitz, M. A. (1995). First admission (1846) of hypnotic testimony in court. *American Journal of Clinical Hypnosis, 37*(4), 326–330.

Gravitz, M. A. (1997). Forensic hypnosis with children. *Australian Journal of Clinical & Experimental Hypnosis, 25*(2), 127–134.

Hall, H. V. (1969). *Hypnosis and memory: The comparable effects of various suggestions, procedures, and susceptibility variables.* Unpublished master's thesis, Brigham Young University, Provo, UT.

Hammer, E. F. (1954). Post-hypnotic suggestion and test performance. *Journal of Clinical and Experimental Hypnosis, 2*, 178–185.

Hilgard, E. R. (1965a). Hypnosis. In P. R. Farnsworth (Ed.), *Annual review of psychology.* Palo Alto, CA: Annual Review.

Kebbell, M. R., & Wagstaff, G. F. (1998). Hypnotic interviewing: The best way to interview eyewitnesses? *Behavioral Sciences & the Law, 16*(1), 115–129.

Kihlstrom, J. F. (1980). Posthypnotic amnesia for recently learned material: Interactions with "episodic" and "semantic" memory. *Cognitive Psychology, 12*, 227–251.

Kinnunen, T., Zamansky, H. S., & Block, M. (1994). Is the hypnotized subject lying? *Journal of Abnormal Psychology, 103*(2), 184–191.

Kirsch, I., & Baker, S. (1993). Clinical implications of expectancy research: Activating placebo effects without deception. *Contemporary Hypnosis, 10*(3), 130–132.

Kroger, W. S. (1963). *Clinical and experimental hypnosis in medicine, dentistry and psychology.* Philadelphia: Lippincott.

Lewis, D. O., & Bard, J. S. (1991). Multiple personality and forensic issues. *Psychiatric Clinics of North America, 14*(3), 741–756.

Lindsay, D. S. (1990). Misleading suggestions that can impair eyewitnesses' ability to remember event details. *Journal of Experimental Psychology: Learning, Memory, & Cognition, 16*(6), 1077–1083.

Miller, R. D., & Stava, L. J. (1997). Hypnosis and dissimulation. In R. Rogers (Ed.), *Clinical assessment of malingering and deception* (pp. 282–300). New York: Guilford Press.

Milne, G. (1992). Investigative hypnosis in clinic and court. *Australian Journal of Clinical & Experimental Hypnosis, 20*(2), 63–78.

Neal, D. E., Scott, E. M., & Grimsbo, R. A. (1993). A case report: Alcohol-induced blackouts during sexual intercourse: Legal responsibility? *International Journal of Offender Therapy & Comparative Criminology, 37*(4), 325–329.

Newman, A. W., & Thompson, J. W. (1999). Constitutional rights and hypnotically elicited testimony. *Journal of the American Academy of Psychiatry & the Law, 27*(1), 149–154.

Orne, M. T. (1979). The uses and misuses of hypnosis in court. *International Journal of Clinical and Experimental Hypnosis, 27*, 311–341.

Orne, M. T., Sheehan, P. W., & Evans, F. J. (1968). Occurrence of posthypnotic behavior outside the experimental setting. *Journal of Personality and Social Psychology, 9*, 189–196.

Parker, P. D., & Barber, T. X. (1964). Hypnosis, task motivating instructions, and learning performance. *Journal of Abnormal and Social Psychology, 69*, 499–504.

Perlini, A., Haley, A., & Buczel, A. (1998). Hypnosis and reporting biases: Telling the truth. *Journal of Research in Personality, 32*(1), 13–32.

Perry, C. (1997). Admissibility and per se exclusion of hypnotically elicited recall in American courts of law. *International Journal of Clinical & Experimental Hypnosis, 45*(3), 266–279.

Perry, C., Orne, M. T., London, R. W., & Orne, E. C. (1996). Rethinking per se exclusions of hypnotically elicited recall as legal testimony. *International Journal of Clinical and Experimental Hypnosis, 44*(1), 66–81.

Perugini, E. M., Kirsch, I., Allen, S. T., Coldwell, E., Meredith, J. M., Montgomery, G. H., & Sheehan, J. (1998). Surreptitious observation of responses to hypnotically suggested hallucinations: A test of compliance hypothesis. *International Journal of Clinical and Experimental Hypnosis, 46*(2), 191–203.

Py, J., & Fernandes, C. (1995). L'hypnose et l'entrerien cognitif: Deux techniques efficaces d'amelioration de la memoire des temoins [Hypnosis and the cognitive interview: Two effective techniques for improving eyewitness memory]. *Psychologie Francaise, 40*(3), 281–294.

Scott, H. D. (1930). Hypnosis and the conditioned reflex. *Journal of General Psychology, 4*, 113–130.

Scheflin, A. W. (1994). Forensic hypnosis: Unanswered questions. *Australian Journal of Clinical & Experimental Hypnosis, 22*(1), 25–37.

Scheflin, A. W. (1997). False memory and Buridan's ass: A response to Karlin and Orne. *Cultic Studies Journal, 14*(2), 207–289.

Sheehan, P. W., Statham, D., & Jamieson, G. A. (1991). Pseudomemory effects and their relationship to level of susceptibity to hypnosis and state instruction. *Journal of Personality and Social Psychology, 60*(1), 130–137.

Spanos, N. (1986). Hypnotic behavior: A social-psychological interpretation of amnesia, analgesia and trance logic. *Behavioral and Brain Sciences, 9*, 449–502.

Spanos, N. P., James, B., & de Groot, H. P. (1990). Detection of simulated hypnotic amnesia. *Journal of Abnormal Psychology, 99*(2), 179–182.

Spanos, N. P., Radtke, H. L., Bertrand, L. D., Addie, D. L., & Drummond, J. (1982). Disorganized recall, hypnotic amnesia, and subjects' faking: More discomfirmatory evidence. *Psychological Reports, 50*, 383–389.

Spanos, N. P., Quigley, C. A., Gwynn, M. I., Glatt, R. L., & Perlini, A. (1991). Hypnotic interrogation, pretrial preparation, and witness testimony during direct and cross-examination. *Law & Human Behavior, 15*(6), 639–653.

Spiegel, D., & Spiegel, H. (1984). Uses of hypnosis in evaluating malingering and deception. *Behavioral Sciences & the Law, 2*(1), 51–65.

Spiegel, D., & Spiegel, H. (1987). Forensic uses of hypnosis. In I. Weiner, & A. Hess (Eds.), *Handbook of Forensic Psychology* (pp. 490–507). New York: Wiley.

Stanley, R. O. (1994). The protection of professional use of hypnosis: The need for legal controls. *Australian Journal of Clinical & Experimental Hypnosis, 22*(1), 39–51.

Tayloe, D. R. (1995). The validity of repressed memories and the accuracy of their recall through hypnosis: A case study from the courtroom. *American Journal of Clinical Hypnosis, 37*(3), 25–31.

Thorne, D. E., & Hall, H. V. (1969). *Hypnosis and memory: The comparable effects of various suggestions, procedures and susceptibility variables.* Paper presented at a meeting of the International Conference on Hypnosis, Palo Alto, CA.

Udolf, R. (1990). Rock v. Arkansas: A critique. *International Journal of Clinical & Experimental Hypnosis, 38*(4), 239–249.

Vingoe, F. J. (1998). Facilitation of sexual pleasure via hypnosis: A case for the court. *Contemporary Hypnosis, 15*(2), 118–124.

Wagstaff, G. F. (1996). Should "hypnotized" witnesses be banned from testifying in court? Hypnosis and the M50 murder case. *Contemporary Hypnosis, 13*(3), 186–190.

Wakefield, H., & Ungerwager, R. (1992). Recovered memories of alleged sexual abuse: Lawsuits against parents. *Behavioral Sciences & the Law, 10*(4), 483–507.

Watkins, J. (1993). Dealing with the problem of "false memory" in clinic and court. *J. Psychiatry & Law, 21*(3), 297–317.

Weitzenhoffer, A. M. (1963). The nature of hypnosis: Part I. *American Journal of Clinical Hypnosis, 5*, 295–321.

Williamsen, J. A., Johnson, J. G., & Eriksen, C. W. (1965). Some characteristics of posthypnotic amnesia. *Journal of Abnormal Psychology, 70*, 123–131.

Worthington, T. S. (1979). The use in court of hypnotically enhanced testimony. *International Journal of Clinical and Experimental Hypnosis, 27*, 402–416.

17 Competency and Deception

The legal requirement of competence to stand trial is an extension of the general rule that no one should be tried for a crime in his or her absence. If a defendant must be physically present to defend against criminal charges, that defendant must also be "mentally present." Disorders that interfere with the psychological participation of a defendant at trial render that defendant incompetent to stand trial and require that the proceedings be postponed until effective participation can be assured.

Reviews of the forensic literature or clinical applications that discuss competence to proceed may be found in Blau (1984); Curran, McGarry, and Shah (1986); Ewing (1985); Gutheil and Appelbaum (1982); Melton, Petrila, Poythress, and Slobogin (1987); Shapiro (1984); Weiner and Hess (1987); and Ziskin and Faust (1988). Works devoted exclusively to competence to stand trial include those of Grisso (1986, 1988); McGarry (1973); and Roesch and Golding (1980). The issue of an accused/defendant's competency threads its way throughout adjudication. The legal definitions of competency are always specific, but clinical application and implications can vary with different populations (e.g., children, adolescents, older people, minorities, and non-English-speaking people). Poythress et al. (1998) investigated the competence-related abilities of women criminal defendants. The various judicial applications of competency have been reviewed by Kagehiro and Laufer (1992) and are outlined in Table 17.1.

There are also many nonjudicial situations where competency is a concern to clinicians. One example is with mentally disturbed patients consenting to treatment. Another example is research involving human subjects where there may be a question about the participant's ability to understand the purpose of participation and render informed consent. Redding (1997) and Appelbaum et al. (1999) described the particular problems involved in the competence of depressed patients to consent to research. Most jurisdictions use a variation of the rule to define competence to stand trial outlined by the U.S. Supreme Court in *Dusky v. United States* (1960). *Dusky* requires that defendants have the ability to (1) understand rationally and factually the legal proceedings and (2) cooperate with their attorney in their defense. A disorder that interferes with either of these capacities is sufficient to render a defendant incompetent to stand trial. However, incompetence to stand trial is not to be equated with the mere presence of mental illness (*Feuger v. U.S.*, 1961), of amnesia (*U.S. v. Adams*, 1969), or of a need for treatment (*U.S. v. Wilson*, 1966). As outlined in *Dusky*, the claimed disorder must be of the kind and severity that impairs the functional capacities.

Grisso (1998) reviewed the specific issues involved in the competency of juveniles to stand trial. The legally assumed age of children developmentally reaching a cognitive level where competency can be assumed remains variable across jurisdictions. Developmental psychologists describe children as achieving the age of reason and responsibility at some point during the 5-to-7-year shift (Sameroff & Haith, 1996). Developmental criteria, however, do not necessarily mesh with legal criteria (see Chapter 7). Grisso, Miller, and Sales (1987) proposed that competency of juveniles should be routinely questioned when any of the following conditions were met:

TABLE 17.1
**Applications of Competency in the
Legal Process**

1. Competency to confess and waive *Miranda* rights
2. Competency to plead guilty
3. Competency to stand trial
4. Competency to waive counsel
5. Competency to refuse an insanity defense
6. Competency to be sentenced
7. Competency to executed

Note: Adapted from *Handbook of Psychology and
Law,* by D. K. Kagehiro & W. S. Laufer, 1992, New
York: Springer-Verlag.

---

1. Age of 12 years or younger;
2. Prior diagnosis/treatment for a mental illness or mental retardation;
3. "Borderline level of intellectual functioning," or history of "learning disability";
4. Observations of others at pretrial proceedings suggest deficits of memory, attention, or interpretation of reality.

Many jurisdictions simply apply the criminal court *Dusky* standard in juvenile court proceedings. Many jurisdictions will assume, by precedent or statutory provision, competence between 10 and 12 years, but the topic of children's competence remains an area of controversy (Grisso, 1998).

Usually the question of competence to stand trial is raised by the defense attorney, who has the most frequent contact with the defendant and who has the professional and legal obligation to raise the question in appropriate cases. However, case law suggests that the question must be raised, even by the prosecution or the court itself, whenever a "bona fide doubt" exists regarding the defendant's capacity to mount a defense (see *Drope v. Missouri,* 1975; *Pate v. Robinson,* 1966). The question of a defendant's competence to proceed may be raised any time from the defendant's first appearance in court to the time of sentencing. The provisions of the Sixth Amendment do not guarantee a "meaningful relationship" between an accused and his counsel (*Morris v. Slappy,* 1982). The Constitution does require that the state provide access to a psychiatric evaluation if the sanity of the accused is likely to be a significant factor at the time of trial (*Ake v. Oklahoma,* 1984). The due process clause of the Constitution permits the state to require that a defendant claiming incompetence to stand trial bear the burden of proving so by a preponderance of the evidence (*Medina v. California,* 1989).

In actual practice, all participants in the criminal process are usually able to identify readily the majority of incompetent defendants. Actively psychotic, demented, and severely mentally retarded persons are usually recognized by arresting officers, jail personnel, or defense attorneys and transferred to treatment facilities prior to any court appearances. However, defendants charged with particularly notorious crimes and defendants who decompensate while awaiting trial often require professional evaluation before criminal proceedings are postponed. In addition, defense attorneys sometimes raise questions of competence to stand trial for their apparently competent clients in order to secure a court-ordered professional evaluation of the defendant, which would otherwise be unavailable. These evaluations may produce evidence relevant to an insanity plea, to the question of diminished capacity (not legally applicable in all jurisdictions), or to mitigating factors, which may be considered at the time of sentencing.

The majority of court-ordered referrals for evaluation of competence to stand trial are competent. The defendant usually readily admits that the evaluation was requested by the attorney, typically cooperates with all assessment tasks, and presents no claims of mental disorder. Everyone understands that the evaluation is really a "fishing expedition" for evidence on questions other than competence to stand trial.

The question of competence to stand trial involves three separate questions

1. Does the defendant have a genuine mental disorder sufficiently severe to justify a finding of incompetence (diagnosis)?
2. Is the defendant unable
   a. To understand rationally and factually the legal proceedings
   b. To assist counsel in defense (incapacity)?
3. Is this incapacity caused by the mental disorder (causation)?

The answers to these three questions lead to eight possible scenarios (Drob, Berger, & Weinstein, 1987), such as (1) a genuine mental disorder causes a defendant to be incapacitated and (2) a genuine mental disorder does not cause a defendant to be incapacitated.

Three of the eight possible causes pose special legal and/or clinical problems. The first involves defendants who have a genuine diagnosis that causes an insufficient incapacity to stand trial (e.g., circumscribed delusions about the "facts" of the alleged crime, but no impairment in trial capacity). The second involves defendants who have a genuine mental disorder whose impaired capacity to stand trial is due to fabrication or exaggeration (e.g., malingering in the context of a genuine disorder). The third involves defendants who have a genuine mental disorder and who are incapable of standing trial, but whose mental disorder is not severe enough to justify a finding of incompetence (e.g., a depressed defendant whose guilt over the alleged crime leads to disinterest or lack of cooperation in putting on a defense).

TARGETS OF DECEPTION

The frequency of faking incompetence to stand trial is unknown. Cornell and Hawk (1989) reported that 8% of 314 consecutive admissions to the Michigan Center for Forensic Psychiatry for pretrial evaluation were diagnosed by staff as malingering. These results suggest that malingering among criminal defendants may occur considerably less often than suggested by popular stereotypes — a suggestion also supported by the authors' experiences in the criminal justice system.

Virtually any target discussed in this book may be faked in an attempt to obtain a better judicial outcome. Two types of faking may be selected (Grisso, 1988): (1) those behaviors directed toward mental conditions and (2) those aimed at specific competency abilities. The targeting of mental conditions is illustrated as follows:

> Defendant Smith, a 28-year-old Caucasian male charged with several counts of bank robbery, presented with a florid psychosis upon evaluation. There was no history of mental problems but a confirmed history of prior arrests, including several for bank robbery. Validity scales on the MMPI and behavioral observations indicated a pronounced tendency to fake bad. During the evaluation, he appeared genuinely ignorant of the competency criteria in spite of his demonstrated understanding of legal proceedings and defense strategies. The accused stated his belief that a psychotic condition would render him incompetent to proceed.

Contrast this with the following case:

> Defendant Arder, a 45-year-old woman charged with the fatal shooting of her husband during a quarrel, exhibited a logical and coherent stream of thought during evaluation. She went over the instant offense in detail. No mental conditions were proffered except for a stress reaction due to the legal proceedings. Her attorney suggested to the court that her recollections of the instant offense were vague and consisted

only of her feelings at the time. Ms. Arder was found competent to proceed with the trial. Eventually, she successfully plea-bargained for manslaughter.

In response to the increased prevalence of certain types of crimes such as aggressive sexual attacks, illicit substance abuse, and repeated offenses, many jurisdictions have legislated mandatory severe sentencing dispositions. California is one such jurisdiction requiring mandatory 25-year sentences for three-time criminal defendants ("Three Strikes and You're Out" law). In response to the requirement, Jaffe and Sharma (1998) described a rash of defendants referred for competency evaluation who exhibited unusual psychiatric symptoms. The symptoms included coprophagia (feces eating), eating cockroaches, and seeing little green men. Of nine defendants evaluated by the investigators, eight were judged competent to stand trial. Kirkish and Sreenivasan (1999) addressed the problem when neurobehavioral symptoms are part of the defendant's justification for not meeting competency criteria.

Thus, targets of distortion can consist of deficits representing a mental condition or the specific ingredients of trial competence. Both approaches have met with success in obtaining long-range goals. With competency issues and especially with misdemeanor offenses, the courts traditionally bend over backward to give the accused "a break." This often results in a finding of incompetence with a recommendation for continued observation and treatment.

RESPONSE STYLES

HONESTY

Honest responding is the norm among defendants referred for evaluation of their competence to stand trial. The vast majority of defendants, even those with extensive criminal backgrounds, are cooperative with the evaluation and try to neither exaggerate nor minimize psychopathology. Many of these honest responders, especially those new to the criminal system, show signs of anxiety and depression. However, these symptoms are rarely so incapacitating that the defendant is found incompetent to stand trial. In addition, many criminal defendants — even those with prior experience in the courts — are ignorant of legal procedures and options (Grisso, 1988). This ignorance is not grounds for a finding of incompetence to stand trial, unless it is due to an incapacity to understand the proceedings when properly explained by the defense attorney.

FAKING GOOD

This style is seen when the defendant desires to go forward with the proceedings, but believes a mental deficit or condition may thwart that goal. It is relatively rare and occurs most frequently among paranoid defendants who are suspicious of the criminal proceedings and of defense counsel, and among defendants who are unaware of their deficits. Faking good is a prevalent problem in domestic cases where parents want to posture themselves in a favorable light with respect to their parenting abilities. These instances of "faking good" must be distinguished from the more common tendency of defendants to minimize or deny wrongdoing. Minimization of psychopathology is relevant to the question of competence to stand trial only when it interferes with the defendant's capacity to understand rationally and factually the criminal proceedings or to cooperate with defense counsel.

INVALIDATION

This response style occurs when an accused tries to invalidate either the entire evaluation or a particular evaluation procedure. It may occur when the subject simply wishes to render the evaluation meaningless or inconclusive. The most common example of invalidation is uncooperativeness.

When a defendant refuses to be interviewed or refuses to be tested, the examiner is left wondering whether the refusal signifies intent to distort the evaluation or an underlying incapacity. Is the lack of cooperation due to fear of being detected as "faking bad" or is it a symptom of genuine paranoia and delusional thinking?

One defendant accused of murdering a female acquaintance and her mother with a machete refused to come out of his hospital room for evaluation and refused to be interviewed about the alleged offense. Although he initially agreed to complete a self-report measure of psychopathology, he consistently failed to answer the questions. His responses to interview questions that did not involve the alleged crime were all coherent and generally rational. Review of an interrogation by police shortly after his arrest, and a social history given by his parents, revealed a long history of paranoid schizophrenia and a delusional justification for the killings. When the evaluator advised the defendant that the court would be informed of his incompetence to stand trial, the defendant unleashed a torrent of psychotic and delusional threats against the examiner. In such cases the evaluator can only rely on historical records, personal observations, and the observations of others to discern the meaning of the uncooperativeness. If such methods are unavailable or are inconclusive, the defendant must be presumed to be competent to stand trial and returned to court as uncooperative.

MIXED STYLES

Mixed styles involve elements of "faking good," "faking bad," "honest responding," and/or "invalidation" in the same evaluation. Certain test patterns may suggest a tendency to exaggerate, while interviews suggest honest responding. Historical records may reveal past problems, which are denied or minimized by the defendant during interviews. A defendant may initially be cooperative with the examiner, only to refuse further participation later in the evaluation. In general, the interpretation of these mixed signals is made easier if the examiner distinguishes between the defendant's capacity and the defendant's willingness. In spite of exaggeration, minimization, or uncooperativeness, is the defendant capable of understanding the legal proceedings and capable of cooperating with defense counsel?

FLUCTUATING STYLES

Fluctuating response styles are most frequently seen when the defendant's goals change, but can also be a sign of mental illness. The accused may, for example, fake bad to gain a trial delay, but then switch to honesty, or even faking good, to have the trial proceed. In one case, a defendant who presented a mixed picture of competence to proceed was told that he would be kept at the hospital for treatment and was moved onto a ward with actively psychotic patients. Before the first day was finished, he begged to be sent back to court and acknowledged that he had not been honest during the evaluation.

CULTURAL CONTAMINANTS

The continued influx of non-English-speaking immigrants to the United States can present as a significant problem in competency assessments. Johnson and Torres (1992) described an evaluation approach in the assessment of two criminal competencies with Hispanic immigrant defendants, neither of whom spoke English. There is a similar but somewhat more complicated problem with immigrants from third-world countries where educational backgrounds can be weak or absent regardless of ability to speak English. Many major metropolitan areas have ethnic minority catchment areas. There are two problems presented by these minority groups in terms of competency assessments. The first is the typical unavailability of qualified forensic clinicians within minority populations. The second and more formidable problem is the general legal assumption that immigrants have the civil and legal responsibility to acclimate themselves to the prevailing legal standards and conform to those standards.

With juveniles and domestic matters, the authors have encountered heartrending situations wherein otherwise law-abiding individuals become caught up in legal quandaries that are the result of conflicts between Westernized values and traditional cultural mores. Likewise, there are situations of immigrants presenting with unintended misunderstanding or ignorance of the law. The adversarial process typically addresses such matters with less than a humanistic approach. The problem is somewhat comparable to the judiciary's long-standing difficulty in adequately coping with mentally ill defendants, but the authors acknowledge that the problems with the two populations are inherently different. A fundamental guideline for forensic practitioners is always to refer to the most competent available resources. Short of that, practitioners must make every effort to work collaboratively with resources that may assist in the most meaningful assessment when cultural issues are a factor. Consider the following case example:

> One of the authors evaluated an African family that had temporarily immigrated to the United States less than a year earlier. The father had been appointed to an Assistant Ambassador position with a local embassy. The parents were native to very rural areas and had minimal formal education. Both had poor to fair spoken English skills. There were three children ranging from 3 to 8 years of age. The 8-year-old was a girl who immediately began attending a local public school upon the family's arrival stateside. Within 6 weeks of beginning school, a report of possible physical abuse was made to authorities regarding the 8-year-old, and during the initial investigation, concerns were raised about the other two children as well.
>
> Competency evaluations of both parents were court-ordered at the request of their attorney who observed the limitations of the parents because of their cultural and language backgrounds. The attorney questioned the parents' abilities to understand the nature of the charges, and their ability to assist in their own defense adequately.
>
> The basis of the abuse charges was barely visible, but still evident — markings on the older child's arms and legs. Subsequent physical examination revealed that the markings covered the child's torso as well. The suspicion was that the child had been physically abused by being beaten with a cordlike instrument or perhaps a piece of botanical cane. The evaluation team by necessity made use of an interpreter who spoke the rare dialect of the parents' native language. The extremely distressed parents appeared to care deeply for the children; they excitedly attributed the markings to some type of ritual involving animals. The interpreter was perplexed and hours of questioning proved indecisive. The children adamantly denied any abusive circumstances and presented as clearly regarding the parents with the utmost fondness.
>
> By happenstance, the interpreter was aware of a person who was from the same South African village; the countryman was a curator with a local museum that had an elaborate exhibit on African cultural artifacts. A visit by the forensic team with the curator at the museum proved very productive. The curator explained that the parents' village had a tribal custom of instilling tribe-characteristic markings on latency-aged children as a prepubescent ritual. The custom took place in the context of a large village ceremony, with as many as 20 to 30 girl inductees; the ceremony was a joyous and festive occasion. The village girls who were of age were softly pummeled with desiccated animal hooves to make characteristic markings essentially all over their bodies.
>
> The curator noted that depending on the child's skin texture and complexion, and no doubt the skill of the person applying the hooves, the marking were, more or less, visible later. Eventually, it was determined that the mother and her four sisters had all undergone the ritual when they were younger and also that the tribal practice had been discontinued approximately 3 to 4 years earlier because of outsider complaints. The findings were presented to the court and the abuse charges were dropped eliminating the issue of the parents' competency to stand trial. This outcome took some 14 months to achieve with the family undergoing considerable turmoil and distress in the interim. Part of that distress was a nearly successful effort to send the father and family back home without compensation, and with the probability of the father being disenfranchised from his government in terms of employability or benefits.

DETECTION METHODS

Any of the methods presented elsewhere in this book may be used for the detection of distorted competence skills. In terms of faked mental conditions or deficits, the following are relevant (with sources for the detection methods listed in the right-hand column):

Syndromes/Symptoms	Chapters
1. Primary disturbance of thought	20, 21
2. Primary disturbance of communication	11, 20
3. Secondary disturbance of communication	11, 20, 21
4. Delusional processes	11, 20
5. Hallucinations	21
6. Unmanageable or disturbing behavior	7, 8, 23
7. Affective disturbances	12, 13, 23
8. Disturbances of consciousness/orientation	11, 12, 13, 19
9. Disturbances of memory/amnesia	19
10. Severe mental retardation	11,
11. General impairment of judgment/insight	6, 18
12. Chronological age	7, 8, 9

A defendant may choose to distort specific trial competencies rather than gross psychopathology. These competencies include the capacity to

1. Know the exact charges,
2. Disclose elements of the instant offense(s),
3. Understand the roles of the court actors,
4. Know the nature and process of the court proceedings,
5. Appreciate the possible consequences of the various legal options,
6. Cooperate with one's attorney, and
7. Present oneself appropriately in court.

The examiner must be prepared to probe each of these areas within a comprehensive evaluation.

Over the course of the past two decades there have been approximately 200 studies addressing competency to stand trial (Ustad, Rogers, Sewell, & Guarnaccia, 1996). A primary interest in this research has been the development of forensic assessment instruments. These instruments have included the Georgia Court Competency Test (GCCT; Wildman et al., 1978); the Georgia Court Competency Test–Mississippi Version Revised (GCCT-MSH, see Ustad et al., 1996); the Competency Assessment Instrument (CAI; Grisso, 1986, 1988); the Interdisciplinary Fitness Interview (IFI; Golding, Roesch, & Schreiber, 1984); and the Competency Screening Test (CST; Lipsitt, Lelos, & McGarry, 1971; McGarry, 1973).

Ongoing validation investigations with these traditional instruments have produced mixed findings and unending adjustment of cutoff scores to accommodate different conditions. The GCCT was used to predict competency in a trial setting in which the ratio of competent to incompetent defendants ($N = 100$) was the same (Wildman, White, & Brandenburg, 1990). The data showed that the GCCT contributed to the prediction of competency better than predictors based on base rates alone. In a factor analysis study comparing several competency instruments with a large outpatient sample of court referrals ($N = 353$), only the GCCT-MSH showed stable independent factors (Bagby, Nicholson, Rogers, & Nussbaum, 1992). Gothard, Rogers, and Sewell (1995) described optimal cutoff scores with the GCCT to screen for defendants feigning incompetence. In a related study, the GCCT-MSH was compared with the SIRS in detecting simulated malingering and suspected malingerers compared with controls. The SIRS had an overall hit rate of 97.8% using three or more primary scales as the criteria for malingering (Gothard, Viglione, Moloy, &

TABLE 17.2
Research Perspectives with the MacSAC-CD and the MacCAT-T

Research Thrust	Instrument	Study
Competence of criminal defendants with and without mental disorder	MacSAC-CD	Bonnie et al. (1997)
Competence of depressed patients for consent to research	MacCAT-T	Applebaum et al. (1999)
Competence-related abilities of women criminal defendants	MacSAC-CD	Poythress et al. (1998)
Depression in jailed women defendants and its relationship to adjudicative competence	MacSAC-CD	Redding (1997)
Effects of state organizational structure and forensic examiner training on pretrial competence assessments	MacSAC-CD	Edens et al. (1999)
Efficacy of specialized forensic assessments	MacSAC-CD	Cruise & Rogers (1998)
Competence to make treatment decisions of matched groups of hospitalized and nonhospitalized patients with schizophrenic or schizoaffective disorder diagnoses	MacCAT-T	Grisso, Applebaum, & Hill-Fotouhi (1997)
Initial MacCAT-T validation study with psychiatric inpatients	MacCAT-T	Grisso et al. (1995)
Initial MacSAC-CD validation study to distinguish competent from incompetent defendants	MacSAC-CD	Hoge et al. (1997)

Sherman, 1995). The GCCT was found to best predict incompetence when defendants carried a diagnosis of psychotic disorder, or a nonpsychotic affective disorder, as well as a measured low IQ. Prior to the introduction of the MacArthur Structured Assessment of the Competencies of Criminal Defendants (MacSAC-CD), the most widely researched instrument was the CAI (Ustad et al., 1997).

Following an 8-year study, the MacSAC-CD was introduced in 1997 (Hoge et al., 1997; Otto et al., 1998). Initial validation studies reflected the MacSAC-CD to meet or exceed accepted indices of consistency and interscorer reliability. The instrument has been touted to distinguish competent from incompetent defendants, to reflect changes in competency status, and to correlate negligibly with scorer cynicism toward the justice system. The MacSAC-CD has received considerable attention since its introduction. It was derived based on face validity considerations for use with legal contexts, psychometric analyses, and input from mental health experts. It was initially validated in an NIMH-sponsored study investigating its psychometric properties (Otto et al., 1998). Notwithstanding criticism of some of the working assumptions of the basic study (Slobogin, 1996), there has been scholarly commentary of the basic social science research effort (Winick, 1996). Table 17.2 depicts the variety of recent research perspectives that have incorporated the MacSAC-CD.

A sister instrument to the MacSAC-CD is the MacArthur Competence Assessment Tool for Treatment (MacCAT-T; Grisso & Appelbaum, 1998). The MacCAT-T is a semistructured interview designed to assist clinicians who are assessing patients' competencies to consent to treatment. It was designed to assess abilities conceptually related to four legal standards for competence to consent to treatment: understanding, appreciation, reasoning, and expression of choice (Grisso, Appelbaum, Mulvey, & Fletcher, 1995). Patients' capacities in four areas are examined by the MacCAT-T: (1) understanding information relevant to their condition, (2) understanding the recommended treatment, (3) reasoning about the potential risks and benefits of their choices, and (4) expressing a choice (Grisso, Appelbaum, & Hill-Fotouhi, 1997).

The MacCAT-T may eventually prove useful in assessing restoration to competency, an issue that has largely been ignored in the research (Ustad et al., 1996). Another use of the MacCAT-T will be with defendants suspected of malingering who are maintained for evaluation in inpatient settings. The instrument will provide an ongoing log of clinical symptoms and lapses or changes in symptoms that are not characteristic of expected clinical course. Roesch, Hart, and Zapf (1996) used the MacArthur Treatment Competence Study model as a framework to analyze the similarities and differences between American and Canadian laws regarding competency to stand trial. The authors noted that the MacArthur model offered an explanatory linkage between psycholegal concepts and forensic assessment procedures.

CONCLUSORY COMMENTS

In a study assessing the reliability of clinical opinions in competency assessments, Rosenfeld and Ritchie (1998) found that misdemeanor defendants were more likely to be found incompetent compared with defendants with more serious offenses. Overall, however, there was a high degree of reliability in clinical determinations of competence. The investigators found that conducting competency assessments jointly increased concordance of competence opinions. In conducting competency assessments, a high index of suspicion should always be engendered with defendants claiming incompetence, but who have no prior history of psychiatric hospitalization or documented complaints of mental health problems (Kucharski, Ryan, Vogt, & Goodloe, 1998). Understanding local system organization and political structures as well as clinician training is a critical variable in conducting valid competency evaluations (Edens, Poythress, Nicholson, & Otto, 1999). Forensic evaluators should utilize validated and current instrument methods within a broadbanded assessment approach, which includes assessment of present psychopathology and response styles. Preparation of reports should involve thoughtful and empirically grounded formulation of ultimate opinions regarding competence as well as malingering/deception dynamics.

LEGAL REFERENCES

Ake v. Oklahoma, 470 U.S. 68 (1984).
Daubert v. Merrell Dow Pharmaceuticals, Inc. 509 U.S. 579 (1993).
Drope v. Missouri, 420 U.S. 162 (1975).
Dusky v. United States, 362 U.S. 402 (1960).
Estelle v. Smith, 451 U.S. 454 (1981).
Feuger v. U.S., 302 F.2d 214 (1961).
Jackson v. Indiana, 406 U.S. 715 (1972).
Lyles v. U.S., 254 F.2d 725 (1957).
Medina v. California, 505 U.S. 437 (1989).
Morris v. Slappy, 461 U.S. 1 (1982).
Pate v. Robinson, 383 U.S. 375 (1966).
U.S. v. Adams, 297 F. Supp. 596 (1969).
U.S. v. Wilson, 391 F.2d 460 (1966).

REFERENCES

Appelbaum, P. S., Grisso, T., Frank, E., O'Donnell, S., & Kupfer, D. J. (1999). Competence of depressed patients for consent to research. *American Journal of Psychiatry, 156*(9), 1380–1384.
Bagby, R. M., Nicholson, R. A., Rogers, R., & Nussbaum, D. (1992). Domains of competency to stand trial: A factor analytic study. *Law & Human Behavior, 16*(5), 491–507.
Blau, T. (1984). *The psychologist as expert witness.* New York: Wiley.
Bonnie, R. J., Hoge, S. K., Monahan, J., Poythress, N., Eisenberg, M., & Feucht-Havier, T. (1997). The MacArthur Adjudicative Competence Study: A comparison of criteria for assessing the competence of criminal defendants. *Journal of the Academy of Psychiatry & the Law, 25*(3), 249–259.
Cornell, D., & Hawk, G. (1989). Clinical presentation of malingerers diagnosed by experienced forensic psychologists. *Law and Human Behavior, 13*, 4, 375–383.
Cruise, K. R., & Rogers, R. (1998). An analysis of competency to stand trial: An integration of case law and clinical knowledge. *Behavioral Sciences & the Law, 16*(1), 35–50.

Curran, W., McGarry, A., & Shah, S. (Eds.). (1986). *Forensic psychiatry and psychology: Perspectives and standards for interdisciplinary practice*. Philadelphia: F. A. Davis.

Drob, S., Berger, R., & Weinstein, H. (1987). Competency to stand trial: a conceptual model for its proper assessment. *Bulletin of the American Academy of Psychiatry and Law, 15*, 1, 85–94.

Edens, J. F., Poythress, N. G., Nicholson, R. A., & Otto, R. (1999). Effects of state organizational structure and forensic examiner training on pretrial competence assessments. *Journal of Behavioral Health Services & Research, 26*(2), 140–150.

Ewing, C. (Ed.). (1985). *Psychology, psychiatry, and the law: A clinical and forensic handbook*. Sarasota, FL: Professional Resource Exchange.

Golding, S., Roesch, R., & Schreiber, J. (1984). Assessment and conceptualization of competency to stand trial: Preliminary data on the interdisciplinary fitness interview. *Law and Human Behavior, 9*, 321–334.

Gothard, S., Rogers, R., & Sewell, K. W. (1995). Feigning incompetence to stand trial: An investigation of the Georgia Court Competency Test. *Law & Human Behavior, 19*(4), 363–373.

Gothard, S., Viglione, D. J., Meloy, J. R., & Sherman, M. (1995). Detection of malingering in competency to stand trial evaluations. *Law & Human Behavior, 19*(5), 493–505.

Grisso, T. (1986). *Evaluating competencies: Forensic assessments and instruments*. New York: Plenum.

Grisso, T. (1988). *Competency to stand trial: Evaluations*. Sarasota, FL: Professional Resource Exchange.

Grisso, T. (1998). *Forensic Evaluation of Juveniles*. Sarasota, FL: Professional Resource Press.

Grisso, T., & Appelbaum, P. S. (1998). *MacArthur Competence Assessment Tool for Treatment (MacCAT-T) Manual*. Sarasota, FL: Professional Resource Press/Professional Resource Exchange.

Grisso, T., Applebaum, P. S., & Hill-Fotouhi, C. (1997). The MacCAT-T: A clinical tool to assess patients' capacities to make treatment decisions. *Psychiatric Services, 48*(11), 1415–1419.

Grisso, T., Appelbaum, P. S., Mulvey, E. P., & Fletcher, K. (1995). The MacArthur Treatment Competence Study: II. Measures of abilities of competence to consent to treatment. *Law & Human Behavior, 192*(127–148).

Grisso, T., Miller, M., & Sales, B. (1987). Competency to stand trial in juvenile court. *International Journal of Psychiatry & the Law, 10*, 1–20.

Gutheil, T., & Appelbaum, P. (1982). *Clinical handbook of psychiatry and the law*. New York: McGraw-Hill.

Hoge, S. K., Bonnie, R. J., Poythress, N., Monahan, J., Eisenberg, M., & Feucht-Havier, T. (1997). The MacArthur adjudicative competency study: Development and validation of a research instrument. *Law & Human Behavior, 21*(2), 141–179.

Jaffe, M. E., & Sharma, K. K. (1998). Malingering uncommon psychiatric symptoms among defendants charged under California's "Three Strikes and You're Out" law. *Journal of Forensic Sciences, 43*(3), 549–555.

Johnson, M. B., & Torres, L. (1992). Miranda, trial competency and Hispanic immigrant defendants. *American Journal of Forensic Psychology, 10*(4), 65–80.

Kagehiro, D. K., & Laufer, W. S. (1992). *Handbook of psychology and law*. New York: Springer-Verlag.

Kirkish, P., & Sreenivasan, S. (1999). Neuropsychological assessment of competency to stand trial evaluations: A practical conceptual model. *Journal of the American Academy of Psychiatry & the Law, 27*(1), 101–113.

Kucharski, L. T., Ryan, W., Vogt, J., & Goodloe, E. (1998). Clinical symptom presentation in suspected malingerers: An empirical investigation. *Journal of the American Academy of Psychiatry & the Law, 26*(4), 579–585.

Lipsitt, P. D., Lelos, D., & McGarry, A. L. (1971). Competency to stand trial: A screening instrument. *American Journal of Psychiatry, 128*, 105–109.

McGarry, A. (1973). *Competency to stand trial and mental illness* (DHEW Publication No. ADM. 77-103). Rockville, MD: Department of Health, Education and Welfare.

Melton, G., Petrila, R., Poythress, N., & Slobogin, C. (1987). *Psychological evaluations for the courts: A handbook for mental health professionals and lawyers*. New York: Guilford.

Otto, R., Poythress, N. G., Nicholson, R. A., Edens, J. F., Monahan, J., Bonnie, R. J., Hoge, S. K., & Eisenberg, M. (1998). Psychometric properties of the MacArthur Competence Assessment Tool–Criminal Adjudication. *Psychological Assessment, 10*(4), 435–443.

Poythress, N. G., Hoge, S. K., Bonnie, R. J., Monahan, J., Eisenberg, M., & Feucht-Havier, T. (1998). The competence-related abilities of women criminal defendants. *Journal of the American Academy of Psychiatry & the Law, 26*(2), 215–222.

Redding, R. E. (1997). Depression in jailed women defendants and its relationship to their adjudicative competence. *Journal of the American Academy of Psychiatry & the Law, 25*(1), 105–119.

Roesch, R., & Golding, S. (1980). *Competency to stand trial.* Urbana-Champaign, IL: University of Illinois Press.

Roesch, R., Hart, S. D., & Zapf, P. A. (1996). Conceptualizing and assessing competency to stand trial: Implications and applications of the MacArthur Treatment Competence Model. *Psychology, Public Policy, & Law, 2*(1), 96–113.

Rosenfeld, B., & Ritchie, K. (1998). Competence to stand trial. *Journal of Forensic Science, 43*(1), 151–157.

Sameroff, A. J., & Haith, M. M., (Eds.). (1996). *The five to seven year shift: The age of reason and responsibility.* Chicago, IL: The University of Chicago Press.

Shapiro, D. (1984). *Psychological evaluation and expert testimony.* New York: Van Nostrand Reinhold.

Slobogin, C. (1996). "Appreciation" as a measure of competency: Some thoughts about the MacArthur Group's approach. *Psychology, Public Policy, & Law, 2*(1), 18–30.

Ustad, K. L., Rogers, R., Sewell, K. W., & Guarnaccia, C. A. (1996). Restoration of competency to stand trial: Assessment with the Georgia Court Competency Test. *Law & Human Behavior, 20*(2), 131–146.

Weiner, I., & Hess, A. (1987). *Handbook of forensic psychology.* New York: Wiley.

Wildman, R. W., Batchelor, E. S., Thompson, L., Nelson, F. R., Moore, J. T., Patterson, M. E., & de Lasoa, M. (1978). *The Georgia Court Competency Test: An attempt to develop a rapid, quantitative measure of fitness for trial.* Unpublished manuscript, Forensic Services Division Central State Hospital, Milledgeville, GA.

Wildman, R. W., White P. A., & Brandenburg. C. E. (1990). The Georgia Court Competency Test: The base rate problem. *Perceptual & Motor Skills, 70*(3, Pt 1), 1055–1058.

Winick, B. J. (1996). Foreword: A summary of the MacArthur Treatment Competence Study and an introduction to a special theme. *Psychology, Public Policy, & Law, 2*(1), 3–17.

Ziskin, J., & Faust, D. (1988). *Coping with psychiatric and psychological testimony* (4th. ed.). Los Angeles: Law and Psychology Press.

18 Criminal Responsibility and Deception

In contrast to the abundance of reports in the literature regarding adjudicative competency, there is a lack of corresponding studies regarding the assessment of criminal responsibility (Borum & Otto, 2000). This is because criminal responsibility assessment is generally a far more involved process than assessment of competency. The suggestion here is not that there are substantive differences of adjudicative importance between competency and criminal responsibility assessment, but rather that competency assessment is generally more straightforward in comparison with criminal responsibility assessment. Competency assessments are also generally less involved in terms of deception detection. These salient differences based on the authors' experiences are outlined in Table 18.1.

Most readers of this book will have a grasp of the all-important history of the insanity defense (for historical reviews, see Shapiro, 1999; Slovenko, 1973). The insanity defense has undergone substantial changes in recent years. Based on the mistaken arguments that the insanity defense is easily "faked" and that many guilty criminals are unjustly spared from punishment by use of the insanity defense, several state legislatures have abolished the defense. Other states and the U.S. Congress have severely curtailed their definitions of legal insanity, and still others have introduced an alternate verdict ("Guilty but Mentally Ill") in hopes of persuading courts to find fewer defendants legally insane.

Among those jurisdictions that retain the insanity defense, there are varying definitions of legal insanity. Some jurisdictions will excuse criminal behavior if it is the product of a mental disorder; others require that the perpetrator, at the time of the offense, was so mentally impaired that he or she could not appreciate the criminality of the conduct or could not conform the conduct to the requirements of law; a few require that the accused could not tell the difference between right and wrong in regard to the criminal act. At least one states that a person's criminal behavior will be excused only if it was the result of a "delusional compulsion" which overpowered the will of the perpetrator.

Shapiro (1999) summarized the impact of the Insanity Defense Reform Act of 1984, which followed the furor over the not-guilty-by-reason-of-insanity defense of John Hinckley in 1982. A year earlier, Mr. Hinckley had attempted to assassinate President Reagan. The Act is the requirement in federal courts and has also been incorporated into the statutory codes of several states. The Act essentially removes the volitional prong (i.e., the lack of substantial capacity to conform one's behavior to the law) of the ALI Model Penal Code (ALI), leaving intact only the cognitive prong (i.e., appreciation of the wrongfulness of one's behavior).

This chapter focuses on distortions during evaluations of criminal responsibility rather than on the insanity defense per se. Specific techniques for evaluating deception are described throughout this book. In this chapter, the fundamental importance of self-control and choice at the time of the instant offense is highlighted. Demonstrating self-regulation — if it exists during the alleged offense — has three important by-products:

TABLE 18.1

Assessment Differences between Competency and Criminal Responsibility

Function	Assessment Type	
	Competency	Criminal Responsibility
Temporal concern	Current level of functioning	Level of functioning, prior to and at the time of the alleged offense
Background database	Prior records helpful and desirable	Access to all prior records critical
Offense circumstances	Not necessarily directly relevant	Constitutes critical information in terms of defendant behavior at the time of offense
Deception potential	Possible to likely	Likely to very high
Probability of deception contaminants (i.e., collusion of others, coaching, researching symptoms)	Low, if defendant is evaluated close to time of arrest; after that, possibilities increase dramatically	High
Probability of deception detection	Reasonably good	Can be very complicated and difficult
Need for appropriate psychometrics	Desirable	Very important and often essential
Multidisciplinary assessment	Desirable	Very important
Need for collaborative contact(s)	Minimal	Extremely important
Evaluation time	Generally 1 to 2 hours	Varies with case and can range from a few to hundreds of clinician hours

1. The defendant's mental condition is clarified in terms of severity (hence its impact on responsibility for the crime).
2. Self-reports by the defendant become less relevant than the abilities and skills evidenced by the defendant during the commission of the crime.
3. The impact of information about self-control on the trier of fact is maximal, since judges and juries typically respond favorably to a description of the defendant's acts which are behaviorally anchored and cross-validated.

PREVIOUS ATTEMPTS TO STANDARDIZE CRIMINAL RESPONSIBILITY EVALUATIONS AND MALINGERING

Various forensic investigators have attempted to standardize criminal responsibility evaluations. Rogers and his colleagues analyzed malingering along the decision path of the evaluator (Rogers, 1984; Rogers & Cavanaugh, 1981; Rogers, Seman, & Wasyliw, 1983). In offering the Rogers Criminal Responsibility Assessment Scales (RCRAS), Rogers (1984) stated the following in the test manual:

> Malingering. The authenticity of the symptoms, presented by the patient-defendant in the retrospective account of the time of the crime, forms a necessary prerequisite to subsequent psycholegal decisions. Although rare, the forensic examiner must consider the possibility that the patient-defendant is both malingering and had a bona fide mental disorder at the time of the crime. (p. 24)

The RCRAS asks the examiner to judge the severity of malingering on the RCRAS five-part Likert scale:

> Reliability of patient's self-report under his/her voluntary control.

> (0) No information.
> (1) Highly reliable self-report; examiner is impressed by the patient's openness and honesty which may include volunteering potentially self-damaging information.

(2) Reliable self-report; the patient reports in a factual, sincere manner. He/she may not volunteer potentially self-damaging information and may gloss over a few incidental details.

(3) Self-report with limited reliability; the patient answers most of the questions with a fair degree of accuracy (volunteers little or nothing and distorts or evades a few specific areas).

(4) Self-report without reliability; the patient, through guardedness, exaggeration or denial of symptoms, convinces the examiner that his/her responses are inaccurate. There may be suspected malingering.

(5) Definite malingering. (p. 24)

The evaluator is then asked to integrate the reliability of self-reports with other information and to compare the total information with the applicable legal definition of insanity. As an illustration, the RCRAS sequentially analyzes (1) malingering, (2) organicity, (3) mental disorder(s), (4) loss of cognitive control, (5) loss of behavioral control, (6) whether the loss of cognitive and/or behavioral control resulted directly from organicity or from a mental disorder, and (7) conclusions regarding "insanity" using the American Law Institute (ALI) and *M'Naughton* definitions of insanity.

Decisions using RCRAS have shown high agreement with actual court outcomes (Rogers, 1984). Rogers's system is databased, is flexible in terms of definition of insanity, and represents a clear advancement in assessment of criminal responsibility. It is therefore puzzling that the RCRAS has received mixed reviews in the courtroom.

Possible reasons for the lack of acceptance include the reluctance of criminal courts to have anyone but themselves define *insanity* (in accordance with the relevant statutes). Moreover, there is a general judicial resistance to accepting criterion-based or statistical approaches in favor of the qualitative analysis of each criminal case (Hall, 1982, 1985, 1987). There is also reluctance by clinicians to embrace actuarial prediction technology even though the accuracy of existing assessment tools improves predictive ability well beyond chance (Steadman et al., 2000)

The RCRAS is confined to malingering (faking bad). Yet, other response styles need also be considered, as this book discusses. The RCRAS procedure considers malingering as preclusion to criminal responsibility. Even though there is a provision in the RCRAS for mentally ill defendants who malinger, many evaluators may not seriously consider that defendants who blatantly malinger can still be genuinely mentally ill. In the authors' experience, and in the literature cited elsewhere in this book, the most disturbed defendants are sometimes the ones most likely to malinger. Generation of false negatives (i.e., those falsely considered to be sane or responsible) is a possible outcome of the RCRAS and needs to be researched.

A RECOMMENDED PROCESS APPROACH TO CRIMINAL RESPONSIBILITY

A heuristic model for criminal responsibility evaluations is presented by Hall (1985, 1987). This involves the sequential and post hoc analysis of the following:

1. Forensic database,
2. Type of distortion and/or deception shown by the accused,
3. Defendant's reconstruction of the instant offense,
4. Long-term (i.e., historical) vs. instant crime behavior,
5. Mental disorder of the accused in terms of whether it is causally connected to the instant offense and sufficiently severe,
6. Self-determination and choice of crime-related behaviors, and
7. Conclusions regarding criminal responsibility.

Step 1: Adequate Forensic Database

The first step involves the creation of a reliable and valid database, multisourced and interdisciplinary in nature, that forms the basis for all opinions regarding criminal responsibility. The content of the database is provided by looking at the perpetrator, victim, and context of the crime and other data relevant to the accused's current and past circumstances.

The most important part of the forensic analysis may be the database upon which the conclusions rely. Criteria for including data in the database are that they are multisourced, interdisciplinary, and based on information drawn from sources other than the client for purposes of cross-validation. Criteria for excluding data from the database include bias, unreliability, and intentional distortion (Hall, 1985, 1987). It is especially important to gather data from sources the defendant wishes to conceal, because of the likelihood of finding unfavorable information (e.g., juvenile records, so-called "expunged" records that may be available in unmodified form at government archives centers, interviews with ex-spouses and mates, military performance reports, information from other states or countries). It is helpful, for the credibility of the examiner, to base the forensic evaluation on as many database sources as possible.

A strong note of caution needs to be sounded regarding use of an interview with the defendant as the principal source of data. Empirical research indicates that the clinical interview is so poor that forensic examiners are frequently unable to repeat their own performances. In this regard, Ziskin (1995) noted the unreliability of the clinical interview and the clinical examination. Ziskin summarized:

> The point can be emphasized that *unless and until adequate methods are provided to control for variation due to examiner and situational effects, the data of the clinical examination are virtually worthless*. It is not necessary to establish that data are always invalid. It is possible that there may be some cases where data obtained are valid. They are virtually worthless, however, because *there is no way of knowing which one has valid data and when one has data that are the product of situation or examiner influence*. (p. 370)

STEP 2: ANALYSIS OF DISTORTION AND DECEPTION

The next step in the decision process consists of ruling out or accounting for nondeliberate distortion within (1) the reporting person and (2) the reported event. Nondeliberate distortion due to anxiety, fatigue, or other factors may largely explain both evaluation and crime behavior and is therefore considered first.

Deliberate distortion, the next step in the evaluation process, should be ruled in by a positive and replicable demonstration of misrepresentation. Deliberate distortion may be shown by the examiner, the client, and all cross-validating sources. Examiners can and do deliberately distort for various reasons. The authors know of some forensic examiners who appear to thrive on the drama and publicity of court work and whose judgment and decisions are clearly influenced by a personal desire to "stir up controversy." It is not inappropriate to look at the evaluator's track record for particular types of forensic assessments (e.g., percentage of time for which he or she testifies for the defense vs. for the prosecution), rate of court agreement with rendered opinions, and whether or not proffered findings can be replicated by equally competent examiners.

The evaluation of the defendant's self-reports should be scrutinized for misrepresentation by examining third-party reports and material evidence of the crime. Psychometric testing is very appropriate for assessing distortion in victims and other parties. Data derived from the input of significant or knowledgeable others, which indicate bias or a given motivational set (e.g., desire for revenge, to rejoin defendant), should be excluded from the data pool or placed into proper perspective by being compared with other known data.

STEP 3: DEFENDANT RECONSTRUCTION OF THE INSTANT OFFENSE

A defendant's recollection of an alleged crime is usually helpful in inferring the defendant's state of mind. Even when the defendant does not testify or when state law shifts the burden of proving sanity to the government after the defendant has raised the possibility of insanity, the defendant's state of mind at the time of the crime is critical to the successful application of the insanity defense.

Although state of mind can often be inferred from eyewitness accounts, from material evidence, and from reports of third parties regarding events before and after the crime, the defendant's own description of events is helpful as one source of data.

Before eliciting a defendant's version of the alleged offense, however, it is critical that the examiner determine the legal admissibility of the defendant's statements. In some jurisdictions, a defendant's statements to an examining professional may be admitted not only as evidence of state of mind (i.e., legal insanity), but also as evidence that the defendant committed the crime (i.e., a confession). In such jurisdictions, the examiner is ethically obliged to inform the defendant of the potential uses of the statements (American Psychological Association Division 41, 1991) and, under some circumstances, is legally obligated to do so (*Estelle v. Smith,* 1981).

STEP 4: ANALYSIS OF HISTORICAL VS. CRIME BEHAVIOR

The next step involves historical analysis of criminal behavior vs. that shown during the instant offense. The goal is to determine whether the instant offense is typical or atypical for the defendant. Rare events are most likely triggered by high stress or by an unusual combination of environmental or internal events. Common events suggest a habitual pattern and are considered more inculpatory.

STEP 5: MENTAL DIAGNOSIS

A diagnosis of the defendant's mental state at the time of the crime usually requires evidence in support of a diagnostic category in an accepted typology of mental disorders (e.g., DSM-IV, ICD-9). The diagnosis requires evidence that the condition existed at the time of the crime, regardless of whether or not it also existed prior to or after the crime. Evidence of a chronic mental disorder (e.g., schizophrenia, mental retardation, organic personality disorder) in existence before the instant offense increases the likelihood that the disorder also existed at the time of the crime, but is not sufficient by itself. Some chronic mental disorders can be in remission or partial remission or can be controlled with psychotropic medications. Evidence of prior episodic explosive incidents is relevant to diagnosis at the time of the instant offense only if the instant offense was also explosive and insufficiently provoked. Evidence of a mental disorder (e.g., depression or anxiety disorder), which arose after the instant crime, is irrelevant to a diagnosis at the time of the offense. Most jurisdictions exclude from their definitions of legal insanity certain mental disorders such as voluntary substance intoxication and antisocial personality disorder.

STEP 6: ANALYSIS OF SELF-REGULATION

The existence of a mental disorder at the time of the instant offense may not shed any light on the (legal) blameworthiness of the defendant. The severity of the disorder and its impairment of critical faculties at the time mediate its exculpatory effect. The analysis of self-control and choice by the accused is central to the determination of criminal responsibility. Intact self-control and choice for the time of the alleged crime often lead to a finding of criminal responsibility. Conversely, impaired self-control frequently results in exculpation or mitigation of responsibility for the instant offense.

Appendix B presents a detailed checklist of discrete behaviors for the times before, during, and after the instant offense. Examiners are encouraged to use this checklist (and/or give it to referring attorneys to fill out and return). It has been refined after application to several cases of evaluation for criminal responsibility.

The following report section presents a self-control analysis of a 25-year-old Caucasian male who was subsequently found guilty of hammering his homosexual lover to death:

Factors suggesting intact self-control for the time of the instant offense included the following:

(a) No reported hyperactivity except during the commission of the homicide; that motor activity was necessary to complete the assault on the victim;

(b) No reported rapid, pressured, perseverative, or incoherent speech;

(c) No reported mental confusion or disorganization of behaviors;

(d) No amnesia for alleged crime-related events;

(e) No other alleged uncontrollable/impulsive behavior aside from the instant offense; the accused showed a wide range of appropriate and controlled behavior for the week previous to the alleged crimes;

(f) No substance intoxication although he did ingest some cocaine and several beers on the night prior to the offense;

(g) No heightened anxiety of maladaptive proportions or of such a nature as would create immobilization; the accused reported anxiety over whether the victim would wake up just prior to the homicide; this elevated anxiety did not prevent the attack;

(h) Intact gross and fine motor skills, suggested by the physical activity engaged in by the accused prior to, during, and after the homicide;

(i) Intact recall of alleged crime events, as shown by later recollection of specific events (e.g., during interrogation) and by reliance on recall in order to carry out the instant offense;

(j) Intact ability to interact verbally with the victim and to utilize auditory feedback, even though his responses may have been maladaptive (i.e., violent);

(k) The ability to delay gratification of anger impulses by waiting until the victim returned to sleep and by starting the sequence of assaultive behaviors (i.e., raising his arm) only to interrupt the chain of behaviors by setting the hammer down for a period of time when the victim moved;

(l) A specific focus on the killing, with a particular victim, a particular weapon which could easily be lethal, a particular method of attack (striking blows to the head) in a manner likely to produce death. Crime photos show the victim's skull caved in on both sides — on the left side, primarily in the temporal lobe area, and on the right side, extending from the prefrontal area back to parietal-occipital sites;

(m) The perceptual-motor skills required to ambulate to a point beside the victim, to aim at a vital spot, and to strike that spot multiple times, killing the victim in the process. Discrete victim behavior was recalled, such as turning on his side after the first blow;

(n) Increasing the severity of the hammer attack after the victim opened his eyes following the first blow;

(o) The ability to monitor and tactily recall the results of the hammer attack (e.g., stating that the victim's head felt like "broken glass" after the attack);

(p) Intact recall, scanning, and other skills required to search the apartment and successfully locate and retrieve valuable items belonging to the victim;

(q) Attempting to avoid apprehension, represented by hiding the murder weapon, leaving the alleged crime scene, traveling away from the crime scene, lying to friends regarding how he acquired the van, eventually hiding the van, and throwing the keys in the bushes. He specifically recalled that he left his blood-stained yellow/blue striped underpants in the apartment of the victim. Each of these self-controlling behaviors was confirmed by cross-validating data.

Step 7: Proffering Conclusions

The last step in the retrospective decision process consists of offering conclusions in regard to criminal responsibility. Adequacy of the database, degree of self-control exhibited, and criminal responsibility are all issues that must be addressed. The report format should conform to the retrospective decision path. Appendix C presents a mental capacity report format that has been developed and refined by the authors. At the very least, use of the format sequence and content factors will communicate to the court that the evaluator has been thorough in his or her assessment of issues relating to insanity.

SYNTHESIS

A heuristic model of seven discrete steps is proposed for evaluating criminal responsibility, which explicitly integrates distortion analysis into the evaluation. The concept of self-control rather than diagnosis is the center point of the evaluation. A self-control checklist (Appendix C) and an Insanity

Report Format (Appendix D) are offered. Appendix E contains an analysis of a criminal case from the perspective of self-control.

LEGAL REFERENCES

Estelle v. Smith, 49 U.S.L.W. 4490 (1981).

REFERENCES

American Psychological Association Division 41. (1991). *Specialty guidelines for forensic psychologists.* Washington, DC: Author.

Borum, R., & Otto, R. (2000). Advances in forensic assessment and treatment: An overview and introduction to the special issue. *Law and Human Behavior, 24*(1), 1–7.

Hall, H.V. (1982). Dangerous predictions and the maligned forensic professional: Suggestions for detecting distortion of true basal violence. *Criminal Justice and Behavior, 9*, 3–12.

Hall, H.V. (1985). Cognitive and volitional capacity assessment: A proposed decision tree. *American Journal of Forensic Psychology, 3*, 3–17.

Hall, H. V. (1987). *Violence prediction: Guidelines for the forensic practitioner.* Springfield, IL: Charles C Thomas.

Rogers, R. (1984). *RCRAS: Rogers Criminal Responsibility Assessment Scales.* Odessa, FL: Psychological Assessment Resources, Inc.

Rogers, R. (1988). *Malingering and deception.* New York: Guilford Press.

Rogers, R., & Cavanaugh, J. (1981). The Rogers Criminal Responsibility Assessment Scales. *Illinois Medical Journal*, 164–168.

Rogers, R., Seman, W., & Wasyliw, O. (1983). The RCRAS and legal insanity: A cross-validation study. *Journal of Clinical Psychology, 39*, 554–559.

Schacter, D. L. (1986). Amnesia and crime: How much do we really know? *American Psychologist, 41*, 286–295.

Shapiro, D. (1999). *Criminal responsibility evaluations: A manual for practice.* Sarasota, FL: Professional Resource Press.

Slovenko, R. (1973). *Psychiatry and the Law.* Boston, MA: Little Brown & Co.

Slovenko, R. (1995). *Psychiatry and criminal culpability.* New York: Wiley.

Steadman, H., Silver, E., Monahan, J., Appelbaum, P. S., Robbins, P. C., Mulvey, E. P., Grisso, T, Roth, L., & Banks, S. (2000). A classification tree approach development of actuarial violence risk assessment tools. *Law and Human Behavior, 24*(1), 83–100.

Ziskin, J. (1995). *Coping with Psychological and Psychiatric Testimony,* Vol. 2 (5th ed.). Los Angeles: Law and Psychology Press.

19 Faked Amnesia and Recall Skills

Memory deficits are found in everyday life and in pathological conditions. They span chronological ages from childhood to old age. They are transient and permanent, specific and global, functional and organic, normal and pathognomonic. Moreover, of course, because they are largely private events, they are fakable and highly subject to distortion. Memory problems can arise from dysfunctions at any stage of information processing: registration, short-term storage, consolidation, long-term storage, or retrieval (McCarthy & Warrington, 1990). Failure of registration, for example, may be due to limits in the span of apprehension (e.g., children may apprehend three items of information, while adults may apprehend seven items) or to deficits in "chunking" or categorizing information. Problems in short-term storage may be due to deficits in the durability of the memory trace or to attentional deficits. Problems in retrieval may be due to a heightened sensitivity to interference or to a failure of consolidation.

These various deficits may have diverse origins. Impaired memory performance per se has no value for differential diagnosis of pathological conditions. Table 19.1 presents examples of conditions that may be associated with mnestic difficulties.

FORENSIC ISSUES

Claimed memory problems are frequent in civil cases involving both tort claims and eligibility claims. Motor vehicle accidents, assaults, industrial accidents, and sporting accidents are leading causes of head injuries that frequently find their way into civil suits for negligence, into Social Security Disability claims, and into workers' compensation claims. Mnestic deficits are the most prevalent residual symptoms of head injuries and therefore figure prominently in civil claims.

> In extreme cases, the injured person is forever bound to an extended present, with recollections of the past and anticipation of the future only fleetingly within awareness. In milder cases, where performance on experimental psychometric memory tasks falls within premorbid expectations, attention and memory difficulties may show as periodic absent-mindedness, especially when dealing with tasks that place a strain on these functions and that rarely can be simulated by conventional assessment procedures. (Grimm & Bleiberg, 1986, p. 500)

Memory problems in cases of closed head injury involve both anterograde and retrograde amnesia. Anterograde amnesia (sometimes called post-traumatic amnesia) refers to memory deficits during the period after a head injury and includes the time of any coma, the time of any confusional period after consciousness is regained, and, in severe cases, a time of varying length thereafter. Retrograde amnesia refers to deficits in the retrieval of memories already consolidated prior to the head injury. In the natural course of recovery from head injury, "anterograde posttraumatic amnesia gradually improves, after which the duration of the retrograde amnesia commonly shows a progressive shrinking to within a few minutes or seconds of the accident" (Cummings & Benson, 1983). This process of salvaging old memories and consolidating new memories is quite variable,

TABLE 19.1
Etiologies of Mnestic Problems

Condition/Event	Mnestic Problem May Be Due To:
1. Neuropsychological	
OBS	Traumatic brain injury, epilepsy, tumor, stroke, dementia
Toxic states	Intoxication, poisoning, neuroleptic syndrome
2. Psychosis	
Schizophrenia	Florid states
Affective disorders	Agitated or depressed periods
3. Psychogenic	
Repression	Intense stress
Dissociation	Hysteria, fugue, multiple personality disorder
Depression	Slowing of cognitive processes
Adjustment disorders	Acute stress
4. Pure malingering	Prevarication not associated with mental disorder or condition
5. Combinations	Malingering associated with genuine deficits/conditions

depending on the severity of the injury and age of the patient, and may range from a few seconds to years.

Even in cases of mild closed head injury, with no loss of consciousness and normal radiological and neurological tests, memory deficits may be apparent in everyday functioning. As Corthell and Tooman (1985) stated:

> After even the mildest of injuries, *incidental* memory, i.e., the ability to recall information not specifically attended to, may be severely impaired. For example, misplaced keys, charge cards, packages, and shoes are common; appointments and commitments are instantly forgotten if not written down, despite every good intention and motivation to carry through. Standard intellectual examinations tend to test familiar, previously learned information and skills.
>
> Very little new learning or extended memory may be required on standard psychological examination. Head trauma clients often score in the "average" range or above on standard mental ability (IQ) tests, and yet can be severely impaired in their capacities for new learning and memory. (p. 15)

In general, there is a positive correlation between the severity of a head injury (as measured, for example, by length of coma) and the severity and duration of both anterograde and retrograde amnesia. There is also a positive correlation between the severity/duration of anterograde amnesia and the severity/duration of retrograde amnesia, although retrograde amnesias tend to be brief. Furthermore, there is a positive correlation between the duration of anterograde amnesia and everyday functioning.

Therefore, the severity of a closed head injury and the duration of anterograde amnesia can provide a rough clue to the genuineness of claimed memory deficits. If a head injury was mild, residual memory deficits should be mild and should be more apparent in incidental memory than in psychometric memory. A patient presenting with a history of mild head injury and complaints of severe mnestic deficits would appear suspicious. If the closed head injury was severe, longer-lasting and more severe anterograde amnesia can be expected. A patient presenting with a history of severe head injury and complaints of mnestic difficulties even years after the injury is more plausible.

When the head injury is caused by penetrating or crushing forces (e.g., a gunshot wound), the duration of anterograde amnesia is a less reliable guide to severity and prognosis. "With penetrating injuries due to missiles or with depressed skull fractures … concussion and amnesia may then be brief or absent, yet focal cognitive deficits can be severe especially if hemorrhage or infection have occurred" (Lishman, 1987, p. 157). These focal deficits include specific amnesias, such as auditory-verbal or visual-mnestic deficits, rather than global amnesia. Depending on the severity of the specific deficits, the degree of everyday impairment may vary from mild to incapacitating. In such clinical cases, there is no "natural course" of recovery against which to assess the genuineness of a patient's complaints.

Similarly, the residual effects of anoxia or exposure to neurochemicals (including prescription medications) are highly variable, depending on such factors as the extent and duration of the anoxia, the toxicity and dosage of the neurochemical, and patient variables such as age and sensitivity. In drowning cases, the extent of central nervous system damage, for example, is mediated by the victim's core body temperature during the period of anoxia. In cases of heavy metal poisoning (e.g., lead, mercury, manganese) and solvent inhalation (e.g., "glue sniffing"), the cumulative dosage level is determinative of any residual effects of exposure. Dosage, individual sensitivity, and length of exposure to phenothiazines (e.g., Haldol) are all critical in producing Parkinsonism, akathisia, and tardive dyskinesia. Global and specific, mild and severe forms of amnesia may be found among survivors of anoxia or neurotoxicity.

In criminal cases, claimed memory problems are most likely to involve substance intoxication or psychiatric disorders. Guttmacher (1955) and Bradford and Smith (1979) reported that amnesia occurred in 30 to 55% of homicide cases. Amnesia associated with violence was generally a short-term, partial, and recoverable phenomenon. Bradford and Smith found that 37% of their sample of 30 arrested for homicide reported amnesia for a period of less than 30 minutes, with 60% claiming some sort of amnesia for less than 24 hours. They also found 44% of the subjects reporting partial (patchy) amnesia, with sudden onset and cessation. This was the largest group, followed by those who claimed no amnesia (37%). Only 3% (one subject) reported a complete amnestic blackout for the entire time. Likewise, only one subject showed lack of complete recovery. Bradford and Smith concluded that malingered amnesia is most likely to be 30 minutes or less in duration.

Taylor and Kopelman (1984) reported no cases of amnesia associated with nonviolent crimes in a sample of 212 men in custody for a variety of offenses. All of their amnesia cases had psychiatric disturbances with substance abuse and depression most frequent. Almost one half (41 out of 98) of young military male patients studied by Kiersch (1962) admitted that they had faked memory problems. These individuals were amnestic for a period of intoxication, but exaggerated the duration of the amnesia into times when they were sober. Psychogenic patients with exaggeration were also found. In a study of 105 males being held on murder charges, Parwatikar, Holcomb, and Menninger (1985) reported that those who faked amnesia may have been more sophisticated in terms of knowing the criminal justice system by having been arrested previously. Those murderers who admitted to responsibility and also claimed amnesia tended to be substance intoxicated at the time of the instant offense, and/or exhibited higher levels of hysteria, depression, and hypochondriasis on the MMPI. For murder suspects the claims of amnesia range as high as 70% (for reviews, see Horton, Smith, Barghout, & Connolly, 1992; Kopelman, 1987; Schacter, 1986)

In a review article, Schacter (1986) suggested that genuine vs. faked recall in criminal cases can be distinguished by examining the accused's behavior in general. For example, was the offense well prepared or impulsive? Second, the amnesia claim itself may help to identify malingered amnesia. Limited recall during the crime with a sharply defined onset and termination is suggestive of faked or exaggerated amnesia. A suspect's "feeling of knowing" may also be used as a detection method. A feeling of knowing is a "subjective conviction that one could retrieve or recognize an unrecalled item, event, or fact if one were given some useful hints or cues" (p. 291). The examiner asks possible fakers to rate their feeling of knowing that they could recall or recognize crime events if given assistance. Fakers tend to discount the chance that their recall would improve. Thus, feigning memory problems is a fundamental concern for forensic professionals in both civil and criminal cases. The essentially private nature of the complaint of amnesia and the possible motive to malinger in legal situations encourage some persons to hide their intentional deception behind the variability and complexity of genuine amnesia. Distinguishing genuine from faked memory problems calls upon the best of psychological, neuropsychological, and forensic skills.

EVERYDAY ASSUMPTIONS ABOUT MEMORY

Faked recall almost always involves assumptions about the way memory normally functions. These assumptions may conform to a commonsense or lay view of memory, but rarely encompass empirical facts about memory processes. The typical person is unlikely to distinguish recognition and recall processes, primacy and recency effects, learning curves and forgetting curves (e.g., Wiggins & Brandt, 1988).

The evaluation of erroneous assumptions made by deceivers should be studied for clues to deception. Herrmann (1982) noted that:

1. People know their memory only to a moderate degree. Fakers may wrongly think, for example, that they can recall their answers to a particular test, yet are unable to repeat their performance when retested.
2. Some types of memory are more stable over time than others; for example, visual experiences involving places (visual memory) are generally recalled more reliably than conversations (auditory-verbal memory). The faker may not know this and perform differentially on various sensory tasks. Information that even true amnesiacs generally do not forget over time also includes word completion. Graf, Squire, and Mandler (1984) found that word completion (cued recall) in amnesic patients declined at a normal rate when subjects were presented with the first three letters of each word presented earlier. They also cite literature that shows that amnesic patients perform normally when (1) given degraded versions of previously presented words, (2) reading words from a mirror-reversed display, and (3) completing puzzles.
3. In most people, recognition appears better than free recall. This is true in normals, those experiencing posthypnotic amnesia, and the brain damaged (Brandt, Rubinsky, & Lassen, 1985; Iverson, Franzen, & McCracken, 1991). In this latter study, subjects feigning amnesia ($N = 10$) performed worse on free recall compared with normals ($N = 12$), those with Huntington's disease ($N = 14$), and those with head trauma ($N = 5$). Recognition performance was above chance levels for both normals and head trauma subjects. Of the 14 subjects with Huntington's disease, 8 performed better than chance, and the rest at chance levels. All of the malingerers performed at chance ($N = 7$) or below ($N = 3$).

Wiggins and Brandt (1988) presented critical questions for which the probability of obtaining wrong answers by both nonsimulating controls and amnesiacs with bona fide organic conditions approaches zero (Table 19.2). Incorrect answers to these questions should be expected only among those with clinically severe retrograde amnesia and, even in those cases, performance might be improved by cueing, prompting, or presenting choices (McCarthy & Warrington, 1990, pp. 307–313).

Any mnestic deficit can be faked. This includes immediate, short-term, and long-term recall problems. Any event that occurred in a person's life can be denied; recollection can be patchy and variable as memory returns.

Fakers tend to distort signs relevant to intended symptoms only on certain tests. Further, mild to moderate deficits appear to be faked more often than severe memory problems (e.g., dementia, global amnesia). Most likely, these types of deficits are selected because of their difficulty in detection. Faking recall should be suspected if (1) there is a loss of crystallized knowledge of skills, which almost never happens; (2) recognition is worse than recall, for example, for lists of words; (3) the person is exhibiting inconsistent organic or psychiatric signs (e.g., DSM-IV conditions).

RESPONSE STYLES

Most fakers show longer latencies in responding to recall questions (Resnick, 1984). This may be because they are simultaneously performing two mental operations — stopping a correct response

---

TABLE 19.2
Suspicious Memory Deficits If Wrong or Implausible Answers Are Presented

1. "What is your …
   a. Name?"
   b. Age?"
   c. Birth date?"
   d. Telephone number?"
   e. Address?"
   f. Mother's first name?"
   g. Mother's maiden name?"
   h. Brother's name and/or sister's name?"
2. "What did you have for breakfast this morning?"
3. Recognizes examiner's name from four choices on Day 2 of evaluation if failed to recall it.

Note: Adapted from "The Detection of Simulated Amnesia," by E. Wiggins & J. Brandt, 1988, *Law and Human Behavior, 12,* 57–78.

---

and presenting another. Many of the faking-bad response styles that depend on memory tasks may be used by the malingerer (see previous chapter). Faking partial deficits may include the following strategies: (1) fractional effort, (2) approximate answers, (3) distributing errors among correct answers, and (4) overall attempt to control error percentage. Fakers often make intentional mistakes early in the evaluation and may change style (Hall & Shooter, 1989; Pankratz, 1988, 1998).

Lande (1993) described an interesting case study depicting a rather unusual and complex malingering response style. The case involved a senior enlisted soldier who worked as a recruiter and made $18,000 worth of unauthorized 900-number telephone calls on a government telephone. Subsequent clinical assessment based on the telephone abuse generated an array of initial differential diagnoses including malingering, dissociative disorder (psychogenic amnesia), depression, obsessive–compulsive disorder, an unusual paraphilia (telephone scatologia), a seizure disorder, and an adult antisocial disorder. In the end, the clinical data did not persuasively suggest the presence of a significant mental disorder. The soldier was found guilty by a military court-martial.

DETECTION STRATEGIES

The development of popular episodic memory tests was the result of traditional neuropsychological measures not satisfactorily discriminating between cerebral brain impairment and malingered impairment (Greiffenstein, Baker, & Gola, 1994). For a review of traditional memory instruments and batteries, see Lezak (1995). Over the years, the efficacy of different instruments to detect malingered memory deficits has received mixed reviews across empirical studies. One problem has been studies using different instruments and/or different clinical populations and then suggesting that the findings generalize to all types of brain injury where malingering may be an issue. Another problem has been validation studies based solely on the performance of normal dissimulators, usually undergraduates. It has become apparent that the detection of malingering from actual brain trauma must involve careful and selective use of assessment instruments, collaborative use of assessment instruments, and selective use of cutoff scores adjusted to brain injury type.

Herrmann (1982, pp. 438–439), in his review, discusses a wide variety of commonly used memory questionnaires. Yet, these tests correlate only moderately with actual recall abilities. A further problem is they have no built-in deception scales and are predicated on the notion that the subject will give his or her best performance. At best, they can be used in parallel fashion if test–retest improvement is taken into consideration. The faker may have difficulty repeating his or her own first (inferior) performance.

Rey (1964) devised a 15-item visual memory test specifically designed to detect feigned memory difficulties. The task consists of five rows of patterned stimuli (e.g., ABC, 123, abc) which give the impression of task complexity (15 items) but which are easily "clustered" into just five memory units. Lezak (1983) and Goldberg and Miller (1986) suggested a cutoff score of nine recalled items was optimal for detecting suspicious mnestic performances. Bernard and Fowler (1990) suggested a cutoff score of 8 and Lee, Loring, and Martin (1992) suggested a cutoff score of 7. Clearly, the optimal cutoff score for detecting malingering will vary from population to population, e.g., demented patients, retarded patients, naive subjects (Flowers, Sheridan, & Shadbolt, 1996; Schretlen, Brandt, Kraft, & Van Gorp, 1991). Greiffenstein, Baker, and Gola (1996) observed that Rey's measures appeared to be valid for assessment of cognitive malingering in situations where litigated disability claims were out of proportion to injury characteristics. They cautioned that Rey's measures were not appropriate for globally and severely impaired patients in clinical settings.

The Wechsler Memory Scale–Revised (Wechsler, 1987) and the Memory Assessment Scale (Williams, 1991) are multifaceted measures of memory functioning. They can be used for adolescents and adults and include tests for verbal and figural stimuli, meaningful and abstract material, and delayed as well as immediate recall. Olfactory and tactile recall, autobiographical memory, and recall of learned skills (such as operating a machine) are not tested with these measures.

Deception on the WMS-R can be assessed by the following:

1. Comparing test scores between retests;
2. Comparing WMS-R subscale scores with those of other tests with the same task (e.g., digit span on WMS-R with WAIS-R, visual reproduction scores with performance on Bender-Gestalt);
3. Comparing test performance with cross-validating sources (e.g., significant others);
4. Comparing the Wiggins and Brandt (1988) list to responses on the information and orientation questions since there is considerable overlap;
5. Comparing easy vs. difficult item scores on the verbal paired associates tasks;
6. Observing behavior during testing (see p. 12 of WMS-R manual) and noting attitude toward testing, motivation, reaction to success or failure, and work habits.

One investigation compared a number of traditional memory instruments with TBI subjects and probable malingerers (Greiffenstein, Baker, & Gola, 1994). All the subjects were actual clinical cases. The probable malingerers were determined by at least two of four criteria:

1. Two or more severe impairment ratings on neuropsychological tests in comparison to expected performance based on age and education,
2. Improbable symptom history,
3. Disability of 1 year or more,
4. Remote memory loss claims.

The findings reflected that the popular Auditory Verbal Learning Test (AVLT), the Wechsler Memory Scale (WMS), and the Wechsler Memory Scale–Revised (WMS-R) did not differentiate the TBIs from the malingerers. In contrast, the probable malingerer group performed poorly on the Rey 15-Item, Rey Word Recognition List, Reliable Digit Span, Portland Digital Recognition Test, and Rey Auditory Verbal Learning Test recognition trial. The probable malingerer group was composed primarily of patients with histories of chronic complaints of mild head injury. The authors concluded that the latter group might have a much higher incidence of malingering than previously recognized because of their adequate performance on instruments erroneously assumed to rule out malingering.

Neurobehavioral Techniques and Amnesia

The neurological substrates of memory continue to be an area of considerable study and controversy (for a review, see Lezak, 1995). New technologies are enhancing our understanding of neurobehavioral functions in general and of memory functioning in particular. One such technology is functional neuroimaging using positron emission tomography (PET). Costello, Fletcher, Dolan, Frith, and Shallice (1998) described the case study of a man in his 40s who suffered a stroke and presented with a dense isolated retrograde amnesia for the 19 years preceding the stroke. The stroke was caused by a left superior dorsolateral prefrontal hemorrhage. The case history reflected that the man's forgotten personal life contained many highly stressful situations such that malingering was at least a suspicion. Functional neuroimaging was used while the man attempted to recall life events using family photographs as stimuli. The findings reflected distinctly different areas of cortical activation depending on whether the man had been present for the stimulus event, had not been present, or if the stimulus presented an analogous event outside the period of amnesia. With the present-for stimuli condition, compared with the other two conditions, activation was greater in part of the precuneus and less in both the right posterior ventrolateral frontal cortex and in a region close to the lesion. The authors concluded that the man's amnesia was not the result of malingering, but, rather, due to the lesion preventing recursive self-cueing of memory traces that were characteristic of the autobiographical retrieval with the not-present-for stimuli conditions.

Another recent area of psychophysiological detection of malingering involves EEG event-related brain potential (ERP) studies. The preliminary research findings have been encouraging. In one study of a series (Rosenfeld, Ellwanger, & Sweet, 1995), 13 undergraduate subjects were instructed to simulate autobiographical amnesia related to head injury. The ERP amplitudes were significant for the main effect of stimulus type. That is, the subjects simulated amnesia, but the ERP findings indicated recognition of the stimuli. A second study using a similar paradigm but measuring intactness of recognition memory with subjects simulating amnesia produced similar findings (Ellwanger, Rosenfeld, Sweet, & Bhatt, 1996). In a third ERP study, the investigators used a forced-choice, matching-to-sample task (Rosenfeld et al., 1998). "Priming" of subjects to achieve (i.e., manipulate) different behavioral hit rates did not adversely affect the ERP amplitudes of simulators, which were essentially comparable to the control group (truth tellers). The authors noted that additional analysis of the data preliminarily suggested evidence for a deception-related amplitude tomography across different paradigms and conditions. A final study in the series attempted to establish a mode of ERP patterns that actual amnestic patients might demonstrate (Ellwanger, Rosenfeld, Hankin, & Sweet, 1999). Undergraduate subjects were exposed to a range of relatively easy recognition memory tests graduated to increasingly difficult match-to-sample recognition memory tests. All the subjects in the modeled amnesia sample maintained intact recognition memory as measured by ERP tracings. These are findings with obvious potential for eventually providing definitive discrimination of malingered amnesia. These laboratory-based findings can only be considered as preliminary data. The findings may eventually prove useful in actual forensic matters. The EEG ERP test is not very portable and at the current time is a rather labor-intensive, costly procedure. With continued research and validation, it is conceivable that it may eventually be worthwhile to conduct ERP examinations of high-profile cases of suspected malingered amnesia. As with any technique or methodology, the ultimate forensic test will be refinement of ERP technology so that it meets scientific standards warranting acceptance of such findings in the courtroom.

Forced-Choice Testing

Explicit Alternative Testing (EAT) is a promising forensic neuropsychological tool that attempts to measure faked sensory and recall deficits (Grosz & Zimmerman, 1965; Pankratz, 1979, 1983, 1988; Pankratz, Fausti, & Peed, 1975; Theodor & Mandelcorn, 1973). Also known as forced-choice, two-alternative, or symptom-validity testing, EAT involves the presentation of stimuli, which the client denies or affirms that he or she can perceive/remember. Almost no one should miss presented items unless a genuine impairment exists, in which case one's performance should approximate chance responding (one half of the items in two-choice formats). Deviation from chance is defined as a total percentage correct, which falls significantly below 50% as defined by the binomial probability distribution (e.g., 1.96 standard deviations below 50% correct). For example, the (one-tailed) probability of obtaining fewer than 40 correct responses in 100 trials of a two-choice task is less than 2%. Obtaining fewer than 36 correct answers in the 100 trials would occur by chance less than two times in 1000. Subjects intent on faking typically make an initial assumption that they must respond correctly less than 50% of the time to demonstrate mnestic difficulties (Haughton et al., 1979; Pankratz, 1988). One advantage of the forced-choice format is avoiding the problem of conventional memory instruments not being useful with malingerers who claim no recollection of previously presented stimuli. As discussed later, the EAT paradigm sets the stage for a generation of new instruments, now generically referred to as *indirect memory tests* (Baker, Hanley, Jackson, Kimmance, & Slade, 1993; Hanley, Baker, & Ledson, 1999; Horton et al., 1992)

Hall and Shooter (1989) achieved a positive hit rate of 84.6% in identifying 52 subjects instructed to "fake bad" on a forced-choice memory recognition task. Shooter and Hall (1990) boosted the positive hit rate to almost 95% ($N = 19$) on the same task. A third study addressed the question of whether 50 or 100 trials are required for successful detection of faking in EAT. In the study, 35 subjects (males = 16, females = 19; mean age = 29.37, SD = 10.46; mixed ethnicity; mixed occupations) were randomly assigned to one of two groups: (1) those administered 100 trials ($N = 10$) or (2) those administered 50 trials ($N = 25$). There were two (20%) successful fakers in the 100-item group and six (24%) in the 50-item group. Chi-square analysis comparing the successful and unsuccessful fakers for the 100- vs. 50-trial group showed no significant differences.

As one would suspect, deception strategies differed between the successful vs. unsuccessful fakers. The most popular strategy used by the unsuccessful fakers was consistently choosing the incorrect response, accounting for 41% of the strategies named. The second most common strategy used by the unsuccessful fakers was giving occasional correct or incorrect responses (accounting for 20% of the strategies used), with attempting to forget being the third most common strategy. It was common for those employing a shift in strategy to switch from consistently choosing the incorrect answer to giving an occasional correct response.

The successful group employed random responding most frequently (accounting for 28%). The second most frequent strategy was consistently using the same response (19%), which necessarily resulted in a total correct of 50%. The third most frequent strategy was consistently choosing the incorrect response (16%), which necessarily involved a strategy shift at some point to produce a total correct greater than 40%. Among those subjects who identified a shift in strategy during the test, 29% named adhering to one response as their first strategy, while 21% reported using random responding as their first strategy. Random responding was used as the second strategy 40% of the time.

Pritchard (1992) has developed a computerized version of EAT, which employs a 72-trial memory recognition task divided into three subsets of 24 trials each. The subject is presented on each trial with a five-digit number ("target") for 5 seconds, followed by a 3 to 5 second delay and then a pair of five-digit numbers from which to select the "target" previously shown. A percentage-correct score is calculated for each subset of 24 trials and for the total 72 trials. Pritchard and Moses (1992) demonstrated that this task was 100% accurate (negative hit rate) in identifying a sample of severely impaired psychiatric and brain-injured patients and was 66% accurate (positive hit rate) in identifying a sample of subjects instructed to "fake bad" without being detected.

Results from EAT studies suggest the following.

1. Forced-choice methodology is indeed promising. The hit rates of EAT studies far exceed other deception-detecting strategies, even when distinguishing "fakers" from severely impaired

patients. Individuals with a high stake in faking — such as defendants facing prison terms or plaintiffs standing to gain monetary compensation for damages — may be even more strongly motivated than volunteer subjects to fake successfully. This would then increase the power of the EAT technique when applied to clinical cases. Indeed, anecdotal examples from the authors' experiences confirm the success of EAT with actual clinical cases.

Case 1. A 45-year-old Filipino male charged with the murder of his wife claimed amnesia for the instant offense. No history of neurological problems was apparent. He presented severe short-term visual and auditory recall deficits on the Wechsler Memory Scale–Revised and other testing. He obtained about 20% accurate responses on EAT and later admitted to exaggerating his recall deficits when confronted with the results. He maintained amnesia for the homicide and was eventually found guilty of manslaughter.

Case 2. A Caucasian, right-handed, 23-year-old ex-stripper at a go-go club was stabbed in the neck by her boyfriend, creating through-and-through puncture wound of the jugular vein and carotid artery. Residual signs included the Brown–Sequard syndrome, a right Horner's pupil, and an ataxic gait favoring the left. Neuropsychological testing several months after the trauma revealed normal functioning except on tasks requiring motor speed, coordination of upper extremities, manual dexterity, and sensitivity to stimulation. Recall abilities were above average for both short- and long-term memory. The victim later sued the nightclub for failure to protect her, claiming pervasive mental deficits stemming from the stabbing. Neuropsychological testing on the same battery two years afterward revealed uniformly poor scores with an impairment index of 1.0, meaning 100% of her scores were in the impaired range. This was in striking contrast to her normal clinical appearance and lack of any event since the stabbing which would explain this deterioration. MMPI testing revealed a pronounced tendency to fake bad. On the EAT, 15% of her responses were accurate, strongly suggesting that she was feigning a visual memory deficit. She did not admit to faking, but was eventually awarded a reduced settlement upon negotiation with the (civil) defendant.

2. Results suggest that as few as three sets of 24 trials or even 50 total trials of EAT can be utilized with no loss of detection accuracy. Thus, EAT can be designed to be both accurate and economical.

3. The use of successive sets of EAT trials, rather than just a total accuracy score based on all trials, appears to make EAT sensitive to fluctuating deception strategies. Fakers may perform poorly in the beginning of EAT testing and switch to honest responding after it is too late to hide their deception. Or subjects may attempt to fake bad after they have adapted to the test and decided on a strategy for deception.

4. EAT may be uniquely adapted to detect deception in individual cases. For criminal cases, this might involve information about an offense that only a perpetrator would know. As suggested by Hall and Shooter (1989), data bits — such as type of weapon utilized, injuries sustained by the victim, and clothing characteristics — could be presented to the suspect with instructions to affirm or deny recognition of them. A suspect with no knowledge of the instant crime should perform at approximately chance levels, while the perpetrator may be (statistically) placed at the scene of the crime. In a practical application of this suggestion, two alternative, forced-choice memory questions were used to assess suspicious complaints of amnesia in three actual cases (Frederick, Carter, & Powel, 1995). Of the three cases, two involved competency to stand trial and the third an insurance medical examination. In each case, the subjects claimed forgotten critical knowledge. Symptom-validity testing was adapted to questions tapping the "forgotten" knowledge in the forced-choice format. The number of correctly answered questions was then compared with the number of questions expected to be correctly answered if no knowledge actually existed. In each of the three cases, the response patterns generated the conclusion that the knowledge claimed to be forgotten was in fact remembered. The clinical circumstances were complex, however, and malingering was not the conclusion in each case.

CONTEMPORARY RESEARCH ON MALINGERED AMNESIA

Rey's Auditory Visual Learning Test (AVLT) was administered to 28 subjects twice using a different version of the test on each trial (Flowers, Sheridan, & Shadbolt, 1996). During the second trial, the subjects were instructed to simulate mild-to-moderate memory impairment. The patterns of scores in the two conditions reflected that the malingered subjects differed from the typical performance of genuine amnesiacs in three respects: they showed a primacy effect in free recall, they overperformed on the delayed recall trial, and they underperformed on the recognition task. The authors suggested that this pattern of findings may be useful in the AVLT distinguishing between genuine and faked amnesia, at least with naive subjects.

A case study described by Pachana, Boone, and Ganzell (1998) highlights the problems encountered by extrapolating from malingering instruments that work well with laboratory populations, but present with problems when used in actual clinical applications. A 32-year-old woman with Wernike–Korsakoff syndrome was administered a series of select neuropsychological tests designed to detect malingering. There was no clinical evidence to suggest that the woman was presenting with exaggeration or feigning of performance. Her performance exhibited mixed results across the instruments indicative of different sensitivity to actual memory impairment. The findings on several measures were contaminated by the presence of organic amnesia and produced false-positive findings of malingering. These measures included the Rey 15-Item and the Rey 15-Word Recognition Test. By comparison, other instruments (e.g., Dot Counting, Portland Digit Recognition) were unaffected by true memory impairment.

In a variety of recent studies, new approaches involving structured indirect measures of malingered amnesia have been introduced. These new studies offer creative paradigms wherein the subjects are not cued at the outset what specific behavior is under scrutiny, or they are distracted from a task explicitly involving memory. Many of the traditional techniques were rather transparent in presentation such that subjects were cued to attempt to engage in more-sophisticated deception. Indirect presentation was one of the features of EAT.

In one indirect memory test, subjects were asked to study a list of words and subsequently performed either a word completion or a fragment completion task (Horton et al., 1992). Genuine amnesics performance on indirect tests was comparable with normals. When the subjects in the study were motivated to simulate amnesia, target completion rates were reliably below baseline rates. Baker et al. (1993) compared simulators to genuine amnesiacs under distraction and no-distraction conditions. The genuine amnesiacs performed significantly worse than controls under distraction conditions. The simulators performed worse than controls under both distraction and no-distraction conditions. Simulators also exaggerated overall memory deficits relative to the genuine amnesiacs.

Kapur (1994) described a nifty and effective "bedside" test for the detection of patients suspected of malingering memory disorders called the coin-in-hand test (CHT). The clinician instructs the patient to observe and recall which hand holds a coin. The test is a simple series of ten trials in which the coin is alternated consecutively right to left. After exposing the coin for 2 seconds, the patient is instructed to close his or her eyes and count backward for 10 seconds. The patient is instructed that no trickery will be employed. In a laboratory study with control subjects, instructed simulators, and patients with amnestic disorders, Baker et al. (1993) found that over the ten trials, controls averaged a score of 9.95 of a maximum score of 10. Amnesic subjects had average scores of 9.65, compared with averages of 4.10 for simulators.

Another investigation utilized the forced-choice model to compare instructed simulators to amnestic patients (Davis, King, Bloodworth, Spring, & Klebe, 1997). A category classification test was used to differentiate between a control group of student subjects, a group of student subjects instructed to simulate amnesia, and a group of amnestic patients. The simulators were instructed to fake a memory deficit for academic credit and possible financial compensation. The subjects studied a list of highly distorted dot patterns and then were asked to choose if a new set of dot patterns belonged to the original category of dot patterns. The simulating subjects (malingerers) performed significantly worse than the controls or the amnesic patients. A discriminant function analysis indicated that the classification test could differentiate the three groups of subjects at an above-chance level. The investigators suggested that the category classification test could be used to supplement standard forced-choice tests in the detection of malingering.

As a lead-in to the next area of discussion, note that one unique aspect of the category classification test is that, while it involves a memory component, the classification task is the focal instruction. Accordingly, malingerers may not be cued to defensiveness from the outset. In one study, Baker et al. (1993) compared the performance of genuine amnesiacs to a group of simulators. One condition involved subjects being distracted by having to count backward between presentation and recall. A second condition involved no distraction in that the retention interval was unfilled. The findings reflected that the genuine amnesiacs performed significantly worse compared with nonsimulating controls under no-distraction conditions. The simulators performed significantly worse than controls under no-distraction as well as under distraction conditions. The simulators also exaggerated the memory deficit overall relative to genuine amnesiacs. The distraction/nondistraction paradigm offers a unique *in vivo* approach to the detection of malingered amnesia.

Greiffenstein, Gola, and Baker (1995) divided 177 subjects referred for neuropsychological assessment into three groups: TBIs, probable malingering, and persistent postconcussions. Comprehensive neuropsychological test batteries (i.e., MMPI-2, Auditory Verbal Learning Test Recognition Word List, Reliable Digit Span, and Rey's 15-Item Memory Test) were administered to all subjects. The findings showed that domain-specific compliance measures were generally more sensitive to noncompliance than were the MMPI-2 measures. Only the Sc scale of the MMPI-2 improved on base rate predictions of probable malingering. The Pd scale had no relationship to malingered amnesia.

Chouinard and Rouleau (1997) described the 48-Pictures Test, a two-alternative forced-choice recognition test designed to detect exaggerated memory impairments. They compared the test to the Rey Auditory Verbal Learning Test (RAVLT) and the Rey Complex Figure Test (RCFT). Three groups of subjects were utilized: 17 suspected malingerers, 39 patients with memory impairments (6 amnesic, 15 frontal lobe dysfunctions, 18 other etiologies), and 17 volunteers instructed to act as simulators. On the 48-Pictures Test, the clinical group showed good recognition performance averaging above 90%. The two simulator groups showed poor performance: suspected malingerers 62% correct; volunteer simulators 68%. The RAVLT and RCFT did not adequately discriminate among the subject groups except on two measures. Both simulator groups tended to show a performance decrement from the last recall trial to immediate recognition of the RALVT and also performed better on the immediate recall of the RCFT. A discriminant analysis utilizing the latter two measures and the 48-Pictures Test correctly classified 94% of the subjects.

Three of the new indirect memory tests that have been reviewed were empirically cross-compared by Hanley, Baker, and Ledson (1999). The findings reflected inherent problems with all three. The tests were the distraction/no distraction test (D/ND; Baker et al., 1993), the coin-in-hand test (CHT; Kapur, 1994), and word fragment completion (WFC; Horton et al., 1992). The D/ND and the CHT were both effective in distinguishing amnestic patients from simulators. The CHT was noted to be particularly effective in reflecting excellent performance by the amnestic patients compared with chance or below-chance performance by the simulators. The WFC effectively discriminated simulators from controls, but was ineffective in discriminating the amnestic patients from simulators. It remains to be seen in future research if these findings can be replicated with subjects who have sophisticated knowledge of performance levels associated with actual memory deficits. As cautioned by Rogers (1988), it also remains to be seen what effect incentives (e.g., financial compensation) will have on simulators' abilities to avoid detection. Most of all, it remains to be seen how the use of indirect memory tests will fare in actual forensic application.

TABLE 19.3
Qualitative Aspects of Malingered Memory Deficits

Malingerers may evidence any of the following:
1. Poor cooperation
2. Increased aggravation
3. Increased frustration
4. Slow response times
5. Frequent hesitations
6. General confusion during testing
7. Asking questions to be repeated
8. Confusing directions during testing
9. Pretending to forget what was asked
10. Fake total amnesia for personal identity
11. Fake total amnesia for past knowledge
12. Fake total amnesia for family
13. Fake total amnesia for friends
14. Fake total amnesia for precipitant trauma

Note: Adapted from "Qualitative Aspects of Malingered Memory Deficits," by G. L. Iverson, 1995, *Brain Injury, 9*(1), 35–40.

QUALITATIVE ASPECTS OF MALINGERED MEMORY DEFICITS

Iverson (1995) investigated qualitative aspects of malingered memory deficits based on interviews generating self-reported strategies of 160 subjects. The subjects were from a variety of backgrounds including adult community volunteers, psychiatric inpatients, federal inmates who participated in analogue malingering studies, and undergraduates. The findings regarding the qualitative characteristics of malingered memory deficits are summarized in Table 19.3.

SUMMARY AND CONCLUSIONS

Feigned memory deficits are essentially private events, which require sensitive psychological and neuropsychological skill to detect. By way of summary of the current state of the art in detecting faked memory problems, Table 19.4 presents an overview of the best signs for the detection of faked memory.

TABLE 19.4
Suspicious Signs for Faked Memory across Detection Methods

Consider faking of recall if any of the following occurs in combination:
1. Loss of crystallized memory with intact anterograde recall
2. Recognition worse than recall
3. Forced choice worse or better than chance on skill for which the assessee claims total impairment
4. "Feeling of knowing" confidence low
5. Misses on critical autobiographical items
6. Increase in latency of verbal response to memory-related queries
7. Memory skill levels significantly change upon parallel or repeat testing
8. Confession of faked recall with recaptured memory
9. Third parties report subject previously discussed the now "lost" memories
10. Faking response style identified and can be reproduced upon retesting

Several concluding observations based on recent studies of malingered memory deficits are offered. The empirical ability to differentiate malingered amnesia from actual amnesia and a thousand gradations of possibilities between these two poles has become increasingly sophisticated. Empirical assessment, however, is still not a definitive science. Lewis, Yeager, Swica, Pincus, and Lewis (1997) described a retrospective case study review of 12 murderers who the writers concluded had "child abuse-based dissociative identity disorder." The investigators concluded that "once and for all" their analysis established a linkage between early severe childhood abuse and dissociative identity disorder; they concluded further that their data demonstrated that the disorder could be distinguished from other disorders to include malingering. In forensic-related matters, it is axiomatic for clinicians to avoid making sweeping conclusory generalizations, and to avoid couching findings in superlatives or absolutes. Klein (1999) soundly rejected the conclusions of the foregoing study citing the inability to determine (1) what data had actually come from the records preceding legal involvement, (2) what prior data clearly pertained to the issues of abuse, and (3) what prior data supported the diagnoses of dissociative identity disorder.

In conducting forensic evaluations, clinicians must always be mindful of clinical presentations that mask another problem. Sundheim and Ryan (1999) described a sobering case example of an emergency room evaluation of a frequently visiting patient who was initially diagnosed as malingering an unusual amnestic syndrome. Further investigation eventually revealed that the patient actually was developmentally disabled (mild mental retardation).

Another caution comes from the literature regarding domestic violence, a phenomenon of increasing occurrence in our society. It has been observed that domestic violence perpetrators do not always remember assaulting family members. Following the violence, the perpetrators have no recollection of their violent behavior but accept full responsibility for it. Swihart, Yuille, and Porter (1999) described that these domestic incidents constitute "red outs" in which there is amnesia for a violent crime carried out in a state of rage. Unlike stranger-to-stranger crime circumstances, domestic violent crime occurs in a context of powerful feelings between the perpetrator and victim. Malingering alone, alcohol intoxication/blackouts, or organic dysfunction cannot explain amnesia in these domestic situations. In the clinical/forensic arena, things may not always be what they initially appear to be.

REFERENCES

Baker, G. A., Hanley, J. R., Jackson, H. F., Kimmance, S., & Slade, P. (1993). Detecting the faking of amnesia: Performance differences between simulators and patients with memory impairment. *Journal of Clinical & Experimental Neuropsychology, 15*(5), 668–684.

Bernard, L., & Fowler, W. (1990). Assessing the validity of memory complaints: Performance of brain-damaged and normal individuals on Rey's task to detect malingering. *Journal of Clinical Psychology, 46*, 432–436.

Bradford, J. W., & Smith, S. M. (1979). Amnesia and homicide: The Padola case and a study of thirty cases. *Bulletin of the American Academy of Psychiatry and the Law, 7*, 219–231.

Brandt, J, Rubinsky, E., & Lassen, G. (1985) Uncovering malingered amnesia. *Annals of the New York Academy of Sciences, 44*, 502–503.

Chouinard, M., & Rouleau, I. (1997). The 48-Pictures Test: A two-alternative forced-choice recognition test for the detection of malingering. *Journal of the International Neuropsychological Society, 3*(6), 545–552.

Corthell, D., & Tooman, M. (1985). *Rehabilitation of TBI (Traumatic Brain Injury)*. Menomonie, WI: Stout Vocational Rehabilitation Institute.

Costello, A., Fletcher, P. C., Dolan, R. J., Frith, C. D., & Shallice, T. (1998). The origins of forgetting in a case of isolated retrograde amnesia following a haemorrhage: Evidence from functional imaging. *Neurocase: Case Studies in Neuropsychology, Neuropsychiatry, & Behavioral Neurology, 4*(6), 437–446.

Cummings, J., & Benson, D. (1983). *Dementia: A clinical approach*. Boston: Butterworths.

Davis, H. P., King, J. H., Bloodworth, M. R., Spring, A., & Klebe, K. J. (1997). The detection of simulated malingering using a computerized category classification test. *Archives of Clinical Neuropsychology, 12*(3), 191–198.

Ellwanger, J., Rosenfeld, J. P., Hankin, B. L., & Sweet, J. J. (1999). P300 as an index of recognition in a standard and difficult match-to-sample test: A model of amnesia in normal adults. *Clinical Neuropsychogist, 13*(1), 100–108.

Ellwanger, J., Rosenfeld, J. P., Sweet, J. J., & Bhatt, M. (1996). Detecting simulated amnesia from autobiographical and recently learned information using the P300. *International Journal of Psychophysiology, 23*(1–2), 9–23.

Flowers, K. A., Sheridan, M. R., & Shadbolt, H. (1996). Simulation of amnesia by normals on Rey's Auditory Verbal Learning Test. *Journal of Neurolinguistics, 9*(2), 147–156.

Frederick, R. I., Carter, M., & Powel, J. (1995). Adapting symptom validity testing to evaluate suspicious complaints of amnesia in medicolegal evaluations. *Bulletin of the American Academy of Psychiatry and the Law, 23*(2), 231–237.

Goldberg, J., & Miller, H. (1986). Performance of psychiatric inpatients and intellectually deficient individuals on a task that assesses the validity of memory complaints. *Journal of Clinical Psychology, 42*, 792–795.

Graf, P., Squire, L. R., & Mandler, G. (1984). The information that amnesic patients do not forget. *Journal of Experimental Psychology: Learning, Memory, and Cognition, 10*, 164–178.

Greiffenstein, M., Baker, W. J., & Gola, T. (1994). Validation of malingered amnesia measures with a large clinical sample. *Psychological Assessment, 6*(3), 218–224.

Greiffenstein, M. F., Baker, W. J., & Gola, T. (1996). Comparison of multiple scoring methods for Rey's malingered amnesia measures. *Archives of Clinical Neuropsychology, 11*(4), 283–293.

Greiffenstein, M. F., Gola, T., & Baker, W. J. (1995). MMPI-2 validity scales versus domain specific measures in detection of factitious brain injury. *Clinical Neuropsychologist, 9*(3), 230–240.

Grimm, B., & Bleiberg, J. (1986). Psychological rehabilitation in traumatic brain injury. In S. Filskov & T. Boll (Eds.), *Handbook of Clinical Neuropsychology: Vol. 2* (pp. 495–560). New York: J. Wiley & Sons.

Grosz, H., & Zimmerman, J. (1965). Experimental analysis of hysterical blindness: A follow-up report and new experiment data. *Archives of General Psychiatry, 13*, 255–260.

Guttmacher, M. S. (1955). *Psychiatry and the Law*. New York: Grune and Stratton.

Hall, H. V., & Shooter, E. (1989). Explicit alternative testing for feigned memory deficits. *Forensic Reports, 2*, 277–286.

Hanley, J. R., Baker, G. A., & Ledson, S. (1999). Detecting the faking of amnesia: A comparison of the effectiveness of three different techniques for distinguishing simulators from patients with amnesia. *Journal of Clinical and Experimental Psychology, 21*(1), 59–69.

Haughton, P. M., Lewsley, A., Wilson, M., & Williams, R. G. (1979). A forced-choice procedure to detect feigned or exaggerated hearing loss. *British Journal of Audiology, 13*, 135–138.

Herrmann, D. (1982). Know thy memory: The use of questionnaires to assess and study memory. *Psychological Bulletin, 92*, 434–452.

Horton, K. D., Smith, S. A., Barghout, N. K., & Connolly, D. A. (1992). The use of indirect memory tests to assess malingered amnesia: A study of metamemory. *Journal of Experimental Psychology, 121*(3), 326–351.

Iverson, G. L. (1995). Qualitative aspects of malingered memory deficits. *Brain Injury, 9*(1), 35–40.

Iverson, G. L., Franzen, M., & McCracken, L. (1991). Evaluation of an objective assessment technique for the detection of malingered memory deficits. *Law and Human Behavior, 15*(6), 667–676.

Kapur, N. (1994). The coin-in-hand test: A new "bedside" test for the detection of malingering in patients with suspected memory disorder. *Journal of Neurology, Neurosurgery & Psychiatry, 57*(3), 385–386.

Kiersch, T. A. (1962). Amnesia: A clinical study of ninety-eight cases. *American Journal of Psychiatry, 119*, 57–60.

Klein, D. T. (1999). Multiples: No amnesia for childhood. *American Journal of Psychiatry, 156*(6), 976–977.

Kopelman, M. D. (1987). Amnesia: Organic and psychogenic. *British Journal of Psychiatry, 150*, 428–442.

Lande, R. (1993). Mental responsibility and 900 phone abuse. *Journal of Psychiatry & Law, 21*(1), 109–121.

Lee, G., Loring, D., & Martin, R. (1992). Rey's 15-item visual memory test for the detection of malingering: Normative observations on patients with neurological disorders. *Psychological Assessment, 4*(1), 43–46.

Lewis, D. O., Yeager, C. A., Swica, Y., Pincus, J. H., & Lewis, M. (1997). Objective documentation of child abuse and dissociation in twelve murders with dissociative identity disorder. *American Journal of Psychiatry, 154*(12), 1703–1710.

Lezak, M. (1983). *Neuropsychological assessment* (2nd ed.). New York: Oxford University Press.

Lezak, M. (1995). *Neuropsychological assessment* (3rd ed.). New York: Oxford University Press.

Lishman, W. (1987). *Organic psychiatry*. London: Blackwell Scientific Publications.

McCarthy, R., & Warrington, E. (1990). *Cognitive neuropsychology: A clinical introduction*. New York: Academic Press.

Pachana, N. A., Boone, K. B., & Ganzell, S. L. (1998). False positive errors on selected tests of malingering. *American Journal of Forensic Psychology, 16*(2), 17–25.

Pankratz, L. (1979). Symptom validity testing and symptom retraining: Procedures for the assessment and treatment of functional sensory deficits. *Journal of Consulting and Clinical Psychology, 47*, 409–410.

Pankratz, L. (1983). A new technique for the assessment and modification of feigned memory deficit. *Perceptual and Motor Skills, 57*, 367–372.

Pankratz, L. (1988). Malingering on intellectual and neuropsychological measures. In R. Rogers (Ed.), *Clinical assessment of malingering and deception* (pp. 169–192). New York: Guilford Press.

Pankratz, L. (1998). *Patients who deceive: Assessment and management of risk in providing health care and financial benefits*. Springfield, IL: Charles C Thomas.

Pankratz, L., Fausti, S., & Peed, S. (1975). A forced-choice technique to evaluate deafness in the hysterical or malingering patient. *Journal of Consulting and Clinical Psychology, 43*, 421–422.

Parwatikar, S. D., Holcomb, W. R., & Menninger, K. A. (1985). The detection of malingered amnesia in accused murderers. *Bulletin of the American Academy of Psychiatry and Law, 13*, 97–103.

Pritchard, D. A. (1992). *Tests of neuropsychological malingering*. Orlando, FL: Paul M. Deutsch Press.

Pritchard, D. A., & Moses, J. (1992). Tests of neuropsychological malingering. *Forensic Reports, 5*, 287–290.

Resnick, P. J. (1984). The detection of malingered mental illness. *Behavioral Sciences and the Law, 2*(1), 21–38.

Rey, A. (1964). *L'examen clinique en psychologie* [The Clinical Examination in Psychology]. Paris: Presses Universitaires de France.

Rogers, R. (1988). Researching dissimulation. In R. Rogers (Ed.), *Clinical assessment of malingering and deception* (pp. 309–327). New York: Guilford.

Rosenfeld, J. P., Ellwanger, J., & Sweet, J. (1995). Detecting simulated amnesia with event-related brain potentials. *International Journal of Psychophysiology, 19*(1), 1–11.

Rosenfeld, J. P., Reinhart, A. M., Bhatt, M., Ellwanger, J., Gora, K., Sekera, M., & Sweet, J. (1998). P300 correlates of simulated malingered amnesia in a matching-to-sample task: Topographic analyses of deception versus truthtelling responses. *International Journal of Psychophysiology, 28*(3), 233–247.

Schacter, D. L. (1986). Amnesia and crime: How much do we really know? *American Psychologist, 41*, 286–295.

Schretlen, D., Brandt, J., Kraft, L., & Van Gorp, W. (1991). Some caveats in using the Rey 15-item memory test to detect malingered amnesia. *Psychological Assessment, 3*(4), 667–672.

Shooter, E., & Hall, H. V. (1990). Explicit alternative testing for deliberate distortion: Toward an abbreviated format. *Forensic Reports, 3*(2), 115–119.

Sundheim, S. T., & Ryan, R. M. (1999). Amnestic syndrome presenting as malingering in a man with developmental disability. *Psychiatric Services, 50*(7), 966–968.

Swihart, G., Yuille, J., & Porter, S. (1999). The role of state-dependent memory in "red-outs." *International Journal of Law & Psychiatry, 22*(3–4), 199–212.

Taylor, P., & Kopelman, M. (1984). Amnesia for criminal offenses. *Psychological Medicine, 14*, 581–588.

Theodor, L. H., & Mandelcorn, M. S. (1973). Hysterical blindness: A case report and study using a modern psychophysical technique. *Journal of Abnormal Psychology, 82*(3), 552–553.

Wechsler, D. (1987). *Wechsler Memory Scale–Revised Manual*. New York: Psychological Corporation.

Wiggins, E., & Brandt, J. (1988). The detection of simulated amnesia. *Law and Human Behavior, 12*, 57–78.

Williams, J. (1991). *Memeory Assessment Scales professional manual*. Odessa FL: Psychological Assessment Resources.

20 Psychosis and Deception

For as muche as sometyme some personnes beinge accused of hyghe treasons, haue after they haue beene examined before the kinges miesties counsayle, confessed theyr offences of hyghe treason, and yet neuer the lesse after the dynge of theyr treasons, and examinations and confessions thereof, as is afore saide, haue falled to madness or lunacye, wherby the condygne punyshemente of theyr treasons, were they neuer soo notable and detestable, hath ben deferred spared and delayed, and whether theyr madness or lunacye by them outwardly shewed, were of trouth or falsely contriued and counterfayted, it is a thing almost impossible certainely to judge or try.

— 33 Henry VIII, c.xx (cited in Diamond, 1956)

Since feedback is rarely obtained on successfully faked psychosis, little is known about its true prevalence or how to detect it in specific cases. The above quote by Diamond (1956), from 1542 during the reign of Henry VIII, suggests that the problem is not new and continues to be vexing. Most probably, malingered psychosis (1) varies according to context — faked psychosis may be more frequent in criminal cases, but low in civil settings; (2) varies in degree within the same individual in his or her attempts to be consistent or inconsistent; (3) is more frequently engaged in by those who are already maladjusted; and (4) is encouraged by widespread dissemination of information on genuine psychosis, the move by deinstitutionalized people to return to the state hospitals, and the increasing mood of the judiciary to imprison felons.

Diverse circumstances and mental conditions are associated with faked psychoses. Ritson and Forrest (1970), in common with others, suggested that the malingering of psychosis is more serious than the condition faked, meaning that faking psychosis can be considered an illness in itself. Their patients had a number of reasons for faking, including (1) not wishing to leave the hospital, (2) being criminally charged, (3) financial problems or seeking a new residence, (4) manipulating unsympathetic doctors, and (5) escaping from an intolerable domestic situation. They proposed going beyond the unconscious vs. conscious dichotomy, in the fashion of Freud and the neodynamically oriented, to focus on the communication or message that the faked behavior represents. The real problem may be the outrage and the indignation shown by the clinician. In the Ritson and Forrest study, most of the 12 fakers originally had personality disorders (or features thereof), but later showed schizophrenic symptoms, a finding cross-validated by Pope, Jonas, and Jones (1982) in their study of factitious psychosis among hospitalized patients. Like Ritson and Forrest (1970), Pope et al. found that their fakers of psychosis had a poor prognosis. Almost one half of their malingering patients were hospitalized 4 to 7 years later. Resnick (1999) offers a different perspective, noting that when the malingerers are defendants, failure to diagnose malingered psychosis causes injustice in the legal system and allows misuse of the mental health system.

TARGETS

The long-range goals of the faker of psychosis may include a desire to avoid the unpleasant (e.g., imprisonment, combat duty) and/or to obtain rewards (e.g., financial compensation in Veterans Administration litigation, drugs, transfer within institutional settings, such as protective custody or the medical unit, admission to agencies for food and lodging).

TABLE 20.1
Targets of Faked Psychosis

Targets	Examples
1. Behavior	Bizarre motor behavior
	Audible self-talk
2. Somatic	Internal body changes
	Physical disease processes
3. Sensation	Vivid hallucinations
	Strange illusions
4. Imagery	Terrifying nightmares
	Uncontrollable flashbacks
5. Affect	Immobilizing fear
	Suicidal depression
6. Cognition	Delusions of persecution, grandiosity; looseness of thought
7. Interpersonal	Inability to respond: mutism
	Sexually inappropriate questions

Feigned behaviors chosen at the time of evaluation include alterations in speech, motor changes, the presentation of unexpected behavior, and the withholding of expected responses. As with all faked conditions, the faker of psychosis selects targets designed to accomplish a particular goal. Responses that the faker chooses should leave him or her blameless or, at least, point to uncontrollable forces beyond the ability to initiate, modulate, or stop. To assist the evaluator, the faker of psychosis often calls attention to faked symptoms. This does not necessarily imply consistency of responding or a desire to be detected. Rather, the examiner must be aware of psychotic symptoms in order to respond to them.

The faker of psychosis may present faked symptoms in writing, only to repudiate the symptoms when questioned orally. Presumably, the stress of verbal inquiry may be greater than with written expression. The evaluator should be prepared for both the presentation of moving targets and a wide variation in response styles. Some fakers will suggest that any variability or inconsistency in their presentation is due to the purported mental illness that they are experiencing. Targets of faked psychosis, with examples, are presented in Table 20.1.

Research on forensic subjects may yield important guidelines to the detection of disingenuous psychosis. A unifying theme of these investigations is that, given motivation to fake, malingerers of psychosis appear to exhibit patterned responses and can be detected by conformance to an inner logic (Bash, 1978; Bash & Alpert, 1980). These investigators determined that increased specificity of response style is associated with less involvement of the faker's own personality. Conversely, the more adaptive and widespread the malingering is to a variety of situations, the greater the likelihood that the faker's own enduring personality traits and lifestyle come into play. As discussed later, this finding has important implications for the assessment of deception.

RESPONSE STYLES

It is important for forensic clinicians to recognize that the foremost, underlying assumption in the assessment of malingering is the fact that malingerers tend to overendorse clinical symptoms when compared with normals and when compared with individuals with specific diagnoses (Bagby, Rogers, Nicholson, Cameron, et al., 1997; Wetter, Baer, Berry, Robison, & Sumptor, 1993). The focus of this chapter is on variations of faking the presence or severity of psychosis. However, malingering is often combined with defensiveness, as when the faker denies symptoms before military service and asserts severe symptoms during or after military service. The evaluator must be aware that clients may deny genuine psychosis for various motives, for example, to preserve the ego. Diamond (1956) speculates that simulating sanity occurs very frequently. He encourages the clinician to investigate simulated sanity actively instead of waiting for the client to inadvertently reveal psychosis.

Even severely maladjusted persons can fake bad or good, depending on their vested interests and opportunities for deception. Braginsky and Braginsky (1967) showed, in a study of 30 patients with long-term schizophrenia, that subjects could present themselves as "sick" or "healthy," depending on their goals. The former response set was presented when the subjects were faced with discharge, while "healthy" behaviors were shown when their open ward status was challenged. Three staff psychiatrists who blindly reviewed tapes of interviews with patients were erroneously convinced by the patients' impressions. The importance of assessing for all response styles, even among persons with well-documented histories of psychopathology, is thus strongly indicated.

A standing question is whether certain diagnostic categories have comorbidity with malingering efforts. Lewis and Bard (1991) described the comorbid relationship of multiple personality disorder (MPD) in a variety of forensic circumstances. Noting a similarity between MPD symptoms and those of antisocial personality disorders, the authors suggested that MPD was often overlooked in forensic assessments. Osran and Weinberger (1994) described the prevalent role of personality disorders in criminal responsibility defenses.

DETECTION STRATEGIES

Hollender and Hirsch (1964) presented five criteria for the detection of "hysterical" psychosis involving schizophrenic symptoms: (1) sudden, dramatic onset; (2) temporally linked to trauma; (3) schizophrenic symptoms in the absence of psychosis or a gross mood disorder; (4) no residual symptoms; and (5) premorbid hysterical personality traits. The authors concluded by suggesting the following criteria for distinguishing faked from genuine psychosis:

1. Delusions or hallucinations as the main symptoms;
2. No derailment of thought or blunted affect;
3. Presence of identifiable causative factors, such as a linkage between critical events and symptom onset, or of secondary gain in terms of avoiding punishment or receiving a reward;
4. Presence of two or more of the following symptoms: visual hallucinations, amnesia, sexual problems, pains or other body distress suggesting loss or change in function, and a histrionic or antisocial personality disorder;
5. No evidence of brain damage, schizophrenia, or a psychotic affective disorder.

By understanding the phenomenology of genuine psychosis, the clinician's skill in detecting fake symptoms is measurably enhanced (Pollock, 1998; Resnick, 1999; Schlesinger, 1996). Resnick (1984, 1988, 1997, 1999) has extensively described baseline techniques for detecting malingered psychosis. Resnick's approach is based on known clinical presentation patterns and prevalence rates of real psychotic symptomatology. This essentially means that the clinician must have a thorough working understanding of real hallucinations, delusions, and affective symptoms. Resnick's clinical signs for detecting faked psychosis are presented in Table 20.2.

Rogers (1984, 1987, 1988) presented a structured interviewing approach to the problem of malingered psychosis. He analyzed the Schedule of Affective Disorders and Schizophrenia (SADS; Spitzer & Endicott, 1978), stemming from a 1978 study on depression but which measures a wide variety of psychiatric symptomatology (Endicott & Spitzer, 1978). He next developed the Structured Interview of Reported Symptoms (SIRS; Rogers, 1992), which is intended for the identification of unreliable or inconsistent presentations during clinical interviews.

The discriminating ability of the SIRS is shown by the frequent and significant differences between malingerers and genuine patients. Symptom combinations are endorsed on Form A of the

TABLE 20.2
Clinical Signs for Detecting Faked Psychosis

Sign of Simulation	Relevant Factor for Client
1. Overplaying psychotic role	Attempts to behave congruently with idiosyncratic view of psychosis
2. Calling attention to symptoms	Rare psychotic conditions
3. Difficulty in imitation of form and style of psychosis	Often focuses on content of psychosis
4. May fit no diagnosis	Unaware of DSM-IV inclusionary and exclusionary criteria
5. Sudden onset and termination	Unaware that delusions usually develop and remit over time
6. Unlikely to conform to delusional content	Discrepancy between delusional content and behavior may not occur to client
7. Far-fetched story	Often seen in naive simulators
8. Contradictions in crime account more likely	Misrepresentation involves remembering and making up a wide range of information

SIRS by only 2.4% of the patient population, but were endorsed by 28.9% of malingerers (Form B, 6.8 and 18.8%, respectively). Symptom combinations in the SADS that were rare (all endorsed by less than 10% of genuine patients) included reporting (1) an adequate appetite together with current feelings of inadequacy, discouragement, distrust, and anger; (2) agitation together with anxiety or discouragement; and (3) persecutory delusions together with worrying, discouragement, insomnia, and anger.

Rogers (1988) suggested a number of criteria for detecting malingering, which formed the basis for the development of the SIRS. The criteria, which are empirically validated, included the following:

Descriptor	Malingerers Endorse
1. Symptom subtlety	More blatant than subtle symptoms
2. Severity of symptoms	Items reflecting extreme or unbearable severity
3. Rare symptoms	Infrequent symptoms
4. Improbable or absurd symptoms	Items of fantastic or preposterous quality
5. Symptom combinations	Symptoms unlikely to coexist
6. Consistency of symptoms	Inconsistent items when repeated
7. Nonselective endorsement	More nonselective in choosing psychiatric symptoms

However, even rare items sometimes are seen in psychotic individuals. These include symptoms such as (1) thought withdrawal, (2) delusions of guilt, (3) somatic delusions, (4) loosening of associations, (5) incoherence during the past week, and (6) neologisms (Rogers, 1988). As Rogers noted, contradictory symptoms are seen in cyclothymic or bipolar disorders such as (1) depressed and elevated mood, (2) worthlessness and grandiosity, (3) insomnia and hypersomnia, (4) decreased and increased energy, (5) decreased and increased appetite, (6) decreased and increased interests, and (7) psychomotor retardation and agitation.

Rogers' approach to structured interviewing has demonstrated impressive discriminant and concurrent validity across a number of follow-up studies and with a number of laboratory and clinical populations (Rogers, Gillis, & Bagby, 1990; Rogers, Gillis, Bagby, & Monteiro, 1991; Rogers, Gillis, Dickens, & Bagby, 1991; Rogers, Kropp, Bagby, & Dickens, 1992). Two primary drawbacks with the SIRS are that it must be administered individually and its administration time is lengthy. Norris and May (1998) described the development of the Screening Structured Interview of Report Symptoms (SSIRS), an abbreviated version of the SIRS. In a counterbalanced design, the SSIRS and the SIRS were administered to 75 inmates. The SSIRS discriminated significantly better than chance when compared with the classification analysis of the SIRS. The authors suggested that the screening procedure may help to facilitate optimal allocation of resources in correctional settings where classification requirements can be demanding.

PSYCHOMETRIC APPROACHES TO FAKED PSYCHOSIS

M Test

A short test for measuring malingering in schizophrenic persons has been developed by Beaber et al. (1985). The M Test consists of three scales: (1) Confusion (C) scale where subjects were expected to respond in a particular way (e.g., "I believe that cancer is a horrible disease"); (2) Schizophrenia (S) scale where items reflect DSM III-R associated features of schizophrenia (e.g., "Periodically, I am bothered by hearing voices that no one else hears"); and (3) Malingering (M) scale or indicators of malingered schizophrenia.

The M scale showed the largest absolute mean difference between normals ($x = 0.36$; SD = 0.83), those with schizophrenia ($x = 2.07$; SD = 2.83), and fakers (x = 8.07; SD = 4.94). The M scale consists of items that cannot be true because they comprise nonexistent entities (e.g., "I believe that God has appointed me to teach the Zolan beliefs to all people that I meet"). Atypical hallucinations, even for genuine experiences, are presented in this scale (e.g., "Sometimes after waking up in the morning, I am bothered by seeing colored triangles in my field of vision"). Items reflecting extreme severity not characteristic of schizophrenia are also included (e.g., "Sometimes my need to be alone and my fear of people are so powerful that I will spend hours in a closed closet by myself"). Other items reflect atypical delusions (e.g., "There have been times when I have found myself thinking that as a teenager, I was the chairman of the board of a major corporation"). The M Test identified 87.3% of 65 individuals with schizophrenia (true negatives) and 78.2% of 104 normal persons who were in fact malingering (true positives).

Smith (1992) attempted to cross-validate the M test with 23 malingerers and 62 inmates referred for a forensic evaluation, but was able to detect only 69.6% of the malingerers. Gillis, Rogers, and Bagby (1992) were able to identify only 40% of suspected malingerers with the M test and therefore the authors proposed a revised M test, which awaits cross-validation.

MMPI

A large field of literature on the MMPI shows that normals who fake psychosis, and psychotics who feign normality or exaggerate their disorder, can be detected with some degree of accuracy. Throughout this literature, however, it is important to distinguish the specific contrasting groups used to support the detection of distorted responding. MMPI scores and indices are better at discriminating between normal MMPI profiles and those of normal subjects instructed to feign psychopathology (normal pseudomalingerers) than they are at discriminating between genuine patients and normal pseudomalingerers (Berry, Baer, & Harris, 1991; Schretlen, 1988).

MMPI indices of malingering are even less accurate in distinguishing genuine, honest patients from genuine, exaggerating patients. Furthermore, some indices of distortion on the MMPI are consistently more effective compared with others. For example, Berry, Baer, and Harris (1991) concluded that "the largest mean effect size [for discriminating genuine from malingered MMPI profiles] was T-scaled F … followed by raw F … the original dissimulation scale … F minus K … obvious item scales … obvious minus subtle scales … subtle item scales … and the revised dissimulation scale" (p. 593).

Berry, Baer, and Harris (1991) noted that the search for a universal cutoff score for distinguishing genuine from faked MMPIs on any of these indices is ill-advised. Cuttoff scores must be locally determined according to the base rate of malingering in the population of interest and according to the costs of classification errors. For example, to achieve a given level of false-positive errors, cutoff scores would need to be higher when differentiating exaggerating patients from genuine

TABLE 20.3
MMPI and MMPI — Validity Indicators

Validity Indicators	MMPI	MMPI-2
1. Item omissions	a. Present	a. Present
2. Consistency	b. Test-Retest (TR) index	b. and c. Replaced with two new scales based on the same rationales: Variable Response Inconsistency (VRIN), 49 pairs of items True Response Inconsistency (TRIN), 20 pairs of items indicating a true or a false set
	c. Carelessness (CLS) scale	
	d. Sum of TR and CLS	d. Eliminated and replaced by above scales
	e. Weiner and Harmon obvious and subtle scales	e. Present
	f. Gough Dissimulation Scale-Rev.	f. Information not available
	g. Lochar and Wrobel Critical Items	g. Present with minor revision (4–5 items)
	h. F Scale	h. Present
	i. Absent	i. F(B) or Back-page F scale. Designed to assess the validity of responses to the latter part of the MMPI (e.g., random responding after tiring)
	j. Positive malingering	j. Present
	k. L and K scales	k. Present
	l. F-K	l. Present
	m. Individual item endorsement vs. cross-validated historical behavior	m. Present

patients than when differentiating malingering normal from genuine normal subjects. Consistent with this observation, Sivec, Lynn, and Garske (1994) assigned undergraduate students ($N = 237$) to three instructed groups (somatoform disorder, paranoid psychotic, and general "fake-bad") and administered the MMPI-2. Each instructed group differed from a control group on the majority of the MMPI-2 clinical and validity scales. The simulated paranoid psychotic and fake-bad groups did not differ from each other, although the somatoform disorder group differed from both. The F scale appeared to be the most effective validity indicator in this study.

The MMPI-2 was introduced in 1989. Shooter and Hall (1989) compared the various validity indicators available on the MMPI and the MMPI-2 (Table 20.3) based upon extant information (Anderson, 1989; Butcher, 1990). A decade later, the MMPI-2 has now withstood the rigors of time and usage. Pope, Butcher, and Sellen (1993, 2000) described the MMPI, MMPI-2, and MMPI-A as widely relied-upon forensic instruments; their reasons for using these instruments in court are summarized in Table 20.4.

During the 1990s, there was an unprecedented increase of studies investigating the application of the MMPI-2 and the MMPI-A in forensic matters. Beginning with the original MMPI, research suggested that the instrument is less useful in discriminating malingering from genuine psychopathology than in discriminating malingering from normalcy (Berry, Baer, & Harris, 1991). In acknowledgment of the central role of malingering in forensic matters, the development of the MMPI-2 involved an effort to retain from the original test a number of measures to assess negative response approaches to the test items. There was also an effort to develop new measures. These MMPI-2 measures are summarized in Table 20.5.

Pensa et al. (1996) described a study investigating the utility of the MMPI-2 and the detection of malingered psychosis. Male subjects ($N = 20$) diagnosed with psychosis were matched in age and education with 20 male volunteers. The volunteers received training materials on psychosis along with instructions and monetary incentives to malinger. All subjects were administered the

TABLE 20.4
The MMPI, MMPI-2, and the MMPI-A in Court

- The MMPI is the most frequently used clinical test. Many courts accept it as a source of personality information about defendants or litigants.
- The instrument is relatively easy to administer and is available in a variety of formats.
- The test is self-administering, under monitored conditions. A minimum of 6th grade reading level is required to understand statements that test-takers simply respond as being "true" or "false" as applies to them.
- The tests are relatively easy to score. The answer sheets can be scored manually or by a number of computerized scoring programs. The computerized scoring programs are quick, provide expanded scoring options, and offer greater reliability with fewer errors.
- The tests are available in a variety of languages (e.g., Spanish, Thai, Vietnamese, Chinese, Norwegian, Japanese), and appropriate national norms are available.
- The tests incorporate a number of response attitude measures.
- The tests are objectively interpreted on empirically validated scales.
- The test scales have been demonstrated to be reliable (stable over time).
- The tests offer valid interpretations of patient symptoms, problems, and characteristics.
- The test scores enable clinicians to predict anticipated responses to treatment and rehabilitation approaches.
- In court, the test findings are reasonably easy to explain, and are reasonably understood.

Note: Adapted from *The MMPI, MMPI-2, & MMPI-A in Court: A Practical Guide for Expert Witnesses and Attorneys* (2nd ed.), by K. S. Pope, J. N. Butcher, & J. Seelen, 2000, Washington, DC: American Psychological Association.

MMPI-2. The results reflected significant differences between the groups on the F-Fb Index, which yielded a hit rate of 70%. Additional t-tests revealed significant group differences on scales Infrequency (F), Bizarre Mentation (BIZ), Obvious-Subtle Difference Score, and the F-Fb Index. Discrimination with the additional t-test scores improved hit rates to the 80 to 90% range. A discriminant function with scales F, Fb, F-K, BIZ, and S-O yielded a hit rate of 92.5%. In a study with a group of forensic psychiatric patients ($N = 353$), Roman, Tuley, Villanueva, and Mitchell (1990) found traditional cutoffs for validity indicators (L, F, K, F-K, and O-S) to be of questionable validity in distinguishing malingerers. In addition to deliberate efforts to deceive, validity indicator elevations could be attributable to a variety of comorbid psychopathology.

An important variable affecting malingering detection with psychological tests is the level of test-taker knowledge of specific psychopathologies. For example, across different studies with the MMPI, subjects are variously asked to fake bad or to simulate a specific psychiatric disorder. Bagby, Rogers, Nicholson, Cameron, et al. (1997) investigated two groups of student fakers who completed the MMPI-2 with instructions to feign schizophrenia. Their responses were compared with the responses of a group of outpatients with schizophrenia. The first group of simulators was undergraduates with no clinical training. The second group comprised clinical psychology graduate students and psychiatry residents. The sophisticated group produced generally lower scores on the clinical scales and validity indicators compared with the undergraduate students. Both groups had higher scores for the clinical scales 6 (Paranoia) and 8 (Schizophrenia) when compared to the sample with schizophrenia. The largest validity indicator effects were observed on F and F-K.

In a follow-up study, Bagby, Rogers, Nicholson, Buis, et al. (1997) investigated this issue with respect to whether divergent validity scales and indicators were differentially effective depending on what psychopathology subjects simulated. The investigators looked at simulated depression and simulated schizophrenia. Overall, the MMPI-2 indicators were better at detecting feigned schizophrenia than feigned depression. The investigators suggested that familiarity with depressive symptoms was probably more commonplace in comparison to schizophrenia. The study also reflected the F, Fb, and F(p) validity scales to best differentiate patients with schizophrenia from subjects feigning schizophrenia and F and Fb to best distinguish depressed patients from subjects feigning depression.

TABLE 20.5
Dissimulation Measures on the MMPI-2

Measure	Assessed Behavior
Cannot Say Score (CS)	Total number of unanswered or answered both true and false; the overall profile is attenuated as the total number increases
Lie Scale (L)	Tendency to deceive the evaluator deliberately
Subtle Defensiveness Scale (K)	Tendency to posture in a socially favorable light; corrects some clinical scales for defensiveness
Superlative Self-Presentation Scale (S) — Scale has five subdimensions: S1 Belief in Human Goodness S2 Serenity S3 Contentment with Life S4 Patience/Denial of Irritability/Anger S5 Denial of Moral Flaws	Tendency to present in a highly virtuous manner
Infrequency Scale (F)	Tendency to exaggerate symptoms
Infrequency Scale (FB)	Derivative of F, but measures F responses only on the last half of the test to provide a comparison between front and rear test performance of symptom exaggeration
Dissimulation Index (F-K)	K > F not empirically useful; F > K empirically demonstrated to indicate faking
Fake Bad Scale (FBS)	Originally designed to measure "fake bad" tendency in personal injury cases; has not been adequately validated for forensic use
F(p) Scale	Tendency to extreme endorsement (symptom exaggeration); most useful with psychiatric inpatients; original F and F(B) scales were not normed with psychiatric population
Variable Response Inconsistency Scale (VRIN)	Tendency not to be consistent in responding to pairs of similar questions
True Response Inconsistency Scale (TRIN)	Tendency to respond inconsistently by endorsing too many items in the same direction (either true or false) when the same response is semantically inconsistent

Note: Adapted from *The MMPI, MMPI-2, & MMPI-A in Court: A Practical Guide for Expert Witnesses and Attorneys* (2nd ed.), by K. S. Pope, J. N. Butcher, & J. Seelen, 2000, Washington, DC: American Psychological Association.

PAI

Like the MMPI, The Personality Assessment Inventory (PAI) is another multiscale inventory; it lacks, however, the many validity referents of the MMPI. The Negative Impression (NIM) scale of the PAI was found successfully to discriminate psychology graduate students with 1-week preparation simulating specific disorders (Rogers, Ornduff, & Sewell, 1993). The NIM cutoff score was found to be effective with feigned schizophrenia, moderately effective with feigned depression, and ineffective with feigned generalized anxiety disorder. Rogers, Sewell, Morey, and Ustad (1996) investigated the effectiveness of the PAI in detecting subjects feigning specific disorders. Two levels of simulating subjects were utilized: 166 naive (undergraduates with minimal preparation), and 80 sophisticated (doctoral psychology students with 1-week preparation). The student subjects' results were compared with those of persons with the designated disorders: schizophrenia ($N = 45$), major depression ($N = 136$), and generalized anxiety disorder ($N = 40$). The PAI was moderately effective with naive simulators but only modestly effective with their

TABLE 20.6
WAIS Approximate Answers and Malingering

Subtest	Criterion
Arithmetic	Answer is + 1 from correct answer
Block design	Answer is correct except for one block, placed 90° or less off
Digit span	Digits reported 1 above or below correct number
Picture arrangement	All pictures are correct except for one, placed as first or last in series (or no change in series)
Information	Total score of "don't know" answers to items 1, 2, 3, 4, 5, 6, 8, 11
Picture completion	"Nothing is missing" response to more than three consecutive items

Note: Constructed with data presented in "The Determination of Malingering," by I. Bash, & M. Alpert, 1980, *Annals of the New York Academy of Science, 347*, 86–98.

sophisticated counterparts. Subsequently, a two-stage discriminant analysis yielded a moderately high hit rate (>80%). This hit rate was maintained in the cross-validation sample, irrespective of the feigned disorder or the sophistication on the simulators.

PSYCHOLOGICAL TESTING BATTERIES

Bash and Alpert (1980) tested four groups of 30 subjects each — (1) suspected malingerers, (2) subjects with schizophrenia who reported auditory hallucinations, (3) subjects with nonhallucinatory schizophrenia, and (4) nonpsychotic subjects with no history of auditory hallucinations. All subjects were tested in two sessions on a variety of neuropsychological and personality measures.

To assess faking on the WAIS, a malingering score based on approximate answers, each scored plus one, was developed (Table 20.6). The total number of approximate answers for each subtest was transformed into a standard score based on the distribution of all subjects. The standard scores were then summed for each individual. The average score of malingerers was 358, with all other groups ranging from 279 to 283.

Although malingerers obtained the lowest scores on every WAIS subtest, they differed significantly from other groups only on Information, Comprehension, Arithmetic, Picture Completion, Verbal, and Full Scale scores. The authors speculated that nonsignificant differences were due to fakers (correctly) believing that individuals with schizophrenia would score worse on those subtests.

The Bender-Gestalt visual-motor test successfully discriminated between malingerers and other subjects. The criteria are shown in Table 20.7. The mean score for known malingerers was 39; the other groups ranged from 11.6 to 12.6.

The Sheehan 1967 form of the Betts test was used successfully to detect fakers. Bash and Alpert (1980) used this test on the assumption that fakers would exaggerate the intensity of their imagery. They also assumed that there should not be substantial differences in intensity across modalities for individual fakers. Using transformed scores based upon the original Sheehan distributions for normal subjects, the mean total score for fakers was 1888, with the other groups ranging from 1388 to 1583. Table 20.8 presents the Betts test items.

The Perceptual Characteristics Questionnaire (PCQ) (Table 20.9) was also utilized by Bash and Alpert (1980). Malingerers obtained a mean score of 900, compared with a mean score of 1161 for those with genuine schizophrenic hallucinators.

TABLE 20.7
Malingering Criteria on the Bender-Gestalt

Targets	Characteristics	Examples
1. Figures	Small and inhibited	Figures all in one corner of page
2. Performance	Uneven quality	Mature mixed with regressed drawings
3. Patterns	Remain unchanged	Squares do not become loops
4. Relationship/direction	Remain unchanged	Diamond shape of parts/details reproduced accurately
5. Symbols	Simplification	Line for series of dots
6. Complexity	Added	Triangle added to Figure A
7. Recall	Low number recalled	0 to 3 figures recalled

TABLE 20.8
Betts Test

Modality	Examples of Requested Imagery
1. Vision	Body image, manner of walking, color of clothing for a known person
2. Hearing	Whistle of a train
3. Touch	Feel of sand, linen, fur
4. Body movement	Running upstairs
5. Taste	Salt in mouth
6. Smell	Fresh paint, cooking cabbage, new leather
7. Body sensations	Hunger, fatigue, sore throat

Note: Vividness of items rated on following scale: 1 = perfectly clear; 2 = very clear; 3 = moderately clear; 4 = not clear, but recognizable; 5 = vague and dim; 6 = very vague and dim; 7 = no image present.

Note: Adapted from "The Determination of Malingering," by I. Bash, & M. Alpert, 1980, *Annals of the New York Academy of Science, 347*, 86–98.

In sum, six of seven tests used by these investigators discriminated fakers from nonfakers (a structured clinical interview failed to discriminate between the two groups). As a general decision rule, subjects who scored in the range of malingering on at least three of the six (valid) tests could tentatively be classified as malingerers. Subjects were considered nonmalingerers if they scored in the range of malingering on fewer than three of the tests. A phi correlation of 0.8872 between diagnosis and performance on three or more tests was reported. It should be noted that the battery used by Bash and Alpert (1980) has not been used in a cross-validation study and the criteria for malingering specified for the component tests of the battery have not been individually cross-validated. Consequently, these results should point the way to additional research rather than be adopted for immediate clinical use.

Schretlen, Wilkins, Van Gorp, and Bobholz (1992) developed and cross-validated a three-test battery on samples of prison inmates and alcoholic inpatients instructed to fake bad and samples of prison inmates, alcoholic inpatients with alcoholism, and psychiatric inpatients who took the tests under standard instructions. The three tests were the MMPI, a specially scored Bender-Gestalt, and a specially developed Malingering Scale (Table 20.10). A discriminant function* of three scores

---

* The discriminant equation was $[2.5 + (0.06 * (MMPI\ F_{(raw)} - K_{(raw)}))] - [0.17 * (VOCABULARY_{(Malingering\ Scale)}) + (0.11 * Bender\ Gestalt\ score)]$. Scores greater than 1 have a 100% probability of faking, while scores less than 1 have a 92% probability of not faking.

TABLE 20.9
Perceptual Characteristics Questionnaire
(PCQ) and Faked Hallucinations

1. Duration of hallucination (3 years or more)
2. Aggressive and hostile messages
3. Occur more than four times per day
4. Visual hallucinations
5. Nonvocal sounds in addition to voices
6. Source localized outside of reporter
7. More frequent with isolation
8. More frequent with emotional arousal
9. More frequent with decreased light
10. Medication does not reduce frequency

Note: Items scored +1 if present, 0 if absent.

Note: Adapted from "The Determination of Malingering," by I. Bash, & M. Alpert, 1980, *Annals of the New York Academy of Science, 347*, 86–98.

---

from these tests correctly classified 80% of the "fakers" with no false-positive errors among their original subjects and 95% of the "fakers" with no false-positive errors among their cross-validation subjects. These results were substantially higher than those obtained from any of the three tests used singly.

In an interesting application of Explicit Alternative Testing (EAT; see Chapter 19), Schretlen et al. (1992) used a two-alternative forced-choice format for their Vocabulary and Abstraction subtests of their Malingering Scale. This permitted them to examine how many of their subjects scored significantly below chance based on the binomial distribution. Since scoring correct on fewer than 18 of the 46 items on these two subtests would occur by chance with $p < 0.05$, they examined how many of their faking and nonfaking subjects scored below this cutoff. Of the faking subjects, 26% scored below 18, and 100% of the nonfaking subjects scored above 18. Thus, this paper-and-pencil application of EAT showed results comparable with other applications of EAT: when a person performs below chance level, one can be confident that he or she is faking, but few genuine fakers do so.

Smith and Burger (1997) described a new instrument called the Structured Inventory of Malingered Symptomatology (SIMS). The SIMS was designed as a paper-and-pencil screening measure to detect malingering. Test items were constructed from a combination of revised validity questions from existing instruments and characteristics of malingerers captured in existing research. The test items were organized on one of five subscales (psychosis, amnestic disorders, neurological impairment, affective disorders, and low intelligence) by experienced clinical psychologists. College students ($N = 476$) were assigned to one of various simulation conditions (each of the subscales, and fake bad) or an honestly responding group. All subjects were administered the SIMS, the F and K scales of the MMPI, 16PF Faking Bad scale, and portions of the malingering scale. The SIMS total score demonstrated the highest sensitivity rating (95.6%) for detection of dissimulation compared with the other indices.

The SIRS instrument alone produced a 95% overall classification accuracy for detecting between a malingered psychiatric and a neuropsychological dysfunction (Hayes, Hale, & Gouvier, 1998). The subjects in this study were initially classified by a multidisciplinary team as nonmalingerers ($N = 12$) and known malingerers ($N = 9$). When scores on the Dot Counting Test, Memory for 15 Items Test, and the M-Test were added to the discrimination function, 100% of the subjects

TABLE 20.10
Malingering Scale

Name _____ Age _____

Vocabulary

Circle the word that means the same thing as the word in CAPITAL letters.

Sample: LAW	book	(rule)
(1) PENNY	money	candy
(2) STEP	write	walk
(3) STREET	road	path
(4) SAUCER	spoon	dish
(5) COUCH	sofa	glass
(6) FABRIC	cloth	shirt
(7) ENORMOUS	huge	gentle
(8) FIDDLE	story	violin
(9) REMEMBER	recall	number
(10) EVIDENT	separate	obvious
(11) HAT	coat	cap
(12) DONKEY	dreadful	mule
(13) THIEF	robber	driver
(14) REPAIR	fix	rest
(15) TUMBLE	dress	fall
(16) FURIOUS	angry	noisy
(17) SHIP	jump	boat
(18) MANY	several	coins
(19) FRY	cook	eat
(20) APPLE	fruit	berry
(21) PARDON	divide	forgive
(22) IMMUNE	diseased	protected
(23) TALK	speak	sleep
(24) GAMBLE	join	bet
(25) DIAMOND	follow	jewel
(26) LIKE	new	same

Abstraction

Circle the answer that should go in the blank (___) space.

(1) A B C ___	D	R
(2) 1 2 3 4 ___	5	4
(3) Scape Cape Ape ___	Ca	Pe
(4) North South East ___	Winter	West
(5) A AB ABC ___	DEF	ABCD
(6) 56/65 24/42 73/___	37	10
(7) Mouth/Eat Eye/See Hand/___	Smell	Touch
(8) AB AC AD ___	AE	BC
(9) Over/Under In/Out Above/___	Below	Behind
(10) A1 B2 C3 ___	D4	E5
(11) White/Black Fast/Slow Up/___	Side	Down
(12) Bus Car Ship ___	Truck	Table
(13) 2 4 6 ___	5	8
(14) Red Blue Green ___	Yellow	Chair
(15) Monday Friday Sunday ___	March	Tuesday
(16) 5 10 15 ___	50	20
(17) Candy/Bar In/Side Light/___	Bulb	Ball
(18) Dog Bird Cat ___	Tree	Horse
(19) Bread Fruit Meat ___	Cheese	Fork
(20) * ** *** ___	****	*

TABLE 20.10 *(continued)*
Malingering Scale

Arithmetic

1. How much is 6 divided by 2?
2. A woman has 2 pairs of shoes. How many shoes does she have altogether?
3. How much does 19 minus 5 equal?
4. How much is 50 cents plus 1 dollar?
5. If you have 3 books and give 1 away, how many will you have left?
6. How much does 1 plus 1 plus 3 equal?
7. If you have 18 dollars and spend 7 dollars and 50 cents, how much will you have left?
8. How much is 20 cents plus 5 cents?
9. How much does 6 divided by 3 equal?
10. A boy had 12 newspapers, and he sold 5 of them. How many did he have left?
11. How much is 4 dollars plus 5 dollars?
12. How much does 1 times 8 equal?
13. If I cut an apple in half, how many pieces will I have?
14. Raffle tickets cost 25 cents each. How much will 6 tickets cost?
15. How much does 3 times 9 equal?
16. If you buy 6 dollars worth of gasoline and pay for it with a 10 dollar bill, how much change should you get back?
17. How much does 7 plus 4 equal?
18. How many hours will it take a person to walk 24 miles at the rate of 3 miles per hour?
19. A girl had 1 dollar in change. She lost 50 cents. How much did she have left?
20. How much does 10 minus 5 equal?

INFORMATION

1. What are the colors of the American flag?
2. How many months are there in a year?
3. How many things make a dozen?
4. What must you do to make water boil?
5. Who discovered America?
6. How many pennies make a nickel?
7. From what animal do we get bacon?
8. Why does oil float on water?
9. What is the capital of Italy?
10. What is a thermometer?
11. How many days make a week?
12. Where does the sun rise?
13. Name the two countries that border the United States.
14. Who wrote Hamlet?
15. Name the four seasons of the year.
16. Who invented the electric light bulb?
17. Name the month that comes next after March.
18. What does the stomach do?
19. What is the shape of a ball?
20. In what direction would you travel if you went from Chicago to Panama?
21. How many weeks are there in a year?
22. Who runs a courtroom?
23. Who was president of the United States during the Civil War?
24. How many legs does a dog have?

Vocabulary _____ Abstraction _____ Arithmetic _____ Information _____ Total _____
Score +1 for each correct answer on each of the four subtests.

Note: Malingering Scale, by D. Schretlen, 1990, Baltimore, MD: Johns Hopkins University. Copyright 1990, David Schretlen, Ph.D. The Johns Hopkins Hospital, Meyer 218, 600 North Wolfe St., Baltimore, MD 21205. With permission.

were correctly classified to the respective groups. As with most forensic assessment efforts using psychometrics, there is wisdom in not relying on any single test or instrument. Although more costly and time-consuming, the advisability of employing a battery of relevant tests in forensic assessments, especially when malingering is suspected, is an often repeated recommendation in the literature (Fauteck, 1995; Hayes et al., 1998; Roman et al., 1990).

PROJECTIVE TESTING AND DETECTION OF MALINGERING

The Rorschach test is one of the few projective techniques that has received some systematic effort to investigate faking. In early studies, the Rorschach technique was presented as an instrument that could not be faked at all (Fosberg, 1938, 1941). Features of this test supposedly lent themselves to detection of malingering (Benton, 1945). Later studies showed that the Rorschach could be faked partially (Carp & Shavzin, 1950; Easton & Feigenbaum, 1967). Belief in the supposed resistance of the Rorschach to faking persisted for years (Ackland, 1990; Exner, 1978, 1991), in spite of studies showing the inability of experts to detect malingering on this technique. By the early 1990s, Exner himself had begun to recognize the problem dissimulation posed for the Rorschach. Exner acknowledged, "It has often been proposed that one value of the Rorschach is its immunity to faking or simulation, but the validity of that axiom seems questionable" (1991, p. 427). Exner cites research supporting successfully dissimulated response sets on the Rorschach, but he suggests, in the end, that if the Rorschach is properly administered it may not be possible to fake psychopathology. Exner (1991) critiqued that the earlier studies contained multiple critical flaws. These flaws included test administration with a group of subjects rather than the recommended one-to-one administration. The earlier studies also employed no formal scoring system and were essentially interpreted on an intuitive basis by panels of "expert" judges. Another significant flaw was the observation that malingered Rorschach protocols were characteristically briefer than with controls. That is, fakers would attempt to abbreviate response production rather than risk overextending their responses. In the Exner system a protocol of <14 responses is considered too abbreviated to be valid.

One investigation with the Rorschach found that Fellows of the Society for Personality Assessment, supposedly representing high competency in Rorschach assessment, were unable to detect malingering of psychosis by normal subjects who were not sophisticated about psychosis (Albert, Fox, & Kahn, 1980). The confidence expressed by these experts in their judgments did not differ between faked and nonfaked protocols. Each protocol was (blindly) judged by six to nine experts. In general, very little malingering was detected, even when malingering was explicitly presented to the judges as an alternative.

In this often-cited study, the ability to fake psychosis was directly related to the information subjects possessed about this mental condition. Fakers to whom a taped description of schizophrenia was presented showed more psychotic disturbance. These subjects were not told, however, how to fake on the Rorschach. A rather disturbing finding involved false positives and false negatives from the two control groups not concerned with faking. Of the normals, 24% were seen as psychotic and only 48% of the psychotics were correctly identified.

Mittman (1983) essentially replicated these findings when 60 clinicians were generally unable to detect faked schizophrenia on the Rorschach. The clinicians did detect uninformed more often than informed fakers, but only small percentages of the protocols were diagnosed as malingered, in spite of the judges possessing formally scored and summarized protocols.

The lack of specific criteria for malingering on the Rorschach has plagued this instrument (Perry & Kinder, 1990), even with Exner's computerized scoring system (Cohen, 1990). Experienced clinicians persist in their false belief that they can detect faking on the Rorschach even when they do not use objective, shareable, teachable criteria. To overcome this problem, Bennett (1988) stated the following in regard to the Exner scoring system and malingering:

Schizophrenics who are attempting to simulate nonschizophrenia are generally not able to produce records that would be judged as "normal." You would still want to analyze the patient's level of cooperation and test-taking attitude, the number of popular responses, the X + %, the X − %, and the special scores. The uninformed schizophrenic would have a difficult time not producing special scores such as malignant FABCOMs or CONTAMs, which would indicate the presence of disordered thinking.

Conversely, most nonschizophrenic patients cannot produce a schizophrenic record, but there are exceptions. Analysis of the same variables of test-taking approach, X + %, X − %, and the special scores will show better reality testing, better form quality, and fewer malignant special scores in a record that "appears" bizarre and detached from the inkblot stimulus. Very long responses and over-elaboration are suggestive of deception. Average response is 15 words, and if the patient responds with about 35 words or more per response, this is often a sign of malingering.

In spite of the lack of a rationale for these criteria, they are at least explicit and testable in properly designed studies.

Seamons, Howell, Carlisle, and Roe (1981) used the Exner system to judge protocols of 48 subjects (36 subjects with schizophrenia) who were asked to take the Rorschach twice — as mentally ill and then as normal individuals. This study clearly showed that the instructions affected the content of responses, but not ratios, percentages, or deviations. More dramatic and bizarre responses were associated with faking particularly those involving sex, blood, mutilation, and fighting. Seamons et al. stated:

> The clinician should exercise caution when response simulation is suspected in a forensic or prison population. For example, if the protocol contains an excessively high number of popular responses, the subject may be attempting to "fake" normal. On the other hand, when X + %, F + %, and L variables are within the normal range, and a high number of dramatic, blood, texture, shading, vista, nonhuman movement, or inappropriate combination responses are observed, it may be indicative of an attempt to appear mentally ill. Finally, it should be noted that the different diagnostic groups accounted for many more significant findings than did the varied instructions, reaffirming the discriminative ability of the Rorschach irrespective of instructions. (p. 133)

The simulation of psychosis was also detected on a multiple-choice group Rorschach (Pettigrew, Tuma, Pickering, & Whelton, 1983). In this study of 75 students and 50 subjects with schizophrenia who selected one of four choices to each of the (miniature) Rorschach inkblots, the 62 student/fakers chose responses with significantly more good form with bizarre wording than did the subjects with schizophrenica. Thus, fakers were exposed by their own perceptual accuracy.

In spite of the limitations of the Rorschach technique in assessment of malingering of psychosis, several criteria are worth further investigation (Stermac, 1988). Good form with dramatic/bizarre wording or dramatic content by itself may indicate faking bad. For faking good, Stermac suggested that no good Rorschach indicators have been presented.

In an effort to overcome some of the flaws in earlier studies (i.e., group administration, abbreviated protocols, no formal scoring, etc.), Ganellen, Wasyliw, Haywood, and Grossman (1996) administered the Rorschach in tandem with the MMPI. The subjects were all defendants accused of serious crimes and therefore all were assumed to be inclined to malinger. Based on MMPI validity scales the subjects were divided into two groups: honest ($N = 35$) and malingered ($N = 130$). The Rorschach protocols of both groups were examined to assess how successfully the malingerers could deliberately produce records that appeared psychotic. This determination was based on empirically derived Rorschach indices of psychosis:

1. Measures of perceptual accuracy (X + %, X − %, Xu %)
2. Measures of thought disorder (Sum 6 Special Scores, Level 2 Special Scores, DRs)
3. Populars

4. Summary measure of dramatic content
5. Number of responses

The results indicated that on the MMPI indicators the malingered group consistently presented as more psychotic compared with the honest group. The malingered group had higher MMPI scale 8 (Sc) elevations than was typical for hospitalized patients with schizophrenia. The two groups did not differ, however, on the Rorschach indicators for psychosis. The suggestion was that the malingerers could successfully accommodate to the validity indicators of the MMPI, but were not successful in being able to accommodate to the more subtle indicators of psychosis on the Rorschach. The malingerers did evidence a greater number of dramatic responses. The investigators noted the importance of clinicians distinguishing between attempts to exaggerate symptoms of a genuine psychological disorder as opposed to conscious, deliberate attempts to claim symptoms that do not exist. This study offered a new breath of life to the use of the (Exner) Rorschach to detect malingered psychosis, particularly when used in the context of a broader psychometric assessment. Undoubtedly, controversy regarding the utility of the Rorschach with malingering of psychosis will persist.

SYNTHESIS

Available research suggests that the following may indicate manufactured or exaggerated psychosis:

1. Production of psychotic symptoms is apparently under voluntary control and is understandable in terms of payoff and environmental circumstances.
2. Psychotic symptoms worsen when being observed or when being interviewed, are bizarre for the circumstances, involve quick shifts to nonpsychotic behavior when not being observed, or cease under mild environmental stimulation.
3. Patient has a history of faked mental problems.
4. Patient admits to faking psychosis and his or her behavior can be explained in terms of environmental events.
5. Patient uses an alias, is unwilling to allow access to old records, displays evidence of a severe personality disorder, has a history of substance abuse, to include possession of paraphernalia, etc., which explain psychotic symptoms.
6. Laboratory testing suggests malingering (e.g., as a factitious disorder).
7. Psychological tests suggest deception in regard to psychosis.
8. Patient has rapid remission of symptoms.
9. Crime is associated with accomplices; crime fits into history of defendant's criminality; defendant has nonpsychotic motives for the crime.

There are caveats for forensic clinicians who conduct evaluation for malingered psychosis. The performance of patients with schizophrenia was investigated on cognitive malingering instruments (Back et al., 1996). The study evaluated the effect of a diagnosis of schizophrenia on test performance and its relationship between severity of psychosis-associated cognitive impairment and psychiatric disturbance. The subjects ($N = 30$) were administered the Rey 15-Item Memory Test (RMT), Rey Dot Counting Test (RDCO), and Hiscock Forced-Choice (FC) method to detect malingering of cognitive symptoms. The subjects also completed the Mini Mental State Exam and the Brief Psychiatric Rating Scale. The results showed that 13% of the subjects failed the RMT and the RDCO, and 27% failed the FC measure. The investigators noted that performance on the RMT appeared to be significantly lowered by lesser educational levels. By comparison, the RDCO and the FC performances were related to the presence of cognitive impairment and the RDCO was also significantly affected by increasing age. The relatively high failure rates of the subjects implicate caution in forensic assessments of malingering when there is any history of schizophrenic symptoms. A number of investigators (Ganellen et al., 1996; Roman et al., 1990) have pointed out that positive psychometric indicators of malingering do not necessarily rule out the presence of a comorbid psychiatric disorder such as characterological features, substance abuse, or acute or severe psychopathology. Any malingering assessment requires careful analysis by the clinician and an appreciation for all possibilities of clinical presentation.

Neuropsychologists are confronted by particular problems with patients who may be malingering (see Chapter 11). Patients may have reported histories of neurological trauma, but also present with varied psychiatric symptoms and/or effects of medications, all of which confound meaningful neuropsychological assessment. When the factors of financial compensation and malingering are added to the clinical mixture, the assessment task is formidable. Schwartz (1991) described the particular problem of neuropsycholgical assessment when the patient presents with possible malingering and/or paranoia approaching psychosis.

Cultural factors can influence the apparent presentation of a malingering effort. In a study with ultraorthodox Jewish military inductees, 24 subjects who had been diagnosed as malingering were reexamined (Witztum, Grinshpoon, Margolin, & Kron, 1996). The reexamination found 21 subjects to evidence severe psychopathology (i.e., psychosis, personality disorder, and mental retardation), but none was diagnosed as malingering. The investigators attributed the discrepancies in diagnosis to the ignorance, cultural bias, and counter-transference of the original examiners.

As a final comment, the extensive use of studies in which subjects are instructed/coached to engage in deception and malingering should be noted. As Ben-Porath (1994) pointed out, it is important for psychologists who interpret psychometric validity to understand the susceptibilities of psychometrics to malingering. Additionally, the use of experimental models of deception is subject to misappropriation and misunderstanding. Forensic psychologists must subscribe to the requirements of professional ethics codes regarding the validity, integrity, and security of tests and test data.

REFERENCES

Ackland, M. (1990). Personal communication.

Albert, S., Fox, H. M., & Kahn, M. W. (1980). Faking psychosis on a Rorschach: Can expert judges detect malingering? *Journal of Personality Assessment, 44*, 115–119.

Anderson, K. (1989). Personal communication.

Back, C., Boone, K. B., Edwards, C., Parks, C., Burgoyne, K., & Silver, B. (1996). The performance of schizophrenics on three cognitive tests, 15-Item Memory Test, Rey Dot Counting, and Hiscock Forced-Choice Method. *Assessment, 3*(4), 449–457.

Bagby, R. M., Rogers, R., Nicholson, R. A., Cameron, S. L., Rector, N. A., Schuller, D. R., & Seeman, M. V. (1997). Detecting feigned depression and schizophrenia on the MMPI-2. *Journal of Personality Assessment, 68*(3), 650–664.

Bagby, R. M., Rogers, R., Nicholson, R. A., Buis, T., Seeman, M. V., & Rector, N. (1997). Does clinical training facilitate feigning schizophrenia on the MMPI-2? *Psychological Assessment, 9*(2), 106–112.

Bash, I. (1978). *Malingering: A study designed to differentiate between schizophrenic offenders and malingerers.* Unpublished doctoral dissertation. New York University, New York.

Bash, I., & Alpert, M. (1980). The determination of malingering. *Annals of the New York Academy of Science, 347*, 86–98.

Beaber, R., Marston, A., Michelli, J., & Mills, M. (1985). A brief test for measuring malingering in schizophrenic individuals. *American Journal of Psychiatry, 142*, 1478–1481.

Ben-Porath, Y. S. (1994). The ethical dilemma of coached malingering research. *Psychological Assessment, 6*(1), 14–15.

Bender, L. (1938). *A visual motor gestalt test and its clinical use.* New York: The Orthopsychiatric Association.

Bennett, M. (1988). Personal communication.

Benton, A. L. (1945). Rorschach performances of suspected malingerers. *The Journal of Abnormal and Social Psychology, 40*, 94–96.

Berry, D., Baer, R., & Harris, M. (1991). Detection of malingering on the MMPI: A meta-analysis. *Clinical Psychology Review, 11*, 585–598.

Braginsky, B., & Braginsky, D. (1967). Schizophrenic patients in the psychiatric interview: An experimental study of their effectiveness at manipulation. *Journal of Consulting Psychology, 31*, 543–547.

Butcher, J. N. (1990). *User's guide to the Minnesota clinical interpretive report for MMPI-2.* Minneapolis, MN: University of Minnesota Press.

Carp, A. L., & Shavzin, A. R. (1950). The susceptibility to falsification of the Rorschach psychodiagnostic technique. *Journal of Consulting Psychology, 14*, 230–233.

Cohen, J. B. (1990). Misuse of computer software to detect faking on the Rorschach: A reply to Kahn, Fox, and Rhode. *Journal of Personality Assessment, 54*(1–2), 58–62.

Diamond, B. (1956). The simulation of insanity. *Journal of Social Therapy, 2*, 158–165.

Easton, K., & Feigenbaum, K. (1967). An examination of an experimental set to fake the Rorschach test. *Perceptual and Motor Skills, 24*, 871–874.

Endicott, J., & Spitzer, R. L. (1978). A diagnostic interview: The schedule of affective disorders and schizophrenia. *Archives of General Psychiatry, 35*, 837–844.

Exner, J. E. (1978). *The Rorschach: A comprehensive system. Vol. 2: Current research and advanced interpretation.* New York: Wiley.

Exner, J. E. (1991). *The Rorschach: A comprehensive system, Volume 2: Interpretation* (2nd ed.). New York: Wiley.

Fauteck, P. K. (1995). Detecting the malingering of psychosis in offenders: No easy solutions. *Criminal Justice & Behavior, 22*(1), 3–18.

Fosberg, I. A. (1938). Rorschach reactions under varied instructions. *Rorschach Research Exchange, 3*, 12–30.

Fosberg, I. A. (1941). An experimental study of the reliability of the Rorschach psychodiagnostic technique. *Rorschach Research Exchange, 5*, 72–84.

Ganellen, R. J., Wasyliw, O. E., Haywood, T. W., & Grossman, L. S. (1996). Can psychosis be malingered on the Rorschach? An empirical study. *Journal of Personality Assessment, 66*(1), 65–80.

Gillis, J., Rogers, R., & Bagby, R. (1992). Validity of the M test: Simulation design and natural group approaches. *Journal of Personality Assessment, 57*, 1, 130–140.

Green, R. L. (1988). Assessment of malingering and defensiveness by objective personality inventories. In R. Rogers (Ed.), *Clinical assessment of malingering and deception* (2nd ed., pp. 169–207). New York: Guilford Press.

Hayes, J. S., Hale, D. B., & Gouvier, W. D. (1998). Malingering detection in a mentally retarded forensic population. *Applied Neuropsychology, 5*(1), 33–36.

Heilbrun, K., Bennett, W. S., White, A. J., & Kelly, J. (1990). An MMPI-based empirical model of malingering and deception. *Behavioral Sciences & the Law, 8*(1), 45–53.

Hollender, M. H., & Hirsch, S. J. (1964). Hysterical psychosis. *The American Journal of Psychiatry, 120*, 1066–1074.

Lewis, D. O., & Bard, J. S. (1991). Multiple personality disorders and forensic issues. *Psychiatric Clinics of North America, 14*(3), 741–756.

Mittman, B. L. (1983). Judges' ability to diagnose schizophrenia on the Rorschach: The effect of malingering. *Dissertation Abstracts International, 44*(4), 2148–B.

Norris, M. P., & May, M. C. (1998). Screening for malingering in a correctional setting. *Law & Human Behavior, 22*(3), 315–323.

Osran, H. C., & Weinberger, L. E. (1994). Personality disorders and "restoration to sanity." *Bulletin of the American Academy of Psychiatry & the Law, 22*(2), 257–267.

Pensa, R., Dorfman, W. I., Gold, S. N., & Schneider, B. (1996). Detection of malingered psychosis with the MMPI-2. *Psychotherapy in Private Practice, 14*(4), 47–64.

Perry, G., & Kinder, B. (1990). The susceptibility of the Rorschach to malingering: A critical review. *Journal of Personality Assessment, 54*(1–2), 47–57.

Pettigrew, C. G., Tuma, J. M., Pickering, J. W., & Whelton, J. (1983). Simulation of psychosis on a multiple-choice projective test. *Perceptual and Motor Skills, 57*, 463–469.

Pollock, P. (1998). Feigning auditory hallucinations by offenders. *Journal of Forensic Psychiatry, 9*(2), 305–327.

Pope, K. S., Butcher, J. N., & Seelen, J. (1993). *The MMPI, MMPI-2, & MMPI-A in court: A practical guide for expert witnesses and attorneys.* Washington, DC: American Psychological Association.

Pope, K. S., Butcher, J. N., & Seelen, J. (2000). *The MMPI, MMPI-2, & MMPI-A in court: A practical guide for expert witnesses and attorneys* (2nd ed.). Washington, DC: American Psychological Association.

Pope, H. G., Jonas, J. M., & Jones, B. (1982). Factitious psychosis: Phenomenology, family history, and long-term outcome of nine patients. *The American Journal of Psychiatry, 139*(11), 1480–1483.

Resnick, P. J. (1984). The detection of malingered mental illness. *Behavioral Sciences and the Law, 2*(1), 21–38.

Resnick, P. J. (1988). Malingering of posttraumatic disorders. In R. Rogers (Ed.), *Clinical assessment of malingering and deception* (pp. 83–103). New York: Guilford Press.

Resnick, P. J. (1997). Malingered psychosis. In R. Rogers (Ed.), *Clinical assessment of malingering and deception* (2nd ed., pp. 47–67). New York: Guilford Press.

Resnick. P. J. (1999). The detection of malingered psychosis. *Psychiatric Clinics of North America, 22*(1), 159–172.

Ritson, B., & Forrest, A. (1970). The simulation of psychosis: A contemporary presentation. *British Journal of Medical Psychology, 43*, 31–37.

Rogers, R. (1984). Towards an empirical model of malingering and deception. *Behavioral Sciences and the Law, 2*, 93–112.

Rogers, R. (1987). The assessment of malingering within a forensic context. In D. N. Weisstub, (Ed.), *Law and psychiatry: International perspectives* (Vol. 3, pp. 209–237). New York: Plenum.

Rogers, R. (1988). *Clinical assessment of malingering and deception* (1st ed.). New York: Guilford Press.

Rogers, R. (1992). *Structured interview of reported symptoms (SIRS).* Odessa, FL: Psychological Assessment Resources.

Rogers, R., Bagby, M., & Gillis, R. (1992). Improvements in the M test as a screening measure for malingering. *Bulletin of the American Academy Psychiatry and Law, 20*, (1), 101–104.

Rogers, R., Gillis, J. R., & Bagby, R. M. (1990). The SIRS as a measure of malingering: A validation study with a correctional sample. *Behavioral Sciences & the Law, 8*(1), 85–92.

Rogers, R., Gillis, J. R., Bagby, R. M., & Monteiro, E. (1991). Detection of malingering on the Structured Interview of Reported Symptoms (SIRS): A study of coached and uncoached simulators. *Psychological Assessment, 3*(4), 673–677.

Rogers, R., Gillis, J. R., Dickens, S. E., & Bagby, R. M. (1991). Standardized assessment of malingering: Validation of the Structured Interview of Reported Symptoms (SIRS). *Psychological Assessment, 3*(1), 89–96.

Rogers, R., Kropp, P. R., Bagby, R. M., & Dickens, S. E. (1992). Faking specific disorders: A study of the Structured Interview of Reported Symptoms (SIRS). *Journal of Clinical Psychology, 48*(5), 643–648.

Rogers, R., Ornduff, S. R., & Sewell, K. W. (1993). Feigning specific disorders: A study of the Personality Assessment Inventory. *Journal of Personality Assessment, 60*(3), 554–560.

Rogers, R., Sewell, K. W., Morey, L. C., & Ustad, K. L. (1996). Detection of feigned mental disorders on the Personality Assessment Inventory: A discriminant analysis. *Journal of Personality Assessment, 67*(3), 629–640.

Roman, D. T., Tuley, M. R., Villanueva, M. R., & Mitchell, W. E. (1990). Evaluating MMPI validity in a forensic psychiatric population: Distinguishing between malingering and genuine psychopathology. *Criminal Justice & Behavior, 17*(2), 186–198.

Seamons, D. T., Howell, R. J., Carlisle, A. L., & Roe, A. V. (1981). Rorschach simulation of mental illness and normality by psychotic and nonpsychotic legal offenders. *Journal of Personality Assessment, 45*, 130–135.

Schlesinger, L. B. (1996). *Explorations in criminal psychopathology: Clinical syndromes with forensic implications.* Springfield, IL: Charles C Thomas.

Schretlen, D. (1988). The use of psychological tests to identify malingered symptoms of mental disorder. *Clinical Psychology Review, 8*(5), 451–476.

Schretlen, D., Wilkins, S., Van Gorp, W., & Bobholz, J. (1992). Cross-validation of a psychological test battery to detect faked insanity. *Psychological Assessment, 4*(1), 77–83.

Schwartz, M. L. (1991). Sometimes safe, sometimes out: Umpire gives split decision. *Clinical Neuropsychologist, 5*(1), 89–99.

Shooter, E., & Hall, H. V. (1989). Distortion analysis on the MMPI and MMPI-2. *Bulletin of the American Academy of Forensic Psychology, 10*, 9.

Sivec, H. J., Lynn, S. J., & Garske, J. P. (1994). The effect of somatoform disorder and paranoid psychotic role-related dissimulations as a response set on the MMPI-2. *Assessment, 1*(1), 69–81.

Smith, G. (1992). Detection of malingering of schizophrenia in male prisoners. Unpublished paper. University of Missouri at St. Louis (as cited in Rogers, Bagby, & Gillis, 1992, p. 102).

Smith, G. P., & Burger, G. K. (1997). Detection of malingering: Validation of the Structured Inventory of Malingered Symptomatology (SIMS). *Journal of the American Academy of Psychiatry & the Law, 25*(2), 183–189.

Spitzer, R. L., & Endicott, J. (1978). *Schedule of affective disorders and schizophrenia*. New York: Biometric Research.

Stermac, L. (1988). Projective testing and dissimulation. In R. Rogers (Ed.), *Clinical assessment of malingering and deception* (pp. 159–168). New York: Guilford Press.

Wetter, M. A., Baer, R. A., Berry, D. T. R., Robison, L. H., & Sumptor, J. (1993). MMPI-2 profiles of motivated fakers given specific symptom information: A comparison of matched patients. *Psychological Assessment, 5*(3), 317–323.

Witztum, E., Grinshpoon, A., Margolin, J., & Kron, S. (1996). The erroneous diagnosing of malingering in the military setting. *Military Medicine, 161*(4), 225–229.

21 Hallucinations and Deception

This chapter suggests three basic methods for assessing misrepresentation in regard to faked hallucinations. These involve assessing (1) violation of base rate expectancies, (2) degree of complex and self-controlled behavior shown by the client, and (3) the details of hallucinatory experiences via a structured questionnaire.

THE UBIQUITY OF HALLUCINATORY EXPERIENCES

Hallucinations are typically defined as false sensory impressions. The "false" part of this definition refers to the lack of an external set of referents, which, to the assessor, would explain and support the assessee's description of the event. Dreaming is considered by some to be a common example of an hallucinatory experience, surrounded at the onset of sleep in some people by hypnogogic hallucinations and waking up with hypnogogic hallucinations (American Psychiatric Association, 1994; Kaplan & Sadock, 1985).

Approximately 12% of the normal population has experienced hallucinations while awake (Coleman, Butcher, & Carson, 1984; Parish, 1914; Slade & Bentall, 1988). In nonpsychiatric populations, hallucinations have been known to be caused by (1) exhaustion, as in the last stage of the General Adaptation Syndrome (Selye, 1980–1983); (2) sleep deprivation; (3) social isolation, as in the "long eye" syndrome caused by rejection by working peers (Coleman, Butcher, & Carson, 1984); (4) severe reactive depression; (5) amputation of limbs, as in the phantom limb experience; (6) heart conditions, secondary to cardiovascular medication or to atropine or its derivatives in hypersensitive persons (Kaplan & Sadock, 1985); and (7) secondary reaction to intoxication by the hallucinogenics, particularly LSD, mescaline, psilocybin, and other drugs such as phencyclidine, opioids, and cocaine. Hallucinatory experience has often been reported by prisoners. Historically, when major mental illness was ruled out, this phenomenon was referred to as Ganser's syndrome, otherwise known as "prison psychosis" (Cocores & Cohen, 1996). Similarly, criminal offenders commonly feign hallucinations when they are attempting to present themselves as being psychotic for the purpose of appearing as either incompetent or as lacking criminal responsibility (Hayes, Hale, & Gouvier, 1997). A particular forensic challenge is posed by offenders who have been previously psychotic, but are currently feigning psychotic symptoms (Pollock, 1998).

In the organic brain syndromes, hallucinations may be caused by a variety of events (see reviews by Lezak, 1983; Strub & Black, 1981) including (1) delirium, (2) tumors associated with increasing intracranial pressure, (3) temporal lobe lesions, (4) seizures of several types, (5) alcohol-related encephalopathy, (6) head injury, as in postcoma experiences and disorientation, and (7) irritation of various sensory pathways, such as the visual pathways transversing the temporal lobes causing Lilliputian hallucinations or the olfactory pathways causing distinctive odors such as burnt rubber.

Not all organic brain-induced hallucinations involve the perception of a separate reality. In organic hallucinosis, for example, the hallucinations (usually auditory) may arise within a full state of alertness and orientation. In Lilliputian hallucinations, the affected person knows the small figures are not real; they are not associated with delusions.

TABLE 21.1

Auditory Hallucinations in Schizophrenia and Acute Alcoholic Psychoses

	Alcoholic Psychoses	Schizophrenia
Onset in illness	Early	Later
Temporality	Continuous or frequent	Episodic, separated by hours, days, or weeks
Type of sound	Nonverbal noises or unintelligible voices	Voices, usually clear
Source	Outside body	Within body
Effect of patterned visual stimulation	Decrease in frequency	No change in frequency
Effect of arousal	Increase in frequency	No change in frequency
Willingness to discuss hallucinations	Eager	Withdrawal response
Insight	Better	Worse
Delusions	Less frequent	More frequent

Note: Adapted from "Perceptual Characteristics Distinguishing Auditory Hallucinations in Schizophrenia and Acute Alcoholic Psychoses," by M. Alpert, & M. Silvers, 1970, *American Journal of Psychiatry, 127,* 298–302.

The major psychotic disorders are often associated with hallucinations (American Psychiatric Association, 1994). Vivid hallucinations can be seen in all the schizophrenic subtypes. Within the affective disorders, hallucinations are encountered. In major depression, for example, the examiner using DSM-IV is asked to determine whether reported hallucinations are mood congruent or mood incongruent. Schizoaffective psychosis, a combination of thought disorder and affective psychosis, often has hallucinations as an associated feature.

Early work suggesting that different mental conditions involve different types of hallucinations is illustrated by Alpert and Silvers (1970). In the study, 80 adult hallucinating inpatients with either alcoholism or schizophrenia were studied. Table 21.1 reveals the differences in hallucinations between the two groups.

The experience of hallucinations is so common that some ascribe that an endogenous hallucinogen will be found, that is, a chemical synthesized within the body due to stress, which in turn creates an hallucination (Slade & Bentall, 1988). Hallucinations may represent an attempt to restructure reality or at least to perceive the stress in a more adaptive fashion.

As a further common feature, most hallucinations can be set off by multiple or indirect combining conditions. Tactile (haptic) hallucinations can be secondary to schizophrenia, withdrawal from alcohol, or drug intoxication. Olfactory hallucinations, the false perception of smell, and gustatory hallucinations, the false perception of taste, are often experienced together in such conditions as temporal lobe epilepsy and schizophrenia. Reflex hallucinations involve irritation in one sense creating a hallucination in another, for example, a toothache might set off an auditory hallucination in a person with schizophrenia. Last, kinesthetic hallucinations involve the sensation of altered states in body organs where no receptor apparatus could explain the experience. This is found in psychotic patients but also among organic patients, as for example, a burning sensation in the brain caused by schizophrenia or a major depression.

In sum, hallucinations are found in a wide variety of unimpaired and impaired individuals. Evaluators of possible deception are thus cautioned to consider hallucinations separately from psychosis. Linking hallucinations to one or two mental conditions neglects the ubiquity of the phenomenon.

TARGETS

Any sensory system can be targeted for hallucinations. These include the chemical sensory (i.e., smell, taste), mechanical (i.e., touch, hearing, vestibular-head movement and orientation, joint position and movement, muscle), photic (i.e., seeing), and thermal (i.e., cold and warmth) systems. The faker may pick a hallucination for a certain time and circumstance (e.g., previous to, during, or after a crime; at the time of an evaluation). Targets may be chosen with distinctive qualities in terms of duration, intensity, form, and frequency. Some aspects are particularly difficult to fake without prior experience or knowledge of hallucinations. These include one's expected response to bona fide hallucinations, the "origin" of the hallucinations, and the normal sequence of prodromal and residual symptoms. The faker often finds himself or herself in a position of having to generate information when questioned and of hoping to maintain consistency. Targets are chosen in the service of a long-range goal, such as exculpation or mitigation in a criminal proceeding.

Hallucinations falsely superimposed on mental disorders such as schizophrenia are most difficult to detect. When a person has a history of genuine hallucinations, but fabricates one for the relevant situation, it is difficult to detect. The best lie is the partial truth, and this applies to faked hallucinations in experienced subjects.

The evaluator should keep in mind that some distortion in falsely describing hallucinations may be nondeliberate. Junginger and Frame (1985) reported a negative relationship between clarity and location. Hallucinations most clearly heard originated inside the head, yet a bimodal distribution was seen in ascribing origination of voices.

RESPONSE STYLES

Various forms of distorting hallucinations with examples follow:

Honesty	A subject with organic disorders shares his/her hallucinations with accuracy
Faking good	A subject with schizophrenia denies hallucinations (e.g., to get out of hospital)
Faking bad	A psychopathic subject makes up hallucinations to avoid imprisonment
Invalidation	No conclusions can be drawn; the faker may have unsuccessfully attempted to fake good or bad
Mixed responding	Admits to hallucinations but denies schizophrenia
Fluctuating	Admits to hallucinations and then changes story as vested interests change when reevaluated

DETECTION METHODS

The use of phenomenological base rate information to detect feigned hallucinations is discussed by Resnick (1984, 1988, 1997, 1999) and involves the assumption that fakers may not be aware of the true nature and quality of hallucinations. For example, they may not know that hallucinations are usually as follows:

1. Related to some psychic purpose.
2. Associated with delusions.
3. Eliminated or reduced when the individual is involved in activity.
4. Perceived as emanating from outside the head — many persons with schizophrenia affirm that the voices could have been due to their imagination.
5. Female and/or male voices with clear, not vague messages. Talking back to voices and perceiving the voices as accusatory occur a minority of the time; persons with schizophrenia usually perceive voices speaking directly to them.
6. Whether with eyes open or closed, no prodromata is typically seen.
7. Perceived as unpleasant in odor (olfactory hallucinations).
8. Consist of normal-size people and are in color.

TABLE 21.2
Base Rates of Hallucinations

	Percentage
1. Overall incidence in psychotic and acute schizophrenia	76
2. Auditory in schizophrenia	66
3. Visual in psychosis	27
4. Associated with delusions	88
5. "Yes" to "Could voices have been due to your imagination?" (schizophrenia)	56
6. Both male and female voices	75
7. Vague voices heard	7
8. Voices are accusatory	33
9a. Originated outside head (all with psychosis and schizophrenia)	88
9b. Originated outside head (schizophrenia only)	50
10. Talking back to voices	45
11a. Voices associated with commands (all patients)	38
11b. Voices associated with commands (schizophrenia only)	47
12. Overall incidence in hospital alcoholics (75% auditory; 70% visual)	84
13a. Command hallucinations in alcoholic persons	35
13b. Command hallucinations in affective disorders	46
14. Content of command hallucinations (all patients)	
a. Suicide	52
b. Nonlethal injury	12
c. Nonviolent acts	14
d. Unspecified	17

Note: Adapted from "Malingered Psychosis," by P. J. Resnick, 1988, in R. Rogers (Ed.), *Clinical Assessment of Malingering and Deception* (pp. 34-53) New York: Guilford Press.

9. Seen in acute schizophrenia by an onset of peculiar tastes (gustatory hallucinations).
10. Composed of vivid figures often discussing the person in the third person (alcoholism). The actions of people with alcoholism are rarely the result of command hallucinations and seem motivated by a desire to avoid threat or disgrace.

Resnick cogently stated, "Detailed knowledge about actual hallucinations is the clinician's greatest asset in recognizing simulated hallucinations" (1988, p. 37). This material is presented in Table 21.2.

Thus, characteristics of reported hallucinations are compared with their overall base rate percentage. Rare responses would thus be the focus of detailed probing by the evaluator, all within a comprehensive assessment to determine possible deception.

Much is owed to Resnick for his base rate approach. In generically addressing the issue of malingered psychosis, Resnick (1993) cites a series of clinical indicators:

1. Overacting
2. Calling attention to illnesses
3. Lack of the subtle signs of residual schizophrenia
4. Sudden onset of delusions
5. Contradictions in patient's account of illness

With specific regard to feigned hallucinations, Resnick suggests a "Threshold Model" (1988, p. 47). Faking hallucinations is suspected if any of the following occur:

1. Continuous rather than intermittent hallucinations
2. Vague or inaudible hallucinations
3. Hallucinations not associated with delusions
4. Stilted language reported in hallucinations
5. Inability to state strategies to diminish voices
6. Self-report that all command hallucinations were obeyed

Item 6 is especially helpful to evaluators because, as Resnick points out, command hallucinations are generally ignored. Further, they can be actively made to disappear altogether temporarily by interpersonal contact, motor activity (e.g., working, exercising), taking psychotropic medication, and even passive activities such as watching TV and lying down.

Some caution is needed with Resnick's approach, however. Hallucinations can occur in the absence of delusions, particularly in organic states and substance intoxication (item 3). Stilted language is occasionally used to describe actual hallucinations (item 4), especially if there is psychotic recall of the hallucinations and the person is reporting a nonverbal event with familiar verbal labels. Similarly, the inability to state strategies to diminish voices (item 5) may be a function of the severity of a mental condition, poor verbal skills, or resistance toward the evaluation.

Congruent with Resnick's findings (1988), instructions to aggress within an hallucinatory experience probably do not contribute to dangerousness (Hellerstein, Frosch, & Koenigsberg, 1987). Contrary to clinical lore, investigators' study of 789 sequentially admitted inpatients showed no significant differences between patients with command and patients without command hallucinations on such variables as assaultiveness, suicidal behavior (or ideation), time in seclusion, use of restraints, and length of hospitalization.

In this important study, Hellerstein, Frosch, and Koenigsberg (1987) found that about 19% of the patients reported auditory hallucinations with about 7% of the total sample (58 of 789 patients) experiencing command auditory hallucinations. About 38% of the patients with hallucinations experienced such commands.

Interestingly, all cases of borderline personality disorder experienced command hallucinations. Of the subjects with schizophrenia, those with command hallucinations ($N = 29$) had significantly shorter (less than 15-day) hospitalizations than those with noncommand hallucinations. Hellerstein, Froesch, and Koenigsberg (1987) opine that command hallucinations may be a risk factor only when superimposed upon a previous history of violence. This last point is repeatedly supported by the literature (e.g., Hall, 1987). The foregoing findings were essentially replicated in a more recent investigation (Kasper, Rogers, & Adams, 1996). This study compared psychotic patients with command hallucinations ($N = 27$) to patients with other hallucinations ($N = 27$) and with other psychotic patients ($N = 30$). The investigators reported that the three groups did not differ on aggressive behavior or most nonhallucinatory symptoms. However, most patients (84%) with command hallucinations reported having recently obeyed the hallucinations. Among those with command hallucinations, almost one half had heard and attempted to obey messages on self-harm during the preceding month.

COMPLEX BEHAVIOR AND HALLUCINATIONS

A clear distinction should be made between alleged hallucinations at the time of the evaluation vs. some other relevant time (e.g., the instant offense). Hallucinations can bear upon competency to proceed if they adversely affect (1) the ability to cooperate with one's attorney, (2) knowing the nature and quality of the legal proceedings, and (3) the possible punitive consequences to oneself. The faker may portray incompetence by presenting hallucinations for the time of evaluation. Feigning hallucinations for the past is more congruent with attempting to escape criminal responsibility rather than with incompetency.

Genuine hallucinations in the present do not imply that previously reported hallucinations were genuine. The two time periods (e.g., offense, evaluation) must be considered separately. One can fake for the present and still have had genuine hallucinations at the time of the alleged crime. Perhaps the accused (now stabilized and not experiencing hallucinations) feels the need to remain consistent with previous behaviors. In sum, both current and previous time periods can involve fake or genuine hallucinations.

For criminal responsibility, the most relevant period is in the past and especially the relevant period of time immediately preceding the offense circumstances. Questions to be asked for past events include the following:

A. According to the victim or witnesses, did the accused
   1. State that he/she was experiencing hallucinations?
   2. Act in a manner congruent with hallucinations (e.g., turn in direction of "voices," continually scratch his/her skin for tactile hallucinations, stare at one spot)?
B. Did the accused exhibit purposeful and self-controlled motor behavior?

Complex, effective, self-controlled performance is antithetical to disorganized behavior typically caused by hallucinations.

Occurring during the violence sequence, effective performance reflects the notion that the accused may simultaneously observe and change his or her behavior in response to a fluctuating environment, all in accordance with the goal or desired object of the action sequence. Hypothesis testing is the highest form of effective performance, as when the accused changes his or her own behavior (e.g., threatens victim, puts key in lock) to see the reaction (e.g., victim acquiescence, door becomes unlocked) and then changes his or her own behavior accordingly (e.g., proceeds to rape victim, goes through door to bedroom). In essence, this skill taps the ability to show a concordance between intentions/plans and actions.

Some of these complex behaviors and abilities suggest that hallucinations were not operative:

1. Demonstration of a variety of acts (flexible behavior as with several weapons);
2. Display multiple sets of simultaneous motor behaviors;
3. Ability to orchestrate multistep, multitask scheme (e.g., long-connected chains of behaviors);
4. Ability to show change in principle (e.g., from robbery to rape);
5. Ability to show self-controlled somatic responses (e.g., sex with ejaculation, eating, drinking; all within violence sequence);
6. Ability to delay responses;
7. Ability to monitor and self-correct ongoing behavior;
8. Hypothesis testing, as illustrated above;
9. Awareness of wrongdoing during violence (e.g., from statements to victim);
10. Ability to stop violence (e.g., response cessation with no perseveration);
11. Ability to regulate tempo, intensity, and duration of behaviors;
12. Systematic obliteration or destruction of evidence during instant violence.

In sum, the evaluator determines whether or not there was a rational motive to the crime (e.g., planning or rehearsal); self-controlled, effective behavior; or attempts to hide or minimize the offense. If so, hallucinations may be absent, low in intensity, or irrelevant to the analysis of criminal responsibility.

Checklist Specifically for Hallucinations

The evaluator may desire to probe particular aspects of hallucinations. The checklist presented in Appendix C may be readministered (1) at another point in time to assess consistency of the client's response, (2) for a particular time period (e.g., before the crime, after it occurred), (3) to significant/knowledgeable others to complete about the accused, returning it directly to the evaluator (significant/knowledgeable others may also fill it out for different time periods); and (4) in both verbal and written form, as some persons affirm in writing what they will not orally and vice versa.

The evaluator must review the answers with the assessee to ensure accuracy and completeness. The assessee may be confronted with contradictions and inconsistencies, which then become part of the database material (see Chapter 3 for confrontation methods).

Signs of Faked Hallucinations

1. The person admits to faking or is inconsistent in symptom presentation, along with confirming evidence (e.g., see Checklist of Sensory Experiences in Appendix C).
2. The hallucination cannot be explained by any known condition or event, along with the ability of the examiner to show faking in testing or observation.
3. Knowledgeable/significant others or the evaluator reports complex, purposeful behavior while the accused is allegedly subject to hallucinations.
4. Alleged command hallucinations occurred when behavior can be explained by secondary gain or an identifiable goal.

REFERENCES

Alpert, M., & Silvers, K. (1970). Perceptual characteristics distinguishing auditory hallucinations in schizophrenia and acute alcoholic psychoses. *American Journal of Psychiatry, 127*, 298-302.

American Psychiatric Association. (1994). *Diagnostic and statistical manual* (4th ed.). Washington, DC: Author.

Coleman, J., Butcher, J., & Carson, R. (1984). *Abnormal psychology and modern life* (7th ed.). Glenview, IL: Scott, Foresman & Co.

Cocores, J., & Cohen, R. S. (1996). Ganser's syndrome, prison psychosis and rare dissociative states. In L. B. Schlesinger (Ed.), *Explorations in criminal psychopathology: Clinical syndromes with forensic implications* (pp. 238–254). Springfield, IL: Charles C Thomas.

Hall, H. V. (1987). *Violence prediction: Guidelines for the forensic professional*. Springfield, IL: Charles C Thomas.

Hayes, J. S., Hale, D. B., & Gouvier, W. D. (1997). Do tests predict malingering in defendants with mental retardation? *Journal of Psychology, 131*(5), 575–576.

Hellerstein, D., Frosch, W., & Koenigsberg, H. (1987). The clinical significance of command hallucinations. *American Journal of Psychiatry, 144*, 219–221.

Junginger, J., & Frame, C. (1985). Self-report of the frequency and phenomenology of verbal hallucinations. *Journal of Nervous and Mental Diseases, 173*, 149–155.

Kaplan, H., & Sadock, B. (1985). *Comprehensive textbook of psychiatry* (4th ed.). Baltimore, MD: Williams & Wilkins.

Kasper, M. E., Rogers, R., & Adams, P. A. (1996). Dangerousness and command hallucinations: An investigation of psychotic inpatients. *Bulletin of the American Academy of Psychiatry & the Law, 24*(2), 219–224.

Lezak, M. (1983). *Neuropsychological assessment* (2nd ed.). New York: Oxford Press.

Parish, E. (1914). *Hallucinations and illusions*. London: Walter Scott.

Pollock, P. (1998). Feigning auditory hallucinations by offenders. *Journal of Forensic Psychiatry, 9*(2), 305–327.

Resnick, P. J. (1984). The detection of malingered mental illness. *Behavioral Sciences and the Law, 2*, 21–38.

Resnick, P. J. (1988). Malingered psychosis. In R. Rogers (Ed.), *Clinical assessment of malingering and deception* (1st ed.; pp. 34–53). New York: Guilford Press.

Resnick, P. J. (1993). Defrocking the fraud: The detection of malingering. *Israel Journal of Psychiatry & Related Sciences, 30*(2), 93–101.

Resnick, P. J. (1997). Malingered psychosis. In Rogers, R. (Ed.), *Clinical assessment of malingering and deception* (2nd ed.; pp. 47–67). New York: Guilford Press.

Resnick, P. J. (1999). The detection of malingered psychosis. *Psychiatric Clinics of North America, 22*(1), 159–172.

Selye, H. (Ed.). (1980–1983). *Selye's guide to stress research* (Vols. 1–3). New York: Van Nostrand Reinhold.

Slade, P. D., & Bentall, R. P. (1988). *Sensory deception: A scientific analysis of hallucination*. London: Johns Hopkins University Press.

Strub, R., & Black, F. (1981). *Organic brain syndromes*. Philadelphia, PA: F. A. Davis Company.

22 Substance Abuse Deception

A vast literature exists on the causes, associated features, and effects of substance intoxication, abuse, and dependence (e.g., see Armor, Polich, & Stanbul, 1976; Bailey, 1961; Bean, 1981; Blane, 1968; Chait & Perry, 1992, 1994; Jellinek, 1952, 1980; Mulhaney & Trippett, 1979; Nace, 1982, 1987; Rutherford, Cacciola, & Alterman, 1999; Sobell, Toneatto, & Sobell, 1994).

In spite of its deleterious medical and psychological effects, incapacitating self-induced ethanol or illicit substance intoxication at the time of an instant offense is not considered a valid argument for claiming impairment. Mitigation can be claimed if substance intoxication removed the criminal intent — *mens rea* — necessary for the offense to have occurred. Information relevant to substance abuse that is to a defendant's advantage can also be presented in regard to sentencing options or dangerousness. The usual argument is that previous violence was a function of substance dependence, a medical condition that is not the entire fault of the defendant. If the substance abuse is controlled through treatment, the argument goes, the future risk of violence is reduced. Prosecutors aim to show that substance use was an independent phenomenon or even operated to make the crime easier, as in building up false courage or lowering the fear to commit robbery, murder, or rape. In most criminal settings, however, denial of substance use is typical. The defendant may wish to avoid the appearance that the instant offense was contributed to by substance use.

Forensic clinicians will encounter the issue of substance abuse denial at any point in criminal adjudication, and beyond. Following criminal sentencing, the issue of substance abuse is a common feature in sentence reconsideration and violation of probation/parole hearings (Bonczar, 1997; Mumola, 1999). A significant percentage of probationers/parolees are stipulated to maintain abstinence and/or be involved in ongoing substance abuse treatment. Clinicians and others who work with these populations on a follow-up assessment and/or treatment basis are constantly confronted with deception regarding substance abuse.

Within the civil arena, the existence of substance use by plaintiff or defendant may affect whether damages are awarded and, if so, how much. Denial is very common by both parties. In most cases, the faker attempts to simulate a nonintoxicated state, or hide symptoms, for some relevant time. A history of substance addiction is typically kept from view. In addition to criminal matters, substance abuse plays a very significant role in juvenile delinquency (Bilchilk, 1998; Poirier, 1999) and in domestic legal matters especially child abuse, spouse abuse, and elder abuse (Poirier, 1996). The social problem of underage drinking is one more example of the magnitude of substance abuse in our culture (McKinney, 1999).

TARGETS

The DSM-IV diagnostic criteria for substance intoxication are known by the lay community. Drug and alcohol intoxication is commonly understood to be characterized as (1) a recent ingestion of a particular substance; (2) maladaptive behavioral changes such as poor judgment, labile behavior, or physical or sexual aggression, without which it would not matter from a legal viewpoint whether the person was intoxicated; and (3) critical physical and psychological signs that will vary according to the substance.

The deceiver may try to hide these symptoms in an attempt to hamper an investigation (e.g., by field testing, urinalysis). Typically, noncooperation with police involving alcohol intoxication takes the form of belligerence and aggressiveness. The range of reactions with drugs other than alcohol is wide, from aggressiveness to almost catatonic immobility.

The person who has a stake in denying or minimizing substance use may selectively hide symptoms. Symptoms chosen for denial depend on the faker's understanding of what constitutes a substance abuse problem. Any of the following for Psychoactive Substance Dependence, Polysubstance Dependence (see DSM-IV, American Psychiatric Association, 1994), or Psychoactive Substance Dependence NOS may be targeted for denial:

1. Substances ingested in larger amounts or over a longer period than the person intended.
2. At least one unsuccessful effort to cut down or control substance use, or continuing desire to quit.
3. Much time devoted to procurement, actually ingesting the substance (e.g., frequent smoking of "ice"), or in recovery from the substance.
4. Interference with work, school, or home obligations when intoxicated or in withdrawal, or when intoxication is imminently dangerous (e.g., while driving).
5. Substance use leading to decreased involvement in work, play, or social activities.
6. Continued use with awareness of a medical or other problem that is created because of it (e.g., alcohol use with cirrhosis, "ice" use with heart problems).
7. Substantial tolerance with at least a 50% increase to attain the same level of intoxication, or a decrease in positive effects as experienced by the individual over time.
8. Withdrawal symptoms with discontinued use.
9. Withdrawal symptoms are avoided on purpose by reuse of substance.

RESPONSE PATTERNS

Faking good is the dominant response style. Exaggeration of substance use occurs in some cases. Mixed styles are common — the faker may deny substance use for drugs but admit to depression, marital problems, and alcohol use. Usually the substance abuse is justified by blaming outside problems (e.g., loss of a job) or other people (e.g., "bad influences").

Fluctuating response styles are also seen. The faker may deny substance use problems during a criminal trial to reduce culpability, but admit or even exaggerate the problems to obtain a sentence to a community treatment setting rather than to prison.

DETECTION METHODS

The traditional method for establishing substance abuse is the gathering of cross-validating material. The data gathering involves a search for substance-related behaviors and events from significant others, neighbors, bartenders, friends, and family. Supporting material should be collected if available (e.g., DUI arrest reports, mental health treatment records). If available, prior and current urinalysis records should be accessed as they provide the most reliable hard data of all. The evaluator should always review the material before questioning the person. The alternative is to return for a second session to ask pinpoint questions about the civil or criminal event.

Critical events that should raise the suspicion that alcohol (or other substance) abuse has occurred are reported by Nace (1987):

1. Any person with a history of substance abuse.
2. Referrals from corporations or industry secondary to job-related problems. Nace cites base rates that suggest that about one half of job-related problems are alcohol related.

Drugs are often interchangeable with alcohol, as some abusers seek different intoxicants after alcoholism has been identified as a problem.

3. Hospital and emergency room consultations. The high rate of substance abuse in hospital populations is well known. Nace states that about 40% of the persons in emergency rooms in urban settings have recent detectable alcohol use, and this is in a setting that generally underdiagnoses substance use.

4. DUI or DWI history. Scrutinizing the actual police reports will often reveal more information relevant to the pattern of abuse.

5. Persons with a history of divorce, especially multiple divorces. Substance abuse generally deteriorates social relationships of all sorts. Separation and divorce occur seven times more frequently among alcoholic than normal individuals (Paolino & McCrady, 1977).

6. Persons who express even minimal concern that they may be substance abusers. In light of the pervasive problem of denial, any admission of substance use should be the springboard for further inquiry.

Chronic alcoholic behaviors can serve as signals (Jellinek, 1952, 1980). The more easily verified ones include (1) drinking a technical product, (2) multiple benders, (3) loss of tolerance, (4) tremors, (5) psychomotor inhibition, (6) verbally admitting defeat, (7) impairment of cognition, (8) alcoholic psychosis, and (9) continued drinking after the problem has been identified.

Laboratory methods and results can be used to indicate substance intoxication. Blood, breath, and urine analyses have long been used to detect substances in the body, despite controversy on their efficacy and intrusiveness. Generally, the tests are carefully controlled and have high accuracy rates. There are several common problems with urinalysis, and clinicians should always be on the lookout for defective specimen collection procedures. Substance abusers can employ ingenious methods to submit false or doctored specimens. For example, specimens from nonusers can be secreted into the collection room using a balloon-type apparatus hidden in the armpit; the specimen bottle can be dipped into the commode, etc. The proper procedure for specimen collection must be the immediately supervised flow of urine into the specimen bottle.

Urine specimens are typically evaluated, for example, by booking facilities in U.S. cities as follows:

Urine specimens are analyzed by EMIT for 10 drugs: cocaine, opiates, marijuana, PCP, methadone, benzodiazepine (Valium), methaqualone, propoxyphene (Darvon), barbiturates, and amphetamines. Positive results for amphetamines are confirmed by gas chromatography to eliminate positives that may be caused by over-the-counter drugs. For most drugs, the urine test can detect use in the prior 2 to 3 days. Exceptions are marijuana and PCP, which can sometimes be detected several weeks after use. (O'Neil, Wish, & Visher, 1990, p. 2)

A relatively new laboratory procedure, but one with considerable promise in terms of accuracy and efficiency, is radioimmunoassay of hair (RIAH; Rogers & Kelly, 1997). The metabolites of illicit substances become embedded in the hair shaft; the shaft is a record of substance abuse and nonuse. The main drawbacks of RIAH are that it is not effective with alcohol abuse and laboratories do not yet use standardized procedures, thereby preventing cross-laboratory comparisons.

BASE RATE APPROACH

One means to assess denial is to compare self-reports to the results of urinalysis. The National Institute of Justice (see O'Neil, Wish, & Visher, 1990) has done exactly that for many metropolitan areas (Table 22.1). They confirmed and extended the results of an earlier study in Washington, DC, and New York in 1984 where self-reports were generally found to have underestimated recent drug use by about one half.

TABLE 22.1
Drug Use by Self-Report and Urinalysis

1. More than 70% of the male and female arrestees in San Diego, New York, Philadelphia, and Washington, DC, tested positive for one or more drugs. San Antonio and Indianapolis had the lowest rates of drug use.
2. More arrestees tested positive for multiple drug use in San Diego than any other city. Arrestees there tended to use cocaine, marijuana, and methamphetamines (speed).
3. PCP is found in about one quarter of arrestees in Washington, DC. The only other city where PCP is prevalent is St. Louis, where 20% of female arrestees tested positive for the drug.
4. The highest rates of cocaine use — above 60% — were found in Washington, DC, New York, and Philadelphia.
5. There is no evidence of an increase in heroin use in male arrestees. In every city, opiates were found in fewer than 20% of tested males. Opiates were more common in females, especially in Washington, DC, Portland, Oregon, and San Antonio, Texas.

Note: From *Drug Use Forecasting: July to September 1989,* by J. O'Neil, E. Wish, & C. Visher, 1990, Rockville, MD: National Institute of Justice. With permission.

Findings included the following:

1. Drug use from arrestee self-report as compared with urinalysis is underreported and different for particular drugs — marijuana, cocaine, and opiates.
2. The least differences between self-report and urinalysis occurred for marijuana and the opiates, with many geographic areas having identical or nearly identical percentages for the two methods.
3. Cocaine was grossly underreported; generally, one third to one half less than what was indicated by urine tests. In Dallas, for example, 14% of arrestees reported cocaine use but 50% tested positive for the drug. Clearly, without urine testing, recent cocaine use would have been greatly undetected.
4. Cocaine was more frequently detected in the urine than the other two drugs, with opiates coming in last. The worst cities in terms of cocaine use as indicated by urinalysis were New York (76% of arrestees) and Philadelphia (74%). In the latter city, males and females had almost equal percentages. The cities with least cocaine use were Indianapolis, Indiana (26%) and San Antonio, Texas (24%).

Results suggest an anchoring strategy as a first estimate that given substances were ingested. Conclusions should not be generalized beyond people arrested for crimes involving substance abuse in reported geographic areas. Additional information can sharpen the speculation that substance intoxication took place by a particular individual. Illicit substances have transitory availability in different geographic regions at a given time. Availability is a complex phenomenon related to a host of determinants, all of which point to the central and underlying role of deception in the widespread social problem of substance abuse. These determinants include:

1. Proximity to coastal sites having proximity to countries producing illicit substances;
2. Local fads and pop interests usually generated surreptitiously by late adolescents/young adults;
3. Media hype particularly to include popular song content and themes;
4. Supply and demand controlled by production activity of clandestine laboratories and by distribution and trafficking of illicit substances;
5. Ethnic subgroup preferences dictated by financial factors and ethnic-based psychological preferences for the effects of certain substances;
6. Effectiveness of local police undercover activity and law enforcement initiatives.

TABLE 22.2
Most Frequently Cited Sources of Drug Indicators

1. National Institute of Drug Abuse (NIDA) national probability sample of high school substance abuse. Conducted annually since 1975 with follow-up sampling. Student response rate is low and survey data are based on self-report.
2. National Household Survey of Drug Abuse (NHSDA) sponsored by the U.S. Department of Health and Human Services Substance Abuse and Mental Health Services Administration (SAMHSA). Conducted periodically from 1971 to 1990 and annually since then. Based on face-to-face interviews with household members. The 70,000 interviews conducted in 1999 will permit prevalence estimates at the state level. Allows good U.S. trend analysis, but known to underreport cocaine and heroin use.
3. Arrestee Drug Abuse Monitoring (ADAM), sponsored by NIJ, conducted quarterly since 1987. Based on anonymous self-report and voluntary urinalysis. Reaches a large fraction of problematic substance abusers at the local level and in a timely manner. Data difficult to integrate with other prevalence indicators.
4. Drug Abuse Warning Network (DAWN), sponsored by SAMHSA, has been collecting data since 1975. DAWN collects data on drug-related admissions to emergency rooms (ER) and drug-related deaths from medical examiners (ME). Data come from national sites in timely manner and provide direct measures of drug-related problems. ER data is known to underreport substantially.
5. Pulse Check developed by the Office of National Drug Control Policy (ONDCP) in 1992. Collects quarterly data from knowledgeable sources such as police, ethnographers, and treatment providers. Less systematic data collection than first four sources above.
6. The Community Epidemiology Work Group (CEWG) is a group of experts from 21 metropolitan areas who report on various local indicators every 6 months and assess developing drug use trends in their local communities. CEWG is sponsored by NIDA and has less systematic data collection than first four sources above.

Note: Adapted from "Drug Use Measures: What Are They Really Telling Us?" R. Reuter, 1999, *National Institute of Justice Journal*, pp. 12–19.

The above general findings are augmented by data relevant to youthful offenders. Urine tests and self-reports were collected for 201 male and female youths tested twice (Dembo, Williams, Wish, & Schmeidler, 1990). In terms of denial, only about one quarter of the youths who tested positive for cocaine reported using it in the prior 2 to 3 days. Racial differences emerged, with blacks underreporting cocaine use substantially more than whites.

A limitation of the self-report data is that these earlier National Institute of Justice (NIJ) statistics were collected under confidential research conditions. In the adversarial system of criminal justice, arrestees may be even less likely to report illicit drug use, for example, when the evaluator is conducting a forensic evaluation. The NIJ is well aware of the limitations of relying on the self-report of psychoactive substance abusers and during the last decade has made an effort to buttress these data with additional collateral source data (e.g., emergency room admissions, drug-related deaths). Reuter (1999) described the most frequently cited NIJ sources of drug indicators and these are outlined in Table 22.2.

In the final analysis, base rates are lacking for many critical groups and, hence, limit the detection strategies that may be employed. Most clients will not have the above characteristics (i.e., arrestees in given areas within certain time periods). In this case, the base rates should not be used as a first estimate of substance abuse. The general minimization of drug usage can be noted, however.

Relying on the spoken word of the assessee is hazardous because of the denial phenomenon. Moreover, in cases of severe/chronic substance abuse, particularly alcoholism, the assessee may not be consciously denying because of (1) blackouts; (2) repression, including the need to protect ego esteem and to stave off hopelessness and despair; and (3) the tendency for euphoric recall (Bean, 1981; Nace, 1987). Commentators point out that piercing denial appears to come in stages, from recognizing that substances have created havoc in one's life to recognizing the need for substances to cope, and, last, to allowing oneself to experience the guilt not expressed during the

TABLE 22.3

Specific Psychoactive Substance Abuse Trends — 1980–2000

- The proportion of offenders under supervision required to participate in substance abuse treatment programs consistently increased between 1987 and 1996 (Adams, Roth, & Scalia, 1998).
- Offender termination from community supervision for drug use increased 47% between 1987 and 1996 (Adams, Roth, & Scalia, 1998).
- It is estimated that each year, of the youth that come in contact with the juvenile justice system, 225,000 evidence diagnosable alcohol or dependence disorders, and 95,000 evidence diagnosable substance abuse or dependence disorders (Bilchilk, 1998).
- Drug trafficking (15%) and possession (13%) were the most common offenses among felons; driving while intoxicated (35%) and assault (11%) among misdemeanants (Bonczar, 1997).
- Drug or alcohol treatment was a sentence condition for 41% of adults on probation; 37% had received treatment. Drug testing was required of 32% (Bonczar, 1997). Overall, three in four state and four in five federal prisoners may be characterized as alcohol- or drug-involved offenders (Mumola, 1999).
- Since 1980, The DAWN ER and ME reports for cocaine and heroin use have increased dramatically (Reuter, 1999).
- The demographics of frequent users of cocaine and heroin indicate that they are getting older and are increasingly likely to be African-American (Reuter, 1999).
- Marijuana use among youth is a weak predictor of future cocaine use; methamphetamine is still primarily a regional drug; and indicators of heroin use are very inconsistent (Reuter, 1999).
- Medical dangers of cocaine have become more apparent and widely known. As cocaine has become cheaper and more addictive in the form of crack, there has been an increased association with cocaine use and health problems and a strong association with crime (Reuter, 1999).

active part of the abuse. Finally, there is some evidence that memories are better produced in a similar physical condition. Termed "state-dependent learning," this means that recall of a previous episode of intoxication may be only possible when the person is in a similar state. Thus, not reporting on previous intoxication may not be denial, rather an inability.

Based on the source indicators described in Table 22.2, the following general trends in psychoactive substance abuse have been identified in the United States over the past 20 years. First-time illicit drug use rose through the late 1970s and perhaps into the early 1980s. Beginning around 1983 there was a sharp decline, which continued until 1992 through 1997 when first-time drug use rose again but still well below the peaks of the early 1980s (Reuter, 1999). Specific psychoactive substance abuse trends based on the Table 22.2 scores for the past 20 years are summarized in Table 22.3.

A new variation of substance abuse involves a number of central nervous system depressants that have been associated with sexual assault and robbery of victims who are surreptitiously given the substances by perpetrators. Examples of these substances are Rohypnol and gamma hydroxybutyrate (GHB) that among other slang terms are called "date rape" drugs. The Drug Induced Rape Prevention and Punishment Act was enacted into federal law in 1996 in response to the abuse of these substances (ONDCP, 1998).

EVALUATING SIGNIFICANT OTHERS

In a study of individuals with schizophrenia, about half of whom were alcoholic as shown on the Self-Administered Alcoholism Screening Test, Smith and Pristach (1990) found that interviews with significant others and chart reviews were extremely helpful. Only half of the alcoholic individuals admitted to their substance abuse problems. The authors conclude that alcoholic individuals with schizophrenia show more denial than those without schizophrenia when compared to findings of earlier studies.

Case managers' ratings, which used reports from collaterals as well as longitudinal observations, were found to be superior to formal clinical evaluations, which frequently missed alcohol problems because of denial (Drake et al., 1990). Interestingly, case managers' ratings were also more accurate

TABLE 22.4
Questions for Significant Others

	Don't Know	Yes	No	Describe
1. Is _____ (Name) a normal drinker in your opinion?				
2. Has s/he reported or acted in a way where part of the previous evening could not be remembered?				
3. Do you worry or complain about his/her substance use?				
4. Once s/he starts using substances, can it be easily stopped?				
5. Does s/he express guilt or remorse about the substance abuse?				
6. Does s/he try to limit the substances to certain times of the day or to certain places?				
7. Has s/he ever attended a meeting of AA, NA, or the like?				
8. Has s/he ever gotten a DUI, DWI, or any arrest related to substances?				
9. Has s/he gotten into physical fights when using substances?				
10. Does s/he mix substances (e.g., drink and smoke marijuana)?				
11. Have his/her substance habits ever created a problem for you?				
12. Have you ever sought help for his/her substance problems?				
13. Has s/he lost friends or turned off people because of substance abuse?				
14. Has s/he gotten into trouble at work because of substance use?				
15. Has s/he ever lost a job because of the same reason?				
16. Has s/he ever neglected the family or work obligations for 2 days or more because of substance use?				
17. Does s/he take substances before noon?				
18. Has s/he ever had physical problems because of substances (e.g., liver, rashes, DTs)?				
19. Has s/he ever been in a general hospital or psychiatric hospital because of substance use?				
20. Has s/he ever seen a doctor or a counselor on an outpatient basis for substance problems?				
21. Was s/he ever put on medication for his/her substance problems?				

than structured research interviews, although the two measures were highly correlated. Drake et al. (1990) point out that a reliable and valid alcohol assessment instrument has not yet been developed, at least for schizophrenia, primarily because these people underreport the extent of their substance abuse.

A closer correspondence between the reports of alcoholic abusers and significant others in nonpsychotic samples is quite possible. Loethen and Khavari (1990) found that there were no significant differences between patients' self-reports compared with reports from collaterals. Further, patients' self-reports showed a direct relationship with both the Self-Administered Alcoholism Screening Test (SAAST) and the Khavari Alcohol Test (KAT).

The evaluator can assess family, friends, acquaintances, and others for information regarding substance use of the assessee. The authors have found this to be a helpful best source of data for a specific individual. The questions in Table 22.4 are adapted from the Michigan Alcoholism Screening Test (Selzer, 1971) and are intended for use with significant others.

The evaluator should probe all positive answers. The original cutoff score for the MAST (> 5 endorsed items indicating alcoholism) cannot be used with this modified questionnaire because of deletions and adaptations and because items are answered by parties other than the client. However, giving the original MAST to the suspected substance abuser and then comparing answers with the answers produced by significant others may be instructive. The suspected abuser can then be questioned about discrepancies. Evaluators must bear in mind that the credibility of all sources of input must be reviewed with discretion. All sources are subject to positive and negative distortion. The authors have evaluated situations where testimony regarding the same individual's substance abuse ranges through the continuum from reports of no substance abuse to reports of addiction such that there is no basis to formulate a reliable impression of actual substance abuse. Such circumstances do, however, raise considerations regarding the manipulative ability of the subject. The authors comment that scenarios of conflicting data are commonplace in family systems and perhaps most common of all with adolescent subjects. Clinicians can attain reasonable headway making a determination of the extent of substance abuse based on collaborative input. All forensic assessments must proceed with a high index of evaluator suspicion with respect to the credibility of all witness-based input. Just as important is the need for the clinician to bear in mind that the *legal* determination of a witness's credibility, whether in regard to substance abuse or other ultimate forensic issue, is the responsibility of the trier of fact.

PSYCHOLOGICAL TESTING

There are a number of substance abuse screening inventories available (for a review see Rogers & Kelly, 1997). Only a small number of these psychometric devices are empirically useful with respect to substance abuse deception and denial. One of these is the Denial Rating Scale (DRS) reported by Goldsmith and Green (1988). This preliminary test is designed to determine whether alcoholism as a condition is denied, or whether particular aspects within the condition, such as loss of control once drinking starts, are denied. Promising interrater reliability and construct and predictive validity are reported.

Denial of substance abuse on testing has sometimes been associated with relatively positive traits. Rohsenow, Erickson, and O'Leary (1978) found that lower levels of psychopathology were related to the use of denial and intellectualization as ego defenses on the Defense Mechanism Inventory (DMI). Reviewing the locus of control research, Rohsenow and O'Leary (1978) found that internality was related to better social functioning and the defenses of denial, intellectualization, and repression. Last, Pekarik, Jones, and Blodgett (1986) found that denial scores on the MMPI were positively correlated with intelligence, but only for completers of an alcohol treatment program.

The MMPI MacAndrew Alcoholism (MAC) Scale (MacAndrew, 1965) has been traditionally considered an index of substance abuse tendencies. However, in a comprehensive review of the empirical literature, Gottesman and Prescott (1989) concluded that the scale makes so many false-positive errors that its use should be suspended. They reviewed 74 studies on the MAC published between 1976 and 1987 and calculated that the positive hit rate (percent of positive scorers who are actually alcoholic) in the general population is only 15% and that 85% of persons called alcoholic by the test are, in fact, not alcoholic.

In a study of 63 white, male forensic patients, Wasyliw, Grossman, Haywood, and Cavanaugh (1990) found that although the MacAndrew Alcoholism scale was a widely used MMPI measure of vulnerability to alcohol abuse, it was susceptible to deception. Patients who were inclined to exaggerate or to minimize substance abuse could positively or negatively affect MAC scores when patients were suspected to be response-biased.

Davis, Offord, Colligan, and Morse (1991) reported the development of a new MMPI scale for alcoholism designed to detect alcoholism among medical inpatients. Using a construction sample of 736 medical inpatients with a diagnosis of alcoholism, a cross-validation sample of 485 medical patients with alcoholism, and three samples of persons without alcoholism totaling 13,120 individuals, the new scale yielded a (cross-validated) valid positive rate of 90 and valid negative rate between 90% and 96%. This scale needs to be investigated further for the possible effects of malingering and denial and for its applicability to nonmedical populations (e.g., psychiatric inpatients/outpatients, criminal offenders).

The MMPI-A incorporates two new scales to assist with the assessment of substance abuse in adolescents (Pope, Butcher, & Seelen, 2000). These scales are the Alcohol or Drug Problem Scale (PRO) and the Alcohol or Drug Problem Acknowledgment Scale (ACK). The validity of these new scales is still pending empirical trials.

There have been studies using psychometrics correlating psychoactive substance abuse with a variety of personality characteristics particularly including personality disorder symptoms (Lather, Vasudeva, & Verma, 1997; Sigurdsson & Gudjonsson, 1995). It is difficult, however, to know precisely what these findings implicate. Correlation is not causation, and once illicit substance abuse becomes an established pattern, the abuser, by necessity, falls into a behavioral pattern that may partially explain the psychometric scale elevations indicative of the personality issues.

The Personality Assessment Inventory (PAI; Morey, 1991) has been touted as having psychometric advantages over other instruments (Rogers, Ornduff, & Sewell, 1993). Fals-Stewart (1996) noted that the PAI items can be answered on a four-point Likert format (e.g., very true, mostly true, slightly true, and false), which offers quantitative response variability as opposed to the more limited dichotomous (i.e., true or false) scale that is most commonly used. Second, the PAI scales do not share like items with the MMPI-2 and MCMI-III. The argument is that this affords more discriminative validity to the PAI. The PAI has two scales relevant to substance abuse deception, Alcohol Problems (ALC) and Drug Problems (DRG). The PAI also has a potentially useful validity scale, the Positive Impression scale (PIM), that is designed to detect the degree of positive impression management by subjects. Fals-Stewart (1996) observed that unlike the nonobvious items on the MMPI-2 and the MCMI-III drug and alcohol subscales, the PAI subscale items were all obviously related to substance abuse issues. This same issue with obvious subscale items was also the case with the popular MAST (Selzer, 1971). The implication is that the PAI and the MAST may be useful in settings where substance-abusing patients are motivated to seek help and whose credibility can be generally assumed. When credibility cannot be assumed, these instruments will have clear limitations. The original PAI normative data (Morey, 1991) was derived exclusively with self-identified substance abusers and this is another significant limitation of the instrument.

Fals-Stewart (1996) investigated the use of the PAI with substance abusers. One treatment group was asked to respond honestly ($N = 59$), another group was instructed to respond defensively ($N = 59$), a third group was a nonclinical control group ($N = 59$), and a fourth group was referred by the criminal justice system ($N = 59$). The findings indicated that the PAI validity scales (DRG and ALC) designed to measure positive dissimulations were prone to making false-positive and false-negative errors depending on the cutoff used. The writer concluded that the findings were expected given the high face validity of the content of the subscale items. The foregoing findings warrant extreme caution when using the PAI with substance abusers when there is any question of deception potential.

In a follow-up study with a similar experimental paradigm, Fals-Stewart (1996) used a classification analysis (i.e., a method similar to discriminant function analysis). An optimally weighted multivariate combination of the DRG, ALC, and PIM was developed to classify more accurately the experimental groups. This analysis resulted in an 82% correct identification of the groups. A third cross-validation study (Fals-Stewart & Lucente, 1997) replicated the design and used two separate sample groups to reduce *validity shrinkage* (i.e., caused by sampling bias and random variability by not using an independent comparative sample). In this study the overall accuracy of the PAI subscales differentiating the experimental groups fell to 68%. The study did identify <80% of the substance abusers with standard instructions (i.e., with subjects in treatment and motivated not to dissimulate). Once again, the findings underscored the difficulties of second-guessing the response of forensic populations who are presumably motivated to dissimulate both in actual forensic application and in empirical studies. In both instances, and assuming no independent source of verification (e.g., urinalysis), there is no way to know with this population when dissimulation is in effect.

SUMMARY OF CRITICAL POINTS

The following criteria should be used for a diagnosis of substance abuse or dependence.

1. A history of maladaptive behavior and substance abuse as suggested by DSM-IV criteria and evidenced by cross-validating sources to include:
   a. Significant/knowledgeable others;
   b. Medical/psychological records of evaluation and/or treatment;
   c. Criminal history data involving maladaptive behavior associated with substance abuse;
   d. Prior, and preferably concurrent, urinalysis records.
2. Psychological test scales if accompanied by a, b, or c.
3. Admission of substance use if accompanied by a, b, or c.
4. Withdrawal symptoms if accompanied by item 1 or 2.

REFERENCES

Adams, W. P., Roth, J. A., & Scalia, J. (1998). *Federal offenders under community supervision 1987–96* (U.S. Department of Justice No. NCJ 168636). Washington, DC: Office of Justice Programs.

American Psychiatric Association. (1994). *Diagnostic and statistical manual of mental disorders* (4th ed.). Washington, DC: Author.

Armor, D. J., Polich, J. M., & Stanbul, H. B. (1976). *Alcoholism and treatment*. Santa Monica, CA: Rand Corporation.

Bailey, M. B. (1961). Alcoholism and marriage: A review of research and professional literature. *Quarterly Journal of Studies on Alcohol, 22*, 81–97.

Bean, M. H. (1981). Denial and the psychological complications of alcoholism. In M. H. Bean & N. E. Zinberg (Eds.), *Dynamic approaches to the understanding and treatment of alcoholism* (p. 55–96). New York: The Free Press.

Bilchilk, S. (1998). *Mental health disorders and substance abuse problems among juveniles* (U.S. Department of Justice OJJDP Fact Sheet #82). Washington, DC: Office of Juvenile Justice and Delinquency Prevention.

Blane, H. J. (1968). *The personality of the alcoholic: Guises of dependency*. New York: Harper and Row.

Bonczar, T. P. (1997). *Characteristics of Adults on Probation, 1995* (U.S. Department of Justice, NCJ-164267). Washington, DC: Office of Justice Programs.

Chait, L. D., & Perry, J. L. (1992). Factors influencing self-administration of, and subjective response to, placebo marijuana. *Behavioural Pharmacology, 3*(6), 545–552.

Chait, L. D., & Perry, J. L. (1994). Effects of alcohol pretreatment on human marijuana self-administration. *Psychopharmacology, 113*(3–4), 346–350.

Davis, L., Offord, K., Colligan, R., & Morse, R. (1991). The CAL: An MMPI alcoholism scale for general medical patients. *Journal of Clinical Psychology, 47*(5), 632–646.

Dembo, R., Williams, L., Wish, E., & Schmeidler, J. (1990). *Urine testing of detained juveniles to identify high-risk youth*. Rockville, MD: National Institute of Justice.

Drake, R. E., Osher, F. C., Noordsy, D. L., Hurlbut, S. C., Teague, G. B., & Beaudett, M. S. (1990). Diagnosis of alcohol use disorders in schizophrenia. *Schizophrenia Bulletin, 16*, 57–67.

Fals-Stewart, W. (1996). The ability of individuals with psychoactive substance abuse disorders to escape detection by the Personality Assessment Inventory. *Psychological Assessment, 8*, 60–68.

Fals-Stewart, W., & Lucente, S. (1997). Identifying positive dissimulation by substance-abusing individuals on the Personality Assessment Inventory: A cross-validation study. *Journal of Personality Assessment, 68*(2), 455–469.

Goldsmith, R. J., & Green, B. L. (1988). A rating scale for alcoholic denial. *Journal of Nervous and Mental Disorders, 176*, 614–620.

Gottesman, I., & Prescott, C. (1989). Abuses of the MacAndrew MMPI Alcoholism scale: a critical review. *Clinical Psychology Review, 9*, 223–242.

Jellinek, E. M. (1952). Phases of alcohol addiction. *Quarterly Journal of Studies on Alchohol, 13,* 673–684.

Jellinek, E. M. (1980). *The disease concept of alcoholism.* New Haven, CT: College and University Press.

Lather, A., Vasudeva, P., & Verma, P. (1997). A study of drug abuse among students as related to personality variables. *Journal of the Indian Academy of Applied Psychology, 23*(1–2), 43–49.

Loethen, G. J., & Khavari, K. A. (1990). Comparison of the self-administered Alcoholism Screening Test (SAAST) and the Khavari Alcohol Test (KAT): Results from an alcoholic population and their collaterals. *Alcohol: Clinical & Experimental Research., 14,* 756–760.

MacAndrew, C. (1965). The differentiation of male alcoholic outpatients from nonalcoholic psychiatric outpatients by means of the MMPI. *Quarterly Journal of Studies on Alcohol, 26,* 238–246.

McKinney, K. (1999). *Enforcing the underage drinking laws program* (OJJDP Fact Sheet No. 107). Washington, DC: U.S. Department of Justice.

Morey, L. C. (1991). *Personality Assessment Inventory: Professional manual.* Tampa, FL: Psychological Assessment Resources.

Mulhaney, J. A., & Trippett, C. J. (1979). Alcohol dependence and phobias: Clinical description and relevance. *British Journal of Psychiatry, 135,* 565–573.

Mumola, C. J. (1999). *Substance abuse and treatment, state and federal prisoners, 1997* (U. S. Department of Justice No. NCJ 172871). Washington, DC: Office of Justice Programs.

Nace, E. P. (1982). The role of craving in the treatment of alcoholism. *National Association of Private Psychiatric Hospitals Journal, 13*(1), 27–31.

Nace, E. P. (1984). Epidemiology of alcoholism and prospects for treatment. *Annual Review of Medicine., 35,* 293–309.

Nace, E. P. (1987). *The treatment of alcoholism.* New York: Brunner-Mazel.

O'Neil, J., Wish, E., & Visher, C. (1990). *Drug use forecasting: July to September 1989.* Rockville, MD: National Institute of Justice.

ONDCP (1998). *Gamma Hydroxybutyrate (GHB)* (NCJ 172867). [ONDCP Fact Sheet]. Washington, DC: National Criminal Justice Reference Service.

Paolino, T., & McCrady, B. (1977). *The alcoholic marriage: Alternative perspectives.* New York: Grune & Stratton.

Pekarik, G., Jones, D. L., & Blodgett, C. (1986). Personality and demographic characteristics of dropouts and completers in a nonhospital residential alcohol treatment program. *International Journal of Addiction, 21,* 131–137.

Poirier, J. G. (1996). Violence in the family. In H. V. Hall (Ed.), *Lethal violence 2000: A source book on fatal domestic, acquaintance, and stranger aggression* (pp. 259–292). Kamuela, HI: Pacific Institute for the Study of Conflict and Aggression.

Poirier, J. G. (1999). Violent juvenile crime. In H. V. Hall & L. C. Whitaker (Eds.), *Collective violence: Effective strategies for assessing and interviewing in fatal group and institutional aggression* (pp. 183–212). Boca Raton, FL: CRC Press.

Pope, K. S., Butcher, J. N., & Seelen, J. (2000). *The MMPI, MMPI-2, & MMPI-A in court.* Washington, DC: American Psychological Association.

Reuter, R. (1999, April). Drug use measures: What are they really telling us? *National Institute of Justice Journal,* pp. 12–19.

Rogers, R., & Kelly, K. S. (1997) Denial and misreporting of substance abuse. In R. Rogers (Ed.) *Clinical assessment of malingering and deception* (pp. 108–129). New York: Guilford Press.

Rogers, R., Ornduff, S. R., & Sewell, K. W. (1993). Feigning specific disorders: A study of the Personality Inventory. *Journal of Personality Assessment, 60,* 554–560.

Rohsenow, D. J., Erickson, R. C., & O'Leary, M. R. (1978). The Defense Mechanism Inventory and alcoholics. *International Journal of Addictions, 13,* 403–414.

Rohsenow, D. J., & O'Leary, M. R. (1978). Locus of control research on alcoholic populations: A review. *International Journal of Addictions, 13,* 231–236.

Rutherford, M. J., Cacciola, J. S., & Alterman, A. I. (1999). Antisocial personality disorder and psychopathy in cocaine-dependent women. *The American Journal of Psychiatry, 156*(6), 849–856.

Sellers, E. M., & Kalant, H. (1976). Alcohol intoxication and withdrawal. *New England Journal of Medicine, 294,* 757–762.

Selzer, M. L. (1971). The Michigan Alcoholism Screening Test: The quest for a new diagnostic instrument. *American Journal of Psychiatry, 127,* 89–94.

Sigurdsson, J. F., & Gudjonsson, G. H. (1995). Personality characteristics of drug-dependent offenders. *Nordic Journal of Psychiatry, 49*(1), 33–38.

Smith, C. M., & Pristach, C. A. (1990). Utility of the Self-Administered Alcoholism Screening Test (SAAST) in schizophrenic patients. *Alcohol: Clinical and Experimental Research, 14*, 690–694.

Sobell, L. C., Toneatto, T., & Sobell, M. B. (1994). Behavioral assessment and treatment planning for alcohol, tobacco, and other drug problems: Current status with an emphasis on clinical applications. *Behavior Therapy, 25*, 533–580.

Wasyliw, O., Grossman, L., Haywood, T., & Cavanaugh, J. (1990). Is the MacAndrew Alcoholism Scale related to response-bias: A forensic study. Paper presented at the American Psychological Association, Boston, MA.

Wish, E., & O'Neil, J. (1989). *Drug Use Forecasting (DUF). Research update.* Rockville, MD: National Institute of Justice.

23 Dangerousness Evaluation and Deception

Dangerousness may be defined as the likelihood of threatened, attempted, or consummated physical harm to others, self, or property within a certain period of time. Typically, a person with a history of violence, the best predictor of future violence, will downplay previous aggression and project blame for acknowledged violence onto victims and contexts. Minimizing and denying dangerousness is a pervasive phenomenon (Hall, 1987; Monahan, 1981).

Risk assessment by mental health professionals continues as a highly controversial area of the law/mental health interface (Borum, 1996; Grisso & Appelbaum, 1992; Grisso & Tomkins, 1996; Lidz, Mulvey, & Gardner, 1993; Link & Steuve, 1995; Monahan, 1992, 1993; Otto, 1992; Steadman et al.,1994). Notwithstanding the controversy, the topic of risk assessment has flourished in terms of studies and investigations reported in the literature (Borum & Otto, 2000). The assessment of dangerousness is a common activity for clinicians who work with the mentally ill (Monahan, 1978, 1992; Mossman, 1994; Shah, 1978). Patients of all ages, in private and public settings, are assessed on a daily basis for any risk presented to self or others. Likewise, formal risk assessment of suicidal and homicidal potential is a mainstay activity for forensic clinicians (Monahan & Shah, 1989) who conduct evaluations for the judicial and correctional systems. Forensic risk assessment is part of a variety of judicial proceedings such as juvenile and domestic matters, civil commitment, pretrial, pre- and postsentencing status of criminal defendants, conditional release of hospitalized patients, and parole and probation status of defendants.

All risk assessments involve a high probability of deception (Hall, 1987; Hall & Pritchard, 1996; Monahan, 1981). Not only is the evaluator challenged with ambiguous professional standards for conducting risk assessments (Appelbaum, 1994), the assessment effort is often confounded by deceptive maneuverings of those being evaluated. Petrilla (1995) and Borum (1996) noted that even managed care is impacted by the dubious empirical status of risk assessments. Managed care is financially driven health care; patients who are at risk for violence are costly liabilities. Patients with histories of violent behavior are actuarially classified as liabilities and can be excluded from full-range coverage or denied coverage altogether. Denial of patient coverage must be based on meaningful risk assessment to reduce company liability. The managed care problem offers an excellent nonforensic illustration of inherent motivation for deceptive efforts in risk assessments.

Regents v. Tarasoff (1976) has been widely viewed as having been a turning point for violence-potential assessment. Grisso and Tomkins (1996) pointed out, however, that *Tarasoff* was, in fact, preceded by 30 years of judicial developments regarding criteria for involuntary civil commitment and also mandatory abuse reporting requirements on behalf of children and elderly people. Civil commitment and abuse reporting both carry assumptions regarding determinations of risk. *Tarasoff* was the culmination of years of changes in the law/metal health interface.

TARGETS

A history of violence, situational and dispositional triggers to violence, and opportunities for violence are the three main factors associated with violence and are commonly the targets of denial and minimization by suspects (Hall, 1982, 1984, 1987). Any of the variables associated with violence may be targeted for denial or minimization. These include features of historical violence (frequency of past violence, arrests, and convictions for violence; recency of violence; severity of violence; targets of violence; frequency of institutional misconduct), and developmental events (felony arrest before age 15, relevant school problems such as truancy, evidence of self-reinforcement for violence).

Dispositional and situational influences on violence may encourage violence in individual cases. The significance of these influences is often denied. These include the subcultural acceptance of violence as a solution to interpersonal problems, perceiving oneself as dangerous, believing that certain types of violence will go undetected or unpunished, violent fantasies, violent friends, substance abuse or dependence, psychiatric conditions, and hostility.

Clients often distort triggering stimuli, short term in duration and intense in impact, that set the violence into motion. Short-term events include, as the two most frequently mentioned triggering events, substance abuse (Petersilia, Greenwood, & Larin, 1977; Wolfgang, 1978) and the breakup of a central love relationship (e.g., Bandura, 1973). Other examples are insults to self-esteem (Toch, 1969) and invasion of body space (Kinzel, 1970).

The presence of opportunity factors, which allow the occurrence of violence or expand the various ways it can be expressed, may also be minimized or denied. Opportunity factors expand the possible severity of exhibited violence or allow its expression. Examples in the former category include availability of a firearm (Berkowitz & Le Page, 1967), presence of a physically weaker potential victim (Bandura, 1973), and elevation to positions of authority where violence toward others is institutionally sanctioned (Fromm, 1973; Milgram, 1963). Variables that allow the expression of violence include release from incarceration into the community (Kelly, 1976) and cessation of taking tranquilizing medication (Stone, 1975). Table 23.1 presents features of violence that are commonly minimized or denied by clients.

Clients typically affirm some associated features of violence. These include easily verifiable associations of violence such as convictions, prison incarcerations, and body tattoos with violent themes. Other associations that are usually affirmed include a preference for violent films (TV, movies), books, etc., release from incarceration, and physical prowess in relationship to the (potential) victim. Some factors are blamed on others or are regarded as irrelevant to violence and hence are not denied. These include physical abuse as a child, praise or reward by parents for aggression, a violent model in the home, substance abuse by the same-sex parents, and a history of reinforcing outcomes for violence.

Perpetrators will typically affirm inhibitory variables that lower the chances that violence will occur. These variables fall into the lower range of frequency, intensity, severity, or duration of any quantifiable factor that is positively associated with violence. A minimal history of violence may be regarded by a client as a sign of dispositional nonviolence, for example, and many subjects will therefore claim a nonviolent basal history. Stabilizing psychotropic medication generally acts as an inhibitor to violence, and most patients will assert compliance with medication.

Dispositional factors associated with a lower propensity to aggress include high socioeconomic status and high educational level (Kelly, 1976; Monahan, 1981) and clients may therefore distort reports of occupational and educational achievement. The opportunity for violence may eliminate or reduce the probability of aggression and subjects may claim, for example, a lack of transportation or a physical disability.

Contextual stimuli include such variables as location of the crime scene and the presence of third parties (Steadman, 1981), architectural features (Atlas, 1982), availability of a weapon at the scene (Boyanowky & Griffith, 1982), and noxious environmental stimuli (Berkowitz, 1983;

TABLE 23.1
Targets of Violence-Related Features Frequently Denied or Minimized

Past multiple violence
Previous "big four" crimes (rape, robbery, aggravated assault, homicide)
Recency within last several years
History of reinforcing results from aggression
Pain cues from victim maintained/intensified perpetrator aggression
Institutional conduct involving threats or violence
Assaults or threats to authority figures
Arrests and hospitalizations for violence
Felony arrest before 15th birthday
Dangerous weapon used in offenses
Possession or recent purchase of firearm
Paraphernalia of weapons or substances
Cessation of stabilizing medication
Substance possession, intoxication, abuse, dependence, withdrawal, organic symptoms, or treatment
Violent or substance-abusing peers
Self-reinforcement for aggression
Insults to the self-esteem leading to violence
Job loss or problems due to aggression
High hostility, low frustration tolerance
Chronic anger toward targeted others
Self-perception as dangerous
Belief that certain types of violence will go unpunished
Violent fantasies and dreams
Reported and unreported spousal abuse
Reported and unreported child abuse
Childhood/adolescent history of animal abuse
Childhood/adolescent history of fire setting

Horowitz & Willging, 1984). Some subjects may therefore emphasize the improbability of violence given eyewitnesses, bright lighting, or other physical "barriers" to violence.

RESPONSE STYLES

Most perpetrators have an interest in a desired legal outcome and, therefore, often distort forensic information. However, if clients only hide violence (i.e., fake good) to escape conviction or punishment, this can and does lead to serious data misinterpretation. Honest responding, invalidation, faking bad, and fluctuating styles are also possibilities (see Hall, 1982, 1985, 1986; Rogers, 1984, 1997). The person may employ these strategies differentially for questions relevant to past violence and to present condition. Thus, there are at least 36 distinct distortion strategies possible, corresponding to six response strategies (faking good, faking bad, honesty, invalidation, mixed styles, fluctuating styles) for two time intervals (past, present). The point is that distortion by a client does not always conform to the strategy that is most obvious to or suspected by the clinician (i.e., faking good).

A defendant may attempt to portray past, but no current, dangerousness. The defendant may be saying that he or she was a dangerous person in the past but is not a risk now. The message communicated may be that it is appropriate to trust this individual or at least to perceive change in a positive direction. The implication for a lesser sentence, release from a state hospital, placement in a witness protection program, etc. may represent the desired outcome. Faking good for both the past and present may occur when the crime was minor and the defendant does not desire to have psychological intervention. If it serves the interests of the defendant, honest responding may be shown, as evidenced by verification from independent facts and sources, and other factors. Faking bad for the present with faking good for the past may be associated with a plea for help, as when the individual has been typically harmless, but is now dangerous due to unusual and highly stressful outside events.

Hall (1987) requested over 1000 military personnel to fabricate in writing acts of violence as well as to relate their genuine accounts of experienced violence. Themes of faked violence fell into four distinct categories:

1. Unlikely behaviors. This included females attacking males, calmness in the face of lethal attack, and smooth execution of behaviors when highly stressed.
2. Symbolic significance of the violence. For example, in the faked accounts, a rapist is struck in the groin with a hat pin, and a "P" (for "prick") is carved on the forehead of a vanquished enemy.
3. Bragging and exaggeration. There appears to be a component of self-esteem to even faked violence. Both of a victim's legs are shot off by the perpetrator in one account. Every bone in the victim's hand is broken by another, and the richest person in the area is kidnapped for ransom.
4. Revenge scenes were common, perhaps as a means to justify the violence. They were accompanied by a large number of acts of self-defense, again possibly to provide a rationale for the aggression. Because of this, the majority of faked accounts involved the use of weapons not designed for attack. A 37-year-old Caucasian female reported the following in her false account:

> I was walking downtown one night, on a very busy road with many people around. Nevertheless I could not feel relaxed.
>
> I was very conscious of my environment and when I left the crowded area to go to a streetcar stop, I felt it almost physically that somebody followed me. I heard footsteps picking up my speed and the heavy breathing of a man behind me. My heartbeat became faster, as my hands formed a fist.
>
> I felt cold sweat on my head, but my conscience and rationality froze up. I was not going to allow this individual to hurt me or even touch me. Without any sign of nervousness, I reached in my purse to get out a letter opener which I always had in there — just in case! It had a wooden handle with a sharp blade. I was also thankful that I had high heels with a metal part. I slowly lifted my knee up to swing my foot back in speed. I heard a moan and felt hands on my hips. That did it! I turned and stared in the face of a man whose face expressed anger and hate. Without hesitation, I raised my arm and ran the blade in him. At the same time I kicked him hard with my knee against his abdomen, while my hands scratched his face and slapped him. I did not stop till he was on the ground — motionless. I had done it and felt no regret.

Response style analysis is in a rudimentary stage of development. Different response styles, conceptualized separately for past and for present violence, appear to represent a fruitful area of study. Knowing how people distort their past violence and their present potential for violence will likely increase the accuracy of predictions of dangerousness. An alternative approach to response style analysis is the profiling techniques used by the FBI; these techniques are described in Chapter 15.

DETECTION METHODS

The empirical status of risk assessment has followed a meandering course for the past 30 or so years. By the mid-1980s, Monahan (1984) suggested a "second generation" of risk assessment studies that had begun to offer more promise than "first-generation" studies. More recently, Borum (1996) suggested a "third generation" of risk assessment marked by the MacArthur Risk Assessment Study (Steadman et al., 1994, 1998, 2000). The MacArthur Study involved a relatively large sample (1000 subjects) of hospitalized patients and investigated a comprehensive array of risk factors. The risk factors were reviewed individually, and in small and large clusters, to determine any predictive patterns of violence risk. This three-generational history of risk assessment studies and the implications for FDA in risk assessment are captured in Table 23.2. These data illustrate some of the significant advances that have been achieved in risk assessment.

As with most evolving research, risk assessment investigations demonstrate controversial and contradictory findings. In time, such differences are usually clarified with new research. The issue of whether or not mental illness is a risk factor in violence is a prime example of such research controversy. There have been a number of reviews of this issue (see Appelbaum, 1994; Borum, 1996; Monahan & Steadman, 1996; Rice, 1997; Rice & Harris, 1997; Teplin, Abram, & McClelland, 1994). Tengström, Grann, Långström, and Kullgreen (2000) noted that the risk for committing violent crimes by individuals suffering from major mental disorders is four to six times higher than that of the general population. Given the fact that violent crimes in the general population are not very common, violence also has a relatively low base rate among individuals with major mental disorders.

The prevailing view appears to be that serious mental illness may be a significant contributing factor to violence, but recent studies have indicated that the basic interactive variables are very intertwined. Teplin, Abram, and McClelland (1994) conducted a 6-year longitudinal study that did not support mental illness as a significantly contributing factor. Rice (1997) also reported a negative relationship between psychotic diagnosis and violent recidivism. One perplexing problem in the foregoing research has been controlling for other suspected high-risk factors. Teplin et al. (1994), for example, did not control for age or prior violence. Other presumed high-risk factors for violence include gender, marital status, victimization history, and especially comorbid personality and substance abuse disorders.

The important role of psychopathic dynamics with violent offenders has been well established. Psychopathy is correlated with early onset of violent offending and a progression of violent and nonviolent acting out through adulthood (Hare, 1991, 1996, 1998a, b; Hare et al., 1990). In a study of criminal offenders with schizophrenia, Hare's Psychopathy Checklist–Revised (PCL-R; Hare, 1991; Hare et al., 1990) was used to test the hypothesis that psychopathy predicted violent recidivism with the subjects (Tengström et al., 2000). As measured by the PCL-R, psychopathy was found to be an important factor in predicting violent recidivism with this group. Other established recidivism risk factors (e.g., prior violent acts, downward social mobility, substance abuse) did not explain as well, or better, the cohort of violence recidivism.

One of the efforts in the ongoing MacArthur Risk Assessment Study (Steadman et al., 1994) has been to identify risk factors comprehensively on a multidimensional basis as opposed to the traditional identification and comparison of single-risk predictor variables. The traditional approach has been to use 2×2 contingency tables that incorporate dichotomous outcome measures and a dichotomous violence predictor (Mossman, 1994; Rice, 1997). Steadman et al. (1994) proposed further that the multidimensional analyses should be conducted at recurrent intervals. Menzies and Webster (1995) reported an effort to adhere to the MacArthur Study proscriptions, but the predictive accuracy of their findings did not produce encouraging results. These writers concluded, "For the time being, the debates continue, the dilemmas persist, and the problem of violence prediction remains one of the most persisting enigmas in the interrelated fields of psychology, medicine and law" (p. 776).

Steadman et al. (2000) noted that the many recent tools developed for violent risk assessment remained primarily research instruments and have not been routinely incorporated into daily clinical/forensic practice. The investigators proposed that this was because most existing actuarial instruments are based on a main-effects regression approach and, as such, do not adequately reflect

TABLE 23.2
Three Generations of Risk Assessment Research

Generation	Critical Issue	FDA
First generation — 1960s to 1981	Clinicians predict risk accurately no more than two out of three times (Monahan, 1981)	Not applicable
	Long-term violence predictions about outpatients usually incorrect (Ennis & Litwack, 1976; Faust & Ziskin, 1988; Monahan, 1978)	
Second generation — 1980s to 1995	At least one in two short-term predictions are accurate (Otto, 1992)	Violence history, triggers, and opportunity are three main factors associated with violence, and are common targets of denial and minimization by perpetrators (Hall, 1982, 1984, 1987)
	"Best estimates" vs. "prediction" (Grisso & Tompkins, 1996)	
	Violence predictions substantially better than chance; second-generation studies more accurate; short-term predictions not better than long-term; past behavior is better long-term predictor than clinical judgment (Mossman, 1994)	
	Research methodology improvement contributed to better predictive accuracy (Borum, 1996)	
	Base of empirical knowledge about risk factors for violent behavior has widely expanded in the last 15 years (Monahan & Steadman, 1996)	
Third generation — 1995 to present	MacArthur Risk Assessment Study comprehensively examines wide range of combinations of violence risk factors in four domains: dispositional, historical, contextual, and clinical (Steadman et al., 1994)	Accurate risk assessment requires:
		1) Multisourced, interdisciplinary forensic database
	Communicate violence risk assessment in probabilistic terms (Monahan & Steadman, 1996)	2) Distortion analysis
	Violence prediction can be analogized to "weather forecasting," violence risk can be communicated as risk "forecasts" (Monahan & Steadman, 1996)	3) Basal violence characteristics
		4) Identification of trigger stimuli
	Several assessment instruments have been developed to improve reliability and validity of risk judgments (Borum, 1996)	5) Examination of opportunity factors (Hall & Pritchard, 1996)
	Mental disorder may be a significant violence risk factor (Appelbaum, 1994; Borum, 1996; Link & Stueve, 1995; Monahan, 1992; Monahan & Steadman, 1996)	
	Violence base rates are higher than previously hypothesized (Borum, 1996; Lidz, Mulvey, & Gardner, 1993; Monahan & Steadman, 1996; Steadman et al., 1994)	
	Research advances have laid the groundwork for developing professional standards for risk assessment (Appelbaum, 1994; Borum, 1996; Monahan, 1993)	

Note: Adapted from "The Prediction of Violent Behavior: Toward a Second Generation of Theory and Policy," by J. Monahan, 1984, *American Journal of Psychiatry, 141,* 10–15, and "Improving the Clinical Practice of Violence Risk Assessment: Technology, Guidelines, and Training," by R. Borum, 1996, *American Psychologist, 51*(9), 945–956.

the evolving and contingent nature of actual clinical assessment processes. To overcome this problem, the authors propose an iterative classification tree model as opposed to main-effects regression procedures. The approach uses two decision thresholds to arrive at a dichotomous risk classification. One classification identifies high-risk cases and the other identifies low-risk cases, leaving a residual group of "unclassified." Classification decisions would be made using current software technologies, which would lead the user through decision tree steps while making and entering threshold decisions.

Borum (1996) reviewed a number of third-generation risk assessment instruments and actuarial methods. These investigations have yet to integrate specifically deceptive behavior as a dependent variable, and, in fact, the normative assumption is that the assessment/actuarial data are credible as gathered.

Accurate prediction of dangerousness in individual cases requires (1) obtaining a multisourced, interdisciplinary forensic database upon which to draw conclusions; (2) analyzing retrospective and current distortion; (3) determining the characteristics of basal violence (frequency, intensity, severity of past dangerousness); (4) determining the presence of triggering stimuli (especially substance intoxication, breakup of a central love relationship, and work conflict) and (5) examining opportunity factors (Hall, 1987).

The instant violence can be represented in a description of the assault cycle of the incident. The typical assault cycle consists of a baseline (past or basal violence), a triggering phase, an escalation phase (where arousal mounts and the perpetrator becomes more threatening), a crisis phase (where the actual violence occurs), and a recovery phase. A typical assault cycle was illustrated in Chapter 15. The following case example is based on an actual forensic assessment by the authors:

> The A.J. family was referred to a forensic evaluation service by the Juvenile Court following a Children in Need of Assistance (CINA) adjudication of the family's five surviving children. The children ranged in age from 18 months to 6 years. The three youngest were still in diapers. The sixth sibling was a 5-month-old boy who had died of mysterious circumstances 3 weeks earlier. The parents had brought the child to a hospital emergency room when the child would not awaken and was having respiratory distress. Hospital records reflected the distraught parents to have reported all the youngsters having recent upper-respiratory ailments.
>
> The distressed infant was initially evaluated for a viral infection, but his condition rapidly deteriorated. A CT scan revealed the infant's brain to be badly swollen and compromising basic bodily functions. Eventually, the mother painfully acknowledged that the child had accidentally fallen to the floor from a dressing table. Tragically, the infant died. An autopsy reflected that the injuries were not entirely consistent with the reported fall. The parents remained steadfast in their explanation; a suspected abuse report was filed leading to an emergency hearing before the Juvenile Court on behalf of the surviving youngsters.
>
> The forensic assessment was ordered on a priority basis. The judge arranged a conference call with the involved attorneys to the Forensic Service and asked to speak to the lead clinician. The judge expressed her deep concern for the surviving children, but acknowledged that the legal evidence was not sufficient to remove the children from the care of the parents. The older children appeared to be doing well; the Protective Services investigation including several home visits had not produced any unusual concerns. The infant's death could have conceivably been accidental. The judge did note that the Protective Services investigation produced vague complaints from the children of their being afraid of the father because of angry outbursts.
>
> A comprehensive forensic assessment determined little new information, and, at best, generated ambiguous clinical-psychological findings regarding the parents. The parents, both individually and together, strenuously maintained that there had never been any remiss behavior toward the children. Records review indicated that a year and a half earlier, there was a Protective Services report from the oldest child's preschool because of "bruises." The child reported she had been disciplined by father; the parents said the child had been fighting with siblings; the matter was closed as "unsubstantiated."

Mrs. A.J. came from a wholesome family background; her developmental history was unremarkable, other than becoming pregnant at the age of 17 and marrying her boyfriend, Mr. A.J. The early marital history was marked by Mr. A.J.'s military stint in Vietnam. Serious shrapnel injuries to the lower torso resulted in Mr. A.J.'s early transfer back to the States. The available military/VA medical records were not entirely clear, but it appeared that Mr. A.J. had acquired a heroin addiction prior to his being wounded. Following multiple surgeries he also became addicted to pain medication. Mr. A.J. reportedly underwent detoxification through the VA and continued in outpatient monitoring including regular urinalysis. The family subsisted on VA disability and other public assistance subsidies. Mr. A.J. was enrolled full-time in a VA-subsidized electronics-training program. Mr. A.J.'s progress as a struggling Vietnam veteran had been the repeated topic of a local newspaper series touting his accomplishments.

Psychological testing reflected the immaturities of both parenting figures, with Mr. A.J. also having multiple soft, characterological signs to include narcissism, impulsivity, anger-management difficulties, and a propensity for substance abuse. The forensic team noted the obvious clinical concerns and recommended stipulated follow-up assessments initially every 60 days. The team also cited the importance of requested, but still not received, treatment records regarding the father from the VA to include especially ongoing urinalysis records.

The matter was complicated by the facts that the parents were African-American and the case had received high-profile attention from the media. The local jurisdiction was very tense because of reported racial discrimination by the local police and the judiciary. During a subsequent CINA proceeding, the parents' attorney underscored the fact that Mr. A.J. was a "wounded-in-action, decorated Vietnam veteran." The attorney dramatically asserted to the bench, "This family has already suffered enough, don't bring further suffering by removing the children or making the father leave the home." The bench maintained the children in the parents' care and ordered a follow-up assessment in 6 months with a status report including further recommendations back to the bench.

From this point on, the circumstances in the case unfolded very quickly. The second-youngest child, a boy, was brought to the emergency room unconscious and with injuries similar to those of the deceased infant. In an emergency hearing, the children were removed from the parents' care and placed in temporary foster care; there were no available family placements. The parents separated with the mother reporting spouse abuse to Protective Service caseworkers. The injured toddler recovered and went with the siblings into foster care. Only the mother and her family exercised court-stipulated, supervised visitation.

Approximately a month later, the media reported that Mr. A.J. had died in a police drug bust. The details were sketchy, but Mr. A.J. and an accomplice were working with police in undercover investigations. Reportedly, Mr. A.J. double-crossed both his civilian accomplice and the police by secreting a large portion of a batch of confiscated heroin following a drug raid. When he was discovered, Mr. A.J. drew a handgun. There was a gunfight with Mr. A.J. incurring immediately fatal wounds. The involved police officers were subsequently exonerated from any wrongdoing in administrative review hearings.

Nearly a year later, the forensic team was ordered to reevaluate Mrs. A.J. who had petitioned the court for return of her children. During that assessment, Mrs. A.J. described that she had been motivated by a strong commitment to her marriage; she described that when Mr. A.J. was not abusing drugs, he was a good husband and father. There had been incidents of Mr. A.J. being verbally and physically abusive prior to the marriage, and now Mrs. A.J. was being told by her husband's family of a long-standing anger problem to include several incidents in which Mr. A.J. had inflicted serious injuries. Mr. A.J. had experimented with street drugs before his military service; he had quickly succumbed to potent, readily available heroin in Vietnam. The first child had died when Mr. A.J. returned home one evening intoxicated and very angry about a street drug sale that had gone sour. The infant was crying, Mr. A.J. took the child from his terrified mother, angrily threw the child to the floor, and stomped the infant's head in a display of his ire. The second child had been similarly injured.

Although not evident at the time of the initial evaluation effort, it is relatively easy, in retrospect, to critique how and why this family situation reached its horrific outcome. The case vividly demonstrates the role of deception in risk assessments. There were unique aspects to the A.J. matter, most notably the subtle but powerful community backdrop of harassment and racial discrimination concerns. Mr. A.J. was clearly a practiced prevaricator; another critical factor was Mrs. A.J.'s passive and active collusion, as well as the collusion of extended family members. The combined collusion only made Mr. A.J.'s deception all the more pervasive and effective. The deception was unwittingly enhanced by the attention of the media. Similarly, the understandable but misdirected community support engendered by media coverage fed into the collusion dynamic.

One can also understand some of the triggering dynamics in the A.J. matter. These included the parental immaturities, Mr. A.J.'s active addiction, and a troubled marital relationship. Mr. A.J. was insecure about his future and continued to rely on his street wiles. Substance abuse exacerbated his insecurities; when frustrated and angry he was unable to refrain from displacing his anger onto his wife and children. Mr. A.J.'s harm to the children was probably more painful to Mrs. A.J. than being physically abused herself. One can only speculate how the children were threats to Mr. A.J.'s narcissism. The violence in the A.J. case involved a family circumstance and did not have the blatantly, inexplicable features that can characterize stranger-to-stranger violence.

COMMON ERORS

Under some circumstances, failure to warn a defendant that information regarding dangerousness may be presented to the court for purposes of sentencing may constitute a violation of the defendant's constitutional rights (*Barefoot v. Estelle*, 1983; *Estelle v. Smith*, 1981; *Powell v. Texas*, 1989). "A criminal defendant, who neither initiates a psychiatric examination nor attempts to introduce any psychiatric evidence, may not be compelled to respond to a psychiatrist if his statements can be used against him at a capital sentencing proceeding" (*United States v. Byers*, 1984). It is ethically, and sometimes legally, incumbent on examiners to inform defendants how the information obtained during an evaluation will be used.

Other common errors in the assessment of dangerousness include (1) the lack of an adequate forensic database, (2) the failure to account for retrospective and current distortion, (3) the prediction of future dangerousness in the absence of previous dangerousness, (4) the reliance on illusory correlations of dangerousness, (5) the prediction of dangerousness solely from clinical diagnosis, (6) the failure to consider triggering stimuli, (7) the failure to take into account opportunity variables, (8) the failure to evaluate inhibitory factors, (9) ignoring relevant base rates, and (10) the failure to formulate circumscribed conclusions.

The FBI recidivism data for 1972 showed that 64% of individuals convicted for homicide, 77% convicted for robbery, 73% convicted for rape, and 70% convicted for aggravated assault committed new offenses within 4 years of release from prison. The PROMIS research project (Institute for Law and Social Research, 1977) showed that with five or more arrests for violent crimes, the probability of similar future arrests approaches certainty. Wolfgang (1977) reported that the probability of future arrests varied directly with the number of previous arrests (e.g., 80% probability with four prior arrests). Guze (1976) found that of male felons released from incarceration: (1) 72% were rearrested and 41% were reimprisoned after 3 years if they had been diagnosed as sociopathic; (2) 90% were rearrested and 67% were reimprisoned over an 8- to 9-year period after release if they had been "flat-timers" (no early release on parole for "good time"). Over a 3-year period after release, 81% were rearrested and 56% were reimprisoned, pointing to the time soon after release as the critical period when most recidivism occurs; and (3) 90% were rearrested and 50% were reimprisoned if they had a diagnosis of drug dependence (3-year follow-up); 74% were rearrested and 45% were reimprisoned if they were primarily alcohol abusers (3-year follow-up).

These statistics may be compared with a relatively low 33% rearrest rate and 21% reconviction rate for released females and a 57% rearrest rate and 28% reimprisonment rate for some types of male parolees, both over 3 years. High rates for reoffending are thus found for some types of individuals (e.g., flat-timers, substance abusers with previous drug dependence) and much lower for others (e.g., females, some types of parolees).

Data that are more recent reflect similar trends, but also some significant differences. Part of these differences may reflect changes in data collection procedures. According to Bureau of Justice Statistics (1999), of the 108,580 persons released from 11 U. S. prisons in 1983, an estimated 62.5% were rearrested for a felony or serious misdemeanor within 3 years. Of these recidivists, 46.8% were reconvicted, and 41.4% returned to jail or prison. The Bureau of Justice (1994) pretrial release of felony defendant statistics for 1992 reflected approximately 14% of all defendants were rearrested while on pretrial release. Of these defendants, 10% were rearrested on a felony charge(s). Released defendants with at least one prior conviction (19%) were about twice as likely to be rearrested compared with those with no prior convictions (9%). Of the released defendants with five or more prior convictions, 29% were rearrested while on pretrial release.

The 1992 misdemeanor rearrest rate (3%) did not differ between the sexes; the felony rearrest rate for males (11%) was higher than for females (6%). About 15% of African-American defendants were rearrested, compared with 11% of Caucasian defendants and 6% of defendants of other races. Hispanic defendants had a rearrest rate of 16%. Defendants under age 21 (16%) had a slightly higher rearrest rate than those 35 or older. Released defendants with ten or more prior convictions had a rearrest rate of 38%, that is, four times more compared with defendants with no prior convictions. About 19% of defendants whose most serious prior conviction was a felony were rearrested for a felony, more than twice the percentage for defendants with no prior felony convictions (7%). For rearrested defendants, the median time from pretrial release to the alleged commission of a new offense was 48 days. About 8% of the new charged offenses occurred within 1 month, and 71% occurred within 3 months of the defendant's release.

In general, there should be compelling reasons for ignoring or disagreeing with the base rate of violence relevant to individuals. Individual predictions of future dangerousness should be "anchored" (Shapiro, 1977) by relevant base rates before adding client-specific data to individualize the prediction. The initial use of baselines also helps avoid the error of overplaying current events and downplaying the violence history.

One of the most important steps in risk assessment is conveying the findings in a meaningful and ethical manner that is empirically supportable. Monahan and Steadman (1996) likened the effort to making a "weather forecast," emphasizing the inherently spurious nature of the very effort. Risk assessment is "future predicting" and therefore an empirically murky process. Based on survey data from a group of psychiatrists and psychologists identified as experts in risk assessment, Heilbrun et al. (2000) described their findings as being very consistent with the weather forecasting analogy. "The most highly valued form of risk assessment communication involved identifying risk factors applicable to the individual and specifying interventions to reduce risk" (p. 137).

LEGAL REFERENCES

Barefoot v. Estelle, 463 U.S. 880 (1983).
Estelle v. Smith, 451 U.S. 454 (1981).
Powell v. Texas, 57 U.S.L.W. 3857 (1989).
Tarasoff v. Regents of the University of California, Cal. 1976 (551 P.2d. 334).
U.S. v. Beyers, 740 F.2d 1104 (DC Cir. 1984) certiorari denied 104 S. Ct. 717, p. 465.

REFERENCES

Appelbaum, P. S. (1985). Tarasoff and the clinician: Problems in fulfilling the duty to protect. *American Journal of Psychiatry, 142*, 425–429.
Appelbaum, P. (1994). New directions in the assessment of dangerousness of the mentally ill. *The Japanese Journal of Psychiatry and Neurology, 48*, 77–83.

Atlas, R. (1982). Crime site selection for assaults in four Florida prisons. *Man–Environment Systems*, *12*, 59–66.

Bandura, A. (1973). *Aggression: A social learning analysis*. Englewood Cliffs, NJ: Prentice-Hall.

Berkowitz, L. (1983). Aversively stimulated aggression: Some parallels and differences in research with animals and humans. *American Psychologist*, *38*, 1135–1144.

Berkowitz, L., & Le Page, A. (1967). Weapons as aggression-eliciting stimuli. *Journal of Personality and Social Psychology*, *7*(2, Part 1), 202–207.

Borum, R. (1996). Improving the clinical practice of violence risk assessment: Technology, guidelines, and training. *American Psychologist, 51*(9), 945–956.

Borum, R., & Otto, R. (2000). Advances in forensic assessment and treatment: An overview and introduction to the special issue. *Law and Human Behavior, 24*(1), 1–7.

Boyanowky, E., & Griffith, C. (1982). Weapons and eye contact as instigators or inhibitors of aggressive arousal in police-citizen interaction. *Journal of Applied Social Contact*, *12,* 398–407.

Bureau of Justice Statistics. (1994). *Pretrial release of felony defendants*. (1992). (Tech. Rep. No. NCJ-148818). Washington, DC: U.S. Department of Justice.

Bureau of Justice Statistics. (1999). *Criminal offenders statistics*. Available at *http://www.ojp.usdoj.gov/bjs/crimoff.htm*.

Ennnis, B. J., & Litwack, T. P. (1976). Psychiatry and the presumption of expertise. *California Law Review, 62,* 693–752.

Faust, D., & Ziskin, J. (1988). The expert witness in psychology and psychiatry. *Science, 241,* 31–35.

Fromm, E. (1973). *The anatomy of human destructiveness*. New York: Holt, Rinehart, & Winston.

Grisso, T., & Appelbaum, P. (1992). Is it unethical to offer predictions of future violence? *Law and Human Behavior, 16,* (6), 621–633.

Grisso, T., & Tomkins, A. J. (1996). Communicating violence risk assessments. *American Psychologist, 51*(9), 928–930.

Guze, S. (1976). *Criminality and psychiatric disorders*. New York: Oxford University Press.

Hall, H. V. (1982). Dangerousness predictions and the maligned forensic professional: Suggestions for detecting distortion of true basal violence. *Criminal Justice and Behavior, 9,* 3–12.

Hall, H. V. (1984). Predicting dangerousness for the courts. *American Journal of Forensic Psychology, 4,* 5–25.

Hall, H. V. (1985). Cognitive and volitional capacity assessment: A proposed decision tree. *American Journal of Forensic Psychology, 3,* 3–17.

Hall, H. V. (1986). The forensic distortion analysis: A proposed decision tree and report format. *American Journal of Forensic Psychology, 4,* 31–59.

Hall, H. V. (1987). *Violence prediction: Guidelines for the forensic practitioner*. Springfield, IL: Charles C Thomas.

Hall, H. V., & Pritchard, D. A. (1996) *Detecting malingering and deception*. Boca Raton, FL: St. Lucie Press.

Hare, R. D. (1991). *Manual for the Hare Psychopathy Checklist–Revised*. Toronto: Multi-Health Systems.

Hare, R. D. (1996). Psychopathy: A clinical construct whose time has come. *Criminal Justice & Behavior, 23*(1), 25–54.

Hare, R. D. (1998a). Psychopaths and their nature: Implications for the mental health and criminal justice systems. In T. Millon, E. Simonsen, M. Birket-Smith, & R. Davis (Eds.), *Psychopathy: Antisocial, criminal, and violent behavior* (pp. 188–214). New York: Guilford Press.

Hare, R. D. (1998b). The Hare PCL-R: Some issues concerning its use and misuse. *Legal & Criminological Psychology, 3*(Part 1), 99–119.

Hare, R. D., Harpur, T. J., Hakstain, R. A., Forth, A. E., Hart, S. D., & Newman, J. R. (1990). The Revised Psychopathy Checklist: Reliability and factor structure. *Psychological Assessment, 2*(3), 338–341.

Heilbrun, K., O'Neil, M. L., Strohman, L. K., Bowman, Q., & Philipson, J. (2000). Expert approaches to communicating violence risk. *Law and Human Behavior, 24* (1), 137–148.

Horowitz, I., & Willging, T. (1984). *The psychology of law*. Boston, MA: Little, Brown, & Company.

Kelly, C. (1976). *Crime in the United States: Uniform crime reports*. Washington, DC: U.S. Government Printing Office.

Kinzel, A. (1970). Body-buffer zones in violent prisoners. *American Journal of Psychiatry, 127,* 59–64.

Lidz, C. W., Mulvey, E. P., & Gardner, W. (1993). The accuracy of predictions of violence to others. *Journal of the American Medical Association, 269,* 1007–1011.

Link, B. G., & Steuve, A. (1995). Evidence bearing on mental illness as a possible cause of violent behavior. *Epidemiologic Reviews, 17,* 1–10.

Menzies, R., & Webster, C. D. (1995). Construction and validation of risk assessments in a six-year follow-up of forensic patients: A tridimensional analysis. *Journal of Consulting & Clinical Psychology, 63*(5), 766–778.

Milgram, S. (1963). Behavioral study of obedience. *Journal of Abnormal and Social Psychology, 67,* 371–378.

Monahan, J. (1978). Prediction research and the emergency commitment of dangerously ill persons. *American Journal of Psychiatry, 135,* 198–201.

Monahan, J. (1981). *The clinical prediction of violent behavior* (National Institute of Mental Health, DHHS Publication No. ADM 81-92). Washington, DC: U.S. Government Printing Office.

Monahan, J. (1984). The prediction of violent behavior: Toward a second generation of theory and policy. *American Journal of Psychiatry, 141,* 10–15.

Monahan, J. (1992). Mental disorder and violent behavior: Perceptions and evidence. *American Psychologist, 47,* 511–521.

Monahan, J. (1993). Limiting therapist exposure to Tarasoff liability. *American Psychologist, 48,* 242–250.

Monahan, J., & Shah, S. (1989). Dangerousness and commitment of the mentally disordered in the United States. *Schizophrenia Bulletin, 15,* 541–553.

Monahan, J., & Steadman, H. J. (1996). Violent storms and violent people: How meteorology can inform risk communication in mental health law. *American Psychologist, 51*(9), 931–938.

Mossman, D. (1994). Assessing predictions of violence: Being accurate about accuracy. *Journal of Consulting & Clinical Psychology, 62*(4), 783–792.

Otto, R. (1992). The prediction of dangerous behavior: A review and analysis of "second generation" research. *Forensic Reports, 5,* 103–133.

Petersilia, J., Greenwood, P., & Lavin, M. (1977). *Criminal careers of habitual felons.* Santa Monica, CA: Rand Corporation.

Petrilla, J. (1995). Who will pay for involuntary civil commitment under capitated managed care? *Psychiatric Services, 46,* 1045–1048.

Rice, M. E. (1997). Violent offender research and implications for the criminal justice system. *American Psychologist, 52*(4), 414–423.

Rice, M. E., & Harris, G. T. (1997). The treatment of mentally disordered offenders. *Psychology, Public Policy, & Law, 3*(1), 126–183.

Rogers, R. (1984). Towards an empirical model of malingering and deception. *Behavioral Sciences and the Law, 2,* 93–111.

Rogers, R. (1997). *Clinical assessment of malingering and deception.* New York: Guilford Press.

Shah, S. (1978). Dangerousness: A paradigm for exploring some issues in law and psychology. *American Psychologist, 33,* 224–238.

Shapiro, A. (1977). The evaluation of clinical prediction: A method and initial application. *New England Journal of Medicine, 296,* 1509–1514.

Steadman, H. (1981). A situational approach to violence. *International Journal of Law and Psychiatry, 5,* 171–186.

Steadman, H. J., Monahan, J., Appelbaum, P. S., Grisso, T., Mulvey, E. P., Roth, L., Robbins, P. C., & Klassen, D. (1994). Designing a new generation of risk assessment research. In J. Monahan & H. J. Steadman (Eds.), *Violence and mental disorder: Developments in risk assessment* (pp. 297–318). Chicago, IL: University of Chicago Press.

Steadman, H., Mulvey, E., Monahan, J., Robbins, P., Appelbaum, P., Grisso, T., Roth, L., & Silver, E. (1998). Violence by people discharged from acute psychiatric inpatient facilities and by others in the same neighborhoods. *Archives of General Psychiatry, 55,* 393–401.

Steadman, H., Silver, E., Monahan, J., Appelbaum, P. S., Robbins, P. C., Mulvey, E. P., Grisso, T, Roth, L., & Banks, S. (2000). A classification tree approach development of actuarial violence risk assessment tools. *Law and Human Behavior, 24*(1), 83–100.

Stone, A. (1975). *Mental health and the law: A system in transition* (National Institute of Mental Health, DHEW Publication No. ADM 76-176). Washington, DC: U.S. Government Printing Office.

Tengström, A., Grann, M., Långström, N., & Kullgreen, G. (2000). Psychopathy (PCL-R) as a predictor of a violent recidivism among criminal offenders with schizophrenia. *Law and Human Behavior, 24* (1), 45–58.

Teplin, L. A., Abram, K. M., & McClelland, G. M. (1994). Does psychiatric disorder predict violent crime among jail detainees? A six-year longitudinal study. *American Psychologist, 49*(4), 335–342.

Toch, H. (1969). *Violent man*. Chicago, IL: Aldine.

Wolfgang, M. (1977). *From boy to man — From delinquency to crime. Serious juvenile offender.* National symposium, Minneapolis, MN.

Wolfgang, M. (1978). *An overview of research into violent behavior.* Testimony before the U.S. House of Representatives Committee on Science and Technology.

24 Conclusions and Expert Testimony

Beginning with the list of quotations at the very beginning, this book has focused on the pervasiveness of deceptive behavior in human nature. Indeed, part of the message of the book has been to emphasize the fundamental importance for those who engage in forensic practice to be ever alert for the possibility of deception. The wealth of studies reviewed in previous chapters can easily lead to a preoccupation with distortions at the expense of sound clinical diagnosis and assessment. Distortion analysis is an integral aspect of the FDA model. Also critical is an appreciation for the role of nondeliberate distortion and the basic existential qualities of sincerity and honesty in human nature.

In an effort to counter the constrictive view of the earlier chapters, the present chapter focuses on broader questions. In particular, the chapter discusses (1) when a distortion analysis is necessary, (2) what methods should be used in such an analysis, (3) what conclusions are justified from such an analysis, and (4) when the clinician should become an expert witness. Finally, the chapter discusses some issues involved in assuming the role of expert witness.

When is a distortion analysis necessary? A distortion analysis is the process of evaluating the effects of intentional and unintentional distortions on the information received from clients during psychological assessments in general and in forensic assessments in particular. It always requires an expenditure of time and resources over and beyond that required for the assessment itself. It is therefore appropriate to ask when such expenditures are proper and necessary.

In general, a distortion analysis is proper whenever the cost of conducting the analysis is less than the cost of making an assessment error and the likelihood of an assessment error is high. If, during intake at a private practice or a mental health clinic, it is routine to collect background information, an MMPI, and a sentence completion test, it would not be justifiable to spend an additional 2 hours assessing the "genuineness" of answers to these instruments. However, if a particular applicant's answers are suggestive of distortion (i.e., the likelihood of an assessment error is increased), then additional testing for distortions may be justified. During psychological screening of police applicants, a distortion analysis may be routinely justified on the basis that most applicants will "put on their best faces" (i.e., the likelihood of missing psychopathology is increased) and that the cost of recommending poor risks for hire outweighs the cost of the additional testing.

However, whenever the cost of an assessment error is greater than the cost of conducting a distortion analysis and the resulting decision is irreversible, then a distortion analysis is necessary. In most clinical situations, assessment decisions lead to treatment decisions, which are subsequently revised based on feedback on the effectiveness of the treatment. Treatment decisions are usually reversible if it appears that the original assessment was in error. In fact, response to treatment is sometimes used as a clinical criterion against which to judge the accuracy of the initial assessment. In addition, most errors in assigning clients to inappropriate psychological and psychiatric treatments are reversible without permanent cost to the client. Switching a patient from one psychotropic medication to another rarely results in serious or irreversible consequences for the patient; substituting behavior therapy for insight-oriented psychotherapy rarely causes a loss to the client.

In other situations, however, the decision resulting from the initial assessment is irreversible. In nearly all forensic situations, for example, a psychological assessment results in an irrevocable report (written or testimonial), which cannot be "taken back." The report becomes a permanent (although not necessarily determinative) factor upon which the judge, jury, hearing officer, appeals panel, or other legal decision maker relies. There is no opportunity for the forensic expert to recall and revise the original assessment, conclusions, or decisions based on new information.* In addition, most forensic evaluations involve an increased risk of assessment errors because of the motivation of the client to influence the outcome in one way or another. In such situations of irreversible decisions with increased risk of assessment errors, an analysis of the distortions, which may have affected the assessment, is not merely proper, but is necessary.

What methods should be used in a distortion analysis? The preceding chapters have reviewed numerous signs, scales, patterns, and other indicators of distortion. The accuracies of these proposed indicators for particular types of distortion (e.g., for detecting denial of substance abuse or exaggeration of memory dysfunction) vary considerably. At one extreme, indicators are merely suggestive of distortion (e.g., indicators of malingered pain), while at the other extreme, indicators are highly probative of distortion (e.g., explicit alternative testing of neuropsychological complaints). Which indicators of distortion are appropriate for use in individual cases depends on the type of decision being made. If the purpose of the original assessment leads to a reversible decision, then less accurate indicators would be acceptable than if the decision is irreversible. Correlatively, if the cost of an assessment error is tolerable, less accurate indicators may be used than if such costs are intolerable. In clinical situations, it would be acceptable to note indicators that suggest denial, minimization, exaggeration, or fabrication, because subsequent treatments can be modified with little cost to the client. In forensic situations, however, the most accurate indicators available should be employed and suggestive indicators should be avoided, both because of the irreversibility of the resulting decision and the costs associated with assessment errors.

Replicated indicators of distortion must be distinguished from experimental indicators of distortion. Both replicated and experimental indicators are associated with rates of error; no prediction is error-free. However, replicated indicators are those shown in multiple studies to distinguish between "malingerers" and other comparison groups relevant to the use for which the indicator was developed. For example, if an indicator has been developed to distinguish between "malingered psychosis" and "genuine psychosis" among criminal defendants, then the indicator would be replicated if there were multiple studies that showed the indicator distinguished between groups of "psychotic defendants" and groups of "nonpsychotic defendants instructed to feign psychosis." The indicator would be experimental if there were only one study showing such discrimination or if there were only studies showing that the indicator distinguished between other groups (e.g., psychotic defendants vs. normal subjects instructed to feign psychosis). Replicated indicators are distinguished from experimental indicators on the basis of their repeatability and their "ecological validity."

This distinction between replicated and experimental indicators does not preclude the possibility that an indicator may be accurate in many different situations. The F-K index on the MMPI, for example, may be accurate in identifying distortions among psychiatric outpatients, medical inpatients, and prison inmates. However, the question is an empirical one. It cannot be assumed that, because an indicator reliably distinguishes between two conditions (e.g., genuine vs. exaggerated back pain) or two groups (e.g., honest vs. malingering parolees), it will also reliably distinguish between other conditions (e.g., headaches) and groups (inpatients).

Multiple indicators are needed in individual cases to assure that the result of any single indicator is generalizable. Given that all indicators are subject to some error no matter how small, it is possible that a single indicator of distortion is not truly representative of either the client's condition or intention. However, a finding of distortion on multiple indicators increases the confidence that

---

* It is legally permissible for an expert witness to repudiate a previously submitted written report during oral testimony at a deposition or trial. However, it requires a special hearing to recant previous testimony once the expert has been dismissed as a witness.

one can place in the final decision that distortion is occurring. The most convincing case occurs when the results of tests are supported by direct observation during the assessment process or in the "real world." For example, one young defendant awaiting trial on multiple charges of breaking and entering and theft (1) refused to be tested by two different forensic psychologists (experimental indicator); (2) answered their questions about the alleged crimes in a tangential, evasive manner while answering other questions responsively (experimental indicator); and (3) failed an explicit alternative test administered by a third psychologist (replicated indicator). The probability that this combination of indicators arose by chance is far less than the probability that any one of the indicators arose by chance and therefore is more convincing.

If multiple indicators of distortion are needed, how are they to be combined into a single decision regarding distortion? What if the indicators are conflicting? There is only limited research on these important questions, but guidelines for the practicing clinician may be taken from the existing literature on clinical vs. statistical prediction. Sawyer (1966) distinguished eight categories of decision procedures involving types of data collection (judgmental, mechanical, both, either/both) and types of data combination (clinical, statistical). Of particular interest is the procedure of clinical synthesis and the procedure of mechanical synthesis. In clinical synthesis, judgmental and/or mechanical (e.g., psychometric, physiological) information is input to an actuarial system, which combines the information and makes a decision. This statistical decision, together with the original input information, is then given to a clinician who can (1) ignore the actuarial decision and make a clinical decision, (2) adopt the actuarial decision, or (3) modify the clinical decision in accord with the actuarial decision. Which choice is made presumably depends on unique features of each case, which are known only by the clinician (i.e., not used as input to the actuarial system). In mechanical synthesis, judgmental and/or mechanical information is given to the clinician, who in turn makes a clinical prediction. This clinical prediction is then input, together with the original data, into an actuarial system, which makes the final decision. The actuary can ignore the clinician's decision entirely, agree with the clinician's decision, or adapt its own decision in accord with the clinical decision. Research suggests that the procedure of mechanical synthesis is more accurate than the procedure of clinical synthesis (Sawyer, 1966; Wiggins, 1973).

The problem is that no actuarial system for predicting distortions from multiple inputs yet exists, although there is continued progress in this direction. For the time being, the practicing clinician is left with the method of clinical synthesis for dealing with multiple indicators of distortion. In the final analysis, the clinician must use personal judgment in weighting, combining, and using multiple indicators of distortion. However, the clinician would be well advised to give greater weight to mechanical than to judgmental information, and to replicated rather than experimental indicators. If indicators of distortion are conflicting, then the more accurate, more mechanical, and more replicated input should prevail. Kleinmuntz (1990) presented many ideas for improving the accuracy of clinical synthesis of assessment data. His suggestions, in combination with the development of new procedures for detecting deception, may contribute significantly to the accurate detection of deception by clinicians in the future.

What conclusions are justified? In clinical situations, decisions regarding distortions are intended for professional use. In-house treating professionals or referring treating professionals are assumed to be the intended audiences for conclusions regarding distortions in a client's self-presentation during assessment. These professionals will presumably use the information to guide their initial treatment plans. However, it cannot be assumed that these intended professionals or future unknown professionals will necessarily be aware of the complexities of a distortion analysis. Therefore, clarity in communicating conclusions regarding distortion is necessary and summary labels should be avoided.

Concluding that a client is "malingering" or "in denial" tells nothing about the scope of the client's distortion (which targets are being distorted? which response style is being used?) or the accuracy of the distortion assessment (which indicators of distortion were used to arrive at the conclusion?). The diagnostic label *malingering*, for example, does not distinguish between conscious exaggeration of a genuine problem and total fabrication of the problem; it does not distinguish between honest reporting of one problem and distorted reporting of another problem; it does not distinguish between honest reporting of a problem on one instrument and distorted reporting of the same problem on a different instrument; it does not distinguish between accurate, replicated indicators of distortion and inaccurate, experimental indicators. Most important of all, a clinician making such absolute determinations about a defendant's credibility preempts what the courts have repeatedly made very clear is the purview of the trier of fact. It is therefore critical to avoid summary or absolute labels in clinical communications regarding malingering by a defendant and instead to use succinct descriptive statements. For example, to state:

> Although his wife expressed concern about his drinking and police records indicate two arrests for driving under the influence, Mr. Jones denied any problems with alcohol both during interview and on self-report measures.

is clearer than to state:

> Mr. Jones appears to be denying his alcohol problems.

Similarly, to state:

> Mr. Jones complained of memory failures which interfered with on-the-job performance. However, explicit alternative testing suggested a gross exaggeration of memory dysfunction and a test of serial learning did not show the pattern of results expected among amnestic patients.

is preferable to stating:

> Mr. Jones's test results suggest malingering.

And, as a final example, stating:

> The assessment findings in the aggregate were consistent with the circumstances of the alleged child sexual abuse charges, and that Mr. Jones's account of his behavior was inconsistent.

is preferable to:

> The findings indicate that Mr. Jones is prevaricating about his involvement in the sexual abuse charges.

The issue of what ultimate matters are the purviews of the trier of fact continues as very sensitive concerns for the judiciary (Mishlove & Heuer, 1999). Two recent appellate decisions (*United States v. Hall* (1999) and *State v. McClendon* (1999), for example, confirmed the continued skepticism of the courts regarding the utility of expert opinion on the reliability of eyewitness testimony. The judicial skepticism in these two cases stood against a substantial body of empirical data regarding the benefits of expert assistance addressing the weak correlation between eyewitness confidence and reliability.

In forensic situations, the intended audience of communications regarding distortions includes the case attorneys and fact-finders (judge, jury, hearing officer). This audience has an even greater need for detailed explanations of procedures and findings than do professional colleagues. Whereas colleagues will use the information to build a tentative treatment plan, attorneys will use the information to support or undermine legal arguments in the case. Fact-finders will use the information as one justification for their verdict in the case. In general, suggestions of distortions should be avoided unless they are based on accurate, replicated indicators. Courts require that an expert's opinions be based on a "professional certainty," which refers to the expert's degree of confidence in the opinion (Black, 1988). Professional standards require that such confidence be empirically based on the accuracy of the techniques used and not merely on the subjective appraisal of the expert. The courtroom is no place to spin hypothetical yarns about what might be happening in a case. If only experimental indicators of distortion exist in a case, the question of distortion should not be addressed at all by the examiner. When questioned about the issue by attorneys, the examiner should then admit the possibility of distortion affecting the examination, but state that no acceptable (accurate, replicated) methods currently exist for detecting distortion in this type of case. While hypotheses and hunches may assist treating professionals in clinical cases, such speculative statements in forensic cases can result in misleading and irreversible outcomes.

Still another consideration is the likelihood of the expert being embarrassed during cross-examination when the attorney challenges empirically unsupportable statements and casts a pall of prejudice or incompetence on the expert. The authors are reminded of a recent experience in which an opposing expert retained by a youth's family became desperate on the witness stand and "guaranteed" the judge that the youth would not reoffend if released to the community on probation. The prosecuting attorney was unrelenting in ridiculing the expert about how any mental health professional could make a "guarantee" about the behavior of another person. The prosecutor's cross-examination was compelling to the judge who placed the youth in a correctional facility.

When should an expert become an expert witness? There are two kinds of witnesses in law: material witnesses and expert witnesses. Material witnesses are allowed to testify about personal knowledge relevant to the legal questions at hand. For example, eyewitnesses to a crime may testify about what they saw or heard at the time of the crime; police officers may relate what they discovered in their investigation of a crime; participants in a situation may explain what transpired in their presence. However, material witnesses are not allowed to express opinions regarding causes, effects, intentionality, responsibility, or other matters outside their personal experience. Expert witnesses, on the other hand, are allowed to testify to professional opinions (within their areas of expertise and competence) on questions that are related to the legal questions at hand, but that are beyond the understanding of the ordinary person. For example, questions about firearms, fingerprints, genetic profiles, accounting procedures, medical diagnoses/treatment, and psychological assessment/treatment generally require information beyond that possessed by the ordinary person. When a legal case involves technical or scientific questions, the court may allow expert witnesses to testify to their opinions regarding those questions.

In routine clinical practice, a mental health professional does not generally anticipate being called as an expert witness in a legal case involving clients. The assessments, treatments, reports, and correspondence that are generated in the course of providing clinical services to clients are not necessarily the best basis for answering technical or scientific questions in a courtroom. As mentioned previously, clinical communications may include hypotheses intended to frame tentative and revisable treatment plans. Such communications, if offered as the basis for a professional opinion in the courtroom, could be misleading and inaccurate in a situation where they cannot be revised. In addition, the clinical professional has an ethical and legal responsibility to the client's best interests, which may conflict with the ethical and legal responsibility to testify truthfully in court.

The best way to protect the flexibility and commitment to the client, which are required for clinical practice, is simply to refuse to become an expert witness in any legal case involving a former or current clinical client. Although the professional may be subpoenaed to testify as a material witness regarding, for example, questions about dates of treatment, types of treatment, diagnoses, the professional cannot be compelled to render a professional opinion regarding any fact in dispute in the case and should not volunteer to do so (American Psychological Association, 1992). For example, if a client currently in treatment is involved in an automobile accident, the treating professional may be called to testify that the client was receiving treatment at the time of the accident, that the focus of treatment was social anxiety, and that the client was making satisfactory progress after seven sessions of treatment. However, the professional should not answer questions regarding the impact of the automobile accident on the client's current functioning, regarding the role of the preexisting social anxiety in causing the accident, or regarding the prognosis for the client.

A professional can be compelled to be a material witness in a trial, just as can any other person, but a professional cannot be compelled to be an expert witness. Principle 7.05 — Prior Relationships of the APA Ethics code (1992) reads, "A prior professional relationship with a party does not preclude psychologists from testifying as fact witnesses or from testifying to their services to the extent permitted by applicable law. Psychologists appropriately take into account ways in which the prior relationship might affect their professional objectivity or opinions and disclose the potential conflict to the relevant parties" (p. 1610). The authors strongly suggest that the most prudent course is for professionals to refuse to become expert witnesses in any case involving former or current clients, even if the client approves it, and that testimony in such cases be limited to the material facts of the professional relationship. Such a position precludes the development of dual relationships (clinical, forensic), avoids the appearance of biased testimony, and safeguards the therapeutic relationship from injurious statements made under oath.

In forensic cases, however, the professional is specifically employed to evaluate a case and render an expert opinion regarding technical/scientific/professional questions. From the very beginning, the professional's responsibilities are clear to the client, the attorneys, and the fact-finder. The forensic expert's job includes conducting a professionally acceptable evaluation, forming expert opinions regarding technical/scientific/professional questions in dispute, and communicating those opinions and their factual bases to the fact-finder.

Whereas material witnesses are allowed to testify if they have personal knowledge of facts in question, the expert witness must first be accepted as an expert by the court. Courts have wide latitude in defining who is an expert, but the *sine qua non* is that the witness possesses professional/scientific/technical knowledge or skill because of experience, training, or education. In mental health matters, the expert witness is usually a psychiatrist, neurologist, or psychologist, but some courts have qualified general physicians, social workers, bachelor-level "psychologists," and even laypeople as experts on mental health questions. In other cases, competent psychologists have been excluded as expert witnesses and not allowed to testify.

Faust and Ziskin (1988; Ziskin & Faust, 1991) have argued that the testimony of mental health professionals should not be admitted on ultimate questions of diagnosis, prediction of future dangerousness, and malingering. In this regard, Faust (1995) has emphasized the tendency of clinicians to underestimate the skill of deceivers. Blau (1998), Brodsky (1989), Hoge and Grisso (1992), and Matarazzo (1990, 1991) have countered that when such testimony is based on reliable and valid methods it can be helpful to fact-finders. McCloskey and Egeth (1983; Egeth & McCloskey, 1984) have argued that expert testimony on the credibility of witnesses is not based on a body of replicable, relevant, and valid facts and therefore should not be admitted in court; Bourg, Connor, and Landis (1995), Loftus (1983; 1984), and Wells (1984) have argued the contrary. In spite of this professional controversy, prior to 1993 the courts continued to admit psychological and psychiatric testimony "for whatever it may be worth." Often the sole qualifying credential of the expert witness was "x years of clinical experience."

In this respect, traditional legal standards for admissibility of expert testimony are far less demanding than professional standards for clinical practice. While professional standards require, for example, that assessment techniques meet certain standards of reliability and validity to assure an acceptable level of accuracy, legal standards of admissibility do not necessarily focus on the accuracy of those assessments (Black, 1988). For many years, the empirical validity of procedures used by expert witnesses was not a primary concern of the courts. Based on credentials and experience alone, clinicians were readily accepted as experts by the courts. The issue of the empirical validity of methods and procedures was managed in terms of how much weight the fact-finder should give to the expert's findings and opinions.

Once a witness is accepted as an expert by the court, then questions arise about the admissibility of the expert's testimony. Since 1923, the applicable standard has been the *Frye* test (*Frye v. United States*). Under *Frye*, expert opinions were generally admitted into testimony if they were relevant and based on generally accepted theories, concepts, or methods in the professional's field of expertise. To be relevant, an opinion must address a fact in question and must have probative or incremental value in the case as a whole. In other words, the opinion must help the fact-finder resolve a professional/scientific/technical question that is in dispute in the case, and must add new information to the case. In cases where the expert's opinions were based on new or novel techniques or theories, under *Frye* they were admitted into testimony as long as other professionals in the field generally accepted the techniques, theories, or concepts. For example, opinions based on polygraph examinations under *Frye* were not typically admissible in court, because polygraphy is not generally accepted by professionals as an acceptable means of detecting "lying" (e.g., Iacono & Patrick, 1987; Lykken, 1981). As described in Chapter 16, there has been a similar problem with the courts ruling hypnotic testimony inadmissible.

One significant problem under the *Frye* test has been the proliferation of "hired gun" expert witnesses in the courtroom (Hjelt, 2000). Hired guns are experts hired by one side in a litigation matter and the testimony of the expert predictably tracks with the interests of the hiring litigant. The Supreme Court addressed this problem in a series of decisions beginning in 1993 with *Daubert v. Merrell Dow Pharmaceuticals*, and culminating most recently in 1999 with *Kumho Tire Co. v. Carmichael* (Hjelt, 2000).

As noted in an earlier chapter, the *Daubert* test applies *only* to federal courts and several state courts that have statutorily incorporated *Daubert*. The clear intent of the Supreme Court in *Daubert* was to add flexibility to trial judges deciding if an expert's opinions are admissible based on actual and demonstrable empirical data. This is in obvious contrast to the former *Frye* test whereby the expert's input was admissible if the data met the "general acceptance" of the respective discipline. *Daubert* continues as the subject of considerable controversy and is not the standard in most local jurisdiction courts, but for the present its implications are very clear for forensic evaluators. Expressed very simply, for the expert's testimony to be admissible, the expert must be prepared to demonstrate to the trial judge that theories, procedures, and methods that will underlie ultimate opinions have sound empirical reliability and validity. The real impact of *Daubert* is still threading its way through various court decisions, but one potential outcome of *Daubert* will be opening the door of admissibility for heretofore-inadmissible psychological approaches. This, of course, is a double-edged sword because approaches and methods having marginal empirical basis will be subjected to intense scrutiny by the trial judge. Another fallout from *Daubert* will assuredly be that hired gun expert and maverick methodologies previously accepted by the courts will now be ruled inadmissible.

Forensic evaluators must exercise great diligence not to expose themselves and psychological procedures to adversarial scrutiny if the result will only be embarrassment for the expert witness and for the profession. For the predictable future, the courts and forensic clinicians will engage in a delicate new courtship with inevitable stepping on each other's toes, until what will be acceptable and unacceptable under *Daubert* endures an initiation period. In the end, clinicians remain ethically responsible to practice within their competence as well as within the competence (i.e., empirical validity) of theories and methods (American Psychological Association, 1992; Committee on Ethical Guidelines for Forensic Psychologists, 1991).

Once a professional has formed professional opinions based on a "professional certainty," has been accepted as an expert by the court, and has communicated those opinions and their bases, the trier of fact (judge, jury, hearing officer) must determine how much weight to give the opinions in disposing of the case. A professional's opinions are never determinative of the ultimate legal questions in a case, but are merely one more piece of evidence to be considered by the fact-finder. The fact-finder may ignore the opinions completely, may give them partial weight, or may endorse them entirely.

THE ROLE OF EXPERT WITNESS

Gutheil (1998), Poythress (1979), Rigling and Russo (1990), Rosen (1983), and Tsushima and Anderson (1996) have highlighted the need for special training in forensics for mental health professionals who become expert witnesses. Attorneys have access to training material to determine the credibility of a witness (e.g., see Aron, Duffy, & Rosner, 1990), which gives clear examples of differentiating between nondeliberate distortion and deception on the part of witnesses. A number of law schools offer courses in handling experts. Temple University in Philadelphia and Southern Methodist University (SMU) in Dallas offer courses to prepare law students to work with experts. The SMU program involves the highly regarded author Shuman and his text, *Psychiatric and Psychological Evidence* (1986). The Association of Trial Lawyers of America offers training in handling expert witnesses. Finally, the widely known texts by Ziskin (1995) and Faust, Ziskin, and Hiers (1991) present attorneys with well-documented lines of attack on mental health professionals in the role of expert witness. In the face of this increasing sophistication by attorneys, clinical training by itself does not well prepare clinicians to become effective expert witnesses.

One of the authors testified in a bitter and protracted disputed custody case. During the cross-examination, the attorney asked his inquiries directly from a dog-eared copy of one of Ziskin's (1995) volumes. The author's familiarity with Ziskin's text made the cross-examination quite straightforward in terms of being able to anticipate the inquiries. After the hearing the attorney commented, "I could tell you have done this a lot, it was like you anticipated everything I asked you." The author graciously accepted the compliment and silently thanked the late Dr. Ziskin.

Professional psychology has experienced an extraordinary growth since the 1980s. Part of this growth has been the number of organizations offering "board certification" in a variety of specialty areas, including forensic psychology. These organizations offer specialty credentials essentially for a fee. They do not require start-to-finish peer review of an applicant's credentials verification, work samples, or formal examination (Otto, 1999). Commenting on the problem, Borum and Otto (2000) observed, "Consequently, the mistakes made in the late 1960s are now being repeated by a new cadre of clinicians foraging into a new area, with certifications and credentials that exceed their demonstrated competence" (p. 2).

THE EXPERT AND SPECIFIC FORENSIC PROCEDURES

The following sections briefly introduce the clinician to selected aspects of the expert role. Brown (1987) and Wellman (1986) discuss cross-examination of witnesses from an attorney's point of view; Blau (1998), Brodsky (1991), and Singer and Nievod (1987) discuss the role of expert witness from a psychologist's point of view.

HEARSAY

Hearsay is a verbal statement made by a person with no personal knowledge of the facts, but offered as evidence to prove the truth of an asserted matter. For example, when a professional quotes another professional about the results of a consultation, the quoted material is hearsay. Mental health professionals in assessing clinical cases frequently use such third-party information. But hearsay is generally inadmissible as evidence in trials and hearings, because the third party is unavailable for direct examination and the reported material is subject to distortion by the witness. Material witnesses can testify only to the personal information they possess.

However, expert witnesses are frequently allowed to base their opinions on hearsay under certain exceptions to the general inadmissibility of hearsay. One such exception allows a witness to rely on records kept in the course of the normal conduct of the business. Consultation reports prepared about a client by another professional would be an example of a routine record prepared in the normal course of clinical assessment. A psychiatrist testifying as an expert witness could rely on a report prepared by a psychologist or a psychologist could rely on a report prepared by a neurologist. Another exception is reliance on the work of an agent of the witness such as a nurse or psychometrician. If it is generally accepted practice for the professional to employ a technician to administer tests, the professional may rely on the results of those tests even though they were prepared by a third party. Finally, if it is customary for the professional to interview or test third parties (e.g., relatives, arresting officers), then the professional may rely on the results in forming an expert opinion. In assessing victim credibility, for example, the authors often evaluate significant/knowledgeable others to determine if the "victim" is exaggerating or fabricating symptoms.

Although hearsay may be legally admissible as the basis for an expert opinion, professionals should be aware of the limitations of such data. The *Specialty Guidelines for Forensic Psychologists* (Committee on Ethical Guidelines for Forensic Psychologists, 1991) states:

> [W]hen hearsay or otherwise inadmissible evidence forms the basis of their opinion, evidence or professional conduct, [forensic psychologists] seek to minimize sole reliance upon such evidence. Where circumstances reasonably permit, forensic psychologists seek to obtain independent and personal verification of data relied upon as part of their professional services to the court or to a party to a legal proceeding.... When using hearsay data that have not been corroborated, but are nevertheless utilized, forensic psychologists have an affirmative responsibility to acknowledge the uncorroborated status of those data and the reasons for relying upon such data. (p. 662)

DISCOVERY

Discovery is the pretrial process by which opposing attorneys exchange information that they believe is supportive to their cases. The exchange can take place in a variety of formats including responding to interrogatory documents between the parties and deposing of witnesses. Courts have developed detailed rules governing the timing and scope of the discovery process. But in all jurisdictions attorneys must declare their intention to call particular experts as witnesses, must make those witnesses available for pretrial deposition, and must share with opposing counsel all documents upon which the expert will rely in testifying.

During a pretrial deposition, the expert may be asked to state all professional opinions relevant to the case and to describe the factual bases for those opinions. The facts supporting the professional opinions would include personal observations, responses to interview questions, results of psychological and medical tests, reports by consultants, observations of ward personnel, and any other information upon which the expert actually relied in formulating the professional opinions. If the evaluation was audio- or videotaped, as recommended by the American Bar Association for certain criminal cases (American Bar Association, 1989, p. 100), copies of such tapes should be produced by the expert. Personal notes of the expert, which may include speculations and hypotheses about the client, are not subject to discovery.

One problem that may arise during discovery is the request for copies of raw data from psychological tests. In general, raw test data should not be released directly to attorneys or to courts, but may be released to another psychologist who agrees not to release the data further. This procedure should satisfy the psychologist's ethical responsibility to "provide appropriate interpretations when test score information is released to ... legal representatives" (American Educational Research Association et al., 1985, p. 84), to "establish procedures for insuring the adequacy of ... explanations [of test results] ... [provided by others]" (American Psychological Association, 1992), and to "ensure that the receiving party is informed that raw scores must be interpreted by a qualified professional in order to provide reliable and valid information" (Committee on Ethical Guidelines for Forensic Psychologists, 1991, p. 664).

Another problem is the request for any self-incriminating statements made during the evaluation by a defendant in a criminal case. In most jurisdictions, statements made by a defendant in the course of a forensic examination are admissible as evidence only on the question of the mental condition of the defendant. They cannot be used as evidence that the defendant actually committed the crime charged. However, in other jurisdictions (e.g., Georgia), statements made by a defendant during a forensic examination can by used as a "confession" to the alleged crime. Therefore, it is imperative that the professional examiner be aware of the rules prevailing in the local jurisdiction. Otherwise, the professional may unwittingly elicit a "confession" from a defendant and be compelled to testify to that confession. It is essential that the professional advise the defendant of the purpose of the evaluation, of the potential uses of the results, and, where appropriate, of the defendant's right to remain silent and to have an attorney present during the evaluation (American Bar Association, 1989; Committee on Ethical Guidelines for Forensic Psychologists, 1991). It should be noted that in all jurisdictions, defendants must be given a warning of their *Miranda* rights prior to a forensic evaluation if the defendant has not raised questions of mental capacity but has been ordered by a court to submit to a pretrial mental evaluation and if the results of the evaluation may used in the sentencing phase of a capital case (*Estelle v. Smith*, 1981; *Barefoot v. Estelle*, 1983). Juvenile defendants are also entitled to know their *Miranda* rights, although with some very young defendants this can become problematic in terms of the youngster's cognitive abilities.

Forensic Reports

Response to a discovery proceeding by a forensic clinician is not the time for hyperbole or pomp. During discovery, the opposing side is exploring and probing. Responses to inquiries should be forthright, but succinct. The nature of the adversarial process demands that the expert plot and strategize with the side retaining him/her as an expert. There is no wisdom in providing opposing counsel with these strategies during discovery proceedings. It is far more advantageous for any strategies to unfold during actual trial when the trier of fact is present. This will maintain the adversarial edge to the advantage of the expert.

The American Bar Association (1989) has offered guidelines for preparation of written forensic reports in criminal cases. With appropriate modifications, these guidelines are applicable to non-criminal proceedings as well:

(a) Requirement of written report. Promptly upon concluding the evaluation, the mental health or mental retardation professional should prepare a complete, written report. However, at the specific request of the defense attorney, a professional who conducted an evaluation initiated by the defense attorney may make only an oral report.
(b) Contents of written report.
　(i) The written evaluation report should ordinarily:
　　(A) identify the specific matters referred for evaluation;
　　(B) describe the procedures, tests, and techniques used by the evaluator;
　　(C) state the evaluator's clinical findings and opinions on each matter referred for evaluation and indicate specifically those questions, if any, that could not be answered;
　　(D) identify the sources of information and present the factual basis for the evaluator's clinical findings and opinions; and
　　(E) present the reasoning by which the evaluator utilized the information to reach the clinical findings and opinions. The evaluator should express an opinion on a specific legal criterion or standard only if the opinion is within the scope of the evaluator's specialized knowledge.
　(ii) Except as limited by standard 7-3.8(a), the evaluator should include in the written report any statements or information that serve as necessary factual predicates for the clinical findings or opinions, even if the statements or information are of a personal or potentially incriminating nature.
(c) Clarification of written report. The attorney who requested the evaluation should not edit, modify, revise, or otherwise compromise the integrity of the report. However, after the report has been completed and submitted, the attorney may correspond in writing with the mental health or mental retardation professional in order to clarify the meaning or implications of the evaluator's findings or opinions. The report and any clarifying correspondence between the attorney and the evaluator should be disclosed at the time established for discovery of written reports. (pp. 109–110)

Standard 7-3.8 of the ABA Standards states, *inter alia*, "The evaluator should prepare a separate report on [the issue of present mental competency] even if other issues have also been referred for evaluation" (American Bar Association, 1989, p. 112).

Once a defendant has proceeded to the trial stage, and all pretrial mental health issues such as competency have been resolved, forensic psychologists may include in their reports or testimony any statements made by the defendant that are directly relevant to supporting their expert evidence, providing that the defendant has "introduced" mental state evidence or testimony within the meaning of Federal Rule of Procedure 12.2(c), or its state equivalent. (Committee on Ethical Guidelines for Forensic Psychologists, 1991, p. 663)

The evaluator's written report is usually not admitted itself as evidence in court, unless opposing attorneys stipulate to its content. The written report cannot be cross-examined and the examining professional is therefore usually required to testify personally. If the expert who prepared the report is unavailable for testimony, the opposing attorneys typically conduct a pretrial deposition, which is then read into evidence at the trial. Otherwise, the written report is used by trial attorneys to frame their line of questioning and, if possible, to impeach the credibility of the testifying witness. Thus, an expert's testimony should not differ in substance from the facts and opinions expressed in the written report or in a pretrial deposition.

Although most state and federal jurisdictions allow for the introduction of testimony regarding the reliability and validity of data obtained during a forensic evaluation, distortion-related data may be attacked because it impugns the credibility of other witnesses and therefore invades the province of the jury to determine the credibility of witnesses.

When the primary focus of the entire examination is itself a question of distortion (e.g., a victim's credibility in a sexual assault case), the examiner may use a two-step process. This would include (1) commenting on any distortion affecting each source of data and (2) offering a separate opinion regarding the subject's deception about the alleged crime. Findings should be circumspect, with descriptors tied to base rates as much as possible. The evaluator is advised to define words, having dissimilar psychological and legal meanings — *credibility, reliability, validity*. Inflammatory words should be avoided in one's reports — *faking, deceitful, lying* — to reduce the impression of bias. Last, ultimate issues should be avoided, if possible. An expert testifying on credibility should not conclude with an opinion on the presence or absence of the (legal) facts. These always involve moral or social value judgments, which are reserved for the court or jury. Appendix E contains a sample report of an evaluation of a violent offender and his victim. Nondeliberate and deliberate distortion emerged as central referral and assessment issues in that case.

LEGAL GUIDELINES FOR DETERMINING CREDIBILITY

Triers of fact have their own criteria for assessing the credibility of witnesses, including expert witnesses. Thus, it is instructive for forensic mental health professionals to understand what jurors and judges employ as factors in determining the believability of witnesses. In one jurisdiction (California), jurors are instructed to consider the following: (1) whether the witness had the opportunity to see, hear, smell, touch, or otherwise become aware of the matter about which the witness has testified; (2) the ability of the witness to remember or communicate the content of events; (3) the general character and quality of the testimony; (4) the demeanor and manner of the witness while testifying; (5) whether the witness has a bias, vested interest in a given outcome, or other relevant motive; (6) whether matters testified to can be or have been corroborated by other evidence; (7) the attitude of the witness toward what he or she has testified to and toward the giving of the testimony itself; (8) inconsistency or consistency of previous statements made by the witness; and (9) the witness's prior conviction of a felony. The trier of fact may apply some of these criteria to the expert witness as well. The lesson for the expert witness is to try to anchor testimony to concrete, observable behavior and then abstract to patterns and attitudes of the subject.

THE EXPERT WITNESS AND THE ADVERSARIAL PROCESS

In recent years, many mental health clinicians have aspired to retread their practice focus to engage in forensic practice. Many clinicians have pursued an interest in forensics, underestimating the realities of the adversarial process. These clinicians enter the courtroom only to leave angry and feeling professionally demeaned. It behooves all clinicians to educate themselves about the adversarial process before entering the courtroom whether or not they intend to adopt a specialty interest in forensics. The expert witness must understand the nature of the adversarial process and be able to cope with it effectively. In the courtroom at least one side, and in some instances more than one side (e.g., child custody, termination of parental rights adjudications), will view the expert's opinions as hostile to their advocacy efforts on behalf of their clients. The substance of the adversarial process is the assumption that vigorous inquiry will reveal weak, bogus, false, and deceptive testimony whether from lay or expert witnesses.

Professional stature, length of resume, sincerity, professional demeanor, and ethical aspirations will all be secondary to the opposing attorneys' efforts to impeach the opposing expert's testimony on behalf of their client's interests. Aggressive defense is, of course, the attorneys' professional responsibility to their client. Some attorneys are very hostile in their manner, others very flamboyant, and others docile and methodical. Attorneys can be baiting, intimidating, demeaning, confronting, devious, misleading, and unfortunately some are even deceptive in their strategic efforts to impeach testimony deemed unfavorable. These strategies are employed all in the name of pursuing their client's interests. The reader is cautioned that the foregoing comments are intended as instructional and not as a categorical castigation of our legal colleagues with whom the authors work respectfully and collegially on a daily basis. The forensic evaluator must understand these litigation styles in the context of the adversarial process and realize that taking such litigation maneuvering personally is a failure to comprehend and respect the adversarial process. It should be of some consolation to forensic evaluators that even the courts recognize the pitfalls of overly aggressive cross-examination of experts. In *Arizona v. Hughes* (1998), the court found the prosecutor's unrelenting attack of a psychiatrist expert for "creating an excuse for the defendant" to be a "masterpiece of misconduct." The court's finding was based on the legal principle of "cumulative error"; the finding of the earlier court that was unfavorable to the defendant was reversed.

A few useful ground rules based on many court appearances by the authors may assist the beginning expert witness. First, the chances of a court's hearing proceeding as scheduled is not very likely in most jurisdictions due to an overcrowded calendar, delaying tactics by attorneys, and other factors. The evaluator may want to take a book or a laptop computer for the waiting, which is sure to follow. Second, even if called to testify, the evaluator may not ever make it to the witness chair for a variety of reasons; this should be accepted with equanimity. Third, when the evaluator testifies, the chances of his or her being cross-examined and attacked approach certainty. The American court system is adversarial in nature.

Once the expert truly grasps the nature of the adversarial process, then a number of strategic assumptions and guidelines fall into place. To begin with, the time for the expert to begin preparation for expert testimony is not when a subpoena is received. The time to begin is with the first awareness of being involved in any forensic matter that will potentially lead to expert testimony. The expert must always bear in mind that if there is no record (written, typed, audiovisual, etc.) of some activity by the expert then the legal principle is that the activity never occurred.

Generally, the expert, as with any other witness, is subject to cross-examination. The attack will in all likelihood come in one or more of three areas:

1. Credibility, with the opposing party attempting to diminish the expert's credibility. Thus, the evaluator's training, experience, personal ethics, and anything the evaluator has done or failed to do professionally may be scrutinized.

2. Database, with the opposing party trying to demonstrate that it is limited, replete with biased input sources, invalid, or deficient in some other way. The evaluator may have to show familiarity with the instant offense or other relevant event.
3. Conclusions. The decision path that the evaluator used to arrive at conclusions may be scrutinized

Usually, the lead expert for one side takes the "heavy hit" and is on the stand for the longest period. The middle expert plays a supporting role and may focus on one aspect of the case. The last expert is the "clean-up batter" and must integrate all previous material, bond with the jury, and, in general, leave the trier of fact with a favorable impression. No cross-examination, or only a few questions, indicates that the other side does not want to interact with the expert witness either because the evaluator's points are too solid or the side considers the input irrelevant. A lengthy attack is directed at vulnerable experts or conducted by desperate cross-examiners. Redirect and recross-examinations may prolong the proceedings, but they focus only on issues covered in the previous interaction with the expert. Five general factors may ease the distress associated with testifying:

1. Data preparation for court. All data relevant to a case should be reviewed. There should be a broad database, and the decision path used to come to decisions should be identified. All data to be used in court should be broken into areas of presentation and anticipated attack. Audiovisual material should be ready for display.
2. Nonverbal and psychological preparation. The witness should assume the role of a teacher, even though this is an adversarial system. This helps put attacks into perspective. It involves a fundamental belief that the evaluator has something to offer the court from a behavioral science perspective. The role of being an objective educator helps avoid the efforts of cross-examining attorneys to posture the expert as being prejudiced and hostile.
3. Credibility factors. The expert witness's background and qualifications (i.e., affiliation with academic, professional, and power organizations, such as the police or the state) and the use of the passive tense (e.g., "My system has been accepted in federal jurisdictions") may be the two most potent determinants of courtroom credibility. Based on courtroom segments of expert testimony, Hurwitz, Miron, and Johnson (1990) stated that the use of the passive tense may create an impression of objectivity.

   Other factors that correlate positively with enhanced expert credibility include the use of words associated with (1) suffering and distress (e.g., *depressed, pain, emotional, trauma, loss*), suggesting empathy on the part of the evaluator; (2) evaluation, as in performing an assessment; (3) certainty (e.g., *correct, really, right, know*); (4) caution (e.g., *some, generally, about, only*); and (5) causes of damage or harm (e.g., *condition, develop, change, start*).
4. Flexibility of response during the proceedings is important. The evaluator may be directed, on purpose, to widely disparate areas of inquiry during questioning. Shifting of conceptual gears may be required to address legal issues.
5. After testifying, the expert should leave and not return to the courtroom, unless invited, as this gives the impression of bias. Feedback on how well the evaluator performed can be obtained from the retaining attorney.

Based on a review of recent forensic literature, Tshuhima and Anderson (1996) described a number of other working guidelines for the expert witness and these are summarized in Table 24.1. Table 24.2 presents a summary of cross-examination tactics, with special regard to the expert's role in commenting on deception.

TABLE 24.1
Expert Witness Guidelines

1. Obtain the proper education and training in forensic practice.
2. Achieve proficiency in your area(s) of expertise and maintain that proficiency by continuing education and training.
3. Be very clear as to your areas of limitation and do not practice beyond them.
4. Be familiar with legal concepts and the specific statutory provisions relevant to your area of expertise and the jurisdiction in which you will testify.
5. Be aware of practice guidelines and ethical codes pertinent to your discipline.
6. Familiarize yourself with the courtroom and courtroom protocol.
7. Maintain objectivity with the referring attorney.
8. Be diligent in requesting and accessing all pertinent background information.
9. Reserve your opinion until the assessment is completed.
10. Obtain a waiver or written fee agreement. Never work on a contingency basis.
11. Have an up-to-date and accurate curriculum vitae (CV) highlighting relevant forensic background.
12. Instruct the examinee regarding the purpose and scope of the assessment and the limits of confidentiality.
13. Complete a thorough and well-documented evaluation.
14. Know precisely the logical chain from amassing the data to generating the conclusions.
15. Consider the potential of faking and malingering and account for discrepancies and distortions.
16. Before trial, prepare attorney.
17. When going to court, wear dark, conservative, semiformal clothing with muted accessories.
18. Allow yourself to relax before court appearance.
19. Listen carefully to each question and strive to look at the trier of fact when making your responses.
20. Explain your conclusions and your rationale in everyday language.
21. Refrain from responding to inquiries regarding ultimate legal questions.
22. Understand the meaning of "reasonable [insert discipline] certainty" in your jurisdiction.
23. During cross-examination listen carefully to each question and direct your response to the trier of fact.
24. During cross-examination, if the attorney demands a "yes" or "no" response, it is appropriate to respond you cannot adequately answer the question in that format.
25. Don't succumb to baiting efforts to argue with the attorney during cross-examination.
26. Acknowledge opposing research data if presented and reaffirm your confidence in your findings.

Note: Adapted from *Mastering Expert Testimony: A Courtroom Handbook for Mental Health Professionals,* by W. T. Tsushima, & R. M. Anderson, 1996, Mahwah, NJ: Lawrence Erlbaum Associates.

TABLE 24.2
Summary of Cross-Examination Tactics

Method	Rationale	Example(s)	Counteraction
1. Attack expert's integrity	Expert may be for sale if he or she (1) charges large fees, (2) spends much time in court, (3) testifies too much for one side	"Aren't you a hired gun? How much do you charge?"	Keep list of court involvements and outcomes.
2. Show controversy in expert's field	Expert's opinion on faking may be one among many	"Isn't there much controversy concerning how alledged malingering should be measured?"	Use as opportunity to educate on recent developments

TABLE 24.2 *(continued)*
Summary of Cross-Examination Tactics

Method	Rationale	Example(s)	Counteraction
3. Show expert ignored literature	Expert's opinion may be personally biased	"Cite some research literature of deception which supports what you just said."	Read and apply literature in area of expertise to specific cases
4. Impeach with authority	Expert may be wrong if disagrees with "giants" in the field	"Do you accept *The Encyclopedia of Psychology* as authoritative?"	Caution: Don't accept any treatise as authoritative unless you wish to take responsibility for its contents
5. Compare expert unfavorably to peers	Expert's impact diluted when he or she disagrees with peer	"Do you concede that the other expert is well respected? Why should we not believe him (her)?"	Refer to wide database and decision rules used in case
6. Attack credentials	Lack of "medical" training may preclude proper commentary	"Do I call you Mister, Doctor, or what?"	Emphasize areas of competence leading to degrees in qualification
7. Attack expert's training experience	Always highlight areas of incompleteness that can be probed	"Are you an expert in psychology or just in the particular field of deception analysis?"	See above; use as basis for educating cross-examiner
8. Show that much of training was irrelevant	Relevant training on deception may be limited or nonexistent	"Why are your observations on 'response style' even relevant? Is this something you made up?"	Show how apparently irrelevant areas illuminate forensic issues
9. Attack methods and tools	Invalid measuring devices render conclusions meaningless	"Why should we believe the results of your faking tests?"	Have reliability and validity data on methods
10. Suggest demand characteristics were not take into account	Poor assessment conditions may redern conclusions meaningless	"Wouldn't you try to put your best foot forward if tested in jail by the prosecution?"	Assess over multiple and varied circumstances
11. Suggest expert is biased due to language or cultural differences	Relying on stereotypes reduces expert's accuracy	"Have you ever before assessed a Western Samoan for believability?"	Demonstrate use of safeguards (e.g., use of interpreter, cross-cultural norm base)
12. Attack second-order conclusions	Experts who rely on investigations of others are vulnerable	"Did you know that a witness you interviewed was convicted for perjury in 1988?"	Directly assess litigants and other parties for deception
13. Show that DSM-IV was not designed to illuminate forensic issues	Weakening the foundation of a diagnosis weakens subsequent conclusions	"Are you aware of the specific disclaimer in DSM-IV for forensic work?"	Agree but add that possible deception is a separate and testable issue
14. Argue that experience/training not connected to accuracy of diagnosis/prediction	Relegates qualification period to waste of time for trier of fact	"Isn't there a body of literature that suggests that experts don't know when they are fooled by defendants?"	Have available your percent of true positives and negatives for deception cases

TABLE 24.2 *(continued)*
Summary of Cross-Examination Tactics

Method	Rationale	Example(s)	Counteraction
15. Vary the hypothesis	Reveals the sometimes flawed decision path of expert	"How would it change your conclusions if you found out the accused concealed past violence?"	Know the criteria at each point of your decision path
16. Make expert your witness	Creat an ally if there is a strong case in causation	"You say he told a lie?"	Anticipate and amplify on leading words/questions of cross-examiner
17. Show inconsistency across trials	Expert may be making up decision rules during questioning	"Aren't you contradicting what you said about deception in *State v. Jones*?"	Use identical decision rules unless change is warranted by data
18. Show database sources are biased	Opinions resting on flawed database sources are flawed	"Describe the tests with results inconsistent with your conclusions on validity."	Advance disconfirming hypotheses in report and in direct examination
19. Challenge evaluator's bias I	Evaluator had preformed opinions	"You believed from the beginning that the defendant was malingering, didn't you?"	The opinion of the defendant presenting with a response style consistent with malingering was not formed until after the assessment and all the data had been reviewed
20. Challenge evaluator's bias II	Evaluator is known and used for bias regarding deception	"Have you ever seen a forensic case that didn't involve deception by someone?"	It is true that forensic cases are very prone to deceptive behavior and must be a consideration in every forensic assessment
21. Challenge evaluator's bias III	Evaluator has history of testifying for prosecution or defense	"How many times have you testified for the (choose prosecution or defense) about a defendant's deception and does that not show a preferential bias?"	My position (e.g., with a court forensic team; private practice) does result in my being called more often by one side, but my opinions are always objective regardless of which side requests the assessment
22. Challenge validity of FDA	Question effectiveness rates of distortion analysis	"Have you ever been deceived by a malingerer?"	Acknowledge the limitations of FDA, but maintain confidence in the integrity of your findings
23. Diffuse opinion of defendant deception	Raise question of other possible explanations	"Are there any other possible explanations of deception by this defendant?"	Acknowledge other explanations including nondeliberate distortion, confusion, memory deficits, mental illness, etc., and reiterate how the analysis strived to rule out each of these

For all the controversy about the use of expert witnesses in the courtroom, the courts continue to rely on experts and this will clearly continue to be the established standard. *Daubert* has ushered in a new era with the courts having greater latitude in deciding what expert testimony will be admissible. In response, prosecutors have become more aggressive in learning about expert witnesses in order to be better prepared during litigation. Most vulnerable to these attorney strategies are experts whose opinions are for "hire" regardless of empirical validity or clinical soundness. May (1999), a staff attorney for the American Prosecutors Research Institute, described "Ten Tips" for prosecutors to obtain information about defense experts. A synopsis of these tips is presented in Table 24.3; they are intended as guidelines for prosecutors, but serve also as a useful forewarning to prospective expert witnesses as to the extent attorneys will proceed to gather impeachment data.

In a study of ability to detect malingered insanity, the findings of a group of clinical psychologists were compared to a group of American Board of Professional Psychology (ABPP) psychologists who were board-certified in forensic psychology (Bourg, Connor, & Landis, 1995). Each subject was given a packet of written case information and asked to determine if the data supported a finding of criminal insanity or malingering. The findings reflected an overall accuracy rate of 86.4% with both groups being equally accurate. Both encouraging and bothersome were subjects' reports of only moderate levels of confidence in their findings. The authors concluded that while psychologists are not poor detectors of malingering, they are not overconfident in their ability to detect it. These findings were encouraging in reflecting the prudent cautiousness of the examiners, but bothersome in that the state of the clinical art does not yet permit greater clinician confidence in deception detection.

This study of malingering and deception concludes perhaps as it began. FDA is a still-evolving system of understanding and detecting deception. Significant technological and theoretical advances since the first edition of this book are apparent. The authors have reviewed those data and have systematically integrated the findings into the Revised-FDA model. In spite of progress, clinical/forensic professionals need to persist with a healthy appreciation for the nature and quality of deception, as well as for ingenuity and adaptiveness of the human deceiver.

TABLE 24.3
Finding Information on Defense Experts.

1. *Ask friendly professional colleagues.* Contacts fellow prosecutors, investigators, medical, and mental health contacts. Ask if they have any information about the expert in question. Contact prosecutor and public defenders in the expert's home jurisdiction.

2. *Ask hostile professional colleagues.* Contact colleagues you would never normally contact for information, you never know what you will find out. The adage of "the enemy of my enemy is my friend" applies here. Ask if copies of transcripted testimony are available.

3. *Ask the expert's enemies.* The academic and clinical worlds are highly competitive. Many experts capitalize on an approach in which they critique other experts. Exploit the adage in tip 2 and contact other experts nationally who may have encountered the expert in question.

4. *Consider retaining the opposing expert.* If funds are available, the opposing expert can be retained to sit through judicial proceedings to coach with cross-examination inquiries.

5. *Ask opposing counsel.* If the state in which you practice does not have a reciprocal discovery rule, file a motion asking the court to require defense counsel to produce all information on any anticipated expert testimony. The legal argument is that the motion is an economical approach to the courts time. As applicable, check if the expert's views lack acceptance in the community (i.e., *Frye*), or if there is a lack of a sound empirical basis (i.e., *Daubert*).

6. *Contact the expert directly.* Call the expert and have the call witnessed. This is a valuable way to obtain valuable impeachment material. It does not matter if the expert is willing to dialogue, or if the expert refuses to speak; either way valuable information is obtained. If the expert chooses to dialogue, ask what the expert expects to disclose in his or her testimony. This may lead to discovery of strengths and weaknesses in the testimony and into the expert's probable demeanor on the witness stand. " For example, you might observe that the expert has a million-dollar vocabulary, is impatient, condescending and pompous and as such, will not be well received by a jury. Remain the polite and humble "student," and take careful notes that you can use later when researching the basis for her opinion or as you prepare for cross-examination of this witness" (p. 2). If the witness refuses to speak over the phone, then there is impeachment material by virtue of the refusal. Later the witness can be questioned, "… is it true that on ___ [enter date] you refused to speak to me by telephone, were you told not to speak to anyone about your theory in this matter, did you refuse to discuss you testimony because the defense paid you for your opinion?" (p. 2).

7. *Contact the library.* Access the professional literature for information about the expert. Use search services to find materials and publications by the expert. Also, conduct searches of the topic areas. The expert's C.V. can be used as a source of publications. Try to find reviews or commentaries on the expert's works.

8. *Search computer databases.* There are a number of search services available for a fee. Lexis-Nexis and Westlaw are two of the most widely used and most readily available. Capitalize on the penchant of many experts to seek their names in print. Do credentials search, as well as case law and reported appellate-level cases in which the expert's name appears?

9. *Surf the Internet.* The more conventional search methods are noted above, but a general search over the net may produce useful information about the expert. The expert may, for example, have a home page. The net also affords worldwide library searches.

10. *Investigate the expert's background.* Under relevant rule or statute, defense counsel is often required to produce pertinent material regarding the expert. Peruse these materials carefully; check out claimed credentials and honors. Watch for puffery and grandiosity. Attempt to document active standing and status of good-standing with professional organizations. Be alert to omissions on the C.V. and determine why there are omissions. "Dr., I notice that there are items missing on your C.V., why were these items left out, were you advised by defense counsel to omit certain information?" (p. 3).

Note: Adapted from "Good Things Come to Those Who Seek: Ten Tips for Finding Information on Defense Experts," by J. D. May, 1999, *National Center for Prosecution of Child Abuse Update, 12*(7),

LEGAL REFERENCES

Arizona v. Hughes, 193 Ariz. 72 *; 969 P.2d 1184, **; 1998 Ariz. Lexis 645, ***; 282 Ariz. Adv. Rep. 31.
Daubert v. Merrell Dow Pharmaceuticals, 125 L. Ed.2d 469, 113 (S. Ct. 2786, 1993).
Barefoot v. Estelle, 463 U.S. 880 (1983).
Estelle v. Smith, 451 U.S. 454 (1981).
Frye v. United States, 293 F. 1013 (DC Cir. 1923).
Kumho Tire Co. v. Carmichael, 119 S. Ct. 1167 (1999).
State v. McClendon, 248 Conn. 572 (Conn. 1999).
United States v. Hall, 165 F.3d 1095 (7th Cir. 1999).

REFERENCES

American Bar Association. (1989). *ABA criminal justice mental health standards*. Washington, DC: Author.

American Educational Research Association, American Psychological Association, & National Council on Measurement in Education. (1985). *Standards for educational and psychological testing*. Washington, DC: American Psychological Association.

American Psychological Association. (1989). Practice directorate: Expert testimony in mental health useful in courtrooms, Newman argues. *Psychological Practitioner, 3,* 12.

American Psychological Association. (1992). Ethical principles of psychologists and code of conduct. *American Psychologist, 47,* 1597–1611.

Aron, R., Duffy, K., & Rosner, J. (1990). *Cross-examination of witnesses: The litigators puzzle*. Colorado Springs: Shepard's McGraw-Hill.

Black, B. (1988). Evolving legal standards for the admissibility of scientific evidence. *Science, 239,* 1508–1512.

Blau, T. H. (1998). *The psychologist as expert witness* (2nd ed.). New York: Wiley.

Bourg, S., Connor, E. J., & Landis, E. E. (1995). The impact of expertise and sufficient information on psychologist's ability to detect malingering. *Behavioral Sciences & Law, 13*(4), 505–515.

Borum, R., & Otto, R. (2000). Advances in forensic assessment and treatment: An overview and introduction to the special issue. *Law and Human Behavior, 24*(1), 1–7.

Brodsky, S. (1989). Advocacy in the guise of scientific advocacy: An examination of Ziskin and Faust. *Computers in Human Behavior, 5,* 261–264.

Brodsky, S. (1991). *Testifying in court: Guidelines and maxims for the expert witness*. Washington, DC: American Psychological Association.

Brown, P. (1987). *The art of questioning: Thirty maxims of cross-examination*. New York: MacMillan.

Committee on Ethical Guidelines for Forensic Psychologists. (1991). Specialty guidelines for forensic psychologists. *Law and Human Behavior, 15,* 655–666.

Egeth, H., & McCloskey, M. (1984). Expert testimony about eyewitness behavior: is it safe and effective. In G. Wells & E. Loftus (Eds.), *Eyewitness Testimony*. Cambridge, MA: Cambridge University Press.

Faust, D. (1995) The detection of deception. *Neurologic Clinics*, 13(2) 255–265.

Faust, D., & Ziskin, J. (1988). The expert witness in psychology and science. *Science, 239.* 1508–1512.

Faust, D., Ziskin, J., & Hiers, J. (1991). *Brain damage claims: coping with neuropsychological evidence* (Vols. I–II). Los Angeles, CA: Law and Psychology Press.

Golding, S., Grisso, T., & Shapiro, D. (1989). *Specialty guidelines for forensic psychologists*. Washington, DC: American Psychological Association, Division 41.

Gutheil, T. G. (1998). *The psychiatrist in court: A survival guide*. Washington, DC: American Psychiatric Press, Inc.

Hjelt, S. (2000). Professional psychology: A view from the bench. *Register Report, 26*(1), 8–13.

Hoge, S., & Grisso, T. (1992). Accuracy and expert testimony, *Bulletin of the American Academy of Psychiatry and Law, 20* (1), 67–76.

Hurwitz, S., Miron, M., & Johnson, B. (1990). *Source credibility and the language of expert testimony*. Paper presented at the 98th Annual Convention of the American Psychological Association, Boston, MA.

Iacono, W., & Patrick, C. (1987). What psychologists should know about lie detection. In I. Weiner & A. Hess (Eds.), *Handbook of forensic psychology* (pp. 460–489). New York: Wiley.

Kleinmuntz, B. (1990). Why we still use our heads instead of formulas: Toward an integrative approach. *Psychological Bulletin, 107*(3), 296–310.

Loftus, E. (1983). Silence is not golden. *American Psychologist, 38,* 564–572.

Loftus, E. (1984). Expert testimony on the eyewitness. In G. Wells & E. Loftus (Eds.), *Eyewitness Testimony* (pp. 273–282). Cambridge, MA: Cambridge University Press.

Lykken, D. (1981). *A tremor in the blood: Uses and abuses of the lie detector.* New York: McGraw-Hill.

Matarazzo, J. (1990). Psychological assessment versus psychological testing. *American Psychologist, 45*(9), 999–1017.

Matarazzo, J. (1991). Psychological assessment is reliable and valid: Reply to Ziskin and Faust. *American Psychologist, 46* (8), 882–884.

May, J. D. (1999). Good things come to those who seek: Ten tips for finding information on defense experts. *National Center for Prosecution of Child Abuse Update,12* (7)

McCloskey, M., & Egeth, H. (1983). What can a psychologist tell a jury? *American Psychologist, 38,* 550–563.

Mishlove, M., & Heuer, L. (1999) Courts continue to exclude expert evidence on witness credibility. *American Psychological Association Monitor, 30*(10), 49.

Otto, R. (1999). Message from the president. *Bulletin of the American Academy of Forensic Psychology, 20,*11.

Poythress, N.G. (1979). A proposal for training in forensic psychology. *American Psychologist, 34,* 612–621.

Rigling, C., & Russo, M. (1990). *Psychologists' attitude survey: Courtroom experience and perceived competence in the court system.* Paper presented at the 98th Annual Convention of American Psychological Association, Boston, MA.

Rosen, R.H. (1983). The need for training in forensic child psychology. *Professional psychology: Research and Practice, 14*(4), 481–489.

Sawyer, J. (1966). Measurement and prediction, clinical and statistical. *Psychological Bulletin, 66,* 178–200.

Shuman, D. (1986). *Psychiatric and psychological evidence.* Colorado Springs: Shepard's.

Singer, M., & Nievod, A. (1987). Consulting and testifying in court. In I. Weiner & A. Hess (Eds.), *Handbook of forensic psychology* (pp. 529–556). New York: Wiley.

Tsushima, W. T., & Anderson, R. M. (1996). *Mastering expert testimony: A courtroom handbook for mental health professionals.* Mahwah, NJ: Lawrence Erlbaum Associates.

Wellman, F. (1986). *The art of cross-examination* (4th ed.). New York: Dorset Press.

Wells, G. (1984). A reanalysis of the expert testimony issue. In G. Wells & E. Loftus (Eds.), *Eyewitness Testimony* (pp. 304–314). Cambridge, MA: Cambridge University Press.

Wiggins, J. (1973). *Personality and prediction: Principles of Personality Assessment.* Reading, MA: Addison-Wesley.

Ziskin, J. (1995). *Coping with psychiatric and psychological testimony,* Vols. I–III (5th ed.). Los Angeles, CA: Law and Psychology Press.

Ziskin, J., & Faust, D. (1991). Reply to Matarazzo. *American Psychologist, 46,* 8, 881–882.

Part V

Appendixes

Appendix A
Pain Survey Checklist (PSCL)

Full name _____

Date _____

Other names used _____

Birth date _____

Reason for referral _____

Soc. Sec. No. _____

Referral source _____

In state since _____

Place of birth _____

Sex _____

Educational level and
  last school attended _____

Race/ethnic group _____

Occupation _____

Employer's name, address and phone no.

_____

_____

_____

Your residential address and phone no.

_____

_____

Attorney's name, address, and phone no. (for pending legal cases or workers' compensation)

_____

_____

_____

PHYSICAL QUESTIONS

1. Your height   _____

2. Your weight   _____

3. Blood type   _____

4. List all disorders or diseases you have had in the past

   _____

   _____

   _____

5. List all significant injuries you have had in the past

   _____

   _____

   _____

6. List all present medical or psychological conditions you have now

   _____

   _____

   _____

7. List operations and dates

   _____

   _____

8. List hospitalizations and dates

   _____

   _____

   _____

9. Who is your primary physician?

   _____

Address _____

Date of last physical exam   _____

10. What other doctor(s) are you seeing?

   _____

11. Have you been treated for a psychological concern? What, when, and by whom?

   _____

   _____

12. Is there a family history of similar pain problems? Please explain.

   _____

   _____

13. Have you ever been treated for this pain condition in the past? Explain.

   _____

   _____

14. What is your overall physical condition?

_____

_____

_____

PAIN QUESTIONS

1. When did your present pain start?

_____

Where was that?

_____

_____

Who was there at the time besides yourself?

_____

What were you doing?

_____

_____

What did you do about the pain?

_____

In your opinion, what do you think was the cause of the pain?

_____

_____

_____

2. Did your pain start gradually? _____ Suddenly? _____ Did it spread? _____
Explain any details _____

_____

_____

_____

3. What is the most frustrating thing about your pain?

_____

_____

_____

4. Can you work? _____ Have you changed jobs? _____
5. What do your relatives or acquaintances do when you show pain?

_____

_____

_____

6. What factors seem to bring on or are associated with the pain?

_____

_____

7. Where do you feel your pain now?

_____

8. Is your pain with you all the time? Or does it change during the day?
    Please explain.

_____

_____

9. Does your pain spread?

_____

_____

10. Does your pain describe a pattern (e.g., continuous, periodic, brief)?

_____

_____

11. How long does it take for the worst pain to develop?

_____

12. How long does your pain usually last?

_____

13. How many times during a typical day do thoughts of pain cross your mind?

_____

_____

14. How would your future life change if your pain went away for good?

_____

_____

_____

_____

When I Experience the Following,

	My Pain Is:			
	Better	**Worse**	**Same**	**Comment**
Coughing or sneezing	_____	_____	_____	_____
Alcohol drinking	_____	_____	_____	_____
Riding in a car	_____	_____	_____	_____
Waking up in the morning	_____	_____	_____	_____
Experiencing tension	_____	_____	_____	_____
Cold	_____	_____	_____	_____
Dampness	_____	_____	_____	_____
Middle of night	_____	_____	_____	_____
Lying on my back	_____	_____	_____	_____
Urinating	_____	_____	_____	_____
Defecating	_____	_____	_____	_____
Having sex	_____	_____	_____	_____
Sitting (straight chair)	_____	_____	_____	_____
Sitting (soft chair)	_____	_____	_____	_____
Being massaged	_____	_____	_____	_____
Talking with people	_____	_____	_____	_____
In whirlpool/jacuzzi	_____	_____	_____	_____
Brushing teeth	_____	_____	_____	_____
Sleeping or napping	_____	_____	_____	_____
Standing	_____	_____	_____	_____
Distracted (TV, etc.)	_____	_____	_____	_____
Hearing loud noises	_____	_____	_____	_____
Middle of the day	_____	_____	_____	_____
Lying on side with knees bent	_____	_____	_____	_____
Doing housework	_____	_____	_____	_____
Exercising	_____	_____	_____	_____
Seeing bright lights	_____	_____	_____	_____
Tired	_____	_____	_____	_____
Weather changes	_____	_____	_____	_____
Drinking coffee or tea	_____	_____	_____	_____
Eating a meal	_____	_____	_____	_____
Swimming	_____	_____	_____	_____

	My Pain Is:			
	Better	**Worse**	**Same**	**Comment**
Working at my job	_____	_____	_____	_____
Standing after sitting	_____	_____	_____	_____
Lifting	_____	_____	_____	_____
Walking	_____	_____	_____	_____
Running	_____	_____	_____	_____
Leaning over	_____	_____	_____	_____
Swallowing	_____	_____	_____	_____
Elevated blood pressure	_____	_____	_____	_____
Certain foods	_____	_____	_____	_____
Boredom	_____	_____	_____	_____
Being alone	_____	_____	_____	_____

1. What medication did you take for any reason before the injury or pain started?

Medication/purpose	**How long did you take it?**	**How effective was it?**
_____	_____	_____
_____	_____	_____
_____	_____	_____
_____	_____	_____

2. What medication have you taken specifically for the pain?

   a. _____ dosage: _____ times a day: _____

   b. _____ dosage: _____ times a day: _____

   c. _____ dosage: _____ times a day: _____

   d. _____ dosage: _____ times a day: _____

3. How well does the medication work?

   _____

   _____

   _____

4. What other medication do you take these days?

   a. _____ dosage: _____ times a day: _____

   b. _____ dosage: _____ times a day: _____

   c. _____ dosage: _____ times a day: _____

   d. _____ dosage: _____ times a day: _____

5. What do you do besides taking pain medication to relieve pain?

   _____

   _____

6. How much alcohol do you drink on the average during the week?

_____

_____

7. What kind of alcohol?

_____

8. Do you mix alcohol with medication (i.e., take at the same time)?

_____

9. What kind of over-the-counter medication do you take?

_____

_____

10. Do you take any illicit drugs? Which kind?

_____

_____

11. Have you ever received a traffic citation for alcohol or drug-related behavior (e.g., DUI)?

What	When	Where	Disposition
_____	_____	_____	_____
_____	_____	_____	_____
_____	_____	_____	_____
_____	_____	_____	_____

12. What other arrests, if any, have you had since 18 years of age?

What	When	Where	Disposition
_____	_____	_____	_____
_____	_____	_____	_____
_____	_____	_____	_____
_____	_____	_____	_____

13. Have you ever received treatment for a drug/alcohol problem?

What	When	Where	Disposition
_____	_____	_____	_____
_____	_____	_____	_____
_____	_____	_____	_____
_____	_____	_____	_____

14. Does drinking coffee or tea bring on or affect the pain?

_____

_____

15. What other factors associated with eating food or drinking liquid affects your pain?

_____

_____

_____

Signs that Accompany My Pain (Mark all that apply)

	Before Pain	During Pain	After Pain
A. Dull ache	_____	_____	_____
B. Sharp pain	_____	_____	_____
C. Burning	_____	_____	_____
D. Steady pain	_____	_____	_____
E. Throbbing pain	_____	_____	_____
F. Deep pain	_____	_____	_____
G. Shooting pain	_____	_____	_____
H. Tingling	_____	_____	_____
I. Pins and needles	_____	_____	_____
J. Tender to touch	_____	_____	_____
K. Vomiting	_____	_____	_____
L. Feeling sick	_____	_____	_____
M. Fear	_____	_____	_____
N. Stress	_____	_____	_____
O. Rapid breathing	_____	_____	_____
P. Dizziness	_____	_____	_____
Q. Heart beating fast	_____	_____	_____
R. Flushed	_____	_____	_____
S. Blurred vision	_____	_____	_____
T. Sweating	_____	_____	_____
U. Fainting	_____	_____	_____
V. Bleeding	_____	_____	_____
W. Skin color change	_____	_____	_____
X. Epileptic seizures	_____	_____	_____
Y. Falling down	_____	_____	_____
Z. Others (specify)	_____	_____	_____

Please give your comments on anything which would help us understand your pain better.

_____

_____

_____

_____

_____

List several people who can be reached for additional information.

Name	**Relationship**	**Address**	**Phone No.**
_____	_____	_____	_____
_____	_____	_____	_____
_____	_____	_____	_____
_____	_____	_____	_____

PAIN CHART

1. Please mark all the locations of pain and numbness on your body. Use two different colors of markers, one for pain and the other for numbness.

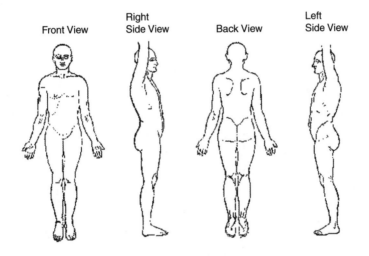

Front View   Right Side View   Back View   Left Side View

My color code for the above drawing:

The _____ color stands for pain.

The _____ color stands for numbness.

2. Now just for the pain locations, please put letters inside the marked areas to indicate any of the following:

    • Write A to indicate a dull ache.
    • Write B to indicate a sharp pain.
    • Write C to indicate a burning pain.
    • Write D to indicate a steady pain.
    • Write E to indicate a throbbing pain.
    • Write F to indicate a deep pain.
    • Write G to indicate a shooting pain.
    • Write H to indicate a tingling pain.
    • Write I to indicate pins and needles.

3. For traveling pain, draw a line from where it starts to where it ends.

4. For pain you feel right now, show where the pain is with the color marker.

Appendix B

Self-Control and Instant Offense Behaviors

CHECKLIST OF DEFENDANT COMPETENCIES

Please take time to fill out this checklist as carefully as you can before drawing conclusions in regard to a particular criminal case. This checklist may be helpful to the forensic professional in assessing different levels of self-control before, during, and after alleged criminal behavior.

In several of the sections, you will be asked to think about the sequence of the alleged behaviors in addition to a number of content factors. The ultimate purpose of this checklist is to illuminate the decision path of the evaluator. Please try to go along with this new perspective because, in doing so, you may be able to gain additional insight into the ability of the defendant to choose and self-regulate instant offense behaviors.

Evaluator's Name _____

Agency _____

PART A: DEMOGRAPHIC AND BACKGROUND FACTORS

Present Date _____

Accused's Full Name _____

Address _____

Contact parties	Relationship to accused	phone number(s)
_____	_____	_____
_____	_____	_____

Aliases _____

Social Security No. _____

Reason for Referral _____

Criminal No. _____

Referral Source _____

Charges _____

Date of Birth _____

Place of Birth _____

In State Since _____

Sex _____

Marital Status _____

Race/Ethnic Group _____

Languages Spoken _____

Educational Level _____

Occupation _____

Hand Dominance _____

Accused's

  Height _____ Weight _____lb Blood Type _____

Victim's

  Height _____ Weight _____lb Blood Type _____

BACKGROUND FACTORS

- History of alcohol abuse or dependence? Specify

_____

- History of drug abuse or dependence? Specify

_____

- Psychiatric/Psychological History

Date of Diagnosis	Diagnosis	Agency	Therapist
_____	_____	_____	_____
_____	_____	_____	_____

Specify if there is a history of critical conditions/events not presented previously (e.g., psychosis, retardation, brain damage, homicidal/suicidal behaviors) _____

_____

_____

- Juvenile Arrest History

Offense	Date of Offense	Disposition	Date of Disposition
_____	_____	_____	_____
_____	_____	_____	_____

- Adult Arrest History

Offense	Date of Offense	Disposition	Date of Disposition
_____	_____	_____	_____
_____	_____	_____	_____

- Physical/mental deterioration for 1 week before alleged offense? Specify

_____

- Physical/mental deterioration for 90 days before alleged offense? Specify

_____

- Physical/mental deterioration for 1 year before alleged offense? Specify

_____

- Anticipated stressors at time of instant offenses? Specify

_____

- Employment in the 3 months before evaluation:

    _____ None _____ Part-time _____ Full-time

    Where and what? _____

- Estimated income from employment in last year $_____/year

CURRENT FACTORS

1. Is accused fit to legally proceed (if no, why not)?

_____

2. Accused's present status

    _____ Incarcerated _____ Outpatient _____ Inpatient

3. Present medications

_____

4. Present alcohol abuse or dependence? _____ Yes _____ No

_____

5. Present drug abuse or dependence? _____ Yes _____ No

_____

6. Significant current psychiatric deficits or problems

_____

7. Relevant medical problems

_____

_____

8. Relevant other current information

_____

_____

_____

_____

PART B: BASAL VIOLENCE ANALYSIS

Previous violence to others is scrutinized to determine whether instant violence is part of a habit pattern or an isolated event. Since attaining adulthood, indicate whether each act of significant violence had the associated feature listed on the left. Threats to do significant violence to another are considered violence and are rated as such. First, threats create psychological trauma in victims. Second, some threats are arrestable behaviors (e.g., robbery, terroristic threatening).

Look at the entire basal history of violence to see if trends emerge. Determine whether these trends are operative in the instant violence and the degree to which they were the result of choice and self-control factors.

Associated Features of Previous Violence	No. of Violent Acts to Others						
	1	2	3	4	5	6	7
1. Date of violence or serious threat	___	___	___	___	___	___	___
2. Description of violence or threat (e.g., assault in the third degree)	___	___	___	___	___	___	___
3. Injury to victim (one or more of following for each act)							
a. Verbal or physical intimidation of victim	___	___	___	___	___	___	___
b. Intimidation by weapon	___	___	___	___	___	___	___
c. Minor harm	___	___	___	___	___	___	___
d. Treated and discharged	___	___	___	___	___	___	___
e. Hospitalized	___	___	___	___	___	___	___
f. Killed	___	___	___	___	___	___	___
4. Forced sex act	___	___	___	___	___	___	___
5. Relationship to victim							
a. Stranger	___	___	___	___	___	___	___
b. Acquaintance	___	___	___	___	___	___	___

Associated Features of Previous Violence	No. of Violent Acts to Others						
	1	2	3	4	5	6	7
c. Family	___	___	___	___	___	___	___
d. Institutional (e.g., police, military)	___	___	___	___	___	___	___
6. Accomplice present	___	___	___	___	___	___	___
7. Instructions to aggress (e.g., military police, contract murder)	___	___	___	___	___	___	___
8. Weapons (one or more of following):							
a. Firearms	___	___	___	___	___	___	___
b. Knife	___	___	___	___	___	___	___
c. Other weapon (e.g., hammer, rope)	___	___	___	___	___	___	___
d. Weapon found at scene	___	___	___	___	___	___	___
e. Use of protected body part (e.g., victim kicked with boots)	___	___	___	___	___	___	___
f. Use of unprotected body part (e.g., hands)	___	___	___	___	___	___	___
g. Use of primitive weapons (e.g., bites or clubs victim with head)	___	___	___	___	___	___	___
9. Substance intoxication							
a. Alcohol intoxication	___	___	___	___	___	___	___
b. Drug intoxication	___	___	___	___	___	___	___
c. Pathological intoxication	___	___	___	___	___	___	___
d. Cessation of prescribed medication	___	___	___	___	___	___	___
10. Pain cues from victim that enhanced violence	___	___	___	___	___	___	___
11. Positive consequences for violence (e.g., money, praise, no incarceration)	___	___	___	___	___	___	___
12. Disrupted central love relationship (e.g., from intimate other)	___	___	___	___	___	___	___
13. Work-related violence	___	___	___	___	___	___	___
14. Characteristics of victims							
a. Female gender	___	___	___	___	___	___	___
b. Weighs less than accused	___	___	___	___	___	___	___
c. Shorter than accused	___	___	___	___	___	___	___
d. Alone before violence	___	___	___	___	___	___	___
e. Victim displayed weapon	___	___	___	___	___	___	___
f. Physical infirmity	___	___	___	___	___	___	___
15. Violence context characteristics							
a. Nighttime occurrence	___	___	___	___	___	___	___
b. Weekend occurrence	___	___	___	___	___	___	___
c. Private residence	___	___	___	___	___	___	___
d. Public building	___	___	___	___	___	___	___
e. Roadway or transportation system	___	___	___	___	___	___	___
f. Property aggression involved	___	___	___	___	___	___	___

Associated Features of Previous Violence	No. of Violent Acts to Others						
	1	2	3	4	5	6	7
16. Acknowledgment of violence (e.g., spontaneous statements; written confession)	___	___	___	___	___	___	___
17. Apologizes for violence	___	___	___	___	___	___	___
18. Suicidal/self-mutilative gestures in response to violence	___	___	___	___	___	___	___

Synthesis: Examine the above tables after completion for behavioral themes. Look for themes that are common both to previous violence and the instant case. Place the common descriptors on the assault cycle.

ESTIMATE OF SELF-CONTROL BY TEMPORAL PERIOD

	Instant Violence		
	Before	During	After
Substantial	_____	_____	_____
Considerable	_____	_____	_____
Moderate	_____	_____	_____
Mild	_____	_____	_____
Minimal	_____	_____	_____
Negligible	_____	_____	_____

Combining all events within a time period, present the overall degree of self-control for *before*, *during*, and *after* the instant violence on the above histogram.

PART C: DAY OF ALLEGED OFFENSE (DATE, TIME, AND DAY OF WEEK)

Event	Defendant Time	Specify Behavior	Victim Time	Specify Behavior
1. Significant events the night before	_____	_____	_____	_____
2. Intoxicating substances ingested before instant violence occurred	_____	_____	_____	_____
3. Procurement of weapons	_____	_____	_____	_____
4. Presence of other people	_____	_____	_____	_____
5. Arrival at instant violence scene	_____	_____	_____	_____
6. First sighting of victim (accused)	_____	_____	_____	_____
7. Verbal interaction with victim (accused)	_____	_____	_____	_____
8. Time of instant violence	_____	_____	_____	_____
9. Time left scene	_____	_____	_____	_____
10. Destination	_____	_____	_____	_____

PERPETRATOR AND VICTIM CHARACTERISTICS AT THE TIME OF THE INSTANT OFFENSE

Please check as many as apply. Fill in the blanks when indicated.

P = Perpetrator V = Victim

P	V	Sex	P	V	Build
___	___	Male	___	___	Skinny
___	___	Female	___	___	Slim
___	___	Unknown	___	___	Medium/average
			___	___	Heavy
___	___	**Known Age**	___	___	Husky
			___	___	Muscular
		Estimated Age	___	___	Fat
___	___	Below 15 years	___	___	Unknown
___	___	15 to 19 years			
___	___	20 to 24 years			**Posture**
___	___	25 to 29 years	___	___	Stooped
___	___	30 to 39 years	___	___	Bowed Legs
___	___	40 to 49 years	___	___	Bent to One Side
___	___	50 to 65 years	___	___	Normal/erect
___	___	Over 65 years	___	___	Stiff
___	___	Unknown			
		Height			
___	___	Under 5'0"			**Gait**
___	___	5'0" to 5'1"	___	___	Slow
___	___	5'2" to 5'3"	___	___	Shuffle
___	___	5'4" to 5'5"	___	___	Limp
___	___	5'6" to 5'7"	___	___	Walks with cane
___	___	5'8" to 5'9"	___	___	Normal
___	___	5'10" to 5'11"	___	___	Fast
___	___	6'0" to 6'1"	___	___	Runs
___	___	6'2" to 6'3"	___	___	Unknown
___	___	6'4" to 6'6"			**Unusual Manners**
___	___	Over 6'6			_____
			___	___	**Unknown**
		Weight			
___	___	Under 100 lb			
___	___	100 to 119 lb			**Accent**
___	___	120 to 139 lb			_____
___	___	140 to 159 lb	___	___	_____
___	___	160 lbs. to 179 lbs.	___	___	Unknown
___	___	180 lbs. to 199 lbs.			

P	V		P	V	
____	____	200 to 219 lb			**Injuries**
____	____	220 to 239 lb	____	____	_____
____	____	240 to 260 lb	____	____	_____
____	____	Over 260 lb	____	____	Unknown
		Ethnicity			**Tattoos**
____	____	Black	____	____	Arm, left
____	____	White	____	____	Arm, right
____	____	Hispanic	____	____	Back
____	____	Chinese	____	____	Chest
____	____	Filipino	____	____	Fingers, left
____	____	Hawaiian	____	____	Fingers, right
____	____	Japanese	____	____	Hand, left
____	____	Polynesian	____	____	Hand, right
____	____	Portuguese	____	____	Leg, left
____	____	Samoan	____	____	Leg, right
____	____	Mixed/Combo			
____	____	_____	____	____	Unknown
____	____	Unknown			
					Head Hair — Length
		Body Scars	____	____	Bald
____	____	Abdomen, left	____	____	Crew Cut
____	____	Abdomen, right	____	____	Neck Length
____	____	Arm, left	____	____	Shoulder Length
____	____	Arm, right	____	____	Long
____	____	Back	____	____	Unknown
____	____	Chest			
____	____	Hand, left			**Facial Hair — Type**
____	____	Hand, right	____	____	Mustache
____	____	Leg, left	____	____	Goatee
____	____	Leg, right	____	____	Beard
____	____	Wrist, left			_____
____	____	Wrist, right	____	____	Unknown
____	____	_____			
____	____	Unknown			
					Facial Hair — Color
		Facial Scars	____	____	Black
____	____	Cheek, left	____	____	Brown
____	____	Cheek, right	____	____	Blond
____	____	Chin	____	____	Red
____	____	Eyebrow, left	____	____	Gray
____	____	Eyebrow, right			

P	V		P	V	
		Facial Scars			**Facial Hair — Color**
_____	_____	Forehead	_____	_____	White
_____	_____	Harelip	_____	_____	_____
_____	_____	Lip, lower	_____	_____	Unknown
_____	_____	Lip, upper			
_____	_____	Nose			**Eyes — Color**
_____	_____	Ears, pierced	_____	_____	Black
_____	_____	_____	_____	_____	Brown
			_____	_____	Blue
			_____	_____	Gray
			_____	_____	Green
		Jewelry	_____	_____	_____
_____	_____	_____	_____	_____	Unknown
		_____			
		_____			
		Other (e.g., hearing aid)			**Eyes — Glasses**
_____	_____	_____	_____	_____	Bifocals
		_____	_____	_____	Other prescription
		_____	_____	_____	Contact lenses
			_____	_____	Sunglasses
		Head Hair — Color	_____	_____	Reflective
_____	_____	Black	_____	_____	_____
_____	_____	Brown	_____	_____	Unknown
_____	_____	Blond			
_____	_____	Dirty blond			**Eyes — Glasses Frames**
_____	_____	Red	_____	_____	Wire
_____	_____	Gray	_____	_____	Plastic
_____	_____	White	_____	_____	Rimless
_____	_____	_____	_____	_____	Clear
_____	_____	Unknown	_____	_____	_____
			_____	_____	Unknown
		Head Hair — Style			**Eyes — Traits**
_____	_____	Straight	_____	_____	Crossed
_____	_____	Curly	_____	_____	Squinted
_____	_____	Wavy	_____	_____	Bloodshot
_____	_____	Afro	_____	_____	Dilated/constricted pupils
_____	_____	Tied back			
_____	_____	Braided	_____	_____	Lazy eye
_____	_____	Neat	_____	_____	Wide
_____	_____	Flat top	_____	_____	Missing, left

P	V		P	V	
		Head Hair — Style			**Eyes — Traits**
_____	_____	Wig	_____	_____	Missing, right
_____	_____	Unknown	_____	_____	
			_____	_____	Unknown
		Complexion			
_____	_____	Pale			**Clothing**
_____	_____	Fair	_____	_____	Aloha shirt
_____	_____	Medium	_____	_____	T-shirt
_____	_____	Ruddy	_____	_____	Pullover
_____	_____	Tanned	_____	_____	Sport shirt
_____	_____	Brown	_____	_____	Dress shirt
_____	_____	Black	_____	_____	Blouse
_____	_____	Clear			
_____	_____	Moles	_____	_____	None
_____	_____	Freckles	_____	_____	Unknown
_____	_____	Blackheads			
_____	_____	Acne/pimples	_____	_____	Sleeve length
_____	_____	Pock-marked			
_____	_____	Birthmark	_____	_____	Markings
_____	_____				
_____	_____	Unknown			
		Teeth			**Clothing — Trousers**
_____	_____	Yellow	_____	_____	Jeans
_____	_____	White	_____	_____	Dress Slacks
_____	_____	Normal	_____	_____	Shorts
_____	_____	False	_____	_____	None
_____	_____	Broken	_____	_____	Casual
_____	_____	Braces	_____	_____	Corduroy
_____	_____	Missing			
_____	_____	Stained	_____	_____	Unknown
_____	_____	Filled	_____	_____	Length
_____	_____				
_____	_____	Unknown	_____	_____	Markings
		Mouth			**Clothing — Shoes**
		Stink breath	_____	_____	Barefoot
_____	_____	Alcohol smell	_____	_____	Slippers
_____	_____	Saliva	_____	_____	Dress shoes
_____	_____	Normal	_____	_____	Work shoes
_____	_____	Unusual lips	_____	_____	Boots
_____	_____	Mouth concealed	_____	_____	Sandals

P   **V**

		Mouth
_____	_____	Unknown

		Hands
_____	_____	Small
_____	_____	Stubby
_____	_____	Large
_____	_____	Spotted
_____	_____	Normal
_____	_____	Hairy
_____	_____	Injured
_____	_____	_____
_____	_____	Unknown

		Clothing — Hat
_____	_____	Baseball cap
_____	_____	Business
_____	_____	Military
_____	_____	None
_____	_____	_____
_____	_____	Color
		_____
_____	_____	Designs

		Type of Weapon
_____	_____	Arson

P   **V**

		Clothing — Shoes
_____	_____	Unknown
_____	_____	Color
		_____
_____	_____	Material
		_____

		Clothing — Dress
_____	_____	Muumuu
_____	_____	Formal
_____	_____	Casual
_____	_____	Work
_____	_____	Unknown
_____	_____	Color
		_____
_____	_____	Length
		_____
_____	_____	Markings
		_____

		Vehicle
_____	_____	Automobile
_____	_____	Bicycle
_____	_____	Motorcycle
_____	_____	Truck
_____	_____	Unknown
		_____
_____	_____	Make
		_____
_____	_____	Color
		_____
_____	_____	Year
		_____
_____	_____	Unusual features
		_____
_____	_____	Decals
		_____
_____	_____	Tag No.
		_____

		Criminal Occupation
_____	_____	Arson

P	V	Type of Weapon	P	V	Criminal Occupation
___	___	Ax	___	___	Burglary
___	___	Blunt instrument	___	___	Fraud
___	___	Firearm	___	___	Gambling
___	___	Handgun ___ Cal.	___	___	Homicide
___	___	Shotgun ___ Ga.	___	___	Larceny
___	___	Rifle ___ Cal.	___	___	Motorcycle gang
___	___	Machine gun ___ Cal.	___	___	Narcotics
___	___	Garrotte/ligature	___	___	Organized crime
___	___	Hatchet	___	___	Pornography
___	___	Knife, large (> 6")	___	___	Prostitution
___	___	Knife, small (< 6")	___	___	Robbery
___	___	Odd/unusual weapon	___	___	_____
___	___	Physical force	___	___	Unknown
___	___	Sharp instrument (other than knife)			
___	___	Vehicle			
___	___	Tire Tool			**Lifestyle**
		_____	___	___	Bisexual
___	___	Unknown			Day person —
___	___	Color	___	___	in early
		_____	___	___	Heterosexual
___	___	Composition	___	___	Homosexual
		_____	___	___	Involved/outgoing
			___	___	Narcotics user
		First Seen by Others			Night person —
___	___	Car	___	___	stays out late
___	___	Club/disco	___	___	Socializes seldom
___	___	Date first seen	___	___	Socializes frequently
		_____	___	___	Withdrawn/shy
___	___	Estimated time			_____
		_____	___	___	Unknown
___	___	Health club			
___	___	Hitchhiking			**Occupation**
___	___	House/apartment			Gas station attendant
___	___	Playground or parks/ yards	___	___	Business professional
___	___	Public conveyance	___	___	Homemaker
___	___	School	___	___	Laborer/services
___	___	Shopping	___	___	Street person
___	___	Walking	___	___	Student
___	___	Work	___	___	None

P	V		P	V	
		First Seen by Others			**Occupation**
___	___	City/state	___	___	Realtor
___	___	_____	___	___	Priest/minister
___	___	Unknown	___	___	Conv. store clerk
___	___	_____	___	___	_____
			___	___	Unknown
		Last See by Others			
		Car			
___	___	Club/disco			
___	___	Date last seen			
___	___	_____			
		Estimated time			
___	___	_____			
		Health club			
___	___	Hitchhiking			
___	___	House/apartment			
___	___	Playground or parks/yards			
___	___	Public conveyance			
___	___	School			
___	___	Shopping			
___	___	Walking			
___	___	Work			
___	___	City/state			
___	___	_____			
___	___	Unknown			

CRIME CONTEXT AND MODUS OPERANDI

	Location Where Occurred		**Modus Operandi**
___	Apartment/house	___	False pretense
___	Building	___	Hitchhiker
___	Construction site	___	Impersonates doctor
___	Field	___	Impersonates police
___	Hotel/motel	___	Newspaper ad
___	Interstate or highway	___	Random
___	Rural	___	Robbery/burglary
___	Street/alley	___	Stalker
___	City/state _____	___	Stranger
___	River/lake	___	Victim knew suspect
___	Woods	___	Arms self at scene
___	Other _____	___	Disables lights/electricity
		___	Disables telephone

Placement/Position of Victim

_____ Buried
_____ Concealed
_____ Displayed
_____ Dumped
_____ Face down
_____ Face up
_____ Fetal position
_____ In receptacle
_____ In water
_____ Moved after injury or death
_____ Nude
_____ Partially nude
_____ Propped-up sitting
_____ Fully clothed

_____ _____

Treatment of Victim

_____ Bound
_____ Body covered
_____ Burned
_____ Face covered
_____ Gagged
_____ Handcuffed
_____ Kidnapped
_____ Raped
_____ Sodomized
_____ Tortured
_____ Duct tape used to bind
_____ Rope/string used to bind
_____ Clothes used to bind
_____ Surgical tape used to bind
_____ Other tape/material used to bind

_____ _____

Modus Operandi

_____ Disables victim's car
_____ Fingerprints removed
_____ Ransacks
_____ Suspect cleans up scene
_____ Suspect injured at scene
_____ Suspect returns to scene
_____ Takes souvenirs
_____ Wears disguises/gloves
_____ Suspect takes victim's vehicle

_____ _____

Vulnerability Analysis

_____ Lighting _____

_____ Security _____

_____ Presence of others _____

_____ Exits _____

_____ Locking system _____

_____ Visibility _____

_____ Noise _____

_____ Temperature _____

_____ History of violence _____

_____ Architecture _____

_____ Concealment _____

HOMICIDE CASES

Cause Of Death

_____ Asphyxiation
_____ Bludgeoning
_____ Burning
_____ Drowning
_____ Drug overdose
_____ Electrocution
_____ Poisoning
_____ Scalding
_____ Shooting
_____ Slashing
_____ Stabbing
_____ Strangling
_____ Unknown
_____ _____

Secondary Wounds

_____ Asphyxiation
_____ Bite marks
_____ Bludgeoning
_____ Burning
_____ Drowning
_____ Drug overdose
_____ Electrocution
_____ Multiple wounds
_____ Poisoning
_____ Scalding
_____ Shooting
_____ Slashing
_____ Stabbing
_____ Strangling
_____ Unknown
_____ Other _____

Condition of Body When Found

_____ Mutilated
_____ Necrophilia
_____ Objects in throat/mouth
_____ Objects in penis
_____ Objects in rectum
_____ Objects in vagina
_____ Objects or symbols placed on body

Technical/physical Evidence

_____ Body X-rays available
_____ Casting available
_____ Composite available
_____ Dental X-rays available
_____ Fibers
_____ Fingerprints available
_____ Fingernail scrapings
_____ Fluids
_____ Footprints available
_____ Hair
_____ Multiple perpetrators
_____ Semen
_____ Tire impressions taken
_____ Weapon found at scene
_____ _____

Articles Left On Body

_____ Clothing
_____ Jewelry
_____ _____

Medical Information (Describe)

_____ Broken bones _____

_____ Blood Type _____

_____ Pregnancy _____

_____ _____

Condition of Body When Found

_____ Penile/anal penetration

_____ Penile/oral penetration

_____ Penile/vaginal penetration

_____ Possible sexual contact

_____ Decomposed/skeletal

_____ Other _____

PART D: SELF-CONTROL DURING THE INSTANT OFFENSE SEQUENCE

Please fill in these items based upon the various database sources relevant to the day of the instant violence.

PHYSICAL AND MENTAL ACTIVITIES

These refer to rudimentary skills and/or homeostatic activities of the defendant. They create the foundation for all self-control behaviors exhibited before, during, or subsequent to instant violence by the accused. Check the appropriate space and present comments when appropriate.

	Insufficient Data	No	Yes	Specify
Ability to sleep	_____	_____	_____	_____
Ability to eat/drink	_____	_____	_____	_____
Responds to autonomic pressure (e.g., urinates)	_____	_____	_____	_____
Self-awareness (e.g., "I" statements)	_____	_____	_____	_____
Long-term memory skills (e.g., visual, auditory, tactile, olfactory)	_____	_____	_____	_____
Short-term memory skills	_____	_____	_____	_____
Reports cognitive activity	_____	_____	_____	_____
Awareness of surroundings (e.g., observations of environment)	_____	_____	_____	_____
Ability to estimate time	_____	_____	_____	_____
Ability to ambulate (e.g., voluntary movements)	_____	_____	_____	_____
Intact sensory skills (e.g., visual, olfactory, hearing)	_____	_____	_____	_____
Ability to express feelings (e.g., verbalizes anger, shows rage or fear)	_____	_____	_____	_____
Intact motor skills (e.g., grasping reflex, biting)	_____	_____	_____	_____
Withdrawal reflex from pain	_____	_____	_____	_____
Voice recognition (e.g., of victim)	_____	_____	_____	_____
Self-grooming	_____	_____	_____	_____
Ability to maintain posture	_____	_____	_____	_____

	Insufficient Data	No	Yes	Specify
Ability to show facial expression	_____	_____	_____	_____
Rudimentary chaining of behaviors (e.g., tracking and moving toward visual stimulus)	_____	_____	_____	_____
Ability to drive	_____	_____	_____	_____
Other signs of basic self-regulation	_____	_____	_____	_____

GOAL FORMULATION

Relevant to the time before the alleged violence, goal formulation taps the ability to systematically analyze and integrate the accused's awareness of self and environment. The capability of productively elaborating from a small number of cues from the crime context is also measured. The ability to think of the violent act before it occurred, as evidenced by behaviors compatible with the idea of the violence to follow, is the central issue of this section.

	Insufficient Data	No	Yes	Specify
Marked cognitive and/or behavioral focus	_____	_____	_____	_____
Ability to link thoughts with adaptive behavior (e.g., walking until entrance is found)	_____	_____	_____	_____
Verbal coherence and verbal fluency	_____	_____	_____	_____
Speaks to victim (e.g., requests money)	_____	_____	_____	_____
Controlled conversation	_____	_____	_____	_____
Appreciation of temporally distant need (e.g., need for more drugs to prevent withdrawal)	_____	_____	_____	_____
Knowledge of steps or elements in violent sequence	_____	_____	_____	_____
Cognitive mapping (e.g., navigating from home to crime scene)	_____	_____	_____	_____
Shows capacity for reflective thought about violence (e.g., verbalizations that involve comparisons)	_____	_____	_____	_____
Ability to think of alternatives to instant violence	_____	_____	_____	_____
Statements to others that he or she would harm the victim (e.g., for socially undesirable behavior)	_____	_____	_____	_____
Victim a targeted individual	_____	_____	_____	_____
Personalizes victim	_____	_____	_____	_____
Other signs of goal formulation	_____	_____	_____	_____

PLANNING AND PREPARATION

Relevant to the time before the alleged crime, this refers to the ability to show cognitive preparation for subsequent behaviors. Routine rehearsals for the alleged crime are the highest form of ability in this dimension.

	Insufficient Data	No	Yes	Specify
Foreknowledge of alleged crime	_____	_____	_____	_____
Creation of time schedules	_____	_____	_____	_____
Temporal ordering of steps to complete task	_____	_____	_____	_____
Ability to revise plan given new information	_____	_____	_____	_____
Completes plan in reasonable time frame	_____	_____	_____	_____
Ability to relate interpersonally to others as planned	_____	_____	_____	_____
Motor or mental rehearsal of crime sequence	_____	_____	_____	_____
Use of ruse to fool victim	_____	_____	_____	_____
Lures victim into defenseless position	_____	_____	_____	_____
Brings weapon and paraphernalia (e.g., "rape kit") to scene	_____	_____	_____	_____
Telephone, lights, security devices disabled	_____	_____	_____	_____
Other signs of planning/preparation	_____	_____	_____	_____

EFFECTIVE PERFORMANCE

Occurring during the violence sequence, effective performance reflects the notion that the accused may simultaneously observe and change his or her behavior in response to a fluctuating environment, all in accordance with the goal or desired object of the action sequence. Hypothesis testing is the highest form of effective performance, as when the accused changes his or her own behavior (e.g., threatens victim, puts key in lock) to see the reaction (e.g., victim acquiescence, door becomes unlocked) and then changes his or her own behavior accordingly (e.g., proceeds to rape victim, goes through door to bedroom). In essence, this skill taps the ability to show a concordance between intentions/plans and actions.

	Insufficient Data	No	Yes	Specify
Able to view environment objectively (takes abstract attitude)	_____	_____	_____	_____
Violence did not occur close to home/work (for planned violence)	_____	_____	_____	_____
Demonstrates a variety of acts (flexible behavior, as with several weapons)	_____	_____	_____	_____

	Insufficient Data	No	Yes	Specify
Displaying multiple sets of simultaneous motor behaviors	_____	_____	_____	_____
Able to orchestrate multistep, multitask scheme (e.g., long, connected chains of behaviors)	_____	_____	_____	_____
Concerted effort to accomplish goal (e.g., despite victim resistance)	_____	_____	_____	_____
Ability to show change in principle (e.g., from robbery to rape)	_____	_____	_____	_____
Ability to show self-controlled somatic responses (e.g., sex with ejaculation, eating, drinking; all within violence sequence)	_____	_____	_____	_____
Ability to delay responses	_____	_____	_____	_____
Ability to monitor and self-correct ongoing behavior	_____	_____	_____	_____
Nonstimulus boundedness (acts independent of environmental influences)	_____	_____	_____	_____
Ability to regulate tempo, intensity, and duration of behaviors	_____	_____	_____	_____
Controlled mood during inflicting of violence	_____	_____	_____	_____
Ability to avoid nonerratic behavior unless planned (e.g., deliberately becomes substance intoxicated)	_____	_____	_____	_____
Hypothesis testing	_____	_____	_____	_____
Awareness of wrongdoing during violence (e.g., from statements to victim)	_____	_____	_____	_____
Ability to hit/penetrate vital body target (e.g., deep knife penetration, shots to head)	_____	_____	_____	_____
Controlled cutting of victim	_____	_____	_____	_____
Ability to stop violence (e.g., response cessation with no perseveration)	_____	_____	_____	_____
Intact self-control (retrospectively reported by accused)	_____	_____	_____	_____
Victim bound or other restraints used	_____	_____	_____	_____
Mouth taped	_____	_____	_____	_____
Mouth gag used	_____	_____	_____	_____
Blindfold placed over victim's eyes	_____	_____	_____	_____
Absence of bite marks on victim	_____	_____	_____	_____
No blood smearing or splattering	_____	_____	_____	_____

	Insufficient Data	No	Yes	Specify
Victim tied to another object	_____	_____	_____	_____
Takes pictures of victim	_____	_____	_____	_____
Perpetrator encourages bystanders to engage in violence to victim	_____	_____	_____	_____
Torture of victim	_____	_____	_____	_____
Other aggressive acts prior to death	_____	_____	_____	_____
Obliteration or destruction of evidence during instant violence	_____	_____	_____	_____
Other signs of effective performance	_____	_____	_____	_____

RECOVERY PERIOD BEHAVIORS

The accused may, after the instant offense, exhibit behaviors suggestive of memory/knowledge that a possible crime had been committed. These include efforts ostensibly directed toward not getting caught for the offense, or of minimizing possible aversive consequences.

	Insufficient Data	No	Yes	Specify
Moves away when help arrives	_____	_____	_____	_____
Disposes of or hides victim's body	_____	_____	_____	_____
Amputation of "ID" body parts (i.e., head, hands)	_____	_____	_____	_____
Disposes of victim's clothing	_____	_____	_____	_____
Other alteration of crime scene	_____	_____	_____	_____
Disposes of weapon used in offense	_____	_____	_____	_____
Disposes of other crime-related material	_____	_____	_____	_____
Takes souvenir from victim/scene	_____	_____	_____	_____
Cleans own body	_____	_____	_____	_____
Washes own clothes used in alleged crime	_____	_____	_____	_____
Cleans/washes other material	_____	_____	_____	_____
Makes verbal statements of crime recall (e.g., spontaneous statements)	_____	_____	_____	_____
Relevant nonverbal gestures (e.g., points to victim's body)	_____	_____	_____	_____
Prevaricates incompatible behavior (e.g., makes up verifiably false story)	_____	_____	_____	_____
Writes confession	_____	_____	_____	_____
Other signs of recall for instant offenses	_____	_____	_____	_____

POSTVIOLENCE DEPRESSION PHASE

For many violent perpetrators, a period of guilt and remorse is experienced after the exhibited aggression. This is especially true for episodic or rare violent offenders. The self-control to avoid self-punitive behavior is the focus of concern here (e.g., suicidal, self-mutilative gestures). Apology and remorseful behaviors are very common here and imply little about self-control or choice at the time of the instant violence.

ROUTINE MENTAL/PSYCHOLOGICAL BEHAVIORS

Eventually, there is a return to baseline functioning for most individuals who perpetrate violence. The new baseline of routine activities and skills would also include that which is a function of violence-related learning, such as increased substance abuse, disturbed sleep patterns, and fashioning of new weapons. Some behaviors may be reduced (e.g., driving after conviction for negligent homicide, social activities that require trust and reciprocity). In the final analysis, an individual is never the same after the perpetration of substantial violence to others.

PART E: SELF-CONTROL MODEL

The rationally-based decision model below can be adapted to a wide range of instant offenses. The model represents the evaluator's post hoc decision path in coming to conclusions relevant to defendant's competencies at the time of the instant offense.

No Forensic Psychological Criteria	Yes	No	Opinion
1. Adequate forensic database; includes historical and instant offense information relevant to the accused, alleged victim(s), and crime context (Part A)	_____	_____	_____
2. Presence of significant basal violence (two or more acts of threatened, attempted, or consummated violence; Part B)	_____	_____	_____
3. Common themes for basal violence and instant offense (Part B)	_____	_____	_____
4. Self-regulation (Part C):	_____	_____	_____
Considerable to substantial goal formation	_____	_____	_____
Considerable to substantial planning and preparation	_____	_____	_____
Considerable to substantial concordance between plans and actions	_____	_____	_____
Considerable to substantial effective performance	_____	_____	_____
(To meet model requirements for substantial overall self-control, the evaluator must score Yes on 1 to 4 above.)	_____	_____	_____
5. The accused had substantial self-control at the time of the instant offense.	_____	_____	_____

Appendix C
Insanity Report Format

MENTAL FITNESS AND CAPACITY REPORT

DATE OF REPORT

Honorable William Smith
First Circuit Court
State Capitol Building   Forensic Psychological Evaluation
Anytown, Anystate 00001   RE: DOE, JOHN NMI
                                      SSN: 000-00-0000
                                      DOB: Month, Day, Year
                                      Charge 1: Unpremeditated Murder
                                      Charge 2: Robbery in the First Degree,
                                             5 counts

Dear Judge Smith:

This is the report of the forensic psychologist [requested/appointed] by [you/the Court/Sanity Board, etc.] to examine and report upon the mental condition of the [defendant/client/patient/subject, etc.], John NMI Doe, SSN 000-00-0000, currently [assigned/residing/incarcerated, etc.] at [location name and address, including zip code].

Forensic Database

The nature of the examination consisted of [clinical interviewing/psychological testing/neuropsychological testing/interview of significant others/ward observation/records review/naturalistic observation/behavioral assessment with a functional analysis of crime-related responses/social-environmental assessment/review of medical findings/developmental assessment/competence assessment/description from relevant demographic data/postdiction or prediction from base rates, etc.] for a total of approximately [N to N] hours of evaluation. Mr. Doe was examined both at the [place, date] and the [place, date] while he was on [pretrial confinement status/in the community on bail, etc.]. In addition to [one/two/N] clinical interviews, he was administered the following psychometric instruments: [list all tests, including multiple administrations and unsuccessful attempts].

The following individuals were interviewed and/or rendered written statements to the undersigned:

[List all persons and their relationship to accused or investigation process; indicate number of interviews and location, if significant]

The following written materials were reviewed:

> [List source and type, include "non-official" materials, such as diaries, notes from the accused to his attorney, etc.]

Assessment Behavior and Database Validity

[Cooperative/uncooperative] and of [normal/disheveled/abnormal] appearance, this [single/separated/divorced/widowed/married], [white/black, etc.], [N]-year-old [vocation and rank or status within vocation] exhibited a [logical and coherent/fragmented/tangential/circumstantial/blocked stream of thought, etc.]. Affect was [appropriate/inappropriate, such as laughter or rage, blandness, lability]. A trend toward [somatic preoccupation/paranoid suspiciousness/rumination about past injustices, etc.] was observed. Orientation was apparent for [time/place/person/circumstance]. Memory for [short/intermediate/remote] events was [intact/impaired] as evidenced by [performance on presented sequences of numbers/inquiries by examiner regarding prior evaluation events/recollection of independently verified historical events], [with/without] a tendency to confabulate. Judgment was [marginal/adequate, etc.], as shown by [appropriate/inappropriate] responses to standardized comprehension questions [give examples — response to finding envelope, discovering theater fire]. Abstraction ability, as reflected by responses to proverbs [give examples — response to glasshouses, striking while the iron is hot] was [appropriate/concrete — if so, give response]. Associational ability, as reflected by responses to similarity items was [concrete/abstract/appropriate], as shown by [give examples — orange, banana; chair, table]. Reading and writing skills are [normally developed/impaired, specify]. Computationally, he had [no difficulty/difficulty] counting backward from 20 [but/and] had [difficulty/no difficulty] in [serial 7s/3s/adding/subtracting/multiplying]. Fund of information was [adequate/inadequate — if so, give responses to four presidents, population of United States, senators in U.S. senate]. Overall, his intelligence appeared [normal/below normal, etc.], which is [congruent/incongruent] with his education [specify years and focus]. Insight into the emotional basis of his present condition was [minimal/apparent, etc.]. No [other, if applicable] pathognomonic features of his clinical appearance were noted.

[If features such as tattoos are present, state "for identification purposes …"]

Distortion analysis of Mr. Doe's evaluation responses revealed, for the time of the interview, an attempt to [fake good/fake bad/invalidate results/present himself in an accurate manner — explain terms]. This is based on [validity scale results/goodness of fit between test profile and clinical behavior/performance on scales or test procedures specifically designed to assess attempts at misrepresentation/discrepancy between response and established events]. Distortion analysis for the time of the instant offense(s) revealed an attempt to [fake good/fake bad/confuse the crime picture/present himself in an accurate manner — explain terms if not done previously]. This is based on [assessment of claimed psychopathological conditions when compared with known data, e.g., BAC/establishing the likelihood of claimed psychopathology with DSM-IV diagnostic criteria/comparing similarity of current distortion to claimed psychopathology].

Interviewed others and written materials were also scrutinized for distortion. Statements by significant others may have been influenced by [a desire to assist the accused because they wish to be rejoined/a sincere desire to represent the facts honestly/the lengthy period between the instant offense(s) and the written recollection of such]. Statements by the victim may have been influenced by [a desire for revenge/stress at the time of the instant offense[s]/a state of intoxication/the lengthy time between the alleged crime and investigation results, etc.].

Generally, evaluation results for Mr. Doe are considered an accurate portrayal of the accused, taking into consideration mental status, test-taking attitude, [psychological/intellectual/neuropsychological, etc.] limitations and competencies, and witnesses'/investigators' input.

Defendant Reconstruction of Instant Offense(s)

[If available, a detailed account of the alleged crime is presented by the accused, e.g., see police investigation report/JAG files].

Generally, the accused stated, during the present assessment, that the killing was [in self-defense/accidental/deliberate, etc.] after the victim [struck him/threatened him, etc.]. After the killing [witnesses stated/the accused self-described] his behavior as [describe], his affect as [describe], his cognitive functioning as [describe], his verbal remarks, in substance, as [paraphrase or quote].

The accused stated that the robbery was [repeat sequence for all charged crimes].

[If amnesia is claimed.] Of particular interest is the claimed loss of memory [following onset of strangulation of the victim/after the second knife thrust, etc.]. This amnesia, if genuine, could be caused by an elevated emotional state such as intense anger or fear, or other condition such as [head trauma/an alcoholic blackout/psychosis/dissociative reaction/substance intoxication/epileptic seizure/other organic states] at the time of the crime. For the instant offense, the claimed amnesia is most compatible with the occurrence of [type or combination, include malingering if conditions for amnesia do not meet DSM-IV inclusionary criteria].

[If auditory hallucinations are claimed.] The accused also stated that he heard a "voice" to the effect that [the victim was trying to kill him, etc.]. Four points are relevant here. First, volunteering that the voice was experienced at the time of the crime [did not take place until long after the accused rendered previous statements about the crime, which did not include auditory hallucinations, took place at the crime scene to investigating officers, etc.]. [One wonders to what extent presenting the "voice" was prompted by the demand characteristics of the accused's legal situation/Presenting the "voice" in such a spontaneous manner while under obvious stress heightens the probability that it was, in fact, genuine, etc.]. Second, if instant offense events were as the accused describes, his acts [may have been in self-defense and therefore the voice is of little relevance/may have indeed been prompted by the auditory hallucination]. Recall that the victim had [describe relevant behaviors] and the context was [describe relevant contextual stimuli]. Third, hearing the "voice" [is/is not] tantamount to obeying it, as the accused [related a number of instances where the voice's command was disregarded; give examples/has acquiesced to it in all reported instances]. Fourth, the "voice" is described as [ego systonic/ego dystonic]. Given the chance to rid himself of the "voice," he [would/would not] do so because of its [describe positive or negative properties]. This means that [describe implications of ego-systonic/dystonic experience].

[Describe and evaluate if other unusual features of defendant's instant offense experience are claimed.]

Historical vs. Instant Offense Behaviors

[If available.]

A general history of the accused is also presented in [Dr. X's report/the presentence evaluation].

The defendant was born and raised in [Anytown, Anystate], the [give ordinal position] of [give number of male and female siblings].

Relevant aspects of his history that may bear upon the alleged crime include conditions that are associated with development of criminal behavior, such as arrest history/a family chronically affected by intramember friction and lack of support/a violent same-sexed parental model/abuse as a child/school problems including frequent fighting and assaults on teachers, etc.].

Medical problems include [relevant diseases/spontaneous loss of consciousness before age 10, etc.]. His substance abuse history was [describe].

[If available.] Apparently, the accused dealt with the above circumstances by [describe strengths and competencies/describe helping relationships with significant others or agencies/describe diversion into areas such as sports, academics, hobbies/mention psychiatric hospitalizations or treatment].

Mental Condition

The diagnosis[es] representing a reconstructed mental condition for the time of the alleged crime is [specify DSM-IV, NNN.NN]. This is based on [specify DSM-IV inclusionary criteria that apply]. The diagnosis[es] for the time of the assessment is [specify DSM-IV, NNN.NN]. This is based on [specify DSM-IV inclusionary criteria].

[If two diagnoses are identical.] The diagnosis of [specify] for the time of the alleged crime [is temporally linked to the identical diagnosis at the time of the evaluation in the sense that both mental conditions have been continually operative during the two time points/even though identical to the diagnosis at the time of the evaluation, represents the mental condition occurring episodically with no implication of continued operation between the two temporal points].

Self-Determination of Instant Offense Behaviors

[If relevant cognitive events operative.] The cognitive capacity of the accused to appreciate the wrongfulness of his acts may have been adversely affected by the following events:

[Specify those which apply.]

1. During a delusion of imminent harm followed by self-defensive behavior [link to history, diagnosis, severity of associated conditions];
2. Other delusions [analyze appropriateness of delusion if it were true];
3. When experiencing hallucinations [specify command auditory hallucinations/visual hallucinations but not illusions; link, as above];
4. In cases of clinical retardation or in borderline conditions where cognitive abilities are especially deficit compared to performance skills [link];
5. Other relevant conditions such as dissociative disorders and some organic states [link].

[If relevant cognitive events operative.] Cognitive capacity to appreciate the wrongfulness of his acts seems to have been present, as evidenced by the following events:

[Specify those that apply.]

1. Flexibility of response, as when the accused brought his [burglar tools/murder weapon, etc.] to the scene of the alleged crime;
2. Interposing a stimulus to a known response, as [when the accused set his alarm clock to meet the victim at a certain time and location, etc.];
3. Attempting to remove potentially aversive stimuli, as [when the accused was caught at the site of the killing attempting to eliminate incriminating evidence, etc.];
4. Recounting the alleged crime to others [specify], which at least suggests image recall;
5. Verbally responding or exhibiting behaviors to others, suggesting he knew his acts were wrong.

[If relevant volitional events operative.] The volitional capacity of the accused to conform his conduct to the requirements of the law may have been adversely affected by the following events:

[Specify those that apply.]

1. All specified cognitive conditions; as that which adversely influences cognition also affects volition [specify];
2. Ingestion of the following substances: [specify];

3. Cumulative stress and other affective experiences operative up to [several months/1 year, etc.] before the instant offense and manifested by [specify and describe];
4. Momentary stress at the time of the crime associated with [victim provocation, describe/social demand traits of the alleged crime, describe];
5. Certain rare organic conditions [e.g., tumor in limbic system/RAS] acting on self-control abilities.

[If relevant events operative.] Events suggesting volitional capacity include the following:

[Specify those that apply.]

1. Changing availability of a stimulus, as when the accused [gave his friend a firearm to keep in his apartment only to retrieve it prior to the alleged crime, etc.];
2. Doing something else, as when one tightens all muscles to avoid a flinch response. For the accused, the similarity is [refusal to respond to police questions after apprehension, etc.];
3. Statements or behaviors by the accused suggesting self-control, as when the accused [stated he "pushed" the gun to the floor before firing to avoid hitting the victim, etc.];
4. Deprivation, as when the accused remained free of intoxicants and socially isolated himself prior to the alleged crime [demonstrate deprivation linked to choice and not other conditions].

Conclusions

[Address all.]

1. In my opinion, the accused is [competent/not competent] to proceed legally. He [has/does not have] an appropriate knowledge of the nature and quality of the legal proceedings, and [is/is not] aware of the possible outcomes and consequences to himself. On the [Competency Screening Test/Competency Assessment Instrument], the accused scored in a range suggestive of [competency/incompetency] to proceed.
2. Concerning the unpremeditated murder charge, it is my opinion that the defendant [did/did not] lack substantial capacity to appreciate the wrongfulness [criminality] of his acts. Concerning the same charge, it is my opinion that the defendant [did/did not] lack substantial capacity to conform his conduct to the requirements of the law.

[For diminished capacity.]

1. Concerning the unpremeditated murder charge, it is my opinion that the accused suffered an impairment in his ability to appreciate the wrongfulness of his acts, corresponding to the highest levels of cognitive intent for this charge. This is based on the simultaneous operation of [specify].
2. Concerning the same charge, it is my opinion that the accused suffered an impairment in his ability to conform his conduct to the requirements of the law, corresponding to the highest level of cognitive control. This is based on the simultaneous operation of [specify].

[For additional charges not linked to an adequate database.]

Concerning the robbery charge, no comments can be proffered regarding mental capacity as those charges are not anchored to an adequate database. That is, the charges [relate to isolated episodes presented long after the alleged acts/were corroborated in most cases by single accusers of doubtful credibility, etc.].

[If applicable, moreover, the accused does not recall his state of mind on the specified dates; therefore, no linkage of the alleged crime to state of mind can be examined].

Thank you for this interesting referral.

        Sincerely,

        [Name]
        [List Specialization] Clinical and Forensic Psychologist
        [License/Certification Status] Certified, State of Hawaii
        [Diplomate Status] Diplomate, ABPP, ABFP

Appendix D

Self-Control Analysis:
A Case Illustration

Re: *State of Hawaii v. Thomas Nakano*
     Criminal Number 12345
     SSN: 123-44-5678

Dear Ms. _____:

This is the report of the clinical/forensic psychologist requested by your agency to conduct a behavioral analysis of instant offense–related behaviors relevant to the defendant in this case, Thomas Nakano, POB Waipahu, Hawaii, DOB January 19, 1957, SSN 123-44-5678, Criminal Number 12345, who is currently on bail status awaiting trial scheduled for May 23, 1987 in the First Circuit Court of Hawaii.

Forensic Database

The nature of the behavioral analysis consisted of clinical interviewing of multiple witnesses, significant/knowledgeable others, review of relevant case materials, and inspection of the alleged crime scene and route.

The Instant Offense and Related Sequelae: Description and Severity of Impact

Alleged facts of the instant offense, including summarized events, have been presented in forensic database sources presented earlier. Briefly, on June 16, 1986 at around 2 a.m. at the Waikiki East Apartment, the accused is alleged to have killed the victim, Edward Kato, by inflicting a single shotgun blast to the left chest area. At about 8 p.m. the previous night, after working at his job as a mechanic, Mr. Nakano had driven the victim and a mutual acquaintance to Mr. Kato's apartment. There, they allegedly consumed about four beers and two "rainbows" (Tuinals) each, and shared a marijuana cigarette. The accused appeared to engage in a verbal disagreement with the victim, arguing possibly about work, drugs, and/or a female known to both of them, an Arlene Gordon, who was due to move into the victim's home the next day. The victim and the accused's disagreement progressed into a physical altercation outside the apartment, with the victim apparently the loser, ending up with minor facial injuries and possibly losing the keys to his vehicle. Irate, agitated, shouting death threats, and stating that he would return, the accused possibly went to this van and obtained a Hawaiian sling, a bayonet, and a stick and headed back toward the victim's apartment.

En route, he was intercepted by a neighbor of the victim, who, forewarned of the earlier fight and later behaviors, was armed with a baseball bat. The accused was disarmed and was accompanied to the victim's apartment, where further argument broke out between Mr. Kato and the accused. The accused left the apartment area to call a friend for assistance. His friend came and the defendant was driven home, where he ingested both beer and marijuana, and obtained several more weapons, to include an axe and a single-shot shotgun with four cartridges. He then had his friend drive him back toward the victim's home. En route, the vehicle stopped and the accused got out and fired his rifle. After discharging it into the air and toward the ocean, he returned to the jeep and was driven to a small part adjoining the neighborhood complex of the victim. He left on foot with his weapons and walked to the vicinity of the victim's apartment until the latter's return from a disco/bar. They entered the victim's apartment together, engaged in an argument, and were told by the victim's roommate to quiet down in order for the latter to get to sleep. The argument continued in a subdued fashion, with the accused terminating the interaction by asking the victim if he could bring his girlfriend into the apartment. He left, obtained his shotgun, returned to the apartment and allegedly shot the victim immediately and without conversation. He was attacked by the roommate after the latter apparently believed he was to be the next victim. The accused's firearm was pulled away from him and he fled the apartment, and returned to the jeep. He was driven to the vicinity of his mother's residence. The accused was arrested several hours later in a vehicle driven by his mother, heading toward the airport area.

The various examiners, although differing in their conclusions in regard to criminal responsibility or whether the accused suffered from a psychosis at the time of the alleged shooting, present data that at the time of the alleged shooting the accused may have been suffering from substance intoxication and possibly an organic brain syndrome, superimposed upon a borderline personality disorder.

An analysis of instant offense events suggests the following may have occurred:

1. Violence toward another is suggested, as opposed to violence to property or self. The violence toward property that may have occurred seemed incidental to violence toward another party.
2. Threatened and attempted violence may have been exhibited to multiple persons at multiple sites. Alleged victims were either in an acquaintance relationship with the accused or were previously known to him. Stranger violence was not suggested.
3. Lethal violence was exhibited, involving the use of a firearm and multiple other weapons; the weapons may have been owned by the accused and involved no recent purchases;
4. Normal inhibitory factors, such as the presence of witnesses or the alleged unwillingness of the victim to resume fighting, did not seem to prevent later alleged violence.
5. Violence may have been related to substance intoxication and/or other assumed mental/behavioral disorders. The key question is to what degree mental capacity was affected by substance intoxication, alone or in combination with other psychological conditions and cumulative/momentary stress.

Relevant History of the Accused

The background of the defendant has been presented in part by others and will not be repeated here. Instead, a few observations regarding the connection between antisocial behavior and mental/psychological conditions are in order.

1. The developmental history of the accused appeared chaotic and psychologically unstable. He may have been born out of wedlock (see April 3, 1975 Honolulu Mental Health Clinic note) and was the oldest of four children, all of whom, except one brother, are half-siblings. The father left the family when the accused was 2 years old and he was raised by his grandmother, whom he reportedly described as strict and who treated him like a "baby." His mother appeared unstable,

worked as a waitress, and was married five times. The defendant reported that he did not feel loved by his mother during his early years.

School grades and test scores were uneven over the years, reflecting upheaval and stress but also an ability to do well academically and to conform appropriately. Entries in the school records during the development period showed at times that he "emotionally and socially seems to feel insecure — very aggressive" (March 5, 1963), was seen as "emotionally insecure" (February 1, 1964) "... car[e]less" but with an improvement in friendliness (November 1965), and needing "encouragement to do well" (April 1966). Other school notes reported good deportment. He graduated from Washington High School in June 1975 in the bottom quartile of his class. The latest year of academic testing revealed uneven performance, with STEP scores for science = 22 (percentile), social studies = 57, and listening = 9 (Fall, 1973). Standardized testing during Spring 1974 revealed average or better scores in quantitative, math, and writing areas, with below-average scores in verbal and reading areas. Emotional problems may have contributed to the uneven performance as the accused performed differently in similar areas over time. The accused was described as always needing to be in control of others, which did not prevent peer bonding during those years.

In general, antisocial behavior during the developmental period is minimal in quantity, except for alleged drug buying (especially marijuana and hashish) during the last several years of high school. An interest in weapons emerged, with at least one incident involving the accidental discharge of a shotgun. An increasingly close relationship with and protectiveness toward his mother was also observed during the high school years.

2. The first few years of the young adult period were characterized by attempts to develop a stable identity and to maintain control over himself and others. He became a Jehovah's Witness for several months. He may have spent about half a year in the Marine Corps, with the defendant claiming to have left because he was a conscientious objector. He returned to polysubstance abuse as part of his young adult lifestyle. Several drug-related treatments were experienced during the period from 1974 to 1977, to include admission to Kaiser Medical Center in May 1974 and King's Medical Center and the State Hospital in March 1978. He received outpatient treatment at the Honolulu Mental Health Clinic (April to November 1975; February to July 1977), Drug Addiction Services of Hawaii (admitted June 5, 1975), and the Downtown Drug Clinic (dates unknown) following inpatient treatment earlier during those years.

The May 1974 Kaiser Medical Center admission was precipitated by a feeling that his mind was leaving his body, fear of loss of control, impulses to hurt himself or someone else, and other symptoms, followed by intense abuse of psychedelic drugs, such as LSD, MDA, and mescaline. A note here is that, as the effect of the drugs wore off, his delusions and agitation increased, suggesting unresolved psychological conflicts with the function of substances to self-medicate and to escape pain (as substance abuse in post-traumatic stress disorders often operate to reduce symptoms) rather than simply to get high or to enjoy the euphoric effects. This suggestion is reinforced by witnesses observing the accused in recent years typically starting off the day with a beer and a marijuana cigarette.

The March 1978 State Hospital admission was precipitated by making out a will after planning to kill himself, followed by kicking out the windows of the police vehicle that was called to the scene. The accused had been smoking heavily and orally ingesting THC for several weeks prior to his admission. This was followed by his boss's accusation that he was stealing from his employer's account.

In general, evidence of antisocial behavior here is minimal, with the accused suffering several mental breakdowns associated with substance abuse.

3. From about 22 years of age, the period of psychiatric upheaval is somewhat subdued, with the accused holding different jobs, such as a manager for a bakery, then as a ramp agent for King Kamehameha Air Service, and then a succession of mechanic jobs. The substance abuse continued, as suggested by a February 8, 1977 arrest for Driving without a License (see police report R-12567) and Possession of Controlled Substance. Marijuana vegetation was also found within his vehicle.

A March 15, 1978 arrest again involved Driving without a License and having marijuana within his vehicle (see police report B-23125). While testifying in regard to a murder trial, the accused admitted that he bought and consumed a quantity of Quaaludes on June 16, 1980. During 1981, he was reportedly involved in buying, selling, and using cocaine. His roommate at the time reported that the defendant once held a shotgun to the roommate's head after accusing him of stealing an ounce of cocaine from him. The roommate ran from the residence after allegedly being threatened repeatedly during the incident and obtained a police escort subsequently to retrieve his possessions.

The substance-abusing lifestyle continued after the instant offense, to include arrests for selling marijuana to an undercover officer (August 1986) and possession of four packets of marijuana in his vehicle (December 1986). An amber-colored vial of cocaine residue was found in the front pocket of his shorts during the last arrest.

In general, antisocial behavior during this last period appeared to have increased, with the accused firmly entrenched in a drug-oriented lifestyle. Rehabilitation efforts to control or eliminate substance abuse and other psychopathological behavior were not successful.

Assessment of Self-Determination for Instant Offense(s) Behaviors

An assessment of mental capacity can be sequentially presented for the temporal flow of the instant offense(s). This will be in terms of events that suggest cognitive and volitional impairments and abilities before, during, and after the instant offenses.

1. Previous to the alleged shooting (several weeks before): In general, witnesses and other data sources suggest a deterioration in behavioral functioning on Mr. Nakano's part prior to the commission of the alleged offenses. Impairments were noted even though he worked at his job as a mechanic, associated with friends and family, continued to maintain his household with renters, and involved himself in other activities.

Several weeks prior to the instant offense, the accused was allegedly abusing methadrine, a stimulant drug, which made him paranoid, hypersensitive, jumpy, and irritable. His renters during these last 2 weeks corroborated the deterioration in behavior at home. They described the accused locking his door even to go to the bathroom, becoming irritated for no ostensible reason, and refusing to talk even when socially appropriate. Other alleged stresses during this time were reported by the various evaluators to include quitting a job as head mechanic to work for another company and reconciling with his girlfriend who had been beaten by her new boyfriend.

2. Previous to the alleged shooting (at the victim's apartment; approximately 10:30 p.m. to 12:30 or 1:30 a.m.): For most of the above time span, the defendant was able to socialize appropriately with co-workers and friends after completing a day's work as a mechanic. Toward the end of this time, some kind of a physical altercation occurred with the victim, the alleged perpetrator having emerged the loser, sustaining minor facial injuries and possibly losing his car keys in the process. Mr. Nakano then became socially inappropriate, verbally loud, agitated, and seemingly indifferent to whether or not witnesses heard multiple threats to return and kill the victim (as reported by several witnesses). His aggression continued after the victim stated he did not want to continue fighting. The victim was overheard by one of the witnesses as saying, "no like fight," or words to that effect. The accused apparently allowed himself to be disarmed after leaving and then returned shortly to the area of the victim's apartment. He went to the victim's apartment, where he engaged in further threats and angry words. Later, at a nearby telephone booth, he continued in his agitation, apparently had difficulty dialing the telephone, dropped coins, and was almost incomprehensible in speech. He allegedly said, "This is what rainbows does to you," or words to that effect. He generalized his anger to the telephone booth, banging on the telephone and yelling, and to persons who offered to help ("If you say one word, I'm going to shoot you, fuck up," and "Leave me alone if you know what's good for you," or words to that effect; other witnesses reported inappropriate behavior at that time, to include a challenge to fight). He was seen to be unsteady on his feet. In general, the limitations and impairments cited above

may have occurred because of the combined effects of substance ingestion (about four beers, several tranquilizers, and possibly a marijuana cigarette), anger, and possibly other factors. The defendant became almost disorganized in speech and nonfunctional in adaptive and motor behavior, and with a pronounced tendency to generalize and displace aggression to other persons and objects in the environment.

Premorbid personality traits may also have contributed to impairments. Abilities demonstrated after the altercation with the victim included:

a. Flexibility of response, as when the defendant attempted to return to the victim's apartment after obtaining and carrying multiple weapons, including a (cocked) Hawaiian sling, a bayonet, and a stick;

b. Long-term recall, as when the accused threatened the intercepting party that the latter would not be going to Maui because the accused was going to kill him; this also shows the displacement tendency of the accused's anger, as discussed above;

c. Intermediate-term recall, as shown by his awareness and knowledge of recently occurring events within the previous hour (e.g., the fight with the victim, the ability to locate the victim's apartment after he left, the memory that he had called for assistance indicated by placing a second call to King's house and asking if help was on its way);

d. Short-term recall, as shown by the ability to respond to what persons were saying a few moments previously, even though the answer may have been aggressive or distancing in nature; short-term recall was also shown by the ability to dial a sequence of telephone numbers; and

e. The ability to influence others, as when the accused on the telephone interacted with and successfully convinced a party to retrieve him from the vicinity of the accused's neighborhood and to take him home.

3. Previous to the alleged shooting (the period of time from leaving until returning to the neighborhood of the victim; between 12:30 or 1:30 a.m. and about 3:30 a.m.): Mr. King, as he related in his statement, picked up Mr. Nakano from the vicinity of the Waikiki East Apartments. He noticed the defendant was hard to understand and slurred his speech, had glassy eyes, smelled a little of alcohol, and was nonresponsive to questions but, when he answered, would perseverate (e.g., the theme that nobody takes advantage of him "like that"). Motor agitation was pronounced, with the accused "shaking up and down," "wobbling all over." Suspiciousness and generalization of anger were evident toward the two local persons and one other who had all allegedly taken his keys and hid them from him. He affirmed taking substances earlier (i.e., "Brah, brah, I took the fucking downers...." "Rainbows, brah, rainbows," or words to that effect). He buried his shirt in a loud and somewhat strange fashion at a service station, indifferent to the appearance he created by emptying trash out of the dumpster and then covering his shirt.

This period of time may have been the most delimiting for the accused from a behavioral point of view and was possibly due to the combined effects of premorbid personality factors, ingested substances, and high emotion caused by the previous interpersonal friction.

He continued to show emotional behavior upon arrival at his house, pounding on the front door and then yelling at the renter to open up. He ingested more substances, including a beer and a marijuana cigarette.

Generalization of the anger was seen, the target of aggression expanding to a small group (e.g., "They like war, they get war," or words to that effect) with lack of insight regarding his own mental condition (e.g., "I'm okay," "I stay sober," or words to that effect). Anger was shown toward the victim and two others for the remainder of the time at the house, and for the trip from the house to the victim's neighborhood. Motor agitation appeared to be reduced toward the middle and end stages of this time period.

Capacities shown by the accused during this period of time included (a) the ability to recognize and signal his friend who picked him up near the telephone booth; (b) the ability to direct others (e.g., going into the service station), count money, and to twice engage in man–machine interface (i.e., to obtain cigarettes), once after the correct amount but incorrect type of coinage was used. This shows gross motor sequencing and memory skills, to include long-term recall (i.e., remembering his brand) and short-term recall (counting money), in addition to modulating successfully his behavior upon negative feedback; (c) the ability to signal for assistance at his house and to display the intermediate-term memory required to let the party know he had lost his means of ingress; (d) at his house, displaying the ability to interact with another party with continuation of intermediate-term memory necessary to relate events concerning the earlier altercation to Mr. King correctly, even if he may have been suspicious of the motivations of the previous actors; (e) at his house, the ability to engage in both fine-motor, short-term sequencing, and long-term recall skills simultaneously, as required when he opened the combination safe in his living room; (f) at the house, displaying the choice to engage in further substance ingestion, drinking a beer, and directing his friend to roll a marijuana cigarette, which the accused subsequently smoked; (g) at the house, the ability to later recall long-term events (e.g., owing his friend money) and the counting skills necessary to parcel out money to pay him back, which he did; (h) the gross motor skills necessary to ambulate and obtain and hold a rifle and later an axe. The carrying of multiple weapons showed further flexibility of method in terms of multiple means of opportunity to aggress; (i) at the house, showing the ability to tell time and to delay gratification of aggression for a period of time until the victim was available, as when the accused was "dillydallying" around the house after obtaining the firearm in question, looking at the clock often, and then, when 3 a.m. came (a short while before "last call" at the disco/bar at which the victim was present), looking at the clock once more and stating, "Oh, we gotta leave," or words to that effect; (j) the ability to state intentions of future behaviors when he stated, "I going get revenge," "I going get those guys," or words to that effect, referring to the parties involved in the earlier altercation; (k) the self-control ability shown by the defendant when he handed his friend the shotgun ("He grabbed the hatchet," "He gave me the gun to pick up the axe," or words to that effect), after telling the friend, "You're the only one can take me there," or words to that effect, previous to ordering the friend out of the house to (first) transport him to the scene of the alleged crime ("He made me walk out first," or words to that effect)*; (1) en route to the neighborhood of the victim, the ability to direct the driver to the specific point (e.g., "Take me to Waikiki East Apartments," or words to that effect) and to modify the usual route to that area from the house of the accused (e.g., "he wanted me to go down to the sewage way"); (m) en route to the neighborhood of the victim, showing vigilant responses by turning around to see if they were being followed; (n) the ability to progress beyond stating intentions to sequences of intended acts (e.g., "I'm going to get the haole first, man" [later] "I don't know where the haole live, but I going to check out Edward first," "I going to be right back," or words to that effect, when parked in the vicinity of the victim's apartment; (o) the continued ability not only to interact with the driver but to control and intimidate him by implied force for noncompliance (e.g., "I know people who squeal and fuck it, I can blow them away," also alluding to relationships with "mafia," "hit man," and people on the mainland, "You better wait right here," or words to that effect), when parked in the vicinity of the victim's apartment; (p) the behavioral ability to rehearse the operation by discharging the firearm prior to entering the neighborhood of the victim and far enough away not to be heard by residents of that area; (q) the attempt to remove and prevent potentially incriminating evidence previous to the alleged shooting, as possibly represented by wiping the

---

* Hall (1985) stated the following in this regard: "Consider changing the availability of a stimulus, as when the accused gives a friend a firearm to hold prior to the commission of a crime. Paradoxically, this may be seen as indicating that loss of self-control is feared when it is in fact operating. The element of choice becomes obvious when the accused retrieves the firearm some time before committing the instant offense" (p. 13).

barrel portion of his firearm with dark or black socks or rags in an up and down motion (the socks or rags were over each hand, with the accused dressed completely in black) and by carrying the rifle around by the barrel with a rag; (r) the ability to locate and retrieve his axe from the back of the jeep; and (s) the directional ability to find the victim's apartment area from the jeep.

4. Several minutes before the alleged shooting, acts during the instant offense, and subsequent immediate behaviors (sometime between 3:30 and 4:15 a.m.): The accused, upon leaving the jeep, was apparently still angry at the victim and the two others, and still very likely was under the influence of multiple intoxicants as described. He may have met with the victim after the latter got out of the taxicab, went up to the room with him, engaged in further argumentation, left for a few moments, returned, and shot the victim. During the struggle with roommate Anthony Kalua, who supplied most of the information in this section, the defendant may have inappropriately yelled for help and lost a slipper. During this period of time, arousal had turned generally from initial agitation to aggressive determination and then to a basic fight-or-flight response. Again, there was an apparent inability to confine the aggression to a single target. This assumes that the accused was not deliberately attempting to get rid of witnesses to the alleged crime (see below).

Abilities during this period included the following: (a) the ability to delay gratification: The accused may have been waiting for the victim after the accused left the jeep and walked to the victim's neighborhood complex (e.g., the victim stated to the cab driver, "That's the guy I was fighting with," or words to that effect); (b) the ability to interact with others and to modulate his verbal behavior just prior to the instant offense, as shown by both the victim and the accused lowering their voices when requested by the roommate at the victim's apartment; (c) the ability seemingly to prevaricate when the accused stated he was going to get his girlfriend and return, instead returning to the room with a shotgun and an axe; (d) the intermediate-term memory ability to relocate his weapons, ambulate back to the apartment, and then allegedly take deliberate aim from a shoulder position, hitting the victim in the chest area; (e) the intermediate-term auditory recall ability represented by telling the roommate, "Now tell me to be quiet," or words to that effect; (f) the ability to initiate another sequence of motor behaviors based upon memory and practice, represented by pointing the shotgun at the roommate, unsnapping the barrel, and attempting to load it before the sequence was interrupted by the roommate wresting the weapon from the accused; (g) the accused's ability to fight off his assailant and to flee the scene of the instant offenses successfully and to elude pursuit by dodging, running, and hiding behaviors (per Smith: "He was running like he was doing a sprint; he looked better than when he was walking earlier;" per Kama: "He was fast, no trouble running," or words to that effect).

5. After the alleged shooting until arrest (approximately 4:15 to 8 a.m.): The accused allegedly returned to the area of the jeep and left the neighborhood of the instant offense. At this point, he was in pain caused by a possible dislocated shoulder suffered during the fight with the roommate.

He was dropped off near his mother's residence and was described by her as being in "bad shape," with his speech difficult to understand. He was difficult to arouse when he went to sleep a short time later. He then asked for a ride to the airport area. En route, he was arrested. He was found with two bullets in his pocket, thus failing to get rid of incriminating evidence. Impairments during this period of time are most likely related to a combination of premorbid factors, physical pain, fear generated by the flight response, the effect of multiple intoxicants, and exhaustion caused by the expenditure of a large amount of energy over the previous few hours.

Abilities during this period included: (a) the ability to relocate the jeep and to once again focally direct the driver (e.g., "Get the fuck out of here, man," "... to the highway," or words to that effect); (b) ability to feel pain, rendering less likely a condition of gross alcohol or drug intoxication where pain signals are partially or completely anesthetized; (c) attempting to avoid aversive stimuli, represented by telling the driver to look straight ahead and to drive slowly as a police car passed them en route to the crime scene; (d) awareness of correct intended direction, as represented by the accused's cursing at his friend when a wrong turn was made (i.e., "Where in the fuck are you going?" or words to that effect); (e) intermediate-term recall of events when responding to his friends' inquiries in regard to what had transpired (to King: "Do you think he's dead?" "history," "I got 'um brah, no worry," or words to that effect); (f) ability to change plans when his friend balked at returning him home; (g) ability to find and ambulate to his mother's residence after being dropped off; (h) awareness and recall that he had done wrong, as represented by telling his mother that he was in trouble and later requesting transportation to the airport area.

Conclusions

1. The database is sufficient to draw some relevant conclusions with a reasonable degree of psychological certainty. Data from other examiners were considered, but all conclusions rendered were derived independently of other psychological/medical examiners who are involved in this case.

2. Database sources were assessed for suggestions of deliberate and nondeliberate distortion. Conclusions rendered are considered an accurate representation of events, taking into account report and witness limitations and competencies, the possible psychological disorder, and substance abuse tendencies of the defendant, biases of input sources, and other factors.

3a. No evidence emerged that the accused has a major psychiatric disorder in that (1) no bizarre behaviors emerged at the time of the alleged crimes; (2) general level of anxiety (not anger) was not significant, except for the period after the alleged shooting; (3) there was not amnesia for alleged events; (4) delusions of a psychotic quality were not operative, even though the accused may have questioned the motives of the victim and relevant others; (5) there were no hallucinations; (6) depression, not the result of substance abuse, was not present; (7) there was no elevated or expansive mood at the time of the alleged crime; (8) the accused was understandable by the victim and others even though, at times, there was an impairment of speech, especially when the accused was emotionally aroused; (9) there was a strong to extreme expression of emotion, primarily anger, during the commission of the alleged crime, but this was appropriate to and congruous with the situation, and not psychotically incongruous. In general, there was no evidence of a formal thought disorder or major psychiatric disorder previous to or at the time of the alleged offense, with all former mental conditions and treatments being associated with substance abuse.

3b. Evidence emerged of polysubstance intoxication at the time of the alleged offense(s) as evidenced by (1) ingestion of alcohol and different psychotropic substances prior to the alleged shooting; (2) maladaptive behavior such as the hyperaggressivity and assaultiveness; (3) other relevant symptoms, to include slurring of speech, impaired judgment, partial incoordination, mood changes, irritability, psychomotor agitation, and limited insight; (4) confirmatory evidence in the form of chemical test results; and (5) the above symptoms not due to any other mental disorder.

3c. Because of the absence of "a" and the voluntary nature of the substance ingestion in "b," the accused does not meet the American Law Institute (ALI) standard for the insanity defense in this jurisdiction.

4. The accused did not lose cognitive control over his behaviors in that he did not lack the ability to appreciate the criminality of his behavior. He appeared aware of transpiring events. Further, he appeared to engage in planning for the alleged shooting, which involved the use of multiple weapons, delays in timetables, movement over distances using several modes of transportation, waiting for the victim, prevaricating to the victim, successfully fleeing the scene of the alleged crime, having backup transportation to take him out of the area, and other factors.

5. The accused was not substantially impaired in his ability to conform his behavior to the requirements of the law. He was able substantially to change, monitor, modulate, and otherwise control not only his behavior, but the behavior of others, as discussed previously. There was a definite behavioral focus and goal orientation in regard to the alleged crime. A behavioral rehearsal of the eventual firing of the homicide weapon was apparent. The level of activity required for the alleged crimes was considerable, requiring a concerted effort on the part of the accused to con-

summate the acts, as discussed above. In general, the accused's impairment in self-control over criminal behavior was at most mild to moderate for the above-stated reasons but not substantial, meaning that the accused had the ability to refrain from the alleged shooting, although the chain of maladaptive behaviors may have been set off in an initially impulsive fashion.

Sincerely,

Appendix E

Interactional Report: A Case Illustration

Re: *State of Hawaii v. Anthony Barnes*
Criminal Number 12-5555
Count I: Attempted Murder
Count II: Assault in the First Degree

Dear Ms. _____:

This is the report of the forensic psychologist requested by your office to examine and report upon the instant case in regard to defendant–victim interaction and related behavior. A primary issue to be addressed in this report is to what extent self-control of the accused was adversely affected by extreme emotion at the time of the alleged offenses. A related issue is to what degree behavioral self-regulation was exhibited during the instant offenses, irrespective of operative emotion, stress, or other arousal factors.

A secondary issue concerns the credibility and mental condition of the victim.

The defendant, Anthony Barnes, DOB February 16, 1953, POB Waipahu, Hawaii, SSN 555-88-9876, is at present in pretrial detainment at the Hawaii Community Correctional Center (HCCC). The victim of the alleged attempted murder and assault is Carole Gordon, DOB October 18, 1962, POB Los Angeles, California, SSN 234-99-8778. The date of the alleged crimes was August 29, 1986, with the incident occurring at the Seaview Lounge on Montgomery Street in Honolulu.

The following analysis sequentially focuses on (1) the forensic database used in terms of perpetrator, victim, and contextual stimuli; (2) an analysis of evaluation validity and victim/witness distortion; the mental condition of the victim is addressed here; (3) an analysis of emotional and self-control aspects of alleged crime behavior in terms of time flow; and (4) conclusions in regard to behavioral self-determination and emotion at the time of the alleged offenses.

FORENSIC DATABASE

Relevant to the alleged perpetrator, the following materials were reviewed and/or individuals interviewed:

1. Central Medical Center records of hospitalization (August 29 to September 17, 1986);
2. Kamehameha Hospital records (September 3 to 5, 1986);

3. Records from T.E. Chang, M.D. (April 2, 1985 to April 10, 1986);
4. Records from the Williams Clinic, Inc., Kailua (May 24, 1984 to September 6, 1985);
5. Mililani Clinic and Hospital records of neurology examination; also containing a history of significant events, handwritten by the accused (September 18, 1986; September 29, 1986);
6. A letter from the Office of the Prosecuting Attorney to HCCC Intake Service Center recommending high bail status (Wayne S. Song, dated September 30, 1986);
7. Preliminary hearing transcript (October 9, 1986);
8. Honolulu Police Department incident reports (K-11111 dated August 30, 1986; S-23232 dated December 10, 1986; P-38889 dated June 9, 1986; R-09876 dated June 12, 1986);
9. Ex-parte petition for temporary restraining order for protection (FC-M, No. 86-0005 of July 30, 1986 for victim; FC-M No. 10029 of May 25, 1984 for wife, Tamara C. Barnes);
10. Letters and drawings by the defendant while at HCCC to the victim (all in 1986: September 6, September 29, October 5, October 15, November 19, November 28, December 8, December 16, December 18);
11. Pretrial Bail Report by Samuel Kane of the Intake Service Center, HCCC (dated September 16, 1986);
12. A letter from the victim's current boyfriend to the defendant (dated November 6, 1986);
13. An interview of Samuel Taft, witness at the crime scene (April 13, 1987, by telephone);
14. An interview of Kevin Nielson, DOB February 5, 1952, witness and worker at the crime scene and acquaintance of the victim (April 17, 1987, by telephone);
15. An interview of Marcus Nishikawa, investigation officer of the instant offense (April 18, 1987, by telephone);
16. An interview of Keith D. Conley, DOB May 25, 1961, acquaintance of the accused and victim, and a witness to the instant offenses (April 18, 1987; April 19, 1987 & April 22, 1987, by telephone);
17. Victim Assistance Program records in relationship to accused-victim interaction; also in regard to Tamara Barnes, the defendant's wife. Interview of Mary Jordan, victim assistance advocate (April 23, 1987);
18. An interview of Dennis King, Ph.D., treating psychologist at HCCC (April 24, 1987, twice by telephone);
19. An interview of Monica Johnson, M.S.W., former director of The Safe House (April 25, 1987, by telephone);
20. An interview of George Kam, employee at Hawaiian Photos, Waialae (April 27, 1987, by telephone);
21. An interview of Susan Fountaine, former employee of the Sky Lounge (April 27, 1987, by telephone);
22. An audiovisual film of the accused and others relating to the issue of family violence ("Abuse in the Family," a four-part series prepared for local television, dated February 2, 1983);
23. HCCC medical and dormitory adjustment records of the accused;
24. An undated letter from the victim to the accused;
25. Honolulu Police Department (HPD) investigation reports of the instant offenses;
26. State of Hawaii educational records reflecting the accused's academic progress, standardized test scores, and behavioral observations;
27. Employment application forms for several previous jobs;
28. U.S. Navy personnel records for the accused for the period from May 30, 1972 to October 7, 1975;
29. Clinical neuropsychological report of Michael Parker, Ph.D. (August 15, 1986); also, test protocols and notes for second examination (February 2, 1987);
30. James Potter, Ph.D., Director of Psychology Workshops (April 23, 1987);

The undersigned's request to examine the defendant psychologically was denied by the defense attorney.

Relevant to the victim, the following materials were reviewed and/or individuals interviewed:

31. See Nos. 2, 3, 5, 6, 7, 8, 9, 10, 11, 12, 13, 14, 15, 16, 17, 18, 21, 24, and 25;
32. Nimitz Medical Center (NMC) records reflecting July 23, 1986 to August 9, 1986 hospitalization of the victim at that facility. NMC outpatient clinic file contained some entries in regard to earlier medical intervention;
33. Certificate of Live Birth of Carol Susan Carter, the victim, from Pennsylvania State Department of Health (certified as a true copy, March 30, 1980);
34. Decree of divorce regarding Mark T. and Carol S. Thompson, (October 30, 1985, Case No. 85-P-999, District Court of King County, Montana);
35. Parkins Medical Center records reflecting August 1 to 9, 1986 hospitalization at that facility;
36. Interview of Paul O. Lowrey, DOB May 29, 1964, who assisted the victim after the alleged stabbing (April 25, 1987);
37. Clinical interviews of the victim (May 10, 19, and 28, June 2, 1987);
38. Bipolar Psychological Inventory (BPI) Lie Scale (administered twice: May 28, 1987, June 2, 1987);
39. Sacks Sentence Completion Test (administered May 28, 1987);
40. Marital Pre-counseling Inventory for the relationship with her current boyfriend (Stuart, R.B. 1973) (administered May 28, 1987;) Marital Pre-counseling Inventory reconstructed for the time of the victim's relationship with the accused (administered June 2, 1987);
41. Fundamental Interpersonal Relationships [with] Others — Behavior (FIRO-B; administered June 2, 1987);
42. Bender-Gestalt Visual–Motor Test (BGVMT, with recall and Koppitz system scoring; administered June 2, 1987);
43. Minnesota Multiphasic Personality Inventory (MMPI) Critical Items List (administered twice: May 28, 1987 and June 2, 1987); MMPI, Form R (June 2, 1987);
44. Slosson Intelligence Test (SIT) for Children and Adults (administered May 28, 1987);
45. Booklet Categories Test (administered May 28, 1987);
46. Wechsler Adult Intelligence Scale–Revised (WAIS-R, administered June 2, 1987);
47. Tactual Performance Test (administered June 2, 1987);
48. Seashore Rhythm Test (administered June 2, 1987);
49. Speech-sounds Perception Test (administered June 2, 1987);
50. Finger Oscillation Test (administered June 2, 1987);
51. Wechsler Memory Test, Form I (administered June 2, 1987);
52. Trail Making Test, A and B (administered June 2, 1987);
53. Reitan–Klove Sensory Perceptual Exam (administered June 2, 1987);
54. Reitan–Indiana Aphasia Screening Test (administered June 2, 1987);
55. Consultation with Robert King, Ph.D., Head, Neuropsychological Department, Hawaii State Hospital (June 9, 1987);
56. Consultation with Ronald Miyake, M.D., neurologist, Central Clinic (June 10, 1987);
57. Writing tasks to include (a) year-by-year presentation of most significant events, from birth to present and (b) list of physical symptoms attributed to the instant offenses;
58. Consultation with David Smith, Ph.D., neuropsychologist (June 10, 1987).

Relevant to the context of the crime, the following records were reviewed or procedures implemented:

59. See Nos. 14, 15, 16, 18, 21, and 25;

60. Physical examination of the crime scene and escape route (May 29, 1987);
61. Examination of photographs of the victim (March 23, 1987). Diagrams and photos of the crime scene were also examined (March 27, 1987 and April 26, 1987).

ASSESSMENT BEHAVIOR AND DATABASE VALIDITY

The victim was cooperative and of attractive appearance. This white, female, 24-year-old vocational school student exhibited a logical and coherent stream of thought. Affect was appropriate, with some emotional behaviors such as muscle twitches and eye reddening when discussing the present incident. A trend toward fear of the accused was observed. Orientation was apparent for time, place, person, and circumstance. Memory for immediate, short-term, and long-term events was intact, as evidenced by performance on passages of words and sequences of numbers on standardized testing, and by accurate responses to inquiries by the examiner regarding prior evaluation events. Episodic long-term memory involved recollection of independently verified historical events without a tendency to confabulate. Judgment was marginal, as shown by history and by some test responses. Abstraction ability was appropriate. Reading and writing skills seem normally developed but were low average in quality. Computationally, she had no difficulty counting backward from 20 or with basic adding, subtracting, and multiplication of math problems. Fund of information and vocabulary skills were marginal, possibly reflecting her eighth-grade education and some cultural–familial factors. Overall, her intelligence was measured as average on a screening test (SIT) and low average on a comprehensive intelligence test (WAIS-R). Overall verbal abilities were low average and performance abilities were average.

Distortion analysis of the victim's evaluation responses revealed, for the time of the interview, an attempt to present herself in an accurate manner. This is based on (1) goodness of fit between test profile and clinical behavior, (2) performance on scales or test procedures specifically designed to assess attempts at misrepresentation, (3) little or no discrepancy between responses and established events, and (4) consistent performance on repeated measures. Distortion analysis for the time of the instant offenses revealed an attempt to present herself in an accurate manner, but was mitigated by loss of recall after the initial knife thrusts, shock effects of the stabbing, and subsequent post-traumatic stress disorder (discussed later). Further, she reported drinking several alcoholic beverages on the night of the instant offenses and affirmed cocaine ingestion on the previous evening (August 28, 1986).

The mental conditions of the victim at the time of the evaluation are as follows.

Axis I: Post-Traumatic Stress Disorder (PTSD), Acute (DSM-IV Code 309.81)

A. Recognizable stressor that would evoke significant distress symptoms in almost anyone

On August 29, 1986 at about 2 a.m., the victim was stabbed 12 times in the back and neck with another stab wound creating through-and-through puncture wounds of the jugular vein and carotid artery, penetrating 3 to 4 inches into the neck. She was unresponsive upon arrival at the emergency room. Deep tendon reflexes in her legs were unobtainable, toes were downgoing to bilateral plantar stimulation, and her blood pressure was 88/41, associated in part with a significant loss of blood. She received 4 liters of crystalloid fluids followed by two units of transfused blood upon admission.

Secondary stressors include loss of work and position, financial problems, and subsequent medical interventions.

B. Reexperiencing the trauma

Following the stabbing, the victim experienced the following: (a) nightmares of being trapped by the accused, (b) frequent flashbacks of the perpetrator dragging her out of the lounge while stabbing her, (c) suddenly acting or feeling as if the traumatic events were reoccurring because of an environmental or ideational stimulus. In regard to the last, responsiveness and memory for ongoing environmental events (e.g., someone talking) has been lost on occasion, with the victim exhibiting fear-related muscle tightening and escape responses (e.g., others noting her almost going off the edge of a chair or couch without realizing it when someone was discussing an unrelated stabbing), and (d) frequent ruminating about the stabbing event. Some of the above symptoms appear to be increasing in frequency and severity as a by-product of current involvement in the instant case.

C. Numbing of responsiveness to, or involvement with, the external world,
beginning some time after the traumatic event

The victim has shown a markedly diminished interest in or outright avoidance of several significant activities (e.g., eating, socializing, drinking alcohol) and sites (lounges, cane fields) where violence involving the use or threatened use of a knife was experienced from the accused. Some constriction of affect is seen compared to descriptions of pre-instant offenses behaviors. Level of distrust has increased, especially toward males.

D. Symptoms of autonomic arousal or suppression and/or related signs.

These include (a) continual scanning of the environment with increased anxiety when by herself, (b) sleep pattern changes with a reduction of several hours in average total sleep time, (c) startle responses, (d) memory and concentration problems with no indication that these problems are of organic etiology, (e) guilt including occasional thoughts that she wished she had died during the knife assault, and (f) body image problems, relating to scarring and disfigurement from the knife wounds.

Axis II: Mixed Personality Disorder (DSM-IV Code 301.9)

At present, the victim is involved in training as a secretary, has a positive and satisfying central love relationship, and has substantially reduced her alcohol intake and eliminated drug abuse. Analysis of her history prior to the instant offenses, however, revealed frequent job changes and periods of unemployment. She showed an inability to maintain enduring attachments to her previous spouses and significant others in her life. There appeared to be a failure to plan ahead and some recklessness, especially when under the influence of alcohol and/or drugs. Previous abuse of alcohol appears to be significant and the substance of choice. Other personality features by history include occasional angry outbursts or tantrums, low frustration tolerance, a need to receive assurance and support from others frequently, and long-term family conflict and discord. Decision-making skills are poor.

Personality features revealed by psychological testing, exclusive of MMPI results, indicate a low to medium expression of affection toward others, with comparable (low to average) needs for involvement from others. This pattern is usually seen as a result of being "burned" in interpersonal relationships. In terms of expressed control, decision skills and perceived behavioral influence over others are low. Dependency needs are elevated. This is usually seen in individuals with low self-esteem. In terms of social interaction, social skills are intact. High anxiety is attached to many social situations where she does not feel accepted by others. Social selectivity is extremely high, meaning that she is "picky" when it comes to choosing others as (emotionally) close associates, another pattern associated with close relationships that have turned out badly. Family relationships are poor, which is congruent with a reported developmental history of frequent corporal punishment, sexual abuse by extended family members, and gross behavioral problems on the part of parents and stepparents.

Minnesota Multiphasic Personality Inventory (MMPI) and MMPI Critical Items List: Her performance yielded the following MMPI profile (015' 8246-739/:L/F'K#). Validity scale results and repeated testing on critical items over time suggested a valid profile with a high degree of consistency. This person admitted to personal and emotional difficulties, is asking for help, and is unsure of her own capabilities in dealing with perceived high current stress. Clinical scale elevations describe a person who is uncomfortable with herself and others, hypersensitive, distrustful of others, concerned about somatic functioning and physical appearance, and withdrawn, and who engages in frequent ruminative behavior.

The type of profile elevation shown by the victim (high point pair 0–1) is rare and usually does not occur except when other scales are elevated, which then reflects possible additional psychopathological conditions. The social style and interactive behavior of the victim prior to the instant offenses can be characterized as active, operating within an individual who knew how to respond interpersonally in an appropriate manner. This suggests that MMPI scales known to be elevated by PTSD symptomatology (see Axis I) contributed to the mild to moderate profile elevations and the overall configuration. Removal of PTSD-related items would then reduce psychopathology to more normal levels. Some character features would undoubtedly remain, reflecting the chronic traits discussed in the first paragraph under Axis II considerations. No suggestions of a thought disorder or other psychotic process emerged upon testing.

Axis III

Physical disorders or conditions related to the instant case include the following. (1) Headaches, generalized or with a burning sensation toward the back of the head. Nerve sensations are occasionally experienced in the chest and arms when the head is leaned forward. (2) Surface numbness, from below the chin to below the knee on the right side of the body, and down the leg on the left side. Focal numbness is also experienced on the back in the area of the stab wounds. Leg stiffness is reported in the morning. (3) Balance problems with falling if she is not concentrating on the synchrony required for ambulation. She loses her balance if she attempts to run. (4) Occasional aphasic signs such as producing "blurred" words, or words switched around in sequence, when those verbal characteristics were not noticed prior to the stabbing.

The above signs appear to be residual symptoms from the sustained trauma. Earlier pathological signs included (1) left hemiparesis (i.e., abnormal neurological; normal CT scan and C-spine at Kuakini); (2) residual central nervous system deficit corresponding to Brown–Sequard syndrome, resulting in loss of sensation and discrimination in certain body sites (i.e., spectrum analysis significant for turbulent flow of right carotid artery; CT scan, arch aortagram, and carotid arteriogram essentially normal; abnormal neurological); (3) right Horner's pupil; (4) equivocal Babinski on the left; (5) ataxic gait favoring the left; (6) relatively weaker left shoulder shrug; (7) weaker left compared with right arm; (8) adequate swallow reflexes with a right pull to uvula; downward left tongue protrusion; (9) positive bilateral Hoffman sign (clawing movement of fingers created by stimulating the index finger); (10) temporary blindness, accompanied by initial visual blurring and later pain on the top of her head (see October 2, 1986 medical note).

To further pinpoint possible neuropsychological impairment, a composite neuropsychological battery plus some focal tests were administered (see Forensic database). Mild severity of cerebral processes was revealed (Halstead Impairment Index = 0.3) primarily on tasks requiring motor speed, coordination of upper extremities, manual dexterity, and sensitivity to stimulation (i.e., impaired performance on Tactual Performance Test, or TPT, finger oscillation, tactile finger recognition). Results suggested a primarily, not exclusively, right hemisphere involvement (i.e., left-handed finger oscillation, nondominant hand performance on TPT, left- vs. right-handed TPT, left-handed tactile finger recognition). The lesion appears static (with deficits improving) as opposed to progressive (i.e., little difference in VWS and PWS weighted scores, no suppressions, intact scores for Seashore Rhythm Test and Speech-sound Perception Test). The overall results are consistent with a cerebral circulatory dysfunction or insufficiency. In general, current neuropsychological deficits are mild and do not involve higher-order cognitive processing, visual perception functioning, or long-term, short-term, or immediate recall skills.

In terms of input from significant/knowledgeable others, statements made during the present evaluation in regard to alleged crime events were generally, but not totally, consistent with earlier versions presented to various investigators; expected errors of omission occurred as a result of forgetting over time and other factors but few errors of commission, as in fabrication, were presented. Several witnesses were reluctant to be interviewed and expressed fear of retaliation from the accused. The accounts of the offenses by significant/knowledgeable others were concrete, clear, and vivid and contained much detailed description within the limitations of their involvement and the brief span during which the instant offenses occurred.

Accounts were original in terms of lack of stereotyping, internally consistent, and embedded in the transpiring circumstances of the crime context and the reporting parties. The accounts contained behavioral chains of events and involved the reporting of subjective experiences and feelings. Unexpected complications and interruptions were mentioned as well as unfavorable behaviors on the part of witnesses. All of the above are fundamental or special semantic criteria that in combination are associated with truthfulness of crime accounts.

The accused's account of the instant offenses is partially presented by spontaneous statements during and subsequent to the alleged crimes. Amnesia was claimed for the actual stabbing but not for immediately preceding events (discussed later) or for the suicidal behavior. Regaining memory for instant offense events was reported in Dr. Chang's assessment records, dated 17 August 1985.

Generally, evaluation results are considered an accurate portrayal of the temporal sequence of the instant offenses and related events, taking into consideration the mental status and condition of the victim; test-taking attitude; psychological, intellectual, and neuropsychological limitations and competencies; and witnesses' and investigators' input.

Sequential Assessment of Emotion and Behavioral Self-Regulation

Emotional level and behavioral self-regulation of the accused can be sequentially analyzed for the temporal flow of the instant offenses, based upon knowledge of the victim, the accused, significant others, and the crime context. This will be in terms of database-reported events which suggest emotional and self-control impairments and abilities before, during and after the instant offenses.

(a) Previous to the alleged offenses: The 6 to 7 months before and violence history

During this period of time, the accused's marital relationship fell apart, with his three children being placed in foster care (March 1986), separation from his wife (April 1986), and his entering into an intimate but stormy relationship with the victim (March 1986). His job of 1 year was lost, with several unsuccessful attempts to reintegrate into the working field. Substance ingestion during this period consisted of alcohol, tobacco (about one pack daily), and daily use of anabolic steroids as an adjunct to his bodybuilding. Social activities consisted in part of frequent dating and socializing with friends. Possession of weapons was observed during this period, to include carrying a knife on his person, keeping a samurai sword behind his truck seat, and owning lethal weapons, including an assortment of knives, "numchuks," "stars," and spears.

Violent or potentially violent activities toward self or others need to be examined as part of the accused's behavioral reaction to stress and placed within a historical perspective. It is important to note that violence in recent times represents a continual pattern, to include previous violence (1) as a victim of child abuse, (2) frequent fighting with peers (e.g., see school records), (3) animal cruelty, (4) a suicide attempt by drug overdose (1982), (5) physical assaults on his wife, Tamara Barnes, especially from 1981 to 1983. Victim Assistance Program files indicate kicking his wife's back, head, and shoulders with threats to kill her (March 2, 1984). Later, his wife was punched in the face and head, resulting in black, swollen eyes, lumps on her head, red marks and bruises by her temple, and severe pains in her head (July 3, 1984). During a conjoint counseling session, the accused threatened to hit her and police were called by the therapist (August 2, 1984). A Temporary Restraining Order was obtained for the period from August 12, 1984 to February 10, 1985.

Violence toward others since 1983 is presented below.

Date	Event	Source
May 3, 1983	Spouse abuse with threats to kill	Victim Assistance Program and Family Court records
June 8, 1983	Spouse abuse	Victim Assistance Program and Family Court records
June 13, 1983	Spouse abuse	Victim Assistance Program and Family Court records
May to June 1986	Threats to kill victim and self if victim tried to leave him	Victim
May to June 1986	Told several acquaintances that if the victim left him, he would kill her	Witness
June 8, 1986	Multiple strikes with fists to victim's face/head	TRO, Victim, HPD report
June 12, 1986	Kidnapping, Assault with a Weapon (knife), and Attempt to do Bodily Harm complaints. Grabbed victim by her hair, put knife to her throat in presence of co-workers, dragged victim into vehicle and left.	HPD report
June 12, 1986	Assault on pregnant wife	Witness, Wife, HPD report
June 27, 1986	Grabbed, yanked by hair, dragged, threw, and choked victim	TRO, Victim
June 28, 1986	Grabbed, punched on head four or five times, restrained victim's head with foot	TRO, Victim
June 29, 1986	Grabbed and swung victim by hair; placed loaded .45 caliber pistol to victim's head; later threatened to kill self	TRO, Victim
July 18, 1986	Took victim to cane field, put knife to her throat, threatened to cut her throat if they did not have sex; victim complied; last contact with victim prior to the stabbing	Victim
July 21, 1986	Stabbing of the victim (instant offenses)	Witnesses

(b) Previous to the alleged stabbing: The week before

In general, data suggest a period of high cumulative stress on Mr. Barnes' part, to include (1) a disrupted relationship with the victim; (2) Mr. Barnes and Carole Gordon were living in separate quarters at this time; the accused was sleeping in his truck and the victim was staying at a friend's apartment; (3) the defendant was not working; (4) he was in poor financial shape; (5) his pickup truck was in danger of being repossessed for nonpayment; and (6) attempts on his part to reconcile with his wife were fruitless. Retrospective self-reported depression and hopelessness were evident. Self-regulation during this period included the ability to drive his vehicle, socialize with acquaintances, and go to recreational spots during the evening, engaging in a wide variety of lounge-appropriate behavior. The accused was aware of and was due to appear in court in connection with a Temporary Restraining Order the victim had filed in an attempt to keep him away from her. A previous arrest for failure to appear at a TRO hearing should be noted.

(c) Previous to the alleged offenses: Before and after arrival at the crime scene

For some hours prior to arrival at the Seaview Lounge, the accused allegedly consumed a large amount of hard liquor at various places with a friend or relative. Between 1:00 and 1:30 a.m. on

August 29, 1986, he entered the bar with this individual and proceeded to the victim's table, where she was seated with three acquaintances. The accused introduced his companion as his brother and asked the victim if he could have his pet dog, a pit bull, back. He was polite, with no unusual behavior noted. The victim, allegedly fearing for her life, went to the lounge manager and told him of her fear. The manager then escorted the accused to the front entrance of the lounge to talk to him. At that point, the accused was observed to show signs of growing agitation and anger. He went to the bar counter area after the 5 to 10 minute talk and had a beer with his "brother." He was observed to be staring at the table where the victim was seated, in what appeared to be an angry fashion, muscles tensed, eyes wide open, and head nodding up and down. The witnesses at the table commented that it was their belief that violence was imminent, but that they believed it would occur outside the bar. The victim left her table to prepare for her dance, stopped by the jukebox to play some songs, and proceeded back to her table. Upon the victim reaching her table, the accused moved toward her.

The accused's reported emotions during the portion of this time period when he was allegedly drinking with his companion were primarily depression and hopelessness. He reported that he did not mention his upset to his companion. Significant emotion, apparently anger, occurred (1) when he was talked to outside the lounge by the manager, and (2) when he was sitting at the bar subsequent to his return. Self-regulation shown during this period included (1) gross motor, fine motor, and recall abilities in order to engage in man–machine interface; (2) ability to locate the bar, ambulate to the interior, scan the environment, spot the victim, leave the bar upon the manager's request, return to the bar, locate his acquaintance, go to him, and later walk to the victim; (3) verbal behaviors and social interactive skills as evidenced by the introduction of his "brother" and other prosocial behavior at that time; (4) ability to conceal the knife; (5) immediate, short-term, and long-term auditory and visual memory, which are necessary for successful execution of the above behaviors. Immediate auditory recall, for example, is required when engaging in verbal conversation, as shown when he first entered the lounge. Long-term recall, as another example, is tapped when mentioning animals the other party presumably has in her possession, or to introduce a relative; (6) the ability to delay the knife attack, if in fact there was such an intent when he was at the bar or at some prior time.

(d) During the instant offenses

At approximately 2 a.m. on August 29, 1986, the accused approached the victim from his position at the bar, stating, "Get over here," or words to that effect. At that point, the victim had arrived at the table and lifted her glass about half way to her mouth. The accused then grabbed the victim by her hair with his left hand and pulled out a double-edged knife from his clothing with his right hand, blade upright (by thumb). He proceeded to stab her multiple times while dragging her toward the bar entrance. The victim collapsed and essentially lost recall after the assault commenced, but witnesses recall her screaming, "No, no, no, don't do this," or words to that effect. The initial thrusts appeared to be in the upper back and neck areas. The final stab in the throat resulted in the carotid artery and jugular vein trauma. The victim was released at a point not far from the entrance and the accused ran off.

Emotion during the instant offenses appeared to be significant for all the preceding reasons regarding cumulative stress. Other events signifying some emotion concern (1) the perseverative nature of the stabbing, (2) that no material gain was realized from the victim (e.g., money, possessions), and (3) that it was unlikely that the accused could get away with the crime as it was perpetrated in the presence of 30 to 40 people.

Self-regulations shown during this period include (1) the ability to verbalize, command, and follow through on statements; (2) simultaneous use of motor behaviors represented by holding, stabbing, and dragging the victim at the same time, all combined with (3) goal-direction, as represented by dragging the victim toward the door, irrespective of what he would do with her once there; (4) ability to multiply stab a relatively circumscribed section of the body; (5) specific focus of attack to a vital area; and (6) attempt to escape, as represented by running off, implying awareness of wrongdoing.

(e) After the alleged crimes until hospitalization

Subsequent to releasing the victim, the accused ran outside the lounge (2:00 to 2:07 a.m.), then toward the mountain across Kapiolani Boulevard, then proceeded in the direction of Hawaii Community College (HCC). Bar patrons were in pursuit in both a vehicle and on foot. He climbed a 6-foot fence at the boundary of HCC and went into a side alley, attempting to conceal himself behind a vehicle. Police arrived shortly afterward and ordered him to come out with raised hands (2:09 a.m.). The accused emerged with his hands above his head, but then fell forward, saying, "Just let me die, I want to die," or words to that effect). While lying face down, the accused stated several times, "I love her," or words to that effect, 2:11 a.m.). He mentioned several times a "Jim Kalanaki" (phonetic). The police noticed lacerations on both of the accused's wrists. The knife was found several feet from his original hiding spot. He became semiconscious and was rendered first aid. He was arrested for Attempted Murder (2:12 a.m.) and shortly after was transported the hospital (2:27 a.m.) At the hospital, he became less stuporous and offered that "They jumped my brother," or words to that effect. His wife, Tamara Barnes, came to the hospital and the accused told her that he loved the victim. He also stated that he attempted suicide because the children were out of the house and that he believed Mrs. Barnes was not planning to reconcile with him (3:00 to 3:20 a.m.). The accused then went to sleep. He entered surgery a short time later for deep cuts to both wrists (4:55 a.m.) and was out later in the morning (6:35 a.m.). Later, he admitted to physically abusing the victim over the previous several weeks (see hospital consultation record). The next day he was formally charged with Attempted Murder and Assault in the First Degree, with the accused declining to make a statement at that time.

Emotional distress during this period appeared to be the highest of all the time blocks. Panic, fear, and self-blame appeared to be the type of emotion rather than the anger of the earlier stage. High emotion during this period was manifested by (1) running away from the bar, and under circumstances likely to result in apprehension; (2) attempting to escape in a disadvantaged manner when other means were available (e.g., he ran past his truck parked on the opposite side of the street; his companion was later seen by the truck with the driver's door open); (3) attempting to kill himself in what appears to be a genuine effort at suicide; (4) spontaneous and repetitious statements in regard to the victim and others; and (5) other behaviors.

Self-regulation during this period appeared to be at the lowest. Yet, running away and hiding behind the vehicle in the alley can be construed as a continuing awareness that he had done wrong, in addition to attempting to escape detection. He had the ability to scale a tall fence, to comply partially with police instructions, and to verbalize. The ability to prevaricate was intact, as evidenced by his false statement that his brother had been "jumped." Recent and remote memory was intact, as shown by a variety of behaviors and his statements to his wife.

(f) After initial medical treatment to the present

The accused was transferred from the hospital to pretrial detainment at HCCC. Multiple psychiatric diagnoses during the hospitalization were given, to include DSM III Adjustment Reaction and Borderline Personality Disorder. The suicide attempt was seen as genuine, but there were many apparent attempts to manipulate the social environment through the use of further suicide threats (see hospital records). Although the defendant denied recall of the instant offenses, he repeatedly expressing remorse for his deeds. At other times, he stated that the victim laughed at him just prior to the attack.

Self-regulation increased with hospitalization. Attempts to control the judicial process and the victim's behavior were shown by the following. (1) Multiple contacts by a family member to the victim in attempts to get her to drop the charges against the accused. (2) A series of letters by the accused with the theme that the victim must share the blame due to her presumed traits of psychological insecurity, distrust, suspiciousness, short-temperedness, greed for money, and playing "mind games" with him (see letters in Forensic Database). He stated that he physically abused her when she made him tense, claimed no insight for the alleged offenses, and asked God to forgive both of them. He affirmed his love for the victim many times. He shared suicide ideation with the victim: "I mite as well hang myself with a strip of my sheet;" "[I'm] depressed," "my body wants to die," "I honestly don't know what I mite do to myself right now." He later told the victim that he hoped she would leave for Alaska because he might then be able to rest his mind. (3) Several pictures drawn by the accused, showing what appeared to be the accused with a large knife cutting through the air, labeled "The Edge," and signed by the accused. Other aggressive drawings were sent to the victim, including one labeled, "Gardenia Gardens Lounge," the scene of a previous knife wielding, assault, and dragging incident by the accused.

On 29 Nov. 1986, Judge James Meyer filed a report indicating that the accused had violated his TRO by contacting the victim through letters and his sister, Trudy King (HPD report # CD-8512).

On 16 Feb. 1987, the accused complained of his transfer to a dormitory and wrote, "Been experiencing harassment because I am gay."

On 14 Mar. 1987, the accused admitted striking another inmate in the face with his fist. Mr. Barnes stated that his wife was struck by a pimp in Waikiki and that he believed the victim-inmate was a pimp and therefore decided to take it out on him. The victim-inmate was transferred out of the HCCC dormitory and the accused was adjudged to have suffered an emotional break. He was placed on a suicide watch by HCCC officials.

On 11 Jun 1987, the victim made a complaint to the HPD indicating that the accused was harassing her by issuing death threats to her and her roommate (HPD report # CD-9112).

Summary of Self-Regulatory Behaviors

Characteristics or behaviors of the accused which indicate both knowledge of wrongdoing and self-regulation for the time of the alleged offenses, when taken in their entirety, are as follows:

1. As a predisposing variable relevant to basal violence, a significant violence history extended over years characterized by choice behaviors and reinforcing outcomes;
2. As a predisposing variable relevant to intentional behaviors, multiple statements to significant others that he would kill the victim if she attempted to dissolve the relationship;
3. As a predisposing variable relevant to opportunity factors, previous instances where the victim was assaulted by the accused where a knife was used as a threat stimulus;
4. As a predisposing variable relevant to triggering stimuli and awareness of vulnerability, breakup in the central love relationship with both his wife and the victim;
5. No indication of impaired intelligence or a major psychiatric disorder. Examination after the instant offenses revealed logical thought processes, no delusions or hallucinations, and present suicidal ideation. History and recent diagnoses suggest a long-standing personality disorder;
6. Suggestions that the accused may have prepared for or at least had foreknowledge of the alleged crimes;
7. Intact orientation, scanning, and sensory skills during the crime time sequence;
8. Intact memory skills for both recent and long-term events;
9. Intact interpersonal skills before the attack;
10. Ability to delay the attack for a significant period of time;
11. The focus of the attempted homicide should be considered specific;
12. At least three sets of motor behaviors were exhibited simultaneously during the attack;
13. Knowledge of wrongdoing and attempting to escape from the crime scene; and
14. Prevarication subsequent to arrest in regard to crime events.

CONCLUSIONS

1. The database is sufficient to draw some relevant conclusions with a reasonable degree of psychological certainty. Available data from other examiners were considered, but all conclusions rendered were derived independently of other psychological/medical examiners who are involved in this case.

2. Database sources were assessed for suggestions of deliberate and nondeliberate distortion. Conclusions rendered are considered an accurate representation of alleged crime events, taking into account report and witness limitations and competencies, the possible psychological disorders of the victim, biases of input sources, and other factors.

The victim emerged as a credible source of information, taking all factors into account. Deliberate distortion in terms of fabrication or lying was not suggested. Nondeliberate distortion created by the trauma of crime events and a subsequent post-traumatic stress disorder was taken into consideration by comparison to both cross-validating information and to the victim's own input over time and across many test procedures.

The perpetrator's credibility for reporting some crime events could not be assessed as some data were not available for cross-validation. Distortion in regard to the manner in which the alleged crime events occurred is suggested by the accused's post-arrest statements. Distortion in regard to evaluation behavior, particularly faking bad (malingering), was suggested by test procedures administered by evaluators in this case.

3. Level of emotion experienced by the accused appeared different as a function of temporal crime sequence. Mild emotion is suggested for the time he entered the crime scene until just before the stabbing. Behavioral self-regulation during this period was high and was characterized by (a) an ability to scan and orient himself to the crime scene, (b) an ability to conceal his knife, (c) normal speech patterns, (d) normal motor and other physical behaviors, (e) an ability to initiate and interact socially in an appropriate fashion, (f) an ability to delay the attack for a significant time span, and (g) adequate short- and long-term memory skills, which were required to execute the above successfully.

Moderate emotion was suggested for the duration of the attack as demonstrated by (a) demanding in an angry tone of voice that the victim come to him, (b) the potentially lethal attack itself, and its occurring in the presence of others, and (c) the perseverative nature of the multiple knife thrusts. Behavioral self-regulation during this period included (a) the ability to verbalize, (b) the simultaneous multiplicity of motor behaviors shown (grabbing and holding, dragging, stabbing), (c) the goal-direction of the dragging, (d) the near-lethal knife thrust in the front part of the victim's neck as a final killing thrust, and (e) the decision to let the victim go and run from the crime scene.

Considerable to substantial emotion was suggested from the point of releasing the victim until his attempted suicide and was demonstrated by panic, escape, and self-destructive behavior. Behavioral self-regulation during this period was lowest and included running and climbing behaviors, an unsuccessful attempt to conceal himself, and partial compliance with police instructions.

In general, extreme emotion was not suggested for the time of the alleged offenses, as shown by a substantial degree of self-control and self-regulation during and especially before the attack. Further, momentary anger and long-standing resentment toward the victim, shown by previous attacks and other relevant behaviors toward her, characterized his behaviors up to the final near-fatal knife thrust. Panic and self-destructive feelings characterized his considerable to substantial level of emotion from the time he released the victim until his arrest. Overall, data suggest that the accused could have refrained from the stabbing if he had so chosen and that the highest level of emotion occurred subsequent to the attack.

4. At the conclusion of the multiple evaluations, a Tarasoff warning was issued to the victim in this case. This was based upon (a) the violence history of the accused in general, (b) the preoccupation with the possession of multiple weapons, particularly lethal weapons, (c) pre-instant offense violence toward women and the victim in particular, (d) the apparent homicidal intent of

the attack in the instant case involving the use of a deadly weapon resulting in near-fatal injuries, and (e) post-arrest intrusive and threatening behaviors toward the victim.

Sincerely,

CC: Presiding Judge
       Defense Attorney
       Prosecuting Attorney

Appendix F
Cutoff Scores for Chance-Level Responding to Tests of Varying Length

Total No. of Items	Cutoff Score (Number Correct)	
	$p \leq 0.05$	$p \leq 0.01$
7	0	0
8	1	0
9	1	0
10	2	1
11	2	1
12	2	1
13	3	1
14	3	2
15	4	2
16	4	3
17	5	3
18	5	3
19	5	4
20	6	4
21	6	5
22	7	5
23	7	5
24	8	6
25	8	6
26	9	7
27	9	7
28	10	7
29	10	8
30	10	8
31	11	9
32	11	9
33	12	9

	Cutoff Score (Number Correct)	
Total No. of Items	$p \leq 0.05$	$p \leq 0.01$
34	12	10
35	13	10
36	13	11
37	14	11
38	14	12
39	15	12
40	15	12

Source: National Bureau of Standards. (1949). *Tables of the Binomial Probability Distribution*. Washington, DC: U.S. Government Printing Office.

Glossary

***Actus reus*:** Guilty act; a wrongful act. As opposed to guilty mind, *mens rea*.

Acute alcoholic hallucinosis: State of alcoholic intoxication characterized by hallucinations.

Adverse witness: A witness who gives evidence that is prejudicial to the party examining the witness at the time. Commonly refers to a witness whose testimony is prejudicial to the party by whom the witness was called.

Alarm and mobilization reaction: First stage of the general adaptation syndrome, characterized by the mobilization of defenses to cope with a stressful situation.

Amicus curiae: Friend of the court; A person who petitions the court for permission to provide information to the court on a matter of law that is in doubt, or one who is not a party to a lawsuit but who is allowed to introduce evidence, argument, or authority to protect one's interest.

Amnestic syndrome: Inability to remember events more than a few minutes after they have occurred, coupled with the ability to recall the recent and remote past.

Attest: To bear witness to; to affirm as true or genuine.

Bona: Good or virtuous.

Burden of proof: In the law of evidence, the duty of a party to prove a fact in dispute affirmatively. The obligation of a party to convince the trier of fact as to the truth of a claim by establishing by evidence a required degree of belief concerning a fact. In civil cases, proof must be by a preponderance of the evidence. In criminal cases, all crime elements must be proved by the government beyond a reasonable doubt. In some equity issues and more recent decisions of the Supreme Court the standard of proof is clear and convincing evidence.

Certiorari: To be informed of; an action or writ issued by a superior court requiring an inferior court to produce a certified record of a particular case tried by the latter. The purpose of said action is to enable the higher court to inspect the proceedings to determine whether or not there were any irregularities. Most commonly used by the Supreme Court of the United States as a discretionary device to choose the cases it wishes to hear.

Civil: Of or pertaining to the state or its citizenry. Relates to an individual's private rights and remedies sought through civil action; in contrast to criminal proceedings.

Clear and convincing: A standard of proof greater than preponderance but less rigorous than reasonable doubt. Proof that should leave the trier of fact with no reasonable doubt about the truth of the matter in issue.

Collusion: The making of an agreement between two or more persons with a view toward avoiding litigation.

Compensation neurosis: Symptoms exceeding physical findings that persist long after expected recovery.

Conduct disorders: Childhood disorders marked by persistent acts of aggressive or antisocial behavior that may or may not be against the law.

Confabulation: Fabrication of information to fill in memory gaps. Associated with organic conditions.

Conspiracy: A combination of two or more persons who propose to commit an unlawful or criminal act, or to commit a lawful act by criminal means.

Deception: Conscious distortion of behaviors or self-report.

Default judgment: A decision of the court against a defendant because of failure to respond to a plaintiff's action.

Delusion: Firm belief opposed to reality but maintained in spite of strong evidence to the contrary.

Direct examination: The initial questioning or examination of a witness by the party who originally called the witness to testify.

Discovery: A pretrial procedure by which one party can obtain vital facts and information material to the case to assist in preparation for the trial. The purpose of discovery is to make for a fair trial and to allow each party to know what documents and information the opponent has in its possession.

Dissociation: Separation or "isolation" of mental processes in such a way that they split off from the main personality or lose their normal thought–affect relationship.

Dissociative disorder. Psychoneurotic disorder characterized by amnesia, fugue, somnambulism, or multiple personality.

Distortion: Unintentional or intentional misrepresentation of events.

Exclusionary rule: The rule that defines whether evidence is admissible in a trial. In cases where evidence has been illegally obtained, it must be removed from consideration by the fact finders.

Fabrication: Relating imaginary events as if they were true without intent to deceive; confabulation.

Factitious disorder: Assuming the role of a patient by the voluntary production of symptoms.

Fiduciary: A person having the duty to act in a relationship of high trust and confidence for another's benefit in the capacity of trustee, executor, or administrator.

Folie a deux: A psychotic interpersonal relationship involving two people; e.g., husband and wife both become psychotic with similar or complementary symptomatology.

Frye test: A test emphasizing that the subject of an expert witness's testimony must conform to a generally accepted explanatory theory. Named after the case in which the determination was made.

Hearsay: A statement made during a trial or hearing that is not based on the personal, first-hand knowledge of the witness.

Hearsay rule: The regulation making a witness's statement inadmissible if it is not based on personal knowledge, unless it falls within certain exceptions.

Hypnosis: Trancelike mental state induced in a cooperative subject by suggestion.

Illusion: Misinterpretation of sensory data; false perception.

In camera: In chambers; in private. The hearing of a case before a judge in private chambers when all spectators are excluded from the courtroom, or where the judge performs a judicial act while the court is not in session.

Incompetency: Lacking the physical, intellectual or moral capacity or qualification to perform a required duty.

Informed consent: A person's agreement to the occurrence of a specified event based on a full disclosure of facts needed to make an intelligent decision.

Insanity: A social or legal term indicating a condition in which a person lacks legal responsibility or capacity due to mental illness. As stated in the American Law Institute Penal Code, "A person is not responsible for criminal conduct if at the time of such conduct as a result of mental disease or defect he lacks substantial capacity either to appreciate the criminality or wrongfulness of his conduct or to conform his conduct to the requirements of the law."

Just-world hypothesis: The hypothesis stating that the world is fair and that victims deserve what happened to them, and therefore, do not deserve help.

Leading question: A question posed that is improper because it suggests to the subject a desired answer.

Malfeasance: The commission of an unlawful, wrongful act; any wrongful conduct that affects, interrupts, or interferes with the performance of official duties.

Mens rea: A guilty mind; having a guilty or wrongful purpose or criminal intent.

Mistrial: A trial that is terminated before its normal conclusion and declared invalid prior to the returning of a verdict. A judge may declare a mistrial due to an extraordinary event (e.g., death of a juror); for a fundamental, prejudicial error that cannot be corrected by instructions to the jury; or because of the jury's inability to reach a verdict (hung jury). In a criminal case, a mistrial may prevent a retrial under the doctrine of double jeopardy.

M'Naghten **rule:** In most jurisdictions, the test applied for the defense of insanity. Under this test, an accused is not criminally responsible if suffering from a mental disease or defect at the time of committing the act and not understanding the nature and quality of the act or that what was done was wrong. To be considered "sane," and therefore legally responsible for the act committed, the defendant must know and understand the nature and quality of the act and be able to distinguish between right and wrong at the time the offense was committed.

Modus operandi: Manner or mode of behavior; a criminal's typical pattern of performing crimes.

Moot: A subject for debate; unsettled; undecided. A case is moot when a determination on a matter is sought, which, when rendered has no practical effect on the matter under dispute.

Moral nihilism: Doctrine that denies any objective or real ground for moral beliefs and holds that the individual is not bound by obligation to others or society.

Multiple personality: Type of dissociative disorder characterized by the development of two or more relatively independent personality systems in the same individual.

Munchausen by proxy: Supplying factitious information on a child's health or manipulation of a child's health.

Non compos mentis: Insane; not sound of mind. A very general term including all varieties of mental derangement.

Path analysis: Statistical technique that takes into account how variables are related to one another through time and how they predict one another.

Perceptual filtering: Processes involved in selective attention to aspects of the great mass of incoming stimuli that continually impinges on the organism.

Perseveration: Persistent continuation of a line of thought or activity once it is under way. Clinically inappropriate repetition.

Posthypnotic amnesia: The subject's lack of memory for the period of hypnosis.

Presumption: An inference resulting from a rule of law or the proven existence of a fact that requires such rule(s) or action(s) to be established in the action. Presumptions can be irrebuttable, such as the presumption of incapacity in a person under 7 years of age to act, or rebuttable, in which case it can be disproved by evidence.

Prima facie **evidence:** Evidence that, in the judgment of the law, is good and sufficient to establish a given fact or a chain of facts making up the party's claim or defense. If such evidence is unexplained or uncontradicted, it is sufficient to sustain a favorable judgment for the issue it supports; may be contradicted by other evidence.

Proximate cause: An occurrence that, in a natural and unbroken chain of events, results in an injury and without which the injury would not have occurred. The event that is closest in the causal relationship to the effect.

Pseudocommunity: Delusional social environment developed by a paranoiac.

Pseudodementia: Faking loss of intellectual abilities. A depressed state confused with brain damage, usually in the elderly people.

Pseudologia fantastica: Pathological and compulsive lying. The motive is unknown or uncertain in many cases.

Reality assumptions: Assumptions that relate to the gratification of needs in the light of environmental possibilities, limitations, and dangers.

Resistance: Tendency to maintain symptoms and resist treatment. Uncovering of repressed material.

Simulation: An intentional imitation of the basic processes and outcomes of a real-life situation, carried out to better understand the basic mechanisms of the situation. In civil law, misrepresenting or concealing the truth, as when parties pretend to perform an act different from that in which they really are engaged.

Sodium pentothal: Barbiturate drug sometimes used in psychotherapy to produce a state of relaxation and suggestibility.

Stare decisis: The legal policy of courts stating that once a principle of law is laid down, it will be adhered to and applied to all future cases in which the facts are substantially the same. Serves to ensure security and certainty of legal principles.

Suppression stage: The retraction of disclosures of sex abuse by the child. Associated with loyalty conflicts and stress.

Tort: A private or civil wrong or injury, excluding a breach of contract, for which the court will provide a remedy in the form of an action for damages.

Voir dire: To speak the truth. The preliminary examination made by the court or by attorneys of one presented as a prospective juror to determine competence to serve or as a witness to determine competence to speak the truth.

Work product: Work done by an attorney while representing a client, such as writings, statements, or testimony on regard to legal impressions, tactics, strategies, and opinions, that are ordinarily not subject to discovery. Discovery may be obtained only when the party seeking it has a substantial need for the material to prepare the case and is unable to obtain the substantial equivalent of the material by other means without undue hardship.

Index